Philosophical Perspectives, 15,
Metaphysics, 2001

Previously Published Volumes
Volume 1, Metaphysics, 1987
Volume 2, Epistemology, 1988
Volume 3, Philosophy of Mind and Action Theory, 1989
Volume 4, Action Theory and Philosophy of Mind, 1990
Volume 5, Philosophy of Religion, 1991
Volume 6, Ethics, 1992
Volume 7, Language and Logic, 1993
Volume 8, Logic and Language, 1994
Volume 9, AI, Connectionism, and Philosophical Psychology, 1995
Volume 10, Metaphysics, 1996
Volume 11, Mind, Causation, and World , 1997
Volume 12, Language, Mind, and Ontology, 1998
Volume 13, Epistemology, 1999
Volume 14, Action and Freedom, 2000

Volumes 1 through 9 are available from Ridgeview Publishing Company, Box 686, Atascadero, CA 93423.
Volumes 10 through 14 are available from Blackwell Publishers, 350 Main Street, Malden, MA 02148.

Additional titles to be announced.

Philosophical Perspectives, 15, Metaphysics, 2001

Edited by
JAMES E. TOMBERLIN

Blackwell Publishers, Inc.
350 Main Street
Malden, MA 02148 USA

Blackwell Publishers, Ltd.
108 Cowley Road
Oxford OX4 1JF
United Kingdom

Library of Congress Cataloging-in-Publication Data has been applied for.

ISBN 0-631-23028-9
ISBN 0-631-23029-7 (P)
ISSN 1520-8583

Philosophical Perspectives, 15, Metaphysics, 2001

Contents

Time and Tense

The Metaphysics of Reference

The Metaphysics of Properties

Conceivability, the Physical, and Theoretical Identity

Actualism: an Exchange

James E. Tomberlin is Professor of Philosophy at California State University, Northridge, where he has taught since completing graduate study at Wayne State University in 1969. He has published more than eighty essays and reviews in action theory, deontic logic, metaphysics, philosophy of language, mind, religion, and the theory of knowledge. He is a co-editor of *Noûs*; and in addition to the editorship of the present series, he has edited *Agent, Language, and the Structure of the World* (Hackett, 1983), *Hector-Neri Castaneda, Profiles* (D. Reidel, 1986) and he co-edited *Alvin Plantinga, Profiles* (D. Reidel, 1985).

THINKING ABOUT THINGS

The Ninth *Philosophical Perspectives* Lecture

Michael Jubien
University of California, Davis

I believe that a good deal of trouble in philosophy—notably in the metaphysics of modality—may be traced to a trio of incompatible tendencies in our ordinary way of thinking and speaking about *things*. Two of these tendencies are virtually harmless in everyday life and I think they would be entirely harmless in philosophy if they were properly understood and accommodated. But I don't think the third tendency is harmless. For one thing, I think it's what misleads metaphysicians into finding harm when the first two are in play. But what's even more important, if I'm right, is that it's the source of a significant body of widely accepted but erroneous philosophical doctrine. In this paper I will try to show how these tendencies figure in both sorts of trouble. I'll also offer a remedy, one that runs strongly against orthodox philosophical practice but nevertheless has its roots in a grand philosophical tradition.

I. Background Assumptions

Metaphysics is not simple, and several different issues could easily muddy the waters of this discussion. But—with one exception—I think these issues are independent of the business at hand. So I'm going to assume a cluster of convenient background positions simply to make the present discussion easier. I hope you will see that the chosen positions don't prejudice things, so that it doesn't matter if you don't actually accept all of them. In fact I don't accept all of them, but adopting the ones I do accept would introduce needless complexity, and matters will be complicated enough anyway.

To begin, I'll assume what I like to call a "naturalistic" conception of physical objects, in particular, the view that any physical object is nothing more nor less than some physical stuff in spacetime, and that any physical stuff in spacetime is a physical object. I'll ignore the question of what physical stuff is, whether it should be taken as primitive, what spacetime is, the status of "fields" and "energy," and the like. These issues are independent of present concerns. The naturalistic view has of course been advocated before, for example by W. V. Quine.[1] Two of its consequences—sometimes viewed with suspicion—are that the realm of physical things includes lots of widely scattered objects, and also objects that lack either extension or duration.[2] But nothing in our discussion will turn on these peculiarities.

A second assumption is that any ordinary thing like a star, a table, or a dog is in fact a physical object, and so is to be found among the objects of this naturalistic ontology. An important consequence is that we may take our physical-object quantifiers to range exclusively over the objects of the naturalistic ontology without worrying that something might be missed. Another matter, not actually an assumption, is that I will try to finesse the question of whether ordinary things are persisting three-dimensional entities or four-dimensional entities with temporal parts. All the main points of concern here could be made more carefully from any coherent three-dimensional or four-dimensional perspective.

The next assumption is that there is a so-called "abundant" realm of Platonic properties. Loosely speaking, any predicate of English that I happen to use, no matter how complicated, will be assumed to express a property. I'm actually agnostic about this abundance. I think the realm of properties might really be quite "sparse." But I don't know how we could ever expect to decide this question. More important, I think that if there really are no properties beyond the sparse, then the supposed instantiation of a nonsparse property must reduce to a complex of instantiations of sparse properties (and perhaps simple relations). So the pretense of abundance does no ultimate harm. But the assumption of at least *some* Platonic properties plays a vital role in dispelling the philosophical trouble. As a result, these proceedings might be seen as a kind of backdoor argument in favor of the Platonism. At any rate, the grand tradition from which the promised unorthodox remedy springs is none other than Platonism about properties.

The final assumption is that a genuine acceptance of Platonic properties includes commitment to what I call the "Doctrine of Constitution." I think most people who accept Platonic properties assume this doctrine is true, but then I think they also routinely forget what it literally says and how thoroughly important it is. According to the doctrine, for a thing *a* to be (say) green, *just is* for *a* to instantiate the property of *greenness*. So *greenness* is every bit as much an intuitive constituent of the proposition *that a is green* as is *a* itself.[3] Intuitively, the proposition asserts that a relation holds between *two* entities (one of which happens to be physical, the other not). Sometimes natural language seems in harmony with this idea, as when we take a sentence like "Sally has courage" to be synonymous with "Sally is courageous."[4] But unfortunately our normal way of thinking about the subject-predicate structure of ordinary language doesn't really serve this conception very well, for we really do think of the two kinds of linguistic entities very differently.

This carries over into our routine application of first-order logic, where we express the proposition *that a is green* by a formula like '*Ga*', with the '*G*' regarded as *attributing* the property of *greenness* but without referring to it. The absence of genuine reference is sealed by the first-order prohibition against quantifying the predicate position. But we can restore reference and remain within the first-order framework simply by dropping the unary predicate symbol in favor of a constant, and adopting a binary relation symbol for instantiation. The simplest application of this strategy would yield a formula like '*Iag*', where both term-positions are of course quantifiable. We'll return briefly to this idea later on. I believe it will ultimately become clear that we cannot deal appropriately with the three tendencies without a significant reform of deeply ingrained habits in deploying logic in philosophy, at both formal and informal levels.

II. Three Tendencies

Now we have the background assumptions, so let's turn to the three tendencies of ordinary thought. I'll illustrate the first with an all-too-familiar "Ship of Theseus" story.[5] But keep in mind that we aren't doing philosophy yet. For now we're just noticing some features of ordinary thinking. Say you own a boat. From time to time you replace a worn part with a similar part. You do this over a long period of time, and you never think that you have a different boat, even after you've replaced many, many parts. It may even occur to you at some point that your boat has none of its original parts. And it may be that a scavenger has collected all the original parts and reassembled them. Even upon learning this you are very likely to think you still have "the same boat" you originally had. And the officials who annually licence the boat surely agree. You certainly don't think the scavenger has "your boat." That, after all, would be grounds for legal action. And you are just as unlikely to think that over this period of time you have owned two or more boats.

But now suppose you think not of boats, but of brute *physical objects*. In other words, suppose you think of things independently of any properties they might have other than the property of being some specific physical thing (that is, some specific physical stuff). You may then notice that a physical object that was once in your possession had exactly the same constituent parts as one that is no longer in your possession. I believe you are very likely to conclude that you no longer have "the same physical object" you once had. To think otherwise would be to flout the very commonsensical idea that a mere physical object is just "the sum of its parts." Of course this conclusion could easily lead you to reevaluate the original opinion that you have "the same *boat*." But if it did, I think *that* would be evidence of the third tendency of ordinary thought, and we'll discuss that topic soon.

I believe the two sides of this story point to a "great divide" in how we think about things: When thought of as an object of a familiar *kind*, like a *boat*, the parts of a thing are not especially important to its "identity." You can change lots of parts of a boat—maybe all of them!—and still have "the same boat." But when the very same entity is thought of merely as a *physical object*, the parts assume much greater—perhaps even definitive—importance. Let's call this two-sided tendency *the parts divide*. It would be a big mistake, I think, to assume that we have to choose sides in the parts divide in order to avoid incoherence, even in the presence of our assumption that an entity like a boat is just a particular physical thing in the naturalistic ontology. I'll say much more about this before long.

The second tendency in our thinking may be illustrated by another story, also of a sort familiar in metaphysics. But again, we're not doing metaphysics yet; we're just noticing some features of everyday thought. Suppose a sculptor has a spherical piece of clay and decides to reshape it as a cube. Later on he decides to make a statue, say of Daffy Duck. Now, no one would think that in reshaping the clay as a cube, the sculptor produced a different physical object from the original. Nor, I think, would most people think that a new physical object emerged with the statue of Daffy. After all, where would the old one have gone? Now let's imagine that the sculptor tires of Daffy, and reworks the clay into a statue of Goofy.[6] Again it seems dead wrong to think there's a new physical object afoot. It's the same physical object, just reshaped. Good. But of course everyone would agree that it's a different *statue* from the statue of Daffy.

Over the period in question, the sculptor has had a clay sphere, a clay cube, and two different statues, but all the while only one physical object. Now, so far these are just our ordinary thoughts, not high-powered metaphysics. Of course many metaphysicians have found these ordinary thoughts to be very unsettling, and have been moved to theorize. But let's not worry about that now. Let's just concede that we've uncovered another divide in our ordinary thinking, one that parallels the parts divide. It's this. When thought of as an object of a familiar *kind*, like a statue, the arrangement of the parts of a thing is very important. But when thought of as a brute *physical object*, the arrangement of the parts isn't important at all. We can call this *the arrangement divide*, and think of the two tendencies together as *the great divide*.

In a nutshell: We are capable of thinking of things either as objects of familiar kinds or merely as brute physical objects, and both the importance of the parts and the importance of their arrangement vary dramatically depending on which way we think.

I've suggested that I don't think the great divide is bad, that it's a mistake to assume it's somehow incoherent. That maybe the boat owner shouldn't let his opinion "about the physical object" cast doubt on his opinion "about the boat." That maybe the metaphysician shouldn't race to theorize just because there were two statues but only one physical object.

What drives the boat owner to doubt and the metaphysician to theory is the third tendency of ordinary thought. For want of a better term, I'll call it *object fixation* (though, as we'll see, *property repression* might do just as well). It's undeniably a very natural tendency, deeply embedded in our thinking. It's this. We tend to think that since a boat or a statue (etc.) *is* a physical object, any truth *about the boat* is just a truth *about the physical object* (and vice versa). In somewhat different terms, we tend to think that a truth about an object *qua* boat is perforce a truth about the object *simpliciter* (and vice versa).

But it just isn't so. The sculptor who made Goofy could very easily say, "Well, I sure like the statue, but I really hate that piece of clay. It's way too hard to work." Now *certainly* this could be true. The challenge is to figure out how. The sculptor has seemingly expressed a favorable attitude toward a thing of a familiar kind (a statue) and an unfavorable attitude toward a thing of another familiar kind (a piece of clay). One easy hypothesis is that there are really two physical objects involved, clear appearances to the contrary notwithstanding. Of course this violates both the naturalistic ontology and common sense. It should be considered seriously only as a last resort, and luckily we won't have to go that far.

I think what's going on is this. The two attitude reports are *not* just about the physical thing, but in each case about a *property* (that is, a *kind*) as well. Since the properties are different—*being a statue* versus *being a piece of clay*—the *thing* doesn't really threaten to be both liked and disliked by the sculptor. Rather, and merely for a vivid illustration, it's *as if* an ordered pair of the thing and a property is the real object of each of the attitudes. It's as if the sculptor likes <x, *being a statue*> but doesn't like <x, *being a piece of clay*>. Since the two pairs are different, the two attitude reports would be perfectly compatible. A more plausible ultimate treatment would avoid pairs and take *liking*, as an "objectual" attitude, to be a multigrade relation, in this instance linking the sculptor, the physical object, and the property of *being a statue*. Then this very same relation would *fail* to link the sculptor, the object and the property of *being a piece of clay*.[7]

Object fixation can crop up in many ways. I'll briefly mention two. Often when we talk about a thing we presuppose that it's an object of a certain familiar kind. Imagine we're discussing a certain small—say pea-sized—object. But alas, it's mounted on a gold ring and it's a diamond. Most discussions of this object will have built in the presupposition that it's a diamond. Someone may exult, "Omigod, it's so *big*!" Of course this remark is true *in the context*. It's true because the object is, as we easily say, "big for a diamond." But if it *were* taken merely as an assertion about the physical object, it would be false, and object fixation would be the culprit. We would have moved from a truth "about a diamond" to a falsehood "about a physical object." Soon we'll see that a very influential metaphysical argument moves in just this object-fixated way from true considerations explicitly about things of familiar kinds, to false conclusions explicitly about mere physical objects.

Closely related but slightly more veiled occasions for object fixation are discussions about things featuring ordinary proper names. Although there isn't space to defend the claim here, I believe that when we use ordinary names we do so with a presupposition that the thing named is of a specific familiar kind, for example a person, a dog, a statue, or a boat. If this is right, then it is a case of object fixation when someone infers from the fact that, say, *Goofy* has a certain property (for example, *being liked by the sculptor*) that the relevant physical object also has that property. We've already seen that it need not be so. And soon we'll consider yet another widely accepted metaphysical argument that proceeds in just this way to a conclusion that I say just isn't so.

III. Five Philosophical Examples

Now that we've seen the tendencies it's time for the metaphysics. I'd like to discuss five examples that I think reveal how these tendencies produce trouble—in some cases troublesome doctrine—when *modality* enters the picture. In each case I'll suggest how the remedy I have in mind removes the trouble. The first couple of cases contain conflicts between object fixation and one or the other aspect of the great divide.

Example 1. The statue and the clay.

The recent *temporal* story about (the statues) Daffy and Goofy is closely related to the infamous *modal* puzzle of the statue and the clay. For simplicity, imagine that a statue and a piece of clay, ostensibly the same physical object, exist over the same interval of time (and, of course, in the same location). We all agree that "the piece of clay" could have been cubical but "the statue" could not. So, on the face of it, the piece of clay appears to have a "modal property"—*possibly being cubical*—that the statue lacks.

Many smart metaphysicians have gone berserk over this. Without pointing fingers, here's a partial recital of familiar responses. (1) Some have proposed restricting Leibniz' Law. (2) Some have plumped for "contingent identity." (3) Some have held that there are "merely conventional" objects over and above the regular ones. (4) Some have fancied nonstandard "counterparts," claiming that what is one thing might have been two. (5) Some have bitten the multiple-object bullet.

Now I think all these responses are implausible overreactions (and there are others I haven't mentioned that I think are no better). So let me offer a more temperate and plausible response, one that is already embedded in our ordinary thinking, though somewhat confusedly. A statue is a familiar kind of thing, and a piece of clay is also a familiar kind of thing. Of course a single physical object may instantiate both the property of *being a statue* and the property of *being a piece of clay*. Now, we know from the arrangement divide that when we think of a thing as a statue, the arrangement of its parts is very important, but when we think of it as a mere physical thing, the arrangement isn't important at all. And similarly when we think of it as a piece of clay versus when we think of it just as a physical object. Of course importance comes in degrees and, as we normally think, the arrangement of parts does happen to be significantly more important for a *statue* than for a *piece of clay*. So far there is nothing wrong with any of this thinking, I think.

But along comes object fixation, seducing us into thinking that whatever is true of the statue is true of the mere physical thing, and similarly for the piece of clay and the mere physical thing. This is real metaphysical trouble. For now we have a physical object that could have been cubical, and we have a physical object that could not have been cubical. We're cornered. All our options are bad. We can say we have two things, or we can tinker with Leibniz' Law, or mess around with identity, or invoke funny kinds of objects, bifurcating counterparts, or what have you. Whatever we do, I think it's going to be a counter-intuitive metaphysical stretch.

But notice what happens if we refuse to be object-fixated in the first place. Then claims about a statue or a piece of clay aren't just claims about a physical object, but claims about a *property* as well. In particular, when we say the statue couldn't have been cubical, I believe we're saying that some physical thing has the property of *being the statue*, *and* that *that* property is incompatible with *being cubical*. And when we say that the piece of clay could have been cubical, we're saying that some physical thing has the property of *being the piece of clay*, *and* that *that* property *is* compatible with *being cubical*. So there's just one thing. It has the property of being a certain statue and the property of being a certain piece of clay. This thing—of course!—could have been cubical, and if it had it would still have been the piece of clay, but it wouldn't have been the statue for the simple reason that *being the statue* is incompatible with *being cubical*. With a nod to the naturalist ontology, we might add that the *thing* could even have been widely scattered, but of course if it had, then it would not have been either a statue or a piece of clay, for neither of these properties is compatible with *being widely scattered*.

I think this solves the puzzle of the statue and the clay and does so with no exotic metaphysics at all. It just requires taking *properties* as seriously as *things*, and recognizing that when we speak of a thing under the presumption that it is of a certain kind, we're not just speaking of the thing, but of the kind as well. I realize that rejecting object fixation and bringing properties to the forefront takes a lot of getting used to. It runs counter to a deeply entrenched tendency of thought, and in some it faces residual resistance to Platonism as well. But even the single example we've just considered shows it may very well be worth the effort.

Example 2. Mereological essentialism

Mereological essentialism is the doctrine that the parts of any thing are essential to it, in other words, that the thing could not have existed without having precisely the parts it actually does have. Many philosophers, perhaps a large majority, believe this doctrine is obviously false, for they think there are clear counterexamples. But I don't think it's obviously false. In fact, I think it's *true*, and—as we'll see—that it's strongly favored by a clear and distinct thought experiment. If this is right, then there's something wrong with the supposed counterexamples. What's wrong is object fixation.

The counterexamples are always objects of familiar kinds, like boats. It's simple common sense that a boat could have had at least some different parts. After all, this is just the familiar-kind side of the parts divide. Since a given *boat* could have had a different sail, we're supposed to conclude that there's at least one *thing* that could have had a different part, and hence that mereological essentialism is refuted. But the move from the boat to the thing is as explicit a case of object fixation as we'll ever find. And the result is strongly at odds with the *other* side of the parts divide, the physical-object side. So we have a case where one aspect of our ordinary thinking—object fixation—is at odds with another aspect—the physical-object side of the parts divide. The opponent of mereological essentialism doesn't typically see things in these terms, but it is nevertheless what is going on.

The counterexample evaporates, or should I say sinks, when we abandon object fixation. The claim that the *boat* could have had different parts concerns the property of *being the boat* as well as the physical thing that happens to have that property. But it doesn't assert of that physical thing that *it* could have had different parts. Rather, it's the proposition that some thing has the property of *being such and such boat*, and that this property is compatible with the property of *having different parts*. For "the boat" to have had different parts, on this view, would be for a *different* physical object to instantiate the property of *being the boat*. Thus mereological essentialism is fully compatible with the ordinary thought that a boat could have had different parts. There's no counterexample. We reject the object fixation and retain both sides of the parts divide.

Let me give this a slight restatement, mostly for emphasis. There is a certain specific *thing* in the world that happens to have the property of being a specific boat. The property of *being that boat* is indeed compatible with the property of *having different parts*, but the property of *being that thing* is *not*. A *boat* could have different parts, in accordance with the familiar-kind side of the divide. But, in accordance with the physical-object side, a *thing* could not. So a situation in which "the boat" would have had different parts is really one in which a somewhat different thing would have been the boat.

It may be even clearer here than in example 1 that avoiding object fixation takes a good deal of getting used to. But now we see another benefit of doing so. For the "counterexample" case against mereological essentialism has always seemed somehow too cheap and easy. After all, the physical-object side of the parts divide really is a tendency of our ordinary thought.

Perhaps we can reinforce it by turning to the thought experiment that I claimed favors mereological essentialism. I do this not only for its intrinsic interest, but also because it closely resembles certain very celebrated thought experiments, soon to be discussed, from which object-fixated conclusions have frequently been drawn.

According to the naturalistic ontology, any physical stuff in spacetime is a *thing*. *The thing* is nothing more nor less than *the stuff*. Now, even if you don't favor this ontology, I think you can see that adopting it doesn't prejudice the question of mereological essentialism. After all, there's nothing *modal* about the ontology. It just says that any actual stuff is an actual thing. So let's try to relax about this and accept the naturalism for the purpose at hand.

Then often some stuff will have a property like *being a statue* or *being a boat* but, in general, any arbitrary stuff is very likely to lack all such familiar properties. Now let's consider stuff—that is, things—under a "veil of ignorance." Since we're doing abstract metaphysics, it would be undignified to worry about whether the stuff is a diamond or a Ferrari anyway, so we won't. In this egalitarian spirit, imagine some specific stuff. Now try to imagine that stuff existing, but without some of it existing. I really don't think you can do this. I think the closest you can come is to imagine *some of* some specific stuff existing, but without *the rest of it* existing. That's not good enough. When we imagine some specific stuff, we imagine all of it. To imagine less isn't to imagine *it*. To imagine more is to imagine something that has *it* as a proper part.

Now, since any physical thing is just some physical stuff, it follows that we can't imagine a *thing* not having some of the parts it actually has. There can be no better evidence that any physical thing has all of its parts essentially. To reject this evidence is to insist on a *mystical* conception of physical objects, according to which under unspecified conditions they might have had more or fewer parts while retaining their "identity." The mysteriousness of such a view is borne out by the fact that it's very hard to entertain it coherently without seeming to rely covertly on mereological essentialism.[8]

Example 3. Modality de re.

That things have certain nontrivial essential properties has become a central tenet of contemporary metaphysics, largely owing to the impressive efforts of Saul Kripke. *Essentialism*, according to Kripke, is the doctrine of modality *de re*, and his famous and influential thought experiments are aimed at establishing this doctrine. Let's examine one and try to see what it does and does not establish.

Kripke often invited us to consider an ordinary wooden table and asked whether we could imagine a situation in which that very table would not have been made of wood. We were supposed to conclude that we really couldn't imagine such a situation, and this was taken as strong evidence that the table really had to be made of wood. Now I think this is entirely correct. And I also think it's reasonable to call it "essentialism." But it isn't modality *de re*. It's merely the claim that it's necessary that if anything is the table, then it's made of wood (and something is the table). In terms I prefer, it's merely the claim that the property *being the table* isn't compatible with the property *not being made of wood*. Or, more simply, that the property *being the table* entails the property *being made of wood*.

But Kripke does not hesitate to infer that there is some *thing* that has the property *being made of wood* of necessity. This really is modality *de re*, but it *doesn't* follow from the "essentialist" conclusion of the thought experiment just mentioned. It's a glaring case of object fixation. Moreover, it isn't even true. Certainly some stuff that was organized at the molecular level so as to be wood could have been otherwise organized. That stuff, in other words, that thing, need not have been wood at all.

We can make this a bit more vivid by changing the example a little. Can we imagine a situation in which we had this very wooden table but didn't have a table? I hope the answer is no, we can't. Then that's evidence that this wooden table is necessarily a table. This is no surprise, but it isn't *de re*. It's just the obvious fact that the property *being this wooden table* entails the property *being a table* (together with the fact that something is this wooden table). Of course it's necessary that if something is a table, then it's a table. But certainly we can imagine having that very *physical object*, but not having a table. Its parts could have been arranged even at the macrophysical level so that it wasn't a table but was maybe a chair instead, or a widely scattered object, etc. So the *de re* claim not only doesn't follow from the legitimate, "essentialist" conclusion of the thought experiment, it's not even true.

Example 4. Modality de re yet another way.

Kripke also argued frequently for the same sort of conclusion as follows. Suppose, as I think we all really do believe, that Al Gore is a human being (and so not an automaton or an alien, etc.). Now we can easily imagine situations in which Gore would not have been married, or a Democrat, or a candidate, and so on. But we can't imagine a situation in which Gore wouldn't have been human. I agree, and this is powerful evidence that *Gore* is necessarily human. But Kripke would infer the *de re* claim that some *entity* is necessarily human. This is object fixation at work, and again, it doesn't follow. *Gore's* being necessarily human merely reflects the incompatibility of the properties *being Gore* and *not being human*.[9] For simplicity, let's assume with the materialists that some purely physical object instantiates the property of *being Gore*. Certainly that physical object need not have been organized so as to be a human being. I have no difficulty myself in thinking it could have been a flock of birds. So *being that physical object* doesn't entail *being human*, and the object-fixated, *de re* conclusion not only doesn't follow, it's false.

Of course there *are* nontrivial *de re* truths about brute physical objects. Mereological essentialism guarantees this. If object A is a proper part of object B, then B necessarily has A as a part, in other words, *being B* entails *having A as a part*. But no physical object is necessarily human or necessarily made of wood.

Together, I think examples 3 and 4 reveal that although Kripke's famous arguments for essentialism show something very important and even worthy of that name, they don't show something that he—and just about everyone else—assumes they show. The identification of essentialism with modality *de re* is the erroneous product of object fixation.

Example 5. Proper names and rigid designation.

The effects of object fixation aren't confined to metaphysics proper. A widely accepted thesis about ordinary proper names, also prominently urged by Kripke, is that they are *rigid designators*. This thesis is presupposed in a large and diverse body of influential work in philosophy of language, for example on the topic of propositional attitudes. These various theories and proposals are so dependent on this presupposition that they would generally be untenable (or incoherent) if it were wrong. And I think it is wrong.

Kripke's official definition of 'rigid designator' is this: a term is "...a *rigid designator* if in every possible world it designates the same object..."[10] And later he adds, "...a designator rigidly designates a certain object if it designates that object wherever the object exists..."[11]

Let's agree at the outset to ignore very legitimate worries about what Kripke means by 'possible world', whether there really are any, and the like. Even if there were no such worries, I don't believe the definition would capture his main motivating idea at all. I think that idea is certainly correct, but that the definition severely distorts it as a result of object fixation. The rather mind-boggling consequence is that proper names are generally *not* rigid designators after all.

To see this, consider the (imaginary) statue I've been calling 'Goofy'. As we've seen, the arrangement of Goofy's parts is very important because Goofy is a statue. But the physical object that instantiates the property of *being Goofy* exists in many "possible worlds" where it isn't a statue at all. If 'Goofy' is a rigid designator, then it designates that object no matter how it may be shaped. But then, for example, "Goofy could have been cubical" comes out true. And so does "Goofy might not have been a statue," and even "Goofy might have been widely scattered." But Kripke thinks all of these are false. They all violate his intuitive essentialism.

What he really wants—or at any rate needs—is not for 'Goofy' to designate the same *thing* in every possible world, but for it to designate the same *statue* in every possible world. In worlds where the thing isn't a statue, or is a different statue—say *Daffy*—the name 'Goofy' shouldn't designate anything. "Goofy might have been Daffy" is false, in fact it flirts with incoherence. For it violates "the necessity of identity," another principle famously (and rightly) espoused by Kripke, since it requires a world where we have Goofy *and* it is

Daffy. But since Goofy isn't Daffy *here*, it isn't Daffy *anywhere*. Thus it is rather stunning that "Goofy might have been Daffy" would not only be perfectly coherent, but would also be *true*, if 'Goofy' and 'Daffy' really were rigid designators!

The Goofy case is one where the definition fails because object fixation conflicts with the arrangement divide. But fixation can just as easily run afoul of the parts divide. Certainly it's true that the *Titanic* might have had some different parts. But if the name designates the same *object* in every "world" where that object exists, then it *doesn't* designate a *ship* in worlds where, intuitively, the *Titanic* exists but has some different parts. Depending on the details of the case, either the name doesn't designate, or else it designates a scattered object that isn't a ship.

Kripke sometimes explains rigid designation in more appropriate terms. In resisting David Lewis's counterparts, he says, "It is *given* that the possible world contains *this man*...[The man in question is Richard Nixon.] We can point to *the man*, and ask what might have happened to *him*, had events been different."[12] I believe that something like this was his main motivating idea, and that unwitting object fixation led him to express it in terms of mere *objects* instead of appropriate *kinds* of objects.

Despite this, it would be a grave error to think the faulty definition was merely a slip of the tongue, and that what's needed is just an adjustment. The definition is actually a symptom of a fatal systemic disorder. What's needed is a completely different view of proper names and modality. The tip of the iceberg is this. Suppose we want 'Nixon' only to designate a certain *man* in other "worlds" (and 'Goofy' only to designate a certain *statue*, and so on). How can we square this reform with Kripke's trademark commitment to the idea that proper names don't have senses, that they are—in Ruth Marcus's apt phrase— "mere tags"? I don't believe we can. I think names must be acknowledged to have senses after all, that there is no other plausible way of involving the *kinds*. Furthermore, having secured this reform (with or without appeal to senses) what becomes of the identification of essentialism with modality *de re*? After all, getting the right modal results is precisely what forced us to bring the *kinds* into view. It can no longer be reasonable to think that a mere *thing* is a man or a statue of necessity.

IV. Concluding Remarks

I'd like to try to characterize the present view from a slightly wider perspective. I've suggested that lots of philosophical trouble can be avoided if we accept and accommodate two tendencies of ordinary thought while rejecting a third. This is essentially the *opposite* of orthodox philosophical practice, in which the third tendency is *unconsciously* taken for granted and, as a direct result, the first two get blamed for the metaphysical trouble. To put the matter another way, the three tendencies *are* incompatible, so *something* has to go. But orthodox thinking doesn't even notice the third tendency, and so concludes that what has to go is one or another aspect of the first two. My view is that what has to go is the third tendency—the unconscious object fixation—and that when it goes the burden of choosing sides in the great divide goes with it, and so does an important and widely accepted corpus of contemporary philosophical doctrine.

I admit that this is a radical conceptual shift, and a very difficult one at that. It's difficult for all of us simply because object fixation is so deeply embedded in our normal thinking that we don't even notice it. And it's difficult for many because it overthrows a cluster of theses thought to have been established beyond a doubt, theses upon which ongoing work often depends very heavily.

To make the shift is to recognize that properties enter into what we think and say in a much more direct way than even the Platonists among us typically contemplate. This recognition, in turn, exerts a very strong influence on how we should deploy logic in philosophy. We had an early glimmer of this with the example "*a* is green." We needed to see the predicate as contributing the property as a full-fledged constituent of the proposition expressed (because the Doctrine of Constitution tells us that "*a* is green" *means* that *a* instantiates *greenness*). So we need a formula more like '*Iag*' than '*Ga*'.[13] Of course this is not a reform of logic itself, but rather a philosophical constraint on how to use it. The standard way of translating even this simple sentence is object-fixated, and so must be replaced.

Of course the same goes for more complex sentences. The usual translation of, say, "Dogs are necessarily canine" is a formula of first-order modal logic with the last variable occurring free in the scope of a box—the classic symptom of *de re* modality. But I've tried to convince you that such a formula expresses a false proposition. Any *thing* that happens to be a dog could have been arranged in such a way that it wasn't a dog, wasn't canine, wasn't an animal, and so forth. But we still want the *English* sentence to be true. After all, a Kripkean thought experiment convinces us it's true: we try to imagine having a dog without having something canine, and we fail. So the *de re* formula isn't the right translation.

To arrive at a better translation we need to think carefully about what's really going on in the thought experiment. This is especially worth doing because it reveals that object fixation isn't embedded in the experiment itself, but rather in the inferences that it typically inspires. So I believe thinking carefully about the experiment can underscore the importance of making the conceptual shift.

The crucial thing to notice is that in this experiment we *don't* imagine any specific *thing* at all. To summon up (say) a dog-like visual image is simply not to imagine a specific *physical object*, though it might create an illusion of specificity. There's absolutely nothing in the image itself (or in the surrounding mental activity) that makes it represent any specific stuff as opposed to any other similar stuff. So in effect we are imagining an arbitrary thing, but under the proviso that it has the property of *being a dog*. This *property* is what is really essential to our imagining. But that doesn't mean we've ruled out the possibility that a thing that has this property might not have.

When we try to conjure a dog that isn't canine, we fail. But exactly why do we fail? We've just seen that it can't be because we imagine some particular *thing* and then go on to intuit *of it* that *it's* essentially canine. For we don't imagine any specific thing in the first place. What's really going on is that we can't imagine *anything* failing to be canine without also failing to be a dog. As I prefer to put it, it's because *being a dog* entails *being canine*, and we know this perfectly well. *The thought experiment is really about relations between properties, and not about specific things at all.* When we realize this it ceases to be a surprise that the experiment has none of the *de re* punch it is generally believed to have.

A reasonable translation of the English must therefore reflect this, and the *de re* candidate cannot. I think the best translation is the usual *de dicto* formula, *but* with the underlying modal semantics based on the relation of entailment between the properties themselves, and having nothing at all to do with "possible worlds" or the like. The thought experiment isn't about "possible worlds" or "possible dogs." It's about one property's entailing another. What makes "Dogs are necessarily canine" true is nothing more nor less than the fact of this entailment. And our evidence that "Dogs are necessarily canine" is true is nothing more nor less than our inability to imagine the failure of this entailment.

In fact I think *all* modality reduces to standing relations between properties, relations that "supervene" on the intrinsic natures of the properties themselves. This view was lurking in the background in the discussion of the five philosophical examples, where various modal claims were analyzed by appeal to relations of compatibility and entailment between properties. Although I'd like to give more motivation and detail, this is really a different topic, one that will have to wait for another occasion. The present and concluding point is that the conceptual shift I've been recommending runs very deep, so deep that it not only puts Platonic properties at the very center of ordinary thinking, it does so in a way that requires a redeployment of elementary logic in philosophy.[14]

Notes

1. See *Word and Object* (Cambridge, MA: MIT Press, 1960), p. 171. For another example see Mark Heller, *The Ontology of Physical Objects* (Cambridge: Cambridge University Press, 1990).
2. In my opinion suspicion about these consequences is entirely unwarranted. I think we are just making a conventional choice about how widely our (singular) individual-quantifiers will be allowed to range in philosophical discussion of the physical stuff that actually happens to exist. In effect, the naturalistic convention is to allow these quantifiers to coincide in range with the mass-quantifiers of ordinary language. This is a decision utterly devoid of ontological import. The wide-open, naturalistic choice simply makes it easier to discuss physical objects in a general theoretical setting.

3. I should say that I don't actually believe that *individuals*, like the imagined *a*, are propositional constituents. In fact I don't even accept *propositions*, but that is quite another matter. (For details, see "Propositions and the Objects of Thought," forthcoming, *Philosophical Studies*.)

4. Of course synonymy is a two-way street, and some might see this as evidence that apparent reference to properties is *merely* apparent.

5. I will stick with ordinary talk and suppress worries about dimensionality.

6. I have it on the authority of Frank McGuinness that Disney's original name for the Goofy character was "Dipsy Dog." Goofy (the character) is a very interesting dog, for he gives little or no ambulatory evidence of being a quadruped.

7. The multigrade character of this relation accommodates more complex possibilities, such as liking the statue in one way, and not liking it in another, etc. I advocate a similar approach to *propositional* attitudes in the above mentioned "Propositions and the Objects of Thought."

8. Since an arbitrary thing could have had different parts, its *parts* could have had different parts too. Now suppose someone proclaims that an actual thing, say A, with actual proper part B, is such that A could have failed to have B as a part. What could support this idea? Is it that we can imagine the *actual* thing *A–B* existing and then somehow think of it as being *A*? This can't be good enough. For how do we know B wouldn't be part of this very thing *unless* we assume that B couldn't have existed without having its *actual* parts? The fact that B isn't *actually* part of A–B is irrelevant, and *calling* this thing "A–B" in the *imagined* situation just begs the question. Moreover, what would "imagining the actual thing A–B in nonactual circumstances" amount to *in the first place* if we didn't assume it to have its actual parts? The (unjustified) initial idea that "A–B" wouldn't have "B" as a part seems to presuppose that both "A–B" and "B" would have their actual parts. (Intimations of both mereological essentialism and the great divide may be found in Locke's remarks on identity in Chapter XXVII, Book II of the *Essay*.)

9. There isn't space to allow for a discussion of properties like *being Gore*. For present purposes the crucial point is that I think this property entails the property *being human* (and *being Goofy* entails *being a statue*, etc.).

10. Saul A. Kripke, *Naming and Necessity* (Cambridge, MA: Harvard University Press, 1972, 1980), p. 48.

11. *Op. cit.*, pp. 48–9.

12. *Op. cit.*, p. 46. Ironically, the emphasis is Kripke's.

13. Actually, I don't believe that physical objects, like *a*, really *are* propositional constituents, so '*Iag*' can't ultimately be right. To put it a little differently, and with doubts about propositions aside, I don't believe '*a* is green' expresses a *singular* proposition ("about the thing *a*"). I think it expresses (what is intuitively) a general proposition, and so it should be translated by a formula like '$\exists x(Ixa^* \& Ixg)$', with 'a^*' denoting the property of *being a*. But such details don't affect the present considerations.

14. This paper was presented as the ninth annual *Philosophical Perspectives* Lecture at California State University, Northridge, in September, 2000. I would like to thank the audience, especially Cindy Stern, Jim Tomberlin, and Takashi Yagisawa, for a lively and beneficial discussion. I am also grateful to Victor Caston and G. J. Mattey for helpful comments on an earlier version.

THE CASE FOR PHENOMENAL EXTERNALISM

William G. Lycan
University of North Carolina

Since Twin Earth was discovered by American philosophical-space explorers in the 1970s, the domain of "wide" or externalist or extrinsic properties has expanded. Putnam (1975) originally focused just on the meanings of people's linguistic utterances, arguing that two perfect twins, an Earthling and that person's molecular duplicate on Twin Earth in parallel physical surroundings, can utter identical sentences that nonetheless have different meanings. Fodor (1980) and Stich (1978) extended this argument to cover the contents of people's propositional attitudes, so far as those contents comprised concepts of certain sorts, s[.] ch as natural-kind concepts. Stich (1980) then argued that Fodor had undere timated the range of the wide ("...what Fodor sees as a bit I see as the tip of an iceberg" (p. 97)).

That far, the discussion had confined itself to standard cognitive and conative propositional attitudes. Block (1990, 1994, 1996) widened the wide further by granting a sense in which perceptual contents are wide—in which, for example, a same-colored object might look red to me but blue to my molecular twin. Yet Block insisted that there is another and perhaps more important sense in which the perceptual contents are "narrow," i.e., in which the object must look the same color to any molecular duplicate of mine. He calls these narrow perceptual contents "qualia," in a special neologistic sense of that fraught word.

I do not believe in "qualia" in Block's special sense,[1] though I insist on the existence of qualia in a more customary and familiar sense. My purpose in this paper is to argue that qualia in the latter sense are wide. I made that claim and defended it a bit in Lycan (1996), but since then a number of arguments have been given for the contrary thesis that qualia are narrow, so it is time to rejoin the debate.

1. The Representational Theory of Qualia[2]

Qualia in my sense are the introspectible qualitative phenomenal features that characteristically inhere in sensory experiences. The color of an after-image would be a good example, as is the color occupying such-and-such a region of your ordinary visual field right now; other examples are the pitch or the volume of a heard sound, and the smell of a smell. I emphasize that these are phenomenal properties. They may be part of normal, veridical sensory experience; or they may be hallucinatory or otherwise purely subjective, and correspond to nothing in the subject's actual environment.

In previous works I have called qualia "introspectible monadic properties of apparent phenomenal individuals," meaning the characteristic properties of what Russell thought were actual phenomenal individuals, i.e., of what he called sense-data; Russell took qualia in my sense to be first-order properties of sense-data. But my reference to "apparent phenomenal individuals" has sometimes confused readers, since it may be hard to think about "characteristic properties of" sense-data without falling in with the assumption that there really are sense-data. Yet it is crucial to see that one need not believe in sense-data to believe in qualia. Most of us reject Russell's idea that an after-image is an actual and nonphysical individual thing, but if you are experiencing a green after-image, you cannot deny that in some sense there is greenness in your visual field; greenness is *somehow* visually exemplified and present to you. If the greenness is (indeed) not a first-order property of an immaterial sense-datum, then of what is it a property, and/or, what kind of property is it? We must relocate it ontologically. And I maintain (Lycan (1987a, 1987b, 1996)) that this is a very difficult metaphysical problem.

To see the difficulty, suppose that while you are experiencing the after-image, there is in reality no green physical object in your environment.[3] Suppose also that there is no green physical object in your brain (if there were one, you would be in big trouble). But there is a green *something* before you, Russellian sense-datum or not. If there is no green physical object outside your head and no green physical object inside your head, it follows that the green something is a nonphysical object. So much for materialism; it seems that the green something might as well be a sense-datum after all.

Enter the Representational theory, to carry us between the horns of the foregoing dilemma: Notice that each disjunct assumes that the green "something" is an *actual* thing (else we could not derive the unwanted conclusion that there actually exists a nonphysical green thing). The Representational theory affords a third alternative, by supposing that qualia are *intentional contents* of sensory states, properties of intentional objects, represented properties of representata. Of course it is characteristic of intentional contents that they may or may not actually exist; and that is how we evade the dilemma. Your visual system quite often portrays, alleges something green. But, vision being not entirely reliable, on a given occasion the green thing may or may not actually exist.

Suppose Ludwig is seeing a real tomato in good light, and naturally it looks red to him. He is visually representing the actual redness of the tomato, and veridically so. But suppose Bertie is experiencing a green after-image as a result of seeing a red flash bulb go off. According to the Representational theory, that is for Bertie to be visually-representing a filmy green blob located at such-and-such a spot in the room. The representation has a truth-condition involving greenness.

There visually appears to Ludwig to be a red tomato; there visually appears to Bertie to be a green blob. The tomato is real and so is its redness, but the blob is unreal, an intentional inexistent, and so is its greenness. The greenness is the color of an illusory, nonexistent thing. If that seems weird to you, think of hallucinating pink rats. Perhaps you know the rats are not real, but they are unquestionably pink. The pinkness is the color of the nonexistent rats. (I take that to be uncontroversial.[4]) Construing intentionality as representation, we can say that the pinkness is the represented color of the represented but nonactual rats, i.e., it is the color they are represented as having.[5]

Nor should it be surprising that Bertie's blob is a nonactual, nonexistent thing. Since in reality there is no green blob in the room with Bertie, his visual experience is unveridical. Remember that after-images are *illusions*; it looks to Bertie as though there is a green blob before him, when there is not anything green before him. Moreover, vision science has an extensively worked out explanation of this particular illusion. It is well understood why it can look to someone as though there is something green even when there is not anything green before that person.

I contend that Russell mistook a nonactual physical individual for an actual nonphysical one.

There are a number of arguments in favor of the Representational theory, but I will (briefly) state only the three most accessible ones.

First: The theory is the only very promising way to preserve materialism while accommodating qualia. For the only viable alternative exegesis of Bertie seems to be belief in actual Russellian sense-data or at least in immaterial properties. (Jackson (1977), Butchvarov (1980) and Lycan (1987a, 1987b) argue at length that the frantic old "adverbial" dodge of Chisholm (1957, Chapter 5) and Sellars (1967) is hopeless.)

Second: We distinguish between veridical and unveridical visual experiences. Ludwig accurately sees a real tomato, but George Edward hallucinates pink rats. I would take it to be fairly uncontentious that George Edward's experience is, falsely, as of pink rats, and has rats and their pinkness as illusory intentional objects. Likewise, Bertie's experience is as of a green blob and has greenness as an intentional object, and what the experience reports is false. Moreover, the experience's veridicality condition, i.e., there being a green blob where there seems to Bertie to be one, seems to exhaust not only the experience's representational content but its qualitative content. Once the greenness has already been accounted for, what qualitative content is left?

Third (Harman (1990)): We normally "see right through" perceptual states to external objects and do not even notice that we are in perceptual states; the properties we are aware of in perception are attributed to the objects perceived. "Look at a tree and try to turn your attention to intrinsic features of your visual experience. I predict you will find that the only features there to turn your attention to will be features of the presented tree, including relational features of the tree 'from here'" (p. 39).

Harman's transparency argument can be extended also to the purely hallucinatory case. Suppose you are looking at a real, bright yellow lemon in good light. Suppose also that you then hallucinate a second, identical lemon to the right of the real one. (You may be aware that the second lemon is not real.) Phenomenally, the relevant two sectors of your visual field are just the same; the appearances are just the same in structure. The yellowness involved in the second-lemon appearance is exactly the same property as is involved in the first.[6] But if we agree that the yellowness perceived in the real lemon is just the yellowness of the lemon itself, then the yellowness perceived in the hallucinated lemon—the yellow quale involved in the second-lemon appearance—is just the yellowness of the hallucinated lemon itself.

On pain of circularity, the Representational theory requires color realism, for it explicates color qualia in terms of the real- (and unreal-)world colors of physical objects; "yellow" means the objective, public property inhering in physical objects. One could not then turn around and explicate the ostensible colors of physical objects in terms of color qualia (e.g., as the disposition to produce yellow qualia in normal human percipients). Of course, color realism has been a minority position in the history of philosophy, so this must be counted as a liability of the Representational theory. What physical property of a lemon is it yellowness supposed to be? For the record, I buy into D.M. Armstrong's Disjunctive Realism, the view that a color is a wildly disjunctive but perfectly real physical property. (See Armstrong and Malcolm (1984). Lycan (1996, Chapter 4) rebuts some objections to the Disjunctive Realist view.)

2. Internalism and Externalism About Qualia

As I have mentioned, Ned Block has defended properties of a type he calls "qualia," distinct from qualia in my more familiar sense, that are narrow properties. But he has also offered a prominent objection to the Representational theory of qualia in my sense, his (1990) Inverted Earth argument (to which we shall return). And that argument depends on assuming that qualia in my sense are narrow also. In print or in conversation, a number of philosophers (including even Dretske (1996)) have since called that assumption a "deep/powerful/compelling intuition."

I reject that judgment utterly. Until the past few years, the assumption that qualia are narrow has been just that, a gratuitous and unexamined assumption. And only recently, to my knowledge, has any philosopher actually tried to motivate it.[7] In the rest of this paper, I shall first defend the opposing thesis, that qualia in my sense are wide, and then survey and rebut the arguments I have heard for their being narrow.

(By the way, I do not myself need phenomenal externalism for my overall Representationalist project, for I have at least two ways of accommodating narrow qualia if I must (Lycan (1996), Chapter 6). But I would prefer to avoid that, and I also enjoy defending phenomenal externalism out of *amor belli*.)

3. Arguments for Phenomenal Externalism

The arguments I shall give are far from conclusive. I believe they create a presumption; but I will be happy if they only show that qualia internalism is not obviously correct.

(A) If the Representational theory is correct, then qualia are determined by whatever determines a psychological state's intentional content; in particular, the color properties represented are taken to be physical properties instanced in the subject's environment, features detected by our visual systems. What determines a psychological state's intentional content is given by a *psychosemantics*, in Fodor's (1987) sense. But every known plausible psychosemantics makes intentional contents wide, explicating them in terms of relations to things external to the subject. Therefore (still assuming the Representational theory), very probably qualia are wide. Of course, the Representational theory is itself contentious; but if one grants that it is plausible or at least defensible, the further step to externalism is not a giant step.

(B) Suppose qualia are narrow. Then Block's Inverted Earth argument is plausible. The argument is based on an example in which a victim is unknowingly transported to a planet which is exactly like Earth except that its physical colors are inverted with respect to ours. But the victim is fitted with compensating lenses so that s/he does not notice the color switch; s/he is now misperceiving, because s/he sees green objects as red, if it is green Inverted objects that correspond to red Earthly objects under the inversion in question. The Inverted Earthlings' speech sounds just like English, of course, so they do not notice anything odd about the victim. But their intentional contents in regard to color are inverted relative to ours: When they say "red," they mean green, and green things *look* green to them even though they call those things "red."

After some period of time, Block maintains, the victim's embedding in the physical and linguistic environment of Inverted Earth would come to dominate, since s/he would be interacting with the local color environment itself, and speaking the Inverted Earthlings' language. Her/his wide intentional color contents would gradually shift to match those of the surrounding population on Inverted Earth. But the victim's qualia (being supposedly narrow) would not shift. If all the intentional properties would shift but the qualia would not, then the qualia are not intentional properties.

Block's argument would show that either qualia are narrow functional properties or they are narrow properties of a very weird kind whose existence is suggested by nothing else we know (see Chapter 6 of Lycan (1996), in which the weird properties are called "Strange Qualia"and their weirdness is exhibited). But qualia are not functional properties, at least not narrow ones. First, qualia are (ostensibly) monadic properties, while functional properties are all overtly relational. Second and more importantly, Functionalism does nothing to resolve the Russellian dilemma aforementioned. So, either qualia are wide or weirdness is multiplied beyond necessity.[8]

(C) Dretske (1996) argues much as follows: So far as qualia are intentional contents, we must concede that they are distinct from belief contents and other conceptually characterized contents (since one can have qualia themselves without possessing the corresponding concepts). Therefore, one can have qualia without being able to know or even have beliefs about what qualia one has. Suppose qualia are narrow. Then two molecular twins whose intentional contents are all different owing to different environmental surrounds must nonetheless have the same qualia. But neither the twins nor anyone else could ever know or even have reason to think that there were those shared qualia, because neither twin has any concept that applies to them. So there is no reason we should believe in them either.

Dretske's argument is flawed, in that it assumes all knowledge is conceptual. Suppose instead that the twins have a more primitive kind of introspective acquaintance with their qualia. Perhaps they, and we, have a nonconceptual "inner sense" that does the acquainting—"nonconceptual" at least in that it does not mobilize concepts possessed by ordinary whole persons. (Unlike Dretske, I believe that we are equipped with an organ of this kind (Lycan (1995; 1996, Chapter 2)).)

But this would not alleviate the epistemic difficulty. As Moore, Harman and others have pointed out, what introspection reveals in the way of sensory qualities are only the qualities imputed (rightly or wrongly) by the senses to external objects. E.g., when I introspect my visual field in regard to the yellow ellipsoidal patch associated with a lemon that is in front of me, the sensory quality that I find in the visual field is the very yellowness that the experience presents as inhering in the lemon, nothing more. If asked, I would report it using the English word "yellow." Of course, introspection presents a much more specific shade, intensity and saturation of yellow than anyone could express in ordinary English words, and in this sense it is non- or subconceptual. But the same is true of vision itself; nonconceptualness of this sort lends no support to the idea that the yellowness is narrow. And notice that the same argument goes for the yellowness of an hallucinated lemon; the argument does not exploit veridicality.

Thus, as before, even if there were shared qualia underlying the twins' differing intentional contents, neither the twins nor anyone else could ever know or even have reason to think so, this time because neither twin's introspective access reveals any sensory property other than the one that is being represented by her/his visual experience.

Before I turn to my official array of objections, I must address a special one.[9] There is a possibility that the Disjunctive Realist theory of color and a particular psychosemantics for vision might interact in such a way as to make color qualia narrow. Suppose that what unites the Realist's disjuncts for a given color is, in fact, that each of the disjoined physical properties causes the corresponding color sensation in a normal human perceiver under standard conditions. (Lycan (1996, Chapter 4) argues that this need not induce circularity in the Representational theory, so long as the disjunctive property could in principle be identified independently of human perception and the color is not metaphysically explicated in terms of perceivers.) Suppose also that a simple causal psychosemantics is correct: A visual brain state represents a given color if it is normally caused by visual contact with an object of that color. Then, depending on the exact formulation of the psychosemantics, it may follow that molecular duplicates always have the same color qualia. Red things always cause, via their respective physical substrata, sensations of red in normal perceivers under standard conditions; what makes a visual neural state a sensation of red is its being normally caused by a red thing. So there is no possibility of varying the environmental surround in such a way as to have the duplicates' corresponding sensations caused by things of distinct natural color-kinds, even if they are caused by different physical substrata, i.e., by different disjuncts underlying redness.

If these things should turn out to be so, then I would accede to the thesis that qualia are narrow, but maintain that they are, so to speak, only accidentally so. That is, a quale would be narrow, not because of the nature of its containing mental state, but only because of the kind of property the state's intentional object happens to be. (And color qualia would still be "wide" in the sense of being externally referential, though the example would show that that does not suffice for wideness in the core sense of nonsupervenience.)

3. Arguments Against Phenomenal Externalism

(1) Block (1996) offers an argument based on the Inverted Earth victim's memories. But I shall not take up the Memory argument here, since I have already dealt with it in Lycan (1996), and Michael Tye (1998) has responded to it more extensively.

(2) Swampman (Tye (1998); cf. Rey (1998, sec. 2.4)): The Representational theory of qualia, interpreted widely, requires some psychosemantics. Representationalists typically appeal to teleological psychosemantics (at least Lycan (1987) and Dretske (1995) do). But teleology is to be explicated in etiological terms. Therefore an organism's teleological properties require a history of some kind.

Now, suppose a creature is freakishly caused to pop into existence in a swamp, or in outer space, and it happens to be a molecular duplicate of some actual or nonactual human being at a given moment. The creature will have all the same internal properties and all the same behavioral dispositions as the human twin; and so we should expect that the creature has the same qualia as the human. But according to the Representational theory, qualia require representation. If externalist representation itself requires teleology and teleology in turn requires having a history, then externalist representationalism is refuted by the historyless swamp creature; the externalist Representational theory counterintuitively rules that Swampman and other accidental spontaneous replicas of normal sentient creatures lack qualitative experiences entirely.

Reply: First, as Millikan (1984) would have it, perhaps Swampman does lack qualitative experiences at first. (To rebut this suggestion by citing his molecular similarity to his original would simply beg the question of externalism in favor of internalism.) But, second, we must take care to distinguish *teleological theories of representation* from *etiological theories of teleology*. One can easily hold either of those without the other, and actual theorists do so. I myself believe pretty firmly in a teleological requirement on representation, but I am not committed to any particular theory of teleology.

Now, the Swampman type of example was originally mobilized against Larry Wright's etiological theory of teleology.[10] If it succeeds against etiological theories generally, then we should abandon such theories. But that does nothing to impugn or even embarrass teleological theories of representation, which per se are not committed to any particular account of teleology in turn. Nor, I assume, could Swampman be taken to count directly against teleological theories of representation, since some accounts of teleology are forward-looking[11] and would award full teleofunctional properties to him.

(3) If qualia are wide, then there must be a relevant sort of twin earth, on which the relevant twin WGL's sensory state has a different representational content from mine even though he is appeared to in the same qualitative way as I am now. Yet if I were spontaneously transported to that twin earth and took the place of my twin, I would notice nothing introspectively, despite a change in representational content; so my qualia must remain unchanged and so are narrow.

Reply: The same goes for propositional attitudes, i.e., the Earthling transported to Twin Earth would notice nothing introspectively, despite the change in her/his belief and desire contents. Yet the attitude contents are still wide. Wideness does not entail introspective change under transportation.

Throughout this paper, I am assuming the standard Putnamian picture of wide propositional-attitude contents. One may reject it, as does Searle (1983). My thesis is only that if one does accept the Putnamian picture of the attitudes, one has no good reason not to accept it for qualia in my sense as well.

(4) Wilebaldo Lara (1995) has complained that if qualia are wide, then then it is hard to see how the qualities of experiences can affect behavior (which they obviously do); what actually causes behavior must be in the head.

Reply: This is just another instance of the problem of wide intentional causation, much discussed for the cases of belief and desire (e.g., Heil and Mele (1993)). It is a vexing problem, but it is not particularly about qualia. (I would argue that it is not even particularly about the mind; wide, though not intentional, causation occurs in biology, in geology, and even in astronomy.)

(5) In the propositional-attitude literature, both the transportation type of argument and the wide-causation problem have been taken as the bases of arguments for "narrow content," as has the problem of self-knowledge given externalism (Cassam (1994); and see Georgalis (1994)). And, come to think of it, any general argument for narrow content will presumably apply to sensory representation as well as to propositional attitudes. If there is narrow content at all, then, probably sensory states have it too, and so qualia can be taken to be the narrow contents of such states.

Reply: The literature features narrow content or "content" of at least three different kinds. Pursuing my comparison to the Putnam-Fodor line on propositional attitudes, I shall focus just on a kind of narrow content that is supposed to underlie an ordinary wide attitude. The idea is that although I and Twin WGL on Twin Earth have different beliefs because mine is about water and his corresponding one is about the different but superficially similar substance XYZ, impacted within each of those beliefs is a narrow content that we share. I am myself very doubtful of that idea; but suppose it is correct. Suppose further that it extends to sensory contents. Now, even if there are such things as narrow contents underlying sensory states, these still would not correspond to qualia in the sense I have defined. For all that has been shown, the yellowness of a patch in my visual field is still a wide property, even if some other, narrow property underlies it in the same way that narrow contents are supposed to underlie beliefs and desires. On the Putnamian model, it is wide properties that are the ordinary contents of mental states, expressed by and ascribed using ordinary public English words; the narrow contents are not, or not easily, so expressed and ascribed. And qualia in my sense are the sensory contents that do go with public English words such as "yellow."

(6) There is no such thing as representation without a mode of presentation. If a quale is a representatum, then it is represented under a mode of presentation, and modes of presentation may be narrow even when the representational content itself is wide. Indeed, many philosophers of mind, myself included, take modes of presentation to be internal causal or functional roles played by the representations in question. Georges Rey (1998) very reasonably wonders aloud (p. 455, footnote 29) why, since I too believe in modes of presentation under which phenomenal states are given in introspection, I did not consider those modes of presentation as candidates for qualitative content. Are they not narrow qualia?[12]

Reply: Remember, the qualia themselves are properties like phenomenal yellowness and redness and greenness, which according to the Representational theory are representata. The mode or guise *under which* redness and greenness are represented in vision are something else again.

It can plausibly be argued that such modes and guises are qualitative or phenomenal properties of some sort, perhaps higher-order properties. I agree that, in particular, they are appealing candidates for constituting the higher-order property of "what it's like for the subject to experience" the relevant first-order quale. (Notice that qualia in my sense and the higher-order "what it's like" are different properties; they must be, since the latter is a property *of* the former.[13]) But, for the record, there is a problem that arises if we make modes or guises into higher-order qualitative properties: If we suppose that those modes can come apart from the qualia they present to the point of switching or inversion, we get the kind of weirdness scouted in Chapter 6 of Lycan (1996).

(7) Rey (1998), "Wide Semantic vs. Qualitative States" (pp. 442–43):

> [Q]ualitative experience...simply doesn't seem to display any of the standard relational links that are usually intuitively obvious when pointed out in the case of genuinely wide states. *Being a parent* is obviously wide, requiring children; *being a knife wound* requires a knife; and *being a thought about Rembrandt* seems to require Rembrandt. But what does a painful, or a phenomenal red[,] experience require? Not clearly any specific external stimulus; there are phantom limb sensations and endogenously hallucinated red experiences.

Reply: It may be that being a thought about Rembrandt requires the existence of Rembrandt, depending on your view of mental proper names. But more generally, being a thought about X-kind does not require the actual current presence of an X. In what seems exactly the same way, a phenomenal red experience "seems to require" at least one red object—and usually is caused by a red object in the immediate vicinity—even though of course red experiences can be hallucinations. A psychosemantics of color vision might well appeal to the property of being-normally-caused-by-light-waves-reflected-by-a-red-object. The phantom limb example is even better: Tinglings and pains in one's foot "seem to require" having a foot with some damage or disorder in it, but not always; the very same tinglings and pains can occur in the absence of any foot (even though they continue to represent disorder in the foot). Unless I have misunderstood him, Rey is way off here.

(8) On p. 442, Rey makes a point additional to (7): that "*phenomenal similarities and differences don't track wide semantic similarities and differences*" (italics original). Intentional contents are environmentally more malleable than are qualitative contents, or at least our intuitions about intentional contents are more liberal in this regard than are our intuitions about qualitative contents. In a transportation example, most of us are willing to believe that a subject's be-

liefs and other attitudes gradually shift their contents in the direction of the new twin planet. E.g., if I am transported to Putnam's original Twin Earth, the beliefs that I express using the sign-design "water" will gradually stop being about water, i.e., H_2O, and be more and more about XYZ. After a month, or a year, or at any rate a decade on Twin Earth (depending on the frequency of my perceptual contact with the waterish stuff XYZ), my beliefs will be about XYZ and mostly true, rather than about H_2O and often false. But it is implausible to think that on Inverted Earth, qualitative contents would shift in this obliging way. It is very unlikely that after a month, or a year, or maybe even a decade, red things would start *looking green* to me, even though I quickly learned to call them "green" and perhaps even came to *believe that* they are green.[14] Color qualia do not change as readily under environmental pressure as color beliefs do.

Reply: It may be true that belief contents are fairly malleable. (I do not respect Block's own reason for thinking that, which presupposes that belief content shallowly and slavishly tracks local word meanings; though I do generally endorse Sellars' view of the priority of public language to thought, I cannot go *that* far.[15]) But belief contents are not the appropriate point of comparison. The Representational theory of qualia does not identify qualia with belief contents, even with the contents of specifically perceptual beliefs. It identifies them with the contents of sui generis perceptual representations.

Perceptual contents differ from cognitive attitude contents in each of a number of respects. It is probable that one such way is grounded in the comparative modularity of sense modalities (Fodor (1983)): Vision, for example, is informationally encapsulated and (at the level of sensory qualities, pace Hanson (1958), Gombrich (1960) et al.) fairly well insulated from the subject's beliefs; this is the lesson of optical illusions. Belief and memory contents might shift under transportation between Twin planets, while visual contents remain determined by nature and by the structure and teleology of the visual system, not by common-sense propositional attitudes. That would explain Block's view (which I share) that the look of a tomato would remain the same even if belief and memory contents changed. And the explanation strikes me as very plausible; and it also explains why we intuitively think that qualia would not shift as easily as attitude contents might.

(9) A problem about modelling a shift of qualia: Even if perceptual contents do not shift in the way attitude contents (arguably) do, perhaps they would eventually shift—say after one or more centuries, if a subject could stay alive that long. After all, they are wide according to me, and environments do change. But how would a distinctive quale even imaginably undergo such a shift? For example, suppose that a quale is supposed to shift from blue to yellow. A shift from blue to yellow might reasonably be supposed to be a smooth and gradual shift along the spectrum that passes through green. But it is hardly plausible that one would experience such a shift, or a period of unmistakable greenness in particular.

Reply: We really have no plausible model for a shift of everyday attitude content either. How would a type of belief state smoothly go from being *about blue* to being *about yellow*? Presumably not by being about green in between.[16] So our presumed quale shift is no worse off than the attitudinal shift in this regard; if the present argument works for the former case, it also works for the latter, contrary to hypothesis.

(10) Rey (1998), "Non-Transparency" (pp. 440–42): Even if the Moore-Harman transparency thesis holds for perceptual states, moods and bodily sensations do not have the same transparent character. "Many have noted that states like that of elation, depression, anxiety, pleasure, orgasm seem to be just overall states of *oneself*, and not 'features of presented objects'" (p. 441, italics original).

Reply: We should grant that the qualia presented by bodily sensations such as orgasm, pains and temperature are narrow in the usual sense. For even if such sensations are intentional—as Lycan (1996) argues—their intentional objects are parts of the subject's own body, and so the subject's molecular duplicates will share them. (Though, n.b., there will be more exacting sense in which they are still wide, if we draw the boundary of where the "subject" leaves off closer to the central nervous system and properly within the skin.) I suspect that this narrowness of bodily-sensation qualia is an important source of the notion that qualia generally are narrow, for it is likely that philosophers extrapolate from the narrowness of bodily-sensory qualia and impute it without thinking to color- and other world-perceptual qualia; it is tempting to assimilate the "feels" of perceptual states to those of sensory states, so far as we consider perceptual states to have feels. But the "feel" terminology suits perceptual states less well than it does bodily-sensory states. Bodily sensations are themselves conceived as *feelings*, while perceptual states are not. Thus, it would be fallacious to infer that since bodily qualia supervene on molecular constitution, perceptual qualia do also.

What about "whole-person" states such as elation, depression, and free-floating anxiety? I agree that their felt phenomenal characters are not "features of presented objects." So they do not have qualia in our strict Lewisian sense (though they can lend phenomenal features to presented objects, and so can be closely accompanied by qualia). The Representational theory does not apply.

For what it's worth, I believe the "whole-person" states are representational nonetheless. Elation represents one's surroundings, or if extreme the whole world, as being beautiful and benign.[17] Depression represents proposed actions as unrewarding and the subject as generally unworthy. Anxiety represents there being some impending harm or disaster. But I do not contend that these representational contents exhaust the overall "feel" or subjective character of the states in question. (Here and elsewhere I distinguish an "overall subjective character" from qualia strictly construed; see Lycan (1998, pp. 484ff.).) Functional and other dispositional elements are crucial to those states as well, probably a good deal more important to their subjective characters as are their representational contents.[18]

(11) In discussion following a presentation of Lycan (1998), Kent Bach and David Chalmers raised a more serious concern: *Natural representation* admits of various indeterminacies. One is in complex Twin-Earth travel scenarios, where there seems to be no fact of the matter about which duplicate a mental symbol refers to (cf. Rey, pp. 443–44). Another might be in a long-term evolutionary process, when for some centuries it is vague whether or not some etiological explicans is satisfied. Now, on the Representational theory of qualia, qualia ought to inherit those indeterminacies and/or vaguenesses. But (version 1) qualia are not vague and indeterminate at all; either you have a red blob in your visual field or you do not. Or even if we agree with Dan Dennett that there is a lot less determinacy in the visual field than philosophers think, (version 2) qualia are not vague and indeterminate *in the same way(s)* that representation is on any going psychosemantics. (Are our biblical beliefs really about Moses, a real person? How about King Arthur? Which twin is my belief about, if I do not realize that there are two of them?)

Reply: Problems of this sort have beset the psychosemantics of belief and thought (since almost all that has been written in the way of psychosemantics has been about belief and thought). But the psychosemantics of sense modalities is going to be different, in each of three ways. First, modularity again; a sense modality like vision is informationally encapsulated and fairly hardwired, processing highly restricted sorts of inputs in comparatively rigid ways; and each module has an identifiable function. Second, more specifically, the function of any sense modality is feature detection, and the proprietary features in question are comparatively few and determinate. Third, as perceptual psychology continues to advance, it is becoming clearer that the main task of a given modality is to map that modality's distinctive quality space. (Cf. Churchland (1989, Ch. 7, sec. 7): Discrimination along each of Edwin Land's three color axes (short wave, medium wave and long wave reflectances) yields a huge 3-space of possible color-visual states; taste has four dimensions generated by the four kinds of receptors found in our mouths, and any humanly possible taste will be represented as a point in the resulting 4-space, more concretely a quadruple of spiking frequencies.)

For each of these three reasons, the psychosemantics of a sense modality can be expected to be far more tightly constrained than that of belief or thought. The teleological job description of a given module will specify a proprietary range of features that the relevant organ is to detect. A module will be (veridically or not) detecting a given feature or not. The determinacy of receptor sets and of the resulting state spaces will not leave much room for indeterminacy as to what is represented. And that, I believe, is why qualia are determinate in ways that belief- and other marshmallow-state contents are not.[19]

(12) Horgan (2000): A brain in a vat whose stream of consciousness is engineered to be exactly like yours would have exactly the sequence of perceptual and other intentional states that you do. Since the brain's external surround would be entirely unlike yours, the intentional contents it shares with you must be narrow contents.

Reply: Non sequitur. From the viewpoint of psychosemantics, brain-in-vat cases have always been seriously underdescribed. Until the scenario is much better fleshed out, we can't say what the brain's intentional contents would be. Simply to assert that they are the same as yours begs the question.

And cf. my reply to (3) above; introspective indistinguishability does not show narrowness.

(13) In a paradigm case of a kind-term having wide content, one can make a direct Twin-Earth argument (cf. Rey, pp. 439–40). E.g., what is called "water" on Twin Earth is not water but XYZ; or the things that look like tigers are not tigers and the tigers look like donkeys. Accordingly, there is a "fool's" distinction: Just as iron pyrites is not gold but fool's gold, so XYZ is only fool's water and the tigerish beasts on Tiger Earth are only fool's tigers. And the contents of our various Twins' thoughts and other representations differ from ours despite the aliens' perfect molecular similarity to us Earthlings. But it is hardly obvious that the green objects on Inverted Earth count as "fool's red" for Block's victim, or that there could be any "fool's red" at all.[20]

Suppose we agree that an object is red iff the object would look red to a normal percipient under standard lighting conditions. (My Armstrongian Disjunctive Realism is committed to that biconditional, even though the theory does not *explicate* redness in terms of looking red.) It follows that if an object looks red to a normal percipient in standard conditions, then the object is red. From which it seems to follow in turn that there can be no such thing as "fool's red."

Reply: To show the wideness of looking-red, the problem is to come up with a case in which two molecular duplicates, say Georges and some twin Georges, experience different color looks, red and, as it might be, green. Let us grant that the twins must be in the same neuroanatomically described visual state N_r (actually I doubt that even neuroanatomy is narrow). So Georges and the twin are both in N_r but supposedly in Georges this constitutes an object's looking red to him while in the twin it constitutes the corresponding object's looking green to him.

For expository purposes let us start with a naïve and casual psychosemantics of "typical causes": A visual state such as N_r will represent redness iff that state is typically caused by irradiation of the retina produced by a red object. Now consider a planet, Light Earth, which is like ours except that on its surface the ambient light is strange. The light is such that green objects almost always cause normal percipients to go into N_r, and N_r is almost always produced in normal percipients by green objects. According to the naïve psychosemantics, then, N_r in Light Earthlings will represent greenness, and green objects will look green to them. If the relevant twin of Georges is Light Georges on Light Earth, we have our example of molecular duplicates visually representing different colors, hence experiencing different color looks. Moreover, if (original) Georges were to be suddenly transported to Light Earth and look at a green object, he would go into N_r, which for him represents red; so the green object would look red to him and he would be fooled. Thus, for Earthlings, green objects on Light Earth would be fool's-red. (The foregoing argument against the possibility of fool's redness is blocked by the stipulation that the lighting on Light Earth is not standard. Nor may it be replied á la Block that the greenness present in Light Georges' visual state is only a shallow matter of word meaning or belief content and really has a red quale underneath it, for that would simply beg the question.)

I myself reject the naïve psychosemantics, for reasons related to what I have said in reply to the previous objection. What happens if we replace it by a psychosemantics based on having feature detection as a function? I do not see that this change would undercut the example. If the light on Light Earth has always been weird in the same way, then we may coherently suppose that in Light Earthlings N_r has the function of indicating green objects, and the argument goes through as before; molecular twins visually represent different colors, and so far as has been shown, that constitutes their experiencing different color looks, period.

There is an obvious further objection to the Light Earth argument: that Light Earth's strange light is standard or normal *for Light Earth*, however weird it may be from the Earthling point of view. So when the original Georges arrives suddenly on Light Earth, sees the green object and goes into N_r, he is a normal percipient in what is locally standard lighting, so (according to our previous biconditional formula) the green object would look green, not red, to him, and so it is not fool's-red after all.

But this is a problem for the present version of Disjunctive Realism about color, not for the wideness of qualia. The problem stems from the biconditional formula, that was licensed by the Disjunctive Realist theory, which would have to be restricted in light of the apparent environment-relativity of "normal," "standard" and such terms. My own view is that we are entitled to take those terms as defined geocentrically, by reference to Earth rather than Light Earth, because they are words of English rather than of Light English. But, granted, this is a large subject.

Conclusion: Not everyone will accept all of the foregoing replies. But I hope no one will continue to find it obvious that qualia are narrow.[21]

Notes

1. See Chapter 6 of Lycan (1996).

2. Lycan (1987a, 1987b, 1996), based on Anscombe (1965) and Hintikka (1969). See also Thomason (1973), Adams (1975), Kraut (1982), Lewis (1983), Harman (1990), Dretske (1995) and Tye (1995).

3. This argument is reprised from Chapter 8 of Lycan (1987a).

4. The *metaphysics of* nonexistence is of course another matter. Another reason that the Representational theory may seem weird is that one cannot go into the metaphysics of nonexistence without getting weird. But that is everyone's problem, not the Representational theory's in particular. For our purposes here, just remind yourself that of course, in some sense, there are things that do not exist, and plug in your own favorite account of the nonactual. (My own view of the nonactual is defended in Lycan (1994).)

5. A surprising but harmless consequence of this view is that qualia are not themselves properties of the experiences that present them: Qualia are represented properties of represented objects, and so they are only intentionally present in experiences. As before, the relevant properties *of* the experiences are, representing this quality or that.

6. Since Moore, Malinas (1975) is the first I know to make this point.

7. Most notably at the SOFIA conference held in Cancun, Q.R., Mexico, in June of 1995. See Villanueva (1996).

8. Of course there may be narrow representational properties. Rey (1998) defends a narrow representationalist theory of items he calls "qualia," but those items, like Block's, are not qualia in my sense (see Lycan (1998), p. 482). Horgan (2000) advocates a narrow representationalist theory also.

9. It was put to me a few years ago by an audience member at York University, and recently by Jesse Prinz.

10. Boorse (1976), Wright (1973). Millikan (1984) entertains a similar example as an anticipated objection to her own etiological theory. The term "Swampman" is Donald Davidson's (1987).

11. E.g., that of Bigelow and Pargetter (1987).

12. Rey goes on to compare experiences' qualitative representational contents to the narrow contents of indexical sentences like "I am ill" and "I am wounded." There is no denying that such sentences have a kind of meaning that is independent of their referential truth-conditions; as Kaplan (1979) has emphasized, any competent English speaker *knows* their meanings without knowing who they refer to or what propositions they express. And I agree that such contents or schmontents—actually I think they are just what Kaplan calls "characters"—carry the kind of ineffability that Rey says they do (p. 450). But by that point in his paper Rey is talking about something other than a quale in my strict sense; see again Lycan (1998), p. 482.

13. For two further reasons why qualia in my sense and "what it's like" are distinct, see Lycan (2000). The distinction is obscured by some writers' using the phrase "what it's like" to mean merely qualia in my sense; Dretske (1995) and Tye (1995) do this. Carruthers (2000) is also good on this topic.

14. As I have noted, Block disagrees, since he thinks as I do that English "looks" expressions such as "looks green" express wide intentional contents. Nonetheless I side with Rey on the present point.

15. Nor as far as to accept Sellars' claim that animals do not have intentional states.

16. One suggestion would be to understand the semantic shift in terms of Hartry Field's (1973) notion of "partial reference." I do not find that notion at all plausible, but there is not space to digress on that here.

17. In Robert Benchley's meditation on dentistry, "The Tooth, the Whole Tooth, and Nothing But the Tooth," he evinces the elation that follows release from the dentist's chair (remember, this was dentistry circa 1920, not the comparatively painless dentistry that we enjoy today):

> Heigh-ho! Here's the elevator man! A charming fellow! You wonder if he knows that you have just had a tooth filled. You feel tempted to tell him and slap him on the back. You feel tempted to tell everyone out in the bright, cheery street. And what a wonderful street it is too! All full of nice, black snow and water. After all, Life is sweet!

(*Inside Benchley*, New York: Harper and Bros., 1921, p. 83.)

18. Rey's "Non-Transparency" argument has a second half, involving an example of a well compensated color-blindness victim. But I do not yet understand the example. It is underdescribed, and in any case I do not see how it is supposed to show that any quale is narrow.

19. Objection: There is still notorious indeterminacy even in the simple perceptual states of lower animals. Does the frog represent flies, food, small dark moving objects, or black blobs? I say, yes. (All of the above.) See the Layering Thesis defended in Chapter 7 of Lycan (1996).

20. Malinas (1975) expresses doubts that here could be Twin-Earth-style examples for color properties. It is salutary that Malinas made that comparison so soon after the publication of Putnam's original article.

21. Thanks to audiences at the University of Arkansas, the North Carolina Philosophical Society (February, 1999), the Australasian Association of Philosophy Conference (July, 2000), Duke University, and Washington University in St. Louis, for their helpful discussion. And thanks especially to Joe Levine and to Güven Güzeldere for their formal commentaries, at Arkansas and at the NCPS respectively, as well as to Dave Chalmers for helpful correspondence.

I am especially grateful to Washington University for appointing me as Clark Way Harrison Visitor in the Fall semester of 2000, during which period I finished this paper. The hospitality of faculty, graduate students and staff was bountiful and is much appreciated.

References

Adams, E.M. (1975), *Philosophy and the Modern Mind*, Chapel Hill, NC: University of North Carolina Press.

Anscombe (1965), "The Intentionality of Sensation: A Grammatical Feature," in R.J. Butler (ed.), *Analytical Philosophy: Second Series*, Oxford: Basil Blackwell.

Armstrong, D.M., and N. Malcolm (1984), *Consciousness and Causality*, Oxford: Basil Blackwell.

Bigelow, J., and R. Pargetter (1987), "Functions," *Journal of Philosophy* 84: 181–96.

Block, N.J. (1990), "Inverted Earth," in Tomberlin (1990).

Block, N.J. (1994), "Qualia," in S. Guttenplan (ed.), *A Companion to the Philosophy of Mind*, Oxford: Basil Blackwell.

Block, N.J. (1996), "Mental Paint and Mental Latex," in Villanueva (1996).

Boorse, C. (1976), "Wright on Functions," *Philosophical Review* 85: 70–86.

Butchvarov, P. (1980), "Adverbial Theories of Consciousness," in P. French, T.E. Uehling and H. Wettstein (eds.), *Midwest Studies in Philosophy, V: Studies in Metaphysics*, Minneapolis: University of Minnesota Press.

Carruthers (2000), *Phenomenal Consciousness*, Cambridge: Cambridge University Press.

Cassam, Q. (ed.) (1994), *Self-Knowledge*, Oxford: Oxford University Press.

Chisholm, R. (1957), *Perceiving*, Ithaca, NY: Cornell University Press.

Churchland, P.M. (1989), *A Neurocomputational Perspective*, Cambridge, MA: Bradford Books/ MIT Press.

Davidson, D. (1987), "Knowing One's Own Mind," *Proceedings and Addresses of the American Philosophical Association* 60: 441–58.

Dretske, F. (1995), *Naturalizing the Mind*, Cambridge, MA: Bradford Books/MIT Press.

Dretske, F. (1996), "Phenomenal Externalism," in Villanueva (1996).

Field, H. (1973), "Theory Change and the Indeterminacy of Reference," *Journal of Philosophy* 70: 462–81.

Fodor, J.A. (1980), "Methodological Solipsism Considered as a Research Strategy in Cognitive Psychology," *Behavioral and Brain Sciences* 3: 63–73.

Fodor, J.A. (1983), *The Modularity of Mind*, Cambridge, MA: Bradford Books/MIT Press.

Fodor, J.A. (1987), *Psychosemantics*, Cambridge, MA: Bradford Books/MIT Press.

Georgalis, N. (1994), "Asymmetry of Access to Intentional States," *Erkenntnis* 40: 185–211.

Gombrich, E.H. (1960), *Art and Illusion*, New York: Pantheon Books.

Hanson, N.R. (1958), *Patterns of Discovery*, Cambridge: Cambridge University Press.

Harman, G. (1990), "The Intrinsic Quality of Experience," in Tomberlin (1990).

Heil, J., and A. Mele (eds.) (1993), *Mental Causation*, New York: Clarendon Press.

Hintikka, K.J.J. (1969), "On the Logic of Perception," in N.S. Care and R.H. Grimm (eds.), *Perception and Personal Identity*, Cleveland, OH: Case Western Reserve University Press.

Horgan, T. (2000), "Narrow Content and the Phenomenology of Intentionality," Presidential Address to the Society for Philosophy and Psychology, New York City (June, 2000).

Jackson, F. (1977), *Perception*, Cambridge: Cambridge University Press.

Kaplan, D. (1979), "On the Logic of Demonstratives," in P.A. French, T.E. Uehling and H.K. Wettstein (eds.), *Contemporary Perspectives in the Philosophy of Language*, Minneapolis: University of Minnesota Press.

Kraut, R. (1982), "Sensory States and Sensory Objects," *Noûs* 16: 277–95.

Lara, W. (1995), commentary on Dretske (1996), SOFIA, Cancun, Q.R., Mexico (June, 1995).

Lewis, D. (1983), "Individuation by Acquaintance and by Stipulation," *Philosophical Review* 92: 3–32.

Lycan, W.G. (1987a), *Consciousness*, Cambridge, MA: Bradford Books/MIT Press.

Lycan, W.G. (1987b), "Phenomenal Objects: A Backhanded Defense," in J. Tomberlin (ed.), *Philosophical Perspectives, 1: Metaphysics, 1987*, Atascadero, CA: Ridgeview Publishing.

Lycan, W.G. (1994), *Modality and Meaning*, Dordrecht: Kluwer Academic Publishing.

Lycan, W.G. (1995), "Consciousness as Internal Monitoring, I," in J. Tomberlin (ed.), *Philosophical Perspectives, 9: AI, Connectionism and Philosophical Psychology*, Atascadero, CA: Ridgeview Publishing.

Lycan, W.G. (1996), *Consciousness and Experience*, Cambridge, MA: Bradford Books/MIT Press.

Lycan, W.G. (1998), "In Defense of the Representational Theory of Qualia (Replies to Neander, Rey and Tye)," in Tomberlin (1998).

Lycan, W.G. (2000), "Representational Theories of Consciousness," in E.N. Zalta (ed.), *Stanford Encyclopedia of Philosophy* (Summer 2000 Edition), URL = http://plato.stanford.edu/archives/fall1999/entries/consciousness-representational/.

Malinas, G.A. (1975), "Sensations and Understanding," *Australasian Journal of Philosophy* 53: 36–45.

Millikan, R.G. (1984), *Language, Thought, and Other Biological Categories*, Cambridge, MA: Bradford Books/MIT Press.

Putnam, H. (1975), "The Meaning of 'Meaning'," in K. Gunderson (ed.), *Minnesota Studies in the Philosophy of Science, Vol. VII: Language, Mind and Knowledge*, Minneapolis: University of Minnesota Press.

Rey, G. (1998), "A Narrow Representationalist Account of Qualitative Experience," in Tomberlin (1998).

Searle, J. (1983), *Intentionality*, Cambridge: Cambridge University Press.

Sellars, W. (1967), *Science and Metaphysics*, London: Routledge and Kegan Paul.

Stalnaker, R. (1996), "On a Defense of the Hegemony of Representation," in Villanueva (1996).

Stich, S.P. (1978a), "Autonomous Psychology and the Belief-Desire Thesis," *Monist* 61: 573–91.

Stich, S.P. (1980), "Paying the Price for Methodological Solipsism," *Behavioral and Brain Sciences* 3: 97–98.

Thomason, R. (1973), "Perception and Individuation," in M. Munitz (ed.), *Logic and Ontology*, New York, NY: New York University Press.

Tomberlin, J.E. (ed.) (1990), *Philosophical Perspectives, 4: Action Theory and Philosophy of Mind*, Atascadero, CA: Ridgeview Publishing.

Tomberlin, J.E. (ed.) (1998), *Philosophical Perspectives, 12: Language, Mind, and Ontology*, Atascadero, CA: Ridgeview Publishing.

Tye, M. (1995), *Ten Problems of Consciousness*, Cambridge, MA: Bradford Books/MIT Press.

Tye, M. (1998), "Inverted Earth, Swampman, and Representationism," in Tomberlin (1998).

Villanueva, E. (ed.) (1996), *Philosophical Issues, 7: Perception*, Atascadero, CA: Ridgeview Publishing.

Wright, L. (1973), "Functions," *Philosophical Review* 82: 139–68.

Philosophical Perspectives, 15, Metaphysics, 2001

NATURALISM: FRIENDS AND FOES

Penelope Maddy
University of California, Irvine

These days, it seems there are at least as many strains of naturalism as there are self-professed naturalistic philosophers. My personal favorite has its primary roots in Quine, though it branches off from Quinean orthodoxy at some fundamental points.[1] Unfortunately, when it comes to spelling out the precise contours of this preferred version, there is an immediate difficulty: naturalism, as I understand it, is not a doctrine, but an approach; not a set of answers, but a way of addressing questions. As such, it can hardly be described in a list of theses; it can only be seen in action.[2] And this is a long-term undertaking.[3]

What I propose to do here is to triangulate on the position in two ways that I hope will be illuminating. For the first perspective, I trace three conspicuous earlier flowerings of this naturalistic impulse; though I won't agree with every opinion of these proto-naturalists, a look at their practices provides us with models of the fundamental naturalistic bent in familiar philosophical settings. For the second perspective, I take up a range of well known objections to 'naturalism'—including its purporting interconnections with the theory of truth, a recurring theme in many discussions, pro and con—and indicate how the naturalist I envision would react. In the end, I hope at least to have clarified the outlines of the position I recommend. If it also comes off as reasonable, so much the better.

I. Roots

The first story I want to tell begins with Kant, not an easy philosopher to discuss briefly.[4] To make things simple, let me suggest, without further discussion, that one attractive way of reading Kant's notorious combination of empirical realism with transcendental idealism is to distinguish two levels of inquiry: empirical and transcendental. In empirical inquiry, we use ordinary scientific methods to investigate an objective world of spatiotemporal objects interconnected by causal relations. So, for example, we might infer the existence of an unobservable because it is related to what we do observe by causal laws. In transcendental inquiry, on the other hand, we recognize that this 'objective' world is in fact partly constituted by our discursive cognitive structures (the pure categories) and our human forms of sensible intuition (space and time); we realize that, viewed transcendentally, certain elements of the world—its spatiotemporality, its causal structure—are not real, but ideal.

To call this ideality 'transcendental' is to distinguish spatiotemporality and causality from mere accidents of human cognition that might be studied at the empirical level; rather, they are necessities for any discursive intellect with our forms of intuition, and the forms of intuition are necessities of human cognition. It follows that we can know a priori that the world of our experience will be spatiotemporal and causally structured, and indeed, that spacetime and causation will satisfy certain a priori principles also gleaned by this transcendental analysis. So the spatiotemporal, causally conditioned world is real, viewed empirically, but ideal, viewed transcendentally, and this transcendental ideality is what makes a priori knowledge possible.

While it is clear that transcendental inquiry must differ markedly from empirical inquiry if results of these sorts are to be achieved, it is not so clear what tools or methods or principles *are* involved, or what justifies them. As commentators have noted, many of the transcendental claims of the *Critique* seem not to qualify as knowledge claims at all by the explicit standards of that work. On top of this comes the further, well known embarrassment that modern science has falsified Kant's supposedly a priori Euclidean geometry and undermined the supposedly inescapable notion of causality.

The task of the many neo-Kantians has been to find a satisfying reaction to these challenges. In the 1920s, those distinctive neo-Kantians who would soon become logical empiricists or logical positivists focused particularly on how Kant could be reconciled with Einstein. Two of these were Reichenbach and Carnap, the one in Berlin, the other in Vienna. Let's begin with the Berliner.

Reichenbach's noble neo-Kantian effort revolved around an attempt to preserve something of the Kantian notion of a priori by dividing it into two notions. The idea was to separate 'certain truth' and 'prior to (partly constitutive of) knowledge', with the thought of preserving only the later. In this way, a priori principles (that is, constitutive principles), like those that produce Euclidean geometry, could be revised on empirical grounds.[5] In reply, Schlick argued that any properly Kantian philosophy must identify these two notions:

> Now I see the essence of the critical viewpoint in the claim that these constitutive principles are *synthetic a priori judgements*, in which the concept of the *a priori* has the property of apodeicticity (of universal, necessary and inevitable validity) inseparably attached to it. (Schlick [1921], p. 323)

In the end, Reichenbach came to agree that claims subject to empirical confirmation or disconfirmation could hardly be considered a priori:

The evolution of science in the last century may be regarded as a continuous pro-cess of disintegration of the Kantian synthetic a priori. ...the synthetic principles of knowledge which Kant had regarded as *a priori* were recognized as *a posteriori*, as verifiable through experience only and as valid in the restricted sense of empirical hypotheses. (Reichenbach [1936], p. 145; Reichenbach [1949], p. 307)

Thus began Reichenbach's move from neo-Kantianism to logical empiricism.[6]

For our purposes, what's most important in all this is the attitude towards philosophizing that Reichenbach developed as he charted his course away from Kant's transcendental method. Consider once again the Kantian scheme: there are the methods of science, at the empirical level, and the methods of transcen-dental analysis, at the transcendental level; the transcendental method produces additional insights, one might even say corrections, to the empirical theorizing of science; ordinary scientific methods are fine for scientific purposes, but for deeper understanding, we must turn to the transcendental. But Reichenbach comes to oppose those who believe

that philosophical views are constructed by other means than the methods of the scientist...(Reichenbach [1949], p. 289)

Instead, he holds that

[M]odern science...has refused to recognize the authority of the philosopher who claims to know the truth from intuition, from insight into a world of ideas or into the nature of reason or the principles of being, or from whatever super-empirical source. There is no separate entrance to truth for philosophers. The path of the philosopher is indicated by that of the scientist...(ibid., p. 310)

Of Kant's two levels, Reichenbach admits the cogency only of the empirical, the scientific. Philosophy is part of science, conducted by scientific means.

This reaction of Reichenbach's to the Kantian two-level system embodies what I consider the fundamental naturalistic impulse: a resolute skepticism in the face of any 'higher level' of inquiry that purports to stand above the level of ordinary science. The naturalistic philosopher is a member of the scientific community; she regards the methods of science as her own, as the best meth-ods we have for finding out what the world is like; until some new method is clearly proposed and defended, she is unimpressed by philosophical systems that place a second level of analysis above that of science. Reichenbach frankly adopts just such a stance in the face of Kantian transcendentalism. In light of scientific progress, he abandons the goal of a Kantian a priori knowledge; he sets out instead, armed only with ordinary scientific methods, to study science itself. In place of the old 'constitutive' quasi-a-priori, he now attempts to sep-arate the definitional or conventional elements from the empirical elements in our scientific theorizing.[7] Whatever we may think of the actual results of his analyses, we must recognize that a distinctive approach has been staked out.

To isolate the second episode of proto-naturalist sentiment, let's return to the neo-Kantian Carnap, back in Vienna.[8] Like Reichenbach, Carnap hoped to preserve the Kantian idea that certain elements of our knowledge are 'constitutive', and again like Reichenbach, he sought these elements in the conventional or definitional. But here the similarity ends. Even in his neo-Kantian phase, Reichenbach favored careful analysis of actual scientific theorizing, but Carnap, inspired in this case by Russell, turned instead to logic.[9] Early on, this orientation produced an attempt to construct ordinary physical objects of everyday experience, by logical means, out of a sensory 'given';[10] later, it produced a focus on language and syntax. To see how this difference between Reichenbach and Carnap plays out, let's turn to Carnap's fully positivistic self, the Carnap of linguistic frameworks and the principle of tolerance.[11]

The general features of Carnap's thinking are familiar. A linguistic framework consists of a set of names, variables, predicates, connectives, quantifiers, etc., a set of formation rules for forming sentences from these, a set of primitive assumptions and deductive and evidential rules. So, for example, there is a linguistic framework for a 'thing language' with classical logic; there is a linguistic framework for arithmetic with intuitionistic logic; there is a linguistic framework for general relativity with complex geometric and mathematical machinery; and so on. Carnap's idea is that we are free to choose any of these linguistic frameworks that suit our purposes:

> *In logic there are no morals.* Everyone is at liberty to build up his own logic, i.e. his own form of language, as he wishes. (Carnap [1934], p. 52)

Once we have selected our preferred linguistic framework and are working within it, some judgments will be part of our adopted language, or follow from parts of our adopted language by our adopted deductive rules. Even if the evidential rules of that language require empirical input for the assertion of many of our sentences,[12] there will some others, like the evidential rules themselves, that are assertable on the basis of the linguistic framework alone. From the point of view of a speaker of the adopted language, these judgments are a priori.

Clearly, Carnap has done Reichenbach one better in the attempt to preserve something from Kant: he has preserved a variety of a priori knowledge. In some linguistic frameworks, like the one for general relativity, even geometric principles will enjoy a priori status. And Carnap achieves this, as Kant achieved it, by distinguishing two levels of inquiry: internal questions asked within a linguistic framework, and prior pragmatic questions about which framework to adopt in the first place. At the level of these pragmatic decisions, we see that the choice of framework is purely linguistic or conventional, but once the decision is made and one framework adopted, at the level of those working inside the framework, the framework's assumptions and evidential rules and what follows from them using the framework's deductive rules—all these are absolute, unrevisable, a priori.

Of course, not all of Kant's valued outcomes are preserved. On Carnap's account, the higher-level, pragmatic decision on which framework to adopt is a pre-scientific, conventional decision on what language to use for science; on Kant's account, what's uncovered at the higher, transcendental level are necessary, absolute truths about the structure of the world as experienced by any discursive knower with human forms of intuition. In other words, while Kant's a priori truths are unrevisable certainties of human knowledge, Carnap's are a priori only in the sense that revising them would constitute a revolutionary change in language, not a garden-variety change in belief.[13]

To view this difference from another angle, notice that Carnap distinguishes sharply between these conventional linguistic decisions and the philosopher's answers to what he calls external questions:

> From these questions [questions internal to the linguistic framework of the thing language, decided by the evidential rules of that framework] we must distinguish the external question of the reality of the thing world itself. In contrast to the former questions, this question is raised neither by the man in the street nor by scientists, but only by philosophers. Realists give an affirmative answer, subjective idealists a negative one, and the controversy goes on for centuries...because it is framed in a wrong way. (Carnap [1950], p. 243)

The problem, as Carnap sees it, is that the philosopher tries to raise the question of reality outside the scientific framework whose evidential rules would give the question sense. The only legitimate question that can be raised outside the framework is that of which framework to adopt, and this question is decided on purely pragmatic grounds:

> The thing language in the customary form works indeed with a high degree of efficiency for most purposes of everyday life. ... However, it would be wrong to describe this situation by saying, 'The fact of the efficiency of the thing language is confirming evidence for the reality of the thing world'; we should rather say instead: 'This fact makes it advisable to accept the thing language'. (ibid., p. 244)

Here the difference is stark: Kant's transcendental analysis is designed to answer the illegitimate external question; his answer is transcendental idealism.

More important for our purposes, however, are the differences between Carnap and Reichenbach. Though both seek to identify some portions of our scientific theorizing as linguistic or definitional or conventional, the structure of this inquiry is very different in the two cases. Reichenbach, as we've seen, undertakes to perform this analysis within science, making full use of scientific methods and theories.[14] Carnap, by contrast, traces the linguistic/conventional elements to a pre-scientific, pragmatic decision to opt for a particular framework for scientific inquiry. Because this deliberation takes place prior to the adoption of the scientific framework, it cannot be carried out as Reichenbach recommends, using scientific methods and the results of its empirical investigations. On the other hand, Carnap's two-level approach does deliver a priori knowledge at the internal level, which Reichenbach's cannot: if our Reichenbachian scientific inquiry into science determines that element x is present in our theory by convention, we can hardly be said to know that the world is x, and ipso facto, cannot be said to know it a priori. So Carnap's two-level approach has advantages and disadvantages when compared with Reichenbach's proto-naturalism: following Kant more closely, Carnap preserves a variety of a priori knowledge; at the same time, Carnap's approach short-circuits Reichenbach's detailed intra-scientific study of the conventional elements in science.

Moreover, Carnap's kinship with Kant leaves his position open to worries parallel to those about Kant's transcendental perspective. At Carnap's higher level, we don't ask or answer external philosophical questions as Kant would have us, but we do make pragmatic, conventional choices between linguistic frameworks, and here, as in the Kantian case, we must face the question of which modes of evidence are applicable: are we then operating within yet another conventionally-chosen linguistic framework, a framework where the principle of tolerance reigns, rather than another, more absolutist framework? If so, why have we chosen the tolerant framework; if not, what is the ground of these non-conventional evidential rules? These questions vex Carnapians much as the corresponding questions vex Kantians.

Still, the most devastating challenge to Kant's two-level scheme was the discovery that some of his synthetic a priori judgments were actually a posteriori (and false). In Carnap's case, the analogous objection comes in one strand of Quine's wide-ranging response to Carnap. In brief, Quine argues that the evidential rules governing decisions at the higher, pragmatic/conventional level of Carnap's model are precisely the same as the rules governing the adoption of ordinary scientific hypotheses at the lower, empirical/theoretical level of that model. For example, where Carnap would distinguish between the methods used to settle an internal scientific question about the combining volumes of various chemicals and those used to settle the external, purely linguistic, question of whether or not to adopt the framework of atomic theory, Quine insists that this is a distinction without a difference.[15] Notice the close analogy between this objection—'there's really no difference between your higher and lower levels'— and the older objections to Kant's transcendentalism—'your cherished synthetic a priori judgments are really just a posteriori'.

Here Quine's reaction is analogous to Reichenbach's; he rejects the two-level model in favor of his own naturalism:

> the recognition that it is within science itself, and not in some prior philosophy, that reality is to be identified and described. (Quine [1981], p. 21)

Metaphysical questions—are there atoms? are there numbers?—epistemological questions—how do we humans come to know the things we do?—all these are to be treated as broadly scientific questions, to be answered using the methods of science and its results. What's ruled out is 'first philosophy', any 'supra-scientific tribunal' (Quine [1975], p. 72) that would justify or criticize science on extra-scientific grounds. The Quinean naturalist 'begins his reasoning within the inherited world theory as a going concern' (op. cit.) and operates 'from the point of view of our own science, which is the only point of view I can offer' (Quine [1981a], p. 181). Here again we meet the fundamental naturalistic impulse.

The third and final episode I'd like to sketch dates to the 1980s, when van Fraassen introduced his 'constructive empiricism': though we have good reason to believe in what we observe, we should refrain from belief in the unobservable posits of our theories. This is not to say that we should give up our theories entirely; rather we should regard them as 'empirically adequate'—that is, as producing truths about observables—while remaining agnostic about their theoretical claims. What, then, are we to say to the practicing scientist who believes in atoms? A first try might be to suggest that she is misstating her actual position—that she actually believes only that atomic theory is empirically adequate—but this is seems untrue to the history of the situation. Before 1905, there *was* an important debate over the reality of atoms, one side of which held that they were only useful fictions, a claim I think we can safely view as a crude version of empirical adequacy.[16] But the calculations of Einstein in 1905 and the meticulous experiments of Perrin on Brownian motion around 1910 proved decisive.[17] Are we to understand van Fraassen as holding that the scientific community was in error when it judged the work of Einstein and Perrin to be conclusive evidence for the actual existence of atoms?

To answer this question, van Fraassen separates it into two. For the practicing scientist, he says,

> the distinction between *electron* and *flying horse* is as clear as between *racehorse* and *flying horse*; the first corresponds to something in the actual world, and the other does not. (van Fraassen [1980], p. 82)

For the scientist immersed in her science, van Fraassen imagines that this distinction might even be a methodologically beneficial one:

> We might even suggest a loyalty oath for scientists, if realism is so efficacious. (ibid., p. 93)

But he insists that

> the interpretation of science, and the correct view of its methodology, are two separate topics. (op. cit.)

As far as methodology goes, the actual practice of science, it is perfectly reasonable for our scientist to take the Einstein/Perrin evidence as establishing the real existence of atoms. But for the proper 'interpretation' of atomic theory, we must adopt a point of view other than that of the practicing scientist; we must use a method different from that of science: 'stepping back for a moment', we adopt an 'epistemic attitude' towards the theory (ibid., p. 82). Only then, answering the question as epistemologists, do we determine that the Einstein/Perrin evidence is not enough, and indeed, that no evidence can be enough to establish the existence of entities that cannot be perceived by unaided human senses. Here we have yet another two-level theory: at the ordinary scientific level, we have good evidence that atoms are real; at the interpretive, epistemic level, we do not.

This time, one voice of dissent comes from Fine. Why should we decide, at the epistemic level, to believe in what we can observe unaided rather than in what we can detect (as Perrin detected atoms)? After all, the method of detection can be put to any number of scientific tests:

> Faced with such substantial reasons for believing that we are detecting atoms, what, except purely a priori and arbitrary conventions, could possibly dictate the empiricist conclusion that, nevertheless, we are unwarranted actually to engage in *belief* about atoms? (Fine [1986a], p. 146)

Fine sees no grounds for this higher-level decision:

> an attitude of belief has as warrant precisely that which science itself grants, nothing more but certainly nothing less...when [the empiricist] sidesteps science and moves into his own courtroom, there to pronounce his judgments of where to believe and where to withhold, he [commits] the sin of epistemology. (ibid., p. 147)

Fine's own position, which he calls the 'Natural Ontological Attitude' or NOA, includes the fundamental naturalistic impulse:

> All that NOA insists is that one's ontological attitude towards...everything...that might be collected in the scientific zoo (whether observable or not), be governed by the very same standards of evidence and inference that are employed by science itself. (ibid., p. 150)

There is only one level at which to evaluate the evidence for the existence of atoms, and that is the ordinary scientific level, where even van Fraassen admits that we are justified in believing in them.

Now we shouldn't imagine that only transcendental idealists (like Kant) or conventionalists (like Carnap) or constructive empiricists (like van Fraassen) are tempted by two-level accounts; even realists occasionally succumb. To see how this might happen, consider again the case of the scientist who believes in atoms on the basis of the Einstein/Perrin evidence. Suppose this scientist is confronted by a constructive empiricist who claims that this evidence is good enough for scientific purposes, but not good enough to establish the actual existence of atoms. The proper naturalistic response would be to ask what other purposes the skeptic has in mind, what other modes of evidence he's applying; until these matters are explained, the scientist is surely within her epistemic rights to continue to adhere to normal scientific standards and to assert the reality of atoms. But given human nature, a scientist confronted with this stubborn agnosticism about atoms, with this condescension towards her cherished evidential standards as merely 'good enough for science'—such a scientist is all too likely to rise to the occasion by trying to defeat the van Fraassenite on his own terms, by insisting that atoms *really* exist.

The fatal flaw in this reaction is that by agreeing (implicitly) to 'step back' with van Fraassen into his 'epistemic attitude', the scientist has forfeited all her actual evidence for the existence of atoms: that evidence has already been declared 'good enough for science' but not 'good enough for epistemology'. Having ascended to the higher level, where her ordinary scientific evidence is no longer relevant, she is left without resources; this is what leads to the foot-stomping *really* of the Realist.[18] Let me distinguish between a lower-case 'realism' about atoms in the ordinary scientific sense, supported by ordinary scientific evidence, and an upper-case 'Realism' about atoms which asserts, at the higher, 'epistemic' level, on who knows what grounds, that atoms *really* exist. Our scientist had perfectly good evidence for her realism about atoms, but in response to van Fraassen's challenge, she sets herself up to defend Realism, an epistemological rather than a scientific view. By the naturalist's lights, this is a fool's errand.

The case of Boyd, van Fraassen's most tenacious philosophical opponent, is somewhat more subtle. Boyd undertakes to show that

> a realistic account of scientific theories is a component in the only scientifically plausible explanation for the instrumental reliability of scientific methodology. (Boyd [1983], p. 207)

Leaving aside the detail of this argument, it is clear that Boyd intends it to take place entirely within science, using ordinary scientific methods:

> The epistemology of empirical science is an empirical science. (Boyd [1990], p. 227)

This certainly has the sound of a purely naturalistic undertaking. But consider again our scientific believer in atoms, the one convinced by the Einstein/Perrin evidence. While van Fraassen challenges this evidence at his higher level of epistemological inquiry, the naturalist remains at the lower level, the ordinary scientific level, and regards it as conclusive, just as the scientist does. Notice that on this contrast, Boyd sides with van Fraassen: he, too, sees the ordinary scientific evidence as standing in need of supplementation, presumably in response to the higher-level considerations raised by van Fraassen. So, though the supplementation Boyd goes on to offer is purely scientific, the perceived need for it is not. In this sense, Boyd, too, has bought into van Fraassen's higher level of evaluation.

Notice also that buying into van Fraassen's perspective tends to push Boyd away from the details of the local debate over atoms and towards global debates over such questions as whether or not the theoretical terms of mature scientific theories typically refer. The naturalist is wary of such blanket assertions, given the complexity of actual science: the particularity of arguments for the existence of individual theoretical entities, like atoms or quarks; the subtle gradations in levels of belief in the various parts of science; the widespread use of idealizations and mathematizations; and so on.[19] At least at the outset, it seems unlikely that a single attitude towards 'the posits of mature science' will be correct across the board.

On this point, Reichenbach agrees.[20] Speaking of the Berlin group, he endorses its

> concrete working-program, which demanded analysis of specific problems in science...(Reichenbach [1936], p. 144)

He writes with approval that

> They concentrated on minute work; and hoped to advance the work of the whole step by step. (ibid., p. 150)

Reichenbach proposes that scientific philosophy proceed by examining particular theories in particular sciences, e.g., 'in logistics, physics, biology and psychology' (ibid., p. 144); he himself concentrated his energies on space, time and geometry in the theory of relativity. While it is possible that this piecemeal approach will lead to a uniform theory of all parts of science, this is neither presupposed nor required as a measure of success. Carnap's fondness for all-inclusive systems was another central point of disagreement between his Viennese positivists and Reichenbach's Berlin empiricists.[21]

These, then, are the three historical episodes that I hope illuminate the fundamental naturalistic impulse. Much as I applaud the reactions of Reichenbach, Quine and Fine, each in opposition to a particular two-level view, I must allow that I cannot agree with all they have to say in their pursuit of their proto-naturalistic projects. In the case of Reichenbach, my own expertise is inadequate for a full accounting, but Friedman has argued persuasively against Reichenbach's later theory of confirmation and in favor of a more naturalistic approach;[22] here, it seems, Reichenbach forsakes the internal, the scientific, in favor of the a priori. In Quine's case, I think the lure of global accounts— of confirmation (holism), of ontology (to be is to be the value of a bound variable)—has overshadowed the detailed analysis of actual scientific theory and practice that's incumbent upon the true naturalist. I've written at length on this and my other departures from Quinean orthodoxy elsewhere, so I won't go into detail here.[23]

My understanding of where and how Fine's NOA differs from the naturalistic stance I'll be espousing is compromised by my uncertainty over precisely what NOA involves. Many passages, like those cited a moment ago, sound naturalistic in spirit:

> we cannot actually do more, with regard to existence claims, than follow scientific practice. (Fine [1986a], p. 132)
>> Trust that science is open to providing all the resources and nourishment that we who study science need. (Fine [1996], p. 176)

And Fine also embraces the secondary naturalistic theme traced in Reichenbach above: a preference for local rather than global analyses in our scientific study of science. In fact, he sometimes goes further, declaring outright that there are no 'general, substantive' (Fine [1996], p. 176) theories of confirmation, explanation, cause, etc., indeed any of 'the concepts used in science' (Fine [1986a], p. 149), but in careful moments, he admits that the question remains open:

> A question that NOA must face is whether going local...means automatically restricting the range of judgments and principles away from the fully general or universal. I think the answer is no. All that NOA urges is that we not impose a universalist framework from the outside as a precondition for trying to investigate or understand a practice. ... It remains to be seen how much universality is actually required for understanding. ... Induction again; let us look and see. (Fine [1996], pp. 179–180)

Fine and the NOAer make an exception to this open-minded policy in the case of the concept truth—insisting outright that there is no theory of truth[24]—but I'll leave that issue for later.

Still, despite this agreement (again leaving truth aside), there are hints that Fine's posture is not quite that of the naturalist. He writes, for example, that NOA means

> to situate humanistic concerns about the sciences within the context of ongoing scientific concerns, to reach out with our questions and interests to scientist's questions and interests—and to pursue inquiry as a common endeavor. (Fine [1996], p. 174)

This suggests that we humanists, which presumably includes us philosophers, begin somewhere else, somewhere outside science, and need to be encouraged to embrace the results and methods of science. In contrast, my naturalist is simply born native to late twentieth-century common sense and the scientific attitude that extends it. The only decision to be made is whether or not to go beyond these means of finding out how the world is, whether or not to add extra-scientific standards of justification to our repertoire. The naturalist, holding to her own standards, will see no reason to do this.

Perhaps these issues come clearest in Fine's rejection of 'essentialism':

> NOA is, therefore, basically at odds with the temperament that looks for definite boundaries demarcating science from pseudo-science, or that is inclined to award the title 'scientific' like a blue ribbon on a prize goat. (Fine [1986a], p. 149)[25]

This passage raises the key questions of demarcation criteria and pseudo-science. On the first, I agree with Fine that it is probably hopeless to search for necessary and sufficient conditions that separate science from the rest. Instead, our naturalist might begin from simple idea that

> Science [is] a method of finding things out. This method is based on the principle that observation is the judge of whether something is so or not. (Feynman [1998], p. 15)

This simple idea brings others in its wake: the importance of falsification in ruling out hypotheses, of precision and thoroughness, of objectivity, of specificity, of theory formation and the rejection of authority, of universality, and so on (ibid., pp. 15–28). As science develops successfully along various paths, so do higher level norms, like the rejection of action-at-a-distance, or the emergence of mechanism, or its over-throw by field theories. But in none of this do we find necessary-and-sufficient conditions. Rather, the moral seems to be that we do best to keep an open mind on the progress of scientific methodology.

Now this conclusion might seem troublesome for the naturalistic approach: after all, isn't naturalism the view that scientific methods are the only legitimate source of evidence, that we should eschew the extra-scientific; doesn't it take a viable demarcation criterion even to state the position?! Perhaps some of my proto-naturalistic precursors would agree to this, but I hope to take a somewhat different line. My naturalist's methodology isn't 'trust only science!'; her methodology just *is* a certain range of methods, which happen to be those we commonly regard as scientific. When asked why she believes in atoms, she says, 'because of the experiments of Perrin' and such-like, not 'because science says there are atoms and I believe the methods of science'. So my naturalist applies no necessary and sufficient conditions; as a native of the contemporary scientific world view, she simply proceeds by the methods that strike her as justified.

Still, though the naturalist can proceed naturalistically without appeal to any demarcation criterion, a new question arises when I attempt to describe her behavior in general terms, when I end up saying things like: the naturalist has internalized the standards and methods of contemporary science. My reading is that in these contexts, terms like 'scientific methods' are informal terms of ordinary language, used in familiar, rough-and-ready fashion, without the backing of necessary and sufficient conditions.[26] I contend that what carries the weight here is not these general terms, but the individual behaviors: e.g., the faith in 'ordinary evidence' like the Einstein-Perrin case for atoms. That's why my efforts to outline this version of naturalism consist largely (and fundamentally) of a list of naturalistic reactions in specific cases to particular challenges. I count on our shared ability to extrapolate from these, with no guarantee that all cases will be beyond controversy.

It's worth noting that in the historical episodes we've just been surveying, the naturalist's opponents have often themselves presupposed a general characterization of science when they grant that such-and-such is acceptable on ordinary scientific grounds (as an empirical matter (Kant), as an internal question (Carnap), for scientific purposes (van Fraassen)). They then introduce an explicitly extra-scientific perspective, from which the view is supposed to be starkly different. Now again, when I describe her, I say that my naturalist, born into the contemporary scientific approach, balks at extra-scientific demands. But what actually happens is not that she insists 'you're proposing methods that go beyond the legitimate range of science', but that she is puzzled: she asks for a better description of the new evidential standards being proposed; she asks to be told why they are needed and how they are justified. Unless some explanation is given that ties into her own methods, the ones her opponents describe as 'ordinary scientific methods', she is unlikely to be persuaded that her original grounds are inadequate. Again, none of this requires her to launch any blanket condemnation of 'extra-scientific methods'.

So far, then, I agree with Fine that we should avoid the losing battle of specifying demarcation criteria, but I don't think this is enough to keep the naturalist from condemning so-called 'pseudo-scientific' practices like astrology. The kind of thing the naturalist might say is once again nicely illustrated by Feynman, our sample naturalist:

Astrologists say that there are days when it's better to go to the dentist than other days. There are days when it's better to fly in an airplane, for you, if you are born on such a day and such and such an hour. And it's all calculated by very careful rules in terms of the position of the stars. If it were true it would be very interesting. Insurance people would be very interested to change the insurance rates on people if they follow the astrological rules, because they have a better chance when they are in the airplane. Tests to determine whether people who go on the day that they are not supposed to go are worse off or not have never been made by the astrologers...

Maybe it's still true, yes. On the other hand, there's an awful lot of information that indicates that it isn't true. We have a lot of knowledge about how things work, what people are, what the world is, what those stars are, what the planets are that you are looking at, what makes them go around more or less...so what are you going to do? Disbelieve it. There's no evidence at all for it. ... The only way you can believe it is to have a general lack of knowledge about the stars and the world and what the rest of the things look like. If such a phenomenon existed it would be

most remarkable, in the face of all the other phenomena that exist, and unless someone can demonstrate it to you with a real experiment, a real test, took people who
believe and people who didn't believe and made a test, and so on, then there's no
point in listening to them.

Tests of this kind, incidentally, have been made in the early days of science.
It's rather interesting. I found out that in the early days, like in the time when they
were discovering oxygen and so on, people made such experimental attempts to
find out, for example, whether missionaries—it sounds silly; it only sounds silly
because you're afraid to test it—whether good people like missionaries who pray
and so on were less likely to be in a shipwreck than others. And so when missionaries were going to far countries, they checked in the shipwrecks whether the missionaries were less likely to drown than other people. And it turned out that there
was no difference. (Feynman [1998], pp. 92–3)

This straightforward sort of thinking requires no general characterization of science to be persuasive. If the NOAer is reluctant to withhold some sort of blue
ribbon in such cases, it would seem that he isn't 'born to the contemporary
scientific world view', that he hasn't 'internalized its methods', and hence, that
he is no naturalist, by my lights.[27]

Let me summarize, then, my description of the naturalist's behavior, using
rough-and-ready general terms that she herself need not: the naturalist begins
her inquiry from a perspective inside our scientific practice, which is, in turn,
an extension of common sense. She approaches philosophical questions as
broadly scientific questions, insofar as this is possible. When faced with a challenge framed in terms of extra-scientific requirements, she is open-minded but
puzzled. Until the motivations and standards for this other style of inquiry are
spelled out and justified, she rests with her own evidential principles, with a
healthy skepticism toward first philosophy. From this perspective, she pursues
a scientific study of science, understood as an undertaking of human beings—as
described by her theories of psychology, physiology, linguistics, etc.—who in-
quire into the structure of the world—as described by her theories of physics,
chemistry, biology, botany, astronomy, etc. In the process, she aims to understand how and why particular principles and practices either help or hinder her
efforts to determine how the world is, and she attempts to fine-tune her overall
methodology in light of this understanding. As simple as that.

II. Putnam Against Naturalism

Having first approached naturalism by describing some of its philosophical roots, I now turn to the objections of Putnam, a prominent contemporary
opponent. The irony here is that Putnam was once himself a proto-naturalist;
e.g., in response to Duhem's fictionalism, he wrote:

it is silly to agree that a reason for believing that *p* warrants accepting *p* in all
scientific circumstances, and then to add 'but even so it is not *good enough*'. Such

a judgment could only be made if one accepted a trans-scientific method as superior to the scientific method; but this philosopher, at least, has no interest in doing
that. (Putnam [1971], p. 356)

Ten years later, the author of 'Why there isn't a ready-made world' and 'Why
reason can't be naturalized' attacks both 'contemporary attempts to "naturalize" metaphysics' and 'attempts to naturalize the fundamental notions of the
theory of knowledge' (Putnam [1982b], p. 229). This is the Putnam I propose
to discuss here.

Unfortunately, despite the simplicity of these declared goals, the target of
Putnam's challenge in these two papers is not always clear.[28] At various points
in the first paper, he uses the terms 'metaphysical realism', 'materialism', 'scientism', and even 'metaphysical materialism'. Here the materialist is said to
view physics as the best source of metaphysical or ontological information, that
is, information about how the world is. Putnam continues

> ...we don't *need* intellectual intuition to do *his* sort of metaphysics: his metaphys-
> ics, he says, is as open ended, as infinitely revisable and fallible, as science itself.
> In fact, it *is* science itself! ... The appeal of materialism lies precisely in this, in its
> claim to be *natural* metaphysics, metaphysics within the bounds of science. (Put-
> nam [1982a], p. 210)

This has a proto-naturalistic ring, and indeed, it seems to me not entirely unfair
to tag naturalism with the pejorative 'scientism'. This last is a view that Putnam considers not only false, but pernicious:

> metaphysical materialism has replaced positivism and pragmatism as the dominant
> contemporary form of scientism. Since scientism is, in my opinion, one of the most
> dangerous contemporary intellectual tendencies, a critique of its most influential
> contemporary form is a duty for a philosopher who views his enterprise as more
> than a purely technical discipline. (Putnam [1982a], p. 211)

For simplicity, I won't attempt to sort out the precise target or targets of Putnam's critique; instead, I propose to consider his arguments as if they were
addressed to the form of naturalism I'm advocating. This may well have no
bearing on their cogency against the view or views Putnam himself has in mind,
but I hope it may suit my goal of clarification.

To begin with, I suspect that the root of Putnam's unhappiness is his conviction that his opponents have failed to learn the lesson of Kant:

> The approach to which I have devoted this paper is an approach which claims that
> there *is* a 'transcendental' reality in Kant's sense, one absolutely independent of
> our minds...*but* (and this is what makes it 'natural' metaphysics) we need no *intelle-
> ktuelle Anschauung*...the 'scientific method' will do... 'Metaphysics within the bounds
> of science alone' might be its slogan. (Putnam [1982a], p. 226)

Earlier, he identifies 'metaphysical realism' with Kant's 'transcendental realism' (ibid., p. 206), the view Kant rejects in favor of 'transcendental idealism'. Now whatever other positions Putnam might have in mind, I hope the previous section has made it clear that this is *not* what I mean to advocate under the label 'naturalism', nor, I would argue, is it what Reichenbach or Quine or Fine advocates. The most fundamental naturalistic impulse, as I understand it, consists in a stubborn resistance to 'transcendental' levels of analysis of any sort; in the Kantian idiom, the naturalist begins and ends in at the empirical level. However strong the human urge towards the transcendental (Putnam [1982a], pp. 210, 226), it is not the naturalist who succumbs.

That much is easy: whatever the naturalist's sins, she has not transgressed against Kant's rejection of transcendental realism, because she hasn't risen to Kant's transcendental level in the first place. But there may be more to the Kantian lesson that Putnam accuses us of having missed, perhaps in some version of what he calls Kant's 'corollary':

> The corollary Kant drew from all this is that even experiences are in part constructions of the mind...the idea that all experience involves mental construction, and the idea that the dependence of physical object concepts and experience concepts goes *both* ways, continue to be of great importance in contemporary philosophy... (Putnam [1982a], pp. 209–210)

Now the idea that human cognizers perform some processing on raw sensory stimulations is a commonplace of contemporary psychology; there is a concerted scientific effort to determine how this is done, to describe the mechanisms involved. Putnam sees more than this in the Kantian corollary; he sees some form of idealism. Before we can offer any naturalistic response, we need to know what sort of idealism is in question.

As we've seen, the trick to understanding any Kantian utterance is to be alert to its level: we shouldn't, for example, try to determine whether or not Kant is an idealist, tout court, for he is an idealist at the transcendental level and a realist at the empirical level. Now Putnam himself so well understands the difficulties of the transcendental level that he is moved to suggest that

> one's attitude to it must, perhaps, be the concern of religion rather than of rational philosophy. (Putnam [1982a], p. 226)

So it seems unlikely that Putnam intends his Kantian corollary to be understood transcendentally.

If, on the other hand, the Kantian corollary is to be interpreted empirically—contrary to Kant's own empirical realism—and if we are to avoid reducing it to the commonplace of empirical psychology—that human cognition adds some processing to raw sensory inputs—then Putnam must tell us more. And he does: it is 'silly' to think that we can have knowledge of objects that goes beyond experience. (ibid., p. 210)

For the 'one idea...definitely sunk by Kant...' is the view that

> We can think and talk about things as they are, independently of our minds. (ibid., p. 205)

Of course, Kant didn't sink this view at the empirical level, he embraced it, but here our concern is with Putnam.

If Putnam's point here is not the commonplace of empirical psychology, then it must be that we cannot hope to know what the world is like independently of our perceptual and conceptual processors or independently of our scientific theories. As a thesis about psychology or science, this seems either false or unproblematic. When psychology tells us that we are prone to certain sorts of perceptual and cognitive mistakes, it is telling us that the world is not as our basic processors tend to see it. Likewise, progress in the physical sciences sometimes takes the form of the discovery that the way the world most naturally appears to us is not the way it actually is: as Einstein showed that our perception of the world as Euclidean was actually a parochial take on a larger non-Euclidean universe, or as quantum mechanics suggests that our everyday ideas of causation are not applicable in the small. In all these cases, careful application of the scientific method allows us to 'see around' our most basic forms of perception and conceptualization, to better understand the world as it is independently of our cognitive structures. And it is clearly possible for us to 'see around' any particular scientific theory; this is how science progresses, by replacing one theory with another. So the complaint can only be that we can't know what the world is like without using scientific methods—something the naturalist is quite ready to grant![29]

In sum, then, it seems that Putnam's Kantian corollary must either be a variety of transcendental idealism that functions at a level rejected by Putnam and beyond the range of the naturalist, or a sort of empirical idealism that's rejected by both Kant and the naturalist and ought to be rejected by Putnam as well. Whatever Kantian lessons Putnam's other opponents may have failed to learn, I don't see that this underlying inspiration for his displeasure with them should carry any weight against the naturalist. So far, my naturalist adheres to an ordinary string of trivialities of science and the common sense it extends: the world is as it is (largely)[30] independently of our modes of perception and conceptualization; by careful application of scientific methods, we can gradually overcome our prejudices and better understand how the world is.

This talk of 'the way the world is' brings us to the doorstep of one of the more specific areas of Putnam's critique, the idea that his opponent is committed to the existence of

> the one true theory, the true and complete description of the furniture of the world. (Putnam [1982a], p. 210)

He elaborates:

> this belief in one true theory requires a *ready-made* world...: the world itself has to have a 'built-in' structure. (ibid., p. 211)

Part of Putnam's resistance to this view is intertwined with his views about truth, which I postpone to the next section, but before delving into that question, we should compare Putnam's notion of 'the one true theory' with our naturalistic commonplaces.

In some sense, the naturalist does think the world has a 'built-in' structure, supposing this to mean that the world is as it is (largely) independently of our cognition. Saying that (most of) the world's structure is 'built-in', in this sense, only means that it isn't imposed by our perception, cognition or thought; this is the part of the world's structure that we're trying to capture in our scientific efforts to screen off our various prejudices and reveal the world as it is. This much I would count as commonplace, but Putnam characterizes his opponent as embracing something more: the assumption that there is one and only one theory that reveals the world as it is. I don't see how the belief that the world has a built-in structure forces one to the conclusion that only one theory can describe that structure. Putnam's case against the 'one true theory' involves purportedly 'equivalent descriptions', but let's not worry about the persuasiveness of his examples; let's simply ask why the bare admission that there might not be 'one true theory' should be troublesome for the naturalist.

There's a hint of one possible worry in another of Putnam's writings:

> Any sentence that changes truth-value upon passing from one correct theory to another correct theory...will express only a *theory-relative* property of THE WORLD. And the more such sentences there are, the more properties of THE WORLD will turn out to be theory-relative. (Putnam [1976], p. 132)

Saying that the world's properties are 'theory-relative' makes it sound as if our theories impose their properties, perhaps even as if the world has no structure of its own and can be imposed upon in any old way we happen to choose. Whether or not Putnam himself intends any of these views, I think the naturalist can be seen to reject them, again with a series of commonplaces.

To see this, consider a crude analogy: suppose the world consists of a deck of cards; then one true theory describes the universe as made up of 52 card-like objects, another describes it as made up of 4 suit-like clump-objects, yet another as consisting of one complex whole. It seems reasonable to say that all these theories are correct, that each of them describes aspects of the way this world is, that each of them ascribes to the world properties that are 'built-in'. Analogously, our naturalist holds that the world our science studies has a built-in structure, that our methods are designed to help us get at this structure, but she needn't insist that there is only one correct way to do this, and she needn't deny that which built-in properties we tend to pick up on is at least partly a function of our cognitive structures and our interests. And to say that there might be several correct ways of describing the world is not to say that *every* way of describing the world is equally good. The history of science is littered with ways of describing the world that didn't work.

But there's another issue lurking in the background of the 'one true theory' discussion, an issue that goes to the heart of our understanding of naturalized metaphysics. In Quine's original version of the view, our ontological commitments were to be assessed by figuring out which things our best scientific theory says 'there are'; we were to imagine an all-inclusive theory T, of 'science' in the broadest sense, and to search through its existential assertions.[31] If there are in fact two equally good theories of the world, two theories that assert the existence of different things, then it seems Quinean naturalized metaphysics is in trouble. To take a simple example, if we have two complete scientific theories of the world, T and T', where T involves points, line segments and lines, and T'; involves line segments, lines and convergent sequences of line segments,[32] the Quinean naturalist seems unable to determine whether or not there are points. Perhaps even worse, this very approach to metaphysics seems to attribute serious ontological import to an issue of theory formulation that strikes most scientists as entirely without significance.[33]

Now it seems to me (as indicated above) that the Quinean picture of scientific theorizing at work here is too simple to do the job he assigns to it: e.g., the existence of atoms was asserted in atomic theory—part of our best theory—before the Einstein/Perrin evidence that convinced the scientific community that atoms are more than useful fictions; the existence of continuous substances is asserted in fluid dynamics, though no one believes there are such things; some mathematical aspects of our theories (like the continuity of space-time) are considered open questions despite the fact that we have no better way to represent the world. The naturalist's scientific study of science will happen upon these and related observations early on, and the moral of the story seems obvious: reading the ontological conclusions off the face of our scientific theorizing is a complex and subtle undertaking, far more complex and subtle than Quine's proto-naturalist would imagine.

Clearly, our scientific study of science will need to address the problem of when and why two theories with superficially different ontologies are in fact two ways of describing the same underlying reality; the problem of differentiating the many varieties of idealizations and some mathematizations from literal claims, and revealing how they work; the problem of understanding how our more complex mathematical machinery is functioning in our most basic theories; and many more. But these important and legitimate inquiries into the structure and function of scientific theorizing in no way undermine the core of metaphysics naturalized, the idea that science is the best way we know of finding out how the world is.[34] We must face the fact that this 'finding out' is a difficult task, not something that can simply be read off the logical form of our theories, but none of this gives our naturalist reason to suppose that this approach is somehow doomed or that there is any better way to proceed.

Turning now to Putnam's epistemological critique of naturalism, let me first take brief note of a common criticism of epistemology naturalized, namely, that in foreswearing the project of answering the Cartesian skeptic, the naturalist also gives up any normative aspirations. Putnam repeats this as a criticism of Quine in particular, while admitting that many naturalized epistemologists do undertake normative analyses (Putnam [1982b], pp. 244–245). I'm not sure this is fair to Quine,[35] but in any case, I hope it is clear that my naturalist's scientific study of science includes the effort to evaluate and improve the methodology of science from within, an explicitly normative undertaking. So let's set this issue aside.

A more central theme of Putnam's epistemological critique paints his opponents as prone to versions of relativism or imperialism, both of which he considers self-refuting. I should grant that the opponents Putnam sometimes has in mind here—the likes of Richard Rorty—inhabit a different intellectual province from the naturalistically-minded, but I think, nevertheless, that an examination of these issues, as they impinge upon the naturalist, might be illuminating. So let's first ask just how the naturalist might come to be accused of relativism or imperialism.

Suppose that our naturalist has begun her scientific study of science: she calls on her physiological and psychological theories of human perception and conceptualization, her linguistic theories of the workings of human language, and her physical, chemical, astronomical, biological, botanical, and geological theories of the world in which these humans live; she uses these, and any other of her scientific findings that seem relevant, to attempt to explain how these humans, by these means, come to know about this world. Now suppose that along the way, she also takes note of other human linguistic practices, practices different from hers. Some of these, say some forms of chanting or story-telling, don't seem to play the characteristic role of bodies of assertions, but others, like astrology and theology, apparently do. Our naturalist also notices that the evidential standards and norms of these assertion-like practices are not the same as the ones she uses in her own investigations.[36] How should the naturalist treat these cases?

We might imagine a brand of quasi-naturalist[37] who reacts by saying: "Clearly their norms are different from mine. I think mine are justified, as I attempt to show in the course of my scientific study of science. Still, I acknowledge that this justification relies on my norms; I can't expect them to be any more impressed by a justification of my norms in terms of my norms than I'm impressed by a justification of their norms in terms of their norms. Given the symmetry of the situation, I must conclude that their practice is as good as mine." Putnam objects that when this quasi-naturalist says something like 'their assertions are justified by their norms', she's using her own norms of assertion, and he argues that this makes it impossible for her claim of symmetry to convey what it ought to convey.[38]

While this relativistic position has perhaps some claim to be called 'naturalism', it is not the version of naturalism I'm attempting to describe and intending to advocate. In some cases, my naturalist might conclude that the seemingly-assertive practice is actually pursued for other reasons: perhaps in hopes of producing a certain spiritual state in the case of theological discourse or perhaps as a tool in a sort of psychoanalytic process in the case of astrological discourse. But suppose the naturalist's scientific analysis, drawing on anthropology, sociology, psychology, etc., determines that one or another of these practices *is* aimed, as the naturalist's scientific practice is aimed, at telling us how the world is; suppose, for example, that the astrologer asserts that human behavior can be predicted from the position of the stars or the theologian asserts that certain phenomena are supernatural miracles. In those cases, my naturalist holds that the norms of these practices are outright incorrect, that they are not effective procedures for supporting the stated claims (recall Feynman's rejection of astrology in the long passage quoted in §I). The others might protest that she reaches these conclusions using her own evidential standards, but this she happily grants. They are her standards, the best standards she knows. Of course, she admits that they are subject to criticism and modification, but only on legitimate scientific grounds, and neither the theologian nor the astrologer has presented any such critique.

But perhaps cases like astrology and theology seem too easy. The sociologists of science draw attention to episodes from the history of science when theories or even 'conceptual schemes' different from ours have held sway, arguing that these alternatives were equally successful at justifying themselves on their own terms and that their eventual demise was not rationally justified. Now the naturalist, with her stubbornly piecemeal approach, will consider such examples case-by-case, with an eye to explicating the details of each, but perhaps one general observation might be offered: the naturalist's scientific study of such episodes will aim to assess the relative merits of the discarded, alternative scheme; in many such cases, existing studies give us reason to suppose that the decisions of the scientific community were considerably less arbitrary than the sociologists would have us believe;[39] still, it is would be foolish for the naturalist to ignore the possibility, indeed the likelihood, that evidentially-irrelevant, irrational factors *have* played an unsavory role in the development of science.

Quine makes a similar point, against the background metaphor of Neurath's boat:

> The ship may owe its structure partly to blundering predecessors who missed scuttling it only by fools' luck.

Ferreting out these improperly-supported passages is a first step towards the naturalist's goal of improving science from within. Still, as Quine goes on to caution:

> ...we are not in a position to jettison any part of it, except as we have substitute devices ready to hand that will serve the same essential purposes. (Quine [1960], p. 124)

Once the weak planks are found, the next job is find more stable replacements. All this is part of naturalism; none of it constitutes relativism.

There remains the logical, as opposed to historical, objection that there might be a methodology completely different from ours that would generate a science completely different from ours, but would nevertheless be as good as our scientific methodology at uncovering the way the world is. I think there is no denying this bare possibility. As Quine puts it:

> Might another culture, another species, take a radically different line of scientific development, guided by norms that differ sharply from ours but that are justified by their scientific findings as ours are by ours? And might these people predict as successfully and thrive as well as we? Yes, I think that we must admit this as a possibility in principle; that we must admit it even from the point of view of our own science, which is the only point of view I can offer. I should be surprised to see this possibility realized, but I cannot picture a disproof. (Quine [1981a], p. 181)

But this bare possibility is methodologically empty.

At this point, it appears that our naturalist is far more susceptible to a charge of imperialism than to a charge of relativism, so it is worth asking why Putnam thinks imperialism is self-refuting. As it happens, the argument turns on Putnam's understanding of what a naturalist like mine, an imperialistic naturalist, would have to say about truth. Thus we are returned to the question set aside in connection with Fine at the end of §1: the question of truth.

III. Naturalism and Truth

What's striking is that the notion of truth enjoys a special status in all these discussions. Putnam thinks that both his materialistic opponent (in [1982a]) and his imperialistic opponent (in [1982b]) are committed by the very structure of their positions to particular views about truth. And though Fine's general approach is summed up in the imperative 'Induction again; let us look and see' (Fine [1996], p. 180), he also thinks that his NOAer is committed at the outset to a particular position on truth. Here the contrast with the naturalism I've been describing is stark: my naturalist isn't committed to any particular position on truth simply on account of her naturalism; she is committed to a scientific approach to the question, but this alone doesn't prejudge or predict how that inquiry will turn out.[40] Let me glance at what I take to be the current state of naturalistic, that is, scientific inquiry into the notion of truth, then return to the arguments of Putnam and Fine.

In fact, I think we've already made one relevant observation in connection with van Fraassen's 'empirical adequacy'. Recall that in a case like that of the post-Einstein/Perrin atomic theorist, it seems incorrect to interpret the claim 'there are atoms' to mean that the assertion of the existence of atoms is empirically adequate: it was considered empirically adequate *before* Einstein and Perrin; afterwards it graduated to another status. I think similar observations of the practice of science will rule out the range of verificationist-style notions of truth. Ordinary scientific practice distinguishes between the claim that 'our meters read so-and-so' and the existence of particles, between 'we have experiences such-and-such' and the existence of medium-sized physical objects, between 'it's useful to act as if there are atoms' and 'there are atoms'. The only hope for such positions is to remove the discussion to a higher level, where the ordinary scientific evidence for existence is judged inadequate, but the naturalist will stubbornly resist any such ascension.

Setting verificationism aside, there remains an ongoing scientific debate about the nature of truth. In the early 70s, Field claimed that Tarski's theory of truth does not do the full job of showing that 'truth' is a scientifically-acceptable notion; Field's thought is that Tarski's account needs supplementation by a robust account of reference (see Field [1972]). In the course of this argument, Field admits that

> this sort of argument...is only as powerful as our arguments for the utility of semantic terms; and it is clear that the question of the utility of the term 'true'...needs much closer investigation. (Field [1972], p. 374)

In a subsequent paper, Leeds ([1978]) undertakes this closer investigation, concluding that the role 'truth' actually plays in science can be filled by something much more modest than what Field has in mind, namely, by a disquotational or deflationary theory of truth, derived from Quine. Thus the question is raised: does science require a robust correspondence theory of truth or can all its explanatory purposes be served by a deflationary theory? The debate continues to this day.[41]

Under these circumstances, what is the proper theory of truth for the naturalist? Given the naturalist's scientific approach, it seems clear that the question remains open. If it should turn out that the purposes of science require a robust correspondence theory, so be it; if not, the naturalist rests content with a deflationary theory. Perhaps it will turn out that both these options are misguided in some fundamental way. The only specifically naturalistic commitment in all this is to follow scientific inquiry wherever it might lead.

With this mundane observation as background, let's return to Putnam's case against the imperialist. Addressed to cultural imperialism, Putnam's argument begins like this:

> He [the imperialist] can say, 'Well then, truth—the only notion of truth I understand—is defined by the norms of *my* culture.' ('After all', he can add, 'which

norms should I rely on? The norms of *somebody else's* culture?') (Putnam [1982b], p. 238)

Thus, the imperialist's notion of truth 'cannot go beyond right assertibility' (ibid., p. 239). The trouble, according to Putnam, is that our culture does not include a norm of the form:

A statement is true...only if it is assertable according to the norms of modern European and American culture. (ibid., p. 239)

So, Putnam concludes:

if this statement is true, it follows that it is not true...Hence it is not true QED. (op. cit.)

Thus imperialism is self-refuting in 'modern European and American culture', though it might not be if

as a matter of contingent fact, our culture were a totalitarian culture which erected its own cultural imperialism into a required dogma, a culturally normative belief. (op. cit.)

Our job is to consider how this style of argument might apply to our naturalistic imperialist. We begin, again, with the notion of truth. To determine whether or not a statement is true, the naturalist applies the norms and standards of her science. From here, the Putnamanian line of thought concludes that she is committed to an account of truth in terms of 'right assertibility' rather than 'correspondence'. But why should this be so? When the naturalist is asked to settle a question of truth, she will indeed appeal to her scientific norms and standards, but she needn't view this as a *definition* of truth; furthermore, we've seen that such a verification-based theory is not likely to emerge from her scientific study of the notion. Indeed, defining truth as 'right assertibility' would convert one important challenge for her scientific study of science—the task of showing that her norms and standards are dependable methods for determining how the world is—into an analytic certainty. Any theory of truth that trivializes this difficult undertaking should certainly be rejected.

So, I think my naturalist is clearly not committed to the Right Assertibility theory that Putnam attributes to the imperialist. But Putnam also has a truth-based argument against his other main opponent, the materialist. Indeed, in his [1982a], Putnam goes so far as to *define* his opponent's position to include a correspondence theory of truth:

What the metaphysical realist holds is that we can think and talk about things as they are, independently of our minds, and that we can do this by virtue of a 'correspondence' relation between the terms in our language and some sorts of mind-independent entities. (Putnam [1982a], p. 205)

We've seen that the naturalist does hold that we can think and talk about mind-independent things; we've also seen that whether or not this involves a robust correspondence theory of truth is still open to debate. This debate will be resolved in terms of the actual role of truth and reference in the explanations of science, an idea that was once clear to Putnam:

> the *success* of [human language use] may well depend on the existence of a suitable correspondence between the words of a language and things, and between the sentences of a language and states of affairs. The notions of truth and reference may be of great importance in explaining the relation of language to the world... (Putnam [1978], p. 100)

If this explanatory role, or some other, is served by a correspondence theory in ways it can't be served by a deflationary theory, we obviously have strong scientific grounds to try to develop a viable correspondence theory. But a correspondence theory is not mandated by naturalism tout court.

That point made, we should consider Putnam's reasons for holding that adherence to the correspondence theory serves to undermine his opponent's position; if what Putnam puts forth is a properly scientific objection, then the naturalist should take note and factor this into the ongoing debate. Alas, Putnam returns instead to the vicinity of his Kantian corollary:

> The problem that the believer in metaphysical realism (or 'transcendental realism' as Kant called it) has always faced involves the notion of 'correspondence'. ... How can we pick out any *one* correspondence between our words (or thoughts) and the supposed mind-independent things *if we have no direct access to the mind-independent things*? (German philosophy almost always began with a particular answer to this question—the answer 'we can't'—after Kant.) (Putnam [1982a], pp. 206–207)

What Putnam disapproves here is not a scientific correspondence theory that attempts to describe a connection between the words humans use—as understood by linguistics, psychology, etc.—and things—as understood by physics, chemistry, biology, etc. Rather, what he has in mind is a transcendental Correspondence Theory—capital 'C', capital 'T'—formulated without the help of ordinary scientific theorizing, connecting our words with transcendental things in themselves.[42] Obviously this is not the sort of correspondence theory—small letters—that interests the naturalist in the first place, so Putnam's critique is irrelevant. In sum, then, I think that the naturalist isn't, and shouldn't be, committed to either of the truth theories Putnam proposes—the Right Assertibility theory or the transcendental Correspondence Theory—and that the jury is still out on what theory she should embrace.

Let me close this discussion of truth with a few words about Fine and the NOAer. While it is sometimes difficult to reconcile this position with other passages in Fine,[43] he clearly takes the NOAer to reject both correspondence and verificationist theories of truth:

> Thus NOA is inclined to reject *all* interpretations, theories, construals, pictures, etc., of truth, just as it rejects the special correspondence theory of realism and the acceptance pictures of the truthmongering anti-realisms. (Fine [1986a], p. 149)

As this passage suggests, Fine's NOAer also rejects deflationary theories; though Fine admits elsewhere to some passing fondness for them, he does not succumb:

> Although I am sympathetic to the deflationary approach to truth defended by Horwich [1990], I still prefer a plain no-theory attitude. (Fine [1996] p. 184)

So the question for us is: why does Fine think the NOAer should eschew all theories of truth?

A partial answer comes in this argument against the correspondence theory:

> The correspondence relation would map true statements...to states of affairs...But if we want to compare a statement with its corresponding state of affairs, how do we proceed? How do we get at a state of affairs when that is to be understood...as a feature of the *World*?...The difficulty is that whatever we observe...or causally interact with...is certainly not independent of us. ...whatever information we retrieve from such interaction is, prima facie, information about interacted-with things. (Fine [1986b], p. 151)

We have here a rerun of Putnam's argument that the correspondence theorist needs but cannot have 'direct access to the mind-independent things' (Putnam [1982a], p. 207), a consequence of his Kantian corollary.[44] In other words, what Fine, like Putnam, is rejecting is a transcendental Correspondence Theory of the sort our naturalist would never so much as consider. Surely we can agree that this is not the sort of theory the NOAer should embrace, but this fact leaves untouched the question of the scientific correctness of the ordinary (small letter) correspondence theory.

A more complete answer to our question begins from this passage:

> If pressed to answer the question of what, then, does it *mean* to say that something is true (or to what does the truth of so-and-so commit one), NOA will reply by pointing out the logical relations engendered by the specific claim and by focusing, then, on the concrete historical circumstances that ground that particular judgment of truth. For, after all, there *is* nothing more to say. (Fine [1986a], p. 134)

So far, this is little more than a reiteration of the claim that the NOAer has no theory of truth, but in a footnote to the final sentence, Fine goes a bit further:

Not doubt I am optimistic, for one can always think of more to say. In particular, one could try to fashion a general, descriptive framework for codifying and classifying such answers. Perhaps there would be something to be learned from such a descriptive, semantical framework. (op. cit.)

This sounds like the sort of scientific study of the role of truth in scientific explanations that the naturalist proposes to undertake. Fine continues:

But what I am afraid of is that this enterprise, once launched, would lead to a proliferation of frameworks not so carefully descriptive. These would take on a life of their own, each pretending to ways (better than its rivals) to settle disputes over truth claims, or their import. What we need, however, is less bad philosophy, not more. So here, I believe, silence is indeed golden. (op. cit.)

In other words, Fine is not holding that a scientific study of truth is impossible, or that it cannot lead to a useful semantic account of language, but that it is also so likely to lead to bad philosophy that it should not be undertaken in the first place. In response to this concern, the naturalist simply trusts to the safeguards of science.

IV. Conclusion

I have tried to illuminate the contours of my post-Quinean version of naturalism first by tracing early occurrences of what I take to be the fundamental naturalistic impulse in Reichenbach, Quine and Fine, and by indicating where my naturalist would disagree with the further elaborations of these proto-naturalists. I then outlined a range of contemporary objections to vaguely naturalistic projects of various sorts and showed how they fail to touch the naturalism I'm recommending. Finally, I sketched Putnam's and Fine's thoughts on the theory of truth and attempted to turn away the suggestion that a naturalist, simply by virtue of her naturalism, is committed to one position or another on this issue. In the end, I hope at least that the position has been clarified. I leave to the reader any further musings on its viability.[45]

Notes

1. For examples, see the treatments of scientific methodology and the status of mathematics in [1997] and [2000].
2. I hope this will come clearer toward the end of §I.
3. [1997] and [2000] are earlier installments in this effort.
4. For a slightly more complete discussion of this approach to Kant, see [2000].
5. See Reichenbach [1920].
6. For an historical discussion, see Coffa [1991], chapter 10.
7. See Reichenbach [1928]. For overview, see Reichenbach [1936], p. 146.

8. The following discussion of Carnap, Quine, the a priori, and naturalism draws on portions of my [2000].
9. See Carnap [1928].
10. Actually, out of the relation that holds between a current experience and a past experience when I recognize them as similar.
11. See Carnap [1934] and [1950].
12. E.g., the 'thing language' presumably includes evidential rules that specify certain experiences as evidence for certain physical object claims. The evidential rule would be a priori in that framework, but the claim that the physical object exists would not follow from the framework alone.
13. See Carnap [1963], p. 921.
14. Reichenbach himself contrasts the work of his group with Carnap's Vienna Circle, emphasizing the intra-scientific approach of the Berlin group: 'In line with their more concrete working program, which demanded analysis of specific problems in science, [the members of the Berlin group] avoided all theoretic maxims like those set up by the Viennese school and embarked upon detailed work in logistics, physics, biology and psychology' (Reichenbach [1936], p. 144).
15. See Quine [1948], pp. 16–19, and [1951], pp. 45–46. For a more complete presentation of the argument in the text, see my [2000].
16. E.g., see the chemist Ostwald in 1904: 'the atomic hypothesis has proved to be an exceedingly useful aid to instruction and investigation...One must not, however, be led astray by this agreement between picture and reality and combine the two'. For references and fuller discussion, see my [1997], §II.6.i.
17. E.g., see Ostwald in 1908: 'the agreement of Brownian movement with the demands of the kinetic hypothesis...which have been proved through a series of researches and at last most completely by J. Perrin, entitle even the cautious scientist to speak of an experimental proof for the atomistic constitution of space-filled matter'. (See op. cit.)
18. See Fine [1986a], p. 129.
19. This is a central theme of my [1997], especially §II.6.
20. Also Fine, see below.
21. See footnote 14 and Reichenbach [1936], pp. 149–150.
22. See Friedman [1979].
23. See my [1997], especially II.2, II.6, III.3, and III.4. There I also disagree with Quine's treatment of mathematics.
24. See Fine [1986a], pp. 149–150.
25. These ideas, Fine says, 'bring NOA in line with certain postmodern and feminist writings' (Fine [1996], p. 174).
26. I hope my general remarks in other parts of this paper will be understood in the spirit described here.
27. I would also disagree with Fine's assessment of the status of the belief that scientific methods are responsive to more than purely social pressures. Fine counts this as an extra-scientific 'add-on' to NOA (Fine [1996], p. 185); I would count it as internal to the scientific theory of science. The process of weeding out methods that are largely responsive to factors like social pressure is part of the process of scientific correction to scientific method.
28. Putnam himself regards naturalized metaphysics as a 'unified movement' and naturalized epistemology as expressed in many 'incompatible and mutually divergent ways' ([1982b], p. 230).

29. Of course this is not to say that we are getting what Putnam dramatically character-izes as 'a coherent theory of the noumena...arrived at by the "scientific method"' (Putnam [1982a], p. 226). What we come to know is the ordinary empirical world, not its transcendental counterpart.
30. Of course, our modes of perception and conceptualization are themselves part of the world, so not everything about the world is independent of them.
31. See the classics, Quine [1948] and [1951].
32. See Putnam [1976], pp. 130–131. The idea, obviously, is that the convergent se-quences of line segments of the second theory take the place of the points of the first theory.
33. See Putnam [1982a], p. 227.
34. As a reminder of the observations at the end of §I, notice that we put the point this way in describing the naturalist's practice; she simply proceeds according to her own methods, unimpressed by proposed alternatives—e.g., philosophical intuition—until their merits can be established by her standards.
35. See, for example, Quine [1981a], p. 181.
36. In [1997], I argue that the naturalist will discover that mathematics is also a seemingly-assertive discourse with norms differing from those of science, but that the naturalist has reason to treat mathematics as a special case (see pp. 203–205). I leave mathematics aside here.
37. This may be Fine's NOAer, but I don't pretend to be sure. The discussion at the end of the previous section even suggests that the NOAer's investigation of science may be undertaken from a perspective other than that of science, but this is not part of the quasi-naturalistic view under consideration here.
38. That is, when she says, 'from their point of view, my assertions are justified by my norms', this claim is justified by her norms, not by theirs. See Putnam [1982b], pp. 237–238.
39. See, for example, Kitcher's skeptical treatment (in his [1993]) of cases studies of Kuhn, Doppelt, Shapin and Schaffer.
40. This goes for other topics as well, e.g., the status of logic.
41. See, for example, Field [1986], Horwich [1990], Gupta [1993], Field [1994], Leeds [1995].
42. Putnam himself distinguishes between 'a "correspondence" between words and sets of things...as part of an *explanatory model* of speakers' collective behavior...[as] a scientific picture of the relation of speakers to their environment' and the Corre-spondence Theory involved in 'metaphysical realism' (Putnam [1976], pp. 123–4).
43. See Musgrave [1989] for discussion.
44. Compare Musgrave [1989], pp. 53–58, discussing Fine: 'Kant is, of course, the phi-losopher who started the rot here' (p. 56).
45. My thanks to my colleagues Jeffrey Barrett and Kyle Stanford for pressing me on these questions (and to an anonymous referee for further critique). I regret that my answers haven't satisfied either of them!

References

Boyd, Richard
[1983] 'On the current status of scientific realism', reprinted in R. Boyd et al, eds., *The Philosophy of Science*, (Cambridge, MA: MIT Press, 1991), pp. 195–222.

[1990] 'Realism, approximate truth, and philosophical method,' reprinted in D. Papineau, ed., *The Philosophy of Science*, (Oxford: Oxford University Press, 1996), pp. 215–255.

Carnap, Rudolf

[1928] *Logical Structure of the World*, R. A. George, trans., (Berkeley, CA: University of California Press, 1967).

[1934] *Logical Syntax of Language*, A. Smeaton, trans., (London: Routledge and Kegan Paul, 1937).

[1950] 'Empiricism, semantics and ontology', reprinted in P. Benacerraf and H. Putnam, eds., *Philosophy of Mathematics*, second edition, (Cambridge: Cambridge University Press, 1983), pp. 241–257.

[1963] 'Replies and systematic expositions', in P. A. Schilpp, ed., *The Philosophy of Rudolf Carnap*, (La Salle, IL: Open Court), pp. 859–1013.

Coffa, Alberto

[1991] *The Semantic Tradition from Kant to Carnap: to the Vienna Station*, (Cambridge: Cambridge University Press).

Feynman, Richard

[1998] *The Meaning of It All: Thoughts of a Citizen-Scientist*, (Perseus Books: Reading MA).

Field, Hartry

[1972] 'Tarski's theory of truth', *Journal of Philosophy* 69, pp. 347–375.

[1986] 'The deflationary conception of truth', in G. MacDonald and C. Wright, eds., *Fact, Science and Morality*, (Oxford: Blackwell), pp. 55–117.

[1994] 'Deflationist views of meaning and content', *Mind* 103, pp. 249–285.

Fine, Arthur

[1986a] *The Shaky Game*, (Chicago: University of Chicago Press).

[1986b] 'Unnatural attitudes: realist and instrumentalist attachments to science', *Mind* 95, pp. 149–179.

[1996] 'Afterward' to *The Shaky Game*, second edition, (Chicago: University of Chicago Press), pp. 173–201.

Friedman, Michael

[1979] 'Truth and confirmation', *Journal of Philosophy* 76, pp. 361–382.

Gupta, Anil

[1993] 'A critique of deflationism', *Philosophical Topics* 21, pp. 57–81.

Horwich, Paul

[1990] *Truth*, (Oxford: Blackwell).

Kitcher, Philip

[1993] *The Advancement of Science*, (New York: Oxford University Press).

Leeds, Stephen

[1978] 'Theories of truth and reference', *Erkenntnis* 13, pp. 111–129.

[1995] 'Truth, correspondence and success', *Philosophical Studies* 79, pp. 1–36.

Maddy, Penelope

[1997] *Naturalism in Mathematics*, (Oxford: Oxford University Press).

[2000] 'Naturalism and the a priori', in P. Boghossian and C. Peacocke, eds., *New Essays on the A Priori* (Oxford: Oxford University Press), pp. 92–116.

Musgrave, Alan

[1989] 'NOA's ark—Fine for realism', reprinted in D. Papineau, ed., *Philosophy of Science*, (Oxford: Oxford University Press, 1996), pp. 45–60.

Putnam, Hilary

[1971] 'Philosophy of logic', reprinted in his *Mathematics, Matter and Method, Philosophical Papers*, vol. 1, second edition, (Cambridge: Cambridge University Press, 1979), pp. 323–357.

[1976] 'Realism and reason', in his [1978], pp. 123–140.

[1978] *Meaning and the Moral Sciences*, (London: Routledge and Kegan Paul).

[1982a] 'Why there isn't a ready-made world', reprinted in his [1983], pp. 205–228.

[1882b] 'Why reason can't be naturalized', reprinted in his [1983], pp. 229–247.

[1983] *Realism and Reason, Philosophical Papers*, vol. 3, (Cambridge: Cambridge University Press).
Quine, Willard van Orman
[1948] 'On what there is', reprinted in his [1953], pp. 1–19.
[1951] 'Two dogmas of empiricism', reprinted in his [1953], pp. 20–46.
[1953] *From a Logical Point of View*, second edition, (Cambridge, MA: Harvard University Press, 1980).
[1960] *Word and Object*, (Cambridge, MA: MIT Press).
[1975] 'Five milestones of empiricism', in [1981a], pp. 67–72.
[1981] 'Things and their place in theories', in [1981a], pp. 1–23.
[1981a] *Theories and Things*, (Cambridge, MA: Harvard University Press).
Reichenbach, Hans
[1920] *The Theory of Relativity and A Priori Knowledge*, M. Reichenbach, trans. and ed., (Berkeley: University of California Press, 1965).
[1928] *The Philosophy of Space and Time*, M. Reichenbach and J. Freund, trans., (New York: Dover, 1957).
[1936] 'Logistic empiricism in Germany and the present state of its problems', *Journal of Philosophy* 33, pp. 141–160.
[1949] 'The philosophical significance of the theory of relativity', in P. A. Schilpp, ed., *Albert Einstein: Philosopher-Scientist*, (La Salle, IL: Open Court), pp. 287–311.
Schlick, Morris
[1921] 'Critical or empiricist interpretation of modern physics?', reprinted in *Philosophical Papers*, H. L. Mulder and B. F. B. van de Velde-Schlick, eds., P. Heath, trans., pp. 322–334.
Van Fraassen, Bas
[1980] *The Scientific Image*, (Oxford: Oxford University Press).

Philosophical Perspectives, 15, Metaphysics, 2001

NOMINALISM, NATURALISM, EPISTEMIC RELATIVISM

Gideon Rosen
Princeton University

1. Two Questions

The problem of nominalism—Do abstract objects exist?—is a problem in metaphysics. But no one knows how to approach this problem directly. Rather in this case as in so many cases in contemporary philosophy, we approach the metaphysical question via a correlative question in epistemology. Instead of asking whether abstract entities in fact exist, we ask whether we are justified in believing that they do.

My aim in what follows is to clarify this epistemological question and its relation to the metaphysical debate. The most important thing to note is that the epistemological question is ambiguous in a sense in which the metaphysical question is not. Some of the ambiguities are quite subtle; indeed we lack a suitably nuanced vocabulary for sorting them out. But let's begin with what ought to be an elementary distinction.

When we ask whether we are justified in believing that abstract objects exist, we might be asking whether we are rationally entitled to believe—whether a commitment to abstract things is rationally permissible for us. But we might also be asking whether we are rationally *obliged* to believe: whether it would be positively unreasonable to reject abstract objects or to suspend judgment on their existence.

These are clearly different questions: as different as the difference between 'must' and 'may': and in my opinion, they have different answers. In what follows I shall try to make it plausible that while a commitment to abstract objects is rationally permissible for us, no such commitment is obligatory. It is rationally permissible, in other words, both to believe that abstract entities exist, and to suspend judgment on their existence and perhaps even to reject them altogether. (*Nota bene*: If these were the answers to the only relevant epistemological questions concerning nominalism, then an epistemological inquiry would leave the original metaphysical question unresolved. You can learn that it's all right to believe and that it's all right not to believe without learning whether abstract objects exist.)

2. The Permissibility of Platonism

There are several ways to argue for the permissibility of platonism, but the case that interests me rests on three main assumptions. (The assumptions are familiar and I shall not defend them here. If the reader doubts them, he should regard the argument of the paper as conditional.)

(1) *The worldview we take for granted entails the existence of abstract entities.* When we say that there are twenty-six letters in the alphabet, or that Shakespeare wrote the Sonnets, or that the laws of motion are Lorentz invariant, what we say entails the existence of objects over and above the ink marks on paper that a nominalist might admit. Letters, languages, poems, laws, the numbers that measure quantities and the quantities themselves, not to mention the sets and functions of higher mathematics: whatever these things may be, they are not concrete objects. So if our considered worldview is roughly accurate, abstract entities exist.

(2) *Not only do we accept a worldview that entails the existence of abstract entities. By ordinary standards as we ordinarily apply them, we are fully justified in doing so.* Consider a striking observation from ordinary botany: the number of seeds in a sunflower is usually a Fibonacci number. By ordinary standards the empirical case for this claim is overwhelming. Sunflowers from all over the world have been examined, and in nearly every case a careful count of the seeds has yielded a term in the famous series. When the result was first announced at the Society for Numerical Botany, the obvious questions were pressed: Was the sample large enough? Were the seed counters reliable? But the authors of the original study were able to answer these questions. And by the standards that normally govern this sort of research, that was good enough. Of course no one asked them how they knew that there were numbers to begin with. (If someone had asked they would presumably have been at something of a loss.) But this just goes to show that by ordinary standards, one may be justified in believing a claim that implies the existence of numbers without being in a position to prove their existence by separate argument. To put the same point another way, this just goes to show that in a normal investigation, the possibility that a mathematical claim might be false because numbers do not exist is not among the possibilities one is obliged to exclude. The standards that govern normal inquiry are simply not that stringent.

This is not just a point about everyday botany. It applies equally to high-stakes research in which the most exacting standards are brought to bear. A novel claim about the rate of global warming may be challenged in many ways. But within geophysics it will never be challenged on the ground that *rates* after all are *numbers*, and numbers might not exist. You might as well object to eye-witness testimony in a criminal trial on ground that the witness cannot prove she's not a brain in a vat. The skeptical possibility may be a genuine possibility. But even if it is, one is normally under no obligation to exclude it—not even in the most demanding precincts of science.

Now so far this is just a point about what is normally allowed to pass, and as such it shows nothing about what we genuinely entitled to believe. But it does show, in my view—and this is the crucial point—that any case for compulsory nominalism must be a skeptical case: a case for revising a pervasive (and by ordinary standards, unproblematic) commitment of common sense and established science. An argument for such revision may take one of two forms. It may exploit epistemic norms internal to the sciences (broadly construed), or it may appeal to some allegedly higher philosophical standard. In the first case what must be shown is that even though abstract objects are freely admitted in every field, they are nonetheless inadmissible *from the standpoint of science itself.* In the second case what must be shown is that whatever the standards of normal science may have to say, claims about the abstract are ipso facto unwarranted *given the real and authoritative superscientific norms governing reasonable belief.*

The case for the permissibility of antinominalism rests on the claim that no compelling skeptical argument of either form can be given. There have been many attempts to undermine our pre-philosophical commitment to abstract entities. But in each case the argument may be shown to rest on one or another dubious claim in epistemology—typically, some version of the causal theory of knowledge.[1] I am not going to argue for this sweeping thesis here, so let this rather stand as my third dogmatic assumption: (3) *There is no compelling case against a commitment to abstract objects as such.* We may legitimately wonder about particular cases: supercompact cardinals, *the* text of *Ulysses.* But there is no compelling case against numbers and the rest simply from the fact that these things would be abstract if they existed.

3. Reasonable Disagreement

If my three assumptions are correct, antinominalism is an option. But is it the only option? Is it also rationally permissible for us to doubt the existence of abstract objects—to suspend judgment on the truth of classical mathematics, for example, simply on the ground that it posits abstract things? Or is the case for antinominalism so profoundly compelling that doubts about the abstract must be reckoned unreasonable?

It should be obvious that reasonable people can disagree, even when confronted with a single body of evidence. When a jury or a court is divided in a difficult case, the mere fact of disagreement does not mean that someone is being unreasonable. Paleontologists disagree about what killed the dinosaurs. And while it is possible that most of the parties to this dispute are irrational, this need not be the case. To the contrary, it would appear to be a fact of epistemic life that a careful review of the evidence does not guarantee consensus, even among thoughtful and otherwise rational investigators.

Our question then comes down to this: Is the debate over nominalism a case in point? William James held that metaphysics is always a matter of temperament, from which he inferred insofar as Reason mandates no temperament in particular, it cannot be expected to resolve debates in metaphysics.[2] A puerile generalization as it stands, no doubt; but there is this much to it: We have no reason whatsoever to assume a priori that metaphysical disagreement can always be resolved by appeal to neutral reasons. We should therefore be open to the possibility that just as reasonable people may disagree about the fate of the dinosaurs, reasonable people may disagree about the existence of abstract objects.

Now when the point is framed in this way, it may seem numbingly obvious. After all, if rational disagreement is to be expected anywhere it's to be expected where the evidence is thinnest and the distance between theory and data most immense. Speculative ontology is sometimes seen as the liming case of this predicament, and so it might be said: "If reasonable people can disagree about what killed the dinosaurs, then *of course* they can disagree about whether abstract entities exist. Speculative ontology is paleontology without the fossils. As constraining evidence goes to zero, scope for disagreement goes to infinity. And that is precisely what we find in this case."

But this is confused. In the first place, it does not follow from the fact that the evidence is thin on some question that reasonable people may disagree about the answer. Sometimes the only reasonable attitude is suspense of judgment. (Is the number of stars odd or even?) More importantly, as Quine pointed out, it is a mistake to view 'ontology' as a limiting case of speculation. Recall our first dogmatic assumption, viz. that the worldview we take for granted is up to its ears in abstract things. To doubt the existence of abstract objects is not just to doubt some bloodless thesis in metaphysics. It is doubt basic arithmetic, settled physics, the solid claims of linguistics and music theory and the rest. The question is not simply whether one may doubt *that abstract objects exist*. It is whether one may reasonably doubt *that Mozart wrote sonatas, that Portuguese is a romance language, that some equations have solutions.* And whatever the ultimate disposition of the issue, it is hardly *obvious* that reasonable people may disagree about such matters given everything else we know about what the world is like.

4. Science and the Limits of Permissible Doubt

We have no settled framework for discussing the scope of reasonable doubt. But we do have intuitions about where doubt is legitimate and where it is perverse, and we may as well begin with them. The most important such intuition concerns the status of science—by which I mean not just the paradigmatic natural sciences, but solid critical thought on any topic: history, music, literature, and so on. If my first assumption is correct, accepted science is entangled with the abstract at every turn. To doubt the abstract is thus to doubt settled science. Moreover this doubt would extend not just to claims that explicitly refer to abstract objects—'The atomic number of helium is 2'—but to claims about the concrete whose only scientific justification proceeds by way of platonistic theory. That the continents are in motion is not a claim about abstract objects. But the case for believing it takes mathematics for granted. Someone with doubts about mathematics should thus have doubts about continental drift (unless he is in a position to supply non-mathematical support for the hypothesis).

The relevant intuition about the scope of reasonable doubt is then as follows: It would be patently unreasonable for an informed citizen of the modern world simply to reject modern science—to suspend judgment on the claims of physics and geology and literary history—simply because it assumes the existence of abstract objects. It would be one thing if there were some positive ground for such doubt: some cogent case against the antinominalist background for science. But we have already stipulated that such a case cannot be made. What we are imagining is someone who dismisses modern science root and branch, simply because its assumptions about abstract objects *might be mistaken*. I submit that in the absence of positive ground for doubt, such an attitude should strike us as pathological. It recalls the skeptical doubt which traditional discussions of induction purport to address, viz., the doubt of the agent who declines to believe that the sun will rise tomorrow *simply because he cannot prove that the future will resemble the past*. This timid Humean freak is a paradigm of unreason, not because he contradicts himself, but rather because his standards for good reasoning are absurdly high. The nominalistically-minded skeptic about science is likewise unreasonable. It may well be that our basic assumptions about abstract objects do not admit of independent justification 'from below'. Still, to take this as grounds for opting out of modern science altogether would be an egregious overreaction—a paradigm case of unreasonable epistemic caution.

This means that any case for the permissibility of suspense of judgment about the abstract must show how nominalism of this sort is compatible with taking science seriously as a source of information about concrete nature. This is of course the point of the familiar 'nominalization' programs.[3] When these programs are not pitched as dubious hermeneutic proposals,[4] they are best understood as attempts to reconcile doubts about the literal truth of extant science with a policy of *accepting* platonistic theories as instruments for description and explanation. I shall not discuss these programs in detail here. Instead I shall describe what I regard as a simple trick for nominalizing at a stroke any theory whatsoever. Given any theory T formulated in the usual mathematical terms, the trick returns a theory that does without abstract objects, but which is nonetheless in a certain sense equivalent to the original. Before I describe the trick, I should emphasize that I do not endorse the novel theories it delivers. The nominalistic version of (say) quantum electrodynamics is in some sense a different theory from standard QED. But it is not a better, more acceptable theory. The nominalistic version is of interest, not as an account of what science actually says, and certain not as an account of what it ought to be saying, but rather as an account of what science might have said, and might have been justified in saying had cultural history gone somewhat differently. (Why it should matter what science might have said will emerge in the sequel.)

5. Bedrock

The dogmatic assumptions with which I began were claims about us as we are. Suppose they are correct: Not only do we indulge in platonistic discourse: we often believe what we say; we harbor no secret reservations; and all of this is rationally permissible by our lights. Indeed for good measure let us make the further assumption that so far as we can see, the cumulative scientific case for certain abstract entities is so utterly compelling that it would be unreasonably cautious to demur. Let us assume, in other words, that so far as we can see, platonism is not just permissible; it is mandatory.

That's how we are, but in Bedrock things are different. They speak English in Bedrock and for the most part they say what we say: "Some poems don't rhyme", "Some numbers are irrational". Bedrocker science and mathematics are indiscernible from ours. Their textbooks, their advanced teaching, the transcripts of their laboratory conversation, and the rest are all thoroughly platonistic, in the sense that the sentences they contain imply the existence of abstract objects.

The difference is that in Bedrock they have reservations about this aspect of what they say—carefully considered and fully articulate reservations. Bedrockers are encouraged from early childhood to suspect that only concrete things exist, and that discourse about the abstract is thus at best a useful fiction. If you ask them how they square this with what they say when they're doing science, they smile as if they've heard the question a thousand times and deliver themselves of a speech along the following lines.

> We admit that our theories imply the existence of abstract objects, and that when we put them forward in the 'assertoric mode', there is a sense in which what we say is at odds with our nominalism. But there is no real conflict. We don't believe what we say. It's not that we're dishonest or hypocritical. It's rather that our practice of 'assertion' differs from yours.
>
> Consider, for example, the following pair of statements:
>
> (1) The number of Martian moons = 2
>
> (2) There are exactly two Martian moons.[5]
>
> These claims are equally 'assertible' in any normal context. But they are distinct claims nonetheless, with distinct truth conditions. Any world in which the first is true must contain at least four items: Mars, its two moons, and their number, the number 2. Worlds in which the second claim is true

include all of these worlds, but also certain worlds in which this fourth thing is missing. But this is just to say that (2) is strictly weaker than (1), and in particular that (2) does not entail the existence of numbers.[6]

The claims are nonetheless clearly very close in content. Intuitively, while they differ in what they say simpliciter, they agree in what they say about the concrete world considered in itself. Let's say the **concrete core** of a world W is the largest wholly concrete part of W: the aggregate of all of the concrete objects that exist in W. What (1) and (2) have in common is simply this: The concrete core of every world at which (1) is true is an exact intrinsic duplicate of the core of some world at which (2) is true, and vice versa. Claims that meet this condition are said to be **nominalistically equivalent**.

Now suppose that ours is a numberless world, and that (1) is therefore false. If we were concerned to speak the truth, we would never countenance its assertion. But the fact is, we are rarely concerned to speak the truth. Our unhedged assertoric utterances normally aspire to a weaker condition we call **nominalistic adequacy**. S is nominalistically adequate iff the concrete core of the actual world is an exact intrinsic duplicate of the concrete core of some world at which S is true—that is, just in case things are in all concrete respects *as if* S were true.[7]

Our beliefs, like yours, are governed by a non-negotiable norm of truth. But for the most part our assertoric utterances do not even purport to be true. We are quite up front about this, and no one is misled. Our children are first introduced to the abstract apparatus by immersion, just as yours are. But in their early required courses in ontological hygiene, they are told explicitly that what they say about the abstract is not to be taken seriously. To drive the point home they are encouraged to prefix their utterances with fictionalizing operators, "According to the best, nominalistically adequate account..." or perhaps, "If there were abstract objects and the concrete world were intrinsically just as it is, then..." But this gets tedious rather quickly, and the prefix soon falls silent. Still, it is always there, tacitly, if you like, and we can always make it explicit when some tourist gets confused.

We should stress that you are familiar with habitual indirection of this sort. When you talk about the movie you saw last night, you may begin very carefully, saying "In the movie, this" and "In the movie, that" But sooner or later you will drop the prefix and begin to regulate your assertions, not by literal truth, but by truth-in-the-story.

This is only the clearest case of what is in fact a widespread phenomenon. Whenever you speak hyperbolically or metaphorically—in short, whenever, you speak figuratively—you 'assert' a sentence without committing yourself its truth. It would not surprise us if non-literal assertion in this sense were the norm, even in a literally-minded culture like yours. But it's certainly the norm with us. You may be cultural platonists. But we're cultural fictionalists. We immerse ourselves in the pretense that the concrete world is embedded in much larger world of abstract objects and then speak from within this pretense as a matter of course. But we have no tendency to believe in the abstract objects that would exist if our claims were true. From our point of view, that is all make-believe.[8]

This indirection would be pointless if every case were like our toy example. In asserting (1) we commit ourselves to the view that (1) is nominalistically adequate. But this is equivalent to the claim that (2) is simply true. So in this case, if we wanted to speak our minds directly, we could just assert (2), bypassing pretense altogether. In other cases, however, this will not be so easy. This is where our fictionalism comes into its own.

Consider the debate over the authorship of Shakespeare's plays. Traditionalists assign the plays to the glover's son from Stratford. Looney and his followers assign them to Edward Devere, the seventh Earl of Oxford.[9] We regard this as an issue of some importance. But of course we don't really believe in *plays* and the like. So when one of our scholars asserts, for example, that Oxford wrote *The Tempest*, he does not commit himself to the opinion that an abstract entity stands in a certain literary relation to the Earl. The question that interests him is a question about how the concrete world is configured. But he has no way to formulate that question or his preferred answer to it without invoking the fiction of abstract entities. No non-parasitic sentence in our language stands to "Oxford wrote the Tempest" as "Mars has two moons" stands to "The number of Martian moons = 2". So the best we can do—and this is quite good enough—is to acquiesce in the pretense that abstract entities exist and conduct our investigation within the scope of that pretense.[10] The real question is not whether Oxford wrote the play. It is whether it is nominalistically adequate that he did.

This phenomenon of the expressive indispensability of the abstract is most pervasive in the natural sciences, where the descriptive apparatus is irredeemably mathematical. We take science very seriously. We teach it; we rely on it. And we do so because we regard it as the only decent way to find out what nature is like. But we do not regard science as a source of information about the abstract. For us the aim of science is (roughly speaking) to produce an account of things that is useful and informative and nominalistically adequate: a strong and explanatory representation that is true insofar as what it says about concrete nature is concerned, but which may be false (for all we care) in what it says about the abstract.

Our practice of theory choice is outwardly just like yours. The considerations that bear upon the assessment of scientific claims—empirical adequacy, simplicity, explanatoriness, and the rest—go over without modification from your culture to ours. This outward similarity conceals a difference, however. For you the resolution to accept a scientific theory is the resolution to believe it (at least tentatively) and in particular, to believe in the real existence of its objects. For us, the resolution to accept a theory is the resolution to use it in certain ways and to believe (at most) that it is nominalistically adequate.[11] What you regard as a reason to believe that T is true, we regard as a reason to believe that T is nominalistically adequate. We stress that this weaker belief can have all the 'empirical content' you like. If you believe that there will be an eclipse tomorrow night because you believe a mathematically formulated theory from which this prediction may be derived, we will form precisely the same expectation. After all, if T is credible by your lights, it is nominalistically adequate by ours. And where P is a claim about the concrete world considered in itself, if T entails P, then so does the weaker claim that T is nominalistically adequate. To the extent that practically relevant conclusions are all claims about the concrete array, it follows that there is no practical difference between believing a theory to be true and believing it to be nominalistically adequate.[12]

Of course there is much more to science than accepting theories on the basis of evidence and deriving predictions from accepted theory. It would be an enormous project to show that every legitimate feature of science in your culture has a defensible analog in ours. To show this would be to establish that nothing essential to scientific practice and application depends for its rationality on believing in abstract entities. We believe this can be done, but it will take some time.[13] Shall we begin?

6. Are the Bedrockers Unreasonable?

Let's not. The point of the story is to make it plausible that there might be a community that rejects our complacent realism about the abstract despite familiarity with all of the evidence and argument we can muster—a community that 'naturally' (as it were) makes the sort of invidious distinction that philosophical nominalists have long urged us to make. It seems to me indisputable that there could be a group of people who respond in the manner indicated to our queries about what they are up to. And given that this is so, we have two questions to ask: Are the Bedrockers rationally entitled to persist in their fictionalism? And is it a rational option for us? In either case a positive answer entails that reasonable people can disagree about the real existence of abstract objects. But a 'yes' to the second question yields a particularly striking result, namely, that despite the pervasive antinominalism of our science and despite the absence of any positive ground for doubt about the abstract, it is not unreasonable for us to maintain a selective skepticism about accepted science by bracketing certain aspects of what our best theories have to say.

Let's begin with the first question. Are the Bedrockers unreasonable? If they are then it should be possible to locate their mistake: to describe a compelling dialectical route from their complacent agnosticism to some form of realism, or at the very least to identify some principle or rule of inference which they reject, the rejection of which strikes us—when we hold it up to the light—as somehow crazy or silly or perverse or unintelligible.

It might be objected, for example, that fictionalism is self-contradictory or self-refuting. Thus Crispin Wright has maintained that certain claims about the concrete—"There are just as many pigs as chickens"—analytically imply claims about abstract objects—"The number of pigs = the number of chickens".[14] And if this is right, agnosticism is not an option. Alternatively, it might be urged that whenever a Bedrocker accepts a claim as nominalistically adequate, he forms a belief that can only be true if abstract objects exist. The belief that T is nominalistically adequate seems to presuppose the existence of the theory T, and it is natural to suppose that theories must be abstract.[15] Less obviously, the belief that T is nominalistically adequate, as I have explained it, is a belief about relations among possible worlds. And one might legitimately wonder whether a commitment to possible worlds (some of which must contain abstracta) is consistent with genuine agnosticism about the abstract.

These are serious objections. I believe they can be answered, but I shall not pursue the matter here. After all, even if the bare coherence of the stance can be secured, this would not be enough to settle the epistemological question. The flat earth hypothesis is not self-contradictory. The evidence does not strictly speaking entail its falsity. And yet knowing what we know, you would have to be crazy to believe it. And so it might be said, "Bedrock-style fictionalism is not self-refuting, nor can it refuted decisively by appeal to evidence. And yet it is unreasonable to suspend judgment about the abstract. We (and they) possess *compelling non-demonstrative grounds* for believing the settled claims of physics and music theory and the rest. The Bedrockers may be able to doubt these claims without contradiction. But they might as well be flat-earthers: consistent but unreasonable."

Of course it's no good just to say this. The Bedrockers I have described are the very picture of lucidity. If their fictionalism is ruled out by some compelling epistemological principle, we should be able to isolate it and so to show them where exactly they go wrong. (Whether they will listen is another matter. There is such a thing as being too far-gone.) When I claim that Bedrock-style fictionalism is not unreasonable, what I mean is that this challenge cannot be met.

7. Epistemic Naturalism: Some Varieties

To get a sense of what is wanted, consider the following from Putnam.

The fictionalist concedes that predictive power and 'simplicity'...are hallmarks of a good theory, and that they make it rational to accept a theory, at least "for scientific purposes". But then[...]what *further* reasons could one want before one regarded it as rational to *believe* a theory? If the very things that make the fictionalist regard [abstract] objects, etc. as 'useful fictions' do not make it rational to believe the [abstract] object 'conceptual system', what could make it rational to believe anything?[16]

Putnam's claim is that fictionalist agnosticism about the deliverances established science is unreasonable. The fictionalist distinguishes between credibility and acceptability for scientific purposes. And that is his mistake. *Reasons to accept a theory for scientific purposes just are reasons to believe that it is true.* The fictionalist is unreasonable because he flouts this basic maxim.

Before we can assess the idea, it will help to fix terms. (What follows is partly stipulative, but I believe it is in the spirit of Putnam's view.) To accept a theory in the relevant sense is use it in certain ways: in giving explanations, deriving predictions, designing experiments, and so on. Acceptance so conceived is a phenomenon of scientific practice. A suitably placed anthropologist can determine which theories a scientist accepts by observing what he does, and in particular, what he says. It is also a fantastically various phenomenon. It comes in degrees as well as kinds, the botanizing of which remains an open problem in the sociology of science. For present purposes we focus on the most serious sorts of acceptance—acceptance without significant scientific reservations. A present-day physicist may rely on Newtonian assumptions in certain contexts. But he knows that the theory is accurate only within certain limits, and when pressed to give his most considered account or to justify his predictions when maximal precision is required, he will typically invoke one or another post-Newtonian theory. This is the theory he *seriously* accepts: the one he appeals to when the chips are down and he is pressed to give his best scientific account of what's what.

Serious acceptance so described is distinct from belief. When the Bedrockers write their textbooks and design their space telescopes, they use the platonistic theories that our scientists use. But of course they do not believe them.

What does it mean to say that T is 'acceptable for scientific purposes'? Here's one way to think of it. The intellectual disciplines are social practices for theory acceptance. As such they embody a batter of norms for theory choice (i.e., acceptance). These norms are rarely made explicit. Rather, to be trained in the practice is to require a practical mastery of what counts as a reason to accept a novel claim. Putnam makes two substantive assumptions about these practice-immanent norms for acceptance. The first is that they are genuine norms: To be justified in accepting a theory by the standards of (say) biochemistry is to be justified in fact in accepting that theory. This is not a tautology. The True Believers embrace an elaborate set of rules for extracting predictions about the End Times from Wittgenstein's laundry lists. But it's one thing to say that S is acceptable *by the standards of crackpot eschatology*, quite another to say that S is genuinely acceptable. As Putnam frames the issue and as I have framed it here, the fictionalist and the realist agree that when it comes to the established, mature sciences, there is no gap between *acceptability by internal standards* and *genuine acceptability*.

This is not to say that scientists cannot make a mistake about acceptance. It is to say that if they do make a mistake, they will have contravened the principles implicit in their own practice. One way to formulate Putnam's first assumption is thus to say that in the established sciences—more on what that might mean in a moment—the only genuine reasons for acceptance are the reasons that function as such within the practice itself.

If we reserve the word **methodology** for the study of acceptance, this is a thesis in normative methodology. It might be called **methodological naturalism** since its motivating thought is that the methodologist must operate as a naturalized citizen of the scientific community, offering only such advice and criticism as may be warranted by the norms somehow implicit in science itself.

Putnam's second assumption, by contrast, is a thesis in normative epistemology, viz., that these internal reasons for serious acceptance are ipso facto reasons for belief. I'll call this **epistemological naturalism**, and of course, the idea is a familiar one. Having shed the bad old foundationalist ambition to justify our practices from without, the naturalist maintains that to regulate one's opinions by the norms implicit in our best cognitive practices is somehow constitutive of full rationality. The skeptic about induction or inference to the best explanation or any of the more specific principles that might be cited to justify an inferential transition within science may not be making a formal mistake. But she is making a normative mistake nonetheless. What she fails to appreciate is simply that when it comes to scientific questions, the only genuine reasons for adopting one opinion rather than another are the reasons that function within science as compelling grounds for acceptance.

Crucially for our purposes, this naturalistic conceit may be read in two ways. There is **permissive** version of the stance, according to which one is always *entitled* to believe what is fully acceptable by scientific standards. This modest view does most of the urgent anti-skeptical work for which naturalism was designed.[17] But it is no threat to fictionalism of the sort I have described. The Bedrockers do not deny, after all, that we are within our rights in believing what science has to say about abstract entities. Their distinctive claim is that they are within their rights in opting out, and permissive epistemological naturalism is consistent with that position.

The view we need to discuss is therefore **restrictive epistemological naturalism**—the thesis that it is unreasonable not to believe what science recommends for serious acceptance. If this is right then fictionalism is clearly untenable. But is there anything to be said for the idea?

8. Against Restrictive Naturalism

The first thing to say is that the Bedrockers don't believe it, and yet they appear to speak the language well enough. This is enough to scotch the neo-Strawsonian thought that to believe what is acceptable is part of what it *means* to be reasonable. Restrictive naturalism may be true, but it is hardly analytic.

But it's really much worse than that. One way to bring this out is to press an issue I have so far ignored. Let's say that an intellectual practice is **authoritative** just in case its internal norms for serious acceptance constitute rationally coercive norms for belief. Where P is an authoritative practice in this sense, it is unreasonable to doubt or deny what a fully acceptable P-theory has to say. Restrictive naturalism is then the view that certain practices—the 'established mature sciences'—are to be reckoned authoritative. But what exactly is an established mature science, and why exactly do they merit authoritative status?

No one believes that every practice is authoritative. It's one thing to say that when it comes to claims about the mass density of the universe, the only relevant standards are those of modern astrophysics. It is something else to insist that when it comes to the interpretation of dreams, the only relevant standards are those of Jungian psychoanalysis. Naturalism in epistemology is a counsel of philosophical deference. But deference has its limits and naturalism owes us an account of them.

It is striking that naturalists have had so little to say on this point. Different naturalists draw the line in different ways. Some take it for granted that the 'hard' natural sciences are the sole authoritative practices, and hence that the credibility of mathematics ultimately depends upon its role in the natural sciences.[18] Others regard pure mathematics as an authoritative practice in its own right.[19] This disagreement can be quite pointed. Do we have reason to believe those axioms of set theory which find no application in the natural sciences? The first sort of naturalist may say 'no'; the second may say 'yes'. Of course it is no objection to a view that its proponents disagree. The objection is rather that we are given no guidance whatsoever as to how the dispute could possibly be resolved. How can we know—or better, what would make it the case—that pure mathematics is an authoritative practice in the relevant sense?

I am inclined to say that in the absence of an answer to this crucial question, epistemological naturalism is not really a theory at all, but rather an incomplete and somewhat unpromising idea for a theory. It's not that I have a better account of where the epistemic norms 'come from'. But the idea that we can proceed in normative epistemology by first locating a set of authoritative practices and then identifying the norms for belief with their internally sanctioned norms for acceptance—that approach strikes me as fundamentally misguided.

Let me try to reinforce this pessimistic verdict by returning to the case in hand. Epistemological naturalism singles out certain practices as authoritative. But we may distinguish two kinds of intellectual practice. Let us say that a practice is **cognitive** with respect to a class of claims if practitioners themselves regard a cogent internal argument for accepting a claim in that class as rationally compelling grounds for believing that it is true. A practice is **instrumental** with respect to a class of claims, on the other hand, if it is rationally permissible to doubt what the practice deems acceptable *from the standpoint of the practice itself.*

Epistemological naturalism as I have formulated does not rule it out that an instrumental practice might be authoritative. It might conceivably be maintained, for example, that even though physicists treat the virtual particles of quantum field theory as mere heuristic fictions, we (and they) are nonetheless obliged to believe in virtual photons precisely because the theory is fully acceptable by their lights. But of course this would be to charge the scientists with a fundamental mistake about what to believe, and this is at odds with the deferential spirit of naturalism. If the experts themselves consistently adopt a fictionalist stance towards certain claims, who are we (we philosophers) to call them unreasonable?

We may therefore assume that the cognitive practices are the only serious candidates for authority, or perhaps better, that a practice is a candidate for authority only to the extent that it is cognitive.

But this raises the Authority Problem in a particularly pointed form. In light of Bedrock the sociological facts are as follows. We have two scientific communities, ours and theirs. By stipulation, our scientists maintain that when it comes to abstract entities, we have rationally compelling grounds for believing whatever we have scientific reason to accept, and hence that anyone who doubts the abstract objects posited in accepted science is impermissibly cautious and thus unreasonable. *Their* scientists, on the other hand, take the ecumenical view that one is required to believe only what science says about the concrete, and that whether you go further is entirely up to you. Our science, in other words is a cognitive practice across the board, whereas theirs is instrumental with respect to claims about abstracta.

How does the naturalist propose to extract the genuine epistemic norms from this clash of opinion? Cultural relativism is an option, but not an attractive one. In some areas—e.g., spelling—it is plausible that one is bound by the norms of one's own group. In this case the relativist's thought would be whereas *we* are obliged to believe in abstract objects, *they* are entitled to suspend judgment on such matters. But this is hard to believe. Once we have been careful to distinguish *blameless* belief from genuinely justified belief, the idea that the epistemic norms extend only to the boundaries of one's community loses whatever plausibility it may once have had.[20] So it will not do to say that the norms embraced by our scientists are binding on us *because they're ours, after all*. The norms may be local for some other reason, but it's hard to see what it could be.

Cultural relativism aside, there are only two possibilities. Either our epistemic practices are authoritative or theirs are. When we consider the claim that the number of Martian moons = 2—a claim that is fully acceptable by everyone's lights—then either we are all rationally obliged to believe it or we are all entitled to doubt it. Naturalism, to my knowledge, provides no guidance whatsoever as to how this conflict should be resolved. It's not that answer is hard to find. It's rather that the theory tells us nothing about what could make it the case that one of these practices is authoritative to the exclusion of the author. So much the worse, in my view, for epistemological naturalism so conceived.

9. For the Permissibility of Fictionalism

Our experts say that certain opinions are required; theirs maintain that these opinions are strictly optional. Forget about naturalism. How shall we decide which side is right?

What we have is a fundamental normative clash, akin in certain respects to basic moral disagreement. Now in the moral case some of us have come to live with view that while the contested moral question must have a single answer, reasonable people may disagree about what that answer is. But it is hard to believe that our epistemological dispute has this character. Rational permission differs from moral permission in the following respect. There is no presumption that when an act is morally impermissible, we should be able to lead any clear-headed, open-minded, intelligent agent to see that it is. That's why rationally irresolvable moral disagreement is a possibility. In the epistemic case, on the other hand, a claim to the effect that one is obliged to follow a certain rule is undermined if we can describe a reasonable-seeming, fully reflective, and fully livable human practice that eschews it. If the foregoing is sound, then a fictionalist stance towards abstract objects is consistent with a serious and reflectively stable engagement both with science and with life. And given this, it strikes me as frankly implausible to insist that this fictionalist stance is nonetheless somehow unreasonable. The Bedrockers are willing to listen and they are not stupid; and they get along as well as we do in every relevant respect. You can charge them with irrationality, and they will listen to the indictment. But what will you say to back it up? When they ask you, "What's wrong with our way of proceeding?", what will you say? If you have nothing to say, then the charge will not stick. Not only will they (quite reasonably) fail to heed you. If you have nothing to say, then in my view the charge is mistaken.

Now even if this is right it does not quite settle the question with which we began. From the fact that it is rationally permissible for *them* to persist in their fictionalism, it does not follow automatically that fictionalism is an option for *us*. By hypothesis, we begin as complacent platonists with no compelling internal reason to change our minds. The question is whether we are rationally entitled to do so anyway—to bracket what we have previously taken for granted about the abstract, and to do so on the basis of no new information.

It is a peculiar question. On the one hand, if you really believe that P, then to abandon that belief for no particular reason is to discard what one presently regards as reliable information, and odd circumstances aside, it is hard to see how that could be rational. On the other hand, anyone who has seriously asked himself whether abstract objects exist has already backed off from his natural complacency about such matters. And for someone in this position, fictionalism may well constitute a genuine rational option. When the complacent theist first asks himself whether or not there is a God, and then notices that there is nothing intrinsically unreasonable in agnosticism, it would be bizarre to insist that he is nonetheless obliged to remain a theist simply because that is where he started out, and he has been given no 'positive grounds' for thinking that he is mistaken. In a case of this sort, retrenchment is obviously an option. The case of nominalism is no different in principle in my opinion.

10. Should We Retreat to Fictionalism?

Bedrock is not real, but it might easily have been. If intellectual history had gone somewhat differently, we might now be fictionalists of just this sort. (Indeed, the overwhelming indifference to questions of abstract ontology among scientists and mathematicians might be taken to show that our natural attitude towards the abstract has a fictionalist element. The best version of this hypothesis, on my view, is that our natural attitude is indeterminate between a simple commitment to the literal truth of standard mathematics and a commitment to something like the nominalistic adequacy of accepted science.) To recognize this modal fact is to acknowledge that our complacent antinominalism is a strongly contingent feature of our worldview. It is not forced upon us: not by the facts; not by a commitment to science; and not by objective principles of rationality.

Should this recognition lead us to reconsider our antinominalism? We've already seen that it may, but *should* it? It can be disconcerting to realize that one's views are strongly contingent in this way. When it first dawns upon the complacent theist that his belief in God is not forced upon him by compelling reasons, but is rather a matter of what he has been raised to take for granted, one response is to say, "There but for the grace of God go I. It's a matter of luck that I wound up believing. But thank goodness for it. If I had been raised differently, I would have been mistaken." But another possible response is to wonder, "With what right do I suppose that I am one of the lucky ones?"

The structure of this familiar predicament is as follows. You have always believed that P for no reason in particular. P is part of the worldview you take for granted: neither inculcated by argument nor supported by argument after the fact. You then encounter someone else who finds it natural to doubt it. Neither of you can offer arguments to sway the other. Nor is it plausible to suppose that you have special access to the truth in the relevant domain (e.g., a special sense for detecting the truths in question). In such circumstances the only thing to think is that the differences between you and them are due to historical contingencies which in themselves favor neither option. Our question about nominalism is then an instance of the question, How should one respond to this sort of predicament?

Al-Ghazali calls this sort of belief *taqlid*—"derivative" or "second-hand" belief. In *The Deliverance from Error* he maintains that *taqlid* is possible only for someone who does not fully realize that he is in it.[21] Once one becomes fully aware that one takes (say) Islam for granted only because one has been raised to take it for granted, and that if one had been raised a Christian, one would have taken it for granted, then, Ghazali says, "the glass of taqlid is broken".[22] Ghazali intends this both as a psychological claim and as a normative one: Not only is it impossible to sustain a commitment in full recognition of its status as *taqlid*; according to Ghazali it would clearly be wrong to do so.

In my view, Ghazali is wrong on both counts: Not only is it psychologically possible for us to maintain a belief in full awareness of its strong contingency. In some cases there is absolutely nothing wrong with doing so. It seems to me, rather, that the most appropriate response to the problem of *taqlid* will vary from case to case and from person to person.

If I had been raised by Ghengis Khan, I would have been much more tolerant of deliberate cruelty than I am, and for all I know, this stance would have been stable upon reflection. But this does not shake my confidence that deliberate cruelty is contemptible, and I don't think it should. If I had been raised by a certain sort of empiricist, I would have been unmoved by the case for atoms. The fact that atomic theory provides the only moderately compelling explanation of the data would have struck me as no reason whatsoever for believing that it is true. And yet the recognition that I might have been unmoved by the explanatory power of the atomic hypothesis does not alter the fact that I find it utterly compelling on the strength of the standard arguments. And again, I do not regard this as a defect in rationality. In this sort of case I can acknowledge the fact that my commitments are contingent without finding myself with anything like a compelling ground for retreating from them.

On the other hand, it seems to me that the complacent theist who is raised to take the existence of an invisible God altogether for granted probably should reconsider when he realizes that this commitment is an accident of history. I should stress that I am imagining a distinctive sort of theist: one who takes himself upon reflection to have no positive grounds for his belief: no arguments, no compelling authority, and most importantly, nothing that he would regard as direct experience of the divine: a theist who believes simply because he has been immersed in a culture in which God's existence is taken for granted. I am prepared to grant that this sort of theist is within his rights in continuing to believe, even when he is made vividly aware of the contingency of his view and the availability of defensible alternatives. He may persist on grounds of doxastic conservatism. (The existence of defensible alternatives does not constitute a "positive ground for doubting the existence of God", as one says.) He may persist simply as an act of faith. But even if such persistence is rationally permissible, it seems to me that there is something admirable in the choice to reconsider. Reconsideration manifests a virtue for which we have no standard name: non-complacency, a concern to be responsive to reasons. Even if it is not strictly required, there is much to be said for it.

Now it seems to me that complacent antinominalism of the sort I have described is more like complacent theism than it is like complacent liberal moralism or scientific realism. To speak only for myself for now: When I reflect on the fact that I might have found it natural to suspend judgment on the existence of mathematical objects and that I have nothing to say to someone who does find this natural, I find my complacency somewhat shaken, and rightly so, in my opinion. I grant that I am entitled to persist on grounds of conservatism, or on the ground that it takes effort and ingenuity to sustain the fictionalist *epoché*. But belief on such a basis strikes me as hollow: as a lamentable concession to necessity or to laziness. It may be permissible, but it is hard to see the virtue in it.

I shall return in a moment to the classification of complacent platonism. The important point for now is that there would seem to be cases in which the recognition that one's commitments are strongly contingent both does and should lead one to reconsider, and cases in which this recognition legitimately leaves one cold. The main challenge in this area is to articulate the norms governing such reconsideration. What (if anything) is the epistemologically relevant difference between (say) complacent liberal moralism and complacent scientific realism on the one hand, and complacent theism (and perhaps complacent anti-nominalism) on the other?

I cannot say with confidence, but here is one relevant difference. The recognition that my moral view is an historical artifact does not destroy the palpable obviousness that attaches to certain claims about right and wrong. I can dwell indefinitely on how I would have felt if I had been raised by Ghengis Khan. I can acknowledge that I would have reveled in deliberate cruelty, and that this stance would been stable upon reflection. And yet this exercise does not lead me to find deliberate cruelty any the less repellant. Similarly in the scientific case, I can recognize that if I had been configured differently by the vicissitudes of culture, I would have been unmoved by the explanatory power of the atomic hypothesis, while continuing to find the abductive case for atoms utterly compelling. By contrast, when I imagine myself in the position of the complacent theist, I imagine myself waking up to find that God's existence no longer strikes me as evident (if it ever did). In this case, the phenomenological impact of the realization of contingency is very different.

"But this is just psychology. In some cases the encounter with the Other dispels the obviousness of the contested commitments (or perhaps reveals that they were never obvious to begin with.) In others it does not. And when the obviousness is gone we are (perhaps) more inclined to retreat from the contested view. But so what? The question was not, 'What are we inclined to do?' It was, 'What should we do?' 'What does it make most sense for us to do?' How do these psychological facts bear on this question?"

My response is a conjecture. It is a familiar thought that perceptual knowledge rests on a principle to the effect that certain non-doxastic 'perceptual seemings' constitute grounds for belief.[23] If it seems to me that there is a cat on the mat, then I have reason to believe that there is a cat on the mat. Its seeming to me that P is not a matter of my believing anything. It is a sui generis propositional attitude that does not stand in need of justification but which is capable of supporting a perceptual judgment that P. The justificatory connection between seeming and believing is immediate. It does not depend on the reliability of the transition. In an evil demon world the dupe is justified believing that the external world is thus and so when it seems to him that things are thus and so. Nor does it depend on the subject's believing that perceptual seemings are reliable. This thought is too sophisticated to enter in to the most basic strata of epistemic justification. To the contrary, insofar as we are justified in believing that perceptual seemings are generally veridical, it is because we are independently justified in accepting a detailed account of the perceptual mechanisms which can only be grounded in particular instances of the transition from 'seems' to 'is'.

This structure is plausibly present in a range of cases not involving sense perception. Mark Johnston has argued that a certain sort of desire is best understood as a matter of being "struck by the appeal of things".[24] This "being struck by the appeal" is a quasi-perceptual matter—it is phenomenologically vivid, for example; but since it is typically directed at hypothetical states of affairs, it is not literally a matter of perception. Like perceptual seeming, evaluative seeming is not doxastic. It is a matter of an object's seeming to one to possess one or another highly determinate evaluative property. There may be other routes to evaluative knowledge. But it is plausible that insofar as perceptual judgment is canonically grounded in perceptual appearances, evaluative judgment is canonically grounded in evaluative appearances. That one finds a certain contemplated course of action appalling is a reason for taking it to be appalling. And once again, it is plausible that this is a basic epistemic norm, ungrounded in further facts (or thoughts) about the reliability of evaluative seeming.

To cite just one more example, Steve Yablo has argued that judgments of metaphysical possibility are typically grounded in intuitions of conceivability.[25] On Yablo's view, to conceive that P in the relevant sense is a compound act: One first imagines a P-world, and that world then *strikes one* as possible. The model is as above. The non-doxastic modal seeming provides a sufficient though defeasible ground for the modal judgment. And in this case in particular there is no thought that the seeming need be a matter of sensitivity to the facts in question.

These cases suggest a pattern. It may be that as a general matter, one's finding it obvious upon reflection that P is the case—its striking one that P; it seeming clearly to be the case that P—amounts to a ground for believing that P. When the encounter with an alien sensibility destroys this felt obviousness—or when it makes it plain that it was never there to begin with—it knocks the ground out from under what one has previously taken for granted. If one has no other ground for believing that God exists, then while one may be entitled to persist in believing on grounds of epistemic conservatism, it will be natural and perhaps laudable for one to think: "Here is something I have taken for granted. And yet upon reflection I find myself with no good reason to believe it." And in this case, there would seem to be some virtue in backing off.

Again, one may not be obliged to do so. The retreat to agnosticism has its costs. One is not obliged to spend a great deal of time policing one's views, shoring up those bits of doctrine whose support has for one reason or another gone by the board. So when the encounter with the Other brings one face to face with the groundlessness of one's commitment one may say, "Fascinating. I'll have to think about that when I don't have more pressing things to worry about." But if one does have the time, and one can see one's way through to a more coherent overall view, then, as I say, there would seem to be virtue in rethinking.

On the other hand, if the obviousness of the contested claim survives the encounter with the Other, then one still has some reason to hold it: the reason provided by the seeming. If, after reflecting on the rational tenability of an ethos that prizes cruelty, cruelty continues to strike me as self-evidently reprehensible, then my conviction that it is reprehensible has a powerful and cogent ground, despite my recognition that others who lack this ground may be fully justified in thinking otherwise.

Now as I say, I am inclined to classify antinominalism with complacent theism in this taxonomy. My reasons are perhaps inevitably idiosyncratic. I believe in one Zero. I believe in the existence of a set with infinitely many members. But when I consider the Bedrockers and what they would say about these commitments, I must say that these claims no longer strike me as obvious. My attachment to them is hollow. It has the feeling of a regrettable concession to necessity. Given my own habits of mind and the intrinsic difficulty of the project, it would take a considerable effort to sustain the fictionalism the Bedrockers find so natural. And there is always the lurking danger that unless one is very careful, one will wind up with commitments to the 'fictional truth' of certain claims about abstracta, which, when unpacked, are incompatible with one's professed agnosticism. Fictionalism is difficult; an ecumenical antinominalism is easy. But even if this is constitutes a legitimate defense of a sort of antinominalism, it is hard not to feel that in persisting on these grounds, one is falling short of an ideal worth pursuing.

But as I say, this may be idiosyncratic. If you can think about the Bedrockers and still find it evident upon reflection that the existential claims of (say) number theory are literally true, then for all I have said, you have no compelling basis for retrenchment.

The upshot is a form of relativism. If the question of nominalism is 'What should I believe about abstract objects? What does it make most sense for me to believe?' then the emerging answer is in part: 'It depends on how things strike you'. The position raises a number of questions, the most urgent of which concern the evidential force of non-doxastic seemings. In each of the cases we have considered, we are presented with what is in effect an array of sensibilities: an array of dispositions that deliver, in response to various sorts of input, a seeming: a non-doxastic appearing-true. In some cases it is possible to imagine wide variation in these sensibilities. We can imagine a community of clear-headed altogether rational-seeming human beings who differ from us in what they find evident in ethics, in mathematics, and perhaps in other areas. I have taken it for granted that other things being equal, one is fully entitled to rely one one's own sensibilities even when one is vividly aware of the alternatives. Not only is it not irrational to do so: in doing so one may constitute a model of epistemic virtue. But it may be wondered whether this is a stable position. After all, there is a sense in which when there are several available sensibilities, it should strike us as *improbable* that the sensibility history happens to have afforded us is just the right sensibility for getting on to the facts. It is manifestly irrational to rely on a method belief fixation while acknowledging that it is probably unreliable. When we rely on how things strike us in full awareness of the fact of contingency, we cannot occupy this detached point of view. We must credit ourselves with a bit of epistemic luck. And while it is possible to say that one is always entitled to take this stance towards one's own sensibilities, it is hard to resist the sense that this is a counsel of desperation—a recoil at the looming threat of skepticism. In any case, if it is an unacceptable counsel of desperation—if we have nothing to fall back on in the encounter with the Bedrockers, not even our healthy sense of what is obviously correct—then the case for agnosticism is all the more compelling. One may still be entitled to persist in one's platonism for reasons of conservatism and the like. But one will be no better off, epistemically speaking, if the existence of abstracta strikes one as evident than if it doesn't—which is to say that one's commitment is bound to have the sort of hollowness described above. And this is clearly an epistemic defect, even if it does not amount to irrationality.

Notes

1. For discussion, see J. Burgess and G. Rosen, *A Subject with no Object*, Oxford, 1997, ch.1.B.
2. "The Sentiment of Rationality", in *The Will to Believe and Other Essays*, Dover, 1956.
3. Locus classicus: Hartry Field, *Science without Numbers*, Princeton, 1980.
4. That is, as accounts of what scientists have meant all along by their words. For discussion, see Burgess and Rosen, op. cit., III.C.2.
5. English for: $\exists x \, \exists y \, (Mx \, \& \, My \, \& \, x \neq y \, \& \, \forall z \, (Mz \rightarrow (z = x \vee z = y)))$.
6. "What do you mean, (2) does not entail (1)? They are necessarily equivalent, so each entails the other?" There are two responses. The first is to say that "entail" does not mean "strictly entail", but rather something more like "analytically entail". The other is to do deny the claim of necessary equivalence, which is tantamount to denying the necessary existence of the numbers. For some discussion of the latter option, see my "A Study in Modal Deviance", in T. Gendler and J. Hawthorne, eds. *Imagination, Conceivability and Possibility*, Oxford University Press, forthcoming.
7. Mark Balaguer employs a similar notion. In his formulation, when the nominalist accepts a platonistic sentence S as adequate, what he believes is that "the concrete world holds up its end of the S-bargain". Balaguer's discussion involves no explanation of this metaphor. See his *Platonism and Anti-Platonism in Mathematics*, Oxford, 1998.

8. I have heard the objection that there could not be an entire linguistic practice in which non-serious, indirect assertion was the norm. The thought is that we must normally or typically mean exactly what we say, and that indirect assertion is therefore necessarily exceptional. But I have never seen a compelling philosophical argument for this principle. And in any case it would seem to prejudge on a priori grounds what ought to be an empirical issue. Do we really know how much ordinary assertion in modern English is intended literally? Can philosophy rule out the possibility that more than half of what we say is meant as some sort of joke?

9. J. Thomas Looney, *Shakespeare Identified*, Kennikat Press, 1975 (reprint).

10. Compare Fuller: "Everyone who has dealt with legal problems must, at one time or another, have had the experience of feeling that a certain doctrine of law was expressed in terms of fiction, and yet have found himself, to his dismay, unable to restate the doctrine without recourse to fiction." *Legal Fictions*, Stanford, 1967, p.10.

11. This difference may be framed as a difference in the fundamental rule of belief revision. We (the Realists in the story) are supposed to accept a version of the Quinean principle of Inference to the Truth of the Best Overall Theory, whereas the Bedrockers accept a weaker rule of Inference to the Nominalistic Adequacy of the Best Theory. The thought is that no matter how one refines the Quinean principle to take into account the real complexities of scientific practice, it will always be possible to describe a weaker principle consistent with agnosticism about the abstract.

12. "But surely it might be important for practical purposes to know (say) the speed of sound in air in units of (say) centimeters per second, and answers to this question are not entirely 'about the concrete'." The response is that in any context in which the question seems urgent, the real question might just as well be whether it is nominalistically adequate that the speed of sound in cm/s $= x$.

13. The task is analogous to the challenge that confronts van Fraassen's constructive empiricism. Van Fraassen's main claim is that agnosticism about unobservables is consistent with immersed participation in science. The claim in the present section is a weaker claim to the same effect, viz. that immersed participation in science is compatible with agnosticism about the abstract. For discussion, see my "What is Constructive Empiricism?", *Philosophical Studies* 74 (1994) and van Fraassen's reply in the same volume.

14. C. Wright, *Frege's Conception of Numbers as Objects*, Aberdeen, 1983. For an altogether different argument for the a priori incoherence of nominalism, see George Bealer, "Universals." *Journal of Philosophy* (January 1993), 90(1): 5–32.

15. For an analogous objection to van Fraassen's fictionalism, see "What is Constructive Empiricism?", *op. cit.*

16. From "Philosophy of Logic," in H. Putnam, *Mathematics, Matter and Method*, Cambridge, 1975, p. 354. The passage from Putnam is an attack on fictionalism about *material* objects. But it is clear from the context that Putnam regards fictionalism about the abstract as untenable for precisely the same reasons.

17. It is possible that in the passage cited earlier, Putnam means only to defend the permissive version of the view against the claim of Vaihinger and others that fictionalism about the posits of accepted science is somehow mandatory.

18. This is the view of the main contestants in the classical debate over nominalism: Quine, Putnam, Field.

19. See Lewis, *Parts of Classes*, Basil Blacwell, 1991, §1.6, and for a related view, Maddy, *Naturalism in Mathematics*, Oxford, 1998. It is unclear to me whether Maddy

is an epistemological naturalist in my sense. For discussion of this issue and the issues raised in this section, see my review in *The British Journal for the Philosophy of Science* 50 (1999).
20. A lousy thinker in a land of lousy thinkers is still thinking badly—his opinions are not warranted—even if he is blameless for his mistakes on the ground that one cannot normally be expected to transcend the universally accepted norms of one's community.
21. In W. Montgomery Watt, ed., *The Faith and Practice of Al-Ghazali* George Allen and Unwin, 1953. I am grateful to Stephen Menn for calling this remarkable text to my attention. For discussion, see Menn's "The *Discourse on Method* and the Tradition of Intellectual Autobiography" (unpublished ms.)
22. Ibid. p.27.
23. For an extensive discussion of this tradition, see James Pryor, "The Skeptic and the Dogmatist", *Nous* 34:4 (2000), §3.
24. "The Authority of Affect", to appear in *Phil. and Phenom. Res.*, 2001.
25. "Is Conceivability a Guide to Possibility?", *Phil. and Phenom. Res.*, 1993.

Philosophical Perspectives, 15, Metaphysics, 2001

THE LIMITS OF HUMAN MATHEMATICS*

Nathan Salmon
University of California, Santa Barbara

I

What, if anything, do Gödel's incompleteness theorems tell us about the human intellect? Do they inform us, for example, about human insight and creativity? Or perhaps about the human mind's capacity for *a priori* certainty? Ernest Nagel and James R. Newman write:

> Gödel's conclusions bear on the question whether a calculating machine can be constructed that would match the human brain in mathematical intelligence. ...as Gödel showed in his [first] incompleteness theorem, there are innumerable problems in elementary number theory that fall outside the scope of a fixed axiomatic method... The human brain...appears to embody a structure of rules of operation which is far more powerful than the structure of currently conceived artificial machines. ... Gödel's proof [of the first incompleteness theorem]...does mean that the resources of the human intellect have not been, and cannot be fully formalized, and that new principles of demonstration forever await invention and discovery. ... The theorem does indicate that the structure and power of the human mind are far more complex and subtle than any nonliving machine yet envisaged.[1]

More recently, Roger Penrose has declared that "from consideration of Gödel's theorem...we can see that the role of consciousness is non-algorithmic when forming *mathematical* judgments, where calculation and rigorous proof constitute such an important factor."[2] J. R. Lucas provided an argument in support of a similar (if slightly stronger) conclusion:

> Gödel's [first incompleteness] theorem must apply to cybernetical machines, because it is of the essence of being a machine, that it should be a concrete instantiation of a formal system. It follows that given any machine which is consistent and capable of doing simple arithmetic, there is a formula which it is incapable of producing as being true—i.e., the formula is unprovable-in-the-system—but which we

can see to be true. It follows that no machine can be a complete or adequate model of the mind, that minds are essentially different from machines.

...The conclusions it is possible for the machine to produce as being true will...correspond to the theorems that can be proved in the corresponding formal system. We now construct a Gödelian formula in this formal system. The formula cannot be *proved-in-the-system*. Therefore the machine cannot produce the corresponding formula as being true. But *we* can see that the Gödelian formula is true: any rational being could follow Gödel's argument, and convince himself that the Gödelian formula, although unprovable-in-the-given-system, was nonetheless—in fact, for that very reason—true. Now any mechanical model of the mind must include a mechanism which can enunciate truths of arithmetic, because this is something which minds can do... But...for every machine there is a truth which it cannot produce as being true, but which a mind can. This shows that the machine cannot be a complete and adequate model of the mind. It cannot to *everything* that a mind can do, since however much it can do, there is always something which it cannot do, and a mind can. ... The Gödelian formula is the Achilles' heel of the cybernetical machine. And therefore we cannot hope ever to produce a machine that will be able to do all that a mind can do: we can never, not even in principle, have a mechanical model of the mind.[3]

Anticipating this argument, Hilary Putnam exposed an apparently fatal fallacy.[4] We are to suppose, for a *reductio ad absurdum*, that we have been given in full detail a complex logistic ("formal") system that adequately and completely formalizes the mathematical abilities of a human mind. It is by no means a foregone conclusion that the mind can prove the proposition expressed by the Gödelian sentence for this system—a sentence that indirectly says of itself (in a well-defined sense) that it is not provable-in-the-given-logistic-system. What is proved is conditional: that the proposition is true *provided the logistic system is consistent*. Indeed, this much is provable within the very logistic system in question. Proving that the system is consistent (free of contradiction) would yield the target proposition as an immediate corollary. Gödel's second incompleteness theorem states that the logistic system, if it is consistent, cannot in this sense prove its own consistency. (The second theorem itself is proved precisely by noting the corollary that would otherwise result.) For some relatively simple logistic systems of arithmetic, we may know with mathematical certainty, even though this is not provable within the system, that its primitive deductive basis (the axioms and primitive rules of inference) does not generate any contradiction. In these cases, there may be a sense in which it is true that the human mind relevantly "sees" the truth expressed by the Gödelian sentence, since this provably follows from the system's consistency. But there are other logistic systems for mathematics with respect to which the system's consistency is anything but obvious. In particular, the second incompleteness theorem calls into serious question whether the human mind is capable of a proof of consistency for a logistic system sufficiently complex to capture all of humanly demonstrable mathematics, i.e. a logistic system adequate to formalize the human capacity for proving mathematical theorems.[5]

Perhaps a more guarded conclusion can be legitimately drawn. In his 1951 Josiah Willard Gibbs Lecture to the American Mathematical Society, Gödel himself derives from his second incompleteness theorem a disjunctive conclusion which, though weaker than the conclusions of Newman and Nagel, et. al., Gödel says is a "mathematically established fact which seems to me of great philosophical interest":

> Either mathematics is incompletable in this sense, that its evident axioms can never be comprised in a finite rule, that is to say, the human mind (even within the realm of pure mathematics) infinitely surpasses the powers of any finite machine, or else there exist absolutely unsolvable diophantine problems of the type specified (where the case that both terms of the disjunction are true is not excluded, so that there are, strictly speaking, three alternatives).[6]

This disjunction is evidently not subject to the same response that Putnam made to Nagel and Newman and company. For Gödel judges only that the human mind surpasses any theorem-proving machine *provided that the mind is in principle capable of solving any purely mathematical problem, including the question of its own mathematical consistency*. This more cautious conclusion is nevertheless philosophically substantive. Gödel proceeds to draw disjunctive philosophical conclusions from it, by inferring consequences of the first disjunct about the human mind's capacity for outperforming any finite computing machine, including whatever theorem-proving machinery there is in the human brain, and consequences of the second disjunct about the independence and objectivity of pure mathematics. If the theorem-proving machinery of the human brain is a computer, then either the human mind surpasses the human brain or humankind does not deserve credit for creating pure mathematics (or as some might see it, humankind does not deserve the blame). Thus, the human mind either surpasses the very organ in which it evidently resides or else it is not responsible for the existence of pure mathematics—or both, as Gödel himself believed (and I agree).[7] Here follows the relevant passage in which Gödel derives the disjunction:

> It is [the second incompleteness theorem] which makes the incompletability of mathematics particularly evident. For, *it makes it impossible that someone should set up a certain well-defined system of axioms and rules and consistently make the following assertion about it: All of these axioms and rules I perceive (with mathematical certitude) to be correct, and moreover I believe that they contain all of mathematics.* If someone makes such a statement he contradicts himself. [*Gödel's note*: If he only says "I believe I shall be able to perceive one after the other to be true" (where their number is supposed to be infinite), he does not contradict himself. (See below.)] For if he perceives the axioms under consideration to be correct, he also perceives (with the same certainty) that they are consistent. Hence he has a mathematical insight not derivable from his axioms. However, one has to be careful in order to understand clearly the meaning of this state of affairs. Does it mean that no well-defined system of correct axioms can contain all of mathematics proper? It

does, if by mathematics proper is understood the system of all true mathematical propositions; it does not, however, if one understands by it the system of all demonstrable mathematical propositions. I shall distinguish these two meanings of mathematics as mathematics in the objective and in the subjective sense: Evidently no well-defined system of correct axioms can comprise all [of] objective mathematics, since the proposition which states the consistency of the system is true, but not demonstrable in the system. However, as to subjective mathematics, it is not precluded that there should exist a finite rule producing all its evident axioms. However, if such a rule exists, we with our human understanding could certainly never know it to be such, that is we could never know with mathematical certainty that all propositions it produces are correct; [*Gödel's note*: For this (or the consequence concerning the consistency of the axioms) would constitute a mathematical insight not derivable from the axioms and rules under consideration, contrary to the assumption] or in other terms, we could perceive to be true only one proposition after the other, for any finite number of them. The assertion, however, that they are all true could at most be known with empirical certainty, on the basis of a sufficient number of instances or by other inductive inferences. ... If it were so, this would mean that the human mind (in the realm of pure mathematics) *is* equivalent to a finite machine that, however, is unable to understand completely its own functioning. [*Gödel's note*: Of course, the physical working of the thinking mechanism could very well be completely understandable; the insight, however, that this particular mechanism must always lead to correct (or only consistent) results would surpass the powers of human reason.][8]

There appears to be the following sort of argument: Suppose that the human mind's capacity for conceiving proofs is an effectively describable phenomenon, like the deterministic workings of a Turing machine, so that the very process by means of which the mind attains, or can attain, purely mathematical knowledge with mathematical certainty is thus fully captured by some finite effective rule (even if it is very long). It is a consequence of the second incompleteness theorem that the mind cannot know with mathematical certainty that this rule generates only correct results, or even that its results are internally consistent. For if the mind can know with mathematical certainty of all the propositions of pure mathematics it is able to prove that all of them are true, then it can also know with mathematical certainty that they are formally consistent—something that is precluded by the theorem. Since the consistency of the system of theorems can be recast as a purely mathematical proposition, it follows that if the mind, in its theorem-proving capacity, is a finite machine, then there are purely mathematical truths it cannot know with mathematical certainty; in particular, it cannot prove its own consistency, and hence cannot completely understand its own functioning.

George Boolos has claimed that Gödel's disjunction—that either the human mind is not equivalent to a finite machine or there exist absolutely undecidable mathematical propositions—though it is weaker than the conclusions of Nagel and Newman, et. al., is still not validly derivable from the incompleteness theorems.[9] Boolos deems the above argument inconclusive owing to obscurity in the idea that "the human mind is equivalent to a finite machine."

Even assuming, for the sake of argument, that the theorem-proving aspect of the human mind is mechanistic, it does not straightforwardly follow that in that case the mind's theorem-proving mechanism meets the conditions for being a Turing machine and is therefore incapable of proving its own consistency. For it is in the first place excessively unclear what is meant by saying (or by denying) that *the* human mind, or even that a single mind, simply *is* a Turing machine. And if what is meant is that the theorem-proving aspect of the mind, or of a single mind, is (or is not) *represented* by a Turing machine, Boolos objects, Gödel does not specify exactly how the representation is supposed to go.

The argument does indeed raise troubling questions of this sort, and more. A Turing machine is the formal counterpart of a deterministic computational process. It does much more than merely represent a recursive function in the abstract, mathematical sense. The function is fully represented by the machine's input and output, and may be aptly represented equivalently by a set of ordered sets of numbers. By contrast, a Turing machine is the program that produces a specific output for a given input; it represents the process of *calculating* the value of the function for any argument. In the opening paragraph of the Gibbs Lecture, just before arguing for his disjunction, Gödel cites Turing machines as providing the most satisfactory way of defining the concept of an effective calculation or algorithm (a "finite procedure")—thereby indicating his acceptance of Church's thesis (at least as restricted to numerical functions, and sets characterizable by numerical functions). Is the "finite machine" of which Gödel speaks in the quoted passage supposed to mirror, in the manner of a Turing machine, the method and procedures by which the human mind is able to construct or discover (as the case may be) mathematical proofs? If so, we need to know exactly how, and exactly to what extent, the finite machine does this in order to assess Gödel's conclusion. Lacking this additional information, the most that can be justified is the supposition that the machine delivers the same theorems that the mind is able to prove, though perhaps by a completely different construction.

Filling in the gaps, Boolos proposes a reconstruction of Gödel's argument culminating in a circumscribed conclusion concerning not the actual process of proving theorems, but just the results thereby obtained. Though still somewhat vague, Boolos grants that the following is a consequence of the second incompleteness theorem: If there is a theorem-proving Turing machine whose output is the set of sentences expressing just those mathematical propositions that can be proved by a mind capable of understanding all polynomials with integer coefficients (and therefore capable of understanding a mathematical sentence tantamount to the meta-theoretic observation that the mind's theorem-proving mechanism is consistent), then there is a true mathematical proposition that can be understood but cannot be proved by that same mind—namely, the mathematically recast assertion of its own consistency. (See note 10 below.) Thus, any mind whose theorem-proving capacity is representable by some Turing machine *in terms of the theorems it proves (as opposed to the proofs it produces and/or the process by which it conceives those proofs)* is in principle incapable of solving certain mathematical problems indirectly about its own theorem-proving capacity. On Boolos's reconstruction, the machine passively represents the mind's potential output of theorems. Boolos's conclusion concerns those theorems only in the sense that it is about that *class* of theorems, not their production. The machine does not necessarily represent the mind's potential proofs of that potential output, let alone the active process by which the mind can generate those proofs.

Boolos's conclusion is comparatively strikingly narrow. It is a trivial, disappointingly anti-climactic restatement of the second incompleteness theorem's corollary that no theorem-enumerating Turing machine prints a sentence tantamount to an assertion of its own consistency. Any possible generating activity whose output coincides, for whatever reason (or for no reason at all), with that of a theorem-enumerating Turing machine fails to produce a mathematical proposition tantamount to the consistency of that output—regardless of whether the activity is teleologically assisted by an understanding of the output, hence even if it is a room full of monkeys at typewriters.[10] One might also point out, in much the same spirit, that anyone whose feats in manipulating geometric figures, as it happens, do not exceed those geometric tasks that can be performed using only a compass and straightedge, does not trisect an angle. In confining his attention to the mathematical theorems themselves, setting aside the epistemological character of their potential proofs by the human mind, Boolos disengages his conclusion from the philosophical issues that drive Gödel's. Gödel's argument does not concern hypothetical minds of a precisely delimited capacity. It concerns the capability of the human mind, such as it is, to attain certainty in mathematics. It is about human mathematics at its edges—both the initial starting points and the ultimate upward limits. Does the obscurity of the very idea that the human mind is equivalent to a machine block us from any such sweeping conclusion, and force a disappointingly restrictive retreat? I believe it does not and that, *contra* Boolos, Gödel's argument about the limits of human mathematics is reasonably secure, or can be made so.

II

Gödel's principal argument does not make any essential detour through Turing machines, or machines of any sort. One can dispense with machines altogether and make an end run for a disjunctive conclusion of just the sort from which Gödel draws philosophical conclusions about the human mind and the objectivity of mathematics.

Following Gödel, let us distinguish between mathematics proper (i.e., all the truths of pure mathematics) and what I have called *human mathematics* (Gödel's "subjective mathematics")—that portion of mathematics that the human mind, or any intelligence (whether biological or artificial) that is epistemologically similarly situated to human intelligence, is capable of knowing with mathematical certainty ("mathematical certitude"). It is useful for this purpose to introduce some artificial terminology. Let '**HuMath**' designate the class ("system") of all true propositions of human mathematics. This is a subclass of the class **Math** of all purely mathematical truths. **HuMath** almost certainly extends well beyond all the mathematics that will ever have been known with mathematical certainty by humans—by some human or other at some time or other. Take note: it is not assumed that **Math** and **HuMath** are distinct, nor is it assumed that they are identical. It is not even assumed that **HuMath** includes every purely mathematical proposition that mathematicians take to be true. **HuMath** is restricted to those purely mathematical propositions that are knowable, hence true. If (contrary to our expectation) there should be any false purely mathematical propositions of which mathematicians have been persuaded (e.g., by a subtly fallacious argument), they are excluded from **HuMath**. Since all of **HuMath** are true, **HuMath** is *a fortiori* consistent, i.e. no contradiction is correctly deducible from it. Notice also that **HuMath** excludes any purely mathematical truths that are only knowable by the human mind to some degree short of mathematical certainty.[11]

HuMath's definition invokes the generic notion of knowability by the human mind, and this notion is somewhat obscure. What is knowable by one human mind may be unknowable by another. It may be that no single, existent human mind (past, present, or future) is capable of knowing everything that the human mind is capable of knowing. It may even be that no *possible* human mind can know all of the facts each of which, taken individually, the human mind is capable of knowing.[12] As Boolos notes, it does not follow that no proposition involving the notion of human knowability is validly deducible from a mathematical theorem. Boolos cites the particular inference: *91 is composite; therefore, it is not humanly knowable that 91 is prime.* This instance depends on the fact that knowledge entails truth. Gödel's derivation of his disjunction, by contrast, depends on the fact that knowledge entails epistemic *justification*. But this does not, in itself, provide a reason to doubt that Gödel's argument is sound. The basic epistemological assumption is that, whatever differences there are among humans, certain epistemic mechanisms—ways of coming to know— are in principle accessible to the human mind.[13] At a minimum, there is an epistemic mechanism that is characteristically human, in this sense, and yields mathematical knowledge with mathematical certainty. The principle does not require that one be able to determine with any certainty whether a particular alleged phenomenon (e.g., telepathy) is a human epistemic mechanism, in this sense, or whether a particular alleged fact is knowable by a human mechanism. It may well be that this fundamental epistemological principle is not itself known with mathematical certainty, and to the extent that Gödel's argument presupposes the principle, the derived disjunction is also not so known. But the principle is known (even if not with mathematical certainty), and is not typically subject to doubt. If a proposition is validly inferred from a mathematical theorem using this epistemological principle, it is not unreasonable to say that the inferred proposition is a mathematically established fact.

The epistemic mechanism by which the elements of **HuMath** are knowable with mathematical certainty by humans is evidently that of mathematical *proof*. Gödel notes that if any purely mathematical knowledge is obtained by proof on the basis of truths antecedently known with mathematical certainty, then some purely mathematical knowledge is not.[14] For proofs must have starting points, and knowledge obtained by proof is derived ultimately from knowledge of those starting points. The latter knowledge Gödel calls the "evident axioms." (It includes axioms of both logic and mathematics proper.) This epistemic mechanism for attaining certainty in pure mathematics is aptly represented by the logistic method.[15] There is a proper subclass **Ax** of **HuMath** consisting of epistemologically foundational axioms—purely mathematical "first truths" each knowable with mathematical certainty by the human mind (i.e., by some possible human mind) without proof from other purely mathematical truths but through direct mathematical intuition or insight ("perception"), or perhaps derived from something more fundamental than pure mathematics (including logic)—while the rest of **HuMath** are knowable with mathematical certainty only by proof, i.e. only by deductive derivation ultimately from the mathematical axioms, using logical (primitive) rules of inference together perhaps with purely mathematical rules of inference over and above the axioms. **HuMath** is the deductive closure of **Ax** under the rules of human mathematical reasoning. In this sense, the union of **Ax** with the rules of human mathematical inference form the deductive basis of human mathematics. Let us call it '**Basis**'.[16]

Ax may extend beyond all those fundamental truths of pure mathematics that will ever have been known by humans with mathematical certainty without independent mathematical proof, i.e. without proof from antecedently known purely mathematical truths. It is not assumed that any particular human mathematician, or even any possible human mathematician, can know all the elements of **Ax**. However, each of the axioms, taken individually, must be humanly knowable with mathematical certainty without independent mathematical proof. If we cannot know an axiom, then we also cannot know anything derived from it—except by some independent epistemological means. Genuinely inferential knowledge requires knowledge of that from which it is inferred. Moreover, each of the rules of inference of human mathematical reasoning must be not only valid (i.e., such as to preserve truth in any model), but also of a sort that transfers, through the cognitive act of immediate inference, the sort of epistemic justification that yields mathematical certainty. It is not independently required that we know each of the inference rules to be valid (let alone that we know this with mathematical certainty), but knowing this may be inextricably bound up with the rules' being such as to transfer mathematical certainty to the immediately inferred conclusion from that from which the conclusion is immediately inferred. In any event, it is reasonable to suppose that we can know of each inference rule of the required sort, with mathematical certainty and without independent mathematical proof, that it is indeed valid.

It is frequently assumed in discussion of Gödel's incompleteness results (especially of their philosophical implications) that they entail that any well-defined deductive basis for arithmetic, if consistent, is incomplete and fails to decide in particular a recast assertion of its own consistency. From this it would follow directly that, contrary to David Hilbert, there are purely mathematical truths the human mind is incapable of proving, including an assertion of its own mathematical consistency. (Recall that **Ax** is a subclass of **HuMath**, which is restricted to truths, and that the rules are valid; hence **Ax** is consistent.) But the assumption often involves a mistake, and Gödel did not believe its conclusion. There exist deductive systems for arithmetic (in a broad sense of 'deductive system') that are both consistent and complete—Gödel's theorems notwithstanding. This simple fact, although sometimes overlooked, is essential to a proper understanding of Gödel's disjunction and the argument for it. One way to obtain a consistent deductive system for arithmetic whose theorems are exactly those sentences of the language that express truths of arithmetic is to take all and only those sentences as axioms.[17] No object-theoretic Gödelian sentence indirectly asserting its own unprovability-in-this-system exists. On the other hand, the axiom set is unwieldy—as unwieldy as possible without allowing for the deduction of falsehoods. It is all over the map. Each expressible truth of arithmetic, regardless of how complex or abstract, is provable in this system in a single line. We are currently in no position to determine whether certain sentences are axioms of this system—for example, the sentence expressing Goldbach's Conjecture. By contrast, the elements of **Ax** are narrowly confined to those purely mathematical truths that are humanly knowable with mathematical certainty without independent mathematical proof. The envisaged complete, consistent system does not come close to adequately representing the way the human mind achieves knowledge with mathematical certainty in arithmetic. Part of the significance of Gödel's incompleteness results derives from the fact that they obtain for deductive systems that do at least approach the way the human mind attains mathematical knowledge.

A requirement that the axioms be written out in full would be excessive, since it excludes the possibility of a logistic system with infinitely many axioms. Instead, it is customary to consider deductive systems whose primitive bases are recursively enumerable (if not indeed primitive recursive)—so that even if there are infinitely many axioms there is an effective procedure by which theoretically one could enumerate them (allowing repetitions) and calculate what the nth axiom is for any natural number n. This condition (or something that entails it, perhaps given Church's thesis) is typically built into the definition of a *logistic* or *formal* system or theory.[18] It is only in that case that the deductive system can be effectively specified (in an intuitive sense) in a finite description. Moreover, if the deductive basis is effectively decidable, then so is the notion of a proof. Suppose that the elements of **Ax** constitute a *recursively enumerable set of propositions*, in the following sense: that there is a recursive numerical function from whole numbers onto a set A of Gödel numbers of sentences of a possible formal language expressing each of the elements of **Ax** in that possible language—so that there is an effective procedure by which theoretically one could calculate what the nth element of **Ax** is for any natural number n.[19] Suppose also that the rules of inference are analogously recursively enumerable. (See note 16.) Gödel showed how, in that case, the notions of a proof-from-**Ax** and of contradiction, and therewith the statement of **HuMath**'s consistency (which is meta-theoretic), can be put into object-theoretic form. Specifically, if the elements of **Ax** form a recursively enumerable set, and so do the inference rules, then there is a purely mathematical binary relation *Proof* which is designated by an open formula $\phi_{Proof}(x, y)$ of a possible formal language suitable for arithmetic and which provably holds between a pair of numbers n and m if and only if n is the Gödel number of a sequence of formulae that collectively express, in that same formal language, a proof from **Ax**, by way of the inference rules, of the proposition expressed, in that language, by the formula whose Gödel number is m. Likewise, there is a purely mathematical relation *Contradict*, designated by an open formula $\phi_{Contradict}(x, y)$ of the same language, which provably holds between a pair of numbers if and only if they are the Gödel numbers of formulae one of which is the negation of the other. There is then a corresponding sentence φ_{Cons} of the form $\ulcorner \sim(\exists x)(\exists y)[\phi_{Contradict}(x, y) \wedge (\exists z)\phi_{Proof}(z, x) \wedge (\exists z)\phi_{Proof}(z, y)\urcorner$, which is mathematical code *via* Gödel numbering for the consistency of the logistic system generated by the set A of axioms and the inference rules. The sentence ϕ_{Cons} expresses a mathematical proposition *Cons* which we know with mathematical certainty to be equivalent to the logistic system's formal consistency.[20] On the assumption that the elements of **Ax** and the rules constitute recursively enumerable sets, Gödel's second incompleteness theorem implies that φ_{Cons} is not provable from **Ax**. For the theorem (as extended by Barkley Rosser) states that if an axiomatic basis suitable for arithmetic is both recursively enumerable and consistent, then the corresponding object-theoretic statement (constructed thus *via* Gödel numbering) of the theory's consistency, though true, is not provable from those axioms.[21] Since each of the propositions expressed by the elements of A is knowable, *a fortiori* each is true. And since all of the them are true and the rules are valid, A is *a fortiori* consistent. Thus, if the elements of **Ax** constitute a recursively enumerable set, and so do the rules, then *Cons* is a purely mathematical truth that does not belong to **HuMath**.

In this sense, either the axiomatic basis of human mathematics (i.e., the purely mathematical truths knowable by the human mind with mathematical certainty without independent mathematical proof, together with the rules of human mathematical inference) is not reducible to a recursively enumerable set (and thus they do not yield a logistic or formal system, in the technical sense), or else some purely mathematical truths—including a mathematical encoding of the consistency of human mathematics—are in principle unknowable by the human mind with mathematical certainty. This result already goes significantly beyond Boolos's conclusion that any mind capable of understanding all polynomials with integer coefficients and whose provable theorems exactly coincide with the output of a theorem-proving Turing machine is incapable of proving a mathematical truth that it apprehends. But Gödel takes matters further still.

Enter the argument about a "finite rule" and the prospect of the human mind being "equivalent to a finite machine." Against the interpretation placed on this by Boolos and others, the imagined rule, as it is understood and intended by Gödel, does not generate proofs of the elements of **HuMath**—let alone does it capture the method or procedure by which the mind constructs or discovers proofs.[22] Whereas Gödel's argument is concerned with the epistemological character of potential proofs by the human mind, the actual cognitive process whereby the human mind might conceive or discover its proofs is irrelevant. Let it be by a mechanistic process or let it be utterly non-mechanistic, by an indescribable mathematical inspiration, by a vital, non-deterministic spark of creativity. Let it be by supernatural revelation, or by divine intervention. It makes no difference to the argument.

Nor is the envisaged "finite rule" merely supposed to produce the mathematical theorems provable by the human mind—the elements of **HuMath**—even if by a potentially different construction. What the speculated rule *is* supposed to generate are the "evident axioms," i.e., not the elements of **HuMath** themselves but their axiomatization in **Basis**. If **Basis** is recursively enumerable, there is an effective procedure that enables one to enumerate its elements (possibly with repetitions). According to Church's thesis (construed so as to include the effective enumeration of a set of propositions), the converse obtains as well. Suppose there is a finite rule that produces all the elements of **Basis**—for example, finite instructions enabling one automatically to write out the sentences of a possible mathematical language, one after another, which express just the elements of **Ax** as well as the inference rules. Mathematical certainty that the rule, properly characterized, generates no inconsistencies would then be unattainable. It follows from the second incompleteness theorem (and Church's thesis) that if there are such instructions, then even though each of the propositions expressed by the sentences they produce is true and humanly knowable with mathematical certainty without proof, and even though each of the generated rules are valid and such as to transfer mathematical certainty *via* the immediate inference, we cannot know of the instructions, with the same certainty, that their product is even consistent. Therefore, either there is no such rule—equivalently, no recursive function that enumerates the elements of **Basis**—or again there are purely mathematical truths of a certain type that are humanly unprovable. This is, nearly enough, Gödel's disjunction. It is, in effect, a trivial transformation in propositional logic of the following: *If the elements of **Basis** constitute a recursively enumerable set, then **HuMath** is a proper subclass of **Math**.*[23]

Gödel expands on his first disjunct—that there is no effective procedure producing exactly the axiomatic basis of human mathematics—by drawing an inference concerning the human mind *vis a vis* a finite machine. If indeed there is no such rule, then the human mind's capacity for attaining certainty in mathematics surpasses that of a theorem-proving computer—at least insofar as the computer's theorem-proving capacity is restricted to procedures that correspond to a recursive notion of proof. There is no assertion here that the theorem-proving mechanism of the human brain is not a computing machine (if 'machine' is the right term to use) whose theorem-proving capacity is not restricted in this way. Boolos's worries about the vagueness of the general notion that "the human mind is equivalent to a finite machine," while they may be an appropriate reaction to an attempt to derive some such more sweeping conclusion than this, are not pertinent here. The difficulty of likening the theorem-proving capacity of the human brain to a computer is not so much that the brain's cognitive processes are not mechanistic. Nor is it that a machine cannot know the fundamental axioms of human mathematics. (Although it cannot. Strictly speaking, it is a person, and not the person's brain, that knows things.) The difficulty comes in the very *design* (let alone the construction) of a theorem-proving machine when there is no effective procedure for delimiting its proofs' admissible starting points. Either there is no such procedure with regard to the human mind's capacity for attaining knowledge with mathematical certainty in pure mathematics, or else there are purely mathematical problems of a certain sort that are in principle unsolvable by the human intellect. This is Gödel's disjunction.

III

Gödel remarks in passing (in effect) that the correctness of a set of propositions (i.e., truth of all the elements) entails their formal consistency, and hence knowledge with mathematical certainty of the former yields knowledge with mathematical certainty of the latter. Call this 'Gödel's thesis'.[24] It follows that knowledge with mathematical certainty of a proposition p (which may be a conjunction of propositions) yields the knowledge, with the same certainty, that p is consistent. Insofar as **Ax** consists of propositions that the human mind is capable of knowing with mathematical certainty, one might expect the mind to be able to know the conjunction of those axioms (perhaps by repeated applications of a familiar logical rule of inference). From the latter, according to Gödel's thesis, we could deduce the conjunction's consistency, and from this the Gödelian undecidable proposition. Does Gödel's thesis provide support for Lucas's assertion that the mind can after all see the truth of Gödel's undecidable proposition, which indirectly says of itself that it is not provable from the axioms?

Not without further argument. **Ax** is presumably infinite. The conjunction of its elements would then be an infinite conjunction. But there is a question of whether there even exist such propositions. If such propositions do exist, there is still a question of whether the human mind can comprehend them. Furthermore, though each element of **Ax** is knowable with mathematical certainty without independent proof, it does not follow that the conjunction of all the axioms is itself knowable with mathematical certainty—even assuming that this conjunction is humanly comprehendible. In order for a proof to confer knowledge with mathematical certainty, one must know each of the axioms employed in the proof with the same certainty. Even if one is thus capable of knowing with certainty the conjunction of axioms used in any proof that one may construct or discover, since proofs are finite this yields knowledge with certainty of conjunctions of finite subsets of elements of **Ax**, not yet knowledge with certainty of the conjunction of *all* elements of **Ax**.[25]

Suppose the human mind were able to know the conjunction of all of **Ax** at once. Suppose the inference rules are finite. According to Gödel's thesis, we could then know with mathematical certainty that if the conjunction of such-and-such axioms is correct, then the conjunction of such-and-such axioms (these same ones) is formally consistent. The fact concerning **Ax**—that if all those propositions are correct then they are consistent—is something we would be able to know with mathematical certainty if we were capable of apprehending **Ax** all at once, and if we are capable of any mathematical knowledge at all. Hence, if we could but know the conjunction of all elements of **Ax** with mathematical certainty, we could infer their consistency by *modus ponens* (an inference rule of just the sort required). But if the elements of **Ax** constitute a recursively enumerable set, then we cannot know *Cons* (which is provably equivalent to the consistency of **Ax**) with mathematical certainty. Therefore, by *reductio ad absurdum*, either the elements of **Ax** are not recursively enumerable, or else their conjunction is not humanly provable. Or to put the point somewhat differently from Gödel: Though each of the elements of **Ax**, taken individually, is humanly knowable with mathematical certainty, if those elements are recursively enumerable, then even though they are, their conjunction is not humanly knowable with mathematical certainty. This result does not advance the position of Nagel and Newman, et. al.

By Gödel's thesis, if the elements of **Ax** are recursively enumerable, then the human mind is barred from knowing their conjunction with mathematical certainty. This does not mean that if the elements of **Ax** are recursively enumerable, then the human mind is barred from knowing with mathematical certainty the general meta-theoretic proposition that *all the purely mathematical propositions knowable with mathematical certainty by the human mind without independent mathematical proof are true*. On the contrary, the latter proposition appears to be something of which we are certain (setting aside worries about the so-called paradox of the knower), on the basis of the analytic truth that whatever is known is true. (See note 25.) What it does mean is that if the elements of **Ax** are recursively enumerable, we are barred from knowing *of* those propositions (*de re*) with mathematical certainty that all are true, by inference from anything of the form ⌜Every x such that $\phi(x)$ is true⌝ where ⌜$\phi(x)$⌝ designates **Ax** in a manner provably equivalent to its designation in ϕ_{Proof} and ϕ_{Cons}. In particular, even if the elements of **Ax** are recursively enumerable, we cannot know with mathematical certainty of any recursive function that enumerates it, that it generates only Gödel numbers of true sentences—with the enumerating function characterized so as to yield a formula ⌜$\phi(x)$⌝ of the indicated sort.

Again suppose there is a finite rule that produces exactly the axioms of human mathematics. Under certain circumstances (e.g., where one fully understands the possible language in question), knowing of the envisioned effective instructions that they produce only sentences expressing truths is tantamount to knowing those propositions expressed to be consistent. It follows that if there are such instructions, then even though each of the propositions expressed by the sentences they produce is true and humanly knowable with mathematical certainty without proof, we cannot know of the instructions, with the same certainty, that their product is correct. If there are effective instructions that produce sentences expressing exactly the axioms of human mathematics, we are incapable of knowing of those instructions with mathematical certainty that they do so. If we were to stumble upon such a rule we could not prove it to be such, or even that it produces only truths.[26]

Lucas, like Nagel and Newman and others who have discussed the philosophical import of Gödel's incompleteness results, evidently tacitly assumes that insofar as the mathematical capabilities of a human mind is represented by a deductive system at all, the axioms constitute a recursively enumerable set, if not indeed a recursive set.[27] It follows from this assumption, taken together with Gödel's thesis, that though each of the axioms is humanly knowable with mathematical certainty, the mind is incapable of deducing their conjunction. This in itself does not refute Lucas's argument. The position of Nagel and Newman, et. al., appears to be that, whatever one's axioms for mathematics may be at a given time, the human mind, unlike the logistic system it instantiates at that time, is capable of augmenting its primitive deductive basis through a non-mechanistic mathematical insight that goes beyond what is strictly provable from those axioms. The mind can both prove that the axioms cannot prove their own consistency, and at the same time *see* (without proving this from the current axioms) that those same axioms *en toto* are correct, hence consistent. The mind thereby expands its deductive basis, empowering itself to prove the incompleteness of the previous axioms from the new set. The mind can then repeat the maneuver with respect to its new deductive basis, and then again with the yet newer basis, and so on in an ongoing dialectic. More important, the vital mathematical faculty or insight that fuels the dialectical progression also yields knowledge with mathematical certainty of its own correctness, and hence consistency, and thereby of the correctness, and consequent consistency, of the entire system generated by the initial axioms and inference rules taken together with the special non-mechanistic faculty itself. The hypothesized vital mathematical insight would strikingly set the human mind apart from any machine or mechanistic process that lacks it.

Unfortunately, this view of human mathematics as a dynamic process of continuing discovery fueled by a unique kind of non-mechanistic and self-validating mathematical insight does not solve the problem. **Ax**, by definition, includes every purely mathematical truth that is humanly knowable without proof from other purely mathematical truths. If there is any special, self-validating faculty or intuition of the sort hypothesized, whatever is humanly knowable by its means is thus already included in **Ax**. The only way for the mind to come to know a purely mathematical truth with mathematical certainty that does not belong to **Ax** is to prove it ultimately from **Ax** (i.e., to prove it from **Ax**, or to prove it from theorems proved from **Ax**, or from theorems proved from theorems proved from **Ax**, etc.). **HuMath** is completely axiomatized by **Basis**, i.e., **Ax** together with the inference rules. In light of Gödel's second theorem, if **Basis** is recursively enumerable, the recast assertion of its consistency is not humanly knowable with mathematical certainty. Rather than making the case for the position of Nagel and Newman, et. al., this result spells trouble for it.

Assume for the moment, with Hilbert, that the human mind is capable, in principle, of solving any purely mathematical problem. It then follows from Gödel's disjunction that the mind's capacity for proving theorems surpasses that of any theorem-proving computer whose primitive deductive basis is recursively enumerable. The mind's superiority over any such machine (in this sense) is explained not so much, or not directly, by the mind's being able to "see" that which cannot yet be proved, but instead by the fact that its primitive deductive basis is essentially richer than the computer's. The richness of human mathematics would in that case result from some human faculty or intuitive insight— which would indeed separate man from those machines without it—but this special mathematical faculty or intuition might be the very same faculty that provides us with even the simplest axioms, not something further and different. Moreover, its consistency may not be reducible to any purely mathematical proposition, and therefore it need not be self-validating to be mathematically complete.[28] In any event, there remains the unproven assumption that the human mind can prove every purely mathematical truth.

IV

Gödel's derivation pointedly places a special focus on a question that is ignored in Lucas's argument: Are the elements of **Basis** recursively enumerable? Or put another way (under the assumption of Church's thesis, applied to the effective enumeration of a set of propositions): Is there an effective procedure for enumerating the rules of human mathematical inference together with those purely mathematical truths that the human mind is capable of knowing with mathematical certainty without independent mathematical proof? If there is not, then the mathematical capacity of the human mind surpasses that of any mathematics machine whose deductive basis is subject to such a procedure; and otherwise, the human mathematical mind is, in a certain sense, in principle incapable of resolving the question of its own consistency.

In particular, could it be that **Ax** is not effectively enumerable? Many logicians would regard this prospect as quite impossible. Church argued, in effect, that nothing should count as a genuine *proof* unless the totality of axioms form a recursively enumerable set, indeed a recursive set. He posed his argument in the context of a logistic system, construed syntactically. Church imposed as an inviolable restriction on any logistic system that "the specification of the axioms shall be effective in the sense that there is a method by which, whenever a well-formed formula is given, it can always be determined effectively whether or not it is one of the axioms."[29] Unless there is an effective procedure for deciding whether a given formula is or is not one of the axioms, the notion of proof itself will not be effective. Church's justification for the restriction is given with characteristic eloquence and force:

> There is then no certain means by which, when a sequence of formulae has been put forward as a proof, the auditor may determine whether it is in fact a proof. Therefore he may fairly demand a proof, in any given case, that the sequence of formulae put forward is a proof; and until this supplementary proof is provided, he may refuse to be convinced that the alleged theorem is proved. This supplementary proof ought to be regarded, it seems, as part of the whole proof of the theorem, and the primitive basis of the logistic system ought to be so modified as to provide this, or its equivalent. Indeed it is essential to the idea of a proof that, to any one who admits the presuppositions on which it is based, a proof carries final conviction.[30]

Lecturing on Gödel's incompleteness theorems in 1974, Church gave the following related argument, as reconstructed from my notes (edited and approved by Church at the time for distribution to the class):

> The initial reaction to an incompleteness proof for a logistic system is to search for additional axioms, postulates, or rules of inference which, when added to the incomplete system, yield a complete system. But there does not seem to be any way of doing this for the logistic system A^2 [a formalization of second order Peano arithmetic]. The Gödel proof does not make great use of the particular axioms, postulates, and rules of inference of A^2. The proof is of such generality that it is easily extended to a logistic system obtained from A^2 by the addition of particular axioms, postulates, and rules of inference.
>
> The reason for the incompleteness of A^2 does not lie in the axioms, postulates, or rules of inference, but rather in the notion of mathematical proof. A proof must carry conviction; one who accepts the axioms and rules of inference, if he has once seen a proof of a particular theorem, must then not be able justifiably to doubt the theorem. But if axiom schemata or rules of inference are non-effective, the situation can arise that one who has seen a proof may still doubt, because he is unable to verify that what is before him is in fact a proof. Thus the notion of proof must be effective, that is, there must be an effective procedure for determining whether an alleged proof is a proof. Presumably this means that the notion of proof must be general recursive, since there is no known effective check which is not general recursive. Even if we were to add an axiom schema to the logistic system A^2, the set of instances of this axiom schema must be general recursive, if not indeed primitive recursive, in terms of their Gödel numbers. One need only show that the notion of mathematical proof which is obtained by adding this axiom schema to A^2 is expressible in A^2 by means of Gödel numbering in order to carry through an incompleteness proof along the lines given above, and this should be possible in virtue of theorems connecting general recursion and primitive recursion (for example, that any general recursive relation can be expressed by means of quantifiers and primitive recursive relations).
>
> Thus in a general way, the Gödel proof is not only a proof of incompleteness, but also a proof of incompletability. Since the only known way of making precise the notion of mathematical proof is the logistic system, the usual conclusion drawn

from the Gödel proof is that any precise formulation of arithmetic cannot be complete—a conclusion which shatters one of the hopes of the Hilbert program.

A genuine mathematical proof is not merely a sequence of formulae satisfying certain purely syntactic conditions (viz., every element of the sequence is either an element of the recursively specified set of "axioms," or else follows from formulae occurring earlier in the sequence by means of one of the recursively specified set of "rules of inference"). Rather, a genuine proof is what such a sequence of formulae semantically expresses: a line of reasoning, consisting of propositions, that conclusively demonstrates a proposition. Church's argument that since a proof must "carry final conviction" the notion of proof must be effective, if sound, applies directly to authentic proofs, and only derivatively, by extension, to their syntactic expression within a logistic system. If sound, the argument supports the broad conclusion that there must be an effective procedure that enables one to decide of any mathematical proposition whether it is or is not an element of **Ax**. In fact, assuming Church's thesis (in the form indicated above), his argument, if sound, supports the conclusion that the elements of **Ax** must *constitute a recursive set of propositions*, in the sense that there is a recursive numerical function that exactly characterizes a set of Gödel numbers of sentences of a possible formal language expressing each of the elements of **Ax**—e.g., a recursive function that yields 1 for the Gödel number of any axiomatic sentence and 0 for the Gödel number of any other sentence of the language in question. (See note 19.)

Church's argument, however, does not itself carry conviction. First, the fact that an auditor may justifiably doubt whether a purported proof is correct (and thus a genuine proof) does not entail that the line of reasoning in question does not after all conclusively demonstrate its conclusion with mathematical certainty (i.e., is not a genuine proof). A proof provides potential epistemic justification for conviction; the carrying of conviction is a horse of a different color. Whether the horse drinks from the water to which it is led is up to the horse. It is not unusual for a theorem to be proved before it is confirmed that the reasoning is thoroughly sound—sometimes well before this is confirmed even to the original author's satisfaction. In such cases, a potential epistemic justification for conviction is provided before conviction is carried—perhaps even before conviction is actually justified by its potential justification. Church's concern is with the auditor who questions whether a purported proof that has been spelled out in full, with a justification provided for each step, is correct. Often one can know that a given object has a given property even in the absence of an effective test for the property in question. Often one can even prove this. In particular, a given proof's correctness can be verified without applying any general test capable of verifying the correctness of any proof whatsoever. It is typically sufficient to re-check each step of the particular proof in question, and to verify that those particular steps are legitimate. One can do this by applying certain sufficient conditions for the justification of a step, even in the absence of a complete set of such conditions, let alone a complete set of effectively decidable necessary and sufficient conditions. Where one auditor may doubt whether a particular piece of reasoning is a proof, another auditor may correctly see, without the benefit of an effective test, that the reasoning is perfectly sound. In that case, the reasoning can decisively establish its conclusion, at least for the second auditor.[31]

For that matter, even if there is an effective test, its mere existence does not put an end to the infinite regress of demanding a proof, then demanding a proof that the first proof is correct, then demanding a proof that the second proof is correct, and so on.[32] Nor does the existence of an effective test for proofs eliminate the possibility of justified doubt in a given case. To quell such doubt the test has to be applied to the proof in question. One may then question whether the test has been applied correctly. And even if one is satisfied that it was, one may justifiably doubt whether the purported test itself is correct. If an auditor wonders whether a particular proposition employed as an axiom in the proof is indeed antecedently known, it is no answer to point out that the formula expressing the proposition in question was written under the heading "AXIOMS" in setting up the primitive basis of a particular logistic system for mathematics (or is generated by an effective procedure for producing the logistic system's "axioms"). The auditor's question is not whether the formula is playing the role of an axiom in the purported proof, or whether it is called an 'axiom'; the question concerns the proposition expressed, whether it is genuinely known with mathematical certainty without independent mathematical proof. The so-called test simply assumes it is so, as it were, by stipulative fiat. The prospects are dim for an effective procedure for deciding whether it really is so. If such a procedure is required for there to be proof, mathematical ignorance is considerably wider than is currently realized.

On the contrary, the general issue of whether the entire line of reasoning in question is a proof is separate from the issue the proof itself is intended to settle: whether the theorem in question is true. The reasoning, if it is correct, enables an auditor to know the theorem with mathematical certainty. This is the purpose of the proof, its *raison d'etre*. To ask whether the purported proof is correct is to raise a separate, further question, an epistemological meta-question related to the issue of whether one knows that one knows—a question that the auditor need not consciously consider in order to gain knowledge of the theorem with mathematical certainty on the basis of the proof. If the assumptions employed in the line of reasoning are *in fact* already known with mathematical certainty, and the inference rules are of the right character (so as to transfer mathematical certainty to the inferred conclusion), the reasoning can be of the right sort to establish its theorem conclusively, and to confer mathematical certainty for an auditor, even if the question of whether it does so is never raised—perhaps even if the question is raised and answered incorrectly, as long as the auditor continues to believe the theorem on the basis of the proof.

Church's argument is fundamentally Cartesian in character. It assumes that knowledge with mathematical certainty precludes the possibility of a certain kind of justifiable doubt. Church supposes that in order genuinely to know something in mathematics one must be able to prove it beyond all possible justifiable doubt, and in order to do this one must be able to prove beyond justifiable doubt that one has done so, by applying an effective test. Descartes took this assumption a step further, requiring that all knowledge, mathematical or otherwise, be obtained by proof that is not subject to doubt of this sort. But the same mistake occurs even when the assumption is restricted to knowledge in mathematics with mathematical certainty. Despite the astounding feats of its champions, the assumption inexorably leads to skepticism. One may legitimately wonder, for example, how one knows (and in particular, whether by direct mathematical insight) that if integers n and m have the same successor then $n = m$. It is doubtful that anything other than Descartes's *Cogito* is completely immune from the kind of doubt raised by demanding indubitable proof that one's proof is a proof. One may even doubt whether the *Cogito* is.

None of this diminishes the epistemological power of mathematical proof. That power is awesome. Though not immune from Cartesian doubt, mathematical proof provides a way—indeed, the only way—to extend human knowledge with mathematical certainty beyond the severely narrow confines of **Ax**. Few epistemological mechanisms can achieve the kind of certainty that mathematical proof confers. In any event, even if Church's argument is not cogent, it does not follow that his conclusion is incorrect.

Though severely narrow, **Ax** may be remarkably diverse. As noted, **Ax** includes fundamental mathematical truths that no one in the entire history of human life will have ever apprehended—let alone believed, let alone known. Some elements of **Ax** involve concepts that are humanly apprehendible but of which no one will have ever formed a grasp. Some elements of **Ax** may be knowable only through modes of thought which are humanly possible but in which no one will have ever engaged. It may be that, though each element of **Ax** taken individually is humanly knowable with mathematical certainty, no possible human mind could apprehend all of them—let alone believe all of them, let alone know all of them with mathematical certainty. As far as Gödel's theorems go, the question is left open whether **Ax** is effectively decidable, or at least effectively enumerable, or enumerable at all—even whether the elements constitute a set. Hao Wang has reported that, though Gödel derives only a disjunction from his second incompleteness theorem, he believed Hilbert was correct in rejecting the second disjunct.[33] In light of Gödel's first theorem (and Church's thesis), Hilbert's optimism that the human mind is capable of solving any purely mathematical problem carries with it the view that the axioms of human mathematics are not effectively decidable. If every purely mathematical problem is humanly solvable in principle, then there is no effective procedure for listing the axioms of human mathematics. This would not mean that the human brain is not (among other things) an organic machine. It does mean that, insofar as Hilbert's optimism is correct, the theorem-proving capacity of the human mind far exceeds that of any theorem-proving mechanism whose deductive basis is effectively enumerable—a restatement of Gödel's disjunction. But one does not have to be optimistic to appreciate that if the human brain is a machine, then it is a remarkable one—or else Gödel was not human (or both).

Notes

*The present essay grew out of meetings of the Santa Barbarians Discussion Group, organized by C. Anthony Anderson. I am indebted to the participants for encouraging my thoughts on the topic and for their comments on an early draft, and especially to Anderson for his valuable assistance.

1. Nagel and Newman, *Gödel's Proof* (New York University Press, 1958, 1967), at pp. 100–102.

2. In *The Emperor's New Mind: Concerning Computers, Minds, and the Laws of Physics* (Oxford University Press, 1989), at p. 416. Penrose revisits some of the issues in *Shadows of the Mind: A Search for the Missing Science of Consciousness* (Oxford University Press, 1994), and "Beyond the Doubting of a Shadow: A Reply to Commentaries on *Shadows of the Mind*," *Psyche*, 2, 23 (1996).

3. Lucas, "Minds, Machines and Gödel," *Philosophy*, XXXVI (1961); reprinted in A. R. Anderson, ed., *Minds and Machines* (Englewood Cliffs, NJ: Prentice-Hall, 1964), pp. 43–59, at 44, 47. A conclusion opposite in thrust from that of Lucas, Nagel and Newman, and Penrose is urged by Judson Webb, *Mechanism, Mentalism and Metamathematics* (Dordrecht: D. Reidel, 1980).

4. Putnam, "Minds and Machines," in Sidney Hook, ed., *Dimensions of Mind: A Symposium* (New York: New York University Press, 1960); reprinted in A. R. Anderson, ed., *Minds and Machines* (Englewood Cliffs, NJ: Prentice-Hall, 1964), pp. 72–97, at 77.

5. Lucas has replied, in "Minds, Machines, and Gödel: A Retrospect," in P. J. R. Millican and A. Clark, eds, *Machines and Thought: The Legacy of Alan Turing, Volume 1* (Oxford University Press, 1996), that the mechanist's claim that the proposed logistic system captures human mathematical reasoning is otiose unless the mechanist concedes that the system is consistent, and it is from this premise that Lucas derives the Gödelian sentence (p. 117). But unless the premise is itself proved mathematically, Lucas's derivation does not constitute a proof, or anything close to a proof. Given Lucas's objective, it is not sufficient for him to argue merely that mechanism cannot be proved.

   An assessment of the arguments and assertions of Lucas and Penrose is provided in Stewart Shapiro, "Incompleteness, Mechanism, and Optimism," *The Bulletin of Symbolic Logic*, 4 (September 1998), pp. 273–302.

6. "Some Basic Theorems on the Foundations of Mathematics and Their Implications," in Gödel's *Collected Works, III: Unpublished Essays and Lectures*, S. Feferman, J. W. Dawson, Jr., W. Goldfarb, C. Parsons, and R. N. Solovay, eds (Oxford University Press, 1995), pp. 304–323, at 310. See also Hao Wang, *A Logical Journey: From Gödel to Philosophy* (Cambridge, Ma.: MIT Press, 1996), especially chapters 6 and 7, pp. 183–246.

7. If the second alternative obtains—that there are purely mathematical questions of a certain sort that the human intellect is in principle unable to prove or disprove—this would seem to indicate that truth in pure mathematics is not reducible to provability (demonstrability), since the two are not even co-extensional. This conclusion relies on the assumption that if there are humanly undecidable purely mathematical

propositions, at least some have truth value. In fact, the propositions that are produced in Gödel's proof as undecidable in the logistic system in question are true (their negations false) provided the system is consistent, and are otherwise false. Any analogous propositions that are undecidable in human mathematics are likewise truth valued, so that truth in pure mathematics would provide no guarantee of certainty, or even potential certainty.

8. *Ibid.*, pp. 309–310.

9. Boolos, "Introductory Note to *1951," in Gödel's *Collected Works, III: Unpublished Essays and Lectures*, S. Feferman, J. W. Dawson, Jr., W. Goldfarb, C. Parsons, and R. N. Solovay, eds (Oxford University Press, 1995), pp. 290–304, at 294.

10. Boolos misformulates his conclusion by saying that if there is a Turing machine whose output is the set of sentences expressing just those mathematical propositions provable by a mind capable of understanding all propositions expressed by any sentence of the form $\ulcorner(\forall x)(\exists y)\phi(x, y) = 0\urcorner$, where x and y are sequences of integer variables and $\phi(x, y)$ is a polynomial with integer coefficients, then there is a true mathematical proposition *of this same technical sort* that cannot be proved by that same mind. It is evident that the conclusion Boolos intends is, rather, that if there is a Turing machine that produces exactly the mathematical truths provable by a mind with such comprehension, then there is a mathematical truth *that such a mind understands* (never mind what technical sort it is) but cannot prove. The latter carries with it the suggestion that the mind's incapacity, under the envisaged circumstances, does not result from a lack of understanding.

The suggestion, however, is misleading. It is built into the case that the mind's theorem-proving capacity, by hypothesis, does not exceed the output of some theorem-enumerating Turing machine or other. This in itself says nothing about *why* the mind's mathematical prowess is thus limited. No logical inconsistency results by adding that the mind's limitations do not result from any lack of understanding. But neither has it been argued that the prospect of such a human mind—whose theorem-proving capacity coincides exactly with the output of Turing machine but nevertheless capable of fully understanding that which, as a consequence of the second theorem, it therefore cannot prove—is a real psychological possibility. These issues are in any case irrelevant. Boolos's intended conclusion follows from the second incompleteness theorem in the same way as the misformulated conclusion. Any possible generating activity whose potential output happens to coincide with the actual output a Turing machine—human or alien, animate or inanimate, with understanding or without—cannot in the relevant sense prove its own consistency.

11. **HuMath** is a proper subclass of the class of propositions, purely mathematical or otherwise, humanly knowable with mathematical certainty (i.e., with the same degree of certainty attainable in pure mathematics). It is not assumed that **Math**, or **HuMath**, is a set in the classical sense. Rather, the use of these terms in bold typeface in a sentence is to be regarded as an abbreviation for statements employing predicates that apply, respectively, to all purely mathematical truths and all purely mathematical truths humanly knowable with mathematical certainty. To say, for example, that a proposition p is one of (or an "element of," or "belongs to") **Math** is to say no more (or less) than that p is one of *these* propositions [the truths of pure mathematics], and to say that **HuMath** is a proper subclass of **Math**, is to say that all of *these* propositions [the truths of pure mathematics that are humanly knowable with mathematical certainty] are among *those* propositions [the truths of pure mathematics] but not vice versa. From the former it follows that *if* there is a set M of all

truths of pure mathematics then $p \in M$, from the latter that again if there is such a set as M then the subset HM consisting of those elements humanly knowable with mathematical certainty is proper. Neither the antecedent of these conditionals nor its negation is presupposed.

12. One may take Heisenberg's Uncertainty Principle to entail this.

13. There may be other epistemic mechanisms, or potential epistemic mechanisms, that are, by contrast, precluded by a mind's being human, i.e. by the nature and biology of humanity. One such may be the ω-rule of inference, which licenses the inference from premises, $\phi(0)$, $\phi(1)$, $\phi(2)$, and so on, to their generalization in $\ulcorner(\forall n)\phi(n)\urcorner$. Unless the human mind can reason with infinitely premises in a finite time span, it may be unable to draw inferences in accordance with this rule.

14. *Op. cit.*, p. 305.

15. This observation is to be taken in a sense in which it is beyond reasonable dispute. Some writers have mistakenly taken the incompleteness results to cast doubt on it. Thus Penrose writes: "Gödel's theorem...established...that the powers of human reason could not be limited to any accepted preassigned system of formalized rules" (*op. cit.*). It is incumbent on one who denies the observation to specify how the phenomenon of proof in mathematics might be otherwise understood while avoiding mathematical mysticism.

     Contemporary holistic empiricism holds that even knowledge of mathematical axioms is inextricably interconnected with all human knowledge taken as a whole, and thus ultimately empirical and fallible. Epistemological holism, however, is not inconsistent (as suggested by Shapiro, *op. cit.*) with the observation—well confirmed by actual practice—that knowledge in mathematics, unlike other disciplines, is furthered by an epistemologically special tool: mathematical proof from axioms, themselves humanly knowable with certainty without proof. Certainty, even mathematical certainty, does not entail immunity from error, let alone the absolute impossibility of human fallibility. (Some holists have proved their own fallibility on the very point in question.) Holistic empiricism maintains that the principles governing mathematical reasoning are ultimately judged, and conceivably might be revised, on ordinary empirical grounds. Whatever the shortcomings of this epistemological stance, it is not committed to denying the obvious role of mathematical proof in extending knowledge with certainty.

16. Axioms may be regarded as special rules of inference permitting inferences *ex nihilo*. On this conception, the deductive basis of a logistic system consists entirely of primitive inference rules. It is common, on the other hand, to minimize the set of primitive (non-axiom) inference rules by taking *modus ponens* as the only such rule, replacing every other inference rule,

     From ϕ_1, ϕ_2,..., and ϕ_n, to infer ψ

     with all instances of the corresponding axiom schema $\ulcorner(\phi_1 \supset (\phi_2 \supset (...(\phi_n \supset \psi))...)\urcorner$.

17. Notice that the resulting axiom set is defined by a precise, finite rule. See note 23 below.

18. Under this restriction, the deductive system that takes all sentences expressing truths of arithmetic as axioms (though it exists) is disqualified as a logistic or formal system or theory. Thus Wang—the expositor who more than any other brought Gödel's philosophical views into the public domain—gives the following informal statement of the first incompleteness theorem (*op. cit.*, p. 3): *No formal system of mathematics can be both consistent and complete*; or alternatively, *Any consistent formal*

theory of mathematics must contain undecidable propositions. Similarly, C. Smorynski, "The Incompleteness Theorems," in J. Barwise, ed., *Handbook of Mathematical Logic* (Amsterdam: North Holland, 1977, 1983), pp. 821–865, states the theorem as follows: *Let T be a formal theory containing arithmetic. Then there is a sentence φ which asserts its own unprovability and is [undecidable by T if T is ω-consistent]* (p. 825).

19. The possible formal language in question should satisfy certain minimal constraints. As a matter of clarity, for example, ambiguity is precluded. The language is assumed to contain denumerably many expressions, to be bivalent (i.e., every sentence is either true or false and never both), and also such that a version of Tarski's theorem about truth holds for it. The language must also include the resources to express any mathematical concept that figures in any element of **HuMath**—including such concepts that have not yet been, or will never be, discovered or apprehended. (It is not assumed that the language contains only a finite number of logical or mathematical primitive constants.)

20. Gödel showed how to construct a formula along the lines of ϕ_{Cons} roughly for any logistic system suitable for arithmetic that includes the resources to designate any recursive function of integers and whose primitive deductive basis is recursive. For details, see Elliot Mendelson, *Introduction to Mathematical Logic* (New York: D. Van Nostrand, 1979), chapter 3, especially pp. 161–162. (See also the following note.) The notion of a mathematical *axiom*, in the sense of a fundamental, purely mathematical truth that is humanly knowable with mathematical certainty without independent mathematical proof, is not itself a purely mathematical notion and is not directly expressible in the language in question. Instead, assuming the elements of **Ax** are recursively enumerable, those propositions may be indirectly specified within the formula ϕ_{Proof}, and hence within ϕ_{Cons}, by means of a direct, purely mathematical specification of the recursive function f that enumerates the Gödel numbers of sentences expressing those very propositions. As a corollary of Gödel's first incompleteness theorem, there can be no expression of the language that extensionally specifies **Math** in an analogous manner. (This is Tarski's theorem about truth; see the preceding note.)

The formulae ϕ_{Proof} and ϕ_{Cons} do not strictly speaking semantically express the notions of proof from such-and-such axioms (those generated by recursive function f) and the consistency of such-and-such axioms and inference rules, respectively. The mathematical notions that are semantically expressed are, however, provably equivalent to these meta-theoretic notions. Indeed, the relationship is closer than mere provable equivalence; in a sense, the formulae are a code for the meta-theoretic notions. It is useful in the present context to think of the language of ϕ_{Proof} and ϕ_{Cons} as consisting of integers (Gödel numbers) functioning directly as expressions, and of the expression of a proof within the language—i.e., of a "proof" in the syntactic sense of a sequence of formulae—as a sequence of such integers-*qua*-formulae (rather than as its encoded representation by a single integer *via* the integer's prime factorization). Then ϕ_{Cons} semantically expresses that there are no such proof-sequences of integers culminating in integers one of which is the number-theoretic negation of the other (or something trivially equivalent to this).

21. Rosser, "Extensions of Some Theorems of Gödel and Church," *Journal of Symbolic Logic*, 1 (1936), pp.87–91. It follows from the result obtained by William Craig in "Axiomatizability Within a System," *Journal of Symbolic Logic*, 18, 1 (March 1953), pp. 30–32, that if **Ax** is recursively enumerable, then even if **Ax** is not itself recur-

sive, **HuMath** is primitive recursively axiomatizable. (Thanks to C. Anthony Anderson for calling my attention to the relevance of Craig's result.)

22. Shapiro, *op. cit.*, explains the first disjunct of Gödel's disjunction as the denial of the thesis that "all human arithmetic procedures are effective algorithms," and says that Gödel inclined instead to hold (with Lucas and Penrose) that "some of the routines and procedures that humans can employ...cannot be simulated on a Turing machine. There are inherently *non-computational* human arithmetic *procedures*" (pp. 277, 290, emphasis Shapiro's).

23. Gödel says in the passage quoted that his second incompleteness theorem "*makes it impossible that someone should set up a certain well-defined system of axioms and rules and consistently make the following assertion about it: All of these axioms and rules I perceive (with mathematical certitude) to be correct, and moreover I believe that they contain all of mathematics.* If someone makes such a statement he contradicts himself. ... [For] no well-defined system of correct axioms can contain-...all true mathematical propositions..." (The thrust of this remark is evidently better conveyed if the italicized phrase 'I believe' is deleted.) A similar remark is reported by Wang (*op. cit.*, p. 187): "There is a vague idea that we can find a set of axioms such that (1) all these axioms are evident to us; (2) the set yields all of mathematics. It follows from my incompleteness theorem that it is impossible to set up an axiom system satisfying (1) and (2), because, by (1), the statement expressing the consistency of the system should also be evident to me.—All this is explicitly in my Gibbs lecture." In order for someone to "set up" (i.e., fully specify) an infinite system of axioms, there would have to be an effective procedure for enumerating them. The term 'well-defined' is evidently a synonym in this context for 'recursively enumerable'.

24. "For if he perceives the axioms under consideration to be correct, he also perceives (with the same certainty) that they are consistent" (*op. cit.*, in the passage quoted above from p. 309). Trivially, no contradiction is validly deducible from a set of truths. The casual manner of Gödel's remark creates the impression that this triviality is sufficient for the thesis, whereas strictly speaking, this justification is incomplete. Given a class of putative inference rules, one must know with mathematical certainty that every element of the class is valid in order to know with the same certainty that no falsehood, and hence no contradiction, is derivable from truths by their means. The validity of each inference rule of human mathematical reasoning is humanly knowable with mathematical certainty. Assuming the inference rules constitute an effectively decidable set, it is reasonable to suppose further that those very rules can be known with mathematical certainty to be one and all valid. Gödel's thesis then follows.

25. The argument I attribute to Gödel is significantly different from that to which Boolos's criticisms apply. Still other interpretations have been proposed. Wang (*op. cit.*, p. 185) apparently construes Gödel as arguing that if the axioms and inference rules of human mathematics were finite in number, then we could not know those very propositions and rules to be the basis of human mathematical knowledge, since otherwise we could know something about that basis (by confirming each element individually) that is not deducible from it—its consistency—and hence they would not be *all* the axioms and rules of human mathematics.

I believe for a variety of reasons that this cannot be Gödel's argument. Curiously, Wang notes that the same line of argument yields another conclusion—one that is, in fact, significantly stronger—namely, that the basis of human mathematics is infinite. Wang might mean to attribute to Gödel a somewhat different argument: We cannot know any finite basis to be the basis of human mathematics; for otherwise we could prove (by individual confirmation) something mathematical that is not deducible from that basis: that the basis (and hence all) of human mathematical knowledge is consistent. But this will not do either. That the basis of human mathematical knowledge—whatever it is, and whatever its size—is internally consistent is trivial and as certain as any mathematical theorem. This, however, is not reducible to a mathematical truth. It is an epistemological truism.

26. This probably yields the intent behind the following remark of Gödel's, reported by Wang (*op. cit.*, p. 186): "The incompleteness results do not rule out the possibility that there is a theorem-proving computer which is in fact equivalent to mathematical intuition. But they imply that, in such a—highly unlikely for other reasons—case, either we do not know the exact specification of the computer or we do not know that it works correctly." If **Ax** is recursively enumerable, so that a computer program might be written for proving theorems from it, then even if we were to write such a program, we could not know that its product is correct; otherwise we would also know what, according to the second incompleteness theorem, we cannot prove: its consistency.

27. Lucas, *op. cit.* (p. 44 of the reprinting in Anderson, *Minds and Machines*), declares that Gödel's results obtain for any formal system that is consistent and contains the natural numbers and the operations of addition and multiplication. In a later footnote (p. 52*n*6), he explicitly mentions the restriction that the primitive deductive basis be recursively enumerable.

28. Gödel evidently believed that the human mind does possess some self-validating insight of this sort. Cf. Wang, *op. cit.*, pp. 187–189.

29. Church, *Introduction to Mathematical Logic, I* (Princeton University Press, 1956), at pp. 50–51. See note 18 above.

30. *Ibid.*, pp. 53–54.

31. C. Anthony Anderson makes a related objection in "Alonzo Church's Contributions to Philosophy and Intensional Logic," *Bulletin of Symbolic Logic*, 4, 2 (June 1998), pp. 129–171, at 130–131.

32. Cf. Lewis Carroll, "What the Tortoise Said to Achilles," *Mind*, N.S. IV, 14 (April 1895), pp. 278–280.

33. Wang, *From Mathematics to Philosophy* (London: Routledge and Kegan Paul, 1974), at pp. 324–326.

Philosophical Perspectives, 15, Metaphysics, 2001

TOUCHING

Hud Hudson
Western Washington University

A *receptacle* is a region of space possibly exactly occupied by a material object. In this essay, I will examine how our beliefs about receptacles can inform our analysis concerning the relation of being in perfect contact.

Assuming that a region of space is a set of points in space, Richard Cartwright has offered a series of definitions that will prove helpful in thinking about our theme.[1]

(C1) R is continuous $=_{df}$ R is not discontinuous.

(C2) R is discontinuous $=_{df}$ R is the union of two non-null separated regions.

(C3) R and R' are separated $=_{df}$ (i) the intersection of R with the closure of R' is null, and (ii) the intersection of R' with the closure of R is null.

(C4) the closure of R $=_{df}$ the union of R with the set of all its boundary points.

(C5) p is a boundary point of R $=_{df}$ every open sphere about p has a non-null intersection with both R and the complement of R.

(C6) R is an open sphere about p $=_{df}$ the members of R are all and only those points that are less than some fixed distance from p.

(C7) The complement of R $=_{df}$ the set of points in space not in R.

(C8) x is an open object $=_{df}$ x exactly occupies a region that has none of its boundary points as members.

(C9) x is a closed object $=_{df}$ x exactly occupies a region that has all of its boundary points as members.

(C10) x is a partially open object $=_{df}$ x exactly occupies a region that has some but not all of its boundary points as members.

Now, whether we are willing to assent to sentences of the form "this object touched that object," often depends on the context—in particular, it often depends on what level of precision we employ in fixing the boundaries of the objects in question. For example, we tolerate quite-crude, perceptually-based standards when we say something such as "the hand touches the desk," but set the bar much higher when we say something such as "the open sphere touches the closed cube." Throughout the present essay, I intend to use the term 'touching' (and its cognates) synonymously with 'being in perfect contact', a phrase that denotes the relation which corresponds to the very highest standards for judgment about such matters.

Well, what is that standard? Suppose we begin with the plausible suggestion that touching is simply a matter of sharing a boundary point,[2] together with the proviso that an object, x, is credited with touching an object, y, whenever one of x's parts touches one of y's parts. (After all, touching something does not require touching each of its parts!) In other words, x might touch y even though x and y do not share a boundary point, provided that some part of x shares a boundary point with some part of y.[3] This suggestion yields

(CONTACT-1) Necessarily, x touches y if and only if $\exists R1$, $\exists R2$, $\exists w$, $\exists v$, $\exists p$ (i) w is a part of x, whereas v is a part of y, (ii) w exactly occupies R1, whereas v exactly occupies R2, and (iii) p is a boundary point of both R1 and R2.

According to (CONTACT-1), then, a perfectly good way for two open objects to touch is to be somewhere separated only by a point that falls between them, for such a scenario will ensure a boundary point common to each. (Imagine, for instance, two open spheres separated by an unoccupied plane that intersects the closure of each at exactly one and the same point-sized region.) Likewise, an open object will touch a closed one when some pair of their respective parts are so positioned that there is no unoccupied space between them, for some outermost point in the region exactly occupied by the relevant part of the closed object will be a boundary point common to each of the parts in question. (Imagine, for instance, an open cube that is limited on one surface by the surface of a closed cube of the same size.) Furthermore, no two (non-overlapping) closed objects will touch no matter how they happen to be positioned, for it would seem that only by way of overlap can two closed objects be so arranged as to guarantee that a part of each shares a boundary point with a part of the other. (Imagine, for instance, two closed hemispheres which overlap by sharing the two-dimensional disc whose perimeter is the equator of their host-sphere. The northern hemisphere, as we may call it, will touch the southern hemisphere, in virtue of one of its partially-open, proper parts—namely, "all-of-the-northern-hemisphere-minus-the-disc"—which certainly seems to be in perfect contact with the southern hemisphere.)

Whether or not (CONTACT-1) strikes one as plausible, however, should turn on just what regions one takes to be receptacles. I think that *any* region (save the null region—should we wish to acknowledge that) is a receptacle. I also think that for any two regions that are (respectively) exactly occupied by two material objects, there is another material object that exactly occupies the union of the two regions. I also think that any material object that exactly occupies a region is such that for any subregion of that region, that material object has a part that exactly occupies that subregion. Others disagree.[4] Cartwright, for instance, thinks that no point-sized region is a receptacle, that no region with finite membership is a receptacle, that no region with countable membership is a receptacle, and that no line, curve, or surface is a receptacle, either. Whereas that collection of intuitions happens to be rather widely endorsed, Cartwright himself proves to be far more restrictive than this when he announces that every receptacle is an open region.[5] Admittedly, disputes over just which regions are receptacles and just which collections of objects have sums are highly controversial and worthy of serious study. Presently, however, I have a more modest aim in mind than attempting to contribute to those disputes. I simply want to highlight their relevance to questions about touching.

Let me make my point first with Cartwright's restrictive view. If one believed (as he does) that only open regions are receptacles, then one should be wholly satisfied with (CONTACT-1). Why? Because on that view, it is not possible that two objects be any closer than are two open objects exactly occupying regions that share a boundary point, and because it would seem that two objects could not have a better claim to being in perfect contact than by being as close as it is possible for two objects to be. (I here ignore the case of overlapping open objects. Although there is some temptation to say that such overlappers would be "even closer still" in virtue of partly being in the same region, this particular kind of overlap is significantly dissimilar from that of the closed, northern and southern hemispheres above. Recall that our current hypothesis declares all objects open, and note that any open part (confined to one overlapper) would be entirely *separated* from any open part shared by the overlappers. Consequently, overlap is not by itself sufficient for the kind of closeness we have in mind when speaking of perfect contact.)

But what should someone believe who agrees with me that points, lines, curves, and surfaces are all perfectly respectable receptacles, and that any union of respectable receptacles is a respectable receptacle? It is interesting to note that we can all begin with the same general methodological strategy apparently employed by Cartwright, namely, to let our highest standards for touching require whatever relation is such that (i) it is possibly instantiated, and (ii) whenever two objects stand in that relation, it is not even possible that any two objects be more deserving of the title 'in perfect contact' than they.

But it would seem that on this rather liberal view of receptacles no two (non-overlapping) open objects can any longer serve as examples of being in perfect contact, since it is clearly possible for two objects to be more deserving of that title than they. Consider again our two open spheres separated by an unoccupied plane that intersects the closure of each at exactly one and the same point-sized region. If we believe that two-dimensional regions are receptacles, then we can fill the portion of that unoccupied plane that separates our two spheres with a type of material object we might call a plane-wall. Admittedly, in one sense it is not possible for any two objects to get any *closer* to one another than are our spheres, for on the standard way of determining closeness (i.e., the minimal distance between their closures), their distance is zero. Nevertheless, our two spheres are not among those objects most deserving of the title 'in perfect contact', since (without changing their positions with respect to one another) they may be separated by a third material object that overlaps with neither of them!

But if not two (non-overlapping) open objects, what will count on the liberal view as an example of some objects that are among the most deserving of the title 'in perfect contact'? Consider again an open cube that is limited on one surface by the surface of a closed cube of the same size. These two objects seem to do the trick. Of course, they are similar to the two open objects insofar as they share a boundary point; but they are significantly dissimilar insofar as no plane-wall can come between them without overlap. The formal difference is that (unlike the two spheres) the two cubes share a boundary point that is itself a member of one of the regions exactly occupied by one of the cubes. Perhaps, then, a proponent of the liberal view of receptacles should maintain that touching is not simply a matter of having parts that share a boundary point; rather it is a matter of having parts that share a boundary point which, in turn, is a member of a region exactly occupied by one of the parts in question. This suggestion yields

> **(CONTACT-2)** Necessarily, x touches y if and only if $\exists R1$, $\exists R2$, $\exists w$, $\exists v$, $\exists p$ (i) w is a part of x, whereas v is a part of y, (ii) w exactly occupies R1, whereas v exactly occupies R2, (iii) p is a boundary point of both R1 and R2, and (iv) p is a member of at least one of R1 and R2.

A proponent of (CONTACT-2) will thus declare that an open object and a closed object can be more deserving of the title 'in perfect contact' than can any pair of (non-overlapping) open objects, which could always be separated by something like a plane-wall. Unfortunately, (CONTACT-2) is subject to a quick (but devastating) counterexample. (CONTACT-2) entails the silly consequence that any point-sized object touches itself merely in virtue of occupying whatever region it exactly occupies, a region that (of course) has the same boundary point as itself. (Note that any point-sized object, S, will be fit to serve as both w and v—since it will be an improper part of itself—thereby ensuring R1 = R2.) Understandably, that consequence need not trouble anyone who doesn't believe in point-sized objects to begin with, but it should certainly seem an undesirable feature of the analysis to those who were attracted to it precisely because they held the liberal view of receptacles, a view which recognizes the possibility of point-sized objects. Perhaps, though, the intuition that touching always relates at least two distinct things need not require us to give up on the main idea inspired by the liberal view of receptacles. Let us just supplement the current analysis by requiring that at least one of the relevant regions be both continuous and non-point-sized.[6] This suggestion yields

(**CONTACT-3**) Necessarily, x touches y if and only if $\exists R1$, $\exists R2$, $\exists w$, $\exists v$, $\exists p$ (i) w is a part of x, whereas v is a part of y, (ii) w exactly occupies R1, whereas v exactly occupies R2, (iii) p is a boundary point of both R1 and R2, (iv) p is a member of at least one of R1 and R2, and (v) at least one of R1 and R2 is a (non-point-sized) continuous region.

Now, we seem to have all the advantages of (CONTACT-2) without the silly consequence that all point-sized objects touch themselves. For quite some time I counted myself among the proponents of (CONTACT-3)—until I realized that the proponent of (CONTACT-3) faces a very curious puzzle, indeed. To entertain this puzzle properly, let us introduce some new terminology:

First let us say that an object is *grainy* if and only if it exactly occupies a region, all of whose non-point-sized subregions are discontinuous. Note that any object which exactly occupies a region that has a finite number of members is grainy and that any object which exactly occupies a region that has a countable infinity of members is grainy. Being non-grainy, then, requires exactly occupying a region that has an uncountable infinity of members. Accordingly, let us acknowledge that any point-sized object is grainy, and that any fusion of countably-many point-sized objects is grainy, as well. Second let us say that two objects are *neighbors* if and only if the first exactly occupies a region that is not separated from the region exactly occupied by the second.

Now, upon reflection on the notions of graininess and being neighbors, I suspect a very common reaction is to assume that no two (non-overlapping) grainy objects touch—perhaps because it seems obvious that any grainy object is closed and because no two (non-overlapping) closed objects touch). And I suspect another very common reaction is to assume that any two neighbors touch, for two such objects will always have parts that share a boundary point which, in turn, is a member of one of the regions exactly occupied by one of the parts in question. Initially, we might even feel confident enough about these common reactions to regard them as adequacy conditions on our attempts to formulate a proper analysis of touching. However (quite surprisingly) we will soon see that we have to choose between this pair of powerful intuitions, for there are clear-cut cases where they come apart.

Let 'A' and 'B' name two point-sized objects that are in an otherwise unoccupied room. At 1:30, point-sized object C is inserted halfway between A and B on the line described by the point-sized regions exactly occupied by A and B. At 1:45, D is inserted halfway between A and C. At 1:52.30, E is inserted halfway between A and D. At 1:56.15, F is inserted halfway between A and E. Zeno the series![7]

Let 'Bits' name the fusion of all of the point-sized objects (excepting A) which are in the room at 2:00. Bits has a (countable) infinity of point-sized parts, each of which exactly occupies a point-sized region on a segment of a particular line that runs through the room. Bits, in turn, exactly occupies that scattered region which is the union of all of those point-sized regions. Thus, Bits is a grainy object. Owing to its lack of any non-point-sized subregions, A is a grainy object, as well. Clearly, A and Bits do not overlap.

So, A and Bits are two (non-overlapping) grainy objects. Thus, if we adhered to the first common reaction reported above, we would be forced to claim that A and Bits do not touch.

Recall now that A exactly occupies a point-sized region, which (as is true of any point-sized region) has its only member as its only boundary point. But then (given our previous description of Bits) we can see that the point-sized region exactly occupied by A contains a boundary point both of itself and of the region exactly occupied by Bits. It then follows that the intersection of the closure of the region exactly occupied by Bits with the region exactly occupied by A is not null. Accordingly, A exactly occupies a region that is not separated from the region exactly occupied by Bits.

So, A and Bits are neighbors. Thus, if we adhered to the second common reaction reported above, we would be forced to claim that A and Bits do touch, after all.

We can't have it both ways! Which common reaction shall we abandon to the misleading-intuitions pile? Well, if our intuitions are in conflict, perhaps it is best to consult our current analysis (which, after all, does have something going for it) for some guidance. Significantly, (CONTACT-3) yields the result that A and Bits do not touch, for A and Bits fail to satisfy condition (v)—(i.e., neither of our grainy objects has a part that exactly occupies a (non-point-sized) continuous region of space). On this resolution of our conflict, then, it turns out that some neighbors don't touch, and *that* is an exceedingly odd consequence to be stuck with. But something has to go; perhaps we should just bite the bullet.

I fear that biting the bullet won't do. There are objects whose prospects for touching Bits should be just as good or bad as are those of our object A. Allow me to introduce one: Consider a one-dimensional material object, line-segment shaped, with a closed interval at exactly one end, hereby named 'Continuous'. Now, remove A from the room containing Bits and carefully place Continuous in the room so that all of its parts fall on the same line where we find all of the parts of Bits and so that the closed end of Continuous now exactly occupies the point-sized region recently vacated by A. Clearly, that point-sized region will now contain a common boundary point of the regions exactly occupied by Continuous and Bits, and that boundary point will also be a member of the region exactly occupied by Continuous itself. To this extent, then, Continuous and Bits resemble A and Bits; each pair is an example of two objects that are as close as it is possible for two objects to be. The only interesting difference between the two pairs seems to depend entirely on a superfluous part of Continuous, a part that doesn't seem to be relevant to whether or not Continuous touches Bits. This particular part (which we might call Continuous' tail) is thoroughly *separated* from Bits by a unique point-sized part of Continuous—namely, by a part that exactly occupies the only region which contains a boundary point of Bits without also containing a member of the region exactly occupied by Bits. Of course, that apparently *relevant* feature was also a characteristic of our object A, and how could "A's not having a tail" (which would be wholly separated from Bits by A itself) be relevant to whether A touches Bits? Accordingly, one expects the same verdict about whether touching occurs between the two objects in each pair. Suspiciously, though, (CONTACT-3)—contrary to expectation—yields the result that Continuous and Bits touch. For unlike the case of A and Bits, one of the objects in our new pairing guarantees that condition (v) is satisfied, after all. Whatever the correct analysis of touching turns out to be, it should generate the same answer to the question "Does A touch Bits?" as it does to the question "Does Continuous touch Bits?" So, much the worse for (CONTACT-3).

Perhaps, then, we should aim for a revision of (CONTACT-3) that won't force us to split our vote on the two cases by way of guaranteeing that neither A nor Continuous touches Bits. This suggestion yields

> **(CONTACT-4)** Necessarily, x touches y if and only if $\exists R1$, $\exists R2$, $\exists w$, $\exists v$, $\exists p$ (i) w is a part of x, whereas v is a part of y, (ii) w exactly occupies R1, whereas v exactly occupies R2, (iii) p is a boundary point of both R1 and R2, (iv) p is a member of at least one of R1 and R2, and (v) both R1 and R2 are (non-point-sized) continuous regions.

A new problem grounded in point-sized objects now arises. Earlier we argued against (CONTACT-2) that it entailed that any point-sized object touches itself. (CONTACT-4) certainly doesn't have that unwanted entailment, but along with its effective ban on (certain kinds of) self-touching (CONTACT-4) has also managed to rule out any and all touching of point-sized objects. For a proponent of the liberal view of receptacles, this isn't credible. A point-sized object that exactly occupies the center point of a sphere is clearly touched by a great number of objects (including the object which is that-sphere-minus-the-object-at-its-center-point). What we need, then, is an analysis that doesn't entail that every point-sized object touches itself, but which permits the touching of a point-sized object by other objects of the right size, shape, and surface.

Such a strategy will inevitably encourage us to resolve the tension between our common reactions concerning grainy objects and neighbors by reversing our former solution. Thus, we will be able to retain the extremely plausible claim that any two neighbors touch (including Continuous and Bits as well as A and Bits). The price we pay this time around is acknowledging that some pairs of (non-overlapping) grainy objects can touch one another, after all! Perhaps, though, this pill will be easier to swallow once we recognize that our previous motivation for denying that any (non-overlapping) grainy objects touch one another may well have been the *mistaken* view that every grainy object is closed. For, as we have seen, Bits exactly occupies a region which contains some but not all of its boundary points, and thus qualifies as partially open. The cost of our new strategy for regaining consistency, then, is not so exorbitant as to force us to grant that two (non-overlapping) closed objects can touch. This suggestion yields

> **(CONTACT-5)** Necessarily, x touches y if and only if $\exists R1$, $\exists R2$, $\exists w$, $\exists v$, $\exists p$ (i) w is a part of x, whereas v is a part of y, (ii) w exactly occupies R1, whereas v exactly occupies R2, (iii) p is a boundary point of both R1 and R2, (iv) p is a member of at least one of R1 and R2, and (v) $w \neq v$.

By way of a quick review of our previous counterexamples to its predecessors, let us note that (CONTACT-5) permits one to say that Continuous touches Bits, that A touches Bits, that whereas point-sized objects never touch themselves they nevertheless can be touched by other objects, and finally that there is no touching between any two (non-overlapping) open objects, since something like a plane-wall could always come between them (without overlap and without changing their positions with respect to one another).

Initially, (CONTACT-5) appears to have some peculiar consequences of its own. A *material simple* is a material object with no proper parts. Whether a material simple could exactly occupy an extended region is currently a controversial question.[8] But (CONTACT-5) seems to rule out the possibility of certain kinds of extended material simples. Here's why: Suppose that there is a (parially-open) extended material simple, say—a spatially continuous object, shaped like a snake, in an otherwise unoccupied room. Once we grant the existence of an object like that, however, it would seem that there would be no reason to suppose that it couldn't coil up head-to-tail, as it were, and touch itself. Perhaps (as a continuous spatial object) it would have to become a little thinner here and there to change from snake-shape to donut-shape, but certainly (one might think) we would have to regard its movement as a clear instance of self-touching. This concession, though, would prove fatal to (CONTACT-5), for (CONTACT-5) requires that all touching (even self-touching) involve two distinct parts in virtue of which the touching occurs. The snake-simple, as I will call it, would violate this condition owing to its utter lack of proper parts. Thus, it would seem reasonable to conclude that if (CONTACT-5) is true, then it is not possible that there be such extended material simples.

Despite initial appearances, (CONTACT-5) is innocent of such charges.[9] The temptation to say that the snake-simple touches itself arises only when we move from thinking of touching as a description of an instantaneous state to thinking of touching as a description of a temporally extended event. Consider each of the moments during which the snake-simple changes from snake-shape to torus-shape. At no moment in the sequence are we compelled to say that the snake-simple is in the state of self-touching, for at some of the moments there is a spatial-gap between "its head and its tail" while at the other moments it simply exactly occupies a torus-shaped region of space without any parts exactly occupying any subregions of that region.

Lest you think there is no controversy to be had, however, here is a genuine consequence of (CONTACT-5) that will lead others to resist it in favor of some competing analysis. Recall our protagonists, A and Bits, and recall that our present analysis yields the verdict that they touch. Here is another character we may introduce into the story—Pieces. Pieces is (like Bits) a scattered material object. Pieces is (like Bits) both grainy and partially open. Pieces has (like Bits) the member of the region exactly occupied by A as its only boundary point which is not also a member of the region it exactly occupies. And, finally, all of the parts of Pieces lie on exactly the same line as do all the parts of Bits. Here's the surprise: Pieces lies entirely between A and the outermost point-sized part of Bits (i.e., that point-sized object we earlier named 'B'). In other words, the outermost part of Pieces lies halfway between the outermost part of Bits and the second-outermost part of Bits, while the second-outermost part of Pieces lies halfway between the second-outermost part of Bits and the third-outermost part of Bits, and so on.

(CONTACT-5) yields the result that *both* Bits and Pieces touch A! Surely, we want to balk at this. Doesn't Bits "get in the way" of Pieces touching A and doesn't Pieces "get in the way" of Bits touching A? After all, for every point-sized part of Pieces, there is an infinity of point-sized parts of Bits closer to A than it, and for every point-sized part of Bits, there is an infinity of point-sized parts of Pieces closer to A than it—and they all fall on the same line! Nevertheless, it is true that you can't so much as slip a point-sized object between (the composite object) Bits and A or between (the composite object) Pieces and A. And when you can't do *that* for objects of this sort, I say they touch. The consequence is surprising—but it's a result not a reductio.

So, as one who can think of no other candidate-analysis more plausible than the five we have already seen, as one committed to the liberal view of receptacles, and as one wholly opposed to some (but not all kinds of self-touching), I recommend (CONTACT-5) to the reader.[10]

Notes

1. Cartwright, Richard. "Scattered Objects," reprinted in *Philosophical Essays* (Cambridge: MIT Press, 1987): 171–186. Note that I say 'continuous' where he says 'connected', I say 'discontinuous' where he says 'disconnected', and I have rewritten the *definiens* of (C3) so as to avoid an ambiguity in the original.

2. As does Cartwright in "Scattered Objects," 172.
3. This may happen, for example, when the relevant parts of x and y are located deep in x's interior. More generally, let us note that not every boundary point of a part of x is automatically a boundary point of x.
4. Lots of others! Many, however, share my commitments to Universalism as a theory of composition and to the Doctrine of Arbitrary Undetached Parts (supplemented by the view that *any* region is occupiable—i.e., a receptacle). For the record, I also am an adherent of Four Dimensionalism (or at least to a variant thereof) although I'm ignoring the complications of that commitment in the present essay.
5. Cartwright, "Scattered Objects," 172.
6. Why say *both* 'continuous' and 'non-point-sized'? Because there is a perfectly good sense in which a region with exactly two elements is non-point-sized, yet also not continuous. (This is also the sense in which an object can count as "bigger-than-point-sized," yet not have extension; e.g., when it is the scattered fusion of two point-sized things.)
7. I am informed that some do not approve of the verb 'to Zeno', but I happily recommend it to you!
8. See Ned Markosian, "Simples," *Australasian Journal of Philosophy* Vol. 76 (1998): 213–226.
9. Although I originally regarded (CONTACT-5) guilty as charged (but didn't care about the crime), the case for the defense was compellingly presented by Michael Bergmann in correspondence, and since he's right, it's worth showing that (CONTACT-5) is innocent for those who do care about the crime.
10. Thanks for cool conversations concerning contact to Ned Markosian, Ted Sider, Mike Bergmann, Dean Zimmerman, John Hawthorne, Kris McDaniel, Andrew Cortens, Saikat Guha, and Achille Varzi.

Philosophical Perspectives, 15, Metaphysics, 2001

HOW TO BE AN ELEATIC MONIST†

Michael C. Rea
University of Delaware

There is a tradition according to which Parmenides of Elea endorsed the following set of counterintuitive doctrines:

(α) There exists exactly one material thing.
(β) What exists does not change.
(γ) Nothing is generated or destroyed.
(δ) What exists is undivided.

For convenience, I will use the label 'Eleatic monism' to refer to the conjunction of α–δ.[1]

Eleatic monism flies in the face of common sense. Scholars of pre Socratic thought rarely have anything to say in its defense beyond what the Eleatic philosophers said themselves, and virtually no one treats it as a serious option in metaphysics today.[2] Jonathan Barnes declares that α by itself (never mind the remaining doctrines) is "at best absurd and at worst unintelligible." (1979a, p. 2) It is not hard to see why. How could anyone possibly look at a sandy beach, witness the birth of a child or the death of a loved one, or gaze into the far reaches of space and believe that there exists exactly one thing that is neither generated nor destroyed, unchanging, and undivided?

The problem is not just that Eleatic monism seems to be false. Rather, the problem is that it seems to be so incredibly wide of the mark, so vastly out of touch with the truth, that it is hard to see what sorts of considerations could have led someone even to take it seriously, much less embrace it. What I offer in this paper is a way into the monist's frame of mind—a model, if you will, for understanding this otherwise apparently unintelligible world view. I will not argue that we should find Eleatic monism plausible; but I will show that, contrary to what many of us might initially have expected, the doctrine does have a legitimate place on the landscape of contemporary metaphysics.

I will argue that the doctrines of Eleatic monism ought to be accepted by anyone who accepts the following four theses:

EXTENSIONISM	There are no unextended material objects.
EXCLUSIVISM	Not every filled region of space at every time is filled by a material object.
ETERNALISM	There are some past objects, there are some future objects, and there neither were nor will be objects that do not exist.
THE PLENUM PRINCIPLE	Spacetime is a connected set of points, and every region of spacetime, no matter how small, is filled by matter.

Exclusivism stands in contrast with what we might call *inclusivism*, the thesis that every filled region of space at every time is filled by a material object.[3] Eternalism is to be understood in contrast with presentism, the thesis that it always has been and always will be the case that there are no actual but non-present objects.[4] Extensionism and the plenum principle are self explanatory.[5]

Though I will not defend this claim here, I believe that each of the four theses can reasonably be attributed to the Eleatics. Furthermore, they are all very well-motivated even from a contemporary point of view. Exclusivism is implied by the common-sense view that (for example) there is no object that fills the scattered region occupied by the Sears Tower and the moon. Eternalism is implied by the special theory of relativity.[6] The plenum principle is consistent with contemporary physical theory, and is often taken for granted as an idealizing assumption.[7] Extensionism is motivated by the notorious paradoxes of Zeno, which continue to be discussed, developed and taken seriously in the contemporary literature.[8] Thus, by showing that Eleatic monism ought to be accepted by anyone who accepts these four theses, I will have done quite enough to show that, counterintuitive or not, it is a live option in contemporary metaphysics that deserves to be taken a lot more seriously than it has been.

My plan will be as follows. I will begin by discussing some technical details. I expect that some readers will be suspicious that talk of times and regions of space in the formulation of exclusivism, and unqualified talk of past and future objects in the formulation of eternalism, is incompatible with current physical theory. I also expect that some readers will wonder about the relations between inclusivism and a very similar view, mereological universalism, which I have defended elsewhere (Rea 1998b). Section 1 will be devoted to addressing these issues. In section 2, I will begin the main argument of the paper by showing that anyone who endorses extensionism, exclusivism, and the plenum principle ought to accept α. In section 3, I will show that anyone who accepts both α and eternalism ought to accept β. In section 4, I will show that anyone who accepts both α and eternalism ought to accept γ. Finally, in section 5, I will show that δ follows directly from α.

1. Technical Concerns

There are diverse views about the nature of times. One natural view is that times are concrete sums of events, or of spatial points. Another is that times are abstract states of affairs—total ways the world is, was, or will be. But one might worry that talk of times is unacceptable from the point of view of contemporary physics. The reason is that such talk might seem to presuppose that time as we know it is an absolute, observer-independent feature of reality, whereas the special theory of relativity seems to imply that space and time are both mere appearances of a more fundamental reality—namely, spacetime. Similar concerns might arise with respect to talk about regions of space and also with respect to unqualified talk about "past" and "future" objects. Thus, it might seem that, at best, the formulations of exclusivism, eternalism, and related doctrines are insensitive to relativity theory and, at worst, they are ontologically loaded in a way that will substantially affect the arguments that follow.

However, there is are ways of understanding talk of times, regions of space, and past and future objects that get around these concerns. We may take a concrete time to be a plane of simultaneity, or a sum of point-sized events in spacetime all of which are simultaneous with one another in some frame of reference; we may take abstract times to be the total state of the universe on such a plane; and we may take regions of space to be regions of spacetime on such a plane. Presentism may then be defined as the view that always there exists exactly one concrete time or, alternatively, that always exactly one abstract time obtains.[9] Eternalism may be defined as the view that every concrete time that ever did or will exist (in any frame of reference) in fact exists or, alternatively, that every abstract time obtains. Exclusivism will be the view that not every filled region at every concrete time is filled by a material object or, alternatively, that not every filled region on every plane corresponding to an abstract time is filled by a material object.

Given what I have just said about exclusivism, one might wonder whether inclusivism is equivalent to the doctrine that every filled region of spacetime is filled by a material object. The answer is no. Inclusivism as I have defined it implies only that every filled region *at every time* is filled by a material object. But some filled regions of spacetime may not exist at a single time. They might instead be regions that span across multiple times without themselves being wholly located on any time.

Despite superficial similarities, inclusivism is also different from *mereological universalism*, the doctrine that the members of every set of disjoint objects compose something. One reason is that inclusivism is, but universalism is not, transparently incompatible with the view that the world contains matter but no material objects.[10] Another reason is that the conjunction of universalism with inclusivism and eternalism implies that every filled region of spacetime is filled by a material object whereas inclusivism and eternalism alone do not. (Here is the argument: Inclusivism implies that every filled spatial region at every time is filled by a material object. Eternalism implies that every time and every object that ever did exist or will exist *does* exist. Now, consider a filled region of spacetime R. Either R is located at a single time or it spans multiple times. If it is located at a single time, then inclusivism implies that R is filled by a material object. On the other hand, if it spans multiple times, then R is the sum of multiple filled sub-regions each of which is located at its own time. By inclusivism, each of those sub-regions is filled by a material object; but it does not yet follow that those objects have a sum. Universalism, however, does imply that those objects have a sum, and so it implies that R is filled by their sum.) Furthermore, if we assume (as seems plausible) that there can be matter only if there are material objects, universalism implies inclusivism but not the other way around. Thus, universalism is a stronger doctrine than inclusivism. So much for technical concerns. I turn now to the main arguments of the paper.

2. Against Plurality

Spacetime exists, and some of it is filled by matter. This much is obvious. Not so obvious, however, are the conditions under which a filled region of spacetime is filled by a material object. Common sense tells us that regions filled by matter arranged treewise, or cellwise, or computerwise, or housewise are filled by material objects, whereas regions such as the scattered region filled by the moon and the Sears Tower are not. But common sense is mistaken on this score.

Consider the question, "Under what conditions is a filled region of spacetime filled by a material object?" I'll call this the "Unity Question" since it effectively asks for the conditions under which the matter filling a region of spacetime composes a single unified thing.[11] In this section, I will argue that, given the plenum principle, the following three claims are the most reasonable answers to the Unity Question: (i) every filled region of space at every time is filled by a material object (and perhaps others are as well), (ii) all and only unextended regions of spacetime are filled by material objects, or (iii) the largest filled spatiotemporal region is filled by a material object, and there are no objects distinct from that one. If I am right, then the common sense beliefs mentioned above about which regions are filled by objects and which are not cannot be correct. Furthermore, and more importantly for our purposes, if I am right, then anyone who accepts exclusivism, extensionism, and the plenum principle should accept (iii) and, therefore, should also accept α.

Here is my argument for the claim that (i-iii) are the most reasonable answers to the Unity Question:

(1) If we believe that there are artifacts, then we should accept inclusivism.
(2) If we reject artifacts, then we should not believe in any composite objects.[12]

(3) However: we should believe that there is *some* material object or other.
(4) Therefore: If we reject artifacts, we should believe in material simples but no other material objects. (From 2, 3)
(5) We should not believe in a plurality of *extended* simples.
(6) Therefore, if we reject artifacts, we should believe either that there are unextended simples but no other material objects or that there exists exactly one extended simple. (From 4, 5)
(7) Therefore: if we accept artifacts we should accept (i), and if we reject them then we should accept (ii) or (iii). (From 1, 6)

This concludes the argument; now I will defend the premises.

2.1. Defense of Premise 1

Consider your dining room table. Now suppose that, by cosmic accident, in a virgin forest some matter appears that is arranged in precisely the same way as the matter of your table. Does the matter in the forest compose an object? If so, presumably it does so because the following general claim is true:

(φ) Whether the matter in a region composes an object depends entirely on how that matter is arranged. It does not depend on how that matter is related to human minds or mental activity.

This general claim is fairly intuitive.[13] However, together with the claim that artifacts (such as tables) exist, it implies inclusivism.[14]

Consider any filled region R of space at some time. Obviously the matter in R will be arranged in some way or other; and, regardless of how it is arranged, had it arranged in just that way *for a purpose*, there would be considerable pressure on those who believe in artifacts to say that R contains an artifact. Of course, some ways of arranging matter are such that no *human* could arrange matter in that way for a purpose. But there seems to be no reason for thinking that there couldn't be purposive agents vastly more creative than we are, and so there seems also to be no reason for thinking that some ways of arranging matter are essentially non-purposive. Thus, there is good reason to think that, for any filled region of space, had the matter in that region been arranged in just the way that it is for a purpose, the region would have contained an artifact. But notice: In accepting φ, we have already conceded that whether the matter in a region composes an object does not depend upon anyone's attitudes, purposes, and so on. Thus, if a region would have contained an object if its matter had been arranged the way that it is for a purpose, that can only be because the region *already* contains an object. Thus, the admission that there are artifacts opens the ontological floodgates. Once we admit artifacts, we admit that purposive arrangement is sufficient for composition; but then the only way to avoid saying that composition depends in some way upon purpose is to accept inclusivism.[15]

Some philosophers reject φ. Those who do are committed to *constructivism about composite objects*—the thesis that the apparent sortal properties of composite objects (properties like *being a horse*, *being an electron*, and even *being a composite object*) are not intrinsic to anything. The reason is obvious: If composition depends on human mental activity, then for any composite object kind K, it is impossible for a K to exist unaccompanied by human beings; thus the property of being a K is not independent of accompaniment; thus it is not intrinsic.[16] But once we see this commitment, we can see also that rejecting φ is of no use in resisting the overall argument of this section. The central question of this section, after all, is not whether we conceive of and describe the world as if it contains a plurality of material objects (obviously we do), but whether *independently of our conceptual and linguistic activity* the world contains such a plurality. Thus, it is a mistake in the present context to think that rejecting φ offers a way of preserving belief in artifacts without commitment to inclusivism, for the person who rejects φ does not really believe in artifacts. One who rejects φ may well *say* she believes in artifacts (and who is to stop her?). But she does not think that artifacts, or any other composite object, are among the denizens of the world as it is independently of our conceptual and linguistic activity.

2.2. Defense of Premise 2

So, if one believes in artifacts, then one ought also to believe inclusivism. But what if one is unwilling to accept inclusivism? What if, in fact, one takes commitment to inclusivism as good reason to reject belief in artifacts? As I see it, one should believe only in simples. I say this because I accept premise (3), defended below, and because I think that there is no non-arbitrary way of excluding artifacts from one's ontology without excluding every other composite object as well.[17] I cannot *prove* that artifacts could only be excluded by an arbitrary principle. But I think that a close look at the two most detailed recent attempts to defend ontologies that include composite objects but not artifacts will reveal that the grounds for optimism about finding a non-arbitrary way of excluding artifacts are shaky at best.

The two attempts that I have in mind are Peter van Inwagen's defense of the claim that there are no composite objects except living organisms and Trenton Merricks's defense of the claim that there are no composite objects except those that have non-redundant causal powers. Both van Inwagen and Merricks reject artifacts. However, their arguments prove either too much or too little: either they speak in favor of eliminating all composite objects or they are insufficient to motivate the rejection of artifacts.

Van Inwagen's view that there are no composite objects other than living organisms follows from what he takes to be the only plausible answer to the

Special Composition Question. The Special Composition Question asks under what conditions the members of a set of objects compose something. After surveying and rejecting various answers, van Inwagen settles on the following: The members of a set of objects compose something just in case the set's only member is a simple or the activity of the members of the set constitutes a life. (1990, sec.9) But the arguments for this view are unconvincing. Van Inwagen offers three reasons for thinking that all and only living organisms deserve a place in our ontology. First, he says that we are forced to believe in at least some organisms—namely, those that think. Second, he expresses pessimism about finding a plausible answer to the Special Composition Question that will let in organisms, artifacts, and natural bodies. Third, he notes that in rejecting artifacts and natural bodies, we avoid all of the problems associated with belief in such things. (1990, pp. 122–3) In fact, however, we are no more forced to believe in organisms than we are forced to believe in computers or various other artifacts; and many of the metaphysical problems that attend belief in organisms also attend belief in artifacts. This is the heart of the problem. Once this is clear, we see that the decision to privilege organisms over artifacts is arbitrary. An answer to the Special Composition Question that lets in (for example) all and only *computing* things will be just as plausible or implausible as van Inwagen's answer; and the prospect of avoiding metaphysical problems will speak just as strongly or weakly in favor of the categorical elimination of organisms as it does in favor of the categorical elimination of artifacts.

According to van Inwagen, we are forced to believe in thinkers because of Cartesian arguments. The Cartesian arguments that he has in mind are arguments like this: "I exist. If I exist, I am a composite material thing. Therefore: some composite material thing exists." The second premise is not Cartesian, but it is entailed by the constraining assumptions listed in the Preface to *Material Beings*.[18] In support of the first premise, van Inwagen points out that he, like everyone else, knows that he exists because he is directly aware of his own existence. To those who would challenge this claim by saying that we are in fact directly aware only of our own mental activity and not of our own existence as a single unified entity, van Inwagen responds by saying that thought seems to require a unified subject. This latter claim is also among the constraining assumptions; but elsewhere he offers a few remarks to motivate it. The activities of artifacts—shelves, automobiles, etc.—are plausibly construed as "disguised cooperative" activities, he says. But thought is different. On his view, it is easy to see how simples might work together without composing anything to hold up books or to move a human being down the road, but it is not easy to see how simples might work together to think without composing anything. Thus, thought seems to require a subject whereas the activities of artifacts do not. (1990, pp. 117–8)

But why the difference? If composition isn't required for simples to cooperate in performing all of the very complicated activities that automobiles perform, why should it be required for simples to cooperate in thinking? Perhaps the answer will appeal to some allegedly relevant difference between automotive functions and the activities of thinking organisms. But if this is the answer, then change the example. The activities of computers are in many relevant respects very similar to the activities of thinking organisms. Thus, if composition isn't required for simples to cooperate in performing all of the complex thought-like activities that my computer performs, it is very hard to see why it should be required for simples to cooperate in thinking. No difference between computers and human beings seems to make a difference with respect to explaining why the activities of one but not the other could be understood as a disguised cooperative activity. But if that is right, then there is no clear reason for thinking that composition is required for mental activity but not for computer activity. Thus, we are forced to believe in organisms only if we are also forced to believe in computers; and so if it is acceptable to eliminate artifacts altogether, it should also be acceptable to eliminate organisms altogether.

One might insist that conscious mental activity is relevantly different even from computer activity, so that (contrary to what I have just said) the activities of computers can be understood as disguised cooperative activities involving simples whereas human consciousness cannot. Perhaps this is right. Perhaps consciousness is *sui generis*. But if so, then it is hard to see why Cartesian considerations should count as evidence in favor of the existence of anything material rather than as evidence against materialism. Granted, such considerations give me evidence of my own existence. But they do not give me evidence of my existence as a material object. Rather, they seem to give me evidence that I am not a material object. Suppose I believe, as van Inwagen does, that all of the activities of alleged artifacts and natural bodies are plausibly construed as disguised cooperative activities involving simples. Suppose I also believe that thought requires a subject, but, like van Inwagen, I have no evidence that any of the other activities of living organisms require a subject. My evidence then points to the conclusion that, apart from thought, all of the activities attributed to objects composed of material simples are plausibly understood as disguised cooperative activities involving simples. Shouldn't I then infer that thinkers are *not* composite material objects? It is hard to see why I would go the other way and infer that thinkers and things relevantly like them are the *only* composite material objects. Certainly nothing *forces* me to go this way. Thus, even if consciousness is *sui generis*, there seems to be no reason to think that Cartesian considerations by themselves force us to believe in any material object. So if we have good reasons for eliminating artifacts, it is hard to see why we wouldn't go the whole distance and eliminate organisms as well.

Of course, Cartesian considerations plus an unwavering commitment to materialism will force us to believe in some material object or other; and let us simply grant that the kinds of material objects we would thus be forced to believe in are human beings. Even still, there is no more reason to expand our ontology to include all and only organisms than there is to expand our ontology to include (say) all and only computing things. After all, computing things have at least as much in common with thinkers as organisms do; and the property of being a computing thing is no more or less vague than the property of being an organism. Thus, the exclusion of artifacts seems arbitrary and unmotivated.

So there seems to be no principled reason in van Inwagen's work for thinking that living organisms exist but artifacts do not. Merricks defends a somewhat similar ontology; but he avoids the charge of arbitrariness by explicitly defending a principle that allegedly supports the ontology. The problem, however, is that the very evidence he points to in support of his ontology seems in fact better to support the conclusion that either his principle is false (in which case it proves nothing) or else it is true but implies that there are no composite objects at all (in which case it proves too much).

Like van Inwagen, Merricks takes his prior commitment to materialism and his view that thought requires a subject as convincing evidence that at least human beings are composite material objects. Also like van Inwagen, he argues that there are no analogous considerations supporting belief in inanimate macrophysical objects and that eliminating such things solves various metaphysical puzzles without doing violence to common sense beliefs about the world. (2001, chs. 2 & 5) Importantly, however, these arguments are supplemented by the following further claim: Human beings, but not inanimate macrophysical objects, have *non-redundant causal powers*, or causal powers that are not exhaustively duplicated by the conjoined causal powers of their microphysical parts. This implies that inanimate macrophysical objects, if they exist at all, are *overdetermining* causes of their effects. Thus, Merricks argues, since we should not believe in overdetermining causes without good reason, and since we have no good reason for believing that the effects commonly attributed to inanimate macrophysical objects are overdetermined, such objects ought to be eliminated. (2001, chs. 3 & 4) Human organisms, however, are to be retained. More generally, *all and only* those things with non-redundant causal powers are to be retained. In light of this principle, Merricks advocates an ontology that includes conscious organisms; but he is officially silent on the question of what exists besides conscious organisms. Strictly speaking, he endorses only the claim: "to be [for material objects] is to have non-redundant causal powers" (2001, p. 115).

But why think that there are *any* composite objects with non-redundant causal powers? In defending the claim that the causal powers of inanimate macrophysical things are redundant, Merricks asks us to consider the example of a baseball. (2001, ch. 3) Everything that a baseball might be said to cause (visual sensations, vibrations in a bat, the shattering of a window) is also caused by the activity of the atoms that allegedly compose the baseball. Moreover, according to Merricks, it is not the case that the baseball and the atoms are in any sense *cooperating* causes of the baseball's effects. The baseball does not cause its atoms to do the things that they do; nor does it work together with its atoms in any other way to cause the effects that it causes. Rather, says Merricks, the causal powers of the atoms working together exhaust the powers of the baseball. And so too for any inanimate macrophysical object. But couldn't the same be said for human beings, or for any other organism? Indeed, wouldn't any reason for thinking that the powers of baseballs are exhausted by the powers of their microphysical parts also be a reason for thinking that the powers of *any* alleged composite object are exhausted by the powers of their microphysical parts? If so, then Merricks's principle proves too much, implying that there are no composite material objects whatsoever.

Merricks does not argue straightforwardly for the conclusion that human beings have non-redundant causal powers. Instead, he argues for the conclusion that we have no reason to think that the causal powers of conscious mental states are redundant. If this is true, he thinks, then Cartesian considerations, in conjunction with various intuitive reasons for rejecting dualism, will be sufficient for our being warranted in believing that we (conscious beings) exist, that we are composite material objects, and (therefore) that our causal powers are in fact not redundant. (2001, chs. 4 & 5) I shall not contest this latter claim. What I am more interested in is Merricks's argument for the conclusion that we have no reason to think that the causal powers of conscious mental states are redundant.

At the heart of his argument is the claim that the property of being conscious is causally efficacious and not supervenient upon the properties and relations obtaining among microphysical objects. There are different kinds of supervenience. The sort Merricks focuses on is what some call 'strong' or 'logical' supervenience: A properties supervene on B properties iff, as a matter of metaphysical necessity, once the B properties are fixed the A properties are fixed as well.[19] Merricks grants that if consciousness *did* supervene on intrinsic microphysical structure, then the fact that a human being causes something by virtue of being conscious might, all by itself, constitute reason for thinking that the relevant effect was non-cooperatively caused by the atoms that compose the human being. But, he argues, given that consciousness does not supervene, the fact that a human being causes an effect by virtue of being conscious does not, all by itself, give us reason to believe that the human's constituent atoms non-cooperatively caused the effect. He then turns to the question of what *else* could give us reason to think that the effects of being conscious are caused by the behavior of our constituent atoms. He considers and rejects three possibilities. I have no substantive quarrel with his rejection of the first two possibilities, so I shall pass over them in silence. But the third possibility merits closer attention.

One would clearly have reason to think that the effects of being conscious are non-cooperatively caused by the behavior of our constituent atoms if one had reason to believe the following claim:

> Microphysical Closure (MC): Every physical effect has microphysical causes to which non-microphysical causes are causally irrelevant.[20]

As I understand it, MC is equivalent to the claim that all effects of alleged macrophysical objects are non-cooperatively caused by the behavior of their microphysical parts. Merricks rejects MC partly on the grounds that it is an empirical claim whose truth has not yet been empirically established. But all by itself, this response is inadequate. In the argument that eliminates artifacts, Merricks relies on something like the following assumption:

> Restricted Microphysical Closure (RMC): All of the effects of alleged inanimate macrophysical objects are non-cooperatively caused by the behavior of their microphysical parts.[21]

But there is no reason to think that this claim is on any better or worse footing empirically speaking than MC. Any empirical reason for thinking that all of the effects of *inanimate* macrophysical objects are non-cooperatively caused by their microphysical parts will also be (or correspond to) an empirical reason for thinking that all of the effects of *all* macrophysical objects are non-cooperatively caused by their microphysical parts. So if Merricks were to rest his rejection of MC entirely on the inadequacy of empirical evidence in support of it, he would be unable to resist someone who rejected the more restricted claim about inanimate macrophysical objects on precisely the same grounds.

In fact, Merricks does not rest his rejection of MC entirely on the dearth of empirical evidence in its favor. He offers two supplemental claims. First, he reminds us of his argument for the claim that consciousness does not supervene on microphysical properties and relations, and he says that this claim counts as evidence that MC is false.[22] Second, he says that MC does not *seem* to be true, since it does not seem that conscious mental events and their effects are sums of atomic events and their effects.[23] Both claims are problematic.

Merricks's defense of the claim that consciousness does not supervene rests on two assumptions: (a) that consciousness is intrinsic and (b) that the same conscious states cannot be tokened in multiple overlapping objects. I do not endorse these assumptions; and so I am not persuaded by Merricks's argument for the conclusion that consciousness does not supervene.[24] But rather than pursue these objections in detail here, I want instead to focus on a deeper problem with his appealing to the anti-supervenience argument as evidence against MC. The problem is just that the claim that consciousness fails to supervene is *not* evidence against MC. Recall that the sort of supervenience Merricks focuses on is *strong* supervenience. But the failure of strong supervenience does not imply the failure of *causal determination*. Property dualists like David Chalmers, for example, deny that consciousness strongly supervenes on the microphysical; but they do not deny that conscious states are non-cooperatively *caused* by microphysical events. (Cf. Chalmers 1996, ch. 4) At most, the failure of strong supervenience only guarantees that conscious mental states are not identical to or logically entailed by microphysical properties. It does not guarantee that MC is false, even on the assumption that consciousness is causally efficacious.

Merricks's second reason for rejecting MC is that it doesn't seem to be true because conscious mental events and their effects don't seem to be sums of atomic events and their effects. This is a straightforward appeal to intuition. As such, it seems rather out of place as evidence against MC in light of his admission that MC is an empirical claim. More importantly, however, this claim suffers from the same problem as the first: to say that conscious mental events are not *identical* to physical events or sums thereof is not the same as saying that the former are not causally determined by the latter. And from a materialist point of view, the intuition that all of the effects of consciousness are *caused by* microphysical events seems to be on much surer footing than opposing intuitions.

Of course, if we *accept* both MC and Merricks's claim that consciousness fails to supervene, it is quite natural to believe that conscious mental states are either overdetermining causes of their effects or not causally efficacious at all. (Chalmers (1996) argues that there is room for other alternatives; but let us leave those aside for now.) Assuming these are the only alternatives, and assuming we have accepted Merricks's assumption that conscious states are causally efficacious, we are left with a choice between rejecting MC and accepting the claim that conscious mental states are overdetermining causes of their effects. Again, as Merricks says, we should not believe in overdetermination without good reason. But science gives us *very* good reason to believe that all of the effects of alleged macrophysical objects (human beings included) are *caused by* the properties and activities of their microphysical parts. Again, it is hard to think of a reason for believing RMC that would not also be a reason to believe MC; and Merricks himself is committed to believing that we have very good reason to accept RMC. Furthermore, it is hard to see how conscious mental states could possibly be *cooperating* causes of their effects if, as Merricks thinks, human beings are material objects composed of microphysical parts. Thus, if we are convinced that human beings exist, are material objects, and have causally efficacious, non-supervenient conscious mental states, it seems that the right conclusion to draw is that the principle "to be [for material objects] is to have non-redundant causal powers" is false.

One further point is worth mentioning. If sound, Merricks's arguments most clearly support the conclusion that consciousness is unique among (alleged) physical properties in failing to be non-cooperatively caused by microphysical events. But then shouldn't we take the proper upshot of those arguments to be that the subjects of conscious mental states are *non-physical* objects? In other words, shouldn't we see in Merricks's work a straightforward argument for *substance dualism* rather than an argument for the conclusion that thinkers and other things with non-redundant causal powers (if there are any such things) are the *only* composite material objects? Merricks, of course, says no. His goal is, among other things, to make room in our ontology for emergent properties with emergent causal powers. But that is a mighty large task with consciousness as his only example and a counterintuitive ontology as the consequence. Much better, it would seem, to accept overdetermination or epiphenomenalism or Chalmers's panpsychism or Cartesian dualism.

Merricks has given no convincing reason for rejecting MC. Hence, he has given no convincing reason for thinking that the causal powers of human beings are any less redundant than the causal powers of inanimate macrophysical objects. We might take this as evidence that human beings are to be eliminated along with everything else and that therefore either thought doesn't require a subject or else it takes place in non-material things. Or we might take this as evidence that the principle 'to be is to have non-redundant causal powers' is false. Either way, Merricks, like van Inwagen, has failed to motivate an exclusivist ontology that eliminates artifacts without eliminating all other composite objects.

I conclude that the prospects are dim for defending an exclusivist ontology that includes composite objects but no artifacts. If there are composite objects, human beings, automobiles, and computers are among them. If some of the paradigmatic examples belong in our ontology, all of them do, and we must accept whatever excess baggage they bring along. On the other hand, if some have to be ruled out, then they all should be ruled out.[25]

2.3. Defense of Premise 3

So if we reject inclusivism, we should believe that there are no composite objects at all. Thus we face two alternatives: We can believe that there is matter but no material objects, or we can believe only in simples. (I assume that believing that nothing at all exists, not even matter, is beyond the pale.) Premise (3) rules out the first alternative. I accept this premise because, even if there are no familiar material objects, it seems clear that at least there is such a thing as the material world or the cosmos, and that it makes sense to ask whether *it* could have been bigger or smaller, whether it could have been propertied differently, and so on. But, as far as I can tell, the only way to understand such talk is to take 'the world' either as a term referring to a particular material object or as a collectively referring term like 'the L.A. Philharmonic Orchestra' or 'the Notre Dame football team'—a term that refers not to a single material object but to many objects collectively. Either interpretation, however, entails that there exists *at least* one material thing. Hence, we should not say that *no* region contains a material object.

2.4. Defense of Premise 5

I have argued so far that if we accept artifacts we should accept inclusivism, and if we reject them then we should believe only in simples. But suppose we do reject artifacts. What kinds of simples should we believe in, and how many should we believe in? Should we believe in unextended simples, or extended ones? And if the latter, then should we believe in many or just one?

I will not attempt to say whether we should believe in unextended simples. But I will argue that we should reject the view that there is nothing but a plurality of extended simples. Consider the question, which Ned Markosian (1998) calls the "Simple Question": What are the necessary and jointly sufficient conditions for an object's being a simple? Answers compatible with extensionism are not abundant in the literature, but there are at least two worth considering.

The first is that an object is a simple just in case it is a self. This answer is inspired (but perhaps not endorsed) by E.J. Lowe.[26] The second answer, defended by Markosian, is that an object is a simple just in case it is a *maximally continuous object*, where the term 'maximally continuous object' is defined as follows:

> *x* is a *maximally continuous object* $=_{DF}$ *x* is a spatially continuous object and there is no continuous region of space, R, such that (i) the region occupied by *x* is a proper subset of R, and (ii) every point in R falls within some object or other. (Markosian 1998, p. 221)

However, as I shall now argue, neither of these answers supports the claim that there exists nothing but a plurality of extended simples; and I am at a loss to imagine any other that would.

The Lowe inspired answer is compatible with the claim that there exist many extended simples; but the underlying view of selves that Lowe defends seems to be incompatible with the claim that there exist *only* extended simples. According to Lowe, selves are simple substances that have physical properties (like *being six feet tall* and *weighing seventy kilograms*). But they are psychological substances rather than biological substances, and their physical properties supervene on the physical properties of the biological substances with which they are associated. (Lowe 1996, pp. 32–41) Whether psychological substances are supposed to be material objects or not is less than clear in Lowe's discussion; nor is it clear what exactly the association between psychological substances and their biological bodies is supposed to be. Lowe in some places talks as if selves are material substances that are somehow located where their bodies are without sharing *any* material parts with their bodies; but in other places he talks as if selves are neither material nor immaterial substances. (1996, pp. 32–41, 7–8) But we needn't resolve these issues here.[27] What is clear is that Lowe thinks that the purely physical properties of selves are had solely by virtue of their association with the biological substances that are their bodies. Though Lowe doesn't say so explicitly, this seems strongly to suggest that even if selves could exist apart from their bodies, they could not have physical properties apart from bodies. But if that is right, then even if Lowe is correct in thinking that selves are in fact extended material simples, it could not be the case that there exist *only* extended material simples.

Whereas Lowe's view fails to support the claim that there exists nothing but extended simples, Markosian's view fails to support the claim that there exists a plurality thereof. According to Markosian's definitions, a spatially continuous object is any object that occupies a connected set of spatial points.[28] This leaves open the question whether a connected set of points might be occupied by matter *without* being occupied by any object at all; but that is no problem for Markosian, who is interested only in addressing the question of what it takes for an object to be simple rather than the question of what it takes for a region to be filled by a simple. Nevertheless, he does take a position on what it takes for a spatially continuous object to exist. On his view, *any* matter-filled connected set of points is occupied by a spatially continuous object. (1998, p. 222) This is certainly a plausible position to take. Moreover, it seems to be the *most* plausible position to take. For to suppose that there are additional necessary conditions for the existence of a spatially continuous object raises difficult questions, analogous to the unity question, about what those conditions might be; and it is hard to imagine a view other than Markosian's that would be even remotely plausible without implying that there are no spatially continuous objects at all. However, once we adopt the view that any occupied connected set of points is filled by a spatially continuous object, Markosian's answer in conjunction with the plenum principle implies that there exists exactly one extended simple.

Are there plausible alternative answers to the Simple Question? Apart from the suggestion that only point-sized regions of spacetime are filled by simples, it is hard to imagine any. Therefore, I conclude that those who accept extensionism, exclusivism, and the plenum principle ought also to accept Markosian's answer to the Simple Question and the attending consequence that there exists exactly one extended simple. However, one loose end remains to be tied. Markosian's answer makes reference to regions of *space* rather than regions of *spacetime*. If we take this fact seriously, the view (in conjunction with the plenum principle) might lead us to conclude that there exists exactly one simple which is *extended* in space but *multiply located* in time. On the other hand, if we take 'space' as equivalent to 'spacetime', we might reach a different conclusion—namely, that there exists exactly one simple which is extended throughout all of spacetime. As it turns out, both views are consistent with the doctrines of Eleatic Monism, and both are consistent with the third answer to the Unity Question mentioned at the outset of this section. However, I think that contemporary philosophers ought to prefer the latter view. The reason is that the former view presupposes that there is some objective, observer-invariant, way of dividing spacetime into space and time; but this presupposition is inconsistent with contemporary physical theory. As I indicated earlier, talk of times and regions of space can be given sense within the context of relativity theory; but relativity theory implies that the way spacetime breaks down into regions of space and times will be different for different observers.[29] Thus, it implies that there is no single frame of reference in which the *whole universe* could possibly count as wholly present. One might choose to reject relativity theory (treating it as empirically adequate, but false); but short of that, there seems to be no way to make room for the claim that there exists exactly one thing which is extended throughout all of space but enduring through all of time.

2.5. Conclusion

I have now finished defending the premises of my argument for the conclusion that, given the plenum principle, the most reasonable answers to the Unity Question are inclusivism, the view that all and only unextended regions of spacetime are filled by material objects, and the view that there exists exactly one material object which fills the largest filled region of spacetime. If the argument is sound then one who accepts exclusivism and extensionism ought to embrace the third alternative and therefore ought to accept α.

3. Against Change

In this section, I will show that anyone who accepts α and eternalism ought to accept β, the claim that nothing changes. I will run the argument first under the assumption (defended above) that the one material thing that exists is extended throughout all of spacetime. I will then drop the assumption and show that the conclusion remains.

Something changes only if it exists at multiple times. But something exists at multiple times only if it is wholly present at multiple times or has proper parts at multiple times. α entails that there exists exactly one material object; hence, it entails that nothing has proper parts—at multiple times or at a single time. Therefore, something changes only if it is wholly present at multiple times. But if eternalism is true, all times exist and (if the times are abstract) all times obtain. So, given eternalism, the largest spatiotemporal region that exists will be a region that spans multiple times. But if this is right, then there is something wholly present at a *single* time only if some region other than the largest spatiotemporal region is filled by a material object. However, on the assumption that the one thing that exists is extended throughout all of spacetime, it follows that the only region that is filled by a material object is the largest filled spatiotemporal region. Thus, nothing is wholly present at a single time. And if nothing is wholly present at a single time, then *a fortiori* nothing is wholly present at multiple times. Therefore, if eternalism and α are true, nothing changes.

One might object that this is a bit hasty. Perhaps we might say that something extended across multiple regions of spacetime changes just in case it is propertied differently at different regions. And if we did say this, wouldn't we then have a basis for saying that the world changes? If this sort of view were coherent, perhaps we would. But as it is, it is hard to see how coherently and precisely to formulate the claim that a *simple* thing extended over multiple regions of spacetime is propertied differently at different regions. The reason is that it is hard to see what it would mean for an extended thing to be propertied *at a region* without either itself exemplifying the property in question *simpliciter* (i.e., in a way that is not relativized to a region) or having a part at the region that exemplifies the property. We might say that an extended simple exists at R just in case some of the simple fills R; but what would it mean to say that an extended simple has at R the property of being F? If we say that it means that some of the simple fills R and, furthermore, the simple has F, then we commit ourselves to the claim that the simple has F *simpliciter*. On the other hand, if we say that it means that some of the simple fills R and, furthermore, *the bit of the simple in R* has F, then we commit ourselves to the claim that there is a *bit* of the simple in R; and it is hard to see why that bit wouldn't count as a part. The problem, in short, is that property exemplification requires a subject; but in the case of properties exemplified *only* at sub-regions of the total region filled by an extended simple, there is no plausible candidate for a subject unless we suppose (contrary to our present hypothesis) that the simple is wholly present at each of the relevant sub-regions.

So, on the assumption that the one thing that exists is extended throughout all of spacetime, α and eternalism together imply β. But suppose we drop this assumption in favor of the view that the one thing that exists is extended in space but multiply located in time. Adopting this view allows us to reject the premise that nothing is wholly present at a single time or at multiple times. It also allows us to say that multiple sub-regions of the total spatiotemporal region filled by the simple are each filled by an object (namely, the simple) which can bear properties. However, we still must face the fact that nothing changes without unqualifiedly having *different* properties at different times.[30] Unfortunately, as many have argued, the only views that are compatible with the claim that objects have, unqualifiedly, different properties at different times are presentism and the doctrine of temporal parts.[31] There are, of course, various ways of accounting for the *appearance* of change that do not involve commitment either to presentism or the doctrine of temporal parts. For example, an object which changes from being F to being G might be said to have the time-indexed properties *being F-at-t_1* and *being G-at-t_2*; or it might be said to *have-$t_1$ly* the property of being F and to *have-$t_2$ly* the property of being G.[32] But, reasonable as these views might be (and I do think they are perfectly reasonable), they are not views according to which one and the same object has, unqualifiedly, different properties at different times. Time-indexed properties (if there are such things) are possessed eternally; and properties that are *had-tly* for some t are not had unqualifiedly. Thus, short of accepting presentism or the doctrine of temporal parts, it appears that genuine change really is impossible—which is just to say, again, that α and eternalism together imply β.

4. Against Generation and Destruction

In this section, I will argue that the conjunction of α with eternalism implies that nothing is generated or destroyed. I assume that generation and destruction are processes that occur in time. More exactly: I assume that for any object x and time t, x is generated at t just in case x exists at t, there are (or were) times prior to t, and at every time prior to t x did not exist; and I assume that for any object x and time t, x is destroyed at t just in case x exists at t, there are (or will be) times after t, and at every time after t x will not exist. Thus, if there is exactly one time and exactly one thing that exists at that time, the thing in question is neither generated nor destroyed; and nothing that exists outside of time is generated or destroyed. More interestingly, this view has the consequence that time (or spacetime) itself is ungenerated. This is consistent with big bang cosmology if we think (as seems reasonable) that the initial spacetime singularity still counts in some sense as spacetime. Furthermore, it is consistent with the view that God created time so long as we understand creation as a process that may or may not involve temporal generation.

The argument for the conclusion that α and eternalism entail that there is no generation or destruction is simple. If eternalism is true, then all concrete times exist and all abstract times obtain. Furthermore, eternalism implies that the world is the total material content of all the times that exist (or, in other words, the total material content of spacetime). Hence, there neither are, were, nor will be times at which the world does not exist. Hence, the world is neither generated nor destroyed. α implies that there is nothing but the world. Thus, nothing is generated or destroyed.

Of course, one might just modify the definitions of generation and destruction. One might say that something is generated at t just in case it exists at t and there is no time prior to t at which it exists; and one might make similar modifications to the definition of destruction. In doing this, we preserve the letter of the claim that generation and destruction occur. But I take it that the spirit underlying the denial of generation and destruction remains: There is exactly one thing—the world; and there neither is, was, nor will be any time at which it did not exist.

5. Against Division

The final doctrine to establish is the doctrine that what exists is undivided. This doctrine follows directly from the thesis that there exists exactly one thing.

Suppose, for *reductio*, that reality is divided. This cannot mean simply that there are holes in reality—"places" where there exists literally nothing at all, not even spacetime. A donut is undivided (in some relevant sense), despite the fact that it has a hole in the middle. Rather, what the division thesis must mean is that there is some bit of reality that is completely separated, or spatiotemporally isolated, from the rest. But to say that there is some bit of reality that is completely separated from the rest is just to say that there is some *thing* (i.e., a bit of reality) that is completely separated from some *other* thing (i.e., the rest of reality). Hence, the division thesis implies that there is more than one thing. But (we are assuming) there is exactly one thing. Hence, the division thesis must be false.

Is there any way to formulate the division thesis in a way that does not presuppose that there is more than one thing? Apparently not. Separation is a two-place relation. A thing cannot be separated from itself except by having parts that are separated. Thus, anyone who accepts α ought also to accept δ.

6. Concluding Remarks

I have argued that anyone who accepts exclusivism, extensionism, eternalism, and the plenum principle ought also to accept Eleatic monism. Since each of these theses is believable and well-motivated, and since two of them are very widely accepted, I take it that this conclusion implies that Eleatic monism is a live (even if somewhat bizarre) option in contemporary metaphysics.

I do not deny that Eleatic monism is counterintuitive. However, I think that the degree to which it is counterintuitive can be mitigated. Eleatic monism denies that there are familiar particulars that come into and pass out of existence, last over time, and so on. But note that denying the existence of familiar particulars is not the same as denying the existence of anything that could give rise to the experiences that help to explain our belief that there are familiar particulars. All of our dog-experiences, tree-experiences, and so on could be caused by non-persisting stuff distributed spatiotemporally in ways just like the spatial and temporal parts of real persisting dogs, trees, and so on would be distributed if there were such things. Of course, given that we exist and that our experiences of the world are in constant flux, Eleatic monism entails that we are not denizens of the material world.[33] But it does not require us to deny anything that is manifest to the five senses. In effect, all Eleatic monism really denies is the claim that what appear to be discrete objects or properties of discrete objects really are discrete things or properties after all. In this respect, the Eleatic monist is not far different from eliminativists like Merricks and van Inwagen who deny that human beings have heads, shoulders, knees and toes as discrete parts. Such a view appears absurd; but once it is understood, we see that, though it might run contrary to our philosophical intuitions, it does not conflict with anything discoverable by empirical observation.

The central question of this paper asks how the Eleatics could have beheld the same world we behold—a world that includes birth and death, apparent multitudes of tiny objects, and so on, without believing that the world also includes plurality, change, generation and destruction, and spatiotemporal division. I take it that the answer is just this: perhaps they were common sense exclusivists, perhaps they were eternalists, and perhaps they accepted the plenum principle and didn't believe in unextended objects. None of these theses is obviously bizarre; and, as far as I can tell, together they imply a coherent (even if counterintuitive, even if false) metaphysic. But that is a big step up from absurd, and a far cry from unintelligible.

Notes

†Work on this project was supported by a University of Delaware General University Research Grant and by a grant from the Pew Evangelical Scholars Program. I am grateful to both institutions. Versions of the paper were read at Purdue University, Indiana University, and the University of Notre Dame. I am grateful to audiences on those occasions for helpful discussion. I am also grateful to Yuri Balashov, Stephen Barr, Michael Bergmann, Jeff Brower, Tom Crisp, Patricia Curd, Alicia Finch, Bruce Gordon, Jeff Jordan, Jared Lessard, Trenton Merricks, Alvin Plantinga, Juliane Rea, Ted Warfield, and Erik Wielenberg for helpful comments and conversations.

1. See, for example, Owen 1960. For references to other philosophers who endorse the traditional reading of Parmenides, see Barnes 1979a and 1979b. Barnes himself

dissents from the tradition, however, arguing that there is no reason to attribute α to Parmenides. A more recent dissenter is Patricia Curd (1998), who argues that in fact Parmenides did not endorse α, but something else which was unfortunately confused with α by subsequent commentators. I should also note that, though at least one follower of Parmenides—Melissus—indisputably endorsed the claim that there exists exactly one thing, Melissus B9 gives good reason to doubt that he believed that the one thing that exists is a *material* thing. So it may well be that what I am here calling Eleatic monism was in fact not endorsed by any Eleatic philosopher at all. But, having acknowledged this possibility, I will not concern myself with it any further. My aim here is not so much to attribute a view to the Eleatics as it is to show that the view commonly attributed to them and dismissed as unintelligible can in fact be motivated by a set of very plausible theses, each of which is endorsed by prominent contemporary philosophers.

2. But see Horgan 1993 for a step in this direction.

3. I assume that if a region is filled at all, it is at least filled by *matter*. The dispute between inclusivists and exclusivists concerns whether every spatial region filled by matter is filled by a *material object*. Exclusivism would be true if, for example, only unextended regions are filled by material objects. Extended regions might then be filled by matter, and they might *contain* many material objects (namely, unextended ones); but, on this view, it would not be the case that any extended region is *filled* (or wholly occupied) by a material object.

4. Presentism and eternalism are not mutually exhaustive views about time. See Rea 2002 for further alternatives and references.

5. Though perhaps the notion of connectedness bears explanation. A set of points is connected iff it is not the union of two disjoint closed sets of points. A set S of points is closed iff every accumulation point of S is in S. P is an accumulation point of S iff every set of points less than some finite distance away from P contains a point that is not in S.

6. On this and other arguments for eternalism see Rea 2002 and references therein.

7. On this topic, see the essays in Saunders & Brown 1991.

8. There are also other arguments available for extensionism. See, especially, Zimmerman 1996.

9. I do not claim that this definition is unproblematic; nor do I claim that this is the only way of trying to define presentism in a relativistic context. But it is a natural definition given what I have just said about times. For deeper exploration of the issues here, and for arguments to the effect that presentism is incompatible with relativity theory, see Rea 2002 and references therein.

10. I say "transparently incompatible" because there is an obvious argument from the premise that inclusivism is true to the conclusion that, if there is matter then there are material objects. But if (as I think) the latter claim is a necessary truth, then, strictly speaking, both universalism and inclusivism are incompatible with its denial.

11. This question closely resembles, but is not the same as, what Peter van Inwagen calls the "Special Composition Question" (discussed below). In a world devoid of mereological simples, the Unity Question might still have an answer that implies that there are extended material objects. It is not so clear that the Special Composition Question could have such an answer in such a world.

12. If (1) is right, one can't accept artifacts without accepting inclusivism; but one *can* accept inclusivism without accepting artifacts. (Cf. Heller 1990 and Jubien 1993). One who does so could then believe in composite objects without believing in arti-

facts. I do not believe that one *should* accept inclusivism without accepting artifacts. But even if I am mistaken, the conclusion of the present argument remains
unaffected. Thus, for convenience, I shall set this sort of view aside without further
argument.

13. But only on the assumption that the facts about how some matter is arranged *include* facts about how that matter is spatially and causally related to matter in relevantly nearby regions. A marble table might be created by chipping stone away
from a block of marble. Thus, one way to arrange marble tablewise is to remove
relevantly nearby marble; and, accordingly, one way to destroy a marble table is to
embed it seamlessly in a larger block. (For more on this, see Rea 1998b, pp. 352–
353. See also Sider (forthcoming).) One might think it odd to talk as if changing
the relational properties of some marble is a way of changing its *arrangement*; but
avoiding such talk would require cumbersome complications in the discussion that
follows. Thus, since nothing substantial hinges on this, I'll accept a little oddity for
the sake of readability.

14. In Rea 1998b, I argue that if we accept artifacts, we ought to accept universalism.
Some, but not all, of what I will say in the next few paragraphs is adapted from that
earlier argument.

15. This implies that either every material object belongs to multiple kinds, at least one
of which is a possible artifact-kind or many, if not all, material objects are co-
located with at least one other object which is a member of a possible artifact-kind.
I am content with this consequence, and have defended it elsewhere (Rea 2000).

16. The definition of intrinsicness as independence of accompaniment is defended in
Langton & Lewis 1998. Sider (forthcoming) raises interesting objections against
this definition; but the objections don't cast doubt on the claim that independence
of accompaniment is *necessary* for intrinsicness.

17. One who accepts inclusivism without accepting artifacts might get an ontology that
includes composite objects without arbitrariness. (Cf. Heller 1990 and Jubien 1993.)
But, as I explained in note 12, I am for convenience setting these sorts of views aside.

18. In particular, it is entailed by assumptions 7 and 8 (van Inwagen 1990, pp. 5–6).

19. Cf. Merricks 2001, p.89, premise 1.

20. Merricks 2001, pp. 110. Note that this claim is different from the one to which
Merricks applies the label 'Microphysical Closure' (Merricks 2001, p.141). But the
label fits this claim and so, for convenience, I'll use it.

21. See Merricks 2001, Chapter 3; see also Chapter 6, pp.145.

22. He writes:

> This chapter argues that the existence of some objects with causally relevant
> properties (viz., objects with conscious mental properties) does not supervene
> on microphysical doings. Because of that, I have argued, we should say that
> some of what those objects cause, in virtue of having those properties, lack
> microphysical causes. (Merricks 2001, p. 110)

23. He writes:

> Yet I endorse the exceptionless existence of microphysical causes with re-
> spect to the effects of (alleged) baseballs. This is, in part, because we have no
> compelling argument for the claim that, if baseballs existed, their existing and
> having some causally relevant property would fail to supervene on the micro-
> physical... .

> Moreover, recall the arguments in Chapter Three (§II) for the claim that the baseball's atoms shatter the window. One such argument was that every atom arranged baseballwise causes something, and when what one of them causes is added to what each of the others causes, the 'sum' is the shattering of the window. And a similar point holds for everything the baseball seems to cause. But it does not seem that, for example, when what one of my atoms does is added to what each of the others does, the "sum" is my consciously deciding. (2001, pp. 111)

24. See Merricks 2001, pp. 89–107. For criticisms which, by and large, I endorse, see Sider (forthcoming).
25. Horgan (1993) arrives at a similar conclusion, though by a different route.
26. Lowe 1996. Officially, Lowe only defends the claim that *all* selves are mereologically simple; he does not defend the claim that selves are the *only* extended simples.
27. For critical discussion of Lowe's view, see Olson 1998.
28. Markosian actually says that a spatially continuous object is one that occupies a *continuous region* of space, rather than a connected set of points in space. But as he uses the terms, a continuous region is nothing more than a connected set of points.
29. On this, see Rea 2002 and references therein.
30. See Rea 1998a and Rea 2002 for further discussion and references. In Rea 2002, I note that some do not analyze change as the unqualified having of different properties at different times; but, I say there, it is not at all clear that this sort of view is intelligible.
31. See, e.g., Merricks 1994 (p. 169), Rea 1998a (p. 244), and Rea 2002 (sec. 1).
32. See Rea 1998a and Rea 2002 for discussion and references.
33. I mentioned in note 1 that Melissus B9 gives good reason for thinking that Melissus believed that there exists exactly one thing, period. But here we have a strong consideration against that interpretation of Melissus. For, given that we experience our own inner lives as a changing sequence of events, it would appear that the view that there exists exactly one thing is incompatible with the doctrine (also clearly endorsed by Melissus) that nothing changes. If there exists exactly one thing, then presumably *we* are that thing (never mind the plurality implied by the pronoun). But we change. Hence, either there is not exactly one thing or else there is change after all.

References

Barnes, Jonathan. 1979a. "Parmenides and the Eleatic One," *Archiv für Geschicte der Philosophie* 61: 1–21.
————. 1979b. *The Presocratic Philosophers*. London: Routledge & Kegan Paul.
Chalmers, David. 1996. *The Conscious Mind*. Oxford: Oxford University Press.
Curd, Patricia. 1998. *The Legacy of Parmenides*. Princeton, NJ: Princeton University Press.
Heller, Mark. 1990. *The Ontology of Physical Objects: Four Dimensional Hunks of Matter*. Cambridge: Cambridge University Press.
Horgan, Terence. 1993. "On What There Isn't." *Philosophy and Phenomenological Research* 53: 693–700.
Jubien, Michael. 1993. *Ontology, Modality, and the Fallacy of Reference*. Cambridge: Cambridge University Press.
Langton, Rae and David Lewis. 1998. "Defining 'Intrinsic'," *Philosophy and Phenomenological Research* 58: 333–345.

Lowe, E. J. 1996. *Subjects of Experience*. Cambridge: Cambridge University Press.

Markosian, Ned. 1998. "Simples," *Australasian Journal of Philosophy* 76: 213–228.

Merricks, Trenton. 2001. *Objects and Persons*. Oxford: Clarendon Press.

———. 1994. "Endurance and Indiscernibility." *Journal of Philosophy* 91: 165–84.

Olson, Eric. 1998. "Human Atoms," *Australasian Journal of Philosophy* 76: 396–406.

Owen, G. E. L. 1960. "Eleatic Questions." Reprinted in *Logic, Science, and Dialectic*, by G. E. L. Owen. Ithaca: Cornell University Press, 1986, pp. 3–26.

Rea, Michael. 2002. "Four-Dimensionalism." *The Oxford Handbook for Metaphysics*, edited by Michael Loux and Dean Zimmerman. Oxford: Oxford University Press.

———. 2000. "Constitution and Kind-Membership." *Philosophical Studies* 97: 169–193.

———. 1998a. "Temporal Parts Unmotivated." *The Philosophical Review* 107: 225–60.

———. 1998b. "In Defense of Mereological Universalism," *Philosoph and Phenomenological Research* 58: 347–360.

Saunders, Simon and Harvey Brown. 1991. *Philosophy of Vacuum*. Oxford: Clarendon Press.

Sider, Theodore. Forthcoming. "Maximality and Intrinsic Properties." *Philosophy and Phenomenological Research*.

Van Inwagen, Peter. 1990. *Material Beings*. Ithaca: Cornell University Press.

Zimmerman, Dean. 1996. "Could Extended Objects be Made Out of Simple Parts? An Argument for 'Atomless Gunk'." *Philosophy and Phenomenological Research* 56: 1–29.

Philosophical Perspectives, 15, Metaphysics, 2001

AGAINST CREATIONISM IN FICTION

Takashi Yagisawa
California State University, Northridge

I. Introduction

Sherlock Holmes is a fictional individual. So is his favorite pipe. Our pre-theoretical intuition says that neither of them is real. It says that neither of them really, or actually, exists. It also says that there is a sense in which they do exist, namely, a sense in which they exist "in the world of" the *Sherlock Holmes* stories. Our pre-theoretical intuition says in general of any fictional individual that it does not actually exist but exists "in the world of" the relevant fiction. I wish to defend this pre-theoretical intuition. To do so, I need to defend two claims: that fictional individuals do not actually exist, and that they exist "in the world of" the relevant fiction. The aim of this paper is to defend the first claim.

There are two mutually exclusive and jointly exhaustive ways of holding the view that fictional individuals actually exist. One way is to hold that fictional individuals actually exist as a result of being created by the author(s) of the relevant story (stories). The other way is to hold that they actually exist but not as a result of being created by the author(s). According to the second way, fictional individuals actually exist either as a result of being created by someone (or something) else or not as a result of being created at all. I shall ignore this second way for its inherent implausibility and lack of supporters. I shall focus on the view that fictional individuals exist as a result of being created by the relevant author(s).[1] Let us call this view *creationism in fiction*, or *creationism* for short. Creationism was always an option for theorists working on the metaphysics of fiction but has recently gained unprecedented popularity among analytic philosophers. I shall attempt to swim against this strong fashionable current. Creationism is the view that fictional individuals exist (i.e., actually exist) by being created by their author(s), and I shall defend the claim that fictional individuals do not (actually) exist by arguing against creationism.

The creationist literature is rich, but the most powerful and most frequently repeated justifications for creationism are to be found in the enormously influential papers by John Searle and Peter van Inwagen. It would be an exaggeration but not an unfair exaggeration to say that creationism in the recent incarnation was born in those papers. I believe it is high time we revisited those classic papers with a critical eye. Seemingly powerful and influential as their arguments are, I believe they are ultimately unsuccessful in establishing creationism. In the case of Searle, it turns out that it is not even clear that his view gives coherent support to creationism. In the case of van Inwagen, though it is clear that his view supports creationism, the support is far from conclusive.

More specifically, my criticism will be directed at Searle's account of how an author of fiction creates a fictional individual and van Inwagen's accounts of the semantic and metaphysical status of fictional individuals. I shall conclude my criticism of creationism with a more general objection based on the very concept of fictionality.

II. Creation by Pretense?

Searle summarizes his main ontological claim about fictional individuals succinctly as follows:

> By pretending to refer to people and to recount events about them, the author creates fictional characters and events.[2]

This connects two apparent platitudes about fiction, namely, that the author pretends to tell a true story and that the author creates fictional individuals. Searle says that the author achieves the latter by doing the former. This claim has been widely accepted. Here is one typical expression of its acceptance by another leading philosopher:

> ...fictional entities are created in a straightforward and unproblematic way by the *pretending* use of names: the fictional entity Jonathan Pine was quite literally and straightforwardly created by John Le Carré's use of 'Jonathan Pine' in order to pretend, in the way definitive of fiction, to refer to a real person.[3]

One cannot help wondering, however, how "straightforward and unproblematic" such creation by pretense is. Searle anticipates this and offers an elaboration in a famous passage. I shall quote the passage in full despite its length, as it is crucial:

> But how is it possible for an author to "create" fictional characters out of thin air, as it were? To answer this let us go back to the passage from Iris Murdoch. The second sentence begins, "so thought Second Lieutenant Andrew Chase-White." Now in this passage Murdoch uses a proper name, a paradigm referring expression. Just as in the whole sentence she pretends to make an assertion, in this passage she

pretends to refer (another speech act). One of the conditions on the successful performance of the speech act of reference is that there must exist an objet that the speaker is referring to. Thus by pretending to refer she pretends that there is an object to be referred to. To the extent that we share in the pretense, we will also pretend that there is a lieutenant named Andrew Chase-White living in Dublin in 1916. It is the pretended reference which creates the fictional character and the shared pretense which enables us to talk about the character in the manner of the passage about Sherlock Holmes quoted above ["There never existed a Mrs. Sherlock Holmes because Holmes never got married, but there did exist a Mrs. Watson because Watson did get married, though Mrs. Watson died not long after their marriage"] ... By pretending to refer to (and recount the adventures of) a person, Miss Murdoch creates a fictional character. Notice that she does not really refer to a fictional character because there was no such antecedently existing character; rather, by pretending to refer to a person she creates a fictional person. Now once that fictional character has been created, we who are standing outside the fictional story can really refer to a fictional person. Notice that in the passage about Sherlock Holmes above, I really referred to a fictional character (i.e., my utterance satisfies the rules of reference). I did not *pretend* to refer to a real Sherlock Holmes; I *really referred* to the fictional Sherlock Holmes.[4]

Searle's reasoning is this:

1. Murdoch pretends to refer to an individual by her use of the proper name 'Andrew Chase-White.'
But 2. A speech act of reference is successful only if there exists an object the speaker is referring to.
So, 3. Murdoch pretends that there is an object she is referring to by her use of the proper name 'Andrew Chase-White.'
So, 4. Murdoch creates Andrew Chase-White.

The move from 1 and 2 to 3 seems acceptable.[5] But the crucial step from 3 to 4 definitely seems abrupt and unwarranted. Murdoch pretends the following situation to obtain: there be an object she is referring to by her use of the proper name 'Andrew Chase-White.' She does this while in fact she is not referring to a fictional individual ("because there was no such antecedently existing character"). How is this supposed to result in her creation of Andrew Chase-White? It is not clear at all. This leaves Murdoch's alleged creation of Chase-White mysterious. It does nothing to explain how the author can possibly create the character "out of thin air."[6]

There is an additional problem with Searle's position. As we noted, he says that a speech act of reference is successful only if there exists an object the speaker is referring to. He also says with emphasis that we do really refer to Sherlock Holmes when we say things like "Holmes remained a bachelor." It follows then that according to Searle, when we say things like "Holmes remained a bachelor," there exists Sherlock Holmes. This accords well with his creationism. However, Searle also says, "Holmes and Watson never existed at all, which is not of course to deny that they exist in fiction and can be talked about as such."[7] This is surprising. Does Searle mean to say that Holmes exists when we say things like "Holmes remained a bachelor" and that Holmes never existed at all? An obvious but facile attempt to make this intelligible would be to say that although referring presupposes existence, talking about does not. Thus, we talk about Holmes when we say "Holmes remained a bachelor," but we do so without referring to Holmes. The problem with this is that it makes the notion of talking about something quite mysterious. If we succeed in talking about Holmes and successful reference presupposes existence, then how can Holmes manage not to exist at all? Also, according to Searle, Holmes never existed at all, and according to Searle, Doyle created Holmes. Searle's position seems hardly coherent.

Perhaps I am being uncharitable to Searle. Perhaps I should interpret him as claiming that Murdoch created Chase-White not in the sense of bringing him into existence in reality but in the sense of bringing him into existence in fiction, and that we can really refer to Chase-White despite his lack of existence in actuality because he exists in fiction. I find such a view attractive myself, but it is not Searle's view and it does not support creationism. It is not Searle's view because it flatly contradicts one of Searle's central theses, viz., that the speech act of reference is unsuccessful if there does not exist an object the speaker is referring to. Here, of course, 'exist' means robust existence, viz., existence in actuality, not any watered-down kind of existence, such as existence in the speaker's mind, existence as an idea, or existence in fiction. The view does not support creationism because creationism asserts the existence of fictional individuals in actuality, not just in fiction.

How should we understand the notion of existence in fiction in the first place? The best way is to start by noting that there is an obvious sense in which it is true to say that Holmes remained a bachelor. It is the "intra fiction" sense. That is, it is true that Holmes remained a bachelor in fiction. The locution "in fiction" here is to be understood as a sentential operator. So we have, "In fiction (i.e., in, or according to, the fictional *Sherlock Holmes* stories), Holmes remained a bachelor." Likewise, to say that Holmes exists in fiction is to say that according to the fictional *Holmes* stories, Holmes exists. Creationism should not be confused with the claim that Holmes exists in fiction in this sense, as most opponents of creationism would agree with the claim.

Another possible way to rescue Searle from incoherence is to have him deny the entailment of existence by creation, or more accurately, to have him deny that necessarily for any x, if x is created, then x comes to exist.[8] There are two problems with this. First, it still does not make Searle's view supportive of creationism, as creationism entails that fictional individuals exist because they are created. To sever the connection between creation and existence is to deny creationism. Second, it makes a mockery of the notion of creation. It is an undeniable conceptual, indeed (I dare say) analytic, truth that for any x, if x is created, x comes into existence. To create something *is* to bring it into existence. If Murdoch really created Chase-White, he must really have come into existence, hence he must really exist.[9] We should be careful enough to distinguish creativity from creation. The creativity with which an author describes a fictional character need not consist in her bringing the character into existence. It may instead consist in an unusually imaginative manner in which she writes the story, for example.

Searle argues from pretense to creation. This is surprising, for many pretense theorists are anti-creationists. Kendall L. Walton is the arch pretense theorist of our time and has done much to popularize the idea of pretense, or make-believe, as he calls it. Gareth Evans follows Walton and takes pretense seriously. Both of these philosophers are anti-creationists. This is not surprising. Not only does creationism seem unnecessary to a committed pretense theorist but it also seems hostile to the centrality of pretense in fictional discourse. In Evans' words, creationism "fails to recognize the undeniable element of pretence present in this kind of discourse [about fictional characters]."[10]

If pretense plays a major role in creating fictional individuals, it is only legitimate to ask what that role is. Incredibly, however, this question has never been seriously addressed beyond the relatively superficial level of Searle's passage above. To see that the question is genuine and requires a substantive answer, let us imagine a purely hypothetical situation. Let us say that unlike Sir Arthur Conan Doyle, another writer, Sarthur Donan Coyle, endeavored to write non-fiction. As it happened by sheer coincidence, Donan Coyle ended up writing stories which contained exactly the same words as Conan Doyle's stories in exactly the same order. Coyle, unlike Doyle, thought he was writing true stories, for whatever twisted and improbable reasons. Coyle thought that there really was a detective called 'Sherlock Holmes,' that he was referring to that detective by his use of the name 'Sherlock Holmes' in his stories, that he himself was a medical doctor named 'John Watson' and a close friend of Holmes, and so on. Doyle was pretending to refer, predicate, assert, etc., in writing his stories, while Coyle thought he was really referring, predicating, asserting, etc., in writing *his* stories. The challenge for the pretense-theoretical creationists is to articulate in an informative way how the presence of pretense in Doyle's writing of his stories gave rise to the creation of fictional individuals and how the lack of pretense in Coyle's writing of *his* stories failed to do so.[11]

III. Abstract Entities?

In supporting creationism, Peter van Inwagen emphasizes the theoretical and abstract nature of fictional individuals. According to the story *Martin Chuzzlewit* by Charles Dickens, Mrs. Gamp is a fat old woman who is fond of gin. Does this mean that if we listed all fat old women in the world who was fond of gin, Mrs. Gamp would be among them? No. There are (in the past, present, and future) many fat old women who are fond of gin, but Mrs. Gamp, the fictional individual from *Martin Chuzzlewit*, is not one of them. Van Inwagen agrees with this and says that Mrs. Gamp is neither, fat, old, a woman, nor fond of gin. This, however, does not mean that when we say, e.g., "Mrs. Gamp is fond of gin," there is no way to interpret our statement so that it comes out true. On van Inwagen's view:

> ...we may *say* "Mrs. Gamp is fond of gin" and be talking *about* a theoretical entity of criticism without thereby *predicating* fondness for gin of that theoretical entity of criticism.[12]

What we may be doing is to be understood by means of a special triadic relation A, which van Inwagen calls "ascription." He says ascription is a primitive relation and does not attempt to defined it. But the idea is clear: '$A(x, y, z)$' is intended to capture what we ordinarily mean by 'According to the fiction z, the fictional individual y has the property x.' Since according to the story *Martin Chuzzlewit*, Mrs. Gamp has the property of being fond of gin, it is the case that A(being fond of gin, Mrs. Gamp, *Martin Chuzzlewit*). And this is what we intend to say when we say "Mrs. Gamp is fond of gin."

This way of thinking about fictional individuals seems to have the consequence that any finished fictional story is a massively false story about existent individuals. For example, Mrs. Gamp is a fat old gin-loving woman according to *Martin Chuzzlewit*, but Mrs. Gamp is none of these things. In fact (in van Inwagen's view), Mrs. Gamp is not human. Worse yet (in his view), Mrs. Gamp is not even concrete! The novel is full of other fictional characters and other fictional individuals, and it is equally massively false about all of them. This poses a serious problem for creationism because it deepens the mysteriousness of the creation of fictional individuals. When Dickens finished writing *Martin Chuzzlewit*, he finished creating Mrs. Gamp, among other fictional beings, according to creationism.[13] The problem is that it is very difficult to fathom how Dickens could create an individual by writing a story which, when finished, would be a massively false story about that individual. If the created individual were a concrete particular, say, a particular word token on a particular sheet of paper, there would be no problem. An author could perfectly well write a massively false story about a particular word token he produced. But in such a case, the fact that the author wrote a story would have nothing to do with the creation of the word token. The token would have been created if the author had not produced any other word token. Fictional individuals are different. Mrs. Gamp's creation is supposed to be essentially tied to Dickens' writing a certain story, not just his producing certain linguistic tokens, and the story Dickens wrote turns out to be massively false not only about Mrs. Gamp but also about all other fictional individuals in the story. The creation of Mrs. Gamp or any other fictional individual in the story seems unfathomable.

A creationist may object to my characterization of a fictional story as being massively false about the fictional individuals its author is supposed to create. It may be said that a fictional story cannot be a false story about fictional individuals because it is neither true nor false about anything. This is a peculiar objection but its motivation is not hard to understand. It comes from the pretense theory of fictional discourse. As we saw earlier, Searle is a representative pretense theorist.[14] According to Searle, an author, in writing fiction, pretends to refer to and say true things about real individuals. Dickens did not in fact refer or assert anything true by using the term 'Mrs. Gamp' but he pretended to refer to a real woman and assert something true about her. Dickens did not make assertions but only pretended to make assertions. So, what he wrote was neither true nor false.

This may be an understandable train of reasoning but it is defective. It conflates pragmatics and semantics. More specifically, it conflates a speech act and its result. Dickens was engaged in a speech act of pretending to (refer and) assert. He did not assert. So he did not commit himself to the truth of the sentences he wrote. This means, among other things, that even if these sentences are not true, Dickens is not to be blamed for it, and even if they are true, he is not to be praised for it. But, of course, this does not at all mean that these sentences are not true or that they are not false. Searle himself puts a relevant point succinctly:

> What they (the conventions of fictional discourse) do rather is enable the speaker to use words with their literal meanings without undertaking the commitments that are normally required by those meanings.[15]

The sentences Dickens wrote retain their literal meanings and therefore are open to semantic evaluations. Dickens' sentence

(1) Mrs. Gamp is a fat old woman who is fond of gin

in *Martin Chuzzlewit* retains its literal meaning. It contains the (apparent) proper name (with a title) 'Mrs. Gamp.' According to creationism, Mrs. Gamp exists, as it is created by Dickens' writing of the story. From this, we must admit, it does not follow by logic alone that, given creationism, 'Mrs. Gamp' in (1) refers to Mrs. Gamp. But it would be very odd indeed, given creationism, if 'Mrs. Gamp,' as it occurs in the very story the writing of which was responsible for creating Mrs. Gamp, did not refer to Mrs. Gamp. We need to take special care here to remember to distinguish the term's reference from the writer's reference. Dickens may not have been referring to anything by 'Mrs. Gamp,' but 'Mrs. Gamp' is an (apparent) referential term and creationism provides the obvious candidate for its reference, namely, Mrs. Gamp. Creationists agree that given the fact that (1) occurs in the story, it is true to say that according to the story, Mrs. Gamp was a fat old woman. The only reason for creationists to be able to say such a thing is that 'Mrs. Gamp' as it occurs in (1) refers to Mrs. Gamp and that (1) says of Mrs. Gamp that it (she) was a fat old woman, among other things. To put it mildly, the burden of proof is on those who insist that Mrs. Gamp was created by Dickens' writing of the novel and that 'Mrs. Gamp' as it occurs in the novel does not refer to Mrs. Gamp.[16]

Thus, according to the story, Mrs. Gamp was a fat old woman. But, given creationism, in fact Mrs. Gamp was not a fat old woman. Therefore, the story is wrong about Mrs. Gamp. Compare this to the following situation. According to Jane, Joe is a philosopher. But in fact Joe is not a philosopher. It then follows that Jane is wrong about Joe. Specifically, Jane is wrong about Joe's being a philosopher. The story is wrong about Mrs. Gamp's having being a fat old woman. Jane may be right about Joe's being other things, like male, human, concrete, etc. But the story is wrong about Mrs. Gamp in virtually every respect.[17] The story is massively wrong about Mrs. Gamp.

A related auxiliary objection is this. If, as creationists say, Dickens created Mrs. Gamp, then Dickens created Mrs. Gamp as being thus and so. In particular, Dickens created Mrs. Gamp as a fat old human female, rather than, say, a slim young reptilian male. If x exists as a result of being created by y, and y created x as an F, then x exists as an F. So, given creationism, Mrs. Gamp exists as a fat old human female. But according to creationism, Mrs. Gamp is neither fat, old, human, nor female.[18]

IV. Theoretical Entities?

Searle more or less confined his remarks to discourse about fictional individuals in the "intra fiction" sense. He did mention some discourse about fiction in the "extra fiction" sense, but without due emphasis or much theoretical mileage. An important contribution by van Inwagen is to go beyond that and concentrate heavily on discourse about fictional individuals in the "extra fiction" sense.

> (2) Mrs. Sarah Gamp was, four-and-twenty years ago, a fair representation of the hired attendant on the poor in sickness (From Dickens's preface to an 1867 edition of *Martin Chuzzlewit*)
>
> (3) Mrs. Gamp...is the most fully developed of the masculine anti-woman visible in all Dickens's novels (Sylvia Bank Manning, *Dickens as Satirist* [New Haven, 1971] p.79).[19]

According to van Inwagen, we should take these sentences "at face value: as assertions about a certain entity called "Mrs. Gamp"."[20] He explicitly asserts that Mrs. Gamp exists: "...there is such a thing as Mrs. Gamp."[21] He then says:

> *Question*: But why do you say there *is* such a thing as Mrs. Gamp? *Answer*: Because there *are* such things as characters in novels. And if there are such things as characters in novels, then Mrs. Gamp is one of them.[22]

So, the argument is this: Characters in novels exist; Mrs. Gamp is a character in novels; therefore, Mrs. Gamp exists. To justify the first premise "Characters in novels exist," van Inwagen invites us to consider the following sentences:

    (4) There are characters in some 19th-century novels who are presented with a greater wealth of physical detail than is any character in any 18th-century novel

    (5) Some characters in novels are closely modeled on actual people, while others are wholly products of the literary imagination, and it is usually impossible to tell which characters fall into which of these categories by textual analysis alone

    (6) Since 19th-century English novelists were, for the most part, conventional Englishmen, we might expect most novels of the period to contain stereotyped comic Frenchmen or Italians; but very few such characters exist.[23]

He says that these are true sentences of literary criticism and have existential implications. For example, (4) entails that there are such things as characters in 19th-century novels. Since (4) is true, characters in 19th-century novels exist. Likewise from (5) and (6), we can conclude that characters in novels that are closely modeled on actual people exist, that characters in novels that are wholly products of the literary imagination exist, and that stereotyped comic Frenchman or Italian characters in 19th-century English novels exist.[24]

This is an ingenious argument and it seems to have convinced many philosophers. I, however, find van Inwagen's exposition here a little muddled. So let us be clear about his reasoning before criticizing it properly. He mentions the sentences (4)–(6) as part of his answer to the question on the existence of Mrs. Gamp. As we have noted, this means that his discussion of (4)–(6) is meant to establish the claim that characters in novels exist. But it appears to fall short of doing so. In order to establish the existence of Mrs. Gamp, van Inwagen resorts to two claims: that Mrs. Gamp is a character in a novel, and that characters in novels exist. For this to work, the second claim has to be interpreted as fully universally quantified, i.e., as asserting that *all* characters in novels exist. However, one might think, the ensuing discussion of (4)–(6) does not establish such a claim. It would at best establish the existence of *some* characters in some 19th-century novels, *some* characters in novels that are closely modeled on actual people, *some* characters in novels that are wholly products of the literary imagination, and *very few* stereotyped comic Frenchman or Italian characters in 19th-century English novels. Or so one might think. If one thought so, since the missing premise is that Mrs. Gamp is one of *those* characters and this implicit premise is not obviously true, one might think that van Inwagen's discussion of (4)–(6) is insufficient to show that Mrs. Gamp, or any particular fictional individual, exists.

If one thought along those lines, one would be misunderstanding van Inwagen's discussion. It is true that (4)–(6) do not establish by themselves that all fictional characters exist. But they are not intended to do so. Nor does van Inwagen's argument for the existence of Mrs. Gamp require them to do so. Sentences such as (2) and (3), when understood correctly, are sufficient for establishing the existence of Mrs. Gamp, according to van Inwagen. (4)–(6) simply provide more sentences of the same pertinent general type as (2) and (3), except that (4)–(6) explicitly contain apparent existential quantification over fictional characters. All of these sentences are meant to be suggestive examples. The general thrust van Inwagen seeks to convey by these examples is that all fictional characters are *"theoretical entities of literary criticism"*[25] and many statements in literary criticism are true when taken "at face value" and have existential implications. He takes literary criticism to "include all "informed" discourse about the nature, content, and value of literary works."[26] So, for example, as long as there is at least one piece of literary criticism in van Inwagen's sense that is true and entails the existence of Holmes when taken "at face value," van Inwagen has an argument for the existence of Holmes. And there appears to be such a piece of literary criticism about Holmes: e.g., "There is a unique fictional individual that is portrayed as a superb detective with the name 'Sherlock Holmes' in Arthur Conan Doyle's *Holmes* stories." Such a sentence appears to be true and have the right existential implication when taken "at face value."

Let us not quibble with van Inwagen's phrase 'literary works.' In distinguishing fiction from literature, Searle says, "The Sherlock Holmes stories of Conan Doyle are clearly works of fiction, but it is a matter of judgment whether they should be regarded as a part of English literature."[27] Let us ignore what Searle says and simply read van Inwagen's 'literary works' as 'fictional works.'

We should also read van Inwagen's word 'discourse' here charitably. His argument does not require that someone utter, even privately, a piece of literary criticism of the relevant kind. What is crucial is the *truth* of the relevant sentence of literary criticism, not its utterance or any other use. Furthermore in this connection, we should not take his word 'character' seriously, either. All fictional characters are fictional individuals but not all fictional individuals are fictional characters. Indeed, most fictional individuals are not fictional characters. Only those fictional individuals which are significant in the story, and perhaps also portrayed as animate, are fictional characters. We should not disregard "informed" discourse about fictional individuals which are not fictional characters. Thus, even if no one utters or even thinks of any piece of literary criticism about a particular insignificant fictional individual, say, the shoe lace on the left shoe Holmes was wearing when confronting Moriarty for the first time, as long as some sentence with the right existential implication is true when taken "at face value," van Inwagen's argument will go through in favor of the existence of that fictional individual, if it should go through in favor of the existence of anything at all.[28]

The idea therefore is that we should accept literary criticism "at face value" and if we do, we should accept the existence of the theoretical entities it postulates, namely, fictional individuals. So, what is really suggested by van Inwagen's (4)–(6) is not a particular argument or arguments. It is instead an argument schema. Let us formulate it explicitly. One may be tempted to put it as follows:

(A) It is a truth of literary criticism that Φ.
(B) That Φ entails that α exists
So, (C) α exists.

Here the Greek letters, 'α' and 'Φ,' are to be replaced with an (apparent) singular term for a fictional individual and a sentence of literary criticism with the relevant existential import, respectively. This is not an adequate formulation, for its invalidity is so obvious that it fails to be sufficiently charitable. What follows from the schematic premises at best is the conclusion schema,

(C′) It is a truth of literary criticism that α exists.

I say "at best," for (C′) follows from (A) and (B) only under the assumption that the truths of literary criticism are closed under entailment, and this is a dubious assumption. The more important point, of course, is that (C′) does not entail (C). Van Inwagen explicitly draws an analogy between literary criticism and physics. He says that just as we should accept the existence of theoretical entities of the theories of physics we accept, we should also accept the existence of theoretical entities of literary criticism we accept.[29] We should take van Inwagen seriously when he says that we should take such sentences as (2)–(6) "at face value." That is, we should understand him as arguing that if some sentence is included in literary criticism as true, then it is true. Taking a sentence "at face value" is tantamount to moving it out of the sentential operator "it is a truth of literary criticism that." This leads us to inserting an additional lemma as a consequence of (A):

(A′) (It is true that) Φ.

(C) follows from (A′) and (B). Thus we now appear to have a valid argument schema. This is the strongest reconstruction of van Inwagen's argument I can think of that is faithful to his text.

Now the criticism: (A′) does not follow from (A). As I indicated, van Inwagen's justification for the move from (A) to (A′) is that we should take sentences of literary criticism, e.g., (2)–(6), "at face value." I see two problems with this justification.

First, it rests on the assumption that literary criticism is a discipline, or activity, that is aimed at discovering truths about the actual world, on a par with physics. This assumption is false. No empirical discipline is on a par with physics as a way of discovering truths. Every natural science is secondary to physics in the sense that it is not allowed to contradict physics. Every social or behavioral science is secondary to natural sciences in the sense that it is not allowed to contradict natural sciences. Literary criticism is not even a social science. It is not a science of any kind. Its main aim is not to discover truths, but to help enhance aesthetic and other kinds of experience by the readers and listeners of literary or fictional works. Sometimes pointing out some truths about the actual world helps, but it is only a means, not an end. Literary criticism is not a discipline or activity aimed at propositional truth at all. Instead it is an activity aimed at practical results. Its main goal is to do something, namely, help the readers and listeners of literary or fictional works appreciate them, in the broadest sense of the word 'appreciate.' Any means by which this may be achieved is allowable in literary criticism. Capturing the actual world as it is has no privileged status.

Apart from this general point concerning the nature of literary criticism, an additional point should be made concerning specific examples. Some sentences in literary criticism indeed express truths about the actual world in the straightforward sense: e.g., 'Dickens lived in the 19th century and wrote in English.' Such sentences, when occurring within literary criticism, should be taken to be true "at face value." But this is so only because their truth is ascertained by other disciplines, history in this case. Unlike such sentences, (2)–(6) are indigenous to literary criticism, and that is why van Inwagen chose them. We should be careful not to take sentences indigenous to literary criticism "at face value." Consider (3), for example. If we take it "at face value," we will assert the sentence, 'Mrs. Gamp...is the most fully developed of the masculine anti-woman visible in all Dickens's novels.' Then by logic, we will be committed to the truth of 'Mrs. Gamp is a masculine anti-woman.' But Mrs. Gamp is not a masculine anti-woman, for Mrs, Gamp is not even concrete, according to creationism. Another example: (4). If we take it "at face value," we will assert the sentence, 'There are characters in some 19th-century novels who are presented with a greater wealth of physical detail than is any character in any 18th-century novel.' Then by logic and the meaning of the relative pronoun 'who,' we will be committed to the truth of 'Some characters are animate.' But no characters are animate, for none of them are even concrete, according to creationism. An insignificant alteration to (4) gives us a slightly more dramatic example: 'There are female characters in some 19th-century novels who are presented with a greater wealth of physical detail than is any female character in any 18th-century novel.' By taking this "at face value," we will be committed to the truth of 'Some characters are female.' But no characters are female, as they are abstract, according to creationism.

This brings out another objection to van Inwagen. He says, and most creationists agree, that we may legitimately refer to Mrs. Gamp by a feminine pronoun and other linguistic devices borrowed from the story, e.g., 'the fat old gin-drinking female,' even though Mrs. Gamp is abstract. So, for example, it is perfectly legitimate for us to say, "Mrs. Gamp is the most fully developed of the fat old gin-drinking female in all English novels. She is well known among the readers of 19th-century English novels. The fat old gin-drinking female is also a fair representation of the hired attendant on the poor in sickness," and thereby refer to the abstract object, Mrs. Gamp, and assert that it is the most fully developed of the fat old gin-drinking female in all English novels, is well known among the readers of 19th-century English novels, and is also a fair representation of the hired attendant on the poor in sickness. But when we do this, our words 'she' and 'the fat old gin-drinking female' are obviously not to be taken "at face value." Mrs. Gamp is abstract, and not at all female, fat, or gin-drinking. Thus, here is a dilemma for van Inwagen: Either we can refer to Mrs. Gamp by 'she,' 'the fat old...,' and the like, or we cannot. If we can, then literary criticism should not be taken "at face value," as the language of literary criticism is not metaphysically straightforward but bound to the host story in such a way that what might appear to be asserted in literary criticism is heavily parasitic on what is true in the story. If we cannot, then most pieces of literary criticism fail to refer to the intended characters. Either way, van Inwagen's argument for the existence of fictional characters is undermined.

Let us assume with the majority of creationists that in literary criticism we can refer to fictional individuals by means of any of the (apparent) singular terms used for those individuals in the host story in which they figure. Then those terms so used in literary criticism should not be taken "at face value." If the (apparent) singular terms are not to be taken "at face value," neither are (apparent) quantifiers. Sentences such as (4)–(6) should be approached cautiously. They contain apparent quantification over fictional individuals. According to van Inwagen, we should take such quantification "at face value" and conclude that literary criticism commits us to the existence of fictional individuals. We now have reason to doubt this. The challenge for us now is to say how such quantification should be taken, if not "at face value." Here "at face value" means "with direct ontic commitment." That is, quantification taken "at face value" is *objectual* quantification. An alternative kind of quantification that suggests itself quite naturally for literary criticism is *substitutional*. Under substitutional quantification, an apparent quantification over fictional individuals is to be interpreted as real quantification over (apparent) singular terms for fictional individuals in the host story. For example, (4)–(6) are interpreted as being true under the conditions along the following lines:

(4′) There be (apparent) singular terms, $t_1, t_2, ..., t_k$ $(1 < k)$, in some 19th-century novels such that for any (apparent) singular term t_m in any 18th-century novel the accompanying predicates for $t_1, t_2, ..., t_k$ exhibit a greater wealth of physical detail than the accompanying predicates for t_m.

(5′) Some (apparent) singular terms in novels be accompanied by predicates that are closely modeled on the predicates for actual people, while others are wholly products of the literary imagination, and it is usually impossible to tell which terms fall into which of these categories by textual analysis alone.

(6′) Since 19th-century English novelists were, for the most part, conventional Englishmen, we might expect most novels of the period to contain (apparent) singular terms accompanied by predicates for stereotyped comic Frenchmen or Italians; but very few such terms exist.

One objection to the idea of substitutional quantification is that there is a mismatch between fictional individuals and (apparent) singular terms for them. Some fictional individuals are not given with sufficient specificity for there to be even one (apparent) singular term for them in the host story: e.g., "A crowd lunged forward." If nothing else is said of the crowd in the story, there is no (apparent) singular term for any member of the crowd. This objection forces us to abandon the strictest substitutional quantification, which requires that the quantification be over terms that explicitly occur in the host story. But we may safely embrace a less strict version. It has a parallel in the account of truth in fiction. So let us consider the latter briefly. Most philosophers, including most creationists, agree that truth in fiction goes beyond what is explicitly said in the story. Even though no sentence to the effect that Mrs. Watson had a liver explicitly occurs in the *Holmes* stories, it is true in the stories that Mrs. Watson had a liver. Likewise what is explicitly stated in the story, "A crowd lunged forward," combined with what is expected of the story yields the truth that in the story each member of the crowd existed. So we can include in the domain of the substitutional quantifiers such terms as 'the first member of the crowd to lunge,' 'the tallest member of the crowd,' 'the heaviest member of the crowd,' etc. But what if the members of the crowd are completely indistinguishable from one another?[30] Is it then not true to say, e.g., that in the story some members of the crowd are indistinguishable? If so, then since no terms are available as the substituents for the variables in 'In the story x_1 is a member of the crowd, x_2 is a member of the crowd, ..., x_n is a member of the crowd, and $x_1 \neq x_2$, $x_1 \neq x_3$, ..., $x_2 \neq x_3$, ...' so as to yield a true sentence, are we not forced to read 'some members' objectually and accept the existence of fictional individuals that are, according to the story, members of the crowd? Not necessarily. The truth condition for the sentence in question need not follow the surface form of the sentence strictly. We can easily see that the following substitutional quantificational truth condition is perfectly adequate: there be a substituent term for the variable in the sentence 'In the story x has indistinguishable members' such that its substitution results in a true sentence. There is indeed such a term, namely, 'the crowd.' This kind of paraphrasing strategy is guaranteed to work as long as there is an (apparent) singular term for the collection whose members are indistinguishable, and it is hard to see how a story could include indistinguishable members of a collection while containing no (apparent) singular term for the collection at least implicitly.[31]

Thus we have found at least one way to mark the sense in which literary criticism differs from physics in ontological seriousness. Quantification in physics is objectual, while quantification in literary criticism is substitutional. There is much more to be said on this matter. But we need to proceed to further issues concerning creationism.

V. Like Other Creations?

As we saw, van Inwagen regards fictional individuals as theoretical entities of literary criticism. Among such entities he also includes "plots, sub-plots, novels (as opposed to tangible *copies* of novels), poems, meters, rhymes, borrowings, influences, digressions, episodes, recurrent patterns of imagery, and literary forms ("the novel," "the sonnet")."[32] Accusing anti-creationists of false parsimony, Amie L. Thomasson follows the spirit of van Inwagen's remark and expands on it. There are two parts to her accusation.

First, she says that one should not eliminate fictional individuals on the basis of their dependence on mental states or their abstractness, for "such things as works of art and scientific theories, churches and schools, and behaviors and social institutions depend on mental states just as fictional objects do" and "[like] fictional objects, ideal entities like numbers (Platonistically conceived) and...universals, laws, and scientific theories,...fail to be located in space-time...[and] are abstract."[33] This is the weaker of the two, for even if we assume for the sake of argument that works of art, scientific theories, churches, schools, behaviors, social institutions, numbers, universals, and laws exist, not all of them are of the same relevant kind as fictional individuals, namely, things that are both created in a certain specific way and abstract. Thomasson herself classifies all of these items except works of art as belonging to different ontological categories.[34] So, the analogy with fictional individuals is weak.

The second part of her accusation does not suffer from this defect, as it concentrates on the analogy with literary works only. She says that fictional individuals and literary works are both abstract entities that are "generically constantly dependent and rigidly historically dependent on real entities" and "rigidly historically dependent on and generically constantly dependent on mental states."[35] Her point is that one should embrace fictional individuals as created existents just as one should embrace literary works as created existents. Plainly, her point is only as strong as the parallelism between fictional individuals and literary works. I think the parallelism is ambiguous, and when taken one way it is rather weak, and when taken the other way it supports anti-creationism.

The story *A Study in Scarlet* is a collection of English sentences, which Doyle wrote in 1886. English sentences are sequences of English words in conformity with the syntactic rules of English. English words are those sequences of letters which are included in the vocabulary of English. The vocabulary of English is a finite list of sequences of letters from the English alphabet. A sequence of sequences of things is a sequence of those things. So, the literary work, *A Study in Scarlet*, is a collection of sequences of the letters of English alphabet in conformity with certain syntactic rules. As such, the work is at least as abstract as any sequence of letters, which in turn is at least as abstract as the letters. The letters are abstract line-shape types. So the work is at least as abstract as line-shape types. Line-shape types, like any type, may be instantiated. To write *A Study in Scarlet* is to produce an instance of the sequence of the line-shape types that is the story without copying another such instance.[36] Doyle did so in 1886. The instantiation he produced is a particular collection of particular ink marks on particular sheets of paper arranged in a particular sequence. Thus, we have two candidates for our comparison with fictional individuals: the story itself and the instantiation of the story produced by Doyle. This is the ambiguity of the parallelism. Let us first compare fictional individuals to the instantiation of the story. The instantiation of the story consists of marks on sheets of paper and therefore is as concrete as anything, having a particular spatial location. Also, once created by Doyle, it needs no further mental goings-on to continue its existence. Fictional individuals, on the other hand, are abstract, lacking spatial location, and dependent on the mental goings-on of the readers for their continued existence, according to Thomasson. This makes the parallelism very weak in crucial respects. Let us then compare fictional individuals to the story itself. The story is abstract, and, according to creationists, so are fictional individuals. So far so good. But the story, as a sequence of line-shape types, did not come into existence when Doyle wrote it. It had existed prior to his writing it. Also, it will continue to exist independently of any mental goings-on. So, if fictional individuals are to be seen as being on a par with the story, creationism is undermined.

Creationists might object that I am being unfair to Thomasson by defining literary works merely syntactically. They might say that a literary work is not a mere collection of sequences of letters but something further that crucially depends on mental goings-on. We should not forget semantics, they might insist. Fair enough. But this merely points to the sense of literary work which calls for interpretation of syntactic items. The story *A Study in Scarlet* under this conception is a certain sequence of letters under interpretation, where the interpretation is in conformity with the semantics of English. What is an interpretation? It is a mapping of syntactic items (e.g., sentences) to contents (e.g., propositions). So the story is a sequence of syntactic items combined with a particular mapping of those items to contents. The "combined with" here may be understood in a variety of ways, but let us go with a handy and fairly standard device of convenience and say that the story is an ordered pair of a sequence of syntactic items and the corresponding contents they are mapped to. The story in this semantically loaded sense then is an abstract object that existed prior to Doyle's writing it and continues to exist independently of mental goings-on. This does not help Thomasson.

Perhaps, I am still not being fair to Thomasson. She writes:

A literary work only comes into existence through the intentional mental states of an author; if a pile of sticks happens to wash up on shore arranged into what looks like a series of letters at the water's edge, we have a remarkable occurrence, but not a work of literature, nor any fictional characters, but only some marks that happen to resemble letters and words.[37]

Here I believe she is confusing how literary works come into existence with how they are written. Doyle wrote *A Study in Scarlet* in 1886. He did so through intentional mental states. If he had not been in intentional mental states, he would not have been able to write the story. In this sense, his intentional mental states played a key role in his writing of the story. In fact, an author's intentional mental states played a similar key role in writing of any story that has ever been written by anybody, and this will probably hold true for any literary work to be written by anybody in the future. But this only shows the causal dependence of the author's writing of a literary work on his/her intentional mental states, not the ontological dependence of the existence of the work on the mental states. Thomasson's example of washed-up sticks underscores this. Such sticks do not constitute an instantiation of a literary work as written by anyone, for no one arranged the sticks that way. The right kind (i.e., intentional mental kind) of causal factors are absent. But this does not mean that the sticks do not constitute an instantiation of a literary work. Not all instantiations of literary works need to be written by someone. The sticks are certainly open to interpretation in accordance with the semantics of English. Whether they are actually so interpreted by someone or not should not affect its ontological status.[38]

VI. Fictionality

Let us conclude with a final objection against creationism. It is devastatingly simple. Unlike you and me, Mrs. Gamp is a fictional individual. To say this entails that Mrs. Gamp does not exist. Fictionality of a thing entails its non-existence. There are two standard creationist replies to this objection. Both use the paraphrase strategy. They say that when we say that Mrs. Gamp does not exist, what we say is not true but what we mean to say is true and that when one says that it is true that Mrs. Gamp does not exist, one is confusing what we say and what we mean to say. The two replies differ on what we mean to say. According to the first reply, what we mean to say is that there is no such woman (or human or...) as Mrs. Gamp.[39] According to the second reply, what we mean to say is that nothing has all the properties ascribed to Mrs. Gamp in the story.[40] The first reply has counterexamples: e.g., 'Boojams do not exist.' When we deny the existence of boojams on the grounds that they are fictional, we need not be able to give a sortal or other kind term to fill the gap in 'There are no such ( ) as boojams,' except for such an empty kind term as 'things' or 'entities.' Since creationists maintain that boojams exist (assuming that boojams are indeed genuinely fictional individuals, i.e., they are real, rather than fictional, according to the relevant story), it is false to say that there are no such things, or entities, as boojams. Another difficulty with the first reply is that it is unable to account for the apparent truth of some general statements: e.g., 'All fictional individuals are unreal,' 'All fictional individuals are non-existent,' 'No fictional individual exists,' 'What distinguishes fictional individuals from you and me is that the former do not exist.' The paraphrasing strategy of the first reply does not apply here. Does the second reply fare better? The second reply entails that what we mean to say when we say 'Mrs. Gamp does not exist' in our attempt to contrast Mrs. Gamp with you and me is false if some existing individual has all the properties ascribed to Mrs. Gamp in the story. But what we mean to say when we say 'Mrs. Gamp does not exist' in our attempt to contrast Mrs. Gamp with you and me is not false if some actual person about whom Dickens was not writing happens to have all the properties ascribed to Mrs. Gamp in the story. So the second reply does not fare any better.

There is no way to understand the fictionality of fictional individuals without making them non-existent.[41]

Notes

1. I take it for granted that if an author creates a fictional individual, s/he creates it by (or, in, or, as a result of) writing the relevant story.
2. P. 73 of John Searle, "The Logical Status of Fictional Discourse," first published in *New Literary History* vol. VI, 1974–75, pp. 319–332, and included in *Expression and Meaning* (Cambridge, Cambridge University Press, 1979), pp. 58–75. Page references are to the latter.
3. P. 157 of Stephen Schiffer, "Language-Created Language-Independent Entities," *Philosophical Topics* vol. 24, no.1, Spring, 1996, pp. 149–167, emphasis his.
4. *Ibid.*, pp. 71–72, emphasis his.
5. Except that we really need a stronger premise than 2, namely, that Murdoch knows that a speech act of reference is successful only if there exists an object the speaker is referring to. And even this is not enough, strictly speaking. Some kind of closure principle on pretense is required. But I shall ignore these minor defects.
6. On page 130 of "The Problem of Non-Existents, I. Internalism," *Topoi* 1 (1982), pp. 97–140, Kit Fine expresses a seemingly different view of creation in fiction when he says of fictional individuals, "...they come into being as the result of [the appropriate activity of the author], in much the same way as a table comes into being as the result of the activity of a carpenter." This analogy, however, does not help. Pretense, and story-telling in particular, plays no essential role in a carpenter's creation of a table. Nor does the appropriate activity of the author essentially involve manipulation and reconfiguration of physical objects. This makes it hard to understand the sameness of the way of creation Fine alleges between creation of a fictional individual and creation of a table.
7. *Ibid.*, p. 71.
8. Kit Fine denies the entailment. He says that fictional individuals are created but non-existent. To create something is to bring it into being but the "being" in question does not have to be existence. It may be actuality instead. For Fine, fictional

individuals are created as actual individuals but they do not exist. Existence entails actuality but actuality does not entail existence. I find this notion of actuality un-intelligible. Fine says that actuality is to be understood in contrast with mere pos-sibility. But to be a possible individual is to be possible to exist. He would probably deny this and say instead that to be a possible individual is to be a possible being. Then I would not understand the notion of a possible being unless it is the same as a possible existent. See his *op. cit.*, pp. 131–132.

9. Of course, he might have come into existence at one time and been annihilated later, so that he does not exist now. I shall ignore such creation-then-annihilation scenarios.
10. Gareth Evans, *The Varieties of Reference* (Oxford: Clarendon Press, 1982), p. 367.
11. Nathan Salmon would say that Coyle did create an individual. Such a view severs the tie between creation and pretense, and therefore is not a version of pretense-theoretical creationism. See his "Nonexistence," *Noûs* 32:3 (1998), pp. 277–319. Mark Richard expresses reservations about Salmon's view, in "Commitment," *Philosophical Perspectives 12, language, Mind, and Ontology, 1998* (ed.) James E. Tomberlin (Boston & Oxford: Blackwell), pp. 255–281.
12. P. 305 of his "Creatures of Fiction," *American Philosophical Quarterly,* 14: 4, 1977, pp. 299–308, emphasis his.
13. If some creationist wants to claim that the creation of Mrs. Gamp was not com-pleted when Dickens finished writing the novel but it came about only when there was enough participation by the readers of the novel, let us be more cautious and say that according to creationism, Dickens did finish doing his obviously rather important part in the creation of Mrs. Gamp when he finished writing the novel. This complication is minor and does not affect the rest of the discussion seriously.
14. As we noted earlier, Kendall Walton has developed an elaborate theory of pretense but he is not a creationist, so I shall not discuss him here.
15. *Op. cit.*, pp. 66–67.
16. Gregory Curry makes a similar point while defending the notion of truth in fiction. See his *The Nature of Fiction* (Cambridge: Cambridge University Press, 1990), pp. 4–9.
17. The story is right about Mrs. Gamp's being an entity, under creationsism.
18. It is possible to be a creationist while maintaining that fictional individuals are con-crete, or even that they are exactly as they are described in the fiction. Though possible, such a position is extremely implausible. I assume that any reasonable creationist would, following van Inwagen, hold that all fictional individuals are abstract.
19. Peter van Inwagen, *op. cit.*, p. 301.
20. *Ibid.*, p.301.
21. *Ibid.*, p. 301. He makes it clear that he takes 'X exists' as equivalent to 'There is X' or 'There is such a thing as X.'
22. *Ibid.*, p. 301.
23. *Ibid.*, p. 302.
24. The last of these implications is odd, thought not totally out of place, for (6) does not only entail existence but entails scarce existence.
25. *Ibid.*, p. 302.
26. *Ibid.*, p. 303.
27. *Op. cit.*, pp. 59–60.

28. The shoe lace example brings up another aspect of the mysteriousness of creation in fiction. If Doyle created Holmes by writing the stories, he must have created a host of other things by writing the same stories, including fictional individuals that are not fictional "characters." The shoe lace in question is such an example. But more interesting examples include fictional individuals that are parts of Holmes according to the stories: e.g., Holmes' right arm, his right hand, his right index finger, etc. It is hard to deny that the creationists are committed to the existence and abstractness of such things as much as the existence and abstractness of Holmes. So, according to creationism, Doyle brought into existence a large number of abstract objects (e.g., Holmes and his body parts) which bear spatial part-whole relations to one another in the stories but not in fact. This is bizarre.

29. See his "Fiction and metaphysics," *Philosophy and Literature* 7:1, 1983, pp. 67–77.

30. See the example of Dee and Dum in Fine, *op. cit.*, pp. 135–136.

31. Even if the story only contains the expression 'some people' for the collection in question, I say that the (apparent) singular term 'the collection of people' occur implicitly in the sense that it is true in the story that there is a unique collection of people in question.

32. "Creatures of Fiction," pp. 302–303.

33. Amie L. Thomasson, *Fiction and Metaphysics* (Cambridge: Cambridge University Press, 1999) pp. 144–145.

34. As belonging to boxes other than the shaded box of Figures 9.1 and 9.2, *ibid.*, p. 131.

35. *Ibid.*, pp. 141, 143.

36. This allows the possibility for someone to write the story independently of Doyle. Some people think that such a story would not be the same story as *A Study in Scarlet*. Cf. Jorge Luis Borges, "Pierre Menard, Author of the Quixote," *Ficciones* (New York: New Directions, 1964). I find their reasoning highly unpersuasive.

37. *Ibid.*, p. 142.

38. Even when instantiations of sentences are produced by someone intentionally, his/her mental states need not determine the interpretation. As George A. Miller observes, "People who know only the rules of pronunciation can read a Spanish text aloud well enough that Spaniards can understand it, even though the readers have no idea what they are saying." See his *The Science of Words* (New York: Scientific american Library, A Division of HPHLP, 1991), p. 56. Also see Herman Cappelen, "Intentions in Words," *Noûs* 33:1, March 1999, pp. 92–102.

39. For example, see Thomasson on Parsons in *op. cit.*, p. 112.

40. For example, see Salmon, *op. cit.*, pp. 303–304. Van Inwagen seems to think that the second reply is a more precise version of the first. I believe they are independent of each other. See van Inwagen, *op. cit.*, p. 308, footnote 11.

41. I thank Amie Thomasson for helpful discussion.

Philosophical Perspectives, 15, Metaphysics, 2001

REALISM ABOUT PERSONAL IDENTITY OVER TIME*

Trenton Merricks
University of Virginia

I shall defend "realism about personal identity over time." Realism is the claim that personal identity over time is never a matter of convention. Realism seems to be true. After all, who really believes that, when facing personal extinction, salvation could be found in effecting linguistic or conceptual revolution? (Cf. Chisholm, 1976, 111–112) And who among us honestly fears death by paradigm shift?

But—in spite of these rhetorical questions!—realism is controversial. Peter Unger, for example, rejects it. He says that any plausible approach to issues of personal identity over time "will treat questions of our existence and identity as being, in large measure, conventional matters" (1990, 66). (See also Unger, 1990, 168, 239, and 257)

And Robert Nozick endorses conventionalism—let's use 'conventionalism' to mean the denial of realism—with:

> What is special about people, about selves, is that what constitutes their identity through time is partially determined by their own conception of themselves, a conception which may vary, perhaps appropriately does vary, from person to person. (1981, 69)

A conventionalist could hold that one's persistence depends on convention only sometimes, perhaps only rarely. Thus Mark Johnston:

> It is important that [the conventionalist about personal identity] can allow that personal identity is not *in general* a matter of conventional fiat and can also allow that the constraints on the identity of human persons—for example, that human persons are in their natural condition constituted by living human bodies—make facts of personal identity more stable and less a projection of context-dependent interests than the facts about the identity of artifacts. (1989, 452)

Note Johnston's intimation that at least sometimes, although not "in general," personal identity is a matter of "conventional fiat."

And, finally, consider Derek Parfit's response to the question of whether I would exist "if half of my body were simultaneously replaced":

> Suppose that I know the facts about what will happen to my body, and about any psychological connections that there will be between me now and some person tomorrow. I may ask, 'Will that person be me?' But that is a misleading way to put my question. It suggests that I don't know what's going to happen. When I know these other facts, I should ask, 'Would it be correct to call that person me?' That would remind me that, if there's anything I don't know, that is merely a fact about our language...Such questions are, in the belittling sense, merely verbal. (1995, 25)

Parfit thinks that in certain "puzzle cases"—such as half-body replacement—personal identity's holding (or not) is itself a fact about linguistic convention. Thus Parfit thinks that there are cases in which the facts of personal identity are conventional.

Conventionalism about personal identity is alive and well.[1] But I shall argue that the metaphysics implied by conventionalism has an unacceptable consequence. Thus we should reject conventionalism and, therefore, accept realism.

I. Plasticity Theory

One attempt at providing a conventionalist metaphysics of personal identity has its roots in the claim that our concepts surrounding personal identity—and the meanings of the words associated with those concepts—are *plastic* or *malleable*. I will call this way of interpreting conventionalism 'Plasticity Theory', and its defenders 'Plasticity Theorists'. Eric Olson (1997) treats (what I have labeled) Plasticity Theory as one reasonable interpretation of conventionalism about personal identity over time. And Mark Johnston (1989) affirms conventionalism on the basis of Plasticity Theory.

Consider the sentence 'P survives teletransportation' and imagine, for the sake of argument, that that sentence has no determinate truth value. Plasticity Theory says that the indeterminacy is explained by 'P''s imprecision. This imprecision explains indeterminacy, Plasticity Theorists would claim, because (at least) one of the candidates for being the referent of 'P' survives teletransportation and (at least) one does not. The Plasticity Theorist would add that we could precisify 'P' in such a way that 'P' would determinately refer to a survivor of teletransportation. Or we could precisify 'P' in such a way that 'P' would determinately not refer to any survivor of teletransportation. Or we could leave it indeterminate.

The account of Plasticity Theory just given makes sense only if we understand what it is to "precisify." Note that to precisify a term is *not* simply to change its meaning. For we could—trivially, setting aside the topic of precisification—change by convention the meaning of 'P' in 'P persists' so that that sentence would express a truth when, say, it actually expresses a falsehood. But this banal observation is irrelevant to conventionalism. For our ability to legislate by convention the meaning of 'p' does not imply that we can similarly legislate whether p is the case. (Zeus would not exist even if we made 'Zeus exists' true by using it to mean that $1+1=2$.)

So to precisify is not simply to change meaning. Precisification, rather, has to do with the idea that the actual meaning of the relevant expression—and that actual meaning is, uncontroversially, fixed by linguistic convention—is somehow *malleable*. So precisification won't change whether 'P' means P; rather, it is supposed to somehow make a difference in whether someone is P. But how can this be?

Mark Johnston offers the best way I know of to make sense of precisification in the context of personal identity. Johnston's account focuses on self-concern and the claim that the object of one's self-concern could reasonably vary (1989, 454). What it is for someone to be P in the future, Johnston seems to say, is for that someone to be the reasonable object of P's future-directed self-concern.

So suppose that P's future-directed self-concern reasonably changed from not being determinately fixed upon one who survives teletransportation to being so fixed. According to Johnston, P will now determinately survive teletransportation; the person emerging at the "other end" of teletransportation will be P. But if that change in concern had not occurred, Johnston would add, P would not determinately survive teletransportation. Moreover, Johnston's position is that certain other changes in concern would have resulted in the survivor's being determinately not the same person as P. In this way, Johnston provides an account of how whether anyone existing after teletransportation is the same person as P could turn on facts about concern, which facts are themselves to some extent up to us, to some extent a matter of convention. And so he thinks that conventionalism about personal identity over time is true.[2]

But, *pace* Johnston, I deny that Plasticity Theory, even if it were true, would imply conventionalism. Indeed, I think Plasticity Theory implies *realism* about personal identity over time. For Plasticity Theory should be understood as implying that the various candidates for being the determinate referent of a name, or for being the determinate object of self-concern, persist non-conventionally. The idea behind Plasticity Theory is *not* that if there are n candidates for being P, then there are n+1 persisters, the candidates plus P. Rather, the idea is that there are exactly n persisters (relevant to the case in question), its being somehow a matter of convention which of them is the same person as P. But, as noted, each of the n candidates—and so every persister—persists non-conventionally. So, given Plasticity Theory, no fact of identity over time is a matter of convention; rather convention governs only things like future-directed self-concern and reference. Thus Plasticity Theory, rather than undermining realism, instead presupposes it.[3]

Now the Plasticity Theorist denies that the 'P' candidates (or the candidates for P's future-directed self-concern) are persons (Johnston, 1989, 449).

He insists that each is only a candidate for being a person. So, he might object, although Plasticity Theory implies realism about the mere identity over time of every entity, it does not imply realism about whether those entities that enjoy identity over time are persons. And in this way, he might charge, Plasticity Theory avoids realism about *personal* identity over time.

I could respond that, supposing the "candidates" exist in the first place, they are really persons. After all, they look, act, think, speak, and behave just like persons. Obviously, this response threatens Plasticity Theory's claim that, in the sort of case we are imagining, although there are many candidates, there is but one person. But this response, even if correct, is misleading. It is misleading because it takes aim at the wrong target. For it is realism about our identity over time—not our being persons—that is at issue between the conventionalist and the realist.

Debates about personal identity almost universally involve cases where the proposed relata of the identity relation are assumed to be persons. For example, Parfit, in the quote at the start of this paper, promotes a conventionalist answer to the question of "Will that person be me?" Here personhood is taken for granted. It is *identity* with himself that Parfit thinks, in certain cases, is "merely a fact about our language." Similarly, the well-worn cases of teletransportation, brain transplant, and fission uniformly involve a person at one "end" of the process and a person (or persons) at the other; the question such cases prompt is always about *identity*.

Perhaps we are persons essentially. If so, then conventionalism about our continuing to be persons would secure conventionalism about our identity over time.[4] But the Plasticity Theorist cannot invoke our essentially being persons to parlay the allegedly conventional nature of personhood into conventionalism about our persistence. For Plasticity Theory requires personhood to be contingent. After all, Plasticity Theory implies that although person-candidates are not persons, each of them *would be* a person given the right precisification. Because the "right" precisification is possible, that implication makes sense only given the contingent nature of personhood.

So Plasticity Theory must concede that realism about our persistence is one thing, realism about our being persons another. It is realism about our persistence or identity over time, not our being persons, that is the primary locus of the realism/conventionalism debate in personal identity. And Plasticity Theory, we have seen, implies realism about the identity over time of every persister and, as a result, about the identity over time of each of us.

Plasticity Theory is a species of realism, given my account of realism. One might grant this, yet object in the following way: "Plasticity Theory seems to deliver *something* like conventionalism. For according to Plasticity Theory there are a number of equally good ways to talk about—and think about and care about—our identity. There are a number of equally good ways to 'carve things up' with respect to our persistence. That is, they are equally good prior to our plumping for one of them. But we can, by convention, render one way 'best' or 'right.' Thus we have *something* here that deserves to be called 'conventionalism about our identity over time'."

I respond that, even given Plasticity Theory, it is false that each of the competing ways of "carving things up" (or of describing the facts) is—setting aside our conventions—equally good. The best description is the most complete. And, if Plasticity Theory is true, the most complete description mentions *all* the candidates for being the person in question.

The best description is the most complete. More carefully, the metaphysically most complete is the best description if we want to know all about identity over time. But not everyone is primarily interested in the facts of identity over time. (And so not everyone is primarily interested in the central topic of this paper.) Some might be more interested in matters of practical concern. Given their interests—and the truth of Plasticity Theory—there may be not always be a single and wholly non-conventional best description of a case of personal identity. I want to elaborate on this point, starting with some comments about ship identity.

Theseus once owned a ship. After Theseus's death, a series of plank replacements resulted in a ship composed of none of the planks that composed Theseus's ship during his lifetime. Suppose it matters, for practical purposes, whether the resultant ship is identical with the one Theseus owned. (Imagine the heirs of Theseus are trying to take possession of the resultant ship, currently in someone else's hands.) Add to all this that the "best description from the metaphysical point of view" is that there are many ship-candidates here, some of which were owned by Theseus, some of which not.

The "best description from the metaphysical point of view" may not be the best from the "practical point of view." Some *other* description might be more useful—might be practically better—such as a description that somehow settles who has rights over the currently existing ship. Given the metaphysics we are here imagining, it seems fair to say that how this should be settled is *up to us*, is a matter of convention. Once it is settled—suppose we find in favor of the heirs—it might be fine to say that, for practical purposes, the resultant ship is Theseus's, but only as a matter of convention. And so it might make sense, for practical purposes, to treat ship identity over time as somewhat conventional. The Plasticity Theorist might insist that something similar is true of persons and personal identity. The Plasticity Theorist might claim that we should, for practical purposes, treat personal identity over time as somewhat conventional.

Now it is not *obvious* that the realist about personal identity over time can blithely accept this "practical conventionalism" about personal identity. Indeed, I claim that if each of us persists non-conventionally, then it is a mistake to treat our identity over time as conventional *even if only for practical purposes.* I realize that my claim here—which perhaps boils down to the assertion that "identity matters in survival"—is controversial. Of course, its denial is likewise controversial. And as a result it is, at the very least, not obvious that "practical conventionalism" is independent of its metaphysical cousin.

At any rate, the metaphysical and the practical theses I've been disentangling are sometimes conflated.[5] Some progress is made simply by clearly distinguishing one from the other. More progress comes with showing that Plasticity Theory fails to deliver metaphysical conventionalism. As far as metaphysics goes—as far as what entities exist and how they persist—Plasticity Theory delivers nothing like conventionalism. Quite the contrary. For, as I have argued, Plasticity Theory presupposes realism.

II. Persons as Conventional Constructs

Hume (1978, 261) famously compared persons to "commonwealths." At least that much of Hume's view of persons—and maybe more—is embraced by many conventionalists about personal identity over time. For one useful summary of a second, more common interpretation of conventionalism about personal identity is as follows: conventionalism about the identity over time of nations is true; persons are relevantly like nations; so conventionalism about personal identity over time is true.

Consider the question of whether the unified Germany of today is identical with the pre-partitioned Germany of 1948. Suppose that those who agree on all the other relevant facts are debating this question. It is plausible that their debate is really over how to speak, which conventions to adopt, or something analogous. And so—here is the conventionalism about identity—it is plausible that if all the relevant parties agreed to adopt conventions that sanctioned the identity, identity would hold; if they agreed to adopt conventions that precluded the identity, it would not.

All that is initially quite plausible. But it remains plausible only given some metaphysical assumptions. This point is illustrated by imagining (absurdly) that a nation persists just so long as its individual, unextended, substantial "nation soul" persists. If this were the case, conventionalism about national persistence and identity over time would imply that our conventions somehow sustain or snuff out a substance. This implication is implausible. So a plausible conventionalism about nations cannot be completely neutral on the metaphysics of nations.

Given this, it is not surprising that a particular metaphysical picture is generally wed to conventionalism about national identity over time. According to this picture, a nation is nothing "in addition to" or "over and above" the persons, territories, and so on that "constitute it." And, according to this picture, such things constitute a nation at least in part because of our conventions. According to this picture, nations are not independently existing entities *discovered* in the way that distant stars are. Rather our social, legal, and linguistic conventions *create* nations.

Let's sum up this view of nations as the claim that nations are "conventional constructs" of persons, territories, and so on. This claim raises a lot of questions, the most central and difficult of which is whether conventional constructs really exist. Rather than defend an answer to that question, I'll suggest two ways to understand the claim that nations are conventional constructs. The first of these "eliminates" nations, the second does not. Either understanding will allow me to proceed with the argument below. And I think everyone should find one, or the other, of these understandings an intelligible account of what it would mean for a nation to be a conventional construct.

One reading of the claim that nations are conventional constructs implies that there really are *no nations*, but rather only the relevant conventions and persons and territories (and so on). Now our eliminativist-cum-conventionalist will say that—properly understood—'Germany exists' is true. But, she will add, this is not true as a result of there being some thing, Germany. Rather, she maintains that this sentence is true only because certain territories and persons (and so on) exist and have certain features and are subject to certain conventions.[6] Similarly, she must say that 'Germany enjoys identity over time' is, if properly understood, true; but, properly understood, that claim does not imply the existence or persistence of Germany, but only the existence—at various times—of the relevant kinds of territories, persons, and conventions. Conventionalism about a nation's persistence, according to this sort of eliminativist, is more literally described as conventionalism about whatever it is that makes sentences like 'Germany enjoys identity over time' true.

Other partisans of the "conventional construct" view of nations will reject eliminativism about nations. Indeed, they might even argue that the eliminativism just noted makes no sense, insisting that if 'Germany exists' is true, then of course Germany exists (cf. Hirsch, 1993). Just disquote! At any rate, some who think nations are conventional constructs also think nations really exist. But, since they believe nations are conventional constructs, they also insist that the existence of nations *consists in* certain persons and territories (and so on) having certain features and, moreover, being involved in the right ways with the relevant conventions.

Both of these interpretations of nations as conventional constructs agree that the *deepest* facts about persisting nations are themselves facts about persons and territories and conventions. That is, both of these interpretations agree that facts about a nation's existence and identity over time *amount to* nothing other than facts about persons, territories, and conventions.

Obviously, given this view of nations, a change in persons or territories could lead to a change in whether a nation exists. Or, better, a change in persons or territories could be what a change in the existence of a nation *amounts to*. For the idea here is not that the change in persons or territories somehow *causes* the change in the existence of the nation. Again, the idea is not that there are two distinct events, one causing the other. Rather the idea is that certain changes in persons or territories *just are* the "corresponding" changes in the existence of the nation. There is nothing more to the second sort of change than the first. Similarly, if what the existence of a nation amounts to includes certain conventions, then a change in those conventions could be a "corresponding" change in whether that nation exists, that is, in whether it continues to exist. And this implies conventionalism about the identity over time of nations.

Such conventionalism about the identity of nations might seem quite plausible.[7] But it lends plausibility to conventionalism about personal identity only if persons are "conventional constructs." A person's existence would then amount to there being the appropriate conventions regarding the "raw material" out of which the person is "constructed." (Candidates for the "raw material" include, among other things, atoms and mental events.) If persons were conventional constructs, then—as in the case of nations—conventionalism about their identity over time would follow.

As we would expect, there are conventionalists about personal identity over time who claim that persons are conventional constructs. Mark Heller (1990, Ch. 4) defends a view of Manhattan along eliminativist conventional construct lines and then uses this to illustrate a similar view about human persons.[8] And Derek Parfit (1984 and 1995) seems to defend the non-eliminativist conventional construct view of nations and an analogous view of persons.

III. The Argument for Realism

During our discussion of Plasticity Theory, we learned that genuine conventionalism requires that facts about persistence or identity over time—as opposed to, say, facts about personhood—can depend on our conventions. But even the staunchest realist should acknowledge that one's enjoying identity over time can be beholden to certain conventions, as when conventions *cause* one to cease to persist. Realism allows, for example, that the conventions of the palace—in cooperation with the Queen's yelling "Off with his head!"—could cause my ceasing to exist, my failing to enjoy identity over time, my no longer persisting.

Conventionalism demands that there is an important, presumably *non-causal*, sense in which facts of identity over time depend of convention. Thus I tender that conventionalism requires that our identity over time somehow *amounts to*, among other things, the relevant conventions. This, in turn, requires that our very existence amounts to, among other things, the relevant conventions.

To see why I say this about existence, suppose that, for all persons and all times, neither a person P's existing at time t nor P's existing at time t* amounts to (among other things) our conventions. This implies that, for all persons and all times, whether P exists at both t and t*, a fact of personal identity over time, does not amount to our conventions. So if personal identity over time amounts to our conventions, then whether a particular person exists at a time likewise amounts to our conventions. I say that to exist at a time is to be such that, when that time is present, one exists *simpliciter* (Merricks, 1994, §IV). And so I conclude that one's existence at a time amounts to our conventions only if one's existence *simpliciter* amounts to our conventions.

To sum up thus far: conventionalism about personal identity requires that personal identity can, in some appropriate way, depend on our conventions; the appropriate dependency requires that personal identity somehow amounts to (among other things) those conventions; this in turn requires that our existence somehow amounts to those conventions. But, of course, to say that our existence amounts to (among other things) the relevant conventions just is to say that we are conventional constructs. And so we can see that conventionalism about our identity over time implies that we are conventional constructs. The view outlined in the last section of this paper is not just one way, among others, to get conventionalism about personal identity over time. It is the only way.

As an aside, note that we must exist before we can establish conventions. So the view that our existence amounts to (in part) our conventions seems to imply that we must exist before we exist. Thus the view that we are conventional constructs seems to be viciously circular. We could break out of this circle if the relevant thinkings and speakings—the ones that constitute the conventions in question—did not depend upon, but rather were "prior to," us thinkers and speakers. I don't think there can be such thinkings and speakings, but I have nothing new to add to that debate.[9] So, although I find the "vicious circularity" objection compelling, I shall defend a different argument against conventionalism. But first I'd like to emphasize that conventionalism commits one to some very controversial metaphysics, complete with persons constructed by (arguably independent) thinkings and speakings. This should give those conventionalists pause who (mistakenly) think a virtue of conventionalism is that it, unlike realism, liberates one from burdensome metaphysical commitments.

To return to the main line of argument, we have seen that conventionalism about personal identity over time implies that persons are conventional constructs. If we are conventional constructs, then the existence of a fully developed conscious human organism would *not* be sufficient for the existence of an entity like you or me, else there would be no work left for conventions to do in bringing that entity into existence by construction. But the existence of a fully developed conscious human organism *is* sufficient for the existence of an entity like you or me.[10] So it is false that we are conventional constructs. As a result, conventionalism, which implies that we are conventional constructs, is false; its denial, realism about personal identity over time, is true.

Note that this argument against conventionalism does not require that the existence of fully functioning human organisms is sufficient for entities like us *being persons*. Nor does it require you or me to be identical with any organism. Nor does it require that facts of our persistence are tied to the persistence of any organism (so the premises of the above argument are consistent with, for example, psychological continuity accounts of personal identity over time). The above argument requires only that the *existence* of a fully developed, conscious, and living human organism is sufficient for the *existence* of an entity like you and me.

One might wonder what exactly an "entity like you and me" is supposed to be. I won't suggest an answer here. For I don't want to beg the question by explicitly presupposing that we are not conventional constructs. Nor do I want to alienate needlessly those who might disagree with me about our nature. The above argument needs only the claim that the existence of a fully functioning conscious human organism is sufficient for the existence of one of us. And that argument is entitled to that claim, its silence on what sort of thing we are not-withstanding. For this claim should be a datum that guides us in any self-ascription of kind-membership, not a casualty of some contentious view about natural kinds and our place within them.

Let's consider some objections to my argument for realism.

Objection One: The conventionalist need not deny that the existence of a human person is entailed by the existence of a fully developed, fully function-ing human organism. Nor need she even deny that the persistence of such an organism, in everyday cases, is sufficient for the persistence of a human per-son. Conventionalism only commits one to the claim that biology under-determines facts of persistence in *some cases*—for example, brain transplant or half-brain transplant or teletransportation.

Response: Right. So this paper could not *start* with the argument above, the argument whose central thesis is that the existence of a fully functioning human organism is sufficient for the existence of a human person. For this the-sis does not directly or immediately or obviously imply the falsity of what many conventionalists say about personal identity over time.

But this thesis does—in a less direct, less immediate, and less obvious way—show that conventionalism is false. For it implies that human persons are not conventional constructs. And, I have argued, conventionalism about per-sonal identity over time implies that we are conventional constructs. Thus con-ventionalism about personal identity over time is false.

Objection Two: Someone who believes that we are conventional constructs will deny your crucial premise: the existence of a human organism is sufficient for the existence of one of us. Because your argument requires a premise that all your opponents will reject, it is uninteresting.

Response: My opponents are not only those explicitly committed to our being conventional constructs. For I am opposed to conventionalism about personal identity over time in all its forms. And some who endorse conven-tionalism—some who think that, for example, our identity over time is a matter of convention only in odd puzzle cases—will not be happy to deny my "crucial premise." Thus it is interesting that the "crucial premise" leads to realism about personal identity.

Perhaps my "crucial premise" will be denied by some initially committed, not just to conventionalism and the mere rejection of realism, but also to the view that persons are conventional constructs. Nevertheless, it is worth noting that the thesis that we are conventional constructs implies such a denial. For this shows that thesis to be less attractive than it might otherwise seem. It shows it to be less attractive than, for example, the claim that *nations* are conventional constructs, a claim that implies no similar denial.

Objection Three: The above argument presupposes that *if* the existence of a human organism is sufficient for the existence of a person, *then* the relevant conventions are not necessary for the existence of a person. But the existence of a human organism's being sufficient for a person's existence does not imply that nothing else (neither oxygen nor electrons nor conventions) is necessary. The above argument is therefore invalid.

Response: My point was not that if a human organism's existence is sufficient for a person's existence, then nothing else is necessary. Other things are necessary. But the existence of such "other things" must be entailed by the existence of the human organism. To see why I say this, suppose that it were possible for a human organism to exist although these "other things" fail to exist. Then it would be false that the existence of the human organism is sufficient for the existence of one of us and also that the "other things" are necessary.

Given this, we can see that my argument would be in trouble if, necessarily, there is a fully functioning human organism only if there are the conventions that construct human persons. But my argument is not in trouble. For the existence of those conventions is not entailed by the existence of a fully functioning human organism. After all, it is surely *possible* that a human organism exist for, say, exactly an hour and yet during that hour fail to be associated with the conventions that (allegedly) construct a person.

Objection to the Response to Objection Three: Maybe human organisms are conventional constructs. If so, then the existence of a human organism would entail the existence of the constructing conventions.

Response: Human organisms' being conventional constructs would threaten my argument only if, necessarily, the conventions that construct those organisms exist only if the conventions that construct human persons exist. Otherwise, the (allegedly) conventionally constructed organisms could possibly exist even if the conventions that (allegedly) construct persons did not. Moreover, if the conventionalist insists that human organisms are conventional constructs, she should—by parity of reason—say the same about their near relatives and evolutionary forbears. But it is hard to see how this could be, since many of these organisms predated the existence of the relevant conventions. (I assume that even if the conventions that construct human persons are *somehow* prior to human persons, they are not *temporally* prior to, did not exist before, the first human organism.)

IV. Conclusion

Conventionalism about personal identity over time implies that persons are conventional constructs. This latter claim comes at one or another high price.

One price involves denying that the existence of a fully functioning conscious human organism is sufficient for—or is a supervenience base for—the existence of one of us. This price seems, at least to me, too high. And it will seem too high for some who would otherwise be inclined to endorse conventionalism about personal identity over time. So, for example, I suspect it will be too high for those who follow Johnston in holding that "human persons are in their natural condition constituted by living human bodies." Moreover, consider conventionalists like Parfit who focus on puzzle cases, never hinting that the existence of a fully functioning human organism in ordinary circumstances fails to secure the existence of one of us. I suppose they too will find the price too steep.

A second way to pay for the claim that we are conventional constructs is to endorse the following. Human organisms are conventional constructs.[11] Our conventions construct some non-human organisms that predated those same conventions. And the existence of the conventions that construct human organisms (but not the existence of those constructing non-human organisms) entails the existence of the conventions that construct human persons. Again, this price seems, at least to me, too high. (Indeed, I would say that such an ontological picture is absolutely incredible.) And again, it will seem too high even to some who might otherwise incline toward conventionalism. For example, consider conventionalists who, like Nozick, are motivated by the belief that something special about persons—but not, I presume, organisms—makes their identity over time a matter of convention.

Conventionalism about personal identity over time has one of the two prices just noted. I say that both prices are prohibitively exorbitant. And so I conclude that conventionalism is false and realism about personal identity over time true.

Even someone who, in spite of the arguments above, embraces conventionalism ought to concede that her position has been shown to be less attractive than it might otherwise seem. To see why I say this, reconsider a claim that conventionalists about personal identity over time will be quick to endorse: conventionalism about the identity over time of nations (or clubs or universities or sports teams) is plausible. Now conventionalism about such entities implies that they are conventional constructs. But this implication about nations (and the rest) does not come at great cost. For nothing like my central argument in terms of human organisms can be run against the thesis that nations are conventional constructs. The existence of nations does not seem to be entailed by the existence of things—such as fully functioning human organisms—whose existence is plausibly independent of the conventions that allegedly construct nations.

So my argument against our being conventional constructs does not tell against the claim that nations are conventional constructs. And we should have expected the claim that we are conventional constructs to be more problematic than a similar claim about nations. For nations are not the source of the conventions that construct them. (That is why the charge of "vicious circularity" applied to nations cannot even get off the ground.)[12] We are the source. If nations exist, it is because we create them by, among other things, our conventions. Thus we should not be surprised to find that it is far more costly—and so far less plausible—to maintain that we are convention's product than to maintain this of our creations. Persons are not remotely like commonwealths.

Notes

*Thanks to Anthony Ellis, Brie Gertler, Eli Hirsch, E.J. Lowe, Andrew Mills, Eugene Mills, Mark C. Murphy, Eric Olson, Michael C. Rea, Theodore Sider, Leopold Stubenberg, and Peter Vallentyne. I presented distant ancestors of this paper at Western Washington University (1996) and El Tercer Coloquio Internacional Bariloche de Filosofía in Bariloche, Argentina (1996). I presented more recent versions at Mighty [sic] Midwestern Metaphysical Mayhem [sic] III at the University of Notre Dame (1998), the College of William and Mary (1998), and the Central Division Meeting of the APA (1999).

1. For references to conventionalists other than those noted here, see Olson, 1997, 142

2. Three worries about Johnston's view that I won't pursue: (1) Johnston analyzes *being the same person as* in terms of self-concern. But I say that the correct analysis—given the thesis that persons endure—is instead wholly in terms of the *identity* relation holding between a person and a person (see my 1999 and 2000). (2) Johnston's analysis implies that Parfit's claim that personal identity is not "what matters" is outright contradictory and so false. But below I suggest that Plasticity Theory might deliver something like conventionalism only if it is read as delivering "conventionalism about what is of practical importance." And so, as will be clear below, I think Johnston's best shot at providing something like conventionalism requires Parfit's claim to be true. (3) Johnston's view, like all forms of Plasticity Theory, implies that now sitting in my chair, now wearing my shirt, are myriad beings that all think and act just like I do. But—I would insist—there is just once such being.

3. This point applies even to versions of Plasticity Theory according to which the identity over time of the *candidates* is a matter of convention. For candidate C's persisting conventionally, according to Plasticity Theory, would turn on the imprecision of 'candidate C'. But no matter how many levels "down" this kind of linguistic imprecision occurs, the number of persisters in the world remains the same. When it comes to the persisters themselves, Plasticity Theory does not imply that they persist conventionally. Indeed, it seems to presuppose just the opposite.

4. Similarly, if one insisted that to be a person just is to have certain persistence conditions, then conventionalism about being a person would lead to conventionalism about personal identity over time. But if conventionalism about our persistence is linked in this way to conventionalism about personhood, my arguments against conventionalism about our persistence are arguments against conventionalism about personhood. Besides, there are independent reasons to reject an analysis of *being a person* in terms of persistence conditions; see my 1998, §IV.

5. Sometimes they are conflated. But not everyone who resists my "disentangling" is guilty of failing to note a distinction. Johnston, for example, doesn't conflate the theses in question; rather, he argues that personal identity should be analyzed in

broadly "practical" terms, in terms of self-concern. In this section, of course, I have claimed that his argument fails.

6. For comparison, consider the eliminativist about holes who thinks 'there is a hole in my sock' is true since it means only that my sock has a perforated shape (see Lewis and Lewis, 1970). Or consider van Inwagen's view according to which there are no chairs, yet 'chairs exist' ordinarily comes out true since it ordinarily means only that there are simples "arranged chairwise" (1990, §10).

7. It seems plausible. But I think it is mistaken. For I think something is wrong with the claim that nations persist conventionally because they are conventional constructs. Let me note, but not pursue, a potential problem with each of the interpretations of what it is for a nation to be a conventional construct and thereby to persist conventionally.

   The non-eliminativist interpretation trades heavily on the relation of *consisting in*. But it is unclear what, exactly, that relation is supposed to be. Admittedly, I characterize the claim that nations are conventional constructs in terms of what their existence "amounts to," which is no clearer than "consisting in." But this is no objection to my characterization, since—so I say here—the view I'm trying to characterize is itself unclear, at least when spelled out in terms of "consisting in."

   If, as the eliminativist interpretation would have it, nations do not really exist, then nations do not persist and, *a fortiori*, do not persist, in part, as a matter of convention. For this reason, I say that one cannot secure conventionalism about a nation's identity over time by eliminating nations. (This objection seems right to me even if certain sentences that *appear* to say a nation exists and persists turn out to be true.) This is not to deny that 'Germany exists'—even if it is just plain false— has a lot more going for it than does 'Avalon exists'. Indeed, I eliminate nations but also think that there is *practical* benefit to speaking and acting as if nations exist and persist and do so in a conventional manner (see my 2001, Ch. 7).

8. See Olson, 1997, §V for more discussion of this method of securing conventionalism about personal identity over time.

9. For familiar arguments against the claim that thinkings and speakings are prior to thinkers and speakers, see Strawson, 1959, Ch. 3; Shoemaker, 1997, 139; Lowe, 1989; and Lowe, 1996, 25ff. Some conventionalists (e.g., Parfit, 1984, 223, 251, and 341) embrace independent thinkings and speakings in spite of those arguments.

10. Even the substance dualist should grant this, since I suppose she'll think there could be a *conscious* human organism only if there is a soul. But if she objects, we can run essentially the same argument on her terms. Suppose substance dualism is true. The existence of a conscious soul would be sufficient for the existence of a person, leaving no work for conventions to do in constructing a person. Thus persons are not conventional constructs.

11. And—given the "solution" to the circularity problem noted above—conventionalism about personal identity over time seems to imply that organisms are constructed out of *independently existing* thinkings and speakings. Perhaps the view that organisms are conventional constructs might be amenable to one who is an anti-realist of a fairly general sort. But that view cannot be absorbed into some sort of universal anti-realism. For it cannot be that each speaking and thinking depends for its existence on *other* speakings and thinkings, or else we face again the sort of circularity that independent speakings and thinkings were introduced to break out of.

12. The conventions that give rise to the existence of nations might make use of the *concept* of a nation (see Searle, 1995, 52–54). But there is no problem with the concept of a nation being prior to both the conventions that invoke it and also the nation that results from those conventions.

References

Chisholm, Roderick (1976) *Person and Object*, La Salle, IL: Open Court Publishing Company.

Heller, Mark (1990) *The Ontology of Physical Objects*, Cambridge: Cambridge University Press.

Hirsch, Eli (1993) "Peter van Inwagen's *Material Beings*," *Philosophy and Phenomenological Research* 53: 687–691.

Hume, David (1978) *A Treatise of Human Nature* (eds.) L.A. Selby-Bigge and P.H. Nidditch, Oxford: Clarendon Press.

Johnston, Mark (1989) "Relativism and the Self" in M. Krausz (ed.) *Relativism: Interpretation and Confrontation*, Notre Dame, IN: University of Notre Dame Press.

Lewis, David and Lewis, Stephanie (1970) "Holes," *Australasian Journal of Philosophy* 48: 206–12.

Lowe, E.J. (1989) *Kinds of Being*, Oxford: Blackwell Publishers.

Lowe, E.J. (1996) *Subjects of Experience*, Cambridge: Cambridge University Press.

Merricks, Trenton (1994) "Endurance and Indiscernibility," *Journal of Philosophy* 91: 165–184.

Merricks, Trenton (1998) "There Are No Criteria of Identity Over Time," *Noûs* 32: 106–124.

Merricks, Trenton (1999) "Endurance, Psychological Continuity, and the Importance of Personal Identity," *Philosophy and Phenomenological Research* 59: 983–997.

Merricks, Trenton (2000) "Perdurance and Psychological Continuity," *Philosophy and Phenomenological Research* 61: 195–198.

Merricks, Trenton (2001) *Objects and Persons*, Oxford: Clarendon Press.

Nozick, Robert (1981) *Philosophical Explanations*, Cambridge, MA: Harvard University Press.

Olson, Eric (1997) "Relativism and Persistence," *Philosophical Studies* 88: 141–162.

Parfit, Derek (1984) *Reasons and Persons*, Oxford: Clarendon Press.

Parfit, Derek (1995) "The Unimportance of Identity" in Henry Harris (ed.) *Identity*, Oxford: Clarendon Press.

Searle, John (1995) *The Construction of Social Reality*, New York: The Free Press.

Shoemaker, Sydney (1997) "Parfit on Identity" in Jonathan Dancy (ed.) *Reading Parfit*, Oxford: Blackwell Publishers.

Strawson, P.F. (1959) *Individuals*, London: Methuen & Co.

Unger, Peter (1990) *Identity, Consciousness, and Value*, Oxford: Oxford University Press.

Van Inwagen, Peter (1990) *Material Beings*, Ithaca, NY: Cornell University Press.

Philosophical Perspectives, 15, Metaphysics, 2001

CRITERIA OF PERSONAL IDENTITY AND THE LIMITS OF CONCEPTUAL ANALYSIS

Theodore Sider
Syracuse University

It is easy to become battle-weary in metaphysics. In the face of seemingly unresolvable disputes and unanswerable questions, it is tempting to cast aside one's sword, proclaiming: "there is no fact of the matter who is right!"

Sometimes that is the right thing to do. As a case study, consider the search for the criterion of personal identity over time. I say there is no fact of the matter whether the correct criterion is bodily or psychological continuity.[1] There exist two candidate meanings for talk of persisting persons, one corresponding to each criterion, and there is simply no fact of the matter which candidate we mean.

An argument schema for this sort of "no fact of the matter" thesis will be constructed. An instance of the schema will be defended in the case of personal identity. But scrutiny of this instance will reveal limits of the schema. Questions not settled by conceptual analysis—in particular, some very difficult questions of fundamental ontology—have answers. So do certain questions that can be settled by conceptual analysis, namely those that would be answered definitively by ideal philosophical inquiry. Whether there is a fact of the matter is not easily ascertained merely by looking to see whether disputes seem unresolvable or questions unanswerable: sometimes the truth *is* out there, however hard (or even impossible) it may be to discover.

1. A Schematic Argument

Consider any metaphysical dispute involving a certain term, T. If the following argument is sound, there is no fact of the matter who is right about T:

1. There exist multiple candidate meanings for T, corresponding to the conflicting theories about T
2. None of these T-candidates fits *use* better than the rest
3. None of these T-candidates is more *eligible* than the rest

4. No other T-candidate combines eligibility and fit with use as well as these T-candidates
5. Meaning is determined by use plus eligibility

6. *Therefore*, T is indeterminate[2] in meaning among T-candidates corresponding to the conflicting theories of T, and so there is no fact of the matter which of these theories is correct.

Let us examine this argument, beginning with premise 5.

2. Meaning, Use, and Eligibility

One lesson from the aftermath of Hilary Putnam's (1981, chapter 2; 1980; 1978, part IV) model-theoretic argument against realism is that meaning is not determined solely by our linguistic or convention-determining behavior. Facts about candidate meanings and our relation to them also play a role. Linguistic/conventional activity alone does not suffice for the semantic determinacy we take there to be, since even for words we take to have determinate meaning, multiple candidate meanings exist that equally fit our meaning-determining behavior.

Here is Putnam's argument. Viewed as a whole, our meaning-determining activity can be viewed as a theory we have: a certain set of sentences. If the theory is consistent it will have many models whose domains consist of objects in the world. Each of these models provides an assignment of semantic values to the predicates and names of the theory *relative* to which the theory turns out true. But surely the existence of these models is not sufficient to make the theory true *simpliciter*, since all that has been assumed about the theory is that it is consistent. One wants to say that many of these models are *unintended*, namely those that assign semantic values to predicates and names contrary to their intended meanings. The theory should turn out true only if it is true in its intended model. But Putnam argues that a "metaphysical realist" is not in a position to rule out some models as unintended. The metaphysical realist cannot rule out unintended models by adopting new conventions about what words are to mean, for this merely adds more sentences to the theory. The theory will still (if it remains consistent) have multiple models, and the problem of saying what makes one of them the intended model remains.

The best response to Putnam, I think, is to say that when multiple candidates equally fit our meaning-determining behavior, meaning may yet be determinate if one candidate is, somehow, more *eligible* to serve as a meaning. One version of this response appeals to a causal theory of meaning: the winning candidate is that one that is causally related (in the right way) to language users.[3] Another version appeals instead to natural kinds—"joints in nature". The winning candidate is the natural kind, or the most natural kind, that fits our meaning-determining behavior.[4] Either way, the determination of meaning is not accomplished solely by us. Meaning is jointly determined by our meaning-determining behavior and facts external to us, whether causal relations between us and meanings or the intrinsic features of the meanings themselves. For short, *meaning is determined by use plus eligibility*.

I will assume the natural kinds response to Putnam (though much of what follows could be recast in terms of the causal response), and accordingly interpret 'eligibility' as naturalness. Moreover, following David Lewis (1983, 1984), I will assume that both fit-with-use and eligibility come in degrees, and that the meaning of a term, T, is that candidate meaning that achieves the best combination of fit with use and eligibility.[5] Let the slogan "meaning is determined by use plus eligibility" be thus understood.

I use the term 'meaning' for that which is jointly determined by use and eligibility. Determining the exact nature of meaning is a task for philosophy of language; all I assume here is that meaning determines truth conditions, both in our world and in counterfactual worlds considered for the purpose of evaluating modal claims. (Meanings are therefore richer than Fregean referents.) A different way of thinking about "meaning" would associate it more closely with use, rather than the joint product of use and eligibility. For this other way of thinking about meaning I use the term 'concept' instead. Twin-Earthians have the same concept of water as do we, though their term 'water' has a different meaning. Thus meanings can differ when concepts do not. (Meanings are therefore not Fregean senses either.) Likewise, concepts can differ when meanings do not. Compare our community, which is enlightened as to the difference between gold and fool's gold, with another community that is not. It is plausible that even though the *use* of the term 'gold' in the unenlightened community fits fool's gold, nevertheless their term 'gold' does not apply to fool's gold. For there is a highly eligible meaning—namely, *gold*—that fits *most* of their use very well, and which does not apply to fool's gold. (That their term 'gold' means *gold* rather than *gold-or-fool's-gold*, or *yellow metal*, is particularly plausible if they encounter fool's gold only very rarely.) Thus these communities share a meaning while differing over its concept.

3. Multiple Candidates

This claim that meaning is determined by use plus eligibility is the fulcrum of the schematic argument of section 1. The meaning of a term, T, is the *candidate meaning* for T that achieves the best balance of eligibility and fit with use. This notion of a candidate meaning appears in premise 1 of the schematic argument: "there exist multiple *candidate meanings* for T, corresponding to the conflicting theories of T". Just what are these "candidate meanings", and what reasons could one have for thinking they exist?

For the sake of concreteness let us focus on our case study: criteria of personal identity. Whether multiple candidate meanings for talk of personal identity exist, and what they are like, depend on what the correct ontology of persistence turns out to be.[6] In what follows I will examine the bearing of several ontologies of persistence on the status of these multiple candidate meanings.

Consider, first, the *worm theory*. Worm theorists identify continuants with aggregates of temporal parts: "space-time worms", which persist through time by "perduring", that is, having temporal parts at different moments. Worm theorists tend to agree with Quine (1976 p. 497) that any filled region of spacetime is occupied by some physical object.[7] Thus, for nearly any criterion of personal identity you like, there exist space-time worms that obey that criterion. There are aggregates of person-stages that are psychologically continuous but not necessarily bodily continuous—the "psychological-persons". But there are also "body-persons": aggregates of bodily continuous but not necessarily psychologically continuous stages. For that matter, there are aggregates of just those stages that are bodily continuous if in North America but psychologically continuous if in some other continent. The debate over criteria of personal identity, for a worm theorist, concerns which of these aggregates we refer to in our talk of persons.

If the worm theory is true, the schematic argument of section 1 for the no-fact-of-the-matter thesis, as applied to the case of personal identity, can be summarized as follows. The disputed term in this debate is the predicate 'person'; the candidate meanings are the properties *being a perduring body-person* and *being a perduring psychological-person*. Since psychological-persons and body-persons both exist, the only question is which of these candidates we mean by 'person'. The winning candidate, in turn, is determined by fit with use and eligibility. So if psychological-persons and body-persons are equally eligible and fit use equally well, then there is no fact of the matter whether our talk of persisting persons is talk about psychological-persons or body-persons, and thus there is no fact of the matter whether the criterion of personal identity is psychological or bodily continuity. The claim that psychological-persons and body-persons are indeed equally eligible and fit use equally well will be argued below; all that is being defended here is that these multiple candidate meanings exist, if the worm theory is true.

There are ontologies of persistence other than the worm theory that support multiple candidates and thus premise 1 of the no-fact-of-the-matter argument. The worm theory is one version of the more general doctrine of temporal parts. I myself defend a different version, according to which persons (and other continuants) are instantaneous stages, not space-time worms (1996; forthcoming, chapter 5). I and the worm theorists accept the same basic ontology—temporal parts and their aggregates—but differ over whether we typically refer to and quantify over temporal parts or aggregates of temporal parts. If typical references to persons are to instantaneous stages, a tensed assertion about what a person did in the past or will do in the future cannot be taken to concern the doings of that person herself in the past or future; otherwise all ordinary statements about our pasts and futures would turn out false. Accordingly, I offer a *temporal counterpart theory* of tensed assertions. To say that I *was* once four feet tall is to say that I have a temporal counterpart in the past that is four feet tall; to say that I *will* have grey hair is to say that I have a grey-haired temporal counterpart in the future. Compare: according to David Lewis's (1968) *modal counterpart theory*, to say that Humphrey *might have* won the election is to say that Humphrey has a (modal) counterpart in another possible world who wins the election.

A temporal counterpart of a person (stage) is another person (stage) to which she is appropriately related. The question of the nature of this counterpart relation is precisely the question of the correct criterion of personal identity. Someone who believes the psychological continuity theory will say that the counterparts of a person stage, *S*, are those stages with which *S* is psychologically continuous; the bodily continuity theorist will say instead that *S*'s counterparts are stages with which *S* is bodily-continuous. The question of who is right is the question of which temporal counterpart relation takes part in the correct truth conditions for the claims about persisting persons we make in ordinary speech.

These counterpart relations are the multiple candidates for the meaning of talk of persisting persons required by the no-fact-of-the-matter argument. One counterpart relation stresses psychological continuity, another bodily continuity; other relations mix these and other factors in countless ways. Just as the worm theorist is a pluralist about spacetime worms, I am a pluralist about counterpart relations between person stages. (Note that for counterpart theory, the multiple candidates are candidate semantic values of tense operators when applied to sentences involving persons, whereas for the worm theorist the candidates are candidate semantic values of the predicate 'person'.)

These first two ontologies of persistence that support multiple candidates have presupposed temporal parts; others do not. Those who reject temporal parts say that continuants "endure", or are "wholly present" whenever they exist. Many friends of endurance think that there are often two things in the same place at the same time—statues and lumps of clay, for example. A clay statue and the lump of clay from which it is made are said to be numerically distinct because they have different persistence conditions: the lump but not the statue is capable of surviving being squashed. The statue and lump can "fit" into a single location in space because they are, at the time, made up of the same matter. The statue and the lump are often said to be "coincident" entities. Now imagine taking this view to an extreme, and postulating in the vicinity of every person a plurality of coincident entities, which share the same momentary properties but differ in their persistence conditions. In my vicinity there is a psychological-person, a body-person, and perhaps other entities corresponding to other criteria of personal identity. Given this "promiscuous" endurance theory, we have multiple candidate meanings for the predicate 'person', much as we did in the case of the worm theory. Whether the bodily continuity theory or the psychological continuity theory is true depends on which candidate is the meaning of the predicate 'person': *being an enduring psychological-person* or *being an enduring body-person*.[8]

Yet another ontology of persistence consistent with the multiple candidates picture is the view that the world consists exclusively of enduring mereological simples—i.e., things with no temporal or spatial parts. Following Peter van Inwagen (1990, chapter 8), call this view *nihilism* (van Inwagen himself does not accept nihilism). According to nihilism, there are, strictly speaking, no composite objects at all, and therefore no persons. Ordinary talk of persons must be interpreted as plural talk of microscopic objects. Though it is strictly speaking false that a person walks, this at least loosely speaking correct, for it is strictly true that a number of microscopic particles stand in a certain multigrade relation we might call the person-walking relation (1990, chapters 10–11). Though the nihilist dispenses with macroscopic objects, many of the traditional questions about macroscopic objects survive, albeit transformed. The question of the criterion of personal identity becomes the question of what multigrade relations particles must stand in, over time, in order for it to be loosely speaking correct to speak of a persisting person. But here again we have multiple candidates, only now they are candidates for being meant by talk of persisting persons understood loosely, not strictly. Two of these candidates are a multigrade relation involving psychological continuity and a multigrade relation involving bodily continuity.

A final ontology of persistence supplying the requisite candidates is mereological essentialism.[9] The mereological essentialist holds that nothing ever gains or loses a part; continuants are mereologically constant over time. Like the nihilist, the mereological essentialist defends an ontology very different from that of ordinary speech and thought. Therefore it is natural for the mereological essentialist to follow the nihilist in paraphrasing ordinary talk about persistence in some way that allows ordinary talk of survival through mereological change to be at least loosely speaking true.[10] The mereological essentialist might say, for example, that a person, P_1, loosely-speaking survives a change of parts iff some person P_2 after the change (not necessarily P_1) bears a suitable relation to P_1. But there are many candidates for what this suitable relation might be; it might involve bodily continuity, psychological continuity, or something else.[11]

Each of these views admits the existence of many "candidates" for being the meaning of talk of persisting persons. Each admits a candidate corresponding to the psychological criterion and a candidate corresponding to the bodily criterion. What sort of theory of persistence would *not* allow multiple candidates? Call the following conjunction of theses "chaste endurantism": i) persons exist, ii) persons have no temporal parts, iii) in uncontroversial cases the (strict and literal) persistence conditions for persons are basically what we ordinarily take them to be, and iv) *distinct entities never coincide* ("one thing to a place at a time"). If chaste endurantism is correct, there seems to be one and only one candidate meaning for talk of persisting persons: a meaning that concerns, with respect to any person, the one and only one enduring object in the vicinity of that person.[12] The ability of the chaste endurantist to reject the "no fact of the matter" view will be discussed below.

I have argued that the truth of premise 1—the claim that there exist multiple candidates—depends on what the true ontology of persistence turns out to be. But it may be objected that candidate meanings are abstract objects whose existence does not depend on the nature of persisting objects. For example, even if there are no such *things* as perduring body-persons and perduring psychological-persons, it may be held that there nevertheless exist such *properties* as *being a perduring body-person* and *being a perduring psychological-person*. Perhaps so; but if there are no perduring body-persons or psychological-persons then these properties will be extremely weak candidates to be meant by talk of persisting persons, for they will have a very poor fit with use. Interpreted in terms of these candidates, nearly all ordinary talk about persons would turn out false. Thus, let the quantifier over "candidates" in premise 1 be restricted to those whose candidacy is reasonably strong—those that have some reasonably high degree of eligibility and fit with use.

4. Inconstant Talk of Persisting Persons

The schematic argument of §1, applied to the case of personal identity, is this:

1. There exist candidate meanings for talk of persisting persons, corresponding to the psychological and bodily continuity theories
2. Neither candidate fits *use* better than the other
3. Neither candidate is more *eligible* than the other
4. No other candidate to be meant by talk of persisting persons combines eligibility and fit with use as well as these candidates
5. Meaning is determined by use plus eligibility

6. *Therefore*, talk of persisting persons is indeterminate in meaning between candidates corresponding to the psychological and bodily continuity theories, and so there is no fact of the matter which of these theories is correct.

The theory of meaning-determination underlying premise 5 was explained in section 2, and a number of metaphysical theories of persistence (including the theory I myself accept) that vindicate premise 1 were introduced in section 3. I turn now to the defense of premise 2. I claim, or at any rate conjecture, that neither bodily continuity nor psychological continuity fits our talk of persons better than the other.[13]

Our use of persistence-talk concerns both actual and counterfactual circumstances. In most actual circumstances the bodily and psychological criteria do not come apart. How we speak in these core circumstances does not favor one candidate over the other. The criteria do come apart in certain extraordinary actual circumstances, but here our talk of persistence is equivocal. When someone dies, we say things like "Grandpa is gone"; but we also say "There's Grandpa, there in the casket".[14] The first corresponds to the psychological criterion of personal identity, the latter to the bodily criterion. Phenomenologically, I detect something like a shift in my thinking when I talk these two ways. When pressed to say which way of speaking is literally correct, non-philosophers typically resist making a choice. They tend to say that in a sense it is Grandpa in the casket, and in a sense it isn't.

Something like the same shift occurs in our talk about cases of amnesia, and perhaps even in cases of extreme personal transformation due to mental illness or radical religious conversion. We say things like: "Jack just isn't the same person he used to be, now that he's been brainwashed by that cult." The less severe the transformation, the more inclined one is to give the standard philosopher's line about these sayings, namely that 'same' here expresses similarity and not numerical identity. One can get undergraduates to retract the sayings by bullying them: "you mean, Jack *never* was a young unbrainwashed boy?" But perhaps the effect of the bullying is just to get the undergraduates to shift to a bodily conception of persons. A strong assertion by a conversational partner, especially one in a position of power, creates pressure for the hearer to shift to a conversational context in which that assertion is true; shifting to an alternate meaning of a semantically indeterminate expression is one way to shift conversational context.[15] There may not be a sharp dividing line between literal talk of personal identity and talk of similarity, but in the more severe cases of psychological transformation a case can be made that it does little violence to ordinary usage to speak of a numerically new person. But neither does it do violence to speak of a person persisting in these cases.

Thus, usage in actual cases of death, amnesia and radical psychological transformation does not support either candidate over the other. Counterfactual cases in which the criteria diverge, for example Locke's (1975, p. 44) cobbler who gets the memories of a prince, are familiar. Philosophers typically appeal to these cases to argue for one or the other criterion. I do not advance any *general* objection to using imaginary cases to investigate meaning, for our dispositions to react to imaginary cases form an important part of what I have been calling "use"—the meaning-determining portion of our linguistic behavior. However, I think our reactions to these cases in the case of criteria of personal identity do not favor either the bodily theory or the psychological theory. Like our descriptions of dead people and amnesiacs, our reactions to imaginary cases are equivocal.

Nowhere is this clearer than in Bernard Williams's classic paper "The Self and the Future". Williams describes an example in which persons A and B take part in an experiment in which A's memories are transferred to B's body, and then A's body is tortured. Williams notes that we have powerful intuitions that appear to favor the psychological view. We imagine waking up in B's body, looking at A's body, and thinking "how lucky I was to be swapped to this body!". But Williams also points out that there is a powerful opposing intuition (1975, pp. 185–186):

> Someone in whose power I am tells me that I am going to be tortured tomorrow. I am frightened, and look forward to tomorrow in great apprehension. He adds that when the time comes, I shall not remember being told that this was going to happen to me, since shortly before the torture something else will be done to me which will make me forget the announcement. This certainly will not cheer me up ... He then adds that...when the moment of torture comes, I shall not remember any of the things I am now in a position to remember. This does not cheer me up either ... He now further adds that at the moment of torture I shall not only not remember the things I am now in a position to remember, but will have a different set of impressions of my past, quite different from the memories I have now. I do not think that this would cheer me up either ... Nor do I see why I should be put into any better frame of mind by the person in charge adding lastly that the impressions of my past with which I shall be equipped on the eve of torture will exactly fit the past of another person now living ... Fear, surely, would still be the proper reaction: and not because one did not know what was going to happen, but because in one vital respect at least one did know what was going to happen—torture, which one can indeed expect to happen to oneself, and to be preceded by certain mental derangements as well.

It appears that we are capable of having either of two intuitions about the case, one predicted by the psychological theory, the other by the bodily continuity theory. A natural explanation is that ordinary thought contains two concepts of persisting persons, each responsible for a separate set of intuitions, neither of which is *our* canonical conception to the exclusion of the other.[16]

The nature of our equivocation here is worth exploring a little more. First of all, we have inconstant intuitions about *personal identity*. Secondly, we have inconstant intuitions about certain *rational and psychological attitudes*. Imagine being in the shoes of A before the experiment. One can imagine feeling *relief*, and not *fear*, when contemplating the upcoming torture of A's body, since one knows that one's psychology will be transferred to a new body before the torture occurs. On the other hand, Williams convincingly argues that A might well fear the upcoming pain to his body, and *not* be comforted at all by the knowledge of the mental transfer that will precede the torture. Which of these apparently incompatible attitudes one has seems to depend on the way the case is described; there seems to be a shift in our thought about fear corresponding to the shift in our thought about personal identity. Insofar as fear of future pain is intimately connected with personal identity, this is further support that use does not favor either candidate over the other.[17]

I should say that although I claim that use does not favor either the psychological or the bodily continuity theory, I make this claim only tentatively.

Perhaps new thought experiments will be devised that tell decisively in favor of one theory or the other. Or perhaps new theoretical distinctions will be made that will make clear that some of the intuitions in question were confused, or mislabeled. (Recall the effect of Saul Kripke's (1972) distinction between epistemic and metaphysical possibility on intuitions about the necessity of identity.) I doubt these things will occur, but it is impossible to know in advance what future philosophical investigation will reveal (more on this below).

5. Eligibility of Psychological and Bodily Continuity

I have argued that, assuming any one of a number of metaphysical theories of persistence, there exist candidate meanings for talk of personal identity based on bodily and psychological continuity (premise 1); and I have argued that neither candidate fits our use of personal identity talk better than the other (premise 2). The argument for the no-fact-of-the-matter thesis requires, in addition, the truth of its premise 3: neither candidate is more *eligible* than the other. Eligibility I understand as naturalness: a candidate meaning is eligible insofar as it "carves nature at the joints".

Given that bodily and psychological candidates both exist, what reason could there be for thinking one to be more natural than the other? We may distinguish two potential reasons, one more radical than the other. The radical reason would be given by someone willing to claim that one candidate is a *perfectly* natural kind, whose naturalness is not explicable in microphysical terms. On this view, seeking the correct criterion of personal identity is a bit like seeking the correct physical theory. Metaphorically, the reason we can expect the question of personal identity to have a determinate answer is that the truth is "out there" in the same sense that it is in physics. This goes against a kind of physicalism: that there are no perfectly natural classifications of objects beyond those studied in physics (in the actual world, at any rate). This physicalism is justified by the past success of physics in accounting for everything else. It is hard to give a definition of just what counts as physics, but on no legitimate definition would high-level kinds corresponding to psychological or bodily continuity count as part of physics.

Might both of the candidates be less than perfectly natural, and yet one be more natural than the other? I would argue that relative naturalness results from one property or relation having a more "complicated" or "disjunctive" basis in the perfectly natural physical properties.[18] (Think of the relative naturalness of *blue* and *grue*, for example.) Given this measure of relative naturalness, surely bodily-continuity and psychological-continuity candidates are on the "same level" of naturalness. Denying this would be like saying that Victorian houses comprise a more natural kind than Tudors.

But perhaps the candidates only appear to have equally complicated bases in the perfectly natural properties because of our inadequate understanding of their nature. Perhaps future philosophical inquiry into the bodily and psychological continuity theories will reveal one to be plagued with internal difficulty. Or perhaps new imaginary cases will be discovered, our reactions to which may be seamlessly incorporated into one theory but which require complicated adjustments to the other. Perhaps a new distinction will show that what we thought were intuitions about a single relatively natural kind were actually intuitions about multiple kinds, the disjunction of which is quite unnatural. In any of these cases, one of the theories would turn out to have a more complicated basis in the natural properties than the other. This is the less radical reason one might give for thinking one candidate more natural than the other.

In essence, the challenge is that philosophical reflection in the ideal limit might favor one of the candidates. For the very theoretical grounds philosophers use to *decide* which theory to believe—simplicity, comprehensiveness and the like—are *constitutive* of which theory provides a candidate that has a more natural basis in the perfectly natural properties and relations. Thus, whether the less radical challenge to premise 3 succeeds depends on the outcome of the debate over criteria of personal identity. I am (tentatively) inclined to doubt that futuristic philosophy will definitely resolve this debate. The fundamental puzzle cases and the supporting intuitions for the competing sides have not changed in hundreds of years. While there has been *refinement* of the competing criteria, there seems to have been no major change in how they are to be understood. We seem to have a genuine impasse.

I do not say that *all* debates involving personal identity are at an impasse. Whether persons have temporal parts, for example, seems an open question. Debate over what to say about cases of fission, fusion, and the like rages on. And the past twenty years has seen much discussion of the role of causation in criteria of personal identity. But both psychological and bodily continuity theories may incorporate a causal element, may be stated with or without temporal parts, and may be augmented with the same bells and whistles to handle fission and fusion. It is only the debate over whether the criterion of personal identity is psychological or bodily continuity that I claim is at an impasse. Even this may be overstating the case, given the important recent work on the subject, even in the past five years.[19] Still, it is interesting to follow out the consequences of the hypothesis that philosophical debate in the ideal limit remains indecisive.

6. A Third Candidate?

Even if candidates corresponding to bodily continuity and psychological continuity are equally eligible and fit use equally well, there would be no indeterminacy in talk of personal identity if some third candidate better combined eligibility and fit with use. Premise 4 denies the existence of such a third candidate. What might such a candidate look like?

One possibility would be a candidate according to which persons are identical iff they are *either* psychologically *or* bodily continuous. But this candidate is slightly less eligible than either pure criterion, given its disjunctive nature. Moreover, it seems to fit use less well than the pure criteria. Granted, any "positive" intuition, to the effect that personal identity *does* hold in a certain case, that is predicted by either the psychological or the bodily continuity theory is predicted by the disjunctive theory. But there are certain "negative" intuitions we have as well. After reading the quotation from Williams, my intuitions say not only that A is the A-body person afterwards, but also that A is *not* the B-body person afterwards. In another frame of mind, the negative predictions of the psychological theory also match intuitions. These negative intuitions clash with the disjunctive candidate. It seems that our intuitions alternate between the psychological and bodily criteria rather than resting in a state in which their disjunction seems correct.

Another possibility for a third candidate would be some criterion entirely unrelated to psychological or bodily continuity. But surely any such criterion matches use significantly worse than either bodily continuity or psychological continuity. If there were a perfectly natural kind corresponding to some such criterion, that would be another story; but the same physicalism that ruled out perfectly natural candidates corresponding to psychological and bodily continuity rules out a perfectly natural kind here as well.

7. The Scope of the Argument and the Scope of Conceptual Analysis

We have examined a schematic argument purporting to show that there is no fact of the matter which theory of a given term, T, is correct. The argument has been defended in the case of personal identity, assuming that one of the ontologies of persistence that support multiple candidates is correct (section 3). The search for *the* correct criterion of personal identity is ultimately in vain, since talk of persisting persons is semantically indeterminate between candidates corresponding to the competing criteria. There simply is no fact of the matter whether the persistence of persons is governed by psychological or bodily continuity. This is not merely a reflection of our linguistic practice, for part of what was argued is that there is no one extremely eligible candidate to be meant by talk of persisting persons.

What is the scope of this sort of argument? Will all philosophical disputes dissolve in this way? Philosophers are notorious for disagreeing, and notorious for their ingenuity in controverting the seemingly uncontrovertable. Isn't the kind of dialectical breakdown to which I appealed in section 4 ubiquitous? If so, wouldn't it follow that there are no genuine philosophical disagreements at all? It is a familiar undergraduate trick to postulate multiple meanings whenever philosophical disagreement arises. Give the fanatical ambiguity-monger her way, and disagreement in any area of philosophy vanishes: disagreement in normative ethics, for instance, turns into conceptual confusion between "utilitarian-obligation", "deontological obligation", "egoistic obligation", and so on. The philosophical community would become a Babel of speakers of different languages who mistakenly think they disagree about a common subject matter.

There may be other areas of philosophy that are like personal identity in this respect, however much we would like this not to be the case. Fortunately, however, there are cases in which the argument does not succeed. These fall into different categories.

There are certainly *scientific* cases in which the argument fails. Dialectical impasse in cosmology would not convince us that there is no fact of the matter as to whether, say, there will eventually be a big crunch; dialectical impasse in particle physics would not lead us to say there is no fact of the matter as to the behavior of electrons. The argument fails in these cases because premise 3 is false—candidates corresponding to rival scientific theories are not in general equally natural. Physics is one place where most of us *do* believe nature has joints.

There are also philosophical cases where the argument fails. First, there are cases in which ongoing philosophical investigation would eventually establish a superior theory. Imagine there are indeed multiple candidates for being meant by a certain term, T, but that there exist vivid and compelling thought experiments waiting to be discovered by future philosophers, in which intuition would tell decisively in favor of one candidate. In that case, premise 2 would be false—one of the candidates would fit use better than the other. Alternatively, imagine there exist new distinctions to be made, which would show one candidate to be far more natural than the other. Then premise 3 would be false.

Perhaps normative ethics is an example. My sense is that the dialectical breakdown in ethics is nowhere near as severe as in the debate over criteria of personal identity. Normative ethics seems richer; there is too much room for unforseen developments to conclude that competing candidates fit use equally well. Even when a particular actual or counterfactual situation in ethics stumps us, or invokes very different reactions in different people, this does not signal the end of argumentation. New cases are often constructed which have more pull on the intellect, and on the basis of those new cases the old ones may be decided. (Deciding the old cases on this basis is justified by the naturalness requirement on meaning: highly natural candidate meanings for T will count T as applying in cases that are natural generalizations of other cases where T applies.) New distinctions cause us to reevaluate our judgments about which theories, and hence which candidate meanings, are more natural than others. I do not claim to be sure that normative ethics is indeed like this, only that there is no compelling reason to suppose it is not.

One cannot say with any certainty in advance where further investigation will lead. Thus, even in cases where the no-fact-of-the-matter argument is sound, there are no shortcuts to hard philosophical work. Even if there is no fact of the matter in a given case, establishing this requires just as much philosophy as establishing one of the competing theories.

For any term, T, say that which theory of T is true is *a matter of conceptual analysis* iff there exist multiple candidates c_1, ..., c_n for being meant by T such that i) all other candidates for being meant by T are far worse candidates than c_1, ..., c_n, and ii) none of c_1, ..., c_n is a perfectly natural kind (and thus, insofar as one of c_1, ..., c_n is a stronger candidate than the rest, this is due either to superior fit with use, or to superior eligibility as a result of having a simpler basis in the perfectly natural properties and relations). What I have been pointing out is that the schematic argument can fail in some cases where which theory is true is a matter of conceptual analysis, namely those in which ideal philosophical inquiry would vindicate one of the competing theories.

But there is a very different way the schematic argument can fail. The argument will fail when multiple legitimate candidates simply do not exist. Recall the theory of chaste endurance mentioned at the end of section 3. On this view, persons exist, have no temporal parts, and persist in basically the way we ordinarily take them to, but distinct entities never coincide. No one accepting this theory will accept anything like premise 1 in the schematic argument. In my immediate vicinity, there is exactly one person-shaped thing. The strict and literal persistence of this sort of thing over time is what is ordinarily meant by talk of persisting persons. We can point to *it*, and meaningfully ask: how long will it continue to exist? Would it be possible for it to continue to exist even after losing all its memories? These questions may well have determinate answers. (Of course, the defender of chaste endurance might for independent reasons claim these questions have no answers; the point is just that the no-fact-of-the-matter argument leaves open the possibility of determinate answers.) Given chaste endurantism, there will be a single correct criterion of personal identity, namely that criterion that gives the correct account of the persistence conditions for things like *the* object I singled out. Moreover, given chaste endurantism, the correctness of the true criterion of personal identity will not be a matter of conceptual analysis. It will be due to the nature of the one and only one candidate meaning we could possibly mean by our talk of persisting persons.

Many of the same remarks apply if substance dualism is true. If every conscious human body is associated with a single simple enduring non-physical soul, the persistence conditions of souls might well be the only live candidate for talk of persisting persons. One criterion of personal identity would be correct (presumably different from both the bodily continuity and the psychological continuity criteria), and its correctness would not be a matter of conceptual analysis.

Thus, the no-fact-of-the-matter thesis is only *conditionally* established: it holds *if* the worm theory or promiscuous endurantism or one of the other ontologies supporting "multiple-candidates" that were discussed in section 4 is correct, but not if chaste endurantism or substance dualism is correct. Whether there is a unique criterion of personal identity depends on which ontology of persistence is correct. Likewise, whether the question of criteria is a matter of conceptual analysis also depends on which ontology of persistence is correct.

Doesn't this just push the question one level back? Might there be no fact of the matter what is the correct ontology of persistence? If so, then the no-fact-of-the-matter thesis for criteria of personal identity would be unconditionally established, and the realm of significant metaphysical questions would shrink further. But as I will argue in the next section, the debate over the fundamental ontology of persistence is special. Given a certain plausible conception about the nature of existence, debates in fundamental ontology—debates about what there is—are intrinsically immune to the no-fact-of-the-matter argument.

8. The Nature of Existence

I say there exist temporal parts; the chaste endurantist disagrees. And each of us disagrees with the nihilist in thinking there exist composites. These disagreements are not merely over how the world should be described; we disagree about what there is. These disagreements cannot, I think, be dissolved. There must be a fact of the matter who is right.

Given any of the "multiple candidates" ontologies discussed in section 3, both psychological continuity theorists and bodily continuity theorists are happy to admit the existence of the multiple candidate meanings for talk of persisting persons. Given the worm theory, for example, both psychological continuity theorists and bodily continuity theorists admit the existence of *both* body-persons and psychological-persons. To establish the no-fact-of-the-matter thesis it was crucial that the existence of the multiple candidates was unproblematic *from the point of view of both sides of the debate*. Otherwise premise 1 of the no-fact-of-the-matter argument would tacitly presuppose the *falsity* of one of the views in question, and so could not establish there was no fact of the matter as to whether that view was correct.

But now consider the debate between the defender of temporal parts, the nihilist and the chaste endurantist. Pretend that nothing exists other than two persisting electrons, which have no proper spatial parts. Then the nihilist, the chaste endurantist and I disagree over which of the following sentences are true, where the quantifiers are intended to range unrestrictedly over absolutely all (concrete) things:

$\exists x \exists y \; x \neq y$ "there are at least two things"

$\exists x \exists y \exists z \; (x \neq y \& x \neq z \& y \neq z)$ "there are at least three things"

$\exists x \exists y \exists z \exists w \; (x \neq y \& x \neq z \& x \neq w \& y \neq z \& y \neq w \& z \neq w)$ "there are at least four things"

The nihilist thinks only the first sentence is true. The chaste endurantist admits the second sentence in addition to the first (provided she is willing to admit the existence of arbitrary fusions). The defender of temporal parts admits all three sentences: assuming she thinks time is dense, she thinks every electron has infinitely many temporal parts. Thus, the defender of temporal parts, the nihilist and the chaste endurantist disagree over sentences stated just with quantifiers, variables, and the identity sign. Given this it is difficult to see how the schematic argument could be made in this case. Since the disagreement between these theorists extends to the logical vocabulary, there is no neutral language in which the existence of multiple candidates could be asserted that would be acceptable *from the point of view of everyone in the debate*. What multiple candidate meanings could there be for unrestricted quantifiers, boolean operators and the identity sign?[20]

Granted, restricted quantifiers can have multiple candidate meanings, corresponding to different possible restrictions. But the quantifiers above were stipulated to range unrestrictedly over absolutely everything, except perhaps non-"concrete" things. Might multiple candidate meanings for these quantifiers creep in via candidate meanings for 'concrete'? No. 'Concrete' is intended to rule out sets, properties, and the like. Any vagueness in this restriction is irrelevant: on any way of fixing on a reasonable candidate meaning for 'concrete', the nihilist, chaste endurantist and temporal parts theorist will still disagree over the truth values of the sentences thus understood.

The only way to defend the no-fact-of-the-matter thesis would be to claim that unrestricted quantificational expressions can indeed have multiple candidate meanings. The best-known version of this appeals to Carnap's (1950) idea that metaphysical questions only have answers within "linguistic frameworks".[21] Quantificational expressions, Carnap might claim, get their meanings from the rules of language adopted by those that use them. The nihilist uses different rules for the quantifiers than do the chaste endurantist or the defender of temporal parts. In the nihilist's linguistic framework, there is no rule allowing one to infer $\ulcorner \exists x \; x$ is made up of a and $b \urcorner$ from the assumption that a and b denote objects. This rule is included in the frameworks of the chaste endurantist and the defender of temporal parts, but only the latter includes as well a rule allowing one to infer $\ulcorner \exists x(x$ is a temporal part of a at $t) \urcorner$ from the assumption that a denotes a continuant and t denotes a time. If the meanings of quantificational expressions are exhausted by rules of this sort, it might then be argued that our meaning-determining behavior does not determinately settle which rules govern quantification. There would be no fact of the matter whether the defender of temporal parts, the chaste endurantist or the nihilist is correct.

The trouble is that the Carnapian view is hard to believe. It is hard to see why the different rules of inference should be regarded as alternate meanings for the quantifier, rather than alternate *beliefs* about what exists. Intuitively, there is nothing the opponents of the nihilist can stipulate about the existential quantifier that will insure that $\ulcorner \exists x \; x$ is made up of a and $b \urcorner$ is true, *provided they use '$\exists$' as a quantifier*, for there simply may not *be* a third object other than those denoted by a and b.[22] Of course, a group of people could agree to use the sentence $\ulcorner \exists x \phi(x) \urcorner$ to mean that Nelson Goodman says that some object satisfies $\phi(x)$. Since Goodman accepts the existence of mereological sums, $\ulcorner \exists x$ (x is made up of a and b)$\urcorner$ will then be true. But in this idiolect '$\exists$' no longer has anything to do with *existence*.

There is a fundamental asymmetry between expressions for unrestricted quantification, on the one hand, and other expressions (like predicates and names) on the other. The existence of multiple candidate semantic values for the latter are relatively uncontroversial, whereas there seems to be only one notion of existence. Think of how the nihilist and the chaste endurantist would regard each other's use of '∃' to describe the world containing only two electrons. The chaste endurantist thinks there exist three things in this world, whereas the nihilist thinks there are only two. Neither will admit the existence of any candidate meaning for '∃' on which the other's assertion is correct. The chaste endurantist does admit the existence of the meaning of the *restricted* quantifier 'is a thing without proper parts', under which the nihilist's claim that there are only two things turns out true. But the nihilist explicitly (and vociferously!) claims not to be using '∃' as a restricted quantifier. And the nihilist does not admit any sort of quantificational meaning on which the chaste endurantist's claim that there exist three things turns out true. This sort of inability of either disputant to accept the other's meaning does not carry over to disputes involving predicates, for example. Consider the debate over whether right action is maximization of utility or conformity to the categorical imperative. Both utilitarians and Kantians are happy to admit the existence of the properties of *conformity to the categorical imperative* and *maximizing utility*; what they disagree over is which property is the property of *being morally right*. Multiple predicate meanings are available to all, whereas multiple quantificational meanings— except for restricted quantificational meanings, which are in the present context irrelevant—simply do not exist.

I claim, then, that if '∃' is to be understood as an unrestricted quantifier, there is just a single meaning for this expression to have: the one and only notion of existence. Relative to this meaning, there are univocal answers to questions of ontology. The temporal parts theorist, nihilist and chaste endurantist share the same notion of existence and make different claims about it; only one of them can be right.

If the "rules of existence" accepted by these theorists are merely different beliefs *about* existence and do not determine the meaning of 'exists', then just what *does* determine its meaning? I would appeal to the existence of *logical joints in reality*. Just as the world comes "ready-made" with natural properties and relations, it also comes ready-made with a domain of objects. This domain is extremely eligible to be meant by quantificational expressions. Provided one's core use of '∃' is reasonably standard, provided one accepts the standard patterns of inference involving '∃', provided one does not introduce bizarre stipulations on '∃' (for example that $\ulcorner ∃x\ \phi(x) \urcorner$ is to be true whenever Nelson Goodman says that some object satisfies $\phi(x)$), and provided one intends '∃' to be utterly unrestricted, then '∃' means this extremely eligible candidate no matter what one believes about existence. This will not convince a determined defender of Carnapian linguistic relativity; it rather shows that the univocality of '∃' is a coherent position.

I discuss this conception of existence and its contrast with the Carnapian picture in somewhat greater detail elsewhere.[23] I only note here that anyone who wants to deny that there is a fact of the matter about these fundamental questions about ontology is committed to a fairly radical conception of the nature of existence. Without a view of existence like Carnap's, questions of fundamental ontology look special. They are not susceptible to the no-fact-of-the-matter argument since there are no multiple candidates for 'exists' to mean. Just as the meaning of 'electron' holds constant through radical changes in scientific belief and hence radical changes in the "concept" of an electron, so the meaning of 'exists' holds constant despite radical differences in opinion about what there is. Just as there is only one thing for 'electron' to mean (provided one wants to mean something remotely in the neighborhood of *electronhood*), there is only one thing for 'exists' to mean.

It is ironic that the questions I claim cannot be dissolved are precisely those some think are most worthy of dissolution. For many, dispute over the existence of composites is a case of metaphysics at its worst. It is certainly a dispute where it is very hard to know who is right. Here, if anywhere, one might think, the dispute results from different conventional decisions about how to use language. It is not surprising that Putnam uses this very debate to motivate his internal "realism" (1987a, Lectures I and II; 1987b). But even Jaegwon Kim takes a similar line about certain questions of ontology:[24]

> Concerning such questions as whether there "really are" events (over and beyond substances and their properties), whether substances are "ontologically prior to" events or vice versa, what the "metaphysical nature" of events is, along with many other similar questions about facts, properties, continuants, time-slices, and so forth, it just seems wrong-headed to think that there are "true" answers, answers that are true because they correctly depict some pre-existing metaphysical order of the world. ...the primary job of ontology should be to work out and purvey ontological options, alternative schemes that will suit our varied activities and aims in science and philosophy. Carnap may have been exactly right with his distinction between "external" and "internal" questions.

But I say that here, where metaphysical questions are as metaphysical as can be, is precisely where those questions have answers.

An important corollary of my conception of existence is that questions of fundamental ontology are in an important sense about the world, not about our concepts. Whether things have temporal parts, whether only mereological simples exist or whether composite objects exist as well, are as much non-conceptual matters as whether electrons exist. This makes fundamental ontology a far more compelling enterprise than mere exercises in conceptual analysis. It also makes its epistemology more difficult. No wonder Putnam and Kim "lose their metaphysical nerve".[25] If ontological beliefs are not based on conceptual analyses of 'there exists', on what are they based?[26]

Notes

1. Psychological continuity theorists say that I go where my mental life goes; bodily continuity theorists say that I go where my body goes. Refinements of these crude formulations will not affect the present discussion.
2. The "indeterminacy" here is not exactly vagueness or ambiguity. It is similar in some ways to Hartry Field's (1973, 1974) notion of partial denotation.
3. Devitt 1984, section 12.4.
4. Lewis 1983, 1984.
5. The exact nature of fit with use, eligibility, and the weighting of each that makes for the best combination, are important matters, but not ones I will discuss.
6. The nature of candidate meanings also depends on the grammatical category of T and on one's semantic theory, but I will suppress these complications.
7. A defender of temporal parts need not believe in arbitrary spacetime worms, for she may reject the doctrine of arbitrary mereological fusions. However, there is a powerful form of argument that can be used to support both temporal parts and arbitrary mereological fusions. See Sider 1997 and Sider forthcoming, chapter 4, §9.
8. Stephen Yablo (1987) holds a modal view somewhat analogous to promiscuous endurance. Note that if one generalizes promiscuous endurance (not Yablo's view) by admitting the existence of objects (not just persons) for absolutely every possible method of trans-temporal tracing, the view turns into the doctrine of temporal parts. See Sider forthcoming, chapter 5, §3.
9. Chisholm 1973, 1975, and 1976, appendix B; van Cleve 1986; Zimmerman 1995.
10. Chisholm's theory of entity successiva (1976, chapter 3) is an example.
11. Another multiple-candidate view seems to have no adherents. *Presentists* say that only present objects are real, and go on to paraphrase talk apparently about merely past and future entities using irreducible tense operators (see Sider forthcoming, chapter 2). Imagine a presentist who thinks there is only one thing in any given place at a time, but postulates multiple primitive tense operators corresponding to various criteria of personal identity.
12. I ignore issues raised by "the problem of the many" (Unger 1980) which cut across the present issues.
13. Even if use favors one candidate *slightly* better than the other, this may not be enough to defang the argument. The word-world meaning relation could plausibly be held to be a matter of degree; we might then want to say that if one candidate wins a very narrow victory over the other, the disputed term is partially indeterminate.
14. See Feldman 1992, chapter 6 for an extensive discussion (note that Feldman does not uphold the no-fact-of-the-matter thesis).
15. See Lewis 1979.
16. For an alternate explanation see Gendler 1998.
17. The connection between personal identity and attitudes like fear of future pain is challenged by Parfit's argument that identity is "not what matters" (1984 pp. 254–266; 1975, p. 200 ff.). Many have replied to Parfit; for my own response see Sider 1996 and Sider forthcoming, chapter 5. But even those convinced by Parfit will surely hold that personal identity and the various attitudes march in step in cases that do not involve fission or fusion or the kinds of complications raised by Parfit's "everlasting bodies" (1975, pp. 217–219).
18. See Lewis 1986, p. 61.

19. See, for example, Olson 1997, Rovane 1998 and Schechtman 1996.
20. Compare van Inwagen (forthcoming).
21. See also Putnam 1987a and 1987b.
22. Compare van Inwagen 1990, pp. 6–12
23. See the introduction to *Four-Dimensionalism*.
24. Kim 1993, pp. ix–x. Kim goes on in the next sentence to say: "I should add, though, that I do not hold this view about metaphysics in general, or even about all ontological issues."
25. The phrase is Alex Oliver's (1996, §7).
26. I would like to thank David Braun, Earl Conee, Matti Eklund, Europa Malynicz, Scott Sturgeon, Achille Varzi, Brian Weatherson, Dean Zimmerman, and especially Tamar Szabó Gendler, for helpful comments.

References

Carnap, Rudolf. 1950. "Empiricism, Semantics and Ontology", *Revue Internationale de Philosophie* **4**: 20–40, reprinted in his *Meaning and Necessity*, 2nd edition (Chicago: University of Chicago Press, 1956).

Chisholm, Roderick. 1976. *Person and Object: A Metaphysical Study*. (La Salle, Illinois: Open Court Publishing Co.).

Chisholm, Roderick. 1975. "Mereological Essentialism: Further Considerations", *Review of Metaphysics* **28**: 477–484.

Chisholm, Roderick. 1973. "Parts as Essential to Their Wholes", *Review of Metaphysics* **26**: 581–603.

Devitt, Michael. 1984. *Realism and Truth*. (Oxford: Basil Blackwell).

Feldman, Fred. 1992. *Confrontations with the Reaper*. (New York: Oxford University Press).

Field, Hartry. 1974. "Quine and the Correspondence Theory", *Philosophical Review* **83**: 200–228.

Field, Hartry. 1973. "Theory Change and the Indeterminacy of Reference", *Journal of Philosophy* **70**: 462–481.

Gendler, Tamar Szabó. 1998. "Exceptional Persons: On the Limits of Imaginary Cases", *Journal of Consciousness Studies* **5**: 592–610.

Kim, Jaegwon. 1993. *Supervenience and Mind*. (Cambridge: Cambridge University Press.)

Kripke, Saul. 1972. *Naming and Necessity*. (Cambridge, MA: Harvard University Press.)

Lewis, David. 1984. "Putnam's Paradox". *Australasian Journal of Philosophy* **62**: 221–236.

Lewis, David. 1983. "New Work for a Theory of Universals". *Australasian Journal of Philosophy* **61**: 343–377.

Lewis, David. 1979. "Scorekeeping in a Language Game", *Journal of Philosophical Logic* **8**: 339–359.

Lewis, David. 1968. "Counterpart Theory and Quantified Modal Logic," *Journal of Philosophy* **65**: 113–126

Locke, John. 1975. "On Identity and Diversity" (chapter 27 of his *Essay Concerning Human Understanding*), in John Perry, ed., *Personal Identity* (Berkeley: University of California): 33–52.

Oliver, Alex. 1996. "The Metaphysics of Properties", *Mind* **105**: 1–80.

Olson, Eric. 1997. *The Human Animal: Personal Identity without Psychology* (Oxford: Oxford University Press).

Parfit, Derek. 1984. *Reasons and Persons*. (Oxford: Oxford University Press).

Parfit, Derek. 1975. "Personal Identity", in John Perry, ed., *Personal Identity* (University of California Press), 199–223.

Putnam, Hilary. 1987a. *The Many Faces of Realism*. (La Salle, IL: Open Court).

Putnam, Hilary. 1987b. "Truth and Convention: On Davidson's Refutation of Conceptual Relativism", *Dialectica* **41**: 69–77.

Putnam, Hilary. 1981. *Reason, Truth and History*. (Cambridge: Cambridge University Press).

Putnam, Hilary. 1980. "Models and Reality", *Journal of Symbolic Logic* **45**: 464–482.

Putnam, Hilary. 1978. *Meaning and the Moral Sciences*. (Boston: Routledge & Kegan Paul).

Quine, W. V. O. 1976. "Whither Physical Objects", in R. S. Cohen, et. al. (eds), *Essays in Memory of Imre Lakatos* (Dordrecht: D. Reidel Publishing Company), pp. 497–504.

Rovane, Carol. 1998. *The Bounds of Agency: An Essay in Revisionary Metaphysics* (Princeton: Princeton University Press).

Schechtman, Marya. 1996. *The Constitution of Selves* (Ithaca: Cornell University Press).

Sider, Theodore. Forthcoming. *Four-Dimensionalism: An Ontology of Persistence and Time*. (Oxford: Oxford University Press).

Sider, Theodore. 1997. "Four-Dimensionalism", *Philosophical Review* **106**: 197–231.

Sider, Theodore. 1996. "All the World's a Stage", *Australasian Journal of Philosophy* **74**: 433–453.

Unger, Peter. 1980. "The Problem of the Many", in French, Uehling, and Wettstein, eds., *Midwest Studies in Philosophy*, V (University of Minnesota): 411–67.

van Cleve, James. 1986. "Mereological Essentialism, Mereological Conjunctivism and Identity Through Time", in P. French, T. Uehling, and H. Wettstein, eds., *Midwest Studies in Philosophy XI*. (Minneapolis: University of Minnesota Press).

van Inwagen, Peter. Forthcoming. "The Number of Things", in Ernest Sosa, ed., *Philosophical Issues, Vol. 12: Realism and Relativism* (Oxford: Blackwell).

van Inwagen, Peter. 1990. *Material Beings*. (Ithaca: Cornell University Press).

Williams, Bernard. 1975. "The Self and the Future", in John Perry, ed., *Personal Identity* (Berkeley: University of California): 179–198.

Yablo, Stephen. 1987. "Identity, Essence, and Indiscernibility", *Journal of Philosophy* **84**: 293–314.

Zimmerman, Dean W. 1995. "Theories of Masses and Problems of Constitution", *Philosophical Review* **104**: 53–110.

Philosophical Perspectives, 15, Metaphysics, 2001

METAPHYSICAL AUSTERITY AND
THE PROBLEMS OF TEMPORAL AND MODAL ANAPHORA*

Peter Ludlow
SUNY Stony Brook

0. Introduction

In Ludlow (1999) I explored the question of whether a presentist can account for temporal anaphora. The problem is this: presentists hold that there are no future or past events,[1] even though we routinely use temporal anaphors, which at least appear to refer to past and future events. So, in example (1) from Partee (1973), there is an intuitive sense in which I am not saying that I turned off the stove once in the past, but rather am saying that I turned it off during a particular temporal interval.

(1) I turned off the stove.

Temporal anaphora is found in other environments as well. For example, Reichenbach (1947) showed that some account of temporal anaphora is crucial to providing a semantics of tense for sentences with complex tenses like the past perfect and future perfect. Reichenbach distinguished three events (or event times) S, R, and E, where S is the utterance event, E is the event under discussion, and R is an understood reference event. The complex tenses were then defined in terms of the relative ordering of S, R, and E. The past perfect, for example, would be the case where E is before R, which is before S. The entire paradigm can be fleshed out as follows:

Pluperfect: ←E—R—S→
Future perfect: ←S—E—R→
Future in Future: ←S—R—E→
Future in the Past: ←R—S—E→ or ←R—E—S→

It has widely been held by semanticists that complex tenses simply cannot be accounted for without Reichenbach's reference event R or some other form of temporal reference.

Additional work by Enç (1986, 1987) has stressed that temporal anaphora can also be argued to hold within *noun* phrases. So, for example, in (2) one intuitively is not talking about current hostages, but rather those individuals who were hostages during a certain time interval.

(2) The hostages came to the White House

The above three arguments do not exhaust the considerations that have been advanced on behalf of temporal reference, and a number of semanticists have developed this general theme, including Hinrichs (1981, 1986), Partee (1984) and Webber (1988). The metaphysical issue, of course, is that if the semantics of natural language is committed to reference to past and future events, then the metaphysics entailed by the semantics of natural language must admit such entities. But then presentism must be false.[2]

In Ludlow (1999) I sketched a theory of "E-type temporal anaphora" which held the promise of doing the necessary semantical work but without temporal reference. There was, however, a class of temporal anaphors that escaped the reach of that theory, so at a minimum the theory needed to be elaborated. In addition, it is now clear to me that presentists are not the only ones with difficulties here—indeed, a whole range of theories of time and tense will need to make use of some non-referential theory of anaphora. In effect, accounting for non-referential temporal anaphora is a problem for nearly everyone, not just presentists.

There is also literature that makes it clear that the concerns raised in the domain of tense have analogous concerns in the semantics of sentences with modals—specifically it has been suggested that the presence of modal anaphora requires that we refer to sets of possible worlds or like objects. In effect, the stakes have been raised because the problem of anaphora infects a wide range of theories of tense and time and also spills over into the semantics and metaphysics of modality. In this note I want to respond to these higher stakes by suggesting a way to extend the theory of E-type temporal anaphora to cover the additional cases, and I further want to suggest an analogous response to the problem of modal anaphora. I will conclude that the phenomena of modal and temporal anaphora do not pressure us into giving up austerity in the metaphysics of time and modality.

I'll proceed as follows: In part 1, I'll argue that the problem of temporal anaphora afflicts a number of positions beyond presentism. In part 2, I'll review the theory of E-type temporal anaphora that I offered in Ludlow (1999). In part 3 I'll discuss some of the constructions that escape the reach of that theory and will explore some possible strategies for handling the additional constructions. In part 4, I'll take up the problem of modal anaphora and will explore the prospects for developing a theory of E-type modal anaphora. I'll summarize in part 5.

1. The Pervasiveness of the Problem of Temporal Anaphora

It's clear enough that temporal anaphora presents difficulties for the presentist—if there are no future or past events, how can we possibly refer to such events?—but it may not be so clear that other positions have apparent difficulties here as well. For example, someone who is a thoroughgoing 4-dimensionalist about time will want to hold that all future and past events exist (and indeed are just as real as present events) but may not want to hold that one can *refer* to all such events. Much recent work on the theory of reference has held that in order to successfully refer to some object one must be in an appropriate causal relation with that object. For example, to refer to some object with either a name or a pronoun it might be necessary to stand in a relevant causal or information-theoretic chain (in the sense of Evans 1982) with the object in question. There are surely many past events which bear no interesting causal or information-theoretic relation to us but which we may nevertheless be able to denote by use of anaphors or descriptions.

The basic point is one that was initially stressed in Russell (1910–11) and by a number of authors since then. In Russell's particular case the idea was that some objects are known by acquaintance and some are known by description. Those objects that are known by description cannot be referred to, but merely denoted by definite descriptions following the theory of descriptions developed in Russell (1905). The headline idea is that referring expressions are used to express singular propositions and denoting expressions are used to express general propositions.[3] When one employs a denoting expression like 'the tallest person in Iowa' in an utterance like 'the tallest person in Iowa is a Freemason' one is not uttering a singular proposition about some individual, but rather one is uttering a general proposition to the effect that there is a tallest person in Iowa and whoever it is, that individual is a Freemason. It is not, strictly speaking, a proposition about some individual but is about the properties of being tall and being a Freemason (or perhaps, in some sense, about the world).

Since Russell, we have come to be more liberal about the kinds of objects one can refer to (as noted above, many would say that a causal chain linking a name to an individual is sufficient for the name to refer to that individual), but it is widely held that there are many noun phrases that are not referring expressions and are rather denoting expressions. In the case of anaphoric pronouns like 'he', 'she', and 'it', there are many instances in which utterances of them are anaphoric on noun phrases that are denoting expressions (like 'the tallest person in Iowa') and not on referring expressions. As Evans (1977) stressed, in these cases we would want to say that the anaphors are not referring expressions but rather stand proxy for descriptions.

So, for example, in (3) the anaphoric pronoun 'He' does not refer to anyone, but rather stands proxy for a description of the form 'the Freemason who entered the room', as in (3′).

(3) A Freemason entered the room. *He* ordered a glass of gin.

(3') A Freemason entered the room. *The Freemason who entered the room* ordered a glass of gin.

In effect both sentences in (3) express general propositions; the pronoun in question is not a referring expression.

If this story is correct for cases of pronominal anaphora it stands to reason that a similar story will hold for event anaphora of the type anticipated by Reichenbach. We simply won't be in the relevant causal relation to refer to many past events (perhaps *most* past events), and the prospects of referring to future events (crucial in the analysis of some complex tenses) will be dim to nonexistent. In effect, even four-dimensionalists need some alternative to reference in providing an account of temporal anaphora.

Between presentism and four-dimensionalism there is room for a number of other positions, including a position in which one rejects the present existence of past events but allows that it is possible to refer to entities that no longer exist.[4] That is, one might hold that one can be in a relevant causal relation to events that were but are no more. Even if one allows this possibility, one wants to hold out that one is not causally related to all such events and hence that it will not be possible to refer to all of the events that one wants to pick out as a Reichenbachian "reference event" R—particularly future events. Accordingly, one is still in need of a theory of temporal anaphora that can dispense with reference. Can such a theory be provided?

2. E-type Temporal Anaphora

In Ludlow (1999) I offered a theory of E-type temporal anaphora on which temporal anaphoric elements are not treated as referring expressions. The basic idea was simple enough: just as E-type nominal anaphors stand proxy for descriptions, E-type temporal anaphors might stand proxy for temporal conjunctions. Consider a case like (4).

(4) I turned off the stove then

Partee (1973, 1984) seemed to assume that 'then' must *refer* to a moment or period of time. However, this assumption was not necessary. It is alternatively possible that 'then' is standing proxy for a temporal conjunction. For example, 'then' could be standing proxy for 'when I finished cooking', or 'when you recently asked me to'. If we represent this elipsed clause as '[$_S$...]', then the logical form of sentence like (4) might be rendered as follows.

(4') [$_S$ [$_S$ PAST [$_S$ I turn off the stove]] when [$_S$...]]

Note the similarity to theories of E-type pronominal anaphora; the key difference is that whereas E-type pronominal anaphors stand proxy for descriptions, temporal anaphors stand proxy for expressions of this form: 'when [s...]', 'before [s...]', 'after [s...]', 'while [s...]', 'during [s...]', etc.

This is the basic idea, but of course the devil is in the details, so a brief exposition of the semantic theory is in order. Since the theory in Ludlow (1999) is embedded in a presentist semantics of tense I'll couch the theory of temporal anaphora in the same framework here, noting that exporting the basic idea to non-presentist ontologies is straightforward.

Presentist Semantics with E-type Temporal Anaphora

Following much recent work in the semantics of natural language, we assume that a semantical theory for natural language involves constructing a truth theory in the spirit of Davidson (1967a). Initial attempts to execute the Davidsonian program involved a translation of natural language into a familiar formal language like first order logic, but subsequent work by Higginbotham (1985), Larson and Ludlow (1993) and Larson and Segal (1995) have offered that one should rather provide a recursive characterization of truth directly for linguistic forms.

To illustrate, consider a simple language that can be described using rewriting rules like the following, where 'S' is understood as "sentence" and 'NP' and 'VP' are understood as "noun phrase" and "verb phrase" respectively.

(5) S → NP VP

A rule of this form would then generate a linguistic "tree" like the following:

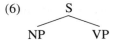

(6)   S
      NP   VP

This same tree structure can be represented in a linear fashion as in (6'),

(6') [s NP VP]

and hereafter we will adopt the linear form of representation for all such trees.

Suppose that we want to give a recursive characterization of truth for a very simple language, L, having the following syntax.

Syntax of L:

S → S1 and S2
S → S1 or S2
S → it is not the case that S1
S → NP VP

NP → 'Dick', 'Sally'
VP → V NP
VP → V
V → 'leaps', 'walks', 'hits'

Our semantics for L will involve the introduction of T-theory axioms corresponding to each of these syntactic rules.

Semantics of L:

We introduce the predicate Val, where Val (A, B) says that A is a semantic value of B.

We begin by providing axioms for the terminal nodes in the language—i.e. those nodes that "terminate" in lexical items.

(7) a. Val(x, 'Dick') iff x = Dick
    Val(x, 'Sally') iff x = Sally

  b. Val(x, 'leaps') iff x leaps
    Val(x, 'walks') iff x walks
    Val($\langle x,y \rangle$, 'hits') iff x hits y

Axioms are then introduced for non-terminal nodes as follows:

(8) a. Val(T, [$_S$ NP VP]) iff
    for some x, Val(x, NP) and Val(x, VP)

  b. Val(x, [$_\alpha$ β]) iff
    Val(x, β) (where α ranges over categories, and β ranges over categories and lexical items)

  c. Val(x, [$_{VP}$ V NP]) iff
    for some x, Val(x, V) and Val(x, NP)

(9) a. Val(T, [$_S$ S1 'and' S2]) iff
    Val(T, S1) and Val(T, S2)

  b. Val(T, [$_S$ S1 'or' S2]) iff
    either Val(T, S1) or Val(T, S2)

  c. Val(T, [$_S$ 'it is not the case that' S1]) iff
    it is not the case that Val(T, S1)

Finally, we introduce derivation rules that can be used to derive T-theories from the axioms:

(10) Derivation Rule (SoE)

$$....\alpha....$$
$$\frac{\alpha \text{ iff } \beta}{....\beta....}$$

therefore

(11) Derivation Rule (SoI)

$$\frac{\phi \text{ iff for some x, x} = \alpha \text{ and ....x....}}{\phi \text{ iff } ....\alpha....}$$

therefore

Let's consider a sample derivation for a sentence like 'Dick walks and Sally leaps'. Recall that this sentence will have the following form in the language:

(12) [$_S$ [$_{S1}$ [$_{NP}$ Dick] [$_{VP}$ walks]] and [$_{S2}$ [$_{NP}$ Sally] [$_{VP}$ leaps]]]

What we want the T-theory to do is to take this sentence as input and to successively apply axioms and rules of derivation until all of the object language material is exhausted and the resulting truth conditions are derived. In the simple semantics for L just defined, the derivation would proceed as follows:

(13) Val(T, [S [$_{S1}$ [$_{NP}$ 'Dick'] [$_{VP}$ 'walks']]
and [$_{S2}$ [$_{NP}$ 'Sally'] [$_{VP}$ 'leaps']]]) iff ...

    i) Val(T, [$_{S1}$ [$_{NP}$ 'Dick'] [$_{VP}$ 'walks']])
       and Val(T, [$_{S2}$ [$_{NP}$ 'Sally'] [$_{VP}$ 'leaps']])
       [instance of 9a]

    ii) for some x, Val(x, [$_{NP}$ 'Dick']) and Val(x, [$_{VP}$ 'walks'])
       and for some x, Val(x, [$_{NP}$ 'Sally']) and Val(x,[$_{VP}$ 'leaps'])
       [from (i) by applications of 8a, SoE]

    iii) for some x, Val(x, 'Dick') and Val(x, 'walks')
       and for some x, Val(x, 'Sally') and Val(x, 'leaps')
       [from (ii) by applications of 8b, SoE]

    iv) for some x, x = Dick and x walks
       and for some x, x = Sally and x leaps
       [from (iii) by applications of 7a, 7b, SoE]

    v) Dick walks and Sally leaps
       [from (iv) by applications of SoI]

In providing a presentist semantics for tense we begin by defining a language LT with the following syntactic rules.

Syntax of LT: To the rules of L, add...

TCP → TP1 'when' TP2
TCP → TP1 'before' TP2
TCP → TP1 'after' TP2
TP → TNS S
TNS → PAST, FUT

Semantics of LT:

We begin with the assumption that verbal stems have an intrinsic present tense that cannot be stripped from the verb. So, for example, in the axiom for 'hits' above (Val($\langle$x,y$\rangle$, 'hits') iff x hits y), we need to regard the right hand side of the axiom as being tensed. This reflects the fact that presentists, along with many others, are so-called "tensers"—they believe that the semantics of tensed sentences cannot be given in an untensed metalanguage. If the verb receives a Davidsonian event-style analysis (Davidson 1967b), then the tense still cannot be stripped from the right hand side of the axiom; it will adhere to the verb 'is' in the axiom, as follows.

(T0) Val($\langle$x,y,e$\rangle$, hit) iff there *is* an e, e *is* a hitting, x *is* the agent of e and y *is* the patient of e

We next introduce a notion of morphological tense, which can handle the basic past and future tense morphemes. We can think of the morphemes as elements that move into prenex position and act like operators, or perhaps more accurately, as predicates that take sentence-like objects as their arguments. Accordingly, the syntactic constructions in which we find these morphemes would be as follows, where TP is a tense phrase containing a tense morpheme and a sentential clause,

Morphological Past: [$_{TP}$ PAST[S]]
Morphological Future: [$_{TP}$ FUT[S]]

and the semantics would be as follows, where we rely upon a tensed metalanguage to state the axioms for the past and future tense morphemes.

(T1) Val(x, PAST) iff x was true
(T2) Val(x, FUT) iff x will be true
(TP) Val(T, [$_{TP}$ TNS S]) iff there is an x, s.t.
        Val(x, TNS) and x = []S[]

In the axiom TP, we use the closed bracket notation '[]' around 'S' ('[]S[]') to indicate a proposition-like object related to S. We say proposition-like because such objects are not "eternal" like standard propositions; their truth value will shift over time. In Ludlow (1999) these objects were taken to be "interpreted logical forms" in the sense of Larson and Ludlow (1993).

The next step is the treatment of relative tense. In the Reichenbachian framework, relative tense involves the temporal position of the reference event R. Since appeal to such reference events is not possible for the presentist, another strategy is required. Accordingly, we rely upon the use of implicit temporal conjunctions to do the work that would otherwise be done via temporal reference.

Relative Present:
On Reichenbach analysis: E,R (simultaneous)
Logical form on a presentist analysis: [S] when [...]

Relative Past:
on Reichenbach analysis: E—R
Logical form on a presentist analysis: [S] before [...]

Relative Future:
on Reichenbach analysis: R—E
Logical form on a presentist analysis: [S] after [...]

Crucially, when we provide the semantics for these temporal conjunctions we cannot take 'when' to mean "at the same time," but rather we must take it as a primitive relation holding between proposition-like objects. Likewise for 'before' and 'after'. Accordingly, we have the following axioms for temporal connectives:

(W1) Val(T, [$_{TCP}$ TP1 'when' TP2]) iff
Val(T, TP1) when Val(T, TP2)

(W2) Val(T, [$_{TCP}$ TP1 'before' TP2]) iff
Val(T, TP1) before Val(T, TP2)

(W3) Val(T, [$_{TCP}$ TP1 'after' TP2]) iff
Val(T, TP1) after Val(T, TP2)

Given these axioms and the analysis of relative tense above, it is now possible to give a straightforward account of the complex tenses without appeal to temporal reference. This can be done by positing an implicit temporal conjunction in each sentence containing a complex tense. The resulting logical forms would be as follows:

Pluperfect
On Reichenbach analysis: E—R—S
Logical form on presentist analysis: PAST[S] before PAST[...]

Future perfect
On Reichenbach analysis: S—E—R
Logical form on presentist analysis: FUT[S] before FUT[...]

Future in Future
On Reichenbach analysis: S—R—E
Logical form on presentist analysis: FUT[S] after FUT[...]

Future in the Past
On Reichenbach analysis: R—E—S
Logical form on presentist analysis: PAST[S] when PAST[...]

To illustrate, given the above logical form for a past perfect sentence and a semantics that incorporated a Davidsonian event theory, we would yield the following truth conditions for a sentence like 'I had walked'.

(14) Val(T, 'I had walked') iff
[][(∃e)(walking(e) & agent(I, e) & culminates(e)][] was true before
[]...[] was true.

What about additional tenses like present perfect? Presumably these involve some aspectual features and we have not had the opportunity to introduce aspect here (notice that perfect aspect *has* been smuggled into (14)). Until incorporated in a fuller theory involving aspect, we can treat them as morphological tenses as follows.

(15) Val(x, PRESPERF) iff x has been true

The reader is referred to Ludlow (1999; ch. 8) for the treatment of a number of other constructions, including calendar names, apparent quantification over times ('I've been to New Jersey 18 times') and so on.

3. Extending the Theory: Temporal Intervals and Apparent Anaphora on Temporal Intervals

One kind of temporal anaphora that was not treated in Ludlow (1999) is temporal anaphora on temporal intervals. Accordingly, one wants to know if the theory sketched in section 2 can be extended to these cases.

The kinds of cases that I have in mind here include the following, where the italicized 'It' and 'then' appear to be anaphors that refer to temporal intervals (the Middle Ages and Henry's—or George's—youth accordingly).

(16) a. Abelard lived during the Middle Ages.
   b. *It* was an interesting period.

(17) a. George W. made many mistakes in his youth
     b. Henry made many mistakes *then* too.

What is the presentist to say about temporal intervals? It seems to me that the natural strategy is to bank on the meaning of temporal conjunctions and their ability to temporally situate events with respect to intervals, not just with respect to time points. Accordingly, (16a) might be taken to have the logical form in (16a′)

(16a′) PAST[Abelard lives] when PAST[(it is) the Middle Ages]

yielding the following truth conditions.

(16a*) [][Abelard lives][] was true when [][(it is) the Middle Ages][] was true

Or alternatively, if this doesn't have the necessary notion of containment, following a suggestion due to Gil Harman (p.c.), we might shift the position of 'when' as follows.

(16a**) when [][Abelard lives][] was true [][(it is) the Middle Ages][] was true

Now, what of the temporal anaphor in (16b)? The suggestion would be that it has the following logical form and truth conditions:

(16b′) PAST[it is an interesting period] when PAST[(it is) the Middle Ages]

(16b*) [][it is an interesting period][] was true when [][(it is) the Middle Ages][] was true

Note that '*It*' is pleonastic and not what many have taken to be the temporal anaphor. A similar sort of story could be told for the cases in (17), thus we have the following logical forms and truth conditions.

(17a′) PAST[George W. is making many mistakes] when PAST[(it is) his youth]
(17b′) PAST[Henry is making many mistakes] when PAST[(it is) his youth]

(17a*) [][George W. is making many mistakes][] was true when [][(it is) his youth][] was true
(17b*) [][Henry is making many mistakes][] was true when [][(it is) his youth][] was true

Note also that this story helps to shed light on the possibility of "sloppy identity" here—i.e. the possibility that (17b) can be either about George's youth or Henry's youth. On an analysis in which there is an anaphor referring to some already-identified interval it is difficult to see how this could be explained.

One construction that is discussed in Ludlow (1999), but not in sufficient detail, involves the different senses of 'since'. It would be an interesting project to tease apart the different senses and to show what elements give rise to them, but for our purposes it will be enough to consider three cases, each involving temporal intervals.

Case 1: Continuously Since

(18) The Red Sox have been cursed since they traded Babe Ruth to NY.

In this case we think of (18) as an explicit temporal conjunction, with the conjunction having a meaning that we might gloss as "ever since." Accordingly, we can posit the following logical form and truth conditions for (18).

(18′) PRESPERF[The Red Sox are cursed] (ever) since PAST[there is an event of their trading Babe Ruth to NY]

(18*) [][The Red Sox are cursed][] has been true (ever) since [][there is an event of their trading Babe Ruth to NY][] was true

Case 2: Once or More Since

(19) The Yankees have won the World Series since they traded for Babe Ruth.

Here there 'since' intuitively has the sense of "once or more since." The treatment of this case parallels (18):

(19′) PRESPERF[There is an event of the Yankees winning] (at least once) since PAST[there is an event of their trading for Babe Ruth]

(19*) [][There is an event of the Yankees winning][] has been true (at least once) since [][there is an event of their trading for Babe Ruth][] was true

Case 3: During the Interval Since

(20) The Yankees have won the World Series 26 times since they traded for Babe Ruth.

Once again, after the sense of the temporal conjunction is fixed the analysis proceeds as above:

(20′) PRESPERF[There is an event/situation/case of the Yankees winning 26 times] (during the interval) since PAST[there is an event of their trading for Babe Ruth]

(20*) [][There is an event/situation/case of the Yankees winning 26 times][] has been true (during the interval) since [][there is an event of their trading for Babe Ruth][] was true

This really only sketches the approach to temporal duration and temporal anaphora that might be pursued within a presentist program. Clearly, handling a full range of linguistic phenomena would involve a much more detailed study. I hope to have shown, however, that this approach is relatively straightforward and that it can do the work of temporal anaphora—even anaphora on temporal intervals—without admitting reference to, or even the existence of past and future events and intervals.

4. Modal Anaphora

Just as a number of semanticists have held that it is necessary to posit widespread reference to past and future events—even events to which we bear no interesting causal relation—a number of semanticists have held that there must be anaphoric reference to possible worlds. For example, some form of the modal reference thesis is advanced in Isard (1974), Portner (1995), Kibble (1994, 1995), Guerts (1995), Frank and Kamp (1997), Stone and Hardt (1997), and Stone (1999). To get a handle on the basic idea, consider a sentence like the following.

(21) A snake might be in those weeds. It would bite you.

According to modal reference theorists, what is happening is that the second sentence has a tacit reference to a set of possible worlds—those nearby worlds in which there is a snake in those weeds.[5] The implicit anaphoric element appears to be made explicit in cases like (22).

(22) That clock might fall on your head. That would certainly be unfortunate.

Once again, the thought would be that the element 'that' is an anaphor that refers to some set of possible worlds.

Clearly a proposal of this nature creates difficulties for those of us who are leery of possible worlds and who would rather not be committed to their existence. And parallel to considerations raised above, even those who are realists about possible worlds may not be prepared to say that we can *refer* to those worlds or to sets of them or to some variation on that theme. But what is the escape route for the metaphysically austere and those who are cautious in their attribution of the reference relation? Is it possible to develop a notion of E-type *modal* anaphora?

Just as E-type pronominal anaphors stand proxy for descriptions and just as E-type temporal anaphors stand proxy for temporal conjunctions, we can argue that E-type modal anaphors stand proxy for the antecedent clauses of conditionals. So, to illustrate, the examples above might be argued to have the following logical forms with implicit conditionals.

(21') A snake might be in the weeds. [(If there were to be a snake in the weeds) It would bite you.]

(22') That clock might fall on your head. [(If that clock were to fall on your head) that would certainly be unfortunate.]

In the second case we see that the element 'that' is not really the modal anaphor, but is rather a pleonastic element, parallel to the pleonastic element in the treatment of (16) above. In both cases the implicit conditional antecedent is recopied from material in the previous discourse. In this respect the treatment follows the theory of "modal accomodation" developed in Roberts (1986, 1989).[6]

If this story is right, then the basic theory of E-type modal anaphora can be grafted onto one's favorite theory of the semantics of conditionals—including those theories that eschew quantification over possible worlds. One such theory, that I only have space to sketch in a toy fragment here, would treat modal predicates disquotationally, parallel to the treatment of tense given in section 2. That is, one could take the language L introduced in section 2 and expand it with the following syntax and semantic axioms. (For the sake of expository simplicity I will not combine LM and LT. Although there are some technical moves necessary, combining the two fragments is relatively straightforward.)

Syntax of LM: to L add

MP → MODE S
MCP → ['if' MP1 'then' MP2]
MODE → 'might', 'would', 'were(to)'

Semantics:

We now introduce a three-place valuation predicate 'Val(A,B,L)', to be understood as "A is a semantic value of B for language L," where we take L to be a particular language that has its properties essentially.[7] We have the following axioms.

(M1) Val(x, 'might', L) iff x might be true in L
(M1') Val(x, 'were (to)', L) iff x were to be true in L
(M2) Val(x, 'would', L) iff x would be true in L
(M3) Val(T, [$_{MP}$ MODE S]) iff
there is an x, s.t. Val(x, MODE) and x = []S[]

(M4) Val(T, [$_{MCP}$ 'if' MP1 'then' MP2]) iff if Val(T, MP1),
then Val(T, MP2)

To illustrate, consider a sentence like 'It would bite you' as considered in example (21′) above. On this analysis, there is an implicit conditional antecedent in this sentence so (abstracting from some detail) the linguistic form of it would be as in (21″).

(21″) [$_{MCP}$ if [$_{MP}$ were [$_S$ there is a snake in the weeds]]
then [$_{MP}$ would [$_S$ it bites you]]] [8]

The truth conditions for this sentence (provided axioms for 'snake', 'weed' etc.) would be as follows:

(21*) If [][$_S$ there is a snake in the weeds][] would be true in L
then [][$_S$ it bites you][] were to be true in L

This is obviously a very rough sketch, and developing a theory of modality in this way (without a possible worlds semantics) is certainly a controversial strategy.[9] Yet, I think the strategy has much to recommend it. Clearly our understanding of what counts as a possible world is dependent on our understanding of the English modals, and not the other way around. There is a genuine worry, however, and it stems from allowing modal operators in the metalanguage, for this arguably amounts to introducing a kind of intensional metalanguage. It may be that talk of constructing T-theories really ought to give way to talk of constructing direct M-theories (meaning theories) as in Davies (1981), or alternatively it may be possible to give this account and remain extensional. However one chooses to develop the theory, the possibility of modal anaphora need not compel us to allow reference to sets of possible worlds.

5. Conclusion

It has long been argued that there are similarities between tense and modality (indeed some have suggested that the distinction between tense and modality collapses altogether) so it is not surprising that the problem of temporal anaphora should have a counterpart in the problem of modal anaphora. Nor is it surprising that there should be similarities in the solution paths that we ultimately choose for the two phenomena. In this paper I have attempted to show that theories of temporal and modal anaphora can be constructed which avoid reference to metaphysically problematic and causally unconnected entities. In particular, I have suggested that by positing implicit temporal conjunctions and implicit conditional antecedents we can develop theories of E-type temporal and modal anaphora, and that these theories of anaphora can be employed in the service of more austere metaphysical theories. There may ultimately be reasons for positing past and future events or for positing possible worlds, but I hope to have shown that temporal and modal anaphora do not provide such reasons.

Notes

*Portions of this paper were presented at Princeton University and at the Rutgers University Center for Cognitive Science. I am indebted to John Burgess, Donald Davidson, Mike Fara, Delia Graff, Gil Harman, Kent Johnson, Ernie Lepore, Stephen Neale, Paul Pietroski, Scott Soames, and Edwin Williams for comments and discussion. I am also grateful to Graeme Forbes for comments on the penultimate draft.

1. See Prior (1967, 1968).
2. One assumption that I make throughout this paper is that there is an interesting connection between semantics and metaphysics, so that if the semantics of natural language requires reference to or quantification over certain entities, then we are committed to the existence of those entities. See Ludlow (1999) for justification of this assumption.
3. See Evans (1982), Neale (1990) for discussion.
4. I am grateful to Scott Soames (p.c.) for suggesting this possibility.
5. This is a simplified version of the proposal. For a more sophisticated treatment see Stone (1999).
6. The phrase 'modal accommodation' is a bit misleading, since Roberts' usage departs in significant ways from the use of the phrase in Lewis (1973). The basic mechanism proposed by Roberts is the same as what I am suggesting here, however.
7. I am grateful to Graeme Forbes for discussion here.
8. Here we should take the pronoun 'it' to be an E-type pronoun that stands proxy for a definite description—e.g. 'the snake in question' (which in turn will have narrow scope with respect to the modal operator).
9. I should also note that this account, as it stands, is only applicable to de dicto modal sentences. As Graeme Forbes reminds me, matters become more complicated when one attempts to construct disquotational T-theories that can handle cases of de re modality.

References

Davidson, D., 1967a. "Truth and Meaning," *Synthese* 17, pp. 304–323. Reprinted in *Inquiries Into Truth & Interpretation*. Oxford: Oxford University Press, 1984.

Davidson, D., 1967b. "The Logical Form of Action Sentences." In *Essays on Actions and Events*. Oxford: Oxford University Press, 1980.

Davies, M., 1981. *Meaning, Quantification, Necessity*. Routlege and Kegan Paul, London.

Enç, M., 1986. "Towards a Referential Analysis of Temporal Expressions." *Linguistics and Philosophy* 9, 405–426.

Enç, M., 1987. "Anchoring Conditions for Tense." *Linguistic Inquiry* 18, 633–657.

Evans, G., 1977. "Pronouns, Quantifiers, and Relative Clauses (I)," *Canadian Journal of Philosophy* 7, 467–536.

Evans, G., 1982. *The Varieties of Reference*. Oxford: Oxford University Press.

Frank, A. and H. Kamp, 1997. "On Context Dependence in Modal Constructions." In *Proceedings of SALT-97*, Stanford, CA.

Guerts, B., 1995. *Presupposing*. PhD thesis, University of Stuttgart.

Higginbotham, J., 1985. "On Semantics." *Linguistic Inquiry* 16, 547–594.

Hinrichs, E., 1981. *Temporale Anaphora im Englishen*. Unpublished Staatsexamen thesis. University of Tubingen, Tubingen, Germany.

Hinrichs, E., 1986. "Temporal Anaphora in Discourses of English," *Linguistics and Philosophy* 9, pp. 63–82.

Isard, S. 1974. "What would you have done if..." *Theoretical Linguistics* 1, 233–255.

Kamp, H., 1971. "Formal Properties of 'Now'." *Theoria* 37, 227–273.

Kibble, R. 1994. "Dynamics of Epistemic Modality and Anaphora." In R. Bunt, T. Muskens, and G. Rentier (eds.), *Proceedings of the International Workshop on Computational Semantics*. Tilburg, NL.

Kibble, R. 1995. "Modal Subordination, Focus and Complement Anaphora." Proceedings of the Tbilisi Symposium on Language, Logic and Computation.

Larson, R., and P. Ludlow, 1993. "Interpreted Logical Forms." *Synthese* 95, pp. 305–356.

Larson, R., and G. Segal, 1995. *Knowledge of Meaning*. Cambridge: MIT Press.

Lewis, D., 1973. *Counterfactuals*. Cambridge: Harvard University Press.

Ludlow, P., 1999. *Semantics, Tense, and Time: An Essay in the Metaphysics of Natural Language*. Cambridge: Cambridge University Press.

Neale, S., 1990. *Descriptions*. Cambridge: MIT Press.

Partee, B., 1973. "Some Structural Analogies Between Tenses and Pronouns in English," *The Journal of Philosophy* 70, pp. 601–609.

Partee, B., 1984. "Nominal and Temporal Anaphora," *Linguistics and Philosophy* 7, pp. 243–286.

Portner, P., 1995. "Modal Discourse Referents and the Semantics-Pragmatics Boundary," *University of Maryland Working Papers in Linguistics*.

Prior, A. N., 1967. *Past, Present and Future*. Oxford: Oxford University Press.

Prior, A. N., 1968. *Time and Tense*. Oxford: Oxford University Press.

Reichenbach, H. 1947. *Elements of Symbolic Logic*. New York: Macmillan.

Roberts, C., 1986. *Modal Subordination, Anaphora and Distributivity*. PhD thesis (Linguistics), University of Massachusettes, Amherst.

Roberts, C., 1989. "Modal Subordination and Pronominal Anaphora in Discourse." *Linguistics and Philosophy* 12, 683–721.

Russell, B., 1905. "On Denoting," *Mind* 14, pp. 479–493.

Russell, B., 1910–11. "Knowledge by Acquaintance and Knowledge by Description," *Proceedings of the Aristotelean Society*. Reprinted in *Mysticism and Logic*, London: George Allen and Unwin, 1917, and New York: Doubleday, 1957.

Stone, M., 1999. "Reference to Possible Worlds." Technical Report TR-49, Rutgers University Center for Cognitive Science.

Stone, M., and D. Hardt, 1997. "Dynamic discourse Referents for Tense and Modals." In R. Bunt, T. Muskens, and G. Rentier (eds.), *Proceedings of the International Workshop on Computational Semantics*. Tilburg, NL.

Webber, B. 1988. "Tense as Discourse Anaphor." *Computational Linguistics* 14, 61–73.

Philosophical Perspectives, 15, Metaphysics, 2001

McTAGGART ON TIME

Judith Jarvis Thomson
MIT

1.

McTaggart's argument for the conclusion that time does not exist is notoriously hard to understand.[1] C. D. Broad says that when properly interpreted, its main part can be seen to be "a philosophical 'howler'."[2] Others see things in it that they regard as true and important, or if not true, then anyway important. But I have not seen any interpretation of it that seems to me to get it exactly right. And I think that it pays to get it right: there are lessons to be learned from consideration of what goes on in it.

By way of reminder, McTaggart's argument has two parts. The first part aims at the conclusion that time does not exist unless the A series exists. The second part aims at the conclusion that the A series does not exist. It follows that time does not exist.

2.

What is the A series? We do better to begin with what McTaggart calls the B series.

Actually, we do best to begin with what McTaggart should be taken to mean when he talks about a series' existing or not existing. He does not say what he means, so we have to supply an interpretation.

McTaggart gives us descriptions of two series.[3] Both descriptions have the following form: the series such that (i) its members are the things that have property P, and (ii) one precedes another in the series just in case the one has the two-place relation Q to the other. It is clear enough that when he asks, rhetorically, whether a series so described exists, what he is asking is whether there is a series that satisfies the description. I suggest that we should take him to think that there is a series that satisfies the description if and only if there are things that have P, and for every pair of things that have P, one has Q to the other. I suggest that we follow him in this usage.

Consider the Happy Lion Series Description: the series such that (i) its members are the lions in my back yard, and (ii) one precedes another in the series just in case the one is happier than the other. Is there a series that satisfies that description? No. That is because there are no lions in my back yard. Consider the Happy Squirrel Series Description: the series such that (i) its members are the squirrels in my back yard, and (ii) one precedes another in the series just in case the one is happier than the other. Is there a series that satisfies that description? Well, there are squirrels in my back yard. Then there is a series that satisfies the description just in case for every pair of squirrels in my back yard, one is happier than the other.

It is worth noticing that opting for this account of the conditions under which there is a series that satisfies a description of the kind we are considering is compatible with opting for a (by now) familiar account of the conditions under which a series S is identical with a series S'. According to that account, S is identical with S' just in case they have the same members, and their order in S is the same as their order in S'. The fact that these accounts are compatible emerges as follows.

Suppose that there are only two squirrels in my back yard, Alfred and Bert, and that Alfred is happier than Bert. Then there is a series that satisfies the Happy Squirrel Series Description. Call it the Happy Squirrel Series. Consider now the Fat Squirrel Series Description: the series such that (i) its members are the squirrels in my back yard, and (ii) one precedes another in the series just in case the one is fatter than the other. Suppose that Alfred is not merely happier than Bert but fatter than Bert. Then there is a series that satisfies the Fat Squirrel Series Description. Call it the Fat Squirrel Series. What is the relation between the Happy Squirrel Series and the Fat Squirrel Series? We are entirely free to say—as the familiar account of the identity conditions for series directs us to say—that they are one and the same series. Indeed, that they are both identical with the ordered pair ⟨Alfred, Bert⟩. Three series-descriptions but only one series.

We must of course allow that the following might have been the case: Alfred is happier than Bert but no fatter or thinner than Bert. If that had been the case, then there would all the same have been a series satisfying the Happy Squirrel Series Description; so on any view, the Happy Squirrel Series would have existed. But there would have been no series satisfying the Fat Squirrel Series Description; would the Fat Squirrel Series have existed? We are free to say that the Fat Squirrel Series would have existed, for we are free to say that it simply would not in that case have satisfied the Fat Squirrel Series Description. We are free to say, more generally, that unless P is an essential property of the things that have it, and Q such that if x has it to y then x necessarily has it to y, a series that in fact satisfies a description of the kind we are considering might have failed to do so.

Would McTaggart have accepted this (by now) familiar identity conditions for series? There is only one place at which it will matter whether he would have accepted it; we will get to it in section 5 below.

3.

Let us now turn to the B series. What are its members? McTaggart introduces us to the B and A series together: he says they are series of what he calls "positions in time"—I take these to be time points or chunks.

But he goes straightway on to say:

> The contents of any position in time form an event. The varied simultaneous contents of a single position are, of course, a plurality of events. But, like any other substance, they form a group, and this group is a compound substance. And a compound substance consisting of simultaneous events may properly be spoken of as itself an event. (10)

Presumably the compounding he has in mind is mereological fusion. And from here on, he throughout writes as if he meant us to suppose that the members of the B and A series are events. For example, he goes straightway on to say: "[t]he first question which we must consider is whether it is essential to the reality of time that its events should form an A series as well as a B series." (11) Let us say that an event is an E event if and only if it is the mereological fusion of all the events that occur at and only at a given time point. And let us say, then, that the members of both the B and A series are the E events.

What fixes which E events precede which in the B series? McTaggart tells us about the B series: "the terms have to be such that, of any two of them, either the first is earlier than the second, or the second is earlier than the first." (10) So we may take it that the following is McTaggart's description of the B series:

> (B Series Description) the series such that (i) its members are the E events, and (ii) one precedes another in the series just in case the one is earlier than the other.

This may well strike us as puzzling, however. It is not, of course, transparent what it is or would be for time to not exist, but it is intuitively very plausible to think that if there are events, some earlier than others, then time does exist.[4] So if there is a series that satisfies the B Series Description, and it is the B series, then doesn't the existence of the B series suffice for the existence of time? But if so, then what are we to make of the first part of McTaggart's argument? Why does the existence of time require the existence of the A series if the existence of the B series would suffice?

McTaggart does not make explicit what his answer is. There are two replies available to him.

He can reply, first, that that intuitively very plausible idea is mistaken. Thus he can say that the existence of events, some earlier than others, does not suffice for the existence of time. He can say that what the existence of time requires is that there be time points. I am sure that many people do so use "Time exists" that it is true if and only if there are such entities as time points.

But it is clear that McTaggart would not make this first reply. If he had said that the B series is a series of events and the A series a series of time points, then perhaps it would be right to think he would make this reply. But as I said, he does not say this. I have pointed to reason to believe he intends the members of both series to be events.

Moreover, there are many places in the text that show that he thinks the existence of the B series really would suffice for the existence of time. For example, having proved to his satisfaction that the existence of the A series is required for the existence of time, McTaggart says that the B series

> cannot exist except as temporal, since earlier and later, which are the relations which connect its terms, are clearly time-relations. So it follows that there can be no B series when there is no A series, since without an A series there is no time." (13)[5]

So I suggest that we should attribute to him the second response available to him, namely that the existence of the B series would suffice for the existence of time. He can also say that the existence of the A series is required for the existence of time: he need merely add that the existence of the B series would suffice for the existence of the A series. We will return to this idea in section 5 below.

4.

The members of the A series, like the members of the B series, are the E events. Under what condition does one member precede another in the A series? There is only one passage that explicitly answers this question, namely: the A series "runs from the far past through the near past to the present, and then from the present through the near future to the far future" (10). Let us help ourselves to the following complex two-place relation:

x has the Temporal Perspective Relation to y just in case
    (1) x is past, and either y is nearer past than x is, or y is present, or y is future, or
    (2) x is present, and y is future, or
    (3) x is future, and y is farther future than x is.

Then we can say that the A series is the series that satisfies the following description:

(A Series Description) the series such that (i) its members are the E events, and (ii) one precedes another in the series just in case the one has the Temporal Perspective Relation to the other.

5.

We now have before us characterizations of McTaggart's B and A series: if there is a series that satisfies the B Series Description, it is the B series, and if there is a series that satisfies the A Series Description, it is the A series. Whether there are series that satisfy these descriptions is a matter we will turn to in the following section. We might well want to ask first, however, how they are related to each other—supposing that they do exist.

Suppose they do exist. They have the same members: each has the E events as its members. Is the order of the events different in the two series? Surely it is obvious that an event x has the Temporal Perspective Relation to y just in case it is earlier than y. (McTaggart himself gives no hint of thinking otherwise.) Then the order of the events in the A series is the same as the order of the events in the B series. So if we opt for the familiar account of the identity conditions for series that I mentioned in section 2—namely that series S is identical with series S' just in case they have the same members, and their order in S is the same as their order in S'—then we are committed to supposing that the A series just is the B series.

I asked, rhetorically, in section 2, whether McTaggart would have accepted this identity condition for series. We should notice now that if he did accept it, he could easily explain why the existence of the B series would suffice for the existence of the A series: the existence of the B series would suffice for the existence of the A series because the A series just is the B series.

On the other hand, he plainly thinks that the A series is not identical with the B series; so he did not accept this identity condition for series. So what should we take him to think marks the one series off from the other?[6] Perhaps that the relation being earlier than and the Temporal Perspective Relation are different relations, and therefore that the series whose order is fixed by the one is different from the series whose order is fixed by the other.

But it is easy to see that this won't do. Suppose there is a series of all E events such that one precedes another in the series just in case the one has the Temporal Perspective Relation to the other; call every such series an alpha series. Suppose also that there is a series of all E events such that one precedes another in the series just in case the one is earlier than the other; call every such series a beta series. Let us grant McTaggart that the Temporal Perspective Relation is not the same as the earlier than relation. Still, an event x is earlier than an event y just in case x has the Temporal Perspective Relation to y.[7] It follows that every beta series is an alpha series. Therefore McTaggart cannot have that every beta series is different from every alpha series in that their ordering relations are different.

So we really had better suppose that if there is such a thing as the A series, it is the B series. This supposition is not going to turn out to have been unfair to McTaggart, since, as we will see, his argument for the nonexistence of time does not anywhere rely on there being a difference between the A series and the B series.

6.

Let us turn now to the first part of the argument; it aims at the conclusion that time exists only if the A series exists.

McTaggart says that time exists just in case some things change, and he argues that things change only if the A series exists.

Is McTaggart right to say that time exists just in case some things change? No doubt there is room to argue that he is not. Let us bypass that question: let us suppose that McTaggart is right to say this.

His argument to the effect that things change only if the A series exists is another matter, and needs a closer look.

What exactly is it for a thing to change? McTaggart invites us to agree that a thing changes just in case it has a property ("quality", "characteristic") at one time and lacks it at another.[8] We may well think this intuitively plausible.

But McTaggart would have us agree that it is not so easy to supply examples. Let us suppose that a certain poker was not hot until a certain Monday, hot on that Monday, and not hot thereafter. We might think that our supposition, together with McTaggart's account of change, entitles us to conclude that the poker changes. Not so, McTaggart says. He says:

> this makes no change in the qualities of the poker. It is always a quality of that poker that it is one which is hot on that particular Monday. And it is always a quality of that poker that it is one which is not hot at any other time. Both these qualities are true of it at any time—the time when it is hot and the time when it is cold. And therefore it seems to be erroneous to say that there is any change in the poker. (15)

McTaggart takes it that for the poker to be hot on and only on that Monday is for the following to be the case:

(S_1) The poker has the two-place relation being hot-at to that Monday and lacks it to all other days.

But he says that the truth of (S_1) does not suffice for the poker to change: after all, the poker always has that relation to that Monday, and always lacks it to all other days.

We might wonder why McTaggart does not take it that for the poker to be hot on and only on that Monday is for the following to be the case:

(S_2) The poker has, on that Monday, the property being hot, and lacks it on all other days.

If that is true, then his account of change yields that the poker does change.

I suggest that we must take McTaggart to think that there is no such property as being hot. Let us call a property a temporary property just in case it is possible that a thing has it at one time and lacks it at another. McTaggart thinks that things change just in case they have a property at one time and lack it at another. Thus things change only if there are temporary properties. I am sure McTaggart would say that if there were such a property as being hot, it would be a temporary property, and the truth of (S_2) would suffice for the poker to change. What I am suggesting is that we must take him to think that being hot is not a temporary property because there is no such property; and (S_2) is therefore false.

Which, on McTaggart's view, are the temporary properties? He says:

> The fact that it [the poker] is hot at one point in a series and cold at other points cannot give change, if neither of these facts change—and neither of them does. Nor does any other fact about the poker change, unless its presentness, pastness, or futurity change. (15)

He had just above said the same of events, thus that the death of Queen Anne, for example, is "in every respect but one" unchanging—the one respect in which it does change is this: it was far future, then nearer future, then present, then past, then further past. "Such characteristics as these are the only characteristics which can change. And, therefore, if there is any change, it must be looked for in the A series, and in the A series alone." (13)

He clearly thinks that the only temporary properties are being present, being past, and being future. (Perhaps we should we add: being far future, being far past, and so on. For brevity, I ignore them.) It follows that a thing changes just in case it has one of these three properties at one time, and lacks it at another.

Which are the things that might be thought to have one or other of the three at a time? Events, and only events.[9] So a thing changes just in case it is an event and has one of the three at a time, and lacks it at another. Consider the event (state of affairs?) that consists in the poker's being hot.[10] If there is such an event, then, given our original supposition, it has the temporary property being present on the Monday, and not on other days. So it is not the truth of (S_1) or (S_2) that would suffice for there to be change; it is rather the truth of

(S_3) The poker's being hot has, on that Monday, the property being present, and lacks it on all other days

that would. We need to keep in mind, however, that the truth of (S_3) would not suffice for change in the poker; what it would suffice for is only change in the event that consists in the poker's being hot.

We have not quite reached McTaggart's conclusion. We have reached the conclusion that a thing changes just in case it is an event that has one of the three temporary properties at a time, and lacks it at another. I take it he would say that if any event has one of the three temporary properties at a time, then all events do, including the E events. I take it he would say that if any E event has one of the three properties at a time, then it has the others at other times. From here it is only a short step to the conclusion that there is change just in case for every pair of E events, one has the Temporal Perspective Relation to the other—and from here an even shorter step to McTaggart's conclusion that there is change only if the A series exists.

Should we accept this argument? Let us begin with temporary properties.

Are there *any* temporary properties? Suppose that "F(x)" stands for a property, and that "A" refers to something, and that in saying

F(A)

you would be predicating that property of A. It is a very natural idea that if you do say "F(A)" you assert a proposition, and moreover, that the proposition you assert if you say it at one time is the same as the proposition you assert if you say it at any other time.[11] For example, suppose that "$\text{Hot}_{3AM,11/2/00}(x)$" stands for the property being hot-at-3AM,11/2/00, and that "the poker" refers to McTaggart's poker, and that in saying

$\text{Hot}_{3AM,11/2/00}$(the poker)

you would be predicating that property of McTaggart's poker. It is very natural to think that if you do say "$\text{Hot}_{3AM,11/2/00}$(the poker)" you assert a proposition, and moreover, that the proposition you assert if you say it at one time is the same as the proposition you assert if you say it at any other time. That is surely very plausible.

Now suppose that there is such a property as being hot. And suppose that "Hot(x)" stands for it, and that "the poker" refers to McTaggart's poker, and that in saying

Hot(the poker)

you would be predicating that property of McTaggart's poker. According to the very natural idea, if you do say "Hot(the poker)" you assert a proposition, and moreover, the proposition you assert if you say it at one time is the same as the proposition you assert if you say it at any other time. But the property being hot—if there is such a property—is a temporary property. That is, it is possible that a thing has the property at one time and lacks the property at another time. Therefore it may be that the proposition you assert when you say "Hot(the poker)" at one time is true and the proposition you assert when when you say it at another time is false. It follows that the proposition you assert at the one time is not the same as the proposition you assert at the other time, and the very natural idea is therefore false.

A devotee of the very natural idea therefore concludes that there is no such property as being hot. And so similarly for all temporary properties: there aren't any. Similar reasoning yields that there are no temporary relations. For example, while there is such a non-temporary three-place relation as "x is taller than y at t", there is no such temporary two-place relation as "x is taller than y".

It may have been something like this very natural idea that led McTaggart to think that there is no such temporary property as being hot, and to say, therefore, that for the poker to be hot on a particular Monday is not for the poker to have, on that Monday, the (temporary) property being hot, but rather for it to have the (non-temporary) two-place relation being hot-at to that Monday.

But perhaps not. For if that very natural idea was what led him to think that there is no such temporary property as being hot, then it is puzzling that he should have failed to notice that the same holds of the (putative) temporary properties being present, being past, and being future. Surely one who says

Present(the poker's being hot)

at different times no more asserts the same proposition on both occasions than does one who says "Hot(the poker)" at a time at which the poker is hot and then again at a later time at which the poker is no longer hot. Thus if the very natural idea had been what led him to think that there is no such temporary property as being hot, then it is hard to see why he rejected being hot out of hand but took being present seriously.

We do not *have to* accept the very natural idea. There are alternatives on offer in the literature.[12] But there remains this to be said for McTaggart: anyone who wants to have that there are temporary properties and relations has to suppose that a satisfactory alternative is available or can be found.

There also remains this to be said against McTaggart: there is no good reason to distinguish among (putative) temporary properties as he does. If there are such temporary properties as being present, being past, and being future, then there is no good reason to reject such temporary properties as being hot.

Should we also say that if there are such temporary properties as being hot, then there is no good reason to reject such temporary properties as being present, being past, and being future? We might think that whether or not there are such temporary properties as being hot, there anyway are no such temporary properties as being present, being past, and being future. Or we might not. Let us not stop over the questions that arise here: let us grant McTaggart his favored temporary properties, and reserve criticism for the use he makes of them. If it helps, we can suppose the following. For an event to be present is for it to be occurring, or going on. For an event to be past is for it to be over, done, completed. For an event to be future is for it to be going to occur or go on.[13]

To return now to McTaggart on change. He invites us to accept two theses. The first, (I), says that a thing changes just in case it has a property at one time and lacks it at another. This yields that the truth of

> (S_1) The poker has the two-place relation being hot-at to that Monday and lacks it to all other days

does not suffice for the poker to change, for the poker always has that relation to that Monday and always lacks it to all other days.

The second thesis, (II), says that the only temporary properties are being present, being past, and being future. This yields that

> (S_2) The poker has, on that Monday, the property being hot, and lacks it on all other days

is false. However (II) leaves open that

> (S_3) The poker's being hot has, on that Monday, the property being present, and lacks it on all other days

may be true.

McTaggart therefore invites us to agree that there is change only if the likes of (S_3) are true.

I have suggested that if there are such temporary properties as being present, being past, and being future, then there is no good reason to reject such temporary properties as being hot. We should therefore reject thesis (II).

We should also reject thesis (I). Suppose you accept the very natural idea that I described, and therefore conclude that there are no temporary properties. Are you really committed to thinking that nothing changes? That is hard to believe. (The very natural idea is an idea about what a person asserts by saying certain sentences. How could it plausibly be thought to yield the metaphysical conclusion that nothing changes?) In particular, you might well say that the truth of (S_1) does suffice for change—indeed, change in the poker. You might well say, more strongly, that for there to be change just is for the likes of (S_1) to be true. It is not in the least obvious why this should be thought a mistake.

A further alternative is available, which some would say is preferable. McTaggart believes that there is no such temporary property as being hot because there is no such property as being hot. Other philosophers would agree with McTaggart that there is no such temporary property as being hot, but for a different reason: on their view, there is such a property as being hot but it is non-temporary. David Lewis is an example.[14] On his view, it cannot be the case that a thing has being hot at one time and not at another. He therefore concludes that we should accept the metaphysic of temporal parts. In particular, that we should say that for the poker to be hot on and only on that Monday is for

(S₄) The poker's that-Monday temporal part has the (non-temporary) property being hot, and the poker has temporal parts prior to its that-Monday part, and temporal parts after its that-Monday part, and all of them lack the (non-temporary) property being hot

to be true, and that the truth of (S₄) suffices for change—once again, change in the poker. Lewis would say that for there to be change just is for the likes of (S₄) to be true.

I find this idea unsatisfactory for a variety of reasons, one of which I will draw attention to in section 9. Meanwhile, however, it supplies us with a second way of understanding change that is incompatible with McTaggart's thesis (I) that a thing changes just in case it has a property at one time and lacks it at another.

In sum, the first part of McTaggart's argument does not succeed.

7.

The second part of McTaggart's argument aims at showing that the A series does not exist. If there is a series that satisfies

(A Series Description) the series such that (i) its members are the E events, and (ii) one precedes another just in case the one has the Temporal Perspective Relation to the other,

where

x has the Temporal Perspective Relation to y just in case
    (1) x is past, and either y is nearer past than x is, or y is present, or y is future, or
    (2) x is present, and y is future, or
    (3) x is future, and y is further future than x is,

then it is the A series. Following McTaggart, we are supposing that the A series exists if and only if there are E events, and for every pair of them, one has the Temporal Perspective Relation to the other. McTaggart now argues for the conclusion that nothing can have the property being present, or the property being past, or the property being future. If that argument succeeds, then nothing has the Temporal Perspective Relation to anything else, and the A series does not exist.

He gives more than one argument for his conclusion. I bypass the first since I am not at all sure I have understood it. McTaggart himself says that the second points to "a more positive difficulty" facing the idea that x might have one or other of the three properties we are concerned with, so let us turn to it.

The argument is a reductio. Let us assume

(1) M is past.

McTaggart says:

> If M is past, it has been present and future. If it is future, it will be present and past. If it is present, it has been future and will be past. Thus all three characteristics belong to each event. (20)

So if (1) is true, so also is

(1*) (a) M is past, and
     (b) M is present, and
     (c) M is future.

But (1*), he says, is self-contradictory.

He knows perfectly well that his opponent has an answer. McTaggart says:

> It is never true, the answer will run, that M *is* present, past, and future. It *is* present, *will be* past, and *has been* future. Or it *is* past, and *has been* future and present, or again *is* future, and will be present and past. The characteristics are only incompatible when they are simultaneous, and there is no contradiction to this in the fact that each term has all of them successively. (21)

Thus (the answer runs): "what follows from (1) is not (1*) but only

(2) (a) M is past, and
    (b) M was present, and
    (c) M was future.

And unlike (1*), (2) is not self-contradictory."

McTaggart asks:

> But what is meant by "has been" and "will be"? And what is meant by "is," when, as here, it is used with a temporal meaning, and not simply for predication? (21)

His answer is:

> When we say that X has been Y, we are asserting X to be Y at a moment of past time. When we say that X will be Y, we are asserting X to be Y at a moment of

future time. When we say that X is Y (in the temporal sense of "is"), we are asserting X to be Y at a moment of present time. (21)

Now "M is (temporal sense) past" is of the form "X is (temporal sense) Y." So (2)(a) says "M is past at a moment of present time." More precisely, it says "M is past at a t such that t is present." But all three characteristics belong to each moment of time just as all three belong to each event; thus if t is present it is also past and future. So if (2) is true, so also is

>   (2*) (a) M is past at a t such that t is present, and t is past and t is future, and
>   (b) M...,

which is self-contradictory.

We can see how it goes on. McTaggart's opponent now says "No, no. What follows from (2) is not (2*), but only

>   (3) (a) M is past at a t such that t is (temporal sense) present and t will be past and t was future, and
>   (b) M...,

which is not self-contradictory." Aha, says McTaggart, the second clause of (3)(a), namely "t is (temporal sense) present", is of the form "X is (temporal sense) Y", so what it says is "t is present at a moment of present time." More precisely, what it says is "t is present at a t' such that t' is present." But all three characteristics belong to each time t'; thus if t' is present it is also past and future. So if (3) is true, so also is

>   (3*) (a) M is past at a t such that t is present at a t' such that t' is present and t' is past and t' is future, and
>   (b) M...,

which is self-contradictory.

As I said, we can see how it goes on. McTaggart now says:

Such an infinity is vicious. The attribution of the characteristics past, present, and future to the terms of any series leads to a contradiction, unless it is specified that they have them successively. This means, as we have seen, that they have them in relation to terms specified as past, present, and future. These again, to avoid a like contradiction, must in turn be specified as past, present, and future. And, since this continues infinitely, the first set of terms never escapes from contradiction at all. (22)

His idea is this. If (1) is true, so also is (1*), which is self-contradictory. We try to escape from contradiction by declaring that what follows from (1) is not

(1*) but only (2). But (2) is tensed; properly interpreted, it can be seen to yield (2*), which is self-contradictory. We try to escape from contradiction by declaring that what follows from (2) is not (2*) but only (3). But (3) is tensed; properly interpreted, it can be seen... .And so on. So we never escape from contradiction.

We must therefore reject our assumption

(1) M is past;

that is, it cannot be the case that M is past. Similar reasoning yields that it cannot be the case that M is present or that M is future. So no event can have any of the temporary properties being past, being present, and being future. It follows that the A series does not exist.

What is crucial to this argument is obviously McTaggart's idea that if an event M, or a time t, is past then it is also present and future. His reason for thinking this lurks in a passage I quoted above, namely

> But what is meant by "has been" and "will be"? And what is meant by "is," when, as here, it is used with a temporal meaning, and not simply for predication? (21)

When we say "M is past", we may be using "is" with a temporal meaning. That is, we may mean "M is now past". But we may instead be using "is" simply for predication. That is, it may be that what we assert is what we would have asserted if we had instead said "Past(M)", in saying which we would simply be predicating pastness of M.

How did he get from here to his idea that if an event M, or a time t, is past then it is also present and future? I suggest that his route went as follows.

In saying "Past(M)" we are simply predicating pastness of M. But that "simply" should be properly understood. In saying "Past(M)" we do assert a proposition. The role of that "simply" is simply to indicate that in saying "Past(M)" we are not asserting that M is past at the time of our speaking. We are not asserting anything about when M is past.

It follows that the proposition we assert if we say "Past(M)" at one time is the same as the proposition we assert if we say it at any other time.

[What has surfaced here is what I called the very natural idea in the preceding section.[15] You might have thought that McTaggart would therefore conclude that there is no such temporary property as being past, and a fortiori, that there is no such thing as predicating 'it' of M. For don't we assert a false proposition if we say "Past(M)" at a time before M is past but a true one if we say it at a time when M is past? (Compare the argument I set out to show that there is no such temporary property as being hot.) Note that there being no such temporary property as being past—and also no such temporary properties as being present and being future—would have been good enough for his purposes: no event would have the Temporal Perspective Relation to any other, and it would follow that the A series does not exist. But McTaggart does not conclude that there is no such temporary property as being past. What he does instead is to deny that we assert a false proposition if we say "Past(M)" at a time before M is past but a true one if we say it at a time when M is past. To return to McTaggart:]

Suppose that M is at some time past. Then the proposition we assert if we say "Past(M)" is true—true whether or not M is past at the time of our saying "Past(M)". For remember: in saying that sentence, we are not asserting anything about when M is past.[16]

But if M is at some time past, it is also at some time present and at some time future. So the propositions we assert if we say "Present(M)" and "Future(M)" are also true. Destination reached: if an event M is past then it is also present and future. Similarly for any time t.

It pays to notice that if McTaggart's reductio succeeded, a similar argument would succeed in showing that nothing that is ever hot and ever cold can be either hot or cold. That is, while I began with "M is past," I could as well have begun with "McTaggart's poker is hot", for a route analogous to the one I suggest that he took to "If an event M is past then it is also present and future" would have taken us to "If McTaggart's poker is hot then it is also cold." It might have been thought (and I think that some people have thought) that what started the regress was the fact that in saying "M is past," we predicate a mysterious property. Not so. Or not so unless a property's being temporary itself suffices for it to be mysterious.

In any case, the combination of ideas at work in McTaggart won't do. If P is a temporary property then there is no such thing as 'simply predicating' it of a thing. And in sum, the second part of McTaggart's argument is no more successful than the first.

8.

Michael Dummett says that those who think McTaggart's argument for the nonexistence of time is a "trivial sophism"—as some people do—have failed to see what is really going on in it.[17] Dummett asks the good question why McTaggart did not go on to supply an analogous argument for the nonexistence of space. Dummett himself thinks that there is an important difference between time and space that emerges when we contrast McTaggart's argument against time with its analogue against space.

What Dummett focuses on in McTaggart's argument is its first part. (He says it contains "the heart of" McTaggart's argument for the nonexistence of time.) As I interpreted it in section 6, McTaggart there argues that there is no change unless things acquire and lose the temporary properties being present, being past, and being future. Dummett interprets it differently. According to Dummett, McTaggart there argues for the following conclusion:

a description of events as taking place *in time* is impossible unless temporally token-reflexive expressions enter into it, that is, unless the description is given by someone who is himself in that time. (354)

Let us call this the Time Thesis. According to Dummett, McTaggart does not argue for the analogous Space Thesis since McTaggart thinks it is not true. What is the analogous Space Thesis? Dummett does not spell it out, but we may take it to say:

a description of physical objects as occupying places *in space* is impossible unless spatially token-reflexive expressions enter into it, that is, unless the description is given by someone who is himself in that space.

According to Dummett, it is because McTaggart thinks the Time Thesis is true and the Space Thesis is not true that McTaggart goes on to argue that time does not exist and does not argue in the same way that space does not exist.

Why does thinking the Time Thesis true lead McTaggart to think that time does not exist? According to Dummett, McTaggart is implicitly appealing to a prejudice that lies very deep in many people, namely that "there must be a complete description of reality; more properly, that of anything which is real, there must be a complete—that is, observer-independent—description." (356) Thus presumably a description that token-reflexive expressions do not enter into.

Dummett himself thinks that the Time Thesis is true and the Space Thesis false. Moreover, he says that he is himself very strongly inclined to accept the prejudice he says McTaggart is appealing to. But he thinks that McTaggart is mistaken in concluding that time does not exist, and that this shows we must abandon the prejudice.

Dummett says that in any case, it is this deep issue that McTaggart's argument for the nonexistence of time draws our attention to, and that McTaggart's argument is therefore quite certainly not a trivial sophism.

Let us bypass the question whether Dummett has interpreted McTaggart correctly. What is more interesting is the question whether the views Dummett attributes to McTaggart are correct.

I think we do suppose that something like what Dummett calls the prejudice is true—that, as Dummett also puts it, "reality must be something of which there exists in principle" a description free of token-reflexives, or that, as he also puts it, "[t]he description of what is really there, as it really is, must be independent of any particular point of view." Surely it is not enough for there to really be a cylindrical gray rock on Cambridge Common that it looks to me, from where I now stand and in the prevailing light, that there is one there.[18]

Let us set the prejudice aside for the time being and return to the Time Thesis and the Space Thesis. You might well think it long over-due that I say something about what Dummett means by them, since that is hardly transparent. To find out what he means we need to look at the reasons he gives for thinking the one true and the other false.

Dummett begins by inviting us to suppose a person is in process of observing a sequence of events. Dummett then says:

> Then even if he knows both what he has observed and what he is going to observe, he cannot give a complete description of his observations without the use of temporally token-reflexive expressions. He can give a complete narration of the sequence of events, but there would remain to be answered the question, 'And which of these events is happening *now*?' (354)

This suggests that what Dummett means by the Time Thesis is: you cannot give a "complete description" of a series of events that you are in process of observing unless it includes "Event M is happening now".

What does he mean by the Space Thesis? He thinks it is false, and we can see what he means by it when we see why he thinks it is false:

> By contrast, the use of spatially token-reflexive expressions is not essential to the description of objects as being in a space. That is, I can describe an arrangement of objects in space although I do not myself have any position in space. An example would be the space of my visual field. In that space there is no here or there, no near or far: I am not in that space. We can, I think, conceive, on the strength of this analogy, of a being who could perceive objects in our three-dimensional physical space although he occupied no position in that space. He would have no use for any spatially token-reflexive expressions in giving a description of the physical universe, ...[19] (354)

This suggests that what he means by the Space Thesis is what was to have been expected, namely that you cannot give a "complete description" of an array of physical objects that you are observing unless it includes "Object O is here". The Space Thesis, then, is the spatial analogue of the Time Thesis, and Dummett thinks the Space Thesis false and the Time Thesis true.

I have flagged Dummett's expression "complete description" in my statement of the two theses for the obvious reason: it is not at all clear what Dummett can mean by it. What could it come to for there to be a complete description of a thing?

There was another place at which Dummett used that expression. His first statement of the prejudice was this: "there must be a complete description of reality; more properly, that of anything which is real, there must be a complete— that is, observer-independent—description." There are two ways of interpreting the final clause of that sentence. We can take the clause to say "there must be a description that is complete in the sense of being observer-independent". But this way of understanding the expression will not do for Dummett's purposes, since there are observer-independent descriptions of events just as there are observer-independent descriptions of physical objects. Alternatively, we can take the clause to say "there must be a complete description that is observer-independent". But this is no help to us: it leaves us still confronted with the expression "complete description".

Perhaps we should give up on that expression, and so also on my interpretations of the Time Thesis and the Space Thesis. Perhaps what Dummett has in mind is not a difference between possibilities of description, but rather a difference that he might express in the following way:

> (i) We can conceive of a being who could perceive objects in our three-dimensional space although he occupied no position in that space,

but

> (ii) We cannot conceive of a being who could perceive events in our one-dimensional time although he occupied no position in that time.

I extracted (i) from the passage I quoted just above. Dummett went on to say there that the being described in (i) "would have no use for any spatially token-reflexive expressions in giving a description of the physical universe"; thus he would have no use for such descriptions as "The poker is here" and "The poker is nearer to me than the piano is." Surely something stronger had better be true: since the being described in (i) is not in the same space as the poker and the piano, those descriptions would be at best false, and perhaps nonsense.

This helps us understand (ii), for we can take it to say that if a being is perceiving a sequence of events that includes event M, then it must be that he speaks truly if he now says either "M took place before now," or "M is taking place now," or "M will take place after now." Never mind whether he must say one or other of those things if he is now to give a complete description of the sequence he is perceiving; it is enough for the difference Dummett is pointing to—on this interpretation of him—that one or other of those descriptions must be true.

It is plausible enough to suppose that (ii) is true. But I can see no good reason to accept (i), and there is good reason to reject it. The being described in (i) is described as *perceiving* objects in our three-dimensional space although he occupies no position in that space. But to be perceiving physical objects, say a poker and a piano, is to be perceiving them from a certain angle, and thus from within the space they occupy.

Dummett had suggested that we should accept (i) on the strength of an analogy with one's visual field: in his visual field, he says, "there is no here or there, no near or far: I am not in that space." Well, I am not in among the things that are in my visual field. (If I am in the dining room looking into the living room, then I am by hypothesis not in among the things in the living room.) But it is nevertheless true that some of the things in my visual field (as, for example, some of the things in my living room) are nearer to me than others are.[20]

It is of course conceivable that there should be an array of physical objects whose space I am not in since I do not exist. But so also is it conceivable that there should be a sequence of events whose time I am not in since I do not exist.

In sum, I have found no way of interpreting the views Dummett attributes to McTaggart under which they could be thought to point to a metaphysically significant disanalogy between time and space—or indeed, to any disanalogy between them at all.

9.

There are plenty of disanalogies between temporal and spatial descriptions, of course; it might pay to mention one that is familiar to all of us but that is nevertheless of interest for present purposes.

What I have in mind is a certain difference between our use of "now" and "here". Suppose that there was, a few years ago, a series of powerful earthquakes in and around Dedham. Standing in Dedham, I say to you "The countryside is hilly here now." Presumably I mean to be telling you that the countryside is hilly in the place in space that I indicate (the Dedham area) at the place in time that I indicate (the time of my speaking). So far so good. Now suppose that standing in Dedham, I say to you "This tomato is soft here now." Do I mean to be telling you that the tomato is soft at the place in space that I indicate (the Dedham area?) at the place in time that I indicate (the time of my speaking)? What would it come to for the tomato to be soft in the Dedham area?

When I say to you "This tomato is soft here now" I typically accompany my remark with a gesture; and what I mean to be telling you is that the tomato is now soft at the place, not in space but on the tomato, that I indicate. What I mean to be telling you, alternatively put, is that a part of my tomato is now soft, namely the part that I indicate.

The countryside has parts too, of course. So perhaps when I say to you "The countryside is hilly here now," I am not indicating a place in space (the Dedham area), and what I mean to be telling you is not that the countryside is now hilly at that place; perhaps I am instead indicating a part of the countryside (its Dedham area part) and what I mean to be telling you is that *it* is hilly now.[21]

There remains a disanalogy. The countryside has a Dedham area part; the tomato has no Dedham area part.

Suppose that the tomato is now lying on the Dedham-Needham line, half in Dedham, half in Needham. Then the tomato has a part that is now in Dedham. But the countryside does not have a part that is *just* now in Dedham. Tomatoes move around, the countryside does not. And the familiar difference between our use of "now" and our use of "here" is due to the very fact that so many of the physical objects that we are interested in do move around.

But how is this 'moving around' to be understood? Motion is a species of change, so we are now brought back to a question about change that I left open at the end of section 6.

Let us focus on motion.[22] Suppose we carried our tomato from Chatham to Dedham. Then our tomato moved from Chatham to Dedham. What marks *it* as having moved from Chatham to Dedham?

A friend of the metaphysic of temporal parts (MTP) says this: the tomato had a series of discrete but spatio-temporally continuous temporal parts, the first of which was in Chatham, and the last in Dedham.

But he needs to do something more: he needs to convince us that none of the members of the series were themselves tomatoes. For consider a series of what according to MTP were discrete but spatio-temporally continuous five-minute temporal chunks of our tomato. Suppose that what really happened was this:

(Story) Each of the five-minute members of the series was itself a five-minute, entirely new tomato—new skin, new tomato-flesh, new seeds, new particles composing it.

If Story is true, then surely no tomato moved from Chatham to Dedham when we thought that ours was doing so.

It won't do for the friend of MTP to say, simply, "Well, if Story is true, then your thought was false: your tomato did not move from Chatham to Dedham." For it had better not be left a chancy business whether or not a tomato (or anything else) ever moves from one place to another.

It also won't do for the friend of MTP to say "No surely about it! Story *is* true since every (cross-sectional) temporal part of a tomato is itself a tomato. So your tomato is the fusion of a great many tomatoes. And it *did* move from Chatham to Dedham since one of the tomatoes was in Chatham and a later one in Dedham." It is an odd idea that a tomato should be the fusion of many tomatoes, and not one offered us by the typical friend of MTP. Not surprisingly. No tomato moved through a short time unless at least some of the skin, the tomato-flesh, the seeds, the particles it was composed of at the start still compose it at the end. If Story is true, however, then the second five-minute tomato shares no skin and so on with the first, and the third shares no skin and so on with the second or the first, and... . So no tomato moved even through the fourth to the sixth minute, much less through all the time it took us to get to Dedham.

The friend of MTP must therefore show that Story is false. We do not have the burden of proving it true or even possible. He has the burden of proof, for he is the one who told us that for our tomato to move from Chatham to Dedham is for new things to be coming into existence throughout that time—new red, bulgy, juicy things, which in all respects other than their short lifespan behave exactly like tomatoes. But I can see no way in which he can show that Story is false.

Similarly for other species of change. A tomato might change from hard to soft. If what followed a five-minute hard tomato was a new five-minute soft tomato, then no tomato thereby changed from hard to soft. Similarly of course for sheer endurance. If what followed one five-minute tomato is another, then no tomato thereby lasted from the one time to the other.

If we reject MTP, we still have three of the four alternatives I drew attention to in section 6. According to McTaggart, only events change, so tomatoes in particular do not. It hardly needs saying that that fact counts conclusively against the alternative he offers us.

That leaves us with two of the four alternatives, each of which allows us to have that the tomato changes. First, we can appeal to temporary properties. We can say that the tomato changes because it has the temporary properties being in Chatham and being hard, at one time and not at another. Second, we can appeal to non-temporary relations. We can say that the tomato changes because it has the non-temporary relations being in-Chatham-at, and being hard-at, to one time and not to another. I suggest that the very fact that these two alternatives allow us to have that the tomato changes counts in favor of them.

10.

McTaggart's dark discussion of time is like a Rorschach blot. Some have seen a frog in it. Others a prince. Still others a clash of armies by night. I have thought it worth trying to be clear about the features of the blot itself.[23]

Notes

1. Until indicated otherwise, numbers in parentheses are page numbers in McTaggart (1927).
2. See Broad (1938).
3. In fact he describes three, but I will discuss the third only briefly, in footnote 5.
4. G.E. Moore famously thought he had refuted McTaggart's thesis that time does not exist by drawing attention to the fact that he had breakfast before he had lunch.
5. Another passage appears later. Having proved to his satisfaction that time does not exist, McTaggart says that there nevertheless exists something he calls the C series, whose members are what we are really observing when we (mistakenly) think we are observing a time-series. The C series, he tells us, includes "as terms everything which appears to us as an event in time, ... And although Mr. Russell's time-series (which is identical with our B series) has a one-to-one correspondence with the C series, still the two series are very different. The terms of the B series are events, and the terms of the C series are not." (31) If he had thought that the B series could exist even though time does not, he would have had no need for the C series.

And what an odd business that C series is! For what are we to suppose its members are? What would an entity be like which "appears to us as an event in time" but is not an event? And which members precede which? McTaggart deals with these questions at length in later chapters; I will not try to summarize his answers.

6. Some commentators fix on a dark footnote (10–11) which suggests that we may think of one of the two series as "sliding along" the other, and if this is true, then the A and B series really are two series. But series don't in fact *slide*. And McTaggart says in the opening sentence of the footnote that the idea that these series do is (mere) metaphor.

7. We might well think that this is not merely true, but necessarily true. On some views, however, even that is compatible with the idea that the Temporal Perspective Relation is not the same as the earlier than relation.

8. Peter Geach says that meeting this condition is sufficient for 'Cambridge' change but not for real change. (For Socrates meets it if Theaetetus grows.) See Geach (1969), pp. 71–2. McTaggart would have been untroubled by that objection. He says: "if anything changes, then all other things change with it. For its change must change some of their relations to it, and so their relational qualities. The fall of a sand-castle on the English coast changes the nature of the Great Pyramid." (11–12) For McTaggart's purposes here, a Cambridge change is as good as a real change.

9. This is not quite right, for McTaggart will later take seriously the idea that time points have them. (See section 7 below.) But our taking that idea seriously now would merely introduce unnecessary complication.

10. McTaggart does not distinguish between events and states of affairs. The poker's being hot is his own example of an event.

11. I think of this as a Fregean idea. My informant on Fregeana, Michael Glanzberg, tells me that while Frege never explicitly asserted it, he would have accepted it without a second thought.

12. I mention two, a stronger and a weaker. The stronger says that there is no such thing as (just) predicating a property of a thing. On this view, to predicate a property (whether temporary or non-temporary) of a thing is always to assert that the thing has it at a time. From this view, however, it follows that we do not know what proposition is asserted by a person who says "F(A)", "(∃x)Fx", and "(∀x)Fx" unless we know what time he meant—the time of his speaking? or 3AM, 11/2/00? Some people might therefore regard this alternative as too costly.

The weaker (and cheaper) alternative says only that to predicate a temporary property of a thing is always to assert that the thing has it at a time.

Sally Haslanger draws attention to alternatives to the very natural idea in Haslanger (1989).

13. Notice that sentences containing these predicates take tenses. We may say of an event M, "M is now occurring" or "M did occur" or "M will occur". So also "M is now over" or "M was over" or "M will be over". So also "M is now going to occur" or "M was going to occur" or "M will be going to occur".

Many of McTaggart's commentators take him to think that once we have helped ourselves to the predicates "past," "present," and "future", then we need nothing further in the way of an account of tense—thus that those predicates could somehow do double duty as tenses. [Michael Dummett is an example. See Dummett (1960), reprinted in Dummett (1978).] They can't, of course; no predicates can. And I think we should agree that McTaggart does not think they can. McTaggart goes on to give an account of tense in terms of those predicates, but it does not consist in mere identification. We turn to it in section 7 below.

14. Lewis believes that the property being hot is a non-temporary property because he thinks it an unintelligible idea that it is a temporary property. See Lewis (1986), pp. 203–4.

15. C.D. Broad, whose interpretation of McTaggart seems to me closest to correct, does not see the attractiveness of that very natural idea. See Broad (1938).

16. We are also not asserting that there is a time at which M is past. If in saying "Past(M)" we were asserting that there is a time at which M is past, then so similarly for "Present(M)" and "Future(M)"; and "Past(M) and Present(M) and Future(M)" would not be self-contradictory. McTaggart's reductio would therefore fail at its first step. I thank Selim Berker for drawing my attention to this point.

17. From here on, numbers in parentheses are page numbers in Dummett (1978).

18. I adapt this example from Dummett's own:

> I can make drawings of a rock from various angles, but if I am asked to say what the real shape of the rock is, I can give a description of it as in three-dimensional space which is independent of the angle from which it is looked at. The description of what is really there, as it really is, must be independent of any particular point of view. (356)

19. The final sentence of the passage reads in toto: "He would have no use for any spatially token-reflexive expressions in giving a description of the physical universe, and yet that description might be a perfectly correct description of the objects of the universe as arranged in space." I omitted its final clause in quoting the passage because of the appearance in it of "correct description" rather than "complete description". The possibility of a (merely) correct token-reflexive free description of the physical objects in an array cannot be what he has in mind, since a (merely) correct token-reflexive free description of the events in a sequence is entirely possible too. What clearly matters to Dummett is complete token-reflexive free description, which he thinks is possible for space but not for time. I go on to comment on Dummett's notion 'complete description' shortly.

20. Can it be that what Dummett intends for us to suppose is in his visual field is not, as it might be, his living room furniture, but rather an array of sense-data? Certainly he is not in their space; but that is because they are not in any space.

21. On one view, that had better be what I mean to be telling you. The view emerges as follows. Let us give the name temporally partial properties to what I have been calling temporary properties. Let us call P a spatially partial property just in case it is possible that a part of a thing has P and another part lacks P. Now as we know, there are people who think that there are no temporally partial properties: thus that while there is such a property as being hot, it is not temporally partial. They may well say, and *for the same reason*, that while there is such a property as being hilly, it is not spatially partial. It follows that when I say "The countryside is hilly here now," I speak truly only if what I mean is that a part of the countryside (the part I indicate) is hilly now. Or indeed: I speak truly only if what I mean is that a certain temporal part of that part of the countryside is hilly.

By contrast, there are people who welcome temporally partial properties. They may be expected to welcome spatially partial properties too.

Still others (McTaggart, perhaps?) may be expected to think that there is no such property as being hilly just as there is no such property as being hot, and that for the countryside to be hilly now in the Dedham area is for the countryside to have the three-place relation hilly-in-at to the Dedham area and the time at which I write.

22. I thank Adam Elga for criticism of an earlier version of the following material on motion.

23. I am grateful to Michael Glanzberg for helpful discussion along the way. I am also grateful to Catherine Elgin for comments on an early draft, and to the members of the seminar in metaphysics given by Ned Hall and me in fall, 2000, for comments on a later draft.

References

Broad, C.D. (1938), *Examination of McTaggart's Philosophy*, Volume II, Part I, Cambridge: Cambridge University Press.

Dummett, M. (1960), "A Defense of McTaggart's Proof of the Unreality of Time," *Philosophical Review*, vol. LXIX.

Dummett, M. (1978), *Truth and other enigmas*, Cambridge MA: Harvard University Press. [This reprints Dummett (1960).]

Geach, P. (1969), *God and the Soul*, New York: Schocken Books.

Haslanger, S. (1989), "Endurance and Temporary Intrinsics," *Analysis*, Vol. 49.

Lewis, D. (1986), *On the Plurality of Worlds*, Oxford: Basil Blackwell Ltd.

McTaggart, J.M.E. (1927), *The Nature of Existence*, Volume II, ed. C.D. Broad, Cambridge: Cambridge University Press.

Philosophical Perspectives, 15, Metaphysics, 2001

RUSSELLIANISM AND EXPLANATION

David Braun
University of Rochester

Russellianism is a semantic theory that entails that sentences (1) and (2) express the same proposition, as long as the names 'Mark Twain' and 'Samuel Clemens' refer to the same person.

(1) Albert believes that Mark Twain is an author.
(2) Albert believes that Samuel Clemens is an author.

Many philosophers think that the *Substitution Objection* decisively refutes Russellianism. This objection claims that sentences (1) and (2) can differ in truth value. Therefore, it says, the sentences express different propositions, and so Russellianism is false.

Russellians have replied at length to the Substitution Objection (McKay, 1979; Salmon, 1986, 1989; Soames, 1988, 1995; Braun, 1998). Indeed, one could easily get the impression that the Substitution Objection is the only criticism to which Russellians need to respond. But, in fact, there are others. For example, Michael Devitt (1996), Mark Richard (1990, 1997a), and Richard Heck (1995) have argued (roughly) that if Russellianism were true, then attitude ascriptions could not explain (certain sorts of) behavior. Call objections that take this sort of line *Explanation Objections*.

Here is a rough version of one Explanation Objection. Suppose that Albert waves, and suppose that we attempt to explain his behavior by uttering (3).

(3) Albert wanted Twain to autograph his book, and he believed that if he waved, then Twain would autograph his book.

A critic might claim that (3) explains Albert's behavior only if it's generally true that people with beliefs and desires like his wave. But consider Bob: he assents to 'I want *Twain* to autograph my book' and to 'If I wave then *Clemens* will autograph my book', but he dissents from 'Twain is Clemens' and so does not wave. Yet according to Russellianism, Bob believes and desires propositions that are like those that Albert does. Therefore, if Russellianism is true, then it's not the case that, generally, those who have beliefs and desires like Albert's wave. So, if Russellianism is true, then (3) cannot explain Albert's behavior. But it can, so Russellianism is false.

In this paper, I formulate a number of Explanation Objections against Russellianism, and provide Russellian replies to each. I argue that some of these objections presuppose unreasonably strict requirements for explaining behavior (and for explaining in general). Other objections rest on mistaken judgments that certain attitude ascriptions do (or do not) explain certain bits of behavior, or that certain ascriptions provide (or fail to provide) certain sorts of explanatory information about the relevant behavior.

Though the Explanation Objections that I consider target a semantic theory, they rely very heavily on assumptions about explanation. As a result, I discuss explanation in this paper at least as much as I do semantics. Unfortunately, the critics I discuss do not make their assumptions about explanation entirely explicit. I therefore formulate some views about explanation that support their objections to Russellianism. I criticize those views, and argue for some alternatives. I show that these alternatives support the claim that attitude ascriptions could explain behavior, even if Russellianism were true. Critics of Russellianism who find the following Explanation Objections attractive might think of this paper as a challenge to them to state and defend their views about explanation explicitly, and to find fault with my alternative views.[1]

Some readers who are familiar with Nathan Salmon's (1986, 1989) and Scott Soames's (1988, 1995) replies to the Substitution Objection might find my replies to the Explanation Objections surprising. Salmon and Soames hold that (1) and (2) really do express the same proposition; speakers who think that (1) and (2) can differ in truth value are confusing the proposition they semantically express with the propositions that they pragmatically convey. Readers who know Salmon's and Soames's work might expect me to argue that utterances of attitude ascriptions pragmatically convey explanatory information that is not semantically expressed by those utterances.[2] But I am skeptical of Salmon's and Soames's attempts to use pragmatics to explain away our antisubstitution intuitions (see Saul, 1998 and Braun, 1998). I am equally worried about using pragmatics to explain away our intuitions about explanation. Therefore, I provide replies to the Explanation Objections that do not force Russellians to rely on Salmon's and Soames's claims about pragmatics (though my replies are consistent with their claims).

There are closely related objections to Russellianism that I do not address here. Some philosophers who press Explanation Objections also argue that attitude ascriptions could not be used to *predict* behavior, if Russellianism were true. Some say that the property of being-a-belief-with-Russellian-content-*P* cannot be *causally relevant* to any effect of a belief (some say similar things about all species of "broad content"). Unfortunately, I do not have space to address such objections here (though I have addressed some of the issues concerning causal relevance in Braun, 1995). In this paper, I focus exclusively on objections concerning explanation.

1. Russellianism and Ways of Taking Propositions

The theory I want to defend might better be called '*neo*-Russellianism', because Bertrand Russell rejects some of its main claims. (Its other popular names—'Millianism', 'the "Fido"-Fido theory', 'the naive theory', 'the direct reference theory'—are misleading in other ways.) I call it 'Russellianism' (following Richard, 1990) because it says that the objects of certain attitudes, such as believing and desiring, are *Russellian propositions*: structured entities whose constituents are individuals, properties, and relations. These propositions are also the *semantic contents* (or simply *contents*) of sentences, *with respect to* (or *in*) contexts, and the objects that sentences *semantically express*, in contexts. The constituents of the proposition that a sentence expresses in a context are the contents of the parts of the sentence in that context. The content of a predicate, in a context, is a property or relation. The content of a proper name, or an indexical such as 'I' or 'she', in a context, is its referent, in that context. The truth value of a sentence, in a context, is the truth value of the proposition it expresses, in that context. So on this view, the sentence 'Mark Twain is an author' expresses a proposition whose constituents are Mark Twain and the property of being-an-author, which can be represented by the following ordered pair.

⟨Mark Twain, being-an-author⟩

The sentence 'Samuel Clemens is an author' expresses exactly the same proposition.[3]

Russellianism says that the content of the predicate 'believes', in any context, is the binary believing relation. The referent, and content, of a 'that'-clause, ⌜that S⌝, in a context, is the proposition expressed by S in that context. So according to Russellianism, (1) and (2) express the same proposition, whose constituents are Albert, the proposition that Twain/Clemens is an author, and the believing relation. It can be represented as follows.

⟨Albert, ⟨Twain, being-an-author⟩, believing⟩

Thus (1) and (2) have the same truth value. Similar remarks hold for attitude sentences whose complements are infinitives with explicit subjects, such as 'Albert wants Twain to smile'. The infinitive clause here refers, in a context, to the proposition expressed by 'Twain smiles', in that context.[4] Its content is its referent. The proposition expressed by the sentence can be represented by the following sequence.

⟨Albert, ⟨Twain, smiling⟩, wanting⟩

There are various reasons to think that Russellianism might be true, despite its unintuitive consequences. It is appealingly simple. It is naturally suggested by the arguments of Keith Donnellan, Saul Kripke, David Kaplan, and others against descriptivist theories of proper names and indexicals. It easily accounts for our free-wheeling use of indexicals in complement clauses of attitude ascriptions. It gives the most straightforward account of quantification into complement clauses of attitude ascriptions. Finally, and very importantly, it avoids many of the difficulties that afflict its rivals. For more details, see Salmon (1986, 1989), Soames (1988, 1995), and Braun (1998).

The Russellian view that I wish to defend includes a certain *metaphysics* of attitudes. According to it, the binary believing and wanting relations are *mediated*: an agent stands in the believing or desiring relation to a proposition in virtue of standing in another psychological relation to an intermediary entity that determines the proposition that the agent believes or desires.[5] The intermediary entity is a *way of taking* the proposition. We could also call it a 'guise' or 'mode or presentation' for, or a 'way of grasping', the proposition; when the relevant attitude is believing or desiring, I shall call such a thing a 'way of believing' or 'way of desiring'. Different Russellians have different views about the nature of this intermediary. It may be said to be a natural language sentence, or a linguistic meaning, or a mental state, or a mental representation. An agent may accept a sentence or linguistic meaning; or be in a certain mental state; or have a certain mental representation in his head in the right way. When he does, he believes the proposition determined by the entity, and we can say that the agent believes the proposition *in a certain way*. A rational agent can believe the same proposition in two distinct ways; he can believe a proposition in one way without believing it in other ways; and he can believe a proposition in one way, while also believing its negation, in another, suitably different, way. Analogous points hold for desiring.[6]

For example, consider (4) and (5).

(4) Mark Twain is an author.
(5) Samuel Clemens is an author.

According to Russellianism, (4) and (5) express the same proposition, but an agent can believe that proposition in various different ways. If an agent believes the proposition in one way, then he will be inclined to assent to sentence (4) and think that (4) is true; but believing the proposition in that way will *not* incline him to assent to (5) or think that (5) is true.[7] There is a second way of believing the proposition that has just the opposite effect. An agent could believe the proposition in the first way but not the second; he would then be inclined to assent to (4) but not to (5). An agent could even rationally believe the proposition *and* its negation, in suitably different ways; for instance, he could believe it in the first way, but believe its negation in a way that "corresponds" to the negation of (5). Such an agent would then be inclined to assent to (4) and dissent from (5), and think that (4) is true but (5) is false.

Similar phenomena can occur when the relevant sentences are attitude sentences, such as (1) and (2).

(1) Albert believes that Mark Twain is an author.
(2) Albert believes that Samuel Clemens is an author.

These sentences express the same proposition. An agent could believe that proposition in a way that corresponds to (1), but fail to believe it in a way that corresponds to (2). She would then be inclined to assent to (1) and think (1) true, but have no such inclinations with respect to (2). In fact, she could believe the proposition in a way that corresponds to (1) and believe that proposition's negation in a way that corresponds to the negation of (2). She would then think that (1) is true, and be inclined to assent to it, while thinking that (2) is false, and be inclined to dissent from it. (These points lie at the core of my response to the Substitution Objection; see Braun, 1998.)

Clearly, the way in which an agent believes or desires a proposition can make a difference to that agent's behavior—for instance, to whether that agent will assent to certain sentences. But according to Russellianism, attitude ascriptions do not semantically express any information about the ways in which agents believe and desire propositions. Thus one might suspect that, if Russellianism were true, then attitude ascriptions could not explain behavior. The following objections to Russellianism attempt to make that suspicion more precise.

2. The Ordinary Explanation Objection

I wish now to turn to the objection that I sketched in the introduction. But I first need to make a few more assumptions explicit.

Suppose that Carol sincerely assents to 'If I wave, then Twain will see me' and 'I want Twain to see me'. Russellians and non-Russellians alike can agree that, under these conditions, (6) and (7) are true.[8]

(6) Carol believes that if she waves then Twain will see her.
(7) Carol wants Twain to see her.

Russellians and non-Russellians can also agree that utterances of (6) and (7), and the propositions they express, are, in a certain sense, *made true* by occurrences of events of certain sorts. They can agree that, necessarily, the proposition expressed by an utterance of (6) is true iff there occurs a certain sort of "believing event" that involves at least Carol, the entity denoted by the 'that'-clause of (6), and a certain relation between them. Call such events *beliefs*.

(Two terminological points: (i) I use the term 'belief' for events of a certain sort, and not for the propositional objects of the believing relation. (ii) Some might prefer to say that beliefs (in this sense) are *states*, rather than events. I use the term 'event' for both events and states; I think of the latter as long-lived events.) Russellians and anti-Russellians can agree on these matters even if they disagree about the denotation of the 'that'-clause of (6) or about the constituents of the propositions expressed by utterances of (6). Similarly, Russellians and their critics can agree that, necessarily, an utterance of (7), and the proposition it expresses, are true iff there occurs a certain sort of "wanting event" that involves at least Carol, the entity specified by the infinitival clause of (7), and a certain relation between them. Call these events *desires*.[9] Since utterances of (6) and (7), and the propositions they express, are made true (in this sense) by events of these sorts, let us say that they *describe* beliefs and desires. Similarly, utterances of (8), and the propositions they express, describe events in which Carol waves.

(8) Carol waves.

Russellians and their critics can also agree that events of the sorts described by utterances of (6) and (7) can cause other events, such as wavings.[10] Let's suppose, then, that Carol has a belief and a desire described by (6) and (7) and that those events are causes of a waving by Carol, so that (8) is true.[11]

Now for the objection. The critic I mention below is a creature of fiction. His objection is modeled on criticisms that are presented by Devitt and Richard, but includes details that theirs do not.[12]

This critic maintains that, in the situation described above, the conjunction of (6) and (7), namely (9), *explains* Carol's waving. So does (10).[13]

(9) Carol wants Twain to see her, and she believes that if she waves then Twain will see her.
(10) Carol waved because she wanted Twain to see her, and she believed that if she waved then Twain would see her.

For convenience, let's concentrate on (10). The critic goes on to say that (10) can explain Carol's waving only if (roughly speaking) it's generally true that people who have attitudes like Carol's wave, other things being equal. More precisely: (10) explains Carol's waving only if *psychological generalization* (11) is true.[14]

(11) If a person wants Twain to see her, and she believes that (if she waves then Twain will see her), then, other things being equal, she will wave.

But, the critic argues, if Russellianism is true, then (11) is false, because it is falsified by cases in which the agent believes and desires the relevant propositions in *mismatching ways*.

To understand this last claim, consider yet another example. Suppose that Diane assents to 'I want *Twain* to see me' and 'If I wave then *Clemens* will see me'. Everyone can agree that, in these circumstances, Diane wants Twain to see her, and that she believes that if she waves then Clemens will see her. But Russellians hold that, if the latter is true, then Diane also believes that (if she waves then *Twain* will see her). So according to Russellians, Diane satisfies the antecedent of (11). But now suppose (further) that Diane dissents from 'I want *Clemens* to see me', and from 'If I wave then *Twain* will see me', and from 'Twain is Clemens'. Then according to Russellians, Diane believes and desires the propositions mentioned in the antecedent of (11) in *mismatching ways*: the way in which she takes the proposition that Twain sees her, when she desires it, is not the same as the way in which she takes that proposition, when she believes the conditional proposition that (if she waves then Twain will see her). In such mismatch circumstances, Diane won't wave. So she will fail to satisfy the consequent of (11). Therefore, the critic says, if Russellianism is true, then Diane satisfies the antecedent of (11), but fails to satisfy its consequent. So if Russellianism is true, then (11) is false.

But, the critic claims, if (11) is false, then (10) does not explain Carol's waving, even if Carol herself happens to believe and desire the relevant propositions in matching ways. Therefore, if Russellianism is true, then (10) does not explain Carol's waving.[15] But (10) *does* explain Carol's waving. Therefore, Russellianism is false.[16]

Let's rearrange and summarize the main points of the objection in a slightly more formal fashion.

(12) a. (10) explains Carol's waving.

b. If (10) explains Carol's waving, then generalization (11) is true.

c. Therefore, generalization (11) is true.

d. If Russellianism is true, then generalization (11) is not true.

e. Therefore, Russellianism is not true.

Call this the *Ordinary Explanation Objection*.[17] My reasons for including the word 'ordinary' in the objection's title will become clear below.[18]

I wish to offer two replies to the Ordinary Explanation Objection (and to a revised version of the objection that will appear later). One reply is perhaps predictable, the other perhaps surprising. My (perhaps) predictable reply criticizes (12d): I say (roughly) that generalization (11) is true, even if Russellianism is correct. I argue for this point in another paper (Braun, 2000), and present only an outline of that argument below. My (perhaps) surprising reply criticizes (12b): I argue that (10) could explain Carol's waving even if generalization (11) were false. I shall start with it.

3. Explanations, Covering Laws, and the Revised
Ordinary Explanation Objection

I say that (10) could explain Carol's waving even if generalization (11) were false. But I admit that premise (12b) is initially plausible. Thus I would like to examine its intuitive support before criticizing it directly.

One might hope to find some arguments for (12b) in the work of Devitt and Richard, the real-life models for my imaginary critic. Unfortunately, they do not explicitly state any assumptions about explanation that support (12b). But their writings *suggest* that they accept some sort of *covering-law theory* of explanation. Theories of this sort say that explanations "depend upon", or are "underwritten by", lawful generalizations. Anyone who holds such a view might well find (12b) plausible. Let's consider whether any reasonable theory of this sort supports (12b).

Let's begin with a simple version of the covering-law theory, which we can call the *D-N theory of ideal explanation*.[19] On this view, an *ideal* (or *complete* or *full*) explanation of a particular event is an *argument* of a certain sort. The conclusion of an ideal explanatory argument is an *explanandum-sentence* that describes the *explanandum-event*. The premises of such an argument (the *explanans-sentences*) include at least one premise describing a particular fact and at least one law sentence. The explanandum-sentence is a deductive consequence of the set of explanans-sentences. Removing any sentence from the set of explanans-sentences results in a deductively invalid argument; in that sense, every explanans-sentence is *essential* to the argument. An argument of this sort is a *deductive-nomological argument* (D-N argument). Every ideal explanation is a D-N argument.[20] A *correct* ideal explanation is a D-N argument with entirely true premises; from here on I shall (usually) use 'explanation' to mean 'correct explanation'.[21]

The D-N theory as it stands would not be acceptable to most critics of Russellianism, for most such critics would judge that (13) is an ideal explanation of Carol's waving.

(13) a. Carol wanted Twain to see her, and she believed that (if she waved then Twain would see her).
   b. If a person wants Twain to see her, and believes that (if she waves then Twain will see her), then, other things being equal, she will wave.
   c. Therefore, Carol waved.

But generalization (13b) (which is just (11) again) is a *ceteris paribus* generalization. Thus the conclusion of argument (13) does not deductively follow from its premises, and so the D-N theory entails that (13) is not an ideal explanation of Carol's waving.[22]

Note, however, that the premises of (13) do, in some sense, *support* its conclusion. So let's say that the premises of ideal explanations need not deductively entail their conclusions, but may, instead, merely support their conclusions.[23] Let's also assume that some psychological *ceteris paribus* generalizations are true, and are either laws, or are law-like enough, to figure in ideal explanations. A theory of explanation that includes these modifications would entail that (13) is an ideal explanation of Carol's waving, and should be acceptable to anti-Russellians.[24]

This modified D-N theory still concerns only *ideal* (or full or complete) explanations. But most *ordinary* explanations are not ideal, in the above sense; (10), for instance, is not an ideal explanation simply because it does not contain a law-like generalization. Yet (10) seems to explain Carol's waving, just as our imaginary critic says.[25] Let's call sentences like (10) *elliptical explanations* and let's suppose that (some) such elliptical explanations are genuine explanations.[26] Clearly any view of explanation that can support premise (12b) must specify some requirements for elliptical explanation, in order to say how the explanatory power of (10) depends on the truth of (11).

Notice that the explanans sentence of (10), namely (9), appears in an ideal explanation of Carol's waving, namely (13).[27] Reflection on this fact, and other similar examples, might lead one to the following view of elliptical explanations.

(14) A sentence, or sequence of sentences, is an *elliptical explanation* of an event iff: (a) it is not an ideal explanation of the event, and (b) its explanans-sentences appear in some ideal explanation of the event.

According to (14), if argument (13) is an ideal explanation of Carol's waving, then (10) is an elliptical explanation of her waving.[28] Moreover, (14) makes clear the sense in which elliptical explanations are "underwritten by" or "depend upon" law-like generalizations: a sentence counts as an elliptical explanation counts iff its explanans-sentences "mesh with" generalizations that appear in some ideal explanation.

Consider now a theory that consists of two parts: (a) the D-N theory, modified so as to allow ideal explanations to be non-deductive arguments containing *ceteris paribus* generalizations; and (b) thesis (14) concerning elliptical explanation. Call this the *Modified D-N theory of explanation*. Notice that we've dropped the term 'ideal' from the title: this is a theory of both ideal and elliptical explanation.[29]

Our imaginary critic might try to use the Modified D-N theory to argue for premise (12b). Suppose that (10) explains Carol's waving. Then clearly it is an elliptical explanation. So, if the Modified D-N theory is true, the explanans of (10) appears in some correct ideal explanation of Carol's waving. The most obvious ideal explanation of Carol's waving is (13). But generalization (11) appears in explanation (13), and must be true if (13) is a correct explanation.

So, the critic might conclude, if (10) explains Carol's waving, then generalization (11) is true.

But this argument for (12b) has a serious flaw. To see this, suppose that (11) is *false*. Then (13) is not a correct ideal explanation of Carol's waving. But there may still be a correct ideal explanation of Carol's waving that contains the explanans of (10), for instance, (15).

> (15) Carol wanted Twain to see her, and she believed that (if she waved then Twain would see her). *Carol had no overriding desires.* If a person wants Twain to see her, and believes that (if she waves then Twain will see her), *and has no overriding desires*, then, other things being equal, she will wave. Therefore, Carol waved.

If (15) is a correct ideal explanation of Carol's waving, then, according to the Modified D-N theory, (10) explains Carol's waving, *even if (11) is false.* So the Modified D-N theory does not justify premise (12b); it does not entail that the explanatory power of (10) depends on generalization (11) in particular.

Our imaginary critic can best respond to this problem by revising the Ordinary Explanation Objection. Notice that, if Russellianism is correct, then there will be "mismatch" Russellian exceptions to the generalization in (15). So our imaginary critic could argue that this generalization is false under Russellianism. Furthermore, he could claim that *any* ideal explanation of Carol's waving that contains the explanans of (10) will also contain an ordinary psychological generalization that is false under Russellianism. (By 'ordinary psychological generalization', I mean a generalization that contains ordinary attitude ascriptions which do not explicitly mention ways of taking propositions.) Thus the critic could argue against Russellianism as follows.

> (12*) a. (10) explains Carol's waving.
>   b. If (10) explains Carol's waving, then some ordinary psychological generalization is true.
>   c. Therefore, some ordinary psychological generalization is true.
>   d. If Russellianism is true, then no ordinary psychological generalization is true.
>   e. Therefore, Russellianism is not true.

Call this the *Revised Ordinary Explanation Objection.* This objection is very much in the spirit of the original (and so in the spirit of Devitt's and Richard's criticisms of Russellianism). The Modified D-N theory supports premise (12b*). So we now have a version of the objection that is well-supported by at least one covering-law conception of explanation. But how plausible is the Modified D-N Theory?

4. Problems with the Modified D-N Theory

The Modified D-N theory says that the explanans of a genuine elliptical explanation must appear in some ideal explanation. But there are apparent counterexamples to this requirement, as we can see by considering the following sentences.

(16) Don is depressed because there is a chemical imbalance in his brain.

(17) Joe died because he ate a wild mushroom.

(18) The tornado caused the building to collapse.

(16)–(18) do not satisfy requirement (14) for elliptical explanations. The explanans-sentence of (16) is 'There is a chemical imbalance in Don's brain'. But not all chemical imbalances in brains cause depression; only certain types do. So an ideal explanation of Don's depression will be more specific about the type of chemical imbalance in Don's brain. Therefore, the explanans of (16) will be redundant to any such ideal explanation, and won't appear in any such explanation. Similarly for (17). Not all wild mushrooms are poisonous, so any ideal explanation of Joe's death will be more specific than (17). (18) presents the same problem, or worse: notice that it does not contain a full explanans-sentence, but rather an "explanans-noun-phrase".

Yet there is a strong intuitive pull to think that (16)–(18) explain their respective events (or, at the very least, that they are elliptical explanations of those events). Thus the Modified D-N theory of explanation is too restrictive.[30]

The problem for the imaginary critic can be roughly summarized in the following way: Many ordinary explanations are *more elliptical* than the Modified D-N theory allows. And yet such ordinary explanations seem to be genuinely explanatory. So the Modified D-N theory is false, and the imaginary critic's argument for (12b*) relies on overly restrictive requirements for elliptical explanation.

5. Some Alternative Theories of Explanation

Further reflection on ordinary elliptical explanations like (16)–(18) will give us reason to think that (10) could explain Carol's waving, even if ordinary psychological generalizations were false.

Sentences (16)–(18) have two salient characteristics. First, they provide information about the causes of their respective explananda-events. Second, they provide some of the information that would be provided by ideal explanations of the events (this is so, despite the fact that their explanans-sentences would not *appear* in those ideal explanations). One might reasonably suspect that (16)–(18) are explanatory because they possess these characteristics. So one might reasonably conclude that an ordinary explanation that has both of these features is a genuine (elliptical) explanation.

This last conclusion is, in fact, supported by two independently plausible theories of explanation, those of Peter Railton (1981) and David Lewis (1986).

Railton's theory relies heavily on his notion of *explanatory information*.[31] An ideal covering-law explanation of an event is an argument, that is, a sequence of sentences. Each sentence in the argument semantically expresses a proposition. Thus corresponding to the argument there is a sequence of propositions expressed by the sentences. Call this the *propositional argument* or *ideal propositional explanation* that is semantically expressed by the (linguistic) argument or ideal explanation. According to Railton, *explanatory information* about an event is information that is *contained* in some ideal propositional explanation of the event. A proposition, or sequence of propositions, can contain some or all of the information contained in an ideal propositional explanation. A sentence or linguistic argument *provides* explanatory information about an event iff it semantically expresses a proposition (or sequence of propositions) that contains some of the information contained in an ideal propositional explanation of the event.[32] A linguistic ideal explanation of an event provides *all* of the explanatory information contained in the ideal propositional explanation that it expresses.

On Railton's view, a sentence (or argument) *explains* an event just in case it provides *some* explanatory information about that event. In other words, a sentence explains an event just in case it semantically expresses a proposition that contains some information that is contained in some ideal explanation of the event. (Similarly, a proposition explains an event if it contains some information in some ideal propositional explanation of the event.) Explanations can vary in how much explanatory information they provide. Some provide more, some less, depending on how much information they provide from their respective ideal explanations.

(16)–(18) count as explanations of their respective events, on Railton's account. Some ideal (propositional) explanation of Don's depression mentions something about the chemistry of Don's brain processes. Thus (16) provides *some* of the information contained in some such ideal covering-law explanation for Don's depression. So (16) counts as an explanation, even though its explanans does not appear in any ideal explanation. Similarly, some sentences about wild mushrooms figure in some ideal explanation of Joe's death, so (17) counts as explaining Joe's death. Similarly for (18).

On Railton's theory, a speaker might utter a sentence that provides explanatory information about an event, and which thus explains the event, even if the speaker does not know enough to provide an ideal explanation, and even if the ideal explanations the speaker might try to provide are incorrect. In fact, this might be the typical case. A person might utter (16), and thus provide some explanatory information about Don's depression, even though she does not know the particular-fact premises that figure in ideal explanations of those events. A speaker might successfully explain Joe's death by offering (17), even if that speaker falsely believes that anyone who eats any wild mushroom will die.

According to Lewis's theory, explanatory information about an event is information about the *causes* of the event. A proposition is an explanation of an event iff it contains information about the causes of the event. A sentence is an explanation iff it semantically expresses an explanatory proposition.[33] Different explanations may differ in the amount of explanatory information they provide. On Lewis's view, (16) counts as explaining Don's depression because it provides information about the causes of his depression. Similarly for (17) and (18).

Railton's theory requires ordinary explanations to be "underwritten" by laws. Lewis's theory does not. But both theories imply that a sentence that provides information about a cause of an event is an explanation of it. This is obviously so on Lewis's view; on Railton's view, such a sentence provides some explanatory information about that event, because some ideal explanation of that event mentions that cause.

Suppose now that a sentence expresses a proposition that (a) contains some information about the causes of a certain event, and (b) contains some information that is contained in some ideal propositional explanation of that event. Then Railton's and Lewis's theories entail that the sentence explains the event. If one or both theories are plausible, then we now have a plausible *sufficient condition* for a sentence's being an (elliptical) explanation of an event.

I shall soon employ a version of this sufficient condition to argue that (10) does explain Carol's waving. Before doing so, however, I should mention that Railton's and Lewis's theories are not entirely uncontroversial, because they are both quite liberal about what counts as an explanation.[34] Consider (16*) and (16%).

(16*) Don is depressed because he has a brain.
(16%) Don is depressed because the Big Bang occurred.

(16*) provides some information about the causes of Don's depression, and also some of the information contained in an ideal explanation of it. Similarly for (16%), for the Big Bang is a distal cause of Don's depression, and there is some (extremely long) ideal explanation that mentions it and concludes that Don (eventually) becomes depressed. So both provide *some* explanatory information, according to both theories. Railton and Lewis can say that (16*) and (16%) provide very little explanatory information about Don's depression, certainly less than (16). Nonetheless, they count as explanations on their theories, and so one might conclude that their theories are too liberal.

I happen to think that the above consequence of Railton's and Lewis's theories is correct. I believe that attempts to draw more restrictive (or substantive) lines than theirs between explanations and non-explanations are doomed to failure. I am persuaded of this by the failures of past attempts, and by the following analogy. Suppose that we tried to formulate necessary and sufficient conditions for a sentence's being a *description* of an object. It's doubtful that any substantive informational requirements would stand up to scrutiny (other than the requirement that the sentence be a true sentence that, somehow, mentions the object). Some descriptions provide more descriptive information, some less, but there is no substantial distinction to be made between descriptions and non-descriptions. But explanations are merely descriptions of a certain sort, ones that focus on events, their causes, and (sometimes) laws.

However, I need not argue this point, for I can modify the above sufficient condition to make it more acceptable to those who find Lewis's and Railton's views too liberal. One intuitive difference between (16), on the one hand, and (16*) and (16%), on the other, is that the former seems to provide a *substantial portion* of the information contained in an ideal explanation, whereas the latter do not. (Don't take the phrase "substantial portion of the information" here to mean "more than fifty percent of the information". Instead, understand it in very roughly the way you do when you speak of a substantial portion of a pie. You provide a diner with a substantial portion of a pie when you give him (say) an eighth or more of it.) This feature of (16) suggests the following *sufficient* condition for explanation.

> (19) Let S be a sentence or sequence of sentences, and let E be an event. If S provides some information about the causes of E, and provides a substantial portion of the information contained in some ideal propositional explanation of E, then S explains E.

Railton's and Lewis's theories entail that (19) is a sufficient condition for explanation (though neither would accept it as a necessary condition). Of course, the expression 'substantial portion' is vague, but we can partially fix its intended extension with the following stipulation: (16)–(18) shall count as providing substantial portions of information from some ideal explanations, and any sentences that provide as much information from some ideal explanations as do (16)–(18) from theirs shall count as providing substantial portions of information from those ideal explanations.

6. First Reply to the Revised Ordinary Explanation Objection

I am now ready to criticize (12b*) directly. But it will be convenient for me first to grant, *for the sake of argument*, that (12d*) is true. That is, I shall grant (*for the moment*) that if Russellianism is true, then no ordinary psychological generalization is true. (I criticize (12d*) in section 8.) Since I wish to defend Russellianism, I shall also assume (for the sake of argument) that no ordinary psychological generalization is true. I shall argue that, even assuming all of this, (10) *does* explain Carol's waving. A bit more intuitively: (10) explains Carol's waving even if Russellianism is true, and all ordinary psychological generalizations are false. Given sufficient condition (19) for explanation, I will be done if I can show that, despite the truth of Russellianism and the falsity of ordinary psychological generalizations, (10) provides information about the causes of Carol's waving and provides a substantial portion of the information contained in some ideal explanation of Carol's waving. I shall argue for these two points in turn.

Recall that (6) and (7) are stipulated to be true in our example.

(6) Carol believes that if she waves then Twain will see her.
(7) Carol wants Twain to see her.

The example also stipulates that (6) and (7) describe causes of Carol's waving. If this is so, then (10) provides information about the causes of Carol's waving. Notice, furthermore, that these stipulations are consistent with Russellianism, for the following situation is consistent with the view: (a) There occurs an event E_1 that is a believing by Carol in the Russellian proposition that (if she waves then Twain will see her); (b) there occurs an event E_2 that is a desiring by Carol in the Russellian proposition that (Twain sees her); and (c) E_1 and E_2 are causes of Carol's waving. In this situation, (10) describes some causes of Carol's waving, if Russellianism is true.

Of course, if Russellianism is true, and the above conditions hold, then Carol believes and desires the Russellian propositions *in certain ways* that are not mentioned by the attitude ascriptions. But (obviously) a sentence like (10) can describe events that are causes of Carol's waving, even if it does not mention all of their properties.

(10) also provides a substantial portion of the information contained in some ideal explanation of Carol's waving—even if Russellianism is true and ordinary psychological generalizations are false. For according to the Russellian metaphysics of attitudes, agents believe and desire propositions via ways of taking propositions. On such a view, there are law-like generalizations that relate believing-in-certain-ways and desiring-in-certain-ways to behavior. So, given these Russellian assumptions, there is a correct ideal explanation of Carol's waving that looks like (20).

(20) a. Carol wants (Twain to see her) in way W_1, and she believes that (if she waves then Twain will see her) in way [W_2 cond W_1].
b. If a person wants (Twain to see her) in way W_1, and believes that (if she waves then Twain will see her) in way [W_2 cond W_1], then, other things being equal, she will wave.
c. Therefore, Carol waves.

'W_1' is a constant that refers to the way in which Carol desires the proposition that Twain see her. '[W_2 cond W_1]' refers to the way in which Carol believes the conditional proposition that (if she waves then Twain will see her). (I use this notation to emphasize that Carol believes and desires these propositions in *matching* ways.) Now (10) clearly provides some of the information provided by premise (20a). So (10) provides some of the explanatory information provided by (20). Intuitively, (10) provides a substantial portion of the information provided by (20)—at least as substantial a portion as (16)–(18) provide from their ideal explanations.

Of course, if Russellianism is correct, then (10) does *not* tell us about the *ways* in which Carol believes and desires the relevant propositions, and so it does not describe *all* of the properties of those events that are mentioned by (20). But as we saw in many examples in previous sections, a sentence may provide a substantial portion of information from an ideal explanation without mentioning all of the properties that are mentioned in the ideal explanation.

Our imaginary critic might reply that if (20) were an ideal explanation of Carol's waving, ordinary speakers would not know it. They would not know that (20a) and (20b) are true, or be able to formulate an ideal explanation like (20). If pressed to formulate an ideal explanation, they would provide something like (13). So, the critic might conclude, an ordinary person's utterance of (10) cannot provide information contained in (20). Reply: as we saw in the last section, a speaker can utter a sentence that succeeds in providing information contained in an ideal explanation of an event, even when he is unable to state an ideal explanation for the event, and even when the ideal explanations he might try to state are incorrect.

Therefore, (10) provides information about some causes of Carol's waving, and provides a substantial portion of the information contained in an ideal explanation of her waving. So (10) explains Carol's waving, even assuming that Russellianism is correct and all ordinary psychological generalizations are false. Thus premise (12b*) of the Revised Ordinary Explanation Objection is false, if ordinary psychological generalizations are false.

I can reformulate the argument of this section in a way that does not rely as heavily on sufficient condition (19). (10) is no more elliptical an explanation than (16)–(18) and many other ordinary explanations, even assuming that Russellianism is true and ordinary psychological generalizations are false. So if (10) is too elliptical to explain Carol's waving, under Russellianism, then (16)–(18), and many other ordinary explanations, are also too elliptical to explain. But (16)–(18), and many other highly elliptical ordinary explanations, are genuinely explanatory. So (10) does explain Carol's waving, even if Russellianism is true.[35]

7. The Ideal Explanation Objection

As I mentioned earlier, I have a second criticism of the Revised Ordinary Explanation Objection. But before turning to that criticism, I want to consider a new objection that might be provoked by my preceding reply. I have been arguing that *ordinary* explanations containing attitude ascriptions could explain behavior even if Russellianism is true. A critic might concede that I am right about ordinary explanations, but argue that Russellianism gets the facts about *ideal* explanation wrong. He might maintain that (13) is a *correct* ideal explanation of Carol's waving, that is, an ideal explanation with true premises. But, the critic might say, if Russellianism is true, then generalization (11) is false, and so (13) is not a correct ideal explanation. Therefore, Russellianism is not true. Call this the *Ideal Explanation Objection*.

I am, for the moment, conceding that (11) is false under Russellianism. So I must (*for the moment*) deny that (13) is a *correct* ideal explanation of Carol's waving. But I can nevertheless explain away any intuition that (13) is a correct ideal explanation. That is, I can explain away any intuition that generalization (11) is true.

Recall that the critic alleges that (11) is false under Russellianism because of certain "Russellian counterexamples". These are cases in which the agent believes and desires the mentioned propositions in mismatched ways: for instance, cases like Diane's, in which the agent assents to 'I want Twain to see me' and 'If I wave then Clemens will see me', but dissents from 'I want Clemens to see me' and 'If I wave then Twain will see me'. If Russellianism is correct, then (the critic thinks) these examples are genuine counterexamples to (11).

But notice that *ordinary speakers* would think that agents like Diane *fail* to satisfy the antecedent of (11). So they would *not* judge the alleged Russellian counterexamples to (11) to be counterexamples. Since they do not recognize the (alleged) Russellian counterexamples to (11), they judge that (11) is true. Thus, even assuming that generalization (11) is really false under Russellianism, Russellians can plausibly explain away any intuitions that (11) is true, and thus any intuitions that (13) is a correct ideal explanation.[36]

8. Second Reply to the Revised Ordinary Explanation Objection

Let's return again to the Revised Ordinary Explanation Objection. I am willing to rest my case against that Objection on my criticism of (12b*); I believe that (10) explains Carol's waving, whether or not ordinary psychological generalizations are true under Russellianism. But, in fact, I think that Russellians should not concede that ordinary psychological generalizations would be false under Russellianism. In another paper (Braun, 2000), I argue (roughly) that such generalizations would be true even if Russellianism were correct. I shall present only a few highlights of that argument here. For simplicity, I concentrate on (11).

Our imaginary critic argued for (12d*) by pointing out that there would be *exceptions* to generalizations like (11), if Russellianism were true. But this argument is weak, for there are *non*-Russellian exceptions to (11) that seem *not* to falsify it. For instance, suppose Eve assents to 'I want Twain to see me' and 'If I wave then Twain will see me'. She may nevertheless fail to wave if she becomes suddenly paralyzed. Exceptions like this, which seem *not* to falsify the generalization, we can call *tolerable exceptions* to the generalization. A critic of Russellianism who wants to argue for (12d*) needs to show that the Russellian *mismatch exceptions* to (11) are not merely tolerable exceptions, but are *genuine counterexamples*.

Tolerable exceptions to *ceteris paribus* generalizations are exceptions that occur when other things are *not* equal, or when *suitable conditions* do *not* hold. But (I argue in Braun, 2000) the suitable conditions associated with a *ceteris paribus* generalization vary from one context to another. Therefore, whether a case counts as a tolerable exception to a generalization can vary from one context to another.[37] Critics who say that the generalizations would be false under Russellianism make their claims in contexts in which distinct ways of taking propositions are salient. The mismatch cases probably are genuine counterexamples to the generalizations in such philosophically sophisticated contexts. But (I argue) they are merely tolerable exceptions with respect to more ordinary contexts in which ordinary, well-informed, non-philosophical speakers consider (11), and judge it to be true (in their contexts). In such contexts, an agent satisfies the suitable conditions associated with (11) only if the agent believes and desires the relevant propositions in *matching ways*. If this is correct, then the mismatch exceptions are merely tolerable exceptions to (11), in ordinary contexts in which it seems true, even if Russellianism is correct. And so (11) is true in such contexts, even if Russellianism is correct.

Now (12d*) says that if Russellianism is true, then all ordinary psychological generalizations are false. Strictly speaking, this is incorrect, simply because the generalizations are context-sensitive: they are true or false only with respect to contexts. The closest we can come to (12d*), while still recognizing the context-sensitivity of the generalizations, is (12d**):

(12d**) If Russellianism is true, then every ordinary psychological generalization is *false with respect to every context*.

When I earlier granted (12d*), for the sake of argument, I was in effect granting (12d**). I argued (in effect) that (10) can explain Carol's waving even if all ordinary psychological generalizations are false in all contexts. But even though I granted (12d**) for the sake of argument, I reject it, for the reasons I give above: ordinary psychological generalizations like (11) are true with respect to some (ordinary) contexts, even if Russellianism is true.

Notice that if (11) is true, in some contexts, then (13) is a *correct ideal explanation* of Carol's waving, in some contexts. If so, then the Ideal Explanation Objection is also unsound.

This completes my replies to the Revised Ordinary Explanation Objection to Russellianism. I now wish to consider three other important objections concerning explanation. Hints of these objections can be found in Devitt and Richard, but they do not explicitly present them.

9. The Explanatory Substitution Objection

Consider (10) and (21).

(10) Carol waved because she wanted Twain to see her, and she believed that if she waved then *Twain* would see her.

(21) Carol waved because she wanted Twain to see her, and she believed that if she waved then *Clemens* would see her.

If Russellianism is true, then (10) and (21) express the same proposition. But a critic might claim that if (10) and (21) express the same proposition, then (10) explains Carol's waving only if (21) does. Yet (21), he might claim, does not explain Carol's waving. Therefore, Russellianism is not true.

This new objection is much like the Substitution Objection that I presented at the beginning of this paper, but with two significant differences. First, the old objection concerns substitution in simple attitude sentences, whereas the new one concerns substitution in attitude ascriptions that are constituents of more complex sentences. Second, and more important, the old objection concerns the truth values of sentences, whereas the new one concerns what I shall call the *explanatory values* of sentences (whether or not they explain certain events, or provide explanatory information about them). In view of this, I call the new objection the *Explanatory Substitution Objection*.

In reply, I deny the last premise of the objection: (21) *does* explain Carol's waving. (21) expresses the same proposition as (10). So (21) semantically provides the same explanatory and causal information as does (10). Therefore, it explains Carol's waving, contrary to the objection.[38] Of course, an ordinary speaker might *think* that (10) explains Carol's waving, but that (21) does not. But I can explain why ordinary speakers have such mistaken intuitions about explanation, by appealing (ultimately) to different ways of taking the proposition they express.

It will be useful to begin with an analogous example that does not involve attitude ascriptions. Consider sentences (22) and (23).

(22) Twain fell because Twain stepped on a banana peel.

(23) Twain fell because Clemens stepped on a banana peel.

Suppose that (22) is true and explains Twain's fall. (23) expresses the same proposition, so it also explains Twain's fall. But clearly a speaker could rationally think that (22) explains Twain's fall and (23) does not. How? There are at least two ways in which a rational speaker can take the proposition that (22) and (23) express. A rational speaker who rejects 'Twain is Clemens' can believe the proposition they express in a way that corresponds to (22) and at the same time believe the negation of that proposition in a way that corresponds to the negation of (23). Such a speaker would think that (22) is true and (23) is false. Thus he would be very likely to think that (22) explains Twain's fall, and very likely to think that (23) does not.[39]

We can press a bit further in our explanation, if we wish. Why would a speaker believe the proposition in a way that corresponds to (22), while believing the negation of that proposition in a way that corresponds to the negation of (23)? There are at least two possibilities. The simpler possibility is that he could believe that (24) is true and (25) is false.

(24) Twain stepped on a banana peel.
(25) Clemens stepped on a banana peel.

That is, he could believe the proposition expressed by (24) and (25) in a way that corresponds to (24), while believing the negation of that proposition in a way that corresponds to the negation of (25). If he believed that (25) is false, he would surely reject (23). But if he believed that (24) is true, he might well conclude that (22) is true. The second possibility is more complex. A speaker could think that both (24) and (25) are true, but think that (24) and (25) "describe different events" involving different people (though he might not put it in those words). He might judge that a stepping-on-a-banana-peel by one person is unlikely to cause the fall of another. And so he might think that (22) is true and (23) is false.

The case of (10) and (21) is similar. A speaker could think that (10) is true while thinking that (21) is false.[40] He could do so because he believes the proposition that they express in one way (a way that corresponds to (10)), while believing the negation of that proposition in a suitably different way (a way that corresponds to the negation of (21)).[41] If he believed that (21) is false, he would naturally think that it fails to explain Carol's waving. But if he believed that (10) is true, he could quite easily think that it does explain Carol's waving.

We can, if we wish, press on for further explanation. Why would a speaker believe the proposition expressed by (10) and (21) in a way that corresponds to (10), but believe its negation in a way that corresponds to the negation of (21)? One possibility is that he thinks that (26) is true and (27) is false.

(26) Carol wanted Twain to see her, and she believed that if she waved then *Twain* would see her.
(27) Carol wanted Twain to see her, and she believed that if she waved then *Clemens* would see her.

That is, a speaker could believe the proposition expressed by (26) in a way corresponding to (26), while believing the negation of that proposition in way corresponding to the negation of (27). If a speaker thought that (27) is false, he would surely think that (21) is false. But if he thought that (26) is true, he might well conclude that (10) is true. The second possibility is more complex. A speaker could think that both (26) and (27) are true, but that they "describe different events" or "different sorts of beliefs and desires" (though he probably would not say this in so many words). He might think that events of the sort described by (26) are likely to cause a waving by Carol, while those described by (27) are not. And so he might judge that (10) is true and explains Carol's waving, while (21) is false and does not explain the waving. (To explain how a speaker could think that (26) and (27) "describe different sorts of belief and desires" would involve explaining why he thinks that (26) and (27) *could* differ in truth value. This would again involve different ways of taking the proposition expressed by (26) and (27). But let's stop here.)

Summarizing: (10) and (21) express the same proposition, so both explain Carol's waving. But, for various reasons, a speaker could rationally believe the proposition they express in a way corresponding to (10), while believing the negation of that proposition in a way corresponding to the negation of (21). Such a speaker would think that (10) is true and (21) is false, and so would naturally think that (10) explains Carol's waving, while (21) does not.

10. The Contrastive Explanation Objections

I want finally to consider two further Explanation Objections to Russellianism. (They are inspired by Lewis (1986) and Heck (1995), though for various reasons I hesitate to attribute the objections to them.[42]) These objections do *not* claim that attitude ascriptions would fail to explain behavior under Russellianism. Rather, they claim that if Russellianism were true, then attitude ascriptions would fail to semantically express a certain specific *sort* of explanatory information.

According to Russellianism, attitude ascriptions do not semantically express information about the *ways* in which agents believe and desire propositions. (Attitude ascriptions on this view semantically express *less* information about beliefs and desires than they do according to Devitt and Richard; see also Crimmins, 1992.) Sometimes, though, this information about ways of taking propositions seems to be the explanatory information that we want, *and seem to get*, from attitude ascriptions. This is (very roughly) the thought behind objections to Russellianism that I call *Contrastive Explanation Objections*. To introduce them, I begin below with a description of *contrastive explanation* in general.[43]

Why-questions are often requests for explanatory information. Usually, the questioner wants explanatory information of a certain type. If a person asks, "Why, in economic terms, did *E* occur?", he wants information about the economic features of the events that caused event *E*, and probably does not want to hear about the physical features of those events. If his auditor nevertheless describes the physical properties of *E*'s causes, and not their economic properties, then the auditor may provide explanatory information about E (and may even explain E), but will not provide the information that the questioner wants.

A person who asks a question of (roughly) the form "Why did E_1 occur *rather than* E_2?" is also usually asking for explanatory information of a certain sort. Typically, there is some sequence of events that led up to E_1 which appears to be very similar to a (possible) sequence of events that led, or would lead, to a different type of event E_2. The questioner wants information about important differences, or *contrasts*, between the actual sequence of events that led up to E_1 and the (actual or counterfactual) sequence of events that led, or would lead, up to E_2.

For example, suppose that on both Monday and Tuesday morning, Oprah wants to eat breakfast, and looks into her kitchen cabinet. On both mornings, she sees a box of sugar-coated Fruity Flakes and a box of sugar-free Bran Bombs. On Monday, she reaches for the Fruity Flakes; on Tuesday, for the Bran Bombs. Rosie knows that Oprah saw both boxes on both occasions, and that Oprah likes Fruity Flakes more than Bran Bombs. So Rosie thinks that the events leading up to Oprah's grabbing the Bran Bombs on Tueday are very much like the events leading up to her grabbing the Fruity Flakes on Monday. If Rosie were to ask "Why did Oprah grab the Bran Bombs on Tuesday, rather than the Fruity Flakes?", she would wish to know about differences between the causal histories of the two events. If her auditor were to say "On Tuesday, Oprah saw the Bran Bombs", he would provide some explanatory information about the events on Tuesday (since Oprah's seeing the Bran Bombs *was* a cause of her reaching for them on Tuesday), and would even explain Oprah's grabbing the Bran Bombs, but he would not offer the sort of information that Rosie wants. If he instead said "Oprah didn't care about eating sugar on Monday, but on Tuesday she wanted to avoid eating sugar", then he would provide some explanatory information about the causes of the Tuesday event, *and also* describe an important difference between the causes of the Monday and Tuesday events. He would then provide Rosie with some *contrastive* explanatory information of the sort she wants.[44]

A critic of Russellianism might claim that attitude ascriptions can be used to provide certain sorts of contrastive explanatory information that they would be unable to provide, if Russellianism were true. He could claim that, on the view, attitude ascriptions could not be used to answer certain questions of roughly the form "Why did x do A_1, but not A_2?".

Imagine that Petra has gone to a bookstore to attend a booksigning by her favorite author.[45] She is milling about the store, waiting for the booksigning to begin. A clerk hangs a sign at one end of the store that reads, "Line up here to have your book signed by Samuel Clemens." Petra sees the sign, but continues to mill about. The clerk then replaces the sign with a second sign that reads "Line up here to have your book signed by Mark Twain." Petra sees the second sign and immediately lines up beside it.

Now consider question (28).

(28) Why did Petra line up after she read the second sign, but not after she read the first?

A critic of Russellianism might say that (29) provides a very good answer to question (28).

(29) Petra wanted Twain to sign her book. When she saw the first sign, she did *not* come to believe that (if she stood in line, then Twain would sign her book). But when she saw the second sign, she *did* come to believe that (if she stood in line, then Twain would sign her book).

In short, a critic might claim that (29) provides relevant contrastive explanatory information. But, the critic might say, (29) does not do so if Russellianism is true, for if Russellianism is true, then the second sentence of (29) is false. When Petra saw the first sign, she came to believe that (if she stood in line, then *Clemens* would sign her book). But then, according to Russellianism, she also came to believe that (if she stood in line, *Twain* would sign her book) when she read the first sign. So if Russellianism is true, then (29) does not describe any relevant difference in Petra between the time when she read the first sign and the time she read the second, and so (29) fails to provide relevant contrastive explanatory information. But (29) does provide contrastive explanatory information. Therefore, Russellianism is false. This is what I call the *Particularized Contrastive Explanation Objection*.[46]

Petra's case crucially involves a *difference in the ways* in which Petra believes a proposition at the two times. When Petra reads the first sign, she comes to believe that (if she stands in line then Twain will sign her book) in a "Clemens"-ish way. She continues to believe that proposition when she reads the second sign, but she then begins to believe it in a new, "Twain"-ish way. Yet according to Russellianism, the belief ascriptions in (29) do not semantically express anything about those ways of believing, or their differences. So a critic could claim that, according to the view, attitude ascriptions do not provide the right sort of contrastive explanatory information about Petra's case.

Notice that the objection does *not* claim that attitude ascriptions cannot be used to explain Petra's behavior, if Russellianism is true. Even if Russellianism is true, attitude ascriptions such as 'Petra believed that if she lined up, then Twain would sign her book' provide information about the causes of her behavior after she sees the second sign, and provide some of the information contained in an ideal explanation of her lining up. So the claim that attitude ascriptions cannot explain her behavior under Russellianism would be incorrect. Rather, the preceding objection claims only that such ascriptions fail to provide *certain sorts* of explanatory information, namely certain *contrastive* explanatory information, if Russellianism is true.[47]

There is a more general version of the above objection that I wish to consider. A critic might claim that if (29) cannot provide contrastive explanatory information about Petra under Russellianism, then *no* attitude ascription can. Therefore, if Russellianism is true, then *no* attitude ascription can provide contrastive explanatory information about Petra's behavior. But, the critic might claim, clearly some attitude ascription can. So Russellianism is false. Call this the *Generalized Contrastive Explanation Objection.*

11. Replies to the Contrastive Explanation Objections

The crucial premise of the Particularized Contrastive Explanation Objection is the claim that (29) provides contrastive explanatory information about Petra's behavior after seeing the second sign. I deny this. (29) may *seem* (to ordinary speakers) to provide such contrastive explanatory information about Petra, but it does not.[48] Of course, I have an obligation to explain why (29) *seems* to provides contrastive explanatory information, even though it does not. I turn to that task below.

According to Russellianism, ordinary speakers' judgments about the truth values of attitude ascriptions are sometimes mistaken, especially in Twain/ Clemens cases. For instance, most speakers would *mistakenly* think that (30) is false at the time when Petra reads the *first* sign.

(30) Petra believes that if she stands in line, then Twain will sign her book.

Furthermore, most ordinary speakers would take (30) to be true with respect to the time when Petra reads the *second* sign (the judgment is correct in this case).[49] Naturally, someone who mistakenly thinks that (30) is false when Petra reads the first sign, but that (30) is true when she reads the second sign, will think that (29) provides contrastive explanatory information about Petra's case (if he understands the notion of contrastive explanatory information). In short, someone who has mistaken intuitions about the truth values of these attitude ascriptions may make mistaken judgments about the explanatory information provided by them.

So the problem for the Russellian "boils down" to the problem of explaining mistaken intuitions about the truth values of attitude ascriptions like (30). But as we've seen before, Russellians have already offered explanations of such mistaken intuitions. Salmon and Soames might claim that an utterance of (30) pragmatically conveys the proposition that Petra would assent to a sentence such as 'If I stand in line, then Twain will sign my book'; ordinary speakers think that (30) is true when they think the conveyed proposition is true. The conveyed proposition is false at the time that Petra reads the first sign, but true after she reads the second sign. Thus ordinary speakers think that (30) is false when Petra reads the first sign, but true when she reads the second sign. Thus they think that (29) is entirely correct.[50]

There is an alternative explanation of the mistaken intuition that avoids claims about the pragmatics of (30). Ordinary speakers think that, when Petra reads the first sign, she understands it and believes what it says. So they come to believe that Petra then believes that (if she stands in line, then *Clemens* will sign her book). Since she doesn't move, they (mistakenly) infer that she does not want Clemens to sign her book. When she reads the second sign, she understands it and believes what it says, and so she believes then that (if she stands in line, then Twain will sign her book). She moves, so they infer that she wanted Twain to sign her book. Ordinary speakers (mistakenly) infer from this that, when Petra read the first sign, she did not then believe that (if she stood in line, Twain would sign her book). Thus they conclude that (29) is entirely correct. These ordinary speakers believe contradictory propositions about Petra's beliefs and desires; but they do so rationally because they believe the propositions mentioned above in suitably distinct ways.[51]

Let's turn next to the Generalized Contrastive Explanation Objection. Its crucial claim is this: if, according to Russellianism, (29) fails to provide contrastive explanatory information, then under that theory, *no* attitude ascription provides contrastive explanatory information about Petra's case. I claim, to the contrary, that it's extremely likely that there are attitude ascriptions other than (29) that can provide contrastive explanatory information about Petra. Let me explain.

Before Petra enters the bookstore, she is disposed to assent to (31) and to dissent from (32).

(31) Twain is my favorite author.
(32) Clemens is my favorite author.

(31) and (32) express the same proposition (in Petra's context). But Petra believes that proposition in a "Twain"-ish way that corresponds to (31); she fails to believe it in a "Clemens"-ish way that corresponds to (32). These facts help determine which propositions she comes to believe when she reads the two signs. When she reads the first sign, containing the name 'Clemens', she does *not* come to believe the proposition expressed by (33) in her context.

(33) If I stand in line, then my favorite author will sign my book.

But she does after she reads the second sign, containing the name 'Twain'. So there is a proposition that she comes to believe after reading the second sign that she does not come to believe after reading the first sign. We can ascribe this belief to her using (34).

(34) Petra believes that if she stands in line, then her favorite author will sign her book.

A belief described by (34) may well have some role in causing Petra to stand in line. If so, then, contrary to the crucial premise of the Generalized Objection, some attitude ascriptions can provide some contrastive explanatory information about Petra's case, even if (29) does not.[52]

The above response to the Generalized Objection relies on the claim that Petra believes some proposition after she reads the second sign that she did not before, namely the proposition expressed by (33). It's unclear, however, whether a similar claim can be made about *all* cases in which an agent changes the ways in which she believes or desires a proposition. That is, it's unclear whether a person always comes to believe new propositions whenever she undergoes a change in the *way* she believes a given singular proposition. There may be some recalcitrant cases in which there is *merely* a change in the ways the agent believes and desires propositions, with no changes in the propositions she believes and desires. There may also be cases in which two distinct agents believe and desire relevantly similar propositions, and yet believe and desire them in different ways, and so behave differently. I won't try to describe such apparently recalcitrant cases here, but they would be close relatives of John Perry's shopper with the torn sugar bag (Perry, 1979), Perry's amnesiac (Perry, 1977), and especially Lewis's two gods (Lewis, 1979) and David Austin's Two Tubes case (Austin, 1990; see Braun, 1997). Thus, if Russellianism is correct, then there may be some unusually recalcitrant cases for which no ordinary attitude ascription can provide contrastive explanatory information about the agent's (or agents') behavior.

A critic might claim, to the contrary, that it is *always* possible to use attitude ascriptions to provide contrastive explanatory information in cases that Russellians would describe as different-ways-of-believing cases. But a Russellian can plausibly deny this, and (again) explain away ordinary intuitions to the contrary (in a way similar to the way I have done several times in this paper). Moreover, the critic's claim does not have much initial plausibility. We are all familiar with cases of pairs of agents who behave differently but for whom attitude ascriptions cannot provide contrastive explanatory information. Suppose that two agents believe and desire relevantly similar propositions in relevantly similar ways, but that one of them suffers from sudden paralysis while the other does not. Suppose that (consequently) one of them waves, while the other does not. A description of the paralysis of one agent would be the most straightforward way of providing contrastive explanatory information about them. No ascription of attitudes to the two agents would provide such contrastive information. Now if Russellianism is true, then there may be extremely recalcitrant different-ways-of-believing cases for which attitude ascriptions cannot provide contrastive explanatory information. But this consequence of Russellianism seems quite acceptable, in view of cases like the paralytic.

Notice, moreover, that even if Russellianism is true, there are always sentences *other than* attitude ascriptions that can provide genuine contrastive explanatory information in different-ways cases. These include sentences that describe the agent's, or agents', dispositions to assent and dissent, and changes in these dispositions; and sentences that explicitly mention the ways in which the agent, or agents, believe and desire the propositions. So in each different-ways case, some sentence can provide some contrastive explanatory information, even if Russellianism is true.

12. Conclusion

The above Explanation Objections to Russellianism rely on ordinary judgments about the *explanatory values* of attitude ascriptions. But Russellians claim that some judgments of well-informed speakers about the *truth values* of attitude ascriptions are mistaken, particularly in Twain/Clemens cases. Now if some speakers' judgments about truth values are incorrect, then (naturally) some of their judgments about the explanatory values of some attitudes ascriptions are likely to be incorrect. So Russellians should be expected to claim that some ordinary judgments about explanatory values are mistaken. Russellians, however, can explain away ordinary speakers' mistaken judgments about the explanatory values of attitude ascriptions, often in a way similar to the way in which they explain away ordinary speakers' mistaken judgments about the truth values of attitude ascriptions.

But many ordinary judgments about the explanatory values of attitude ascriptions are correct, according to Russellianism. Russellianism is consistent with the fact that beliefs and desires sometimes cause behavior (and other events). Thus attitude ascriptions sometimes describe genuine causes of behavior, according to Russellianism. They also provide some of the information contained in ideal explanations of behavior. So, on any plausible view of explanation, those ascriptions qualify as (elliptical) explanations of behavior. Thus, attitude ascriptions can explain behavior, even if Russellianism is true.[53]

Notes

1. Presentations of Explanation Objections (in the literature with which I am familiar) tend to be very brief and thus tend to raise real interpretive difficulties. Thus I cannot reasonably claim to have replied to every Explanation Objection that might be extracted from this literature. (In particular, there may be further objections that are based on cases like those that I describe in sections 10 and 11 below.) My hope here is to present, clarify, and distinguish among some initially plausible Explanation Objections, and to present some plausible Russellian replies to these objections.
2. Richard (1997a, p. 202) assumes that Russellians must appeal to pragmatics to account for the explanatory power of attitude ascriptions. Richard himself, when he was more favorably inclined towards Russellianism, tried to provide such a pragmatic account (Richard, 1987).
3. Because sentences (1) and (2) are tensed, it would be reasonable to think that one of the constituents of the proposition they express, with respect to a context, is a time. See, for instance, Salmon, 1986. But I shall ignore all matters of tense and time throughout this paper.
4. I am ignoring the difference in tense between 'Twain smiles' and 'Twain to smile'. See note 3.

5. See Salmon, 1986 and 1989; and Soames, 1988 and 1995. The intermediary determines the proposition believed or desired only relative to a context or a causal/historical chain.

6. It's sometimes useful to speak of a *ternary* relation that holds between an agent *A*, a proposition *P*, and a way of taking that proposition *W*, when *A* stands in the right psychological relation to *W* (e.g., accepting) and *W* has *P* as its content. Following Salmon (1986), we could use '*BEL*' to refer to this relation. An agent *A* believes proposition *P* iff there is some way *W* of taking *P* such that *BEL*[*A*, *P*, *W*]. In more ordinary English, we can speak of an agent believing a proposition in a certain way. Similar points hold for desiring.

7. I often use numerical indices of sentences as abbreviations for their quotation names, especially within complement clauses of attitude ascriptions. For example, I use (i) as an abbreviation for (ii).

> (i) Albert believes that (4) is true.
> (ii) Albert believes that 'Twain is an author' is true.

8. Richard (1990) holds that attitude ascriptions are context-sensitive. Thus he might hold that, even given the facts about Carol, (6) and (7) are true only with respect to certain sorts of contexts. Let's assume below that we are discussing the truth values of (6) and (7) with respect to contexts in which they are true, according to Richard; thus, we will be concerned with whether (6) and (7) can explain Carol's waving in such contexts. Devitt (1996) thinks that (6) and (7) have opaque and transparent readings. Devitt can agree that, given the facts about Carol, (6) and (7) are true on both of their readings.

9. Richard (1990) thinks that the verbs 'believe' and 'want' express different relations in different contexts; thus there is no such thing as *the* believing relation or *the* wanting relation. But he could agree that (6) is true, with respect to a context *c*, only if there occurs a certain sort of "believing event" that involves Carol, the relation expressed by 'believes' in *c*, and the proposition denoted by the 'that'-clause in *c*. Similarly for (7). Devitt (1996) could agree with the claims in the main text, though he holds that the denotation of the 'that'-clause is a property, rather than a proposition.

10. A critic might argue that if Russellianism is true, then (6) and (7) cannot describe events that are genuine causes of Carol's waving. Such a critic might simply dislike my explication of the describing-relation that (I claim) can hold between events and sentences like (6) and (7). More interestingly, such a critic might agree with my explication of this notion, but have strong views about causation or causal relevance of properties. For instance, he might hold that the property of being-a-believing-by-Carol-in-*Russellian*-proposition-*P* is causally irrelevant to behavioral events. He might hold that any event that has this property fails to be a cause of Carol's waving. So he might conclude that (6) and (7) cannot describe causes of Carol's waving, if Russellianism is true. I find the last premise of this argument very implausible. In any case, I do *not* claim that this property is causally relevant to Carol's waving; I claim only that, if Russellianism is true, then some events that have that property might be among the causes of Carol's waving. I do not have the space to consider objections that rely heavily on claims about the nature of causation or causally relevant properties. I have not detected such arguments in Devitt and Richard (my main targets here).

11. There are a number of further assumptions that I shall make; not all of them are acceptable to anti-Russellians, but they could accept analogous assumptions. First, I assume that if Carol understands 'If I wave, then Twain will see me' and 'I want Twain to see me', and sincerely and reflectively assents to them, then she believes the propositions that they express, in the context in which she assents. I assume that, in the context under discussion, 'I' refers to Carol. Thus I assume that Carol believes the propositions that (if Carol waves then Twain will see Carol) and (Carol wants Twain to see Carol). Second, I assume that she believes these propositions in "first-person" ways. Third, I assume that if she believes (in a first-person way) the proposition that Carol wants Twain to see Carol, then she really does want (in a first-person way) the proposition that Twain sees Carol. Fourth, I assume that (if Russellianism is true) the occurrences of 'she' and 'her' in (6) and (7) are singular terms whose contents are Carol herself. Thus, (under Russellianism) the contents of the complement clauses of (6) and (7) are propositions that have Carol herself as a constituent. (There are alternative theories about the functions of the pronouns that are consistent with Russellianism; see Salmon 1992 and Soames 1994; but the issues about these pronouns are tangential to my concerns here.)

12. See notes 16 and 17 for some further qualifications. Devitt seems to press an objection roughly like the one that follows in Devitt 1996, pp. 151–3, 182–4, 243, and 304 (but see note 17 below). There are other places where he is not particularly concerned with Russellianism, but where he emphasizes the role of "supporting" laws and generalizations in explanation of behavior; see Devitt 1996, pp. 174–5, 220–1, and 230–7; and Devitt 1997, p. 117. Richard (1997a, p. 202) seems to admit that Russellians have reasonable replies to substitution objections; he seems willing to rest his case against Russellianism on explanation objections. He presses an explanation objection roughly like my imaginary critic's in Richard 1990, pp. 126 and 173–6. (In Braun 2000, I discuss one aspect of the argument that Richard presents on p. 174.) Richard says (or implies) that ordinary psychological explanations of behavior are "underwritten by" or "implicitly invoke" psychological generalizations (1990, pp. 260–3; 1997b, p. 90); he also sometimes speaks of the premises of belief-desire explanations (1990, pp. 176, 219). He also assumes in several places (1987; 1990, pp. 44, note 16, and 260–3) that complete psychological explanations are covering-law arguments that include psychological generalizations.

13. Similarly, some critics might maintain that sentences (i) and (ii) also explain Carol's waving.

> (i) Carol waved because she wanted Twain to see her.
> (ii) Carol waved because she believed that if she waved then Twain would see her.

But for convenience, let's imagine that our critic concentrates on the explanatory status of (10).

Since I shall often talk about (10) in what follows, I shall sketch a Russellian view about its content and truth conditions. I assume that (10) expresses a proposition of the form $\langle P, Q, BECAUSE \rangle$, where P is the proposition expressed by 'Carol waves' and Q is the proposition expressed by (9), and *BECAUSE* is a relation that holds between two propositions just in case (roughly) one is true because the other is. I won't try to provide a metaphysical analysis of the *BECAUSE* relation, but I do want to assume the following: if there are some events that make Q true (in the sense explicated in the main text) and an event that makes P true, and the Q-events are causes of the P-event, then the *BECAUSE* relation holds between propositions P and Q.

14. A "more general" generalization, such as (i), would also subsume the sentences on both sides of the 'because' in (10).

    (i) If a person wants Q, and she believes that [if P then Q], then, other things being equal, she will make it the case that P.

But notice that if (11) is false, then so is (i). Therefore, I will concentrate on the more specific (11). I shall assume that, if Russellianism is true, then (a) the pronouns that occur in these generalizations function as variables bound by 'a person', (b) the ranges of those variables are ordinary individuals (not, e.g., senses), (c) the complement clauses in the generalizations refer to singular propositions, relative to assignments of values to the pronouns/variables, and (d) instantiating one of these generalizations to a name of an agent results in ascriptions of attitudes towards singular propositions to the agent. See also note 11.

15. Devitt might also conclude that (10) is *false*, if Russellianism is true; see Devitt 1997, pp. 118–121, especially p. 121. See note 13 for a Russellian theory of the content and truth conditions of (10).

16. My imaginary critic's objection is a *generic* anti-Russellian objection that many anti-Russellians could endorse. Richard and Devitt might want to qualify it, to better fit their views about attitude ascriptions.

    Richard (1990, pp. 133–54) holds that attitude ascriptions express different propositions in different contexts. In some contexts, (10) is true only if Carol believes and desires the propositions in matching ways; but in other contexts, it is true even if Carol believes and desires in mismatching ways (Richard 1990, pp. 174–6, 234–44). Similarly for (11): in some contexts, an agent satisfies the antecedent of (11) only if he believes and desires the propositions in matching ways; in other contexts, this is not required. Richard (1990, p. 175–6) seems to hold that (10) explains Carol's waving, in a context, only if its truth, in that context, requires Carol to believe and desire in matching ways. Now according to Russellianism, there is no context in which the truth of (10) requires Carol to believe and desire in matching ways. Thus (10) fails to explain Carol's waving in any context under Russellianism, according to Richard (1990, pp. 173–6).

    Devitt (1996, esp. pp. 151–3) holds that (10) and (11) are ambiguous: each attitude ascription has an opaque reading and a transparent reading. If (11) is true when all of its attitude ascriptions are read opaquely, then (10), on this "fully opaque" reading, can explain Carol's waving. (10), on its fully transparent reading, can also explain Carol's waving, but only if it follows from true opaque ascriptions and true identities (Devitt 1996, p. 184). Ultimately, then, it seems that attitude ascriptions can explain behavior only if they have opaque readings. But according to Russellianism, they do not have opaque readings. See also note 17.

17. In personal correspondence about an earlier draft of this paper, Devitt says that he thinks that (10) does not *fully* explain Carol's waving, if Russellianism is true, because its explanatory power depends on the truth of opaquely construed attitude ascriptions that are unavailable under Russellianism (see note 16). But he thinks

(10) may explain her waving in some less-than-full sense, under Russellianism. In addition, Devitt claims not to have asserted a premise like (12d), and is unsure whether he agrees with it. Nevertheless, he agrees that the Ordinary Explanation Objection can be constructed from elements of his view, and that it is suggested by some of his comments about the explanatory failures of Russellianism. I think the objection is well worth considering, whether or not it exactly captures Devitt's, or Richard's, intentions.

18. The Ordinary Explanation Objection is distinct from, but easily confused with, another Explanation Objection that some anti-Russellians might endorse. According to it, an explanation of an event must describe events whose occurrence is *nomologically sufficient* (other things being equal) for the explained event. (10) does not describe such events, if Russellianism is true; for on this view, it's nomologically possible for (9) to be true, and for other things to be equal, even though Carol believes and desires the relevant propositions in mismatched ways, and so does not wave. Therefore, (10) does not explain Carol's waving if Russellianism is true. But (10) does explain the waving, so Russellianism is false. Call this the *Nomological Sufficiency Objection*. The Ordinary Explanation Objection assumes (i), while the premises of the Nomological Sufficiency Objection imply (ii).

    (i) If Russellianism is true, then (11) is false.
    (ii) If Russellianism is true, then (11) is not a nomologically necessary truth.

    If (i) is true, then so is (ii), but not vice versa. Thus the Nomological Sufficiency Objection might be sound, even if the Ordinary Explanation Objection is not. But the first premise of the Nomological Sufficiency Objection is implausibly strong; see note 30.

19. I have relied heavily on the work of Carl Hempel to construct the following covering-law theories. See Hempel, 1962 and 1965b, and Hempel and Oppenheim, 1965. But I do not wish to imply that Hempel accepts any of the following theories.

20. Hempel (1962, 1965b) rejects the claim that every ideal explanation is a D-N explanation, for he allows there to be other (covering-law explanations) of particular events that are not deductively valid, including *inductive-statistical explanations*.

21. The D-N theory has at least two well-known problems that may be relevant to what occurs below. Eberle, Kaplan, and Montague (1961) show that a D-N theory of the above sort entails that just about any law can appear in a D-N explanation of just about any particular event. Kaplan (1961) proposes some additions to the theory that may solve this problem; his additions should be acceptable to anti-Russellians. For further discussion, see these articles and the postscript to Hempel and Oppenheim (1965). Other counterexamples point to the need for another modification. Suppose that it is a law that a star's spectrogram displays a red-shift to an observer if and only if it is receding from the observer. Then one can formulate a D-N argument such that (i) its premises include this law and a sentence saying that a certain star's spectrogram displayed a red-shift to an observer, and (ii) its conclusion says that the star is receding from the observer. On the D-N theory, this argument explains the star's recession. But this is obviously wrong; if anything, the star's recession explains the red-shift. This problem with the D-N theory can be fixed in a way that is acceptable to anti-Russellians by requiring that the particular fact premises of an explanatory argument describe causes of the explanandum event.

22. The problem with the D-N theory is not confined to psychological explanations; it also entails that (i) is not an ideal explanation, for similar reasons.

> (i) Match *m* was struck. If a match is struck, then (other things being equal) it lights. Therefore, match *m* lit.

In fact, the D-N theory may well entail that only arguments stated in the vocabulary of basic physics qualify as ideal explanations. Hempel (1962, 1965b) seems to think that *ceteris paribus* generalizations of the sort that appear in (13) and (i) are statistical generalizations. He presents a theory of inductive-statistical explanations of particular events that makes use of such generalizations. But his theory seems unacceptable, for reasons that I will not go into here (see Railton, 1981).

23. Here's one very rough attempt to analyze the support-relation. Let *A* be an argument that contains at least one *ceteris paribus* generalization. For each generalization (and context) there is a *suitable condition* that holds when "other things are equal" (in the sense required by that generalization, with respect to that context). Say that the premises of *A support* its conclusion iff: for every context *c*, if the premises were true in *c*, and the suitable conditions associated with its generalizations in *c* held, then the conclusion would be true in *c*. This analysis of the supports-relation fits well with the semantic analysis of *ceteris paribus* generalizations that I (tentatively) provide in Braun (2000).

24. There are difficulties with these requirements that may be important to what follows. First, the original D-N theory requires the premises of an explanatory argument to be essential to it (that is, dropping any premise from the explanation should result in a deductively invalid argument). It seems that a new theory should have an analogous requirement in order to exclude explanatorily irrelevant premises. But it is unclear how to state an analogous requirement for the theory, given that ideal explanations on this view need not be deductively valid. Second, there may be problems with the modified theory analogous to those that Eberle, Kaplan, and Montague raise for the original theory; see note 21. Kaplan's proposed modifications (Kaplan 1961) do not seem suitable for the modified theory, mainly because explanations need not be deductively valid on the latter view. See also note 30.

25. Similar points hold for ordinary non-psychological explanations like 'The match lit because it was struck'.

26. The term 'elliptical explanation' comes from Hempel (1962, 1965b). Hempel distinguishes between different sorts of explanations that deviate from full or ideal explanations: some he called 'elliptical', some 'partial', and some 'explanation sketches'. Hempel admits that it is often difficult to tell whether a given explanation is elliptical, partial, or merely a sketch. We need not distinguish between them for our purposes.

27. I use the term 'explanans-sentence' much more loosely when I discuss elliptical explanation than when I discuss ideal explanations. I won't try to make this use more precise, for I suspect that the critics of Russellianism would agree with my judgments about which sentences in ordinary elliptical explanations are explanans-sentences.

28. So is 'The match lit because it was struck'. See note 22.

29. An alternative to the Modified Theory might hold that a sentence is an elliptical explanation of event *E* iff it describes some events that are *nomologically sufficient*

(other things being equal) for *E* to occur. See note 18. Notice that this theory would be stricter than the Modified theory, for on the latter view, a sentence can qualify as an elliptical explanation even if the events it describes are not nomologically sufficient for the explained event.

30. A defender of the Modified Theory might reply by asking me to justify my claim that the sentence 'There is a chemical imbalance in Don's brain' does not figure essentially in any ideal explanation of Don's depression. I think my claim is intuitively plausible, but defending it further would require me to rely on some explication of the notion of an *essential premise* that is appropriate for arguments that are not deductively valid; as I mentioned earlier (note 24), no such explication has been given, and formulating one is not easy. (See Hempel and Oppenheim 1965, Eberle, Kaplan, and Montague 1961, and Kaplan 1961 for discussions of similar issues that arise for *deductive* explanatory arguments. The issue arises there because there there are various "logician's tricks" that can make nearly any premise essential to some ideal explanation of an event.) But an advocate of the Modified Theory must assume that there is such an explication that is consistent with intuition, so that he can rule out certain arguments that (intuitively) have premises with no explanatory relevance (including those that rely on "logician's tricks"). I believe that any such explication of 'essential premise' would entail that the explanans of (16) is inessential to arguments that contain enough specific information to qualify as ideal covering-law explanations of Don's depression.

    Notice that (16)–(18) do not describe events that are nomologically sufficient for their respective explananda-events. Since (16)–(18) (nevertheless) explain their respective events, the Nomological Sufficiency Objection is unsound (see notes 18 and 29).

31. In what follows, I distinguish more carefully than Railton does between (a) sentences, arguments, and linguistic explanations, on the one hand, and (b) propositions, propositional arguments, and propositional explanations, on the other. Doing so is much more important for my purposes than for Railton's.

32. I deviate from Railton in at least two ways. First, I use the primitive *x contains information that is contained in y*, which holds between (sequences of) propositions and propositional explanations, rather than Railton's notion *x provides information about y*, which holds between a sentence (or linguistic argument) and an ideal (linguistic) explanation. Second, because of this difference, Railton's theory may be more liberal than the version of his view that I present here, for it may be possible for a sentence to provide information *about* an ideal explanation, even though the proposition it expresses does not *contain* information that is contained in some ideal propositional explanation. For instance, a sentence may provide peculiarly *negative* information about an ideal explanation; it may tell us that all ideal explanations of the event *lack* certain features. (See Lewis, 1986, p. 220.) Thus the proposition the sentence expresses may not contain information that is contained in an ideal propositional explanation of the event. However, this difference will not affect the issues under discussion here.

33. This last sentence is an addition to Lewis's view, but one that conforms with its spirit. Lewis says that, in one sense of the term 'explanation', an explanation of an event is an act of providing causal information about the event. In another sense of the term, an explanation of an event is a proposition that might be expressed in such an act, that is, a proposition that contains information about the causes of that

event. Lewis does not speak of explanatory *sentences* or arguments (though he does mention theories).

34. Thanks to Jeffrey King and Brendan Jackson for persuading me that I need to address this issue.

35. I am grateful to Jeffrey King for discussion of this last argument.

36. There are two other features of (13) that are worth noticing. First, (13a) is true, and describes causes of Carol's waving. So argument (13) provides some true explanatory information about Carol's waving, even if one of its premises is false. Second, (11) is *approximately true*, under Russellianism, in a relatively clear sense: (11) need only be modified to mention *matching ways* of believing and desiring the relevant propositions in order to be strictly true. An ideal explanation that contains one premise that is (only) approximately true may easily appear to be (strictly) correct. It's conceivable that some speakers' judgments that (13) is a correct ideal explanation might be explained by these features of (13).

37. The recognition of the context-sensitivity of (11) and other psychological generalizations would require some further complications in covering-law theories of explanation. If (11) is true in some contexts and false in others, then the premises of the ideal explanatory argument (13) would vary in their truth values from context to context. Thus (13) may be a correct explanation in some contexts, but not others. Perhaps a covering-law theorist should hold that (10) explains Carol's waving in some contexts, but not in others.

38. There is an entirely different response to the Explanatory Substitution Objection that is consistent with Russellianism. According to this response, two sentences that express the same proposition can have different explanatory values. This response would accept that (10) explains Carol's waving and that (21) does not; but it would deny the premise that (10) explains Carol's waving only if (21) does. This response would require a view of explanation on which the explanatory value of a sentence may depend heavily on its wording. It would be consistent with Russellianism, but inconsistent with the views about explanation that I endorsed in section 5.

39. A speaker could perhaps think that (10) and (21) are *both* true, and yet think that (10) explains Carol's waving while (21) does not. Such speakers would have to accept views about explanation that entail implausibly strong requirements for explanation (e.g., the Modified D-N theory). Thus I will ignore them here.

40. There is one salient difference between the case of (22) and (23) and the case of (10) and (21): a person who assents to 'Twain is Clemens' could rationally think that (10) is true and (21) is false, whereas it's not clear that such a person could rationally think that (22) is true and (23) is not. I discuss this difference between attitude ascriptions and simple sentences in Braun, 1998.

41. I suspect that Salmon and Soames would be inclined to appeal to a difference in the pragmatic implications of (10) and (21) to explain ordinary speakers' intuitions that they differ in truth value. Perhaps they would wish to give an account like that of Richard (1987), but I won't speculate about that any further here.

42. See note 47 for my reasons for my hesitation. Thanks to Theodore Sider for suggesting that I discuss objections and examples like those that follow below.

43. My account of contrastive explanation relies heavily on Lewis, 1986, sec. VI. For a critical discussion of Lewis's view, see Lipton, 1990.

44. Often, a person who asks about the *non*-occurrence of a type of event also wants contrastive explanatory information. Questions of this sort often take the form "Why

didn't *x* do *A*?" For instance, suppose that Sally is ignorant of the Monday events, but knows that on Tuesday Oprah liked the taste of Fruity Flakes better than Bran Bombs. Thus Sally thinks that the events leading up to Oprah's taking the Bran Bombs on Tuesday should have caused Oprah to reach for the Fruity Flakes instead. So Sally might ask "Why didn't Oprah take the Fruity Flakes on Tuesday?" Again, it seems that Sally would want information about the causal chain leading to Oprah's reaching for the Bran Bombs that differentiates it from a (counterfactual) causal chain leading up to Oprah's reaching for the Fruity Flakes. She would, again, be seeking constrastive explanatory information.

45. This example is inspired by Lewis (1986b, pp. 58–59); it resembles an example given by Heck (1995, pp. 79–80), and also examples that John Perry (1977, 1979) uses for other purposes.

46. A similar objection could be framed around the question "Why didn't Petra line up when she saw the first sign?". See notes 44 and 47.

47. I can now say in what way the Particularized Contrastive Explanation Objection is inspired by Lewis and Heck, and why I hesitate to ascribe it to them. Lewis (1986, pp. 58–59) presents an example like that of Petra in a discussion of whether Russellian singular propositions are objects of the attitudes. But Lewis does not use his example to argue against Russellian theories of attitude *ascriptions*, and does not mention contrastive explanation in connection with his example. Heck (1995, pp. 79–80) gives a similar example, and *does* explicitly use it to argue against Russellianism. However, he does not mention *contrastive* explanation. Instead, he argues that, if Russellianism were true, then attitude ascriptions could not be used to explain why certain agents (like Petra) do *not* behave in certain ways (e.g., do not line up after seeing the first sign). I think that attempts to explain such *non*-occurrences are best understood as attempts to provide certain sorts of contrastive explanatory information; see notes 44 and 46. If I am correct, then a reply to the Particularized Contrastive Explanation Objection should also constitute a reply to Heck's criticism.

48. It's important to recall that I am using the expression 'provide' in a technical, semantic sense that I defined in section 5. In this sense of 'provide', a sentence provides contrastive explanatory information iff it *semantically expresses* a proposition that contains such information. In another, looser sense of the term 'provide', a sentence or utterance may provide such information without semantically expressing it. See below, especially notes 50 and 51. (Thanks to John Bennett for discussion of this.)

49. I am speaking very loosely here about sentences' and propositions' being true at times. To speak more accurately about these matters would require me to introduce many distracting complications concerning time and tense that are not directly relevant to my replies to the Contrastive Explanation Objections (see Salmon, 1986).

50. Salmon and Soames might claim that an utterance of (30) at the second time "provides" contrastive explanatory information, in a non-semantic, pragmatic sense of 'provide' different from the semantic sense of the term that I earlier stipulated. It's important to distinguish my technical, semantic sense of 'provide' from this looser sense of 'provide'.

51. See sections 1 and 9, and Braun, 1998. A fuller explanation of these ordinary speakers' inferences would mention the ways in which they take the various propositions about Petra's beliefs and desires. Some ordinary speakers might use further commonsense psychological reasoning to infer that Petra would dissent from 'If I stand

in line then Twain will sign my book' at the first time, but that she would assent to it at the second. (They can reason their way to this conclusion even if an utterance of (29) does not pragmatically convey any proposition about Petra's assents and dissents.) This conclusion would be correct. Thus (29) might sometimes, in some loose sense, "provide" some correct contrastive explanatory information to some speakers, but not in the semantic sense of 'provide' that I earlier defined (and which is under discussion here), and perhaps not even in a pragmatic sense (via pragmatic implications).

52. This response to the Generalized Contrastive Explanation Objection is inspired by some remarks by Lewis (1986b, p. 58), though he may well disagree with it.

53. Thanks to John G. Bennett, Michael Devitt, Richard Feldman, Graeme Forbes, Tamar Szabo Gendler, Brendan Jackson, Jeffrey King, Thomas McKay, Mark Richard, Theodore Sider, Zoltan Gendler Szabo, Gabriel Uzquiano, and Edward Wierenga for helpful comments, criticisms, and advice. I presented abbreviated versions of this paper at Syracuse University and the University of Rochester. I am grateful to the audiences at those talks for the discussions that followed.

References

Austin, David. 1990. *What's the Meaning of "This"?*. Ithaca, NY: Cornell University Press.

Braun, David. 1995. "Causally Relevant Properties." *Philosophical Perspectives* 9, pp. 447–475.

Braun, David. 1997. Review of Austin (1990) and Yourgrau (1990). *Minds and Machines* 7, pp. 247–302.

Braun, David. 1998. "Understanding Belief Reports." *Philosophical Review* 107, pp. 555–595.

Braun, David. 2000. "Russellianism and Psychological Generalizations." *Noûs* 34, pp. 203–226.

Crimmins, Mark. 1992. *Talk About Beliefs*. Cambridge, MA: MIT Press.

Devitt, Michael. 1996. *Coming to Our Senses: A Naturalistic Program for Semantic Localism*. Cambridge: Cambridge University Press.

Devitt, Michael. 1997. "Meanings and Psychology: A Response to Mark Richard." *Noûs* 31, pp. 115–131.

Eberle, Rolf, Kaplan, David, and Montague, Richard. 1961. "Hempel and Oppenheim on Explanation." *Philosophy of Science* 28, pp. 418–428.

Heck, Richard G., Jr. 1995. "The Sense of Communication." *Mind* 104, pp. 79–106.

Hempel, Carl G. 1962. "Explanation in Science and in History." In R. G. Colodny (ed.), *Frontiers of Philosophy*, pp. 7–33. London and Pittsburgh: Allen & Unwin and University of Pittsburgh Press. Reprinted in Ruben 1993, pp. 17–41.

Hempel, Carl G. 1965a. *Aspects of Scientific Explanation and Other Essays in Philosophy of Science*. New York: Free Press.

Hempel, Carl G. 1965b. "Aspects of Scientific Explanation." In Hempel 1965a, pp. 331–496. Portions reprinted in Ruben 1993, pp. 42–55.

Hempel, Carl G., and Oppenheim, Paul. 1965. "Studies in the Logic of Explanation." In Hempel 1965a, pp. 245–290. Originally appeared in *Philosophy of Science* 15 (1948), pp. 135–175.

Kaplan, David. 1961. "Explanation Revisited." *Philosophy of Science* 28, pp. 429–436.

Lewis, David. 1979. "Attitudes *De Dicto* and *De Se*." *Philosophical Review* 88, pp. 513–543. Reprinted in his *Philosophical Papers, Volume I* (1983), pp. 133–156. Oxford: Oxford University Press.

Lewis, David. 1986a. "Causal Explanation." In his *Philosophical Papers, Volume II*, pp. 214–240. Oxford: Oxford University Press. Reprinted in Ruben 1993, pp. 182–206.

Lewis, David. 1986b. *On the Plurality of Worlds*. Oxford: Blackwell.

Lipton, Peter. 1990. "Contrastive Explanation." In D. Knowles (ed.), *Explanation and Its Limits.* Cambridge: Cambridge University Press. Reprinted in Ruben 1993, pp. 207–227.

McKay, Thomas. 1979. "On Proper Names in Belief Ascriptions." *Philosophical Studies* 39, pp. 287–303.

Perry, John. 1977. "Frege on Demonstratives." *Philosophical Review* 86, pp. 474–497.

Perry, John. 1979. "The Problem of the Essential Indexical." *Noûs* 13, pp. 3–21.

Railton, Peter. 1981. "Probability, Explanation, and Information." *Synthese* 48, pp. 233–256. Reprinted in Ruben 1993, pp. 160–181.

Richard, Mark. 1987. "Attitude Ascriptions, Semantic Theory, and Pragmatic Evidence." *Proceedings of the Aristotelian Society* 87, pp. 243–262.

Richard, Mark. 1990. *Propositional Attitudes: An Essay on Thoughts and How We Ascribe Them.* Cambridge: Cambridge University Press.

Richard, Mark. 1997a. "Propositional Attitudes." In Bob Hale and Crispin Wright (eds.), *A Companion to Philosophy of Language*, pp. 197–226. Oxford: Blackwell.

Richard, Mark. 1997b. "What Does Commonsense Psychology Tell Us About Meaning?" *Noûs* 31, pp. 87–114.

Ruben, David-Hillel (ed.). 1993. *Explanation.* Oxford: Oxford University Press.

Salmon, Nathan. 1986. *Frege's Puzzle.* Cambridge, MA: MIT Press.

Salmon, Nathan. 1989. "Illogical Belief." *Philosophical Perspectives* 3, pp. 243–285.

Salmon, Nathan. 1992. "Reflections on Reflexivity." *Linguistics and Philosophy* 15, pp. 53–63.

Saul, Jennifer. 1998. "The Pragmatics of Attitude Ascription." *Philosophical Studies* 92, pp. 363–389.

Soames, Scott. 1988. "Direct Reference, Propositional Attitudes, and Semantic Content." In Nathan Salmon and Scott Soames (Eds.), *Propositions and Attitudes*, pp. 197–239. Originally published in *Philosophical Topics* 15 (1987), pp. 47–87.

Soames, Scott. 1995. "Beyond Singular Propositions?" *Canadian Journal of Philosophy* 25, pp. 515–550.

Soames, Scott. 1994. "Attitudes and Anaphora." *Philosophical Perspectives* 8, pp. 251–272.

Yourgrau, Palle (ed.). 1990. *Demonstratives.* Oxford: Oxford University Press.

Philosophical Perspectives, 15, Metaphysics, 2001

REMARKS ON THE SYNTAX AND SEMANTICS
OF DAY DESIGNATORS*

Jeffrey C. King
University of California, Davis

I shall call an expression such as 'January 24, 2001' a *day designator*. The purpose of the present work is to discuss the syntactic and semantic properties of day designators.[1] Because my topic may seem very narrow to some, let me begin by discussing a few of the broader issues that thinking about the proper semantics of day designators brings to the fore. First, if one views semantics, as I do, as being at least in good part about how language attaches to reality, it becomes very important in formulating a semantic theory of an expression to think about the bit of reality that expression is used to talk about and how we interact with it. We shall see that giving careful consideration to how time is measured leads us to a semantic theory of day designators that we would be otherwise unlikely to propose. Thus I view the present work as a sort of case study illustrating the importance of attention to such details, which are much too often neglected, in proper semantic theorizing. Second, some philosophers think that all noun phrases in natural languages are either quantifier phrases or rigid referring expressions.[2] In what follows, I shall argue that day designators are non-rigid; I shall also argue (somewhat more tentatively) that day designators are not quantificational. If I am right, then natural languages contain non-rigid, non-quantificational expressions, contrary to the claim mentioned above. Further, and perhaps more importantly, the present study illustrates how to go about determining whether an expression is non-rigid and non-quantificational; and how delicate the issues are that one must face in making such a determination.

Let us begin by discussing the syntax of day designators and some of their syntactic constituents. First, there are the words 'January', 'February', and so on. Though these expressions are often called "names of months", there is good reason to hold that they are not names at all. Syntactically, these words behave as count nouns. They combine with determiners such as 'every', 'many', 'exactly three' etc. to form restricted quantifiers:[3]

(1) Every January I go skiing.

(2) I spent many Januarys at Squaw Valley.

(3) I wasted exactly three Januarys in Bakersfield.

Like other count nouns, they can take relative clauses in constructions such as (1)–(3):

(1a) Every January that you visited we went skiing.

(2a) I spent many Januarys that I will never forget at Squaw Valley.

(3a) I wasted three Januarys that seemed interminable in Bakersfield.

They also combine with the copula, indefinite article and adjectival modifiers to form predicates in the way that other count nouns do:

(4) The first full month I lived in Northern California was a pleasant July.

Further, it is generally held that only constituents of the same syntactic category can be conjoined. And as the following example shows, 'January' can be conjoined with other count nouns:[4]

(5) All Januarys and funerals last too long.

Thus distributional evidence strongly suggests that 'January', 'February', etc. are count nouns.

Since in general we take count nouns to express properties, we ought to take 'January', 'February' etc. to express properties as well.[5] We shall return to the question of what properties such words express below. For now, we shall stick with syntax.

Let us turn to the other syntactic constituents of day designators and the syntactic structure of day designators generally. Of course, numerals occur in day designators: one immediately following 'January' etc.; and another following the first and a comma. There is evidence that 'January 24' is a syntactic constituent of 'January 24, 2001', as the placement of the comma in day designators suggests. First, it is generally held that only "phrasal constituents" of sentences can serve as sentence fragments. Thus the acceptability of:

When will you be out of your office in 2001?
January 24.

suggests that 'January 24' is a phrasal constituent of 'You will be out of your office January 24, 2001.' And since 'January 24, 2001' is itself a noun phrase and so a syntactic constituent of the sentence, this suggests that 'January 24' is a phrasal constituent of the noun phrase 'January 24, 2001'. Further, only syntactic constituents can undergo coordination or conjunction. Thus, the acceptability of:

I will be out of my office January 23 and January 24 2002.

suggests that 'January 24' is a syntactic constituent of the above sentence, and hence of 'January 24, 2002'. Thus it would appear that 'January 24' is a syntactic constituent of the noun phrase 'January 24, 2002.' But what is *its* syntactic category?

As with the word 'January' itself, such phrases can be used to form restricted quantifiers ('Every January 24 is a holiday.'). And again like 'January', they can take relative clauses in such constructions ('Every January 24 that you visited was a holiday.'). Finally, once more like 'January', they can be used with the copula and modifiers to form a predicate ('The day you last visited was a very pleasant January 24.'). Other syntactically complex expressions that occur in constructions of this sort, such as 'woman who lives in St. Paul', are of the syntactic category N'. Thus, the distributional evidence suggests that phrases like 'January 24' are N' constituents and so, like other N' expressions, express properties. Finally, phrases like 'January 24' combine with "year numerals" to form day designators: noun phrases that designate days.

Syntactically, then, the picture that emerges is that the "month words" (e.g. 'January') are count nouns and so express properties. The concatenation of a month word and a "day numeral" (between 1 and 31) is a syntactically complex N' expression and so once again expresses a property. The concatenation of such a "complex day expression" (e.g. 'January 24') with a "year numeral" ('1','2',...e.g. '2001') yields a noun phrase that designates a day: a day designator (e.g. 'January 24, 2001').

We must now address the much more difficult questions concerning the precise semantics of (some of) the syntactic constituents of day designators, and the semantics of day designators themselves. Let us begin with the month words 'January', 'February', etc. We have said these words express properties. Perhaps it would be best to ask what sorts of things are in the extensions of such words before turning to the question of what properties determine those extensions.

It seems to me that the things that possess the properties of being a January, being a February, etc. are certain (continuous 28–31 day long) intervals of time. For just as the sentence 'Every skier is happy' intuitively quantifies over skiers, and in so doing makes a claim about them, in virtue of the fact that skiers are in the extension of the property expressed by 'skier', so in (1)–(3) intuitively we seem to be quantifying over intervals of time and making claims about them. Intuitively, (1) claims that during all intervals of time of a certain sort ("Januarys"), I go skiing. Intuitively, (2) claims that I spent many intervals of time of a certain sort at Squaw Valley, and so on. If these intuitions are correct, and they certainly seem to be, 'January' etc. express properties of intervals of time, and these properties deliver sets of such intervals of time as the extensions for 'January', etc.

This view is supported by the fact that the following seems true:

(6) A January is a thirty-one day long interval of time.

But for this to be true, each thing in the extension of 'January' must have the property of being a thirty-one day long interval of time.[6]

An additional reason for thinking that 'January', etc. express properties of intervals of time is that sentences such as the following seem to be true:

(7) Every January is 31 days long.

Thus the things in the extension of 'January' have the property of being 31 days long. Now what sorts of things have this type of property? It seems that only time intervals and events or states have properties like this. Could the things in the extension of 'January' be states or events? Following Jaegwon Kim [1969, 1973], let us assume that events (and states) are objects instantiating properties at (or over) times (or objects standing in relations at (or over) times, etc.). Now what sort of events could be Januarys? That is, what object possessing a property at a time (or what objects standing in relations at a time) could be a January? Certainly no natural candidate suggests itself. By contrast, that Januarys are intervals of time *does* seem the natural view. Since there are no events that are natural candidates for being Januarys, since time intervals are natural candidates for being Januarys, and since the truth of (7) suggests that Januarys are events or time intervals, we have reason to adopt the view that they are indeed time intervals.[7]

Actually, this is not *quite* correct and a qualification is in order. Because of the different time zones on Earth, the exact thirty-one day time intervals that are Januarys, Februarys, etc. vary from time zone to time zone.[8] It was January 2000 in Oswego New York before it was January 2000 in Lake Tahoe California, and it was January 2000 in Lake Tahoe after February had already begun in Oswego. Thus the time interval that is January 2000 in Oswego is slightly different from the time interval that is January 2000 in Lake Tahoe. Hence, 'January' doesn't really express a property of time intervals; rather 'January in Lake Tahoe' does. Thus 'January' itself expresses a relation between locations on Earth (or time zones) and thirty-one day time intervals. Because of the small discrepancy between Januarys at any two locations on Earth, for most purposes we don't worry about this and act as though 'January' expresses a property of time intervals.

Having said all this, in the interest of simplicity I choose to ignore it and pretend that 'January' expresses a property of time intervals. Thus, what I say about 'January' etc. actually applies to expressions like 'January in Lake Tahoe'. So far as I can see addressing this complication by really treating 'January' as expressing a relation between locations on Earth and time intervals would be tedious but straightforward. Hence my opting to ignore the complication and pretend 'January' etc. express a property.

Returning to our main theme, what property of time intervals is expressed by 'January' and exactly what intervals of time are in its extension? We can get some idea of the property 'January' expresses by considering how 'January', 'February' etc. came to have the extensions they currently have. This, in turn, requires saying a bit about the history of the Gregorian calendar and the evolution of international time standards.

Pope Gregory XIII undertook to reform the Julian calendar shortly after he was elected Pope in 1572. He managed to implement his reform in 1582. That year, the day after October 4 was stipulated to be October 15, 1582. This was to counter the cumulative effect of the discrepancy between the average length of the Julian calendar year (including leap years every four years = 365.25 days) and the length of the "tropical year" (number of days required for Earth to move from the vernal equinox back to the vernal equinox again = 365.2422 days). This discrepancy had resulted in the vernal equinox occurring earlier and earlier in the Julian calendar year, occurring on March 21 in 325 A.D. and having moved back to March 11 by 1580. Stipulating that the day following October 4, 1582 would be October 15, 1582 insured that the vernal equinox would occur on March 21, 1583. Further, since the discrepancy between the average Julian calendar year and the tropical year was the result of the average Julian calendar year being too long, Pope Gregory XIII decreed that only centennial years (1600, 1700, 1800, etc.) whose numeral designations are divisible by four hundred are leap years. This has the effect of eliminating three leap days every four hundred years, rendering the discrepancy between the Gregorian calendar year and the tropical year quite small, (though future "corrections" will still be required to keep the vernal equinox on March 21!).

What does all this mean? Pope Gregory fixed the extensions of 'January', 'February' etc. by: 1) stipulating a "starting point": that a particular day is October 15, 1582; 2) implicitly specifying the number and order of the months in a year (by taking them over from the Julian calendar); 3) implicitly specifying the lengths (in days) of all months except February (by taking them from the Julian calendar); and 4) specifying an algorithm for determining the length (in days) of any subsequent February.[9] These four things suffice to determine which (future and past) time intervals are Januarys, Februarys, etc.

At least they *did* until very recently.[10] In the mid-1800's a standardized time was established for the United Kingdom. This time standard, Greenwich Mean Time (GMT), came to serve as the international time standard until 1972. From its establishment (along with the establishment of an international system of time zones) until 1972, GMT served as the basis for so-called "civil time", the "official" time in different time zones.

With the development of extremely accurate clocks in the mid-1900's it became clear that the rate of rotation of the Earth was not uniform.[11] Not only does it fluctuate during a given rotation, but the Earth is decelerating due to "tidal friction". GMT, of course, had been based on the rate of rotation of the Earth. In 1972, Coordinated Universal Time (UTC) displaced GMT as the international standard on which civil time is based. UTC is determined by read-ings from a variety of atomic clocks around the world and runs at a rate determined by those clocks. Since, as mentioned, the rate of rotation of the Earth fluctuates over time and in general has been slowing, the time taken for one rotation of the Earth has been increasing slightly. Currently, the Earth takes 86,400.002 seconds to rotate. One day, twenty four hours, as measured by an atomic clock, is 86,400 seconds. If UTC were never adjusted, the discrepancy between the time taken for the Earth to rotate once and twenty-four hours as measured by atomic clocks would accumulate day after day. The result would be that as time passed "official times", as determined by UTC, would occur at different points in the Earth's rotation. Thus, noon (at a given location), as mea-sured by the rotation of the Earth, would not occur at the official civil time, based on UTC, of 12:OOP.M. (at that location). This discrepancy would, of course, get larger and larger over time. The increasing discrepancy would make UTC a poor basis for civil time. To avoid this, when UTC was adopted as the basis for civil time, it was decided that it would never differ from universal time (UT1—more or less what used to be called 'GMT'), which is based on the rate of rotation of the Earth, by .9 seconds. The mechanism for keeping UTC within less than .9 seconds of UT1 is the "leap second".

The International Earth Rotation Service (IERS) anticipates when the ab-solute value of UTC-UT1 will be .9 seconds. They then add a leap second to UTC to prevent this from happening. The rate of rotation of the Earth is not predictable, being influenced by a number of complex factors.[12] Thus, the IERS must constantly observe and monitor the rate of rotation and on that basis pre-dict when in the near future |UTC-UT1| would be .9 seconds were correction (via leap second) not to occur. In principle, a leap second can have a positive or negative value, depending upon whether the atomic clock-based UTC is ahead of rate-of-Earth's-rotation based UT1 (so that the Earth rotated "too slowly"— hence a positive value for the leap second) or whether UT1 is ahead of UTC. All leap seconds added to this point have had positive values, (UTC currently runs "too fast" relative to the rotation of the Earth by approximately .73 sec-onds per year and, as mentioned earlier, Earth is slowly decelerating).

When a (positive) leap second is added to the last day of a month, the last minute of the day has sixty one seconds, and the day itself lasts twenty three hours, fifty nine minutes, and sixty *one* seconds.[13] Thus the month is one sec-ond longer than the same month would be in a "non-leap second version" of the month. I wish to emphasize that a (positive or negative) leap second in principle can be added to the end of any month, depending on the observed and anticipated discrepancy between UT1 and UTC, (though the end of June and December are the favored times for adding leap seconds).

It is important to note that *both* as a result of the Gregorian reform of the Julian calendar *and* as a result of the adoption of UTC and the accompanying device of leap seconds, the words 'January' etc. came to have different exten-sions than they would have had had these events not occurred. The result of the

Gregorian reform was that e.g. time intervals in the extension of 'November' have subintervals that would have been part of what *would have been called* 'October' had the reform not occurred. And even after the Gregorian reform, the adoption of UTC and the device of leap seconds changed the extensions of 'January', 'February' etc. For consider the Gregorian calendar when UT1 (formerly GMT, more or less), rather than UTC, is used as the international time standard. Though UTC is kept within .9 seconds of UT1 by the device of leap seconds, there are generally small, variable discrepancies (< .9 second) between UTC and UT1. Thus, UT1 and UTC will often disagree as to *exactly* when certain days, and hence months, end. Thus, time intervals in the extensions of 'January' etc. when used with the Gregorian calendar and UT1 (GMT) will differ slightly from the time intervals in the extensions of 'January' etc. when used with the Gregorian calendar and UTC. Thus, when UTC displaced GMT as the international time standard, the extensions of 'January' etc. changed slightly.

Thus the Gregorian reform of the calendar together with the adoption of UTC served to determine what now are the extensions of the terms 'January', 'February', etc. Given this account of the determination of the extensions of the terms 'January', etc., what *properties* ought we to say are expressed by 'January', etc.?

Since the principles introduced by the Gregorian calendar reform, (1)–(4) above, together with UTC and the accompanying device of leap seconds comprise the means by which 'January', 'February', etc. came to have the extensions they have, and since the properties expressed by these terms must determine their extensions, it is reasonable to think that (1)–(4) together with UTC and the accompanying device of leap seconds must in some sense characterize the properties expressed by 'January', 'February', etc. But in what sense do they do this? Suppose we spelled out (1)–(4) more explicitly, while adding to them features resulting from adopting UTC and the device of leap seconds, in the following way. Let 't' rigidly designate the second immediately following 11:59:59 P.M. on October 4, 1582 (Julian calendar). Then:

1′) October 15, 1582 is the twenty-four hour period (as measured by the rotation of the Earth) beginning at t.

2′) & 3′) A January prior to 1972 consists of 31 consecutive 23 hour 59 minute and 60 second intervals (as measured by the rotation of the Earth), and after 1972 consists of 31 consecutive time intervals the first 30 of which are 23 hour 59 minute and 60 second intervals and the 31st of which is a 23 hour 59 minute and 60 second time interval plus or minus 1 second (as measured by atomic clocks) depending on whether the discrepancy between UTC and UT1 would exceed .9 seconds were a positive or negative leap second not added to correct the discrepancy; and a January precedes a February, which in non-leap years prior to

1972 consists of 28 23 hour 59 minute and 60 second intervals (as measured by the rotation of the Earth), and after 1972 consists of 28 consecutive time intervals the first 27 of which are 23 hour 59 minute and 60 second intervals and the 28th of which is a 23 hour 59 minute and 60 second time interval plus or minus 1 second (as measured by atomic clocks) depending on whether the discrepancy between UTC and UT1 would exceed .9 seconds were a positive or negative leap second not added to correct the discrepancy; and which in leap years prior to 1972 consists of 29 consecutive 23 hour 59 minute and 60 second intervals (as measured by the rotation of the Earth), and after 1972 consists of 29 consecutive time intervals the first 28 of which are 23 hour 59 minute and 60 second intervals and the 29th of which is a 23 hour 59 minute and 60 second time interval plus or minus 1 second (as measured by atomic clocks) depending on whether the discrepancy between UTC and UT1 would exceed .9 seconds were a positive or negative leap second not added to correct the discrepancy; and which precedes a March, which...and which precedes a December, which... ; and which precedes a January.

4') Any non-centennial year whose numeral's last two digits designate a number that is evenly divisible by four is a leap year. Centennial years are leap years iff their entire numerals designate numbers that are evenly divisible by four hundred.

Though somewhat unwieldy, 1'), 2') & 3') and 4') together specify the extensions of 'January', etc.[14]

Given the way in which 2') & 3') characterizes Januarys, Februarys, etc. by reference to each other (Januarys precede Februarys etc.), it would seem that our "calendar theory" 1')–4') "implicitly defines" the month terms 'January', 'February', etc. in terms of each other and all at once. But then if we ask how to characterize e.g. January *by itself*, surely the strategy that suggests itself is to "define" 'January' (and 'February' etc.) *a la* David Lewis [1970, 1972]. We begin by (i) rewriting 1')–4') turning 'January' etc. into names (e.g. by replacing 'A January' by 'Something that has January-hood', etc.) and taking their conjunction; and (ii) replacing all the resulting "month names" ('January-hood', etc.) in this conjunction with distinct free variables.[15] Representing the result of (i) as T[January-hood, February-hood, ... , December-hood], the result of (ii) can be represented as $T[x_1,...,x_{12}]$. Then, still following Lewis, define 'January-hood', etc. as follows:

(J) January-hood=$\imath x_1 \exists x_2 ... \exists x_{12} \forall y_1 ... \forall y_{12}(T[y_1,...,y_{12}]$ iff
   $x_1=y_1 \& ... \& x_{12}=y_{12})$

This says that January-hood is the first element of the twelve-tuple that uniquely realizes the theory $T[x_1,...,x_{12}]$. Thus we would hold that 'January-hood' names (and so 'January' expresses) the property denoted by the definite description on the right side of (J).

But how do we know that there is a *unique* twelve-tuple of properties that realizes $T[x_1,...,x_{12}]$ in the actual world? After all, any twelve-tuple of properties whose members have the "right" time intervals (as dictated by $T[x_1,...,x_{12}]$) in their extensions *in the actual world* will realize $T[x_1,...,x_{12}]$ in the actual world, even if they fail to realize $T[x_1,...,x_{12}]$ in other possible worlds. If there is more than one such twelve-tuple, the description on the right side of (J) has no denotation (in the actual world) and (J) fails to supply a property for 'January' to express.

Further, even if we convinced ourselves that only one twelve-tuple of properties realizes $T[x_1,...,x_{12}]$ in the actual world, how could we show that only one twelve-tuple of properties realizes $T[x_1,...,x_{12}]$ in all (relevant) possible worlds? If different twelve-tuples of properties (uniquely) realize $T[x_1,...,x_{12}]$ in different possible worlds, then the description on the right side of (J) denotes different properties in different possible worlds. But then 'January-hood' *names* different properties in different worlds, and so 'January' *expresses* different properties in different worlds. This seems unwelcome.

We could do one of two things to address these worries about multiple realizations of $T[x_1,...,x_{12}]$ both in the actual world and across possible worlds. The first thing we might do is to "beef up" the right side of (J) to insure that the description denotes in the actual world. The formulation that immediately comes to mind is:

(JN) January-hood$=\imath x_1 \exists x_2 ... \exists x_{12} \, \forall y_1 ... \forall y_{12} \, (\text{Nec}(T[y_1,...,y_{12}])$ iff $x_1=y_1 \& ... \& x_{12}=y_{12})$

This say roughly that January-hood is the first element of a twelve-tuple of properties that uniquely realizes $T[x_1,...,x_{12}]$ in all possible worlds. Recall that the description on the right side of (J) would fail to denote (in the actual world) if more than one twelve-tuple of properties had the "right" extensions (as dictated by $T[x_1,...,x_{12}]$) in the actual world. By contrast, the description on the right side of (JN) would fail to denote (in the actual world) if more than one twelve-tuple of properties gets the "right" extensions (as dictated by $T[x_1,...,x_{12}]$) across all possible worlds.

But how can we be sure that only one twelve-tuple of properties realizes $T[x_1,...,x_{12}]$ in all possible worlds? At this point, we might wish to junk (J), (JN) and their ilk and "go second order". That is, we could say that to be a January is to possess *some property or other* x_1 such that $\exists x_2 ... \exists x_{12} T[x_1,...,x_{12}]$. On this way of doing things, familiar from philosophy of mind, being a January would be a "second order property" that may well have different first order "realizers" in the actual world and in different possible worlds.

Going second order in this way is bound to solve the "multiple realization problem" (if there is one). And *perhaps* (J), (JN) or some other beefed up version of (J) will do in any case. Since we know we can get around the problem, I propose to ignore it henceforth and to talk as though (J) is fine as it is.

Whatever one may think of Ramsey-Lewis style definitions generally, it seems to me that this type of account of the properties expressed by 'January', etc. has a number of things to recommend it. First, $1'$)–$4'$) is an account of the stipulations made by Pope Gregory and the features of UTC that secured the current extensions of 'January', 'February', etc. As we said, since these things together in fact secured extensions for the "month words", it is reasonable to think that they in some sense characterize or determine the properties expressed by these terms. The Ramsey-Lewis style account gives content to the idea that $1'$)–$4'$) determine the properties expressed by the month terms. For their conjunction essentially is our calendar theory (T[January-hood, February-hood, ... , December-hood]—except that the latter contains 'January-hood', etc. instead of 'January'). Clearly, this theory plays a central role in specifying the properties expressed by the month words, as a glance at (J) will confirm.

Second, the month words, and presumably the properties they express, seem "interconnected" in some way. This is reflected in the fact that we use the month words to characterize each other ('February follows January...', etc.) and so e.g. teach them to children as a group. Further, it seems plausible that to be competent with any one month term requires competence with them all. Finally, there is some inclination to think that one cannot be competent with month words or grasp the properties they express without having *some* grip on the calendar theory (T[January-hood, February-hood, ... , December-hood]) or $1'$)–$4'$). Because the calendar theory plays the same central role in characterizing each of the properties expressed by the month terms and in effect implicitly defines them, we capture the intuitive "interconnectedness" of properties expressed by 'January', etc. and the idea that to grasp such properties requires having some grip on the calendar theory.

Third, the account delivers the right extensions for the month words in the actual world.[16] If we consider (1)–(3) again, it does seem plausible that we are quantifying over continuous thirty-one day intervals that bear particular temporal relations to other continuous 28–31 day intervals and to the twenty-four hour period stipulated to be October 15, 1582. So our account of the properties expressed by the month terms seems to pick out the intervals of time that we in fact quantify over in (1)–(3).

Further, assuming that times are common to all worlds and that temporal relations between specific times remain the same in them (or at least restricting our attention to such worlds), and for the moment restricting our attention to worlds that are not too remote from our own in relevant respects (discussed below), definitions like (J) characterize properties that deliver the intuitively correct extensions in such possible worlds.[17]

First, consider a counterfactual situation in which the Gregorian reform of the calendar never occurred, (but which "contains" the same times that the actual world contains; and in which those times bear the same temporal relations to each other as they do in the actual world; and in which the Earth's rate of rotation at a given time is the same as in the actual world). In describing such a situation we would still take the extension of 'January' to be what it is in the actual world. Thus we would describe the situation as one in which e.g. they called part of January 'December'. But it is of course part of *January* that they are *calling* 'December'. And this is what our account predicts. It therefore correctly predicts that the sentence "If the Gregorian reform of the calendar had never occurred, we would have called part of January 'December'" is true.

Second, consider a counterfactual circumstance in which the Earth's position relative to the sun in what we call 'January' is exactly the same as the Earth's position relative to the sun when it is July in the actual world (and vice versa—and in which the Earth's orbit is otherwise the same as in the actual world; and again which "contains" the same times that the actual world contains; and in which those times bear the same temporal relations to each other as they do in the actual world; and in which the Earth's rate of rotation at a given time is the same as in the actual world). How would we describe this counterfactual situation? It is one in which in *January*, the Earth occupies the position relative to the sun that in the actual world it occupies in July; and in which in July, it occupies the position relative to the sun that in the actual world it occupies in January. Thus the extensions of 'January' and 'July' are the same set of time intervals in this counterfactual situation as they are in the actual world, just as our account predicts.

Thus far we have considered counterfactual situations in which the rate of rotation of the Earth at a given time is the same as it is in the actual world (and which "contains" the same times that the actual world contains; and in which those times bear the same temporal relations to each other as they do in the actual world). Thus, in the worlds considered thus far, 'January' etc. have had the same extensions as they do in the actual world. However, our account predicts that in worlds in which the Earth's rate of rotation is (slightly!—see below) different from what it is in the actual world, 'January' etc. will have (slightly) different extensions from their actual extensions. For exactly which intervals prior to 1972 are in the extension of 'January', and their lengths, depends on the rate of rotation of the Earth. And exactly which intervals after 1972 are in the extension of 'January' depends on the discrepancy between UT1 and UTC, where UT1 is based on the rate of rotation of the Earth and UTC is based on atomic clocks. But this means that our account predicts that in worlds in which the rate of rotation of the Earth is different than it is in the actual world, the extensions of the month words will be different. Thus we ought to see whether this prediction is borne out.

So consider a world that is just like ours with one exception: the rate of rotation of the Earth since 1972 has been completely uniform and unchanging, (or the world is as much like ours as is possible, given the difference described). Each rotation takes *exactly* 86,400 seconds as measured by an atomic clock.[18] Thus, there is never a need to add any leap seconds to atomic clocks keeping track of UTC in this world. Our account of the property expressed by 'January' predicts that in this world all time intervals from 1972 on that are in the extension of 'January' are *exactly* 2,678,400 (31 × 86,400) seconds long. Of course, in the actual world, some time intervals between 1972 and now that are in the in the extension of 'January' are 2,678,401 seconds long, since (positive) leap seconds have in fact been added to the last days of some Januarys. Thus, our account predicts that the time intervals in the extension of 'January' in this world are slightly different from the time intervals in the extension of 'January' in the possible world under consideration, (assuming, as seems undeniable, that intervals of time possess their lengths essentially, so that one and the same interval of time could not have different lengths in different possible worlds). Now that you have been apprised of the facts, if you did not already know them, I think you will agree that the sentence

(8) Every January since 1972 has been exactly 2,678,400 seconds long.

expresses a proposition that is false in the actual world, but true in the possible world under consideration. Now this requires that every thing (time interval) that possesses the property of being a January since 1972 in the possible world possesses the property of being 2,678,400 seconds long there; and that some thing that possesses the property of being a January since 1972 in the actual world fails to possess the property of being 2,678,400 seconds long. But then (again, assuming that intervals of time possess their lengths essentially), it follows that the extension of 'January' is different in the possible world in question than in the actual world. And this is, of course, what our account predicts about this case.

Similarly, the following sentence seems true:

(9) If every rotation of the Earth since 1972 had taken exactly 86,400 seconds, every January since 1972 would have been exactly 2,678,400 seconds long.

On one standard account of counterfactuals, for (9) to be true, the consequent must be true in the "nearest" possible world in which the antecedent is true. The nearest possible world in which the antecedent is true is the one described above. Thus, the consequent must be true in this world. For the reasons given above, this again requires 'January' to have a different extension in the world in question than it does in the actual world.

There is a final bit of evidence that suggests that our account is correct in predicting that in worlds in which the Earth's rate of rotation is slightly different than it is in the actual world the extensions of month words are different.

Kevin and Teresa are "time geeks". They carefully track differences between UT1 and UTC and eagerly anticipate the addition of leap seconds, throwing parties when this occurs. They knew that a leap second was to be added to the end of December 31, 1998. At precisely 11:59 and 60.5 seconds of December 31, 1998, in front of their hushed party guests who are viewing a clock precisely synchronized with UTC and registering official civil time (in their time zone), Kevin and Teresa clap their hands together once. As cheers and applause break out, Teresa gleefully screams:

> (10) That event of clapping occurred in December, but had the Earth rotated slightly more quickly it could have occurred at exactly the same time but been in January.

Intuitively, what Teresa said is true! But this means that the instant of time at which the clap occurred is part of January in some world in which the Earth rotated slightly more quickly. And this in turn means that the extension of 'January' is different in that world than it is in the actual world.[19]

If we were to consider a possible world in which the Earth currently rotates slightly *faster* than it does in the actual world, considerations similar to those just canvassed would show that the extension of e.g. 'January' would be different in this world from what it is in the actual world.

Thus our account of the properties expressed by 'January', 'February' etc. delivers the correct extensions for these terms in this world and in various possible worlds which "contain" the same times that the actual world contains; and in which those times bear the same temporal relations to each other as they do in the actual world; and in which the Earth's rate of rotation (and "history of rotation") is close to what it is in the actual world.[20] But what about worlds that are more remote from ours? For example, what about worlds in which the Earth's rate of rotation and orbit are *very* different? Or worlds that don't contain the times of the actual world and in which those times are differently related to each other? I believe that we don't have clear intuitions about the extensions of our month words in such possible worlds. Our counterfactual talk about months and our evaluation of propositions about months takes place against the background of (if only tacitly) assuming that things are much like they are in the actual world in relevant respects (such as the rate of rotation of the Earth, etc.). To be sure, the properties we claim are expressed by the month words deliver extensions for these words in some worlds that are remote from ours in relevant respects.[21] But because we do not have clear intuitions about the extensions of these terms in such worlds, consideration of them will not provide evidence for or against the present account. Thus, I ignore such remote worlds here.

We now turn to the semantics of another syntactic constituent of day designators: N′ constituents such as 'January 24'. Let us begin as we did with the semantics of the month words, and ask what is in the extension of an N′ phrase like 'January 24'. Considerations exactly similar to those that suggested that 'January', etc. express properties of time intervals suggest that phrases like 'January 24' also express properties of time intervals. Consider the following sentences:

(11) Every January 24 is a holiday.
(12) I spent many July 4ᵗʰs at the beach.

Intuitively, in (11) one is quantifying over certain twenty-four hour periods and in so doing making a claim about them to the effect that they are holidays. Similarly, in (12) I am quantifying over certain twenty-four hour periods and making a claim to the effect that many such periods were spent by me at the beach. This suggests that the concatenation of a month word and a numeral (between 1 and 31) is an N' phrase that has as its extension a set of twenty-four hour periods and so expresses a property had by certain twenty-four hour time intervals.

Another reason for thinking this is that sentences such as

(13) Every January 24 is a twenty-four hour interval of time.

are true. But this requires things in the extension of 'January 24' to have the property of being a twenty-four hour interval of time.

In addition, sentences such as the following

(14) Every January 24 is twenty-four hours long.

are true. But this requires things in the extension of 'January 24' to have the property of being twenty-four hours long. And as we said earlier, it seems that only time intervals and events or states have properties like this. Since there are no events that are natural candidates for being January 24ᵗʰs and time intervals are natural candidates for being January 24ᵗʰs and the truth of (14) suggests that January 24ᵗʰs are events or time intervals, we have reason to adopt the view that they are indeed time intervals. So, as was the case with 'January', this provides reason for holding that 'January 24' expresses a property of time intervals.

Intuitively, 'January 24' expresses the property of being the twenty-fourth consecutive continuous twenty-four hour period that is a subinterval of a time interval possessing the property of being a January. Thus in a "complex day expression" like 'January 24', the numeral tells us which consecutive continuous twenty-four hour time periods that are subintervals of a time interval that is a January are in the extension of the term.

From the fact that 'January' etc. have different extensions in different possible worlds it follows that 'January 24' etc. have different extensions. For consider a possible world, call it w, that is exactly like the actual world except that from July 1997 to January 1999 the rotation of the Earth speeded up slightly so that on average it took exactly 86,400 seconds to rotate once during that period. Since a leap second was added to the end of June 1997, the discrepancy between UT1 and UTC was negligible at that point in both worlds. Thus, in January 1999 the discrepancy was still negligible in the possible world in question. In the actual world, the discrepancy was approaching .9 seconds by the end of December 1998. Thus a leap second was added to the end of December that year. But this means that there is a second, call it s, which was part of a December in the actual world and part of a January in w, (thus the extension of 'January' is different in the actual world than it is in w—in w there is a time interval containing s in the extension of 'January'; not so in the actual world.) Now consider 'January 1'. It has in its extension in w a twenty-four hour time interval that includes s. But no such time interval is in its extension in the actual world. Thus, 'January 1' has a different extension in w than in the actual world.

Further, this means that *all* complex day expressions have different extensions in w and the actual world. For s is the first second of a time interval in the extension of 'January 1' in w, whereas $s+1$ is the first second of the "corresponding" time interval in the extension of 'January' in the actual world.[22] Thus, the twenty-four hour time interval beginning with s and ending with, say, the second t is in the extension of 'January 1' in w; whereas the twenty-four hour time interval beginning with $s+1$ and ending with $t+1$ is in the extension of 'January 1' in the actual world. But then in w a twenty-four hour time interval beginning with $t+1$ is in the extension of 'January 2'; but not so in the actual world. Obviously, the same argument can be made for any complex day expression.

As was the case with 'January', intuitions about the truth and falsity in various possible worlds of the propositions expressed by certain sentences suggests that we are right in claiming that 'January 24' etc. have different extensions in different possible worlds. So consider again a world that is just like ours except that each rotation of the Earth since 1972 took *exactly* 86,400 seconds as measured by an atomic clock, (or the world is as much like ours as is possible, given the difference described). Thus, there has never been a need to add any leap seconds to atomic clocks in this world. Now consider the sentence:

(15) Every December 31 since 1972 has been exactly 86,400 seconds long.

The proposition expressed by this sentence is false in the actual world, because leap seconds have been added to some December 31st's making them 86,401 seconds long. But in the possible world in question, the proposition expressed by (15) is true! Again, (assuming time intervals have their lengths essentially) this means that 'December 31' has a different extension in this world and the actual world. For every time interval since 1972 in the extension of 'December 31' in the possible world has the property of being 86,400 seconds long and something in its extension in the actual world lacks this property.

Further, the following conditional seems true:

(16) If every rotation of the Earth since 1972 had taken exactly 86,400 seconds, every December 31 since 1972 would have been exactly 86,400 seconds long.

But this means that in the "nearest" possible world in which the antecedent of the conditional is true (i.e. the one under discussion), the consequent must be true. And, as we have seen, for this to be the case, the extension of 'December 31' must be different in the possible world in question than it is in the actual world.

At long last we turn to day designators themselves. The concatenation of a complex day expression ('January 1') with a year numeral ('1999') yields a noun phrase that designates a day: a day designator ('January 1, 1999'). Intuitively, it designates a twenty-four hour period that has the property of being a January 1 and that is a subinterval of the time interval (year) designated by '1999'. That 'January 1, 1999' designates a twenty-four hour interval of time is supported by the fact that the following sentence is true:[23]

(17) January 1, 1999 was a twenty-four hour interval of time.

The truth of (17) requires January 1, 1999 to possess the property of being a twenty-four hour interval of time. The claim that 'January 1, 1999' designates a twenty-four hour interval of time is also supported by the fact that if on December 31, 1998
I say:

(18) The twenty-four hour time interval beginning with the next occurrence of 12:00 A.M. and ending with following occurrence of 12:00 A.M. is January 1, 1999.

what I have said is true. But (18) appears to be an identity claim.[24] Thus its truth requires what 'January 1, 1999' designates to be identical with what the definite description denotes. And the description denotes a certain twenty-four hour interval of time. And of course, if 'January 1, 1999' designates a certain twenty-four interval of time, it certainly seems plausible that it is a twenty-four hour period that has the property of being a January 1 that is a subinterval of the time interval (year) designated by '1999'.

Now if what we have said to this point is correct, *different* twenty-four hour time intervals have the property of being a January 1 that is a subinterval of the time interval (year) 1999 in different possible worlds, and so 'January 1, 1999' designates different time intervals in different worlds. For consider again a possible world, w, that is exactly like the actual world except that from July 1997 to January 1999 the rotation of the Earth speeded up slightly so that on average it took exactly 86,400 seconds to rotate once during that period. Recall that since a leap second was added to the end of June 1997, the discrepancy between UT1 and UTC was negligible at that point in both worlds. Thus, in January 1999 the discrepancy was still negligible in the possible world in question, and so there are no further leap seconds to be added. In the actual world, the discrepancy was approaching .9 seconds by the end of December 1998. Thus a leap second was added to the end of December that year. As we noted above, this means that there is a second, *s*, which was part of a December in the actual world and part of a January in w. Now consider 'January 1, 1999'. In w, this day designator designates a twenty-four hour time interval that includes *s*. In the actual world, it designates a twenty-four hour time interval that does not include *s*. Thus, 'January 1, 1999' designates different time intervals in these worlds. That day designators designate different time intervals in different possible worlds is supported by the fact that the following sentence expresses a proposition that is false in the actual world and true in the possible world in question:

(19) December 31, 1998 was exactly 86,400 seconds long.

But for that to be so, 'December 31, 1998' must designate intervals of time of slightly different lengths, and so slightly different intervals of time, in the actual world and the possible world in question. In addition, the following is true:

(20) If the rotation of the Earth had taken a constant and uniform 86,400 seconds from July 1997 to January 1999, December 31, 1998 would have been exactly 86,400 seconds long.

The truth of (20) requires that in the nearest possible world in which the antecedent is true (the one under discussion), the consequent is true. And as we have seen, this requires 'December 31, 1998' to designate a slightly different time interval in that world than it does in the actual world. Thus, as promised, we have established that day designators are not rigid designators.

There is additional evidence that supports the claim that day designators are modally non-rigid.[25] If what I have said is correct, there are worlds in which the interval of time d that 'December 31, 1998' *actually* designates exists and is not designated by 'December 31, 1998' (a slightly different interval being so designated). But then the following is true:[26]

(21) $(\exists x) (x = $ December 31, 1998 & Possibly(x exists & $\sim(x = $ December 31, 1998)))

And it does appear that English analogues of this are true:

(21a) There is something/some interval of time that is December 31, 1998 and it is possible that it should have existed and not have been December 31, 1998 (some slightly different interval being December 31, 1998).

Further, the following sentence also seems true:

(22) December 31, 1998 was 86, 401 seconds long, but it is possible that December 31, 1998 should not have been 86,401 seconds long, (but 86,400 seconds long instead)

Now this sentence has the form

(22a) December 31, 1998 is F but Possibly (December 31, 1998 is not F)

where, if we are correct that day designators designate time intervals and that time intervals have their lengths essentially, 'F' expresses a property that is an essential property (being 86,401 seconds long) of what 'December 31, 1998' designates in the actual world. But then the truth of (22)/(22a) requires 'December 31, 1998' to be non-rigid. The second occurrence of 'December 31, 1998' must pick out a different time interval (one that is not 86,401 seconds long) in another possible world than the first picks out in the actual world. So here again, we have more evidence of the non-rigidity of day designators.

I suspect that many philosophers have thought that day designators are rigid.[27] Why have day designators seemed rigid? I think this illusion has at least three sources. First, I think many are not aware of, or have not thought about the implications of, the non-uniform rate of rotation of the Earth, UTC, leap seconds and so forth. Of course, the conclusion that day designators are not rigid depends heavily on considerations involving these things. Second, the overlap between the twenty-four hour time intervals designated by a day designator in this world and in worlds that are not too remote in the relevant respects is quite significant. It is plausible to suppose that the difference between the intervals designated in such worlds would not exceed, say, ten minutes.[28] And, as I mentioned earlier, our counterfactual talk about months and days takes place against the background of assuming that we are only considering worlds that are very similar to our in terms of the Earth's rate of rotation, etc. Thus, the very large overlap and small difference between the intervals designated by day designators in such worlds can reinforce the illusion that the *same* interval is designated in all such worlds.[29] Third, and related to the previous point, many have thought that the first of the two following sentences is necessary and the second is false (when uttered on February 21, 2001):[30]

(23) Today is February 21, 2001
(24) Today might not have been February 21, 2001.

The necessity of (23) and the falsity of (24) would be explained by holding that 'February 21, 2001' is rigid. For if 'today' rigidly designates February 21, 2001 when uttered on that day, and if 'February 21, 2001' is rigid, and if the 'is'/ 'have been' in the sentences express identity, then (23) expresses a proposition that is true iff February 21, 2001 is self-identical, and (24) expresses a proposition that is true iff February 21, 2001 might not have been identical to itself.

Of course, if the present view is correct and *if* 'today' as uttered on February 21, 2001 rigidly refers to the *exact* twenty-four hour time interval that in the actual world is February 21, 2001, then (23) is contingently true and (24) is true. I'm not sure how one would go about showing that 'today' when used on February 21, 2001 does or does not *semantically* (rigidly) refer to the *exact* twenty-four hour time interval that in the actual world is February 21, 2001. But what is clear is that 'today' when uttered on a given day is often used to *convey information* about a time interval bigger than or smaller than the exact twenty-four hour time interval that is the day in question. For example, suppose that I stay up until 12:05 A.M. on (the morning of) February 21, 2001, eat some food at that time and then go to bed. Feeling guilty when I wake up, I eat no more food that day. That evening, my friend, who was with me when I had my post-midnight snack and who has noticed that I haven't eaten since rising, says:

(25) You haven't eaten anything today.

This remark would be naturally interpreted by all parties as true in the situation as described, but I did eat during the twenty-four hour time interval that constitutes the day on which 'today' was uttered. Thus in (25) 'today' is used to convey information about a smaller time interval than that. Further, when I say:

(26) Today the United States is the most powerful nation on Earth.

my remark is naturally interpreted as about a time interval greater than the twenty-four hour time interval constituting the day on which (26) was uttered. So there is a certain looseness in what time interval an utterance of 'today' is used to talk about.

Further, as already mentioned, in any possible world very "close" to ours in relevant respects (and these are the worlds we concern ourselves with in evaluating our talk about months and dates in counterfactual circumstances), the twenty-four hour time interval that is February 21, 2001 overlaps very significantly with the time interval that in the actual world is February 21, 2001. These will differ by only a few minutes and so have twenty-three and fifty-some minutes in common. This means that over ninety-nine percent of the two intervals will be the same! The looseness of 'today' combined with the fact that any two time intervals designated by 'February 21, 2001' in worlds close to our in relevant respects will be over ninety-nine percent the same makes (23) seem necessarily true and (24) seem false. A further fact that contributes to this appearance is that when we ask e.g. how (24) could be true we tend to try to imagine how the *entire* time interval that 'today' refers to (when used on February 21, 2001) could have been some day other than February 21, 2001. But the *entire* time interval that 'today' refers to when used on February 21, 2001 (whatever this time interval is exactly) could not have been (or been part of) some day other than February 21, 2001 in any world very close to ours in relevant respects. And so we tend to think that (24) is false.

That something like these explanations of why (23) seems necessarily true and (24) seems false are correct is supported by the following consideration. When we eliminate the looseness of 'today' and make clear that even small differences in largely overlapping time intervals matter, the intuitions cut the other way. Thus, suppose after explaining all the things I have explained about, leap seconds, UTC etc., I say (on February 21, 2001)

(27) So, we see that the *exact* actual twenty-four hour time interval that is the present day might not have been February 21, 2001 and some time interval differing from it by a second might have been.

It seems to me that this is clearly true! But it differs from (24) only in employing the (rigid) definite description 'the *exact* actual twenty-four hour time interval that is the present day' in place of 'today', thereby eliminating the looseness of 'today' and, by talking about exact (stressed!) twenty-four hour time intervals and intervals differing by only a second, making clear that small differences in time intervals matter. Similarly, in light of all I've said, the following seems only contingently true:

(28) The *exact* actual twenty-four hour time interval that is the present day is February 21, 2001.

Hence, we have an explanation of why (23) seems necessarily true and (24) seems false that is consistent with our claim that 'February 21, 2001' is not rigid.

Before turning to other matters, let us briefly and informally describe the contribution day designators make to propositions on the present view. Let m be a month word, d be a "day numeral" (1–31) and y be a "year numeral" (1,2,...2001,...). Then [md] is a complex day expression and [[md]y] is a day designator. [[md]y] contributes to propositions [m*d*]y*], where m* is the property expressed by m, d* is the number referred to by d and y* is a property that is uniquely possessed by the year long time interval that is the year y.[31] When a proposition containing [[m*d*]y*] is evaluated at a world w, this complex propositional constituent denotes the unique twenty-four hour time interval that in w possesses the property of being the dth consecutive continuous twenty-four hour time interval that is a subinterval of a time interval possessing m* and that in w is a subinterval of a time interval possessing y*. Alternatively, we could have [[m d] y] contribute to propositions the (uniquely instantiated) *property* of being the dth consecutive continuous twenty-four hour time interval that is a subinterval of a time interval possessing m* and that is a subinterval of a time interval possessing y* (note that this is distinct from [[m* d*] y*], which is a complex "sub-propositional constituent" that has as constituents the property m*, the number d* and the property y*—see King [1995] and [1998] for discussion). The important point is that day designators contribute to propositions entities that determine which day they denote at a world. The *exact nature* of the entity is not important for present purposes.

Having argued that day designators are not rigid, a further question arises about their semantics. Philosophers of language who adopt an account of propositions according to which they are structured, sentence-like entities, an account of the sort that I presuppose here and have defended elsewhere, have suggested at least three ways in which noun phrases function semantically.[32] First, a noun phrase may be a device of direct reference, contributing only its referent (in a context) to the proposition expressed (in that context) by a sentence in which it occurs. Second, a noun phrase may a quantifier. General accounts as to the propositional contributions of quantifiers vary, but for present purposes we need not worry about this. Third, some hold that a noun phrase may contribute *both* its referent (in a context) to the proposition expressed (in that context) by a sentence in which it occurs *and* some descriptive condition that the referent (in that context) must satisfy at a circumstance of evaluation for the proposition to be true there.[33]

Now if the argument of the present paper is correct, day designators cannot function in the first or third ways just mentioned. Clearly, if day designators are not rigid, they cannot be directly referential. Nor can they function in the third way, again, because they are non-rigid and pick out different referents in different circumstances of evaluation. This means that the truth of propositions expressed by sentences containing them at different circumstances of evaluation cannot require some *one and the same* referent to satisfy some descriptive condition at the *different* circumstances in question. Thus, given the three ways of functioning outlined so far, this leaves only the option that day designators are quantifiers. And here an interesting question arises.

Quantifiers can have varying scope with respect to other scoped elements, whereas neither directly referring expressions nor expressions that function in the third way mentioned above ("articulated terms"/"partially descriptive names") admit of variable scope.[34] It is generally held that the explanation as to *why* natural language quantifiers can have variable scope is that in the mapping from surface structure to the level of syntactic representation whose representations are the syntactic input to semantics, quantifiers undergo "movement" and often can be "moved" to different sites, resulting in different scopes for the quantifiers. Names are generally held not to undergo such movement. Thus quantifiers have variable scope and names and "articulated terms"/"partially descriptive names" do not.

The question then arises whether there is any evidence that day designators undergo movement and have variable scope. If there is, then we have good reason to hold that they are quantifiers. However, if there is not such evidence, then it appears that day designators would be non-rigid designators that do not undergo movement and have variable scope. I shall call (still hypothetical) expressions of this sort *non-rigid terms* (henceforth *NRTs*). So far as I know, there are no non-controversial examples of NRTs in the literature. Indeed, as I mentioned at the outset, many philosophers of language lean toward the view, discussed by Neale [1993], that all natural language NPs are rigid singular referring terms or generalized quantifiers, ("articulated terms"/"partially descriptive names", if there are such, are rigid and refer; so they are rigid referring expressions).[35] Of course if day designators are NRTs, this view is incorrect. Thus, it is worth looking to see if there is evidence that suggests that day designators are quantificational or that they are NRTs. As we will see, it is surprisingly difficult to find evidence that definitively supports either claim. This, in turn, suggests that the question as to whether natural languages contain NRTs is a surprisingly subtle one.

Let us begin by looking at syntactic tests for movement of noun phrases. As suggested above, many philosophers and linguists subscribe to the view that the syntactic representations that are the inputs to semantics are distinct from, and somewhat more abstract than, the surface structures of sentences. Following the usage of Chomskyans, let us call the latter *S structure representations* and the former *LF representations*.[36] As noted above, one of the main differences between LF representations and S structure representations is that in the mapping to LF quantifier phrases are "moved" out of their argument positions and are adjoined to an S node, whereas names are not. So, for example, consider the following two S structures:

(29) $[_s[_{np}Glenn] [_{vp}[_v loves] [_{np}Tracy]]]$
(30) $[_s[_{np}Every\ skier] [_{vp}[_v skis] [_{np}some\ steep\ chute]]]$

Since names do not undergo movement, the LF representation underlying (29) is not really any different from (29). However, in (30)'s LF representation, both quantifiers will have been moved out of their argument positions surrounding 'skis', and will have been adjoined to an S node. This can occur is two ways, as follows:

(30') $[_s[_{np}some\ steep\ chute]_2 [_s[_{np}Every\ skier]_1 [_s\ e_1 [_{vp}[_v skis]\ e_2]]]]$
(30") $[_s[_{np}Every\ skier]_1 [_s[_{np}some\ steep\ chute]_2 [_s\ e_1 [_{vp}[_v skis]\ e_2]]]]$

These LF representations correspond to the two readings of (30) resulting from the quantifiers taking different scope with respect to each other.

Now it is thought that verb phrase deletion is only allowed where neither the missing verb nor its antecedent c-commands the other.[37] But examples like the following violate this condition at S structure:

(31) JC skied every chute that Shane did.

Here 'skied' c-commands 'did' (and hence the missing verb). But if quantifier phrases undergo movement in the mapping to LF, neither 'skied' nor 'did' will c-command the other at LF.[38] Thus if we assume that our condition on VP deletion must be satisfied only at LF, and that quantifiers move in the way indicated in the mapping to LF, (31) no longer constitutes a counterexample to the condition.

Since day designators do not take restrictive relative clauses, we cannot form a sentence of the form of (31) with a day designator in the place of the quantifier.[39] However, we can use non-restrictive relative clauses, and the result is unacceptable:

*(35) Albert dreaded July 12, 2001, which John did.

This would appear to suggest that day designators do not undergo movement in the mapping to LF as quantifier phrases do. However, instead it might be thought that the contrast between (31) and (35) reflects some difference between restrictive and non-restrictive relative clauses and not some difference in the behavior of quantifier phrases and day designators in the mapping to LF. This claim gains support from the unacceptability of the following sentence in which we have a definite description, which most philosophers take to be a quantifier phrase, instead of a day designator:

*(36) Jay feared the mayor of Chicago, who Erik did.

However, it is thought by some that the unacceptability of examples like (35) involving *names* (instead of day designators) does show that names do not undergo movement:[40]

*(37) Albert hated Alan, who John did.

Thus, either (35) and (37) show that names and day designators do not undergo movement (and some other explanation is given of (36)), or the contrast between them and (31) must be explained in terms of some difference between restrictive and non-restrictive relatives. So *perhaps* we have a slight bit of evidence that day designators do not undergo movement and so are NRTs, though it isn't entirely clear.

Another test used to detect the movement of NPs is to look for so-called "weak crossover effects". To illustrate, in the following sentences, the pronouns cannot be interpreted as anaphoric on the quantifier phrases:

(38) Its owner loves every ski.
(39) Their parents love all children.

(38) cannot be interpreted to mean that every ski is such that its owner loves it; and (39) cannot mean that all children are such that their parents love them. By contrast, in the following sentence, 'his' can be interpreted as anaphoric on 'Albert':[41]

(40) His mother loves Albert.

I shall not discuss the details of the explanation of the contrast between (38) and (39) on the one hand and (40) on the other. But it is generally held that the explanation makes essential reference to the fact that quantifiers undergo movement in the mapping to LF and names do not. Consider now examples containing day designators:

(41) Its events distinguished December 7, 1944.
(42) Its detractors who think the millennium begins in 2001 dismissed January 1, 2000.

(41) and (42) do seem to allow readings on which 'Its' is read as anaphoric on the day designators, (or at least co-referential with them). So this initially appears to show that day designators do not exhibit weak crossover effects and so do not undergo movement. This, again, would suggest that they are NRT's. The problem is that again we can find examples in which definite descriptions exhibit the same behavior:

(43) His appointees despise the governor of California.
(44) Its fierce winds distinguished the first hurricane of 2000.

Here too, we seem to get readings on which the pronouns are anaphoric on the definite descriptions, (or at least co-referential with them). As a result, again, it isn't clear how much evidence the data (41) and (42) provide in favor of the view that day designators do not undergo movement and so are NRTs. In considering lots of examples, it seems to me that sentences containing day designators almost never display weak crossover effects and that sentences containing definite descriptions sometimes do. This, if true, would support the view that day designators are NRTs. But the intuitions here are subtle.

Thus, the syntactic tests involving VP deletion and weak crossover effects *may* provide some evidence in favor of the view that day designators are NRT's. How strong that evidence is remains unclear.

Let us now turn to more "semantic" considerations. If day designators are quantificational, they should exhibit scope interactions with other quantifiers. In simple cases in which day designators occur with other quantifiers, we fail to detect scope ambiguities. Thus, the following sentences appear to have only one reading:

(45) Every American looks forward to July 4, 2005.

(46) Many professors dread October 1, 2007.

The lack of multiple readings in such cases might suggest to some that day designators are not scoped elements and so are non-quantificational. However, of course, there is another explanation of the lack of multiple readings in (45) and (46). If we suppose that day designators function somewhat like definite descriptions do, designating the unique thing satisfying certain descriptive conditions, then we should not expect multiple readings with different truth conditions in examples like (45) and (46). For neither do we get such readings in the following sentence:

(47) Every person in the restaurant stared at the man wearing the pink tie.

The reason, of course, is that whether the description takes wide or narrow scope relative to the quantifier 'Every person in the restaurant', we get the same truth conditions.[42] Thus the fact that we don't get readings with different truth conditions in (45) and (46) does not show that day designators don't have scope and so aren't quantifiers. Of course, neither does the lack of readings with different truth conditions support the view that day designators do have variable scope.

There is other data that might be thought to indicate that day designators engage in scope interactions with other scoped elements. On the view we have defended, the truth of the propositions expressed by sentences such as:

(48) July 4, 1998 was a holiday.

(49) Virginia went skiing on August 6, 1997.

requires there to be a unique day, satisfying certain descriptive conditions. In particular, (48) is true iff there is a unique day satisfying the descriptive conditions specified by 'July 4, 1998' and it was a holiday. Now consider sentences of the following form:

(50) September 3, 2000 is not F.

Since negation is an element with scope, if day designators have scope, we would expect instances of (50) to have two readings: one where negation takes wide scope and one where the day designator takes wide scope. These readings of (50) can be represented as follows:

(50a) Not [[September 3, 2000 x] x is F]

(50b) September 3, 2000x [Not[x is F]]

Because the day designator 'September 3, 2000' in fact designates a day, instances of (50a) and (50b) won't diverge in truth value. Both will be true iff the day designated fails to be F.[43] However, for designators like 'September 31, 2000' that don't designate anything, one might think that instances of the following analogues of (50a) and (50b) *would* diverge in truth value:[44]

(50a′) Not [[September 31, 2000 x] x is F]
(50b′) September 31, 2000x [Not[x is F]]

For (50b′)'s truth requires a day to possess the property of being September 31, 2001 and not to be F. Whereas (50a′)'s truth merely requires it not to be the case that a day possesses the property of being September 31, 2001 and is F. But then (50a′) should be true since no day possesses the property of being September 31, 2001; and (50b′) should be false.

Thus if we could find instances of (50) containing a "non-denoting" day designator, some of which seem true and some of which seem false, that would provide evidence that such sentences have two readings corresponding to (50a′) and (50b′). But then this would be evidence that day designators have variable scope.[45] And we do seem to find such evidence. Both of the following seem true:

(51) September 31, 2000 is not next week. (spoken the week before October 1, 2000)
(52) September 31, 2000 is not a holiday.

And both of the following do not:[46]

(53) September 31, 2000 is not a day I will forget.
(54) September 31, 2000 was not sunny.

Thus (51)–(54) appear to provide some evidence that day designators have variable scope.

Similar remarks apply to the pair

(55) No person died on September 31, 2000.
(56) No hour passed quickly on September 31, 2000.

(55) seems true and (56) does not. This would be explained if (55) strongly favored wide scope for 'No person' and (56) favored narrow scope for 'No hour'. But this explanation assumes that day designators have variable scope.

Though the data comprising (51)–(56) initially appear to provide evidence for the claim that day designators have variable scope and so are quantificational, I don't think the data ultimately support this claim. For non-referring names exhibit behavior exactly like that of 'September 31, 2001' in (51)–(56). Such expressions do not have variable scope. But then data like (51)–(56) cannot provide evidence of variable scope. Thus consider:

(57) Vulcan is not behind the sun right now.
(58) That is not Vulcan. (pointing at Venus)
(59) No one has ever set foot on Vulcan.

All these sentences seem to have true readings and they are analogues of (51), (52) and (55). By contrast, the following sentences do not seem true and they are the analogues (53), (54) and (56):

(60) Vulcan does not have a molten core.
(61) Vulcan is not over 25,000 miles in diameter.
(62) No life exists on Vulcan.

Thus in (57)–(62) we have data that is exactly analogous to (51)–(56). Since the former is not taken to show that names have variable scope, the latter should not be taken to show that day designators do. Thus, (51)–(56) apparently do not, as they initially seemed to, provide evidence that day designators are quantificational.

There is other data that similarly may initially appear to provide evidence for the view that day designators undergo movement and have variable scope. When day designators combine with verbs of propositional attitude, they may seem to exhibit scope interactions with respect to such verbs. For example, imagine that Jay, who knows nothing of the Gregorian calendar, has been stranded on a remote island for years. He takes (what he thinks of as) various divine signs to mean that in twenty-one days, a ship will arrive to rescue him. Thus he believes on what is in fact August 2, 2001 that twenty-one days hence, he will be rescued. However, ignorant of the Gregorian calendar as he is, he has no beliefs about what the current month is, nor what month it will be in twenty one days. Now consider the following belief ascription:

(63) Jay believes that he will be rescued on August 23, 2001.

Is it true? It seems to me that we are ambivalent about its truth value. This ambivalence would have an explanation on the hypothesis that day designators can take wide or narrow scope relative to verbs of propositional attitude. On the wide scope reading of the day designator, arguably the belief ascription is true: concerning the day that satisfies the descriptive condition specified by 'August 23, 2001', Jay believes he will be rescued on it. But on the reading on which the day designator takes narrow scope relative to 'Jay believes', the ascription is false. For on that reading, the descriptive condition specified by 'August 23, 2001' is said to be part of the content of Jay's belief. And it is not.

By contrast, if day designators are NRTs, (63) in the situation described is false. For if day designators do not undergo movement, then (63) *must* attribute to Jay a belief whose content includes the descriptive condition expressed by

'August 23, 2001'. By hypothesis, Jay's belief includes no such thing. But then it appears that the view that day designators are NRTs has no explanation of our ambivalence about (63) in the case as described. It looks like we should be inclined to judge (63) straightforwardly false. In particular, then, to defend the view that day designators are NRTs, some explanation must be offered as to why we have some tendency to think (63) is *true*, and so end up ambivalent.

In defending the view that day designators are NRTs, it will not do *here* to respond that the same phenomenon (i.e. ambivalence in cases of the sort described) arises with *names*, which do not undergo movement or have variable scope. Let us see why. In our example, Jay has a belief about a certain day, which is in fact August 23, 2001, where he doesn't think of the day in question as August 23, 2001. Similarly, people sometimes have beliefs about a person who is in fact Ed, without thinking of that person as Ed. In such a case, we may be ambivalent about the truth value of a belief ascription ascribing a belief to such a person using a sentence containing the name 'Ed'. So if Virginia sees a man, Ed, running every morning and comes to believe he is healthy, but doesn't know his name and would not assent to the sentence 'Ed is healthy', we may be ambivalent about the truth value of:

(64) Virginia believes Ed is healthy.

Even if this right, the problem with appealing to this fact in defense of the claim that our ambivalence in the case of (63) doesn't cut against the view that day designators are NRTs is that on the dominant view of names, they are directly referential. So the embedded sentence in (64) expresses a singular proposition. If we assume that 'believes' expresses a relation between a person and a proposition, then (64) is true iff Virginia stands in the belief relation to the singular proposition that Ed is healthy. And in our story she does appear to believe this. So (64) is true. Thus, if we are really ambivalent about (64) in this case, since it is true, what is needed is an explanation as to why we have some tendency to think that (64) is *false*.[47]

And this is why to defend the claim that day designators are NRTs it does no good to appeal to our ambivalence about (64) in the situation as described. For since (64) is true, explaining the ambivalence here will require offering an explanation as to why we have some tendency to think it is false. But if day designators are NRTs, (63) is false in the situation described. And so explaining our ambivalence in this case requires offering an explanation as to why we have some tendency to think (63) is true. But presumably the sort of explanation offered for our tendency to think that (64) is false will be of no use in explaining our tendency to think (63) is true.

To be sure, we are assuming here that names are directly referential and that 'believes' expresses a relation between people and propositions. If we replaced these assumptions by others, the explanation of our ambivalence about (64) in the situation described could well be quite different; and perhaps we could appeal to it in explaining our inclination to think (63) is true on the hypothesis that day designators are NRTs. But I shall not take this route, since I do not want the defense of the view that day designators are NRTs to rest on controversial claims about the semantics of names and 'believes'.

So assuming day designators are NRTs, why would we have some inclination to judge (63) true in the situation described? Well, 'August 23, 2001' designates a day, and Jay believes that he will be rescued on that day. (63), in spite of its literal falsity, conveys this truth. It is easy to see how (63) could convey this truth. We in effect ignore the descriptive conditions expressed by 'August 23, 2001' and focus on the day those conditions pick out. This is particularly easy to do, since we don't think of 'August 23, 2001' as having descriptive content in the way that 'the inventor of four buckle ski boots' does. The sentence then conveys true information about the day in question; and this gives us some inclination to think the sentence is true.

But why would we use literally false things like (63) to convey such truths? The answer is that day designators are the canonical expressions we use in talking about days. There are many reasons for this. First, they are relatively short expressions, and so convenient to use. Second, by means of these expressions, we can designate any day we wish. Third, day designators are not contextually sensitive so we can carry them across contexts and continue to designate the same day. Fourth, we all have calendars and we use them, or our knowledge of them, in planning our lives, talking about past and future events, etc. We count on the fact that others around us do the same. Thus, the use of a day designator "locates" the day being talked about relative to other days and makes that day easy to remember. For example, if five weeks and four days ago someone told me that he was leaving for Europe in exactly seven weeks and four days, even if I now remember exactly what he said, I may not be able to determine what day he is leaving. However, if he told me he was leaving on December 22, 2000 and if I now remember what he said, I know the exact day of his departure.[48] Fifth, and related to the previous points, day designators are particularly useful in describing sequences of events and the temporal relations between them. Imagine how history books would read if day designators were banned!

Given the fact that day designators are our canonical expressions for talking about days, in part because they serve to locate days in a way that allows us to retain and easily use information about the day, and because they are particularly useful in describing sequences of events and the temporal relations between them, it isn't at all surprising that we would use day designators in false sentences like (63) to convey truths about certain days by ignoring the descriptive content of the day designator. Indeed, to literally express the truth conveyed by (63) using non-contextually sensitive expressions (which we will often want to do, since e.g. we might be relating the facts in writing or wish to make Jay's beliefs easy to reconstruct in another context) we would have to resort to some awkward, cumbersome thing like 'The day we designate by 'August 23, 2001' is such that Jay believes he will be rescued on it.'[49] That this is so makes it even less surprising that we would resort to the false (63) to convey the truth in question.

So I think that assuming that day designators are NRTs, we can see why we would use the strictly false (63) to convey the truth in question. In so doing, we end up ambivalent about (63)'s truth value. It is strictly false, but it is conveying something true.

Thus I don't think that considerations having to do with sentences containing verbs of propositional attitude provide much evidence for or against the view that day designators are NRTs. On both the hypothesis that day designators are quantificational and the hypothesis that they are NRTs, we can explain our ambivalence about (63) in the situation described. I would also add that given the flexibility and vagaries of our intuitions about the truth and falsity of belief ascriptions, I don't think such intuitions by themselves are very useful as evidence for or against semantic theories of the sort under consideration.

Let us summarize what the data considered thus far suggest. The syntactic tests involving VP deletion and weak crossover *perhaps* provided some evidence that day designators do not undergo movement and so are NRTs. There initially appeared to be evidence of scope interaction between negation and day designators, as well as between monotone decreasing quantifiers, such as 'No person', and day designators. But names exhibit behavior that is similar to day designators here, and so the behavior of day designators cannot be taken as evidence that they are quantificational and take variable scope. There also initially appeared to be some data providing evidence of scope interaction between day designators and verbs of propositional attitude. However, it turned out that the view that day designators are NRTs could explain the data as well. Thus, the range of data considered to this point probably slightly favors the view that day designators are NRTs. Still, it is perhaps surprising that the data have not come down more firmly on one side or the other.

However, at last we consider some solid evidence that day designators are NRTs. Consider sentences of the following form, where 't' is a singular term:[50]

(65) t might not have been t.

Some philosophers seem to think that Kripke's [1980] intuitive test for rigidity amounts to asking whether for a given singular term 't', instances of (65) have a true reading.[51] If not, so the story goes, 't' is rigid. If so, it isn't. Though there are passages in Kripke [1980] that *might* suggest such a thing (in particular, footnote 25 page 62), it is very unclear to me that Kripke endorses *this* test. His "official" formulations/examples of the intuitive test for rigidity make use of more complex sentences, such as 'No one other than Nixon might have been Nixon'; or 'Although the man (Nixon) might not have been president, it is not the case that he might not have been Nixon.', (Kripke [1980] pps. 48 and 49). These more complex sentences, because they contain quantifiers or anaphoric pronouns, raise issues not raised by sentences of the form (65). But I have not found passages in Kripke [1980] that justify attributing to him the "test for rigidity" mentioned above involving the more simple (65).

In any case, given certain plausible and widely accepted assumptions, that (65) has no true reading for a given 't' does not show that 't' is rigid. In particular, assume that the modal element in (65) can be treated as a sentence operator (or at least something quantifiers can take wide or narrow scope with respect to), and that the element of negation is a unary sentence operator (that expresses the truth function of negation). So (65)'s "regimented surface structure" is:[52]

(65a) Possibly(not (t=t))

Now instances of (65) involving non-rigid definite descriptions have true readings, as witnessed by Kripke's example:

(65D) The teacher of Alexander might not have been the teacher of Alexander.

But the crucial point here is that this is as much a consequence of the fact that descriptions undergo movement and have scope (and so are quantifiers) as it is a consequence of the fact that the description here is non-rigid. *One* LF representation for (65D) (given the above assumptions about the modal element and negation) is:

(65D′) (The teacher of Alexander: x) Possibly (the teacher of Alexander: y (not (x = y)))

Since one occurrence of the description occurs outside the modal operator and one occurrence occurs inside, the different occurrences are allowed to choose their denotations from different worlds.[53] Given the description is not rigid, different individuals may be chosen in the different worlds, and in such a case we get a true reading of (65D). But it is only the fact that descriptions qua quantifiers undergo movement that yields an LF representation like (65D′) in which one occurrence of the description occurs inside the scope of the modal operator and the other occurs outside. Since descriptions undergo movement, they leave their argument places surrounding the identity predicate (leaving behind the "traces"/variables 'x' and 'y') and can end up at various sites, including those they occupy in (65D′).[54]

Now suppose 't' in (65) is an NRT. Since, by hypothesis, it doesn't undergo movement in the mapping to LF, (65)'s only LF representation will be no different from its (regimented) surface structure. Thus it will be

(65NRT) Possibly(not (t=t))

The occurrences of 't', since they do not undergo movement, must remain in their "argument" positions flanking the identity sign. But of course, (65NRT) is false, despite the non-rigidity of 't'! So for 't' an NRT, (65) will have no true reading.[55] Obviously, then, the fact that (an instance of) (65) has no true reading cannot show that 't' is rigid.

We have already established that day designators are non-rigid. The question that remains, and the one we are addressing, is whether they are quantifiers or NRT's. Consider the following sentence:

(66) January 24, 2001 might not have been January 24, 2001.

I cannot get a true reading of this sentence, even when I rehearse all the facts about leap seconds etc, that we have discussed. But if 'January 24, 2001' were non-rigid *and* a quantifier, (66) should have a true reading just as (65D) does. However, as we have seen, if 'January 24, 2001' were an NRT, (66) would have no true reading. Thus, the lack of a true reading for (66) provides evidence for the view that day designators are NRT's, (again, given that we have established that they are non-rigid). This is rather ironic, since, as mentioned, some have taken the lack of a true reading in a sentence like (65) (of which (66) is an instance) to indicate rigidity!

Interestingly, when we replace the first occurrence of 'January 24, 2001' in (66) by the description 'the time interval that is (identical to) January 24, 2001', the result has a true reading:

(66D) The time interval that is January 24, 2001 might not have been January 24, 2001.

After what we have covered regarding leap seconds etc., (66D) clearly seems to have a true reading, since some time interval slightly different from the one that was January 24, 2001 might have had that honor. But this again supports the view that the reason for the lack of a true reading for (66) is that day designators are NRTs and so don't move. For one would think that 'The time interval that is January 24, 2001' and 'January 24, 2001' co-refer in every possible world. And of course they are both non-rigid, if the present view is correct. Thus, the only difference between them is that 'The time interval that is January 24, 2001', being a quantifier, undergoes movement. This, in turn, makes possible the following LF representation underlying (66D):

(66D') The time interval that is January 24, 2001:x (Possibly (not (x= January 24, 2001)))

And this, of course, is true when evaluated in the actual world. Thus, the data (66)–(66D') appear to provide solid evidence that day designators are NRTs.

Similarly, consider

(67) December 31, 2000 might have been 86,401 seconds long.

Given everything I have said about UTC, leap seconds, etc., (67) seems obviously true. Though December 31, 2000 was 86,400 seconds long, if the Earth had rotated slightly more slowly (and so a leap second needed to be added), December 31, 2000 would have been slightly longer. By contrast, I cannot get a false reading for (67). But if 'December 31, 2000' were a quantifier and underwent movement, one LF representation corresponding to (67) should be

(67') December 31, 2000: x (Possibly (x is 86,401 seconds long).

But (67') is false! The time interval that in fact is designated by 'December 31, 2000' has its length essentially and so could not have had a different length from its actual length. So again, the fact that (67) appears to have *only* a true reading suggests that day designators do not have variable scope and so are NRTs. This claim again appears to be supported by the fact that the following sentence *does* appear to have a false reading

(67D) The time interval that is December 31, 2000 might have been 86,401 seconds long.

(67D) appears to have a reading on which it expresses the false claim that the interval that in fact is December 31, 2000 might have had a length other than its actual length. Again, since descriptions can have variable scope, the following should be one of the LF representations associated with (67D)

(67D') The time interval that is December 31, 2000: x (Possibly (x is 86,401 seconds long))

And (67D') is of course false. As before, the fact that the sentence containing a description instead of a day designator, where both are non-rigid and coreferential in all possible worlds, has a reading where the sentence containing the day designator has no corresponding reading, and that supposing descriptions have variable scope and day designators don't would allow the former to have an LF representation that yields the reading but not the latter, provides strong evidence that day designators are NRTs. So it does appear as though the interaction of day designators and modal elements at last provides solid evidence that day designators are not quantifiers but NRTs.[56]

In closing, I wish to again emphasize the broader issues highlighted by the present case study. First, as we saw, that day designators are non-rigid is something we would not have noticed had we not payed careful attention to how time is measured, etc. Thus the present case highlights the importance, in constructing a semantic theory for a certain expression, of thinking about the portion of the world that the expression attaches to. Second, we saw that contrary to what a lot of philosophers believe, natural language contains NRTs. And we saw how subtle the data was that ultimately showed this and so how difficult this fact was to establish. Finally, I hope the present work illustrates a methodological point that has always been close to my heart: sound conclusions in philosophy of language require careful attention to detail.

Notes

*Thanks to the members of the Bay Area Philosophy of Language Discussion (BAPHLD) Group for reading an earlier version of this manuscript and making helpful suggestions. A (much shortened) version of this paper was presented to the Rutgers Semantic Workshop on the autumnal equinox 2000. I thank the participants in the workshop and my commentator Philippe Schlenker for their helpful comments. Thanks also to Kent Bach, David Copp, Mark Crimmins, Ron Pritchard, Mark Richard, Jason Stanley and George Wilson for helpful comments. Finally, thanks to Mark Wilson, whose way of thinking about semantics has influenced me deeply.

1. Henceforth I ignore the fact that such designators designate different intervals of time at different places on Earth. Hence what I subsequently say is more applicable to expressions such as 'January 24, 1999 in Los Angeles'. I don't think ignoring this complication affects any of the substantive issues I shall discuss. Below in the body of the text I discuss ignoring the analogous feature of the month terms 'January' etc. Finally, I ignore relativistic considerations in what follows.

2. E.g., Neale [1993] discusses and tentatively endorses this view. See my note 35 below.

3. Of course, as is the case with other quantifiers, context generally further restricts the range of quantification in some sense. When I say 'Every student did well on the exam' I generally don't intend to, and am not taken to, make an assertion about every student in the universe.

4. Any oddness one may find with (5) results from the fact that the sorts of things in the extensions of 'January' and 'funeral' are very different. For similar reasons, sentences like the following may sound slightly odd too:

   All virtues and country singers are overrated.

   The problem here is that it is hard to find a (clear case of a) count noun that has in its extension things that are (in some sense) similar to the things in the extension of 'January' (where the count noun isn't 'February', etc). Mark Richard suggested to me that the following is fine:

   'Most Januarys and (other) months I find depressing I snort Prozac.'

   It seems clear that 'months I find depressing' is a "count N'" (i.e. N' whose head noun is a count noun) and 'Januarys' is coordinated with it. Thus 'Januarys' must be a count N' whose head noun ('Januarys') is a count noun.

5. In saying this I am simply assuming that properties are the sorts of things that are the semantic values of count nouns. Some will suggest that 'January' sometimes

functions as a "name" of a *particular* period of time, as when I say 'In January, I am going to Lake Tahoe'. It seems to me that in such uses 'January' is in some sense a proxy for or elliptical for something like 'the upcoming January'. Indeed, when we look at larger prepositional phrases of which 'In January' is a part, it appears that 'In January' may have an additional argument place that needs to be filled by an expression specifying which January or Januarys are being talked about and which is elided in the sentence 'In January, I am going to Lake Tahoe'. The expression in question can specify a year ('In January 1979'; 'In January next year'; 'In January two years from now'; etc.) or quantify over them ('Every year in January'). If something like this is right, then it obviously supports the view that in the sentence 'In January, I am going to Lake Tahoe', 'In January' is elliptical for something like 'In the upcoming January'. It is also worth noting that month words seem to have something like "generic" uses, as in 'January is warm in New Zealand.' Such uses seem similar to uses exhibited by other count nouns, as in 'Man is a rational animal'. This provides more evidence that the month terms are count nouns.

6. Ron Pritchard pointed out to me that we take sentences like: 'Every January in Waterloo is cold' to be true. But on the present theory, the quantification here is over time intervals and so we are saying that these time intervals have the property of being cold. But it isn't clear that time intervals can have this property and so on the present theory it isn't clear why we should take such sentences to be true. However, Mark Richard notes that we also say things like 'Summer days in Davis are hot', (and take them to be true) but there doesn't seem to be any candidate for being a day that is a more plausible candidate for being hot than are time intervals. Perhaps what is going on in both cases is that we use expressions that pick out time intervals and contain expressions that refer to places (e.g., 'Every January in Waterloo' picks out time intervals (intervals that are Januarys-in-Waterloo) and contains a name that refers to a place ('Waterloo')) to convey claims about the air or environment in the place in question during the time interval in question.

7. For ease of exposition, I am assuming a theory of time according to which there really are instants of time and intervals of time that are independent of the events occurring in time. I believe that the main conclusions I wish to defend do not depend on this assumption, though without it the arguments I give for those conclusions would be somewhat different.

8. See note 1.

9. Pope Gregory simultaneously fixed the extensions of the "year numerals" '1583', etc., by these means. E.g. '1584' would have had as its extension a slightly different interval of time had it not been for Pope Gregory's reform.

10. Information on the topics I go on to discuss including UTC, leap seconds etc. is available on the websites of the United States Naval Observatory, the National Institute of Standards and Technology and the International Earth Rotation Service. These groups also have paper publications on these topics. I have benefited from these sources and from e-mail correspondence with Dennis McCarthy, Director of the United States Naval Observatory's Directorate of Time.

11. Here and throughout, when I talk about a rotation of the Earth, I am talking about a rotation of the Earth relative to the sun. Further, when I talk about the rotation of the Earth taking a certain amount of time, I am talking about the *average* time taken for the Earth to rotate once relative to the sun (a mean solar day), as measured by an atomic clock (where the seconds used as units are defined in terms of the

duration of a certain number of cycles of radiation corresponding to two hyperfine levels of the ground state of cesium 133). Similarly, *general* remarks about the Earth's rate of rotation are about the average rate of rotation relative to the sun.

12. In e-mail correspondence, Director of the United States Naval Observatory's Directorate of Time Dennis McCarthy characterized the rate of rotation of the Earth as "inherently unpredictable", apparently even being influenced by weather!

13. I *believe* that days that are twenty three hours fifty nine minutes and sixty one seconds long are properly said to be twenty four hours long. For the sixty one second interval that includes the leap second is said to be a minute (so that some minutes are sixty one seconds long, and were a negative leap second ever to be used, we would have a fifty nine second minute). But then such days are twenty-three hours sixty minutes long, and so, one would think, are twenty-four hours long. At any rate, henceforth, when I talk of days as twenty-four hour time intervals, I mean to include days that are twenty three hours fifty nine minutes and sixty one (or fifty nine) seconds long.

14. Or rather, $1')–4'$) specify the extensions of 'January', etc. given the rate of rotation of the Earth over time. If these facts are not "fixed" in the future, if it is *now* undetermined at what rate the Earth will rotate in the future, then it isn't clear that $1')–4'$) specify the *future* time intervals that are in the extension of 'January', etc. Here we encounter very deep issues in metaphysics that I will henceforth ignore; and so I will suppose that $1')–4'$) do specify which past, present *and future* time intervals are Januarys, etc.

15. (i) requires us to replace 'A January...' etc. by 'Something that has January-hood' etc. But $1'$) introduces a complication because here we have 'October' occurring without the indefinite article ('October 15, 1582'). So we really should rewrite this as 'the 15th day in an October in 1582'. Further, for reasons having to do with what we want the Ramsification of our theory to do, we need to change $1'$) in another way. As before, letting 't' rigidly designate the second immediately following the last second of October 4, 1582 (Julian calendar), what we need is something like this:

> $1''$) October 15, 1582 is the twenty four hour period (as measured by the rotation of the Earth) beginning at 12:00 A.M. (as measured by the rotation of the Earth) closest to t.

I mention below why we need a formulation like this.

16. Except that we have to decide what to do about the odd October of 1582. My inclination is to think that the "October" of that year was an odd amalgamation of a Julian October and a Gregorian October. Thus, the "pure" Gregorian October of that year includes part of a Julian September. If this is correct, we need do nothing. Note that once we have implemented the Gregorian calendar, there is no reason not to count time intervals prior to its implementation as (Gregorian) Januarys, etc. Our theory in fact does this, and so makes good sense of sentences like: 'One million years ago, Januarys in the Finger Lakes region of New York were arctic-like'.

17. It was because we wanted the Ramsification of $1')–4'$) to play a role in delivering the correct extensions for our month words in other possible worlds that we had to alter $1'$) in the way discussed in note 15 above. For we want to consider worlds in which the Earth behaved very much like it did in the actual world through October 4, 1582 (Julian calendar) except that it rotated *slightly* more slowly or more quickly. Though in the actual world, October 15, 1582 begins with the second t, in other

possible worlds it may begin at a somewhat different time. This is why in 1″) (note 15) we talk about the twenty-four hour period beginning at 12:00 A.M. *closest to t*. I assume here that we restrict our attention to worlds in which the twenty-four hour period beginning at 12:00 A.M. closest to t begins within, say, ten minutes of t and that this rotation of the Earth "corresponds" to the rotation of the Earth that in the actual world occurs on October 15, 1582. That is, in both worlds the Earth rotated the same number of times to this point. Below I briefly discuss the reason for this restriction.

18. As mentioned above, in the actual world the Earth presently takes 86,400.002 seconds to rotate, (and is slowing). This gives rise to a discrepancy between UT1 and UTC of approximately .73 seconds per year (365x.002). Thus a leap second needs to be added about once every 1.23 years.

19. Thanks to Mark Crimmins for suggesting this sort of example. It might be better to imagine Teresa saying, instead of (10), simply: 'That clapping event might have occurred at exactly the same time but been in January'. Perhaps intuitions are more robust with respect to this simpler sentence.

20. One sometimes reads things such as the following in books about the Roman, Julian and Gregorian calendars: 'December is the twelfth month, but its name tells us it was once the tenth, from the Latin 'decem'. Likewise, September, October and November were originally the seventh, eighth and ninth months, respectively.' (from *Pictorial Astronomy* (fifth revised edition), 1983, Climinshaw et al, Harper and Row, New York). And Mark Richard noted that it is natural to say things like 'If Gregory had put a leap year adjustment at the end of January, January would sometimes be 32 days long' and 'If Gregory hadn't changed the calendar, it would be December now (not January)', (spoken in the first week of January). Yet such things come out false on the current view. My temptation is to think that such remarks should be construed as "implicitly metalinguistic" Thus, the first sentence above should be construed as: 'The tenth month of the old Roman calendar was called "December".' And Richard's examples ought to be construed along the lines of: 'If Gregory had put a leap year adjustment at the end of the month he called 'January' (instead of the month he called 'February'—and left everything else the same), the month we would have called 'January' would sometimes be 32 days long'. I suspect that one of the reasons ordinary folk are so inclined to use (as opposed to mention) month terms in conveying metalinguistic assertions is that they think of month words as part of a system for talking about time that is completely arbitrary in the sense that it doesn't get at anything in the nature of time intervals (nor would any different system). There is no "correct way" to divide up time intervals. But ordinary folk tend not to think of many other property terms in this way. They tend to think that some things are really dogs and some are really cats, and so using the terms 'dog' and 'cat' to divide certain individuals up is far from arbitrary (though of course that we use the particular words 'dog' and 'cat' is arbitrary). Given that there is no correct way to divide up time intervals, it is easy to slip into thinking that in some deep sense there is nothing more to being a January than being called 'January'. But having slipped this far, it is easy to see why one would convey claims about what things are (or would be) called 'January', by talking about what things *are* (or would be) January.

21. Perhaps an account that simply didn't assign extensions to 'January' etc. in such worlds would be better. For one might think that if our counterfactual talk about

months and our evaluation of propositions about months really does take place against the background of assuming that things are much like they are in the actual world in relevant respects, then there is no fact of the matter about what the extensions of our month terms are in remote worlds. I am sympathetic to this idea, which is similar in spirit to ideas in the excellent Wilson [1982].

22. I use '$s+1$' and similar notation to designate the second immediately following s.

23. (17) is a bit pedestrian, and so may sound slightly odd. It helps to imagine it being uttered in response to someone *completely* unfamiliar with the Gregorian calendar, and perhaps calendars generally (say, a Venutian), asking 'What is/was January 1, 1999?'.

24. As Frege noted, identity statements are "reversible", whereas predications in which 'is' is used as the copula in general are not. Thus, 'Shane is the world extreme skiing champion' and 'The world extreme skiing champion is Shane.' are both fine; but the second of the pair 'Shane is happy' and 'Happy is Shane' sounds at least odd. And (18) is clearly reversible:

> (18') January 1, 1999 is the twenty-four hour time interval beginning with the next occurrence of 12:00 A.M. and ending with following occurrence of 12:00 A.M.

25. Day designators *are* temporally rigid. That is, within a given world, a given day designator designates the same interval at all times in that world, (if we set aside worries about whether e.g. *now* 'January 24, 2444' designates a specific time interval, given that it is not now determined how fast the Earth will rotate for the next 444 years or so). So temporal and modal rigidity come apart in the case of day designators. Henceforth, talk about rigidity should be understood as being about modal rigidity.

26. Jason Stanley [1997] notes that the truth of sentences like the one to follow suffices to show that the expression occurring where 'December 31, 1998' does is not rigid.

27. Stephan McCaffery [1999], for example, explicitly defends the view that day designators are rigid.

28. This allows for worlds in which the rate of rotation of the Earth is currently a constant and uniform 86,400 seconds, worlds in which only negative leap seconds have been used, etc.

29. Though as Kent Bach pointed out to me, on the present view there are possible worlds which are very similar to the actual world in terms of the Earth's rate of rotation (and rotational history), but for which a *very* slight current discrepancy between the rate of rotation of Earth there and in the actual world would result in day designators designating different, *non-overlapping* twenty-four hour intervals in the two worlds in the far future.

30. For example, McCaffery [1999] claims this.

31. For simplicity, here we suppose that "day numerals" directly refer to numbers. This, of course, may not be the case for at least two reasons. First, numerals may not be mechanisms of direct reference. And second, there may not be any numbers; that is, it may turn out that the best way to understand what mathematics is about precludes our holding that numbers are "things" that can be referred to by singular terms. On the other hand, the considerations we have raised suggest that "year numerals" are non-rigid and so cannot directly refer to years. E.g. if two possible worlds differ only in that in one December 31, 1998 was 86,401 seconds long and ended with

second *s*, whereas in the other December 31, 1998 was 86,400 seconds long and ended with second $s-1$, '1998' designates slightly different year long intervals of time in the two worlds. Thus, we must have year numerals contribute to propositions properties of year long time intervals that are uniquely satisfied by different time intervals in different worlds.

32. See King [1995] and references there for the account of structured propositions I favor. I don't mean to suggest that all philosophers who adopt the structured proposition approach agree that each of the three semantic ways of functioning I discuss is such that some noun phrase functions in that way. I mean that in this tradition, for each of the three ways I shall discuss, someone in the tradition has claimed that some noun phrase or other functions in this way.

33. Scott Soames [2000] calls such expressions *partially descriptive names*. See Chapter Three. Mark Richard [1993] calls such expressions *articulated terms*, and holds that complex demonstratives are examples of articulated terms. Strictly, for Richard, in the general case, articulated terms contribute to propositions a referent, an "articulated content", and a relation. The truth of the resulting proposition at a circumstance of evaluation e requires the referent to bear the relation to the articulated content at e. In the case of complex demonstratives, the articulated content is something like a property (expressed by the N' constituent of the complex demonstrative) and the relation is instantiation. Thus, the truth at a circumstance of evaluation e of a proposition expressed by a sentence containing a complex demonstrative (in a context) requires the referent (in that context) to instantiate the property that is the articulated content at e. So *in the case of complex demonstratives*, Richard's view amounts to saying that such a noun phrase contributes *both* its referent (in a context) to the proposition expressed (in that context) by a sentence in which it occurs *and* some descriptive condition that the referent (in that context) must satisfy at a circumstance of evaluation for the proposition to be true there. And this is the view under discussion in the body of the paper.

34. Or at any rate, I read Soames and Richard this way and so as holding that "articulated terms"/"partially descriptive names" do not have variable scope.

35. Neale [1993] actually defends the stronger claim that 'Every meaningful noun phrase (NP) in natural language is either a semantically unstructured, rigid referring expression (singular term) or else a semantically structured, restricted quantifier." (p. 90). In fairness to Neale, though he defends this claim in various ways, he only ends up endorsing the view that it is "...very much closer to being correct than many people think." (p. 91), and admits that it may ultimately be false (see pps. 91 and 109).

36. This isn't quite right, since for Chomskyans S structure is itself slightly more abstract in certain ways than real surface structure. But these subtleties don't matter here.

37. Roughly, α c-commands β iff the first branching node that dominates α dominates β and α does not dominate β.

38. If such movement occurs, the tree for the LF representation of (31) looks as follows:

every   chute that Shane did₁   JC   skied   e₁

It should be clear that neither 'skied' nor 'did' c-commands the other here.

39. That day designators don't take restrictive relative clauses might itself be taken as an indication that day designators are not quantifier phrases, since names and some other non-quantificational NP's do not take restrictive relatives:

> (32) *Al Gore who Jane admires is happy.
> (33) *I will ski tomorrow that is a holiday.

However, quantifiers sometimes will not take restrictive relatives, as the following example shows:

> (34) *The current president of the United States who Jane loves is happy.

It seems to me that the reason that day designators will not take restrictive relatives is that these relative clauses are always gratuitous. Day designators are guaranteed unique designations without such clauses. Thus the addition of gratuitous relatives clauses is infelicitous. This appears to be the problem with (34) as well.

40. E.g. Robert May [1985] claims this in Chapter 1.

41. Or, more cautiously, 'his' and 'Albert' can be understood as coreferring.

42. Of course if a definite description contains a pronoun, we can get truth conditional differences resulting from differences of scope. E.g. with respect to 'Every male skier loves the steepest run at his favorite mountain' there is a reading of the sentence on which 'Every male skier' binds 'his', so that the sentence is true iff every male skier loves the steepest run at that skier's favorite mountain (possibly different runs for different skiers). Here of course the description must take narrow scope with respect to 'Every male skier' so that the latter can bind the pronoun in the description. If the description is read as taking widest scope, then the pronoun cannot be bound by 'every male skier'. Thus the pronoun can be assigned a referent in context. Say it is assigned Greg. Then the sentence will be true iff every male skier loves the steepest run on Greg's favorite mountain. So here we get a truth conditional difference between wide scope and narrow scope readings of the description with respect to the universal quantifier. But this is only possible because definite descriptions allow restrictive relative clauses, and so can contain pronouns that can get bound by higher quantifiers. Day designators do not, and so there is no way to get a pronoun into a day designator. Hence we cannot get truth conditional differences of this sort with day designators.

43. For ease of exposition, I here and below talk sloppily of the truth of things like (50a) and (50b) rather than the truth of their instances.

44. Of course, one might hold that (50a′) and (50b′) don't express propositions at all. Perhaps one could hold that there is some sort of presupposition failure that has this result. I ignore such views here.

45. I shall not attempt to show that *one sentence* of the form of (50) (containing a non-denoting day designator) seems to have both a true and a false reading. Rather, I shall attempt to find an instance of (50) (containing a non-denoting day designator) that seems true and another instance that seems false (or at least doesn't seem true). See next note.

46. I don't say that the following sentences seem *false*. But this is similar to the case of definite descriptions. Certain sentences containing non-denoting descriptions and negation seem true, such as 'The present King of France is not under this table' (indicating a particular table), and so presumably the description is read as taking narrow scope. Others do not seem true, though it is a bit strong to say they seem

false, such as 'The present King of France is not bald'; and so presumably the description is read as taking wide scope. Apropos my remarks in the previous note, it is hard to find cases in which one and the same sentence of this sort seems to have both a true and a not true (or false) reading. But still, Russellians about descriptions take the fact that some sentences of this sort seem true and others not to indicate a scope ambiguity.

47. And direct reference theorists have offered such explanations. Scott Soames [1987], for example, in discussing a similar example notes that when we are inclined to judge (64) false in a situation of the sort I have described, it is because of the attitude the agent of the ascription has toward the embedded *sentence* in the ascription. Soames holds that the ascription is true in a case of the sort described, because Virginia does stand in the belief relation to the proposition expressed by the embedded sentence in (64). But (64) *suggests*, though it does not assert, that Virginia has a pro attitude towards the embedded *sentence* in (64). And of course she does not in the case as described. This inclines us to say that (64) is false in the situation described.

48. Sometimes there are reasons for favoring other day designating expressions. For example, sometimes I wish to locate a day relative to the present, as when I am trying to convey to you how long it will be from now until I leave for Europe. I might then say 'I leave in two weeks.' But if you are simply trying to say something concise about a day (other than today or yesterday) and you want your audience to retain and make use of what you say, and to locate the day you are talking about relative to other days, nothing beats a day designator.

49. It might be thought that 'August 23, 2001 is such that Jay believes he will be rescued on it' does the job. Of course, this is pretty cumbersome and awkward too. But if, as we are assuming, day designators are NRTs there is some reason to think that pronouns anaphoric on them are not rigid referring expressions. Let me cryptically remark that the fact the following sentence seems true suggests this: 'Concerning December 31, 1998, it is possible that it should have been 86,400 seconds long'. Thus, it is not at all clear that the above sentence says of the day designated by 'August 23, 2001', that Jay believes he will be rescued on it.

50. By 'singular term', I mean an expression that purports to designate (not refer to!) an individual. Thus, e.g. both names and definite descriptions are singular terms.

51. I have heard this many times in conversation. It appears in many, many places, including, for example, Dummett [1981], p. 580; Laporte [2000], p. 307; and More [1980], p. 327.

52. (65a) isn't really a surface structure, since scope relations between negation and the modal operator are explicitly represented. (65) might have another regimented surface structure. See note 55 below.

53. Of course, if we are evaluating (65D′) in the actual world, the first occurrence chooses its denotation from the actual world, and the second from another possible world. For simplicity, I talk here and below about evaluating LF representations like (65D′) at various possible worlds. I think that it is *propositions* that are evaluated at possible worlds, but I think sentences express propositions that are structurally identical to their LF representations, (see King [1995] and references there). So talking this way does no harm.

54. The descriptions could be moved to other sites as well. Thus there are other LF representations underlying (65D) and so it has other readings.

55. (65) might have another "regimented surface structure" corresponding to negation taking wide scope over the modal element as follows:

   (65b) not(Possibly(t=t))

   If 't' is an NRT and so doesn't move, then (65b) will be another LF for (65). But clearly (65b) cannot be true, and so will not yield a true reading for (65) (for 't' an NRT) either. So, again, if 't' is an NRT, (65) will have no true reading.

56. My argument that day designators are NRTs here involving (65)–(67D') depends on a number of assumptions that some might deem false, in particular that the modal element in instances of (65) is a sentence operator, and that the only way for the NP in subject position in an instance of (65) to be outside the scope of the modal element at LF is for it to have been moved there by a movement rule that applies only to quantificational NPs (i.e. quantifier raising). If one denied this second assumption, one might hold that the subject NP in an instance of (65), *whether quantificational or not*, must appear outside the scope of the modal element at LF (on at least one reading of the instance of (65)). But then even if 't' is an NRT, this would yield a true reading of (65) contrary to what is claimed in the text, (since one occurrence of the NRT would be outside the scope of the modal element and one would be inside). Rather than debate these points, let me simply say that we could re-run my entire argument using the sentence:

   (65') It is possible that t should not have been t.

(and replacing each of (65)–(67D') with its (65') analogue). Here the modal element is explicitly a sentence operator; and it is very plausible to suppose that the only way for an occurrence of 't' to be outside the scope of the modal operator at LF is for it to undergo quantifier raising. The argument for the conclusion that day designators are NRTs that is exactly like the one given in the text except that it uses (65') and its analogues thus doesn't depend on the controversial assumptions mentioned. Hence the conclusion stands even if these assumptions are rejected.

Finally, if the assumptions in question are rejected and certain other views adopted (e.g. that the subject NP in an instance of (65) whether quantificational or not must appear outside the scope of the modal element at LF on at least one reading of the instance of (65)), perhaps whether instances of (65) have true readings or not could be resurrected as a legitimate test for rigidity, (though this would still not be true of (65')). But these are all controversial questions! Thus, those who endorse testing for rigidity by asking whether instances of (65) have true readings or not should not simply blithely state and endorse the test, but should note that the claim that it is a good test rests on a number of controversial assumptions in linguistics. I thank Jason Stanley for raising questions that helped me get clear on these points.

References

Dummett, Michael, 1981. *The Interpretation of Frege's Philosophy*, Gerald Duckworth and Co. LTD, London

Kim, Jaegwon, 1969. 'Events and their Descriptions: Some Considerations', *Essays in Honor of Carl G. Hempel*, N. Rescher et al. (eds.), Reidel, Dordrecht

Kim, Jaegwon, 1973. 'Causation, Nomic Subsumption, and the Concept of Event', *The Journal of Philosophy* 70, 217–236

King, Jeffrey C., 1995. 'Structured Propositions and Complex Predicates', *Nôus* 29(4), 516–535.

King, Jeffrey C., 1998. 'What is a Philosophical Analysis?' *Philosophical Studies* 90: 155–179.

King, Jeffrey C., 1999. 'Are Complex 'that' Phrases Devices of Direct Reference?', *Nôus* 33:2 155–182.

King, Jeffrey C., 2000. 'On the Possibility of Correct, Apparently Circular Dispositional Analysis', *Philosophical Studies* 98, 257–278.

King, Jeffrey C., 2001. *Complex Demonstratives: A Quantificational Account*, forthcoming MIT Press.

Kripke, Saul, 1980. *Naming and Necessity*, Harvard University Press, Cambridge, MA

Laporte, Joseph, 2000. 'Rigidity and Kind', *Philosophical Studies* 97 (3), 293–316.

Lewis, David, 1970. 'How to Define Theoretical Terms', *Journal of Philosophy* 67: 427–446.

Lewis, David, 1972. 'Psychophysical and Theoretical Identifications', *The Australasian Journal of Philosophy*, 50, 249–258.

May, Robert, 1985. *Logical Form*, The MIT Press, Cambridge, Massachusetts

McCaffery, Stephan J., 1999. 'Compositional Names', *Linguistics and Philosophy*, volume 22, no. 4.

More, M.J., 1980. 'Rigidity and Scope', *Logique et Analyse*, 23, 327–330.

Neale, Stephen, 1993. 'Term Limits', in *Philosophical Perspectives, 7, Language and Logic*, James E. Tomberlin (ed.), Ridgeview Publishing, Atascadero, CA.

Soames, Scott, 1987. 'Direct Reference, Propositional Attitudes and Semantic Content', *Philosophical Topics* (15) 47–87.

Soames, Scott, 2000. *Beyond Rigidity: The Unfinished Semantic Agenda of Naming and Necessity*, manuscript.

Stanley, Jason, 1997. 'Names and Rigid Designation', in *A Companion to the Philosophy of Language*, B. Hale and C. Wright (eds.), Blackwell Publishers Ltd., Oxford

Wilson, Mark, 1982. 'Predicate Meets Property', *The Philosophical Review*, XCI No. 4, 549–589.

Philosophical Perspectives, 15, Metaphysics, 2001

FREGEAN SENSES, MODES OF PRESENTATION, AND CONCEPTS*

Edward N. Zalta†
Stanford University

Ever since Frege postulated senses in [1892] and conceived of them as (containing) modes of presentation, serious studies in the philosophy of language have often appealed to these entities. In the recent philosophy of language and mind, however, the notions of 'mode of presentation' and 'concept' have become more important. It seems fair to say that much of the theorizing involving senses, modes of presentation, and concepts has taken place at a very general level. Frege never told us what senses are; they were simply stipulated to be entities that play certain roles in his philosophy of language. Philosophers today still work with both senses and modes of presentation without having a systematic and viable theory of them. And although the notion of a concept has been employed in various ways, there are not all that many precise theories of concepts.

In this paper, I try to clear away some of the mystery surrounding these three kinds of entities by offering a precise theory of them. The theory of Fregean senses developed in my previous work will be extended to yield a more general theory of modes of presentation and concepts. Modes of presentation and concepts will be identified, therefore, in terms of my axiomatic theory of abstract objects.[1] The theory asserts the existence not only of ordinary properties, relations, and propositions, but also of abstract individuals and abstract properties and relations. The concepts by which ordinary individuals, properties, and relations are conceived will be analyzed as abstract individuals, properties, and relations, respectively.[2] In what follows, we take the denotation of a predicate to be a property or relation (intensionally conceived), and we analyze the sense of that predicate, relative to some person, as a *concept* by which that person conceives of the property or relation denoted by the predicate. We shall, therefore, be distinguishing properties and concepts. Moreover, our theory of concepts will predict that the concepts of individuals can combine with concepts of properties and relations so as to form complex concepts. These complex concepts are entities by which ordinary 'Russellian' propositions (or states of affairs) can be conceived.

In Section 1 of the paper, I'll focus on senses and modes of presentation, and explain why the more general notion of a mode of presentation may be more useful for the analysis of propositional attitude reports than the notion of the sense of a term. In Section 2, I explain how to extend my earlier work on senses to produce a theory of modes of presentation and concepts. Since the resulting theory offers precise existence conditions for modes of presentation and for concepts, we'll see that it addresses Schiffer's [1990] 'candidate problem' for modes of presentation.

In Section 3 of the paper, our theory will be used to 'plug the theoretical gap' which exists in the work of those philosophers who employ senses and/or modes without having a precise theory of them. (I'll reserve, for another occasion, a similar study of some of the work on concepts which has been conducted in the absence of a precise theory.) The work of the following four philosophers will be discussed in more detail in that section. The first is D. Kaplan, who acknowledged the elegance of Frege's theoretical explanation of intensional contexts, but pointed out that we must continue looking for the 'peculiar' intermediate entities involved.[3] The second is G. Forbes, who acknowledges at the end of a recent essay that his neo-Fregean theory of attitude reports awaits a more precise theory of modes of presentation.[4] Despite this absence of theory, Forbes introduces ([1987], 8; and [1990], 548) the variables $\alpha, \beta,...$ to range over senses and uses the uninterpreted notation $\alpha \wedge \ulcorner F \urcorner$ to indicate that α is a mode of presentation which has somehow combined with the sense of the predicate 'F' to form a complex sense or Fregean thought. Not only does this notation need interpretation, but also modes of presentation need a precise identification if we are to accept that they can be combined in this way. The third example is N. Salmon, who in [1986] eschews senses in his analysis of belief reports as 2-place relations between persons and Russellian propositions, but appears to employ modes ('ways of taking a proposition') as the third relatum of his theoretical *BEL* relation.[5] But he then admits that he has said very little about what this third relatum is.[6] The final example is M. Crimmins, who in [1998] develops a pretense-theoretic analysis of modes of presentation and belief ascriptions. Crimmins agrees that an account of modes of presentation is required for his analysis of belief reports to succeed,[7] but suggests that his view is not committed to standard conceptions of modes of presentation. Nevertheless, he quantifies over, individuates, and introduces notation for modes in his paper.[8]

In Section 4 of the paper, I'll discuss, but not resolve, a technical issue about how to best enhance our formalism so that we can refer to modes of presentation in the analysis of belief reports. We will work within a theory of belief reports on which they are analyzed as asserting 2-place relations.[9] In Section 5 of paper, we conclude with a few remarks about concepts.

Let me emphasize before we begin that the theory of modes of presentation and concepts developed in what follows is *neutral* with respect to the different analyses of belief reports that various authors have proposed. The theory that I offer here provides a theoretical underpinning for any theory of belief or belief reports which appeals to modes of presentation or concepts. Even if the analysis of belief reports discussed here turns out to be flawed, the underlying theory of modes of presentation could still ground the other analyses of attitude reports that invoke these entities.

Finally, I should mention that my earlier work on the theory of abstract objects will be presupposed in what follows. I shall assume that the reader is familiar with the typed theory of abstract individuals and abstract relations, with our previous discussions of how these abstract individuals and abstract relations can play the roles that Frege assigned to senses in his philosophy of language, with the special notation we have introduced into intensional logic for denoting the sense of a term with respect to an individual, and with our previous approach to the analysis of belief reports, in which such reports are treated as ambiguous and in which any of the terms within the scope of propositional attitude verbs can be given either a *de re* or a *de dicto* reading depending on the facts about substitution. I'll refer to this overall theory as 'ILAO' ('the intensional logic of abstract objects') in what follows.[10]

1: From Fregean Senses to Modes of Presentation

In this section, we examine the reasons why the appeal to the more general modes of presentation, as opposed to Fregean senses, might give one more flexibility when analyzing propositional attitude reports. It is important to understand just how far the notion 'the sense of a term' can take you, and where the more general notion 'mode of presentation' becomes useful. Before we look at examples where the more general notion becomes important, let us look at an example which, it has been claimed, cannot be analyzed in terms of Fregean senses. Schiffer [1992, 507-508] describes a case that he claims is problematic for the Fregean. He begins his discussion of the problematic case by first pointing out how the Fregean would represent the following, unproblematic sentence:[11]

(1) Ralph believes that Fido is a woodchuck.

On behalf of the Fregean, Schiffer offers the following representation:

(S) $B(\text{Ralph}, \langle m_f, m_w \rangle)$

Schiffer uses '$\langle m_f, m_w \rangle$' to denote the "mode-of-presentation-containing proposition" referred to by the occurrence of 'that Fido is a woodchuck' in (1), where m_f and m_w are the ways Ralph has of thinking of Fido and the property of being a woodchuck, respectively. With this understanding of the Fregean analysis, Schiffer then says the following sentence poses a problem:

(2) Everyone who has ever known her has believed that Madonna was musical.

Schiffer points out [1992, 507]:

> According to the Fregean proposal, there is a particular mode of presentation m of Madonna and a particular mode of presentation m' of the property of being musical such that the foregoing utterance of (2) is true only if everyone who has ever known Madonna has believed the proposition $\langle m, m' \rangle$. Yet this is surely too strong a requirement on the truth of (2). It requires that everyone who has ever known Madonna shared a single way of thinking of her and a single way of thinking of the property of being musical....

Since there is no single mode of presentation by which those who know Madonna conceive of her, Schiffer concludes that the classic Fregean view cannot successfully represent (2).

Clearly, Schiffer is correct when he says that there is no single mode of presentation by which people who have known Madonna conceive of her. To make the example even harder, we can replace 'known' in (2) by 'seen'. Even if someone were to argue that people who have known Madonna do have a single way of thinking of her, it is hardly likely that something similar can be said about everyone who has ever seen Madonna. Moreover, in what follows, we accept the claim that there is no single *sense* of the term 'Madonna' in terms of which everyone conceives of the person denoted by the name. We assume, in general, that the sense of a name varies from person to person.[12]

However, we've developed a more flexible notation and theory of senses than the one Schiffer offers on behalf of the Fregean. Consider first how it differs from Schiffer's representation of the *unproblematic* case of (1). (1) is ambiguous from the point of view of ILAO, and among the possible readings of (1), there is a pure *de re* reading and a pure *de dicto* reading. These are as follows, respectively:

(1′) $B(r, [\lambda Wf])$ (pure *de re*)
(1″) $B(r, [\lambda \underline{W}_r \underline{f}_r])$ (pure *de dicto*)

(In (1′) and (1″), we read the λ-notation of the form $[\lambda\phi]$ as 'that-ϕ', and since (1′) and (1″) are supposed to disambiguate the English, they read exactly the same when read back in *ordinary* English.) Clearly, (1″) is the counterpart of Schiffer's (S), but notice the difference in the notation for representing the thought to which Ralph is related. (1″) relates Ralph to a Fregean thought containing the sense of 'woodchuck' for Ralph ($\underline{W}_r$) and the sense of 'Fido' for Ralph ($\underline{f}_r$) as constituents. This notation acknowledges the fact that the sense of a term may vary from person to person.

This is the key to a representation of (2) which doesn't require that everyone who has known Madonna share a single way of thinking about her. In ILAO

([1983], 144; [1988], 178), we allowed our special sense-denoting terms like '$\underline{W}_r$' and '$\underline{f}_r$' to be indexed by variables as well as names. Contrast (i) Schiffer's notation 'm_M', in which 'm' is a variable ranging over modes and in which the whole expression 'm_M' denotes the sense of the name 'Madonna', with (ii) our notation '$\underline{m}_x$', in which 'm' names Madonna, '$\underline{m}$' is a term that ranges over possible senses of the name 'Madonna' and the subscripted index 'x' serves to identify the particular sense the term 'Madonna' has for x. So relative to an assignment to the variable x, '$\underline{m}_x$' denotes the sense of the name 'Madonna' for person x.[13]

Similarly, we symbolize the mode of presentation that x associates with the predicate 'is musical' as: $\underline{M}_x$. So a Fregean with a formalism that can represent how the sense of a term may vary, could use the following representation for Schiffer's sentence (2):

(2a) $\forall x(Kxm \rightarrow B(x, [\lambda \underline{M}_x \underline{m}_x]))$

On this analysis, (2) is true just in case each person x that has known Madonna stands in a relation to a certain Fregean thought, namely, $\underline{M}_x \underline{m}_x$. This thought is a proposition-like logical complex in which $\underline{M}_x$ and $\underline{m}_x$ are constituents. Note that from a formal point of view, such an analysis is immune to Schiffer's objection, for it doesn't imply that there is a single mode of presentation under which everyone thinks of Madonna, or a single mode under which everyone thinks of musicality, or a single complex Fregean thought by which everyone thinks that Madonna is musical.

Of course, it seems reasonable to suggest that (2) has a reading on which it includes people who in some sense know Madonna and think she is musical but who don't know her name or know her as 'Madonna'. Such a reading becomes even clearer if we replace 'known' by 'seen' in (2); many people have seen Madonna and believe that she is musical without having learned the name 'Madonna' as the name of the woman they have seen. There is, at present, one way to represent this reading in ILAO. On that reading, the terms in the context of attitude verbs denote their ordinary denotation. Let us say that the occurrence of a term τ in an ordinary language attitude report is a *de re* occurrence whenever substitutions of codenotational terms for τ are truth preserving. When such substitutions for τ are not truth preserving, we say that the occurrence of τ is a *de dicto* occurrence. Therefore, in addition to the above reading of (2), ILAO also permits the following *de re* reading:

(2b) $\forall x[Kxm \rightarrow B(x, [\lambda Mm])]$

On this reading, (2) is true iff every person x that has known Madonna stands in the belief relation to a certain singular proposition, namely the one having the property of being musical and Madonna as constituents. This gives us one reading of (2) on which it quantifies even over those acquainted with Madonna without knowing her name. On this reading of (2), if we substitute for 'Madonna' any term that has the same denotation, truth is preserved. This analysis survives even when we replace 'known' by 'seen' in (2), and replace 'K' by 'S' in (2a).

However, this second reading (2b) raises a question about the first reading (2a). One might wonder whether (2a) can cover even those people who don't know Madonna by name. Right now, (2a) asserts that for any person x that knows Madonna, x is belief-related to the Fregean thought which has the following constituents: x's sense of the name 'Madonna' and x's sense of the predicate term 'is musical'. But what if we replace 'known' by 'seen' in (2) and consider those people who have seen Madonna (say on a video) and think she is musical, but who don't know her by name and, indeed, have never heard the name 'Madonna' used to refer to Madonna? By hypothesis, such people won't have a sense for the name 'Madonna', or if they do, it won't be a sense which represents Madonna. But such people will have at least one mode of presentation for Madonna, since there will be such modes in connection with their past episodes of seeing Madonna. Shouldn't there be reading of this variant of (2), in which every such person has a belief about Madonna's musicality which is effected by way of their mode of presentation for Madonna? Can we produce a variant of (2a) and regard it as asserting: for any person x that has known or seen Madonna, x is belief-related to a Fregean thought which has as constituents some mode of presentation that x has for Madonna and some mode of presentation that x has for the property of being musical?

This is, in fact, one of the reasons for adding flexibility to ILAO so that we may analyze belief reports in terms of the more general notion of a mode of presentation. Although ILAO addresses the problem Schiffer raised for the Fregean, it is still not quite flexible enough. In Section 4, we'll consider the technical issues that arise in when we consider adding new notation to our formalism, to obtain the needed flexibility. Our goal will be to extend the formalism, so that it can be used in analyses (of attitude reports) that are tied less closely to the notion of a sense and more closely to the notion of a mode of presentation.

Here is another kind of example which makes the point. We often report the beliefs of a person x in terms of proper names and predicates which x would not or could not have used. For example, we might reasonably report either of the following:

(3) Hammurabi believed that Hesperus is not made of water.

(4) Hammurabi didn't believe that Hesperus is not made of H_2O.

Given that the the property of being made of water is identical to the property of being made of H_2O, and that the Russellian proposition denoted by "that Hesperus is not made of water" is identical to the one denoted by "that Hesperus is not made of H_2O", we'll have to appeal to the distinct modes of presentation by which Hammurabi conceived of the property of being made of water, if we are to represent these belief reports as consistent. From the terms 'W' ('is made of water'), 'H' ('is made of H_2O') and 'b' ('Hammurabi'), ILAO allows us to create special terms '$\underline{W}_b$' and '$\underline{H}_b$'. We have interpreted these latter terms respectively, as the sense of the predicate 'is made of water' for Hammurabi and the sense of the predicate 'is made of H_2O' for Hammurabi. But clearly, we don't want to analyze the belief reports in terms of the senses of these expressions for Hammurabi, since Hammurabi would not have used the expressions 'is made of water' and 'is made of H_2O'. Instead, the analyses of the reports should be in terms of the modes of presentation by which Hammurabi conceptualized the property of being made of water.

For these reasons, then, we plan to investigate the more general notion of a 'mode of presentation' within the context of ILAO. Our background theory of abstract objects doesn't need to be changed, for abstract individuals and abstract relations can just as easily play the more general role of modes of presentations. In the next section, we see one of the reasons why this is so.

2: Modes of Presentation and Concepts

In Frege's theory, the sense of a term is, or contains, a mode of presentation. Since the category *mode of presentation* is wider than the category *sense* (given that not all modes of presentation function as the sense of some term of natural language), it is possible to tease them apart. Modes of presentation are not introduced to explain problems in the philosophy of language such as the informativeness of identity statements or substitution failures in attitude reports, but rather to explain problems in the philosophy of mind such as our frequent recognition failures of familiar objects and properties and the apparent contradictory attitudes we sometimes have with respect to one and the same object. Modes of presentation may therefore be introduced and connected with the different ways by which we can conceive of an object or property (relation). One and the same object or property (relation) can be conceived in different ways and the various conceptions need not be recognized as conceptions of the same entity. Moreover, our conceptions of objects combine somehow with our conceptions of properties (relations) to form various complex conceptions. One and the same Russellian proposition or state of affairs can be conceived via different complex conceptions but these complex conceptions need not be recognized as conceptions of the same Russellian proposition or state of affairs.

It should come as no surprise to readers familiar with my work that my candidates for the role of modes of presentation are the abstract individuals and abstract relations of our typed intensional logic ILAO.[14] Recall that this logic is based on the following typing scheme: where 'i' is the type for individuals, and where $t_1,...,t_n$ are any types, then '$\langle t_1,...,t_n \rangle$' is the type for relations having arguments of type $t_1,...,t_n$, respectively. We sometimes let 'p' stand for the type

$\langle\,\rangle$ (i.e., where $n = 0$); this is the type for propositions, or 0-place logical complexes. In terms of this scheme, the typed comprehension principle for abstract objects asserts the existence not only of abstract individuals, but also of abstract properties and abstract relations (at every relational type).[15] Abstract objects of type t may encode the same properties that ordinary objects of type t exemplify. So abstract properties encode properties of properties, and abstract relations encode properties of relations, etc. In particular, abstract properties can encode properties that ordinary properties exemplify, and abstract relations encode properties that ordinary relations exemplify. In what follows, I'll sometimes refer to 'A-individuals' and 'A-properties' ('A-relations') to talk about these abstract entities, and refer to them generally (both A-individuals and A-relations) as 'A-objects'.

In our previous work, we used this typed theory of abstract objects as follows. If a term of natural language is a term of type t (i.e., denoted an object of type t), then we represent the sense of that term (with respect to some individual) as an A-object of type t. For example, the sense of a term denoting an individual is an abstract individual; the sense of a term denoting a relation is an abstract relation. So the sense of a term of natural language was analyzed as an abstract object of the very same logical type as denotation of the term.[16] We showed that this identification would explain how Fregean senses could be modes of presentation.

But, in present essay, we are interested in showing more generally that modes of presentation can be identified as A-objects. There are two basic reasons for thinking that modes of presentation can be identified as A-individuals and A-relations. The first is the fact that an A-object of type t can *represent* an ordinary object of type t, and the second is that ILAO predicts that A-individuals and A-relations can combine to form logical complexes which can represent structured (Russellian) propositions or states of affairs. In the remainder of this section, we examine the first reason, and we take up the second reason in the next section.

The first reason for thinking that modes of presentation can be identified as A-objects is that there is a clear sense in which A-objects can *re*present ordinary individuals and properties, namely, by encoding properties that ordinary individuals and properties exemplify. By saying that A-objects 'represent' ordinary objects, I do not mean to imply that A-objects are 'in the head'. A-objects are *not* in the head, though they can be used to classify what is in the head. As we shall see, A-objects can objectify the cognitive content of the mental tokens that are in the head. Of course, philosophers often suppose that the (intrinsically meaningless) mental tokens in our brains are the entities which 'represent' ordinary individuals and properties, and certainly there is a sense of 'represent' on which this may be true. But I am not using this sense of 'represent'. I am using 'represent' to mean a *way* of conceiving an object or property, and though an intrinsically meaningless mental token can be a vehicle by which an object or property is conceived, it is not a *way* of conceiving them if it is intrinsically contentless. I am using a sense of 'represent' on which the object which is doing the representing does so in virtue of some *content* which it has. A *way* of conceiving an ordinary individual or property involves some cognitive content by which that individual or property is conceived.

Let's look at an example of how an A-object can represent. Consider a person x having a veridical perception of some ordinary individual, say d, in x's visual field. In x's brain, some (intrinsically meaningless) mental token, call it '$\mathbf{d}$', becomes a mental symbol of d. In the perceptual encounter with d, certain properties strike x's cognitive apparatus as features of d. Just which properties strike x depend on the situation in which x encounters d, on how attentive x is, and on x's capacity for observation and discrimination. So the mental token $\mathbf{d}$ gets cognitively *linked* to (mental tokens of) those properties that x registers in the perceptual encounter.

Now I claim that the A-individual that encodes those properties, call it μ_1, just is the cognitive content of x's mental token $\mathbf{d}$, whereas d itself is the objective content of $\mathbf{d}$.[17] The objective content of a mental token is the object that is causally responsible for the token's existence and which stands at the beginning of the chain leading back to the first perceptual encounter. But whereas the token $\mathbf{d}$ is in the head, μ_1 is not. The A-individual μ_1 represents d for x because it objectifies the (cognitive) content that the mental token $\mathbf{d}$ has or plays in x's mental life. The token $\mathbf{d}$ then represents d to x both in the sense that it denotes d (d is its objective content), and more importantly for the present investigation, in the sense that μ_1 is one way by which x conceives of d (namely, the way which is defined by the particular group of properties it encodes).

Note that the A-individual μ_1 can represent the ordinary individual d for person x even though μ_1 encodes properties that d does not exemplify! Indeed, μ_1 may encode properties which individuate nothing, or which individuate something other than d. In cases of misinformation, such as non-veridical perceptions, properties which d doesn't really exemplify are presented in the context in which a mental token for d is created. Person x may take these properties to be characteristic of d and so these properties can be encoded by the A-individual μ_1 that is a mode of presentation of d for x. It is an *extrinsic* fact about μ_1 that it represents d for x; this fact is not a result of μ_1's intrinsic (encoded) properties. But note that since A-objects encode properties, they have an intrinsic content. For example, the properties that μ_1 encodes constitute its intrinsic content. That is what allows it to *be* a mode of presentation. It re-presents d to x by encoding properties that x takes to be characteristic of d. The more vivid the properties that are encoded, the more vivid a mode of presentation it is.

Before we extend these ideas to modes of presentation for properties and relations, it is worth pausing for a moment to note how easy it is to introduce the language of 'concepts' at this point by just identifying *concepts* with A-objects. Concepts of individuals may be identified as A-individuals that encode properties of individuals. (We'll see, in just a few paragraphs, that concepts of properties may be identified as A-properties that encode properties of properties.) Returning to the example we have been developing, we could say that μ_1 is one of the concepts that x has of d, namely, the concept of d that associated with the mental token **d**. If x encounters d (without knowing it is d) in some completely different situation, some new mental token **d$'$** could become created in x's cognitive architecture. The cognitive content of **d$'$**, call it the concept μ_2, would encode different properties from those encoded by μ_1. x might fail to recognize d because μ_2 would bear little resemblance to μ_1 (i.e., they would encode few properties in common). This identification of concepts has the added virtue that the precise existence and identity conditions for A-individuals now become existence and identity conditions for possible concepts.

We now extend these ideas to modes of presentation, and concepts, of properties and relations. Recall that we will be distinguishing ordinary properties and relations, conceived intensionally, from the hyperintensional modes of presentation, and concepts, by which we represent these entities.[18] Consider a being x that has the mental architecture to detect or perceive instances of some particular property, say P. Suppose x has perceptually encountered an exemplification instance of P for the first time and has registered that P is involved in the perception or is cognizing that the perception involves P. It seems that x's cognitive architecture must take steps to represent the property P by first creating a mental token, say '**P**'. Since various properties of properties will strike x's cognitive architecture as being characteristic of P, we can take the cognitive content of the mental token **P** to be the A-property which encodes these properties of properties. This A-property serves to represent P to x by encoding some of the properties that P itself may exemplify. For example, consider the property of being a circle, and let '**C**' denote the mental token for this property in x's brain, and let ξ_1 be an A-property that encodes one or more of the following properties of properties (all of which might have been cognized by x when x was becoming acquainted with the property of being a circle): being a shape that involves no straight lines, being a shape that is always uniformly curving, being a shape which can be inscribed with the help of a compass, being the geometric property exemplified by this particular figure on this particular printed page, etc. ξ_1 is clearly a mode of presentation for x of the property of being a circle. It is one of the concepts that x has for the property of being a circle.

Now of course, x may subsequently cognize the property of being a circle in a different way, say by a description, without realizing it. For example, x might learn some geometry, and encounter the shape which, in analytic geometry, is defined by the equation $a^2 + b^2 = c^2$, or the shape which, in Euclidean geometry, is defined as being a closed, plane figure every point of which lies equidistant from some given point. Now the properties in question (being a circle, being defined by the equation $a^2 + b^2 = c^2$ in analytic geometry, being a closed, plane figure ...) are all identical. But x may have different conceptions (i.e., different concepts) of this property. Each conception is a different mode of presentation, a different way of representing the property of being a circle in x's cognitive architecture. Consider, for example, the A-property, call it 'ξ_2', which encodes the following properties of properties: being a property F which can be defined by a certain equation in analytic geometry, being a property F which can be defined by a certain condition in Euclidean geometry, etc. Here we might have a case of 'recognition failure'; x may not recognize that the concept ξ_1 and the concept ξ_2 are concepts of the same property. Notice our switch here to the language of concepts. It seems natural to suppose that A-properties serve as our concepts of ordinary properties.

The foregoing remarks should be sufficient to establish that A-individuals and A-relations can represent ordinary objects and relations. This, you may recall, was the first reason for analyzing modes of presentation and concepts as A-objects. Before we turn to the second reason for doing so, we may summarize our analysis explicitly by way of the following equivalences:

> z^t is a *mode of presentation* [*concept*] *of* y^t *for* person x^i iff z^t is an abstract object of type t, y^t is an object of type t, and z^t is the cognitive content of some mental token in x^i's cognitive architecture which has y^t as its objective content

> z^t is a *mode of presentation* [*concept*] iff $\exists y^t \exists x^i (z^t$ is a mode of presentation [concept] of y^t for x^i)

Note that by supposing x's cognitive architecture to contain mental tokens that correspond to the linguistic expressions in x's vocabulary, then the cognitive content of a linguistic expression for x can be identified with the cognitive content of the corresponding mental token. It would follow that the sense of a linguistic expression for an individual is a mode of presentation.

It is important to point out that our analysis satisfies what Schiffer calls the 'Intrinsic Description Constraint' ([1990], 253; and [1992], 511). The entities in terms of which modes of presentation have been identified can be characterized independently of their role. As abstract objects, modes and concepts are intrinsically characterized by the axioms of our theory, and these are stated in terms of the notion of encoding. Encoding is the central notion of object theory, just as set membership is the central notion of set theory. If one accepts (as Schiffer does) that the notion of set membership and the axioms of set theory suffice to intrinsically characterize sets, one should accept that the notion of encoding and the axioms of object theory intrinsically characterize A-objects.[19]

3: Plugging the Theoretical Gap

The second reason for thinking that modes of presentation, and concepts, of individuals and relations can be identified with A-individuals and A-relations, respectively, is that under such an identification, ILAO predicts that modes of presentation (concepts) of relations can be combined with modes of presentation (concepts) of individuals to yield modes of presentation (concepts) of propositions or states of affairs. The formal semantics developed for ILAO in previous work makes use of a logical operation, the **PLUG** operation,[20] which can take objects $o_1,...,o_n$, having types $t_1,...,t_n$, respectively, and 'plugs' them into a relation of type $\langle t_1,...,t_n \rangle$, producing a 0-place logical structure (of type p). The relation here need not be a primitive relation (it maybe complex) and the objects here need not be individuals (but they have to be objects of a type which is appropriate for a given argument place of the relation). In the simplest case, the **PLUG** function can combine ordinary individuals and an ordinary relation among individuals to produce an ordinary 'Russellian' proposition (or, if you prefer, a 'state of affairs').[21] It can also combine A-individuals and an A-relation to produce a logical complex which is structurally identical to a Russellian proposition yet which contains only abstract constituents. But note that an A-object of type t can occupy any place of a 0-place logical complex that an ordinary object of type t can occupy. So **PLUG** can even combine any individuals, ordinary or abstract, with either an ordinary or an abstract relation to produce a logical complex which is structurally identical to a Russellian proposition but which has a mixture of abstract and ordinary constituents. These 'mixed' complexes will prove to be useful.

The point here is that by identifying modes of presentation (and concepts) with A-objects, ILAO predicts the existence of complex modes of presentation (and complex concepts). These latter can be used to analyze 'ways of conceiving' Russellian propositions or states of affairs; they are structurally identical to Russellian propositions but they may have an abstract constituent of type t where the Russellian proposition has an ordinary constituent of type t. In terms of the language of concepts, we could say that a way of conceiving an (atomic) proposition is defined whenever **PLUG** combines the concepts of individuals with a concept of a relation.

In previous work, this analysis gave us a clear theory of Fregean thoughts. The Fregean sense of a predicate was identified as an A-relation, and the Fregean senses of individual terms were identified as A-individuals. So the existence of Fregean thoughts was predicted by ILAO.[22] Since Frege never told us what senses and thoughts were, our identification fills the theoretical gap in his work.

Notice also, that if we focus on ILAO's analysis of Fregean senses as A-objects, we can easily interpret, and fill the theoretical gap, in the works of Kaplan and Forbes cited at the outset. These two philosophers discuss Fregean senses (as modes of presentation) in their work without providing a theory of them. Consider first Kaplan's work, in which we find the following analyses of a 'relational' (as opposed to 'notional') belief ([1969], item (44)):

(K) $\exists \alpha [\mathbf{R}(\alpha, \text{Ortcutt}, \text{Ralph}) \ \& \ \text{Ralph } \mathbf{B}^\ulcorner \alpha \text{ is a spy}^\urcorner]$

In this analysis, $\mathbf{R}(\alpha, \text{Ortcutt}, \text{Ralph})$ asserts that α represents Ortcutt to Ralph. Although the variable α at this point in Kaplan's paper stands for an expression, Kaplan later admits that this is inadequate to the task ([1969], Section XII):

> When earlier I argued for Frege's method—seek the intermediate entity—it was on the grounds that a clarified view of the problem was worth at least momentary ontological risk. But now it appears that to give adequate expression to the epistemological situation requires explicit quantification certification of the status of such entities. I am undismayed and even would urge that the conservative course so far followed of taking expressions as the intermediate entities is clearly inadequate to the task.

Kaplan then discusses the cases in which the mode of presentation involves not words but sensory images, impressions, sounds, etc. These are part of what makes names *vivid*.

We can now identify the 'missing intermediate entities' which Kaplan discusses if we take the variable α to range over our A-individuals. We've seen how these objects can *represent* ordinary objects to individuals. That gives us an interpretation of the clause '$\mathbf{R}(\alpha, \text{Ortcutt}, \text{Ralph})$' in (K) above. Moreover, we can interpret the clause 'Ralph $\mathbf{B}^\ulcorner\alpha$ is a spy$^\urcorner$' in (K) as follows. Let $\mathbf{S}$ be the A-property which serves as the sense of 'is a spy'. Then, given our previous identification of α in (K) as A-individual, the second clause simply relates Ralph to the proposition $\mathbf{PLUG}(\mathbf{S}, \alpha)$. This is the propositional complex which has α plugged into Ralph's sense of the predicate 'is a spy'. Finally, Kaplan's talk of *vivid* names now makes more sense—if the mode of presentation Ralph associates with a name of Ortcutt is an A-individual that encodes vivid (i.e., visual or other perceptual) properties, then that name will become a 'vivid name' of Ortcutt for Ralph.

The theory also provides an interpretation for the uninterpreted notation used by Forbes. Recall that Forbes uses the variables α, β to range over modes of presentation and represents the fact that a mode of presentation α has combined with the sense of the predicate 'F' to form a complex sense by using the notation: $\alpha^{\wedge\ulcorner}F^\urcorner$. There is a natural interpretation of this on the present view. The variables α, β may be interpreted to range over A-individuals. We may take $^\ulcorner$F$^\urcorner$ to be the A-property which serves as the sense of the predicate 'F'.[23] Then the notation $\alpha^{\wedge\ulcorner}F^\urcorner$ can be interpreted as representing the Fregean thought $\mathbf{PLUG}(^\ulcorner F^\urcorner, \alpha)$. With these suggestions, then, we eliminate a theoretical gap in this recent work in defense of Frege's theory of senses.

We next consider how ILAO now provides a framework for those analyses of attitudes and attitude reports which appeal to modes of presentation without appealing to Frege's notion of sense. Salmon, for example, eschews senses and works directly with modes of presentation in analyzing attitudes. Although Salmon uses a 2-place 'B' relation to analyze belief reports, he uses a 3-place *BEL* relation to analyze beliefs. Our identification of modes of presentation fills the theoretical gap in Salmon's analysis since it offers a precise understanding of the 'ways of taking Russellian propositions' which serve as one of the arguments to the *BEL* relation. Here is how.

Consider, for example, the following claims:

(3) Hammurabi believed that Hesperus is not made of water.

(5) Hammurabi didn't believe that Phosphorous is not made of H_2O.

The pure *de re* readings of (3) and (5), in ILAO, are:

(3a) $B(b,[\lambda \neg Wh])$

(5a) $\neg B(b,[\lambda \neg Hp])$

Given the identity statements '$W = H$' and '$h = p$', these are inconsistent reports. But Salmon analyzes the underlying beliefs as consistent. Consider how we can develop further analyses of (3a) and (5a) which are very much in the spirit of Salmon's analysis ([1986], 111) even if they don't follow it to the letter. In ILAO, Salmon's *BEL* relation would be of type $\langle i, p, p \rangle$ and so holds between an individual and two 0-place logical complexes of type p. $BEL(x,q,r)$ holds just in case the person x believes q by means of the complex mode of presentation r. Now, following Salmon's basic idea, we could claim that (3a) and (5a) respectively entail such claims as (6) and (7), respectively, where $ModeOf(z^t, y^t, x^i)$ is a predicate representing the notion "z^t is a mode of presentation (concept) of y^t for x^{i}" (which we analyzed at the end of Section 2):

(6) $\exists z^i \exists F^{\langle i \rangle} \exists q(ModeOf(z,h,b)$ & $ModeOf(F,W,b)$ & $q = [\lambda \neg Fz]$ &
     $BEL(b,[\lambda \neg Wh],q))$

(7) $\exists z^i \exists F^{\langle i \rangle} \exists q(ModeOf(z,p,b)$ & $ModeOf(F,H,b)$ & $q = [\lambda \neg Fz]$ &
     $\neg BEL(b,[\lambda \neg Hp],q))$

These assert, respectively:

(8) There exists a concept z of type i, a concept F of type $\langle i \rangle$, and a logical complex q of type p such that (i) z is a mode of presentation of Hesperus for Hammurabi, (ii) F is a mode of presentation of being made of water for Hammurabi, (iii) q is the complex *that z doesn't exemplify F*, and (iii) Hammurabi stands in the *BEL* relation to the proposition *that Hesperus exemplifies being visible in the evening* by means of the complex q

(9) There exists a concept z of type i, a concept F of type $\langle i \rangle$, and a logical complex q of type p such that (i) z is a mode of presentation of Phosphorus for Hammurabi, (ii) F is a mode of presentation of the property of being made of H_2O for Hammurabi, (ii) q is the complex *that z doesn't exemplify F*, and (iii) Hammurabi fails to stand in the *BEL* relation to the proposition *that Phosphorus doesn't exemplify being made of H_2O* by means of the complex q.

(6) and (7) are clearly formulable in ILAO, and they show how an analysis similar to the one proposed by Salmon, reflecting the consistency of Hammurabi's beliefs, can be spelled out in precise detail.

So it remains for us to examine the recent work by Crimmins. Here is where our hybrid, or 'mixed' logical complexes, in which A-individuals are plugged into the argument places of ordinary relations, come into play. In [1998], Crimmins considers Hammurabi's belief that Hesperus is visible in the evening. He says ([1998], 11):

> Where m_H is the mode of presentation in question, the fictional truth turns on the claim diagrammed in (10):
>
> (10) Hammurabi believed: $[m_H]$ is visible in the evening.

... In (10), we are using the bracket notation in a formula that, in describing a belief, partly describes what is allegedly believed to be so, and also describes the agent's alleged way of thinking of the subject matter of the belief. The formula (10) portrays a state of affairs that obtains just in case Hammurabi had a belief ascribing evening visibility, and this belief involved the mode of presentation m_H in the "subject position." (It does not entail that Hammurabi's belief is *about* the mode of presentation.)

Crimmins then notes that (10) is not the most perspicuous notation, and that a more perspicuous (and more complex) notation would make it clear that the mode of presentation is not part of the propositional object of belief. But I am intrigued by the fact that Crimmins uses the simpler notation in his paper to regiment belief reports (cf. Zalta [1983], 130; [1988], 161-173; and [1989], 461). Let us consider whether we might take this simpler regimentation at face value and address Crimmins' reasons for not doing so.

Using the simpler notation, Crimmins analyzes the truth conditions of (11) as (12) ([1998], 12):

(11) Hesperus, but not Phosphorus, was thought by Hammurabi to be visible in the evening.

(12) Hammurabi believed: $[m_H]$ is visible in the evening, but Hammurabi did not believe $[m_P]$ is visible in the evening.

Now, as we've said, Crimmins explicits disavows the idea that modes of presentation are constituents of thoughts. Nevertheless, we can interpret (12) directly in ILAO! Since the notation Crimmins uses doesn't index the mode of presentation to Hammurabi, let us use $\underline{\mathbf{h}}$ as the semantic name of the mode of presentation Crimmins refers to as '$[m_H]$', and use $\underline{\mathbf{p}}$ as the semantic name of the mode of presentation Crimmins refers to as '$[m_P]$'. Then if we use '$\mathbf{V}$' as a semantic name of the property of being visible, ILAO asserts the existence of the propositions $\mathbf{PLUG(V,\underline{h})}$ and $\mathbf{PLUG(V,\underline{p})}$. The most straightforward interpretation of (12), then, is to regard it as asserting that Hammurabi is related to the first, and not the second, of these two propositions.

Of course, it is essential here not to confuse these truth conditions of the belief report with the truth conditions of the beliefs being reported. The truth conditions of the beliefs being reported have to be stated in terms of the ordinary Russellian proposition having the property of being visible and Venus itself as constituents. We can say Hammurabi's belief is 'about' these entities, and this respects Crimmins' injunction that Hammurabi's belief is not *about* the mode of presentation. So whereas the truth of the belief report in (12) relates Hammurabi to $\mathbf{PLUG(V,\underline{h})}$, the belief of Hammurabi's which is being reported is true iff the proposition $\mathbf{PLUG(V,h)}$ is true, i.e., iff Venus is visible in the evening. This distinction, between the truth of the belief report and the truth of the belief reported, will come up again in the next section.[24]

It is important to point out here that Crimmins developed the analysis (12) from within the context of a 'pretense-theoretic' account of belief reports, one which extends the ideas in Walton [1990]. Crimmins certainly does not regard modes of presentation as abstract objects ([1998], 8). Instead, he supposes that a pretense-theoretic account of modes can be given. But even though it might seem that our understanding of (12) in ILAO is inconsistent with Crimmin's own understanding of (12), this may not be the case. In [2000b], we develop a rapprochement between object theory and pretense theory. Abstract objects can be understood as entities which the pretense theorist accepts and over which she quantifies, namely, patterns of pretense behavior and manners of speaking. This rapprochement may be consistent with Crimmins' own pretense-theoretic conception of modes of presentation.[25] I won't, however, pursue this question any further in the present paper.

4: An Unresolved Technical Issue

There is an interesting technical issue that arises concerning the best way of developing a new analysis of attitude reports *within the logic* ILAO. In previous work, we have represented such reports as having multiple readings. Reconsider (3) and (5), for example.

(3) Hammurabi believed that Hesperus is not made of water.

(5) Hammurabi didn't believe that Phosphorous is not made of H_2O.

According to the plan developed in our previous work, (3) and (5) could each have up to four readings. However, given that Hesperus is Phosphorus ($h = p$) and that being made of water just is being made of H_2O ($W = H$), the readings on which (3) and (5) are consistent are the pure *de dicto* readings:

(3b) $B(b, [\lambda \neg \underline{W}_b \underline{h}_b])$

(5b) $\neg B(b, [\lambda \neg \underline{H}_b \underline{p}_b])$

The relation denoted by 'B' is of type $\langle i, \langle \rangle \rangle$ and therefore relates an individual to a 0-place logical complex. The '$\underline{W}_b$' and '$\underline{H}_b$' denote distinct A-properties, while an '$\underline{h}_b$' and '$\underline{p}_b$' denote distinct A-individuals.

But the expressions '$\underline{W}_b$', '$\underline{H}_b$', '$\underline{h}_b$' and '$\underline{p}_b$' represent the senses of the expressions 'is made of water', 'is made of H_2O', 'Hesperus', and 'Phosphorus' for Hammurabi, respectively. As we noted at the end of Section 1, we should like to find a way to avoid representing the truth conditions of reports like (3) and (5) in terms of Hammurabi's senses of English expressions. So, the question is whether we can introduce notation that picks out appropriate modes of presentation for the analysis of (3) and (5) *without* further identifying them as the Fregean senses of the terms in question. This is an interesting question because a problem of uniqueness arises. For example, if we cannot consider the sense of the expression 'Hesperus' for Hammurabi, how are we to understand 'Hesperus' in (3) so that it both picks out one of the many modes of presentation by which Hammurabi conceived of Venus and contributes that mode to the truth conditions of the belief report? The problem becomes even more acute in the case of predicates. How are we to pick out the relevant concepts by which Hammurabi conceived of the property of being made of water without incorrectly treating those concepts as the senses, for Hammurabi, of the English expressions 'is made of water' and 'is made of H_2O'? Can we introduce notation which somehow picks out the relevant modes of presentation, either by using a choice function to interpret the notation or by supposing that the context in which the report is uttered will suffice to isolate the relevant modes of presentation by which Hammurabi conceived of Venus and the property of being made of water?

To summarize, then, we are now interested in the question of whether we can develop in ILAO a *new reading* of belief reports which invokes modes of presentation without invoking senses. To present the question in a maximally explicit way, consider the notation '$\underline{h}_x$', where this is supposed to pick out a mode of presentation by which x conceives of Hesperus. Suppose that we interpret this notation as follows: if given assignment function f to the variable x, a choice function g maps '$\underline{h}_x$' to one of the modes of presentation by which $f(x)$ conceives of Hesperus (i.e., Venus). If we enhance our formalism with ϵ-expressions, we might even consider such notation as abbreviations of formal expressions of ILAO as follows. That is, we might introduce:

$\underline{h}_x =_{abbr} \epsilon z(ModeOf(z, h, x))$

We would read the ϵ-term as "an individual z such that z is a mode of presentation of h (Hesperus) for x". (We may suppose that if there is no object z that is a mode of presentation of Hesperus for x, then the ϵ-term denotes the null abstract object of type i, i.e., the A-individual which encodes no properties.) Now suppose, further, that 'p_x' is introduced in the same way. Similarly, if 'W' denotes being made of water and 'H' denotes being made of H_2O (i.e., the same property), we might introduce:

$$\underline{\underline{W}}_b \ =_{abbr} \ \epsilon F^{\langle i \rangle}(ModeOf(F, V, b)),$$

and do something similar for '$\underline{\underline{H}}_b$'.

In terms of this new notation, we might offer the following as a new analysis of (3) and (5):

(3c) $B(b, [\lambda \neg \underline{\underline{W}}_b \underline{\underline{h}}_b])$

(5c) $\neg B(b, [\lambda \neg \underline{\underline{H}}_b \underline{\underline{p}}_b])$

On this analysis, the (3) is true just in case Hammurabi stands in the 2-place belief relation to the negation of a logical complex in which some mode of presentation of Hesperus for Hammurabi is 'plugged' into some mode of presentation of the property of being made of water for Hammurabi. Similarly, (5) is true iff Hammurabi fails to stand in the 2-place belief relation to the negation of a logical complex in which some mode of presentation of Phosphorus for Hammurabi is 'plugged' into some mode of presentation of the property of being made of H_2O for Hammurabi.[26] And, if we generalize our new notation in the obvious way, we could return to Schiffer's problem case (2) and offer the following new reading:

(2c) $\forall x(Kxm \rightarrow B(x, [\lambda \, \underline{\underline{M}}_x \underline{\underline{m}}_x]))$

On this analysis, the truth conditions of (2) would be that every (person) x who has known (seen) Madonna stands in the belief relation to a logical complex which has as constituents some mode of presentation of the property of being musical and some mode of presentation of Madonna.

Even though these new analyses look promising, there is a problem. Under their present interpretations, there is no guarantee that '$\underline{\underline{h}}_b$' and '$\underline{\underline{p}}_b$' will be assigned *distinct* modes of presentation. Without such a guarantee, we cannot rest assured that (3c) and (5c) are consistent. An analogous problem holds for '$\underline{\underline{W}}_b$' and '$\underline{\underline{H}}_b$'. Is there some other way of interpreting '$\underline{\underline{h}}_b$' and '$\underline{\underline{p}}_b$' (and '$\underline{\underline{W}}_b$' and '$\underline{\underline{H}}_b$') which ensures that these pairs of expressions pick out different modes of presentation? Or can we relativize the interpretation of ϵ-terms to a context, and legitimately suppose that such a relativization can ensure that distinct modes of presentation will be assigned whenever appropriate?

It is unclear to me, at present, whether this technical issue can be nicely resolved, and if so, what is the best resolution. So I am uncertain about what is the best way to extend ILAO so as to develop analyses of attitude reports which appeal to modes of presentation that aren't conceived as senses. (At least, we have found a new reason to appreciate the tight theoretical connection between senses and modes in Frege's theory.) Although further study is in order, it should be reiterated that even if no nice resolution can be found, our identification of modes of presentation and concepts as A-objects nevertheless provides a framework for other possible analyses of attitude reports which appeal to these entities, as we have seen.[27]

5: Concluding Remarks on Concepts

The present theory of concepts treats concepts of individuals as A-individuals and treats concepts of properties and relations as A-properties and A-relations. This gives us a *new* understanding of what it is to 'possess a concept'. Consider the example of the property of being red. A sighted person with an ordinary visual system, assuming they haven't been enclosed in a colorless room since birth, etc., will become acquainted with the property of being red and be able to learn properly how to use the predicate 'is red'. When philosophers say that such a person 'posseses the concept red', they usually mean that the person in question has had visual experiences of red things, is (thereby) acquainted with the property of redness, and/or can properly use the term 'red'. In the present essay, however, we are distinguishing properties and concepts. The present theory allows us to give a new explanation of how a blind person or individual deprived of red stimuli can understand and use the term 'red' and even be said to 'possess the concept red'. This new explanation involves our theoretical notion of a concept and goes as follows.

Although the blind person, or person deprived of red stimuli, has no acquaintance with property *being red*, he or she can nevertheless have one or more concepts of the property of being red. Each concept is something that encodes properties that the property of being red may exemplify, such as being the color of fire engines, being the color of traffic lights which indicate 'stop', Bill's favorite color, being the color of ultraviolet light with a certain frequency, etc. The properties of properties encoded can characterize the property of being red to a blind or sensory-deprived person who has had no visual experiences of red things. Concepts that encode such properties may serve as the cognitive content of some mental token for the property of being red. Now suppose that a blind or sensory-deprived person, say x, has such a mental token, say $\mathbf{R}$, and that $\mathbf{R}$ has a certain cognitive content, say ξ_3. If the A-property ξ_3 comes to serve as the cognitive content of a term of natural language, say the term 'red', then x can understand and use the term on the basis of the conception that x has of the denotation of the term. Similarly, a blind mathematician, with no visual experiences of circular objects, might possess several

concepts of the property of being circle, one by way of the Euclidean definition and one by way of the definition in analytic geometry. Each definition
yields distinct properties of the property of being a circle, and these distinct
properties of properties are encoded by distinct A-properties.

This new explanation suggests that 'possessing a concept' can be a matter
of degree. Our judgement that x does 'possess the concept red', for example,
should be based on (i) the degree to which the properties of properties encoded
by x's concept of red are properties that are in fact exemplified by the property
of being red, and (ii) the degree to which the properties of properties encoded
reflect intrinsic properties of being red. Similarly, in the case where F is a more
abstract property, such as being a brother, being a number, etc., then the question of whether x 'possesses the concept' will depend on the degree to which
the A-property which serves as x's 'F'-concept encodes defining or other properties of properties which are exemplified by the property F. This can be tested,
since these A-properties will ground x's propositional attitudes about the property F. By this I mean that the properties encoded by x's concepts of y are the
source of the beliefs x has about y.

Philosophers can define several notions here. One might be said to 'possess the concept F' simply by having a concept of F (in the present sense)
which encodes a single, defining property of properties. Or one might 'possess
the concept F' by having a concept of F (in the present sense) which encodes a
sufficient number of properties of properties all of which the property F in fact
exemplifies. Thus, the *failure* to 'possess the concept F' can come about in
various ways. This will often be a matter of degree, since our concepts of a
property F may be inaccurate if they also encode properties of properties that
F *fails* to exemplify. As the number of such properties becomes greater, the
more inaccurate the concept becomes. In such cases, there may come a point
where we have to say that x just fails to have the concept of F.

Notes

*This paper originally circulated, and may have been cited, under the titles 'Modes
of Presentation and Belief Reports' and 'Modes of Presentation and Fregean Senses'.
Even though these earlier versions have been revised in numerous ways, some of
the work in them survives in this final version.

†I would like to acknowledge the support I've received from the Center for the
Study of Language and Information as well as my indebtedness to John Perry, Mark
Textor, and Jonathan Berg for conversations on the topics discussed in the paper. I
am also indebted to the Philosophy Department at the University of Alberta, where
I received many interesting comments after presenting this work.

1. The axioms for the theory have been presented in various works, including Zalta
   [1983], [1988], [1993b] and [1999].
2. It is important to note that the notion of 'concept' we consider in the present paper
   is to be distinguished from the notion that was the subject of Zalta [2000a]. In the
   present paper, I am interested in the notion that comes to us from the contemporary

tradition in the philosophy of mind and language. In [2000a], I was interested in systematizing the Leibnizian notion of a concept.

3. In Kaplan [1969], we find (p. 119):

> My own view is that Frege's explanation, by way of ambiguity, of what appears to be the logically deviant behavior of terms in intermediate contexts is so theoretically satisfying that if we have not yet discovered or satisfactorialy grasped the peculiar intermediate objects in question, then we should simply continue looking.

It should be mentioned, however, that in recent years, Kaplan has changed his view on these matters.

4. In [1987], Forbes says (p. 31):

> My overall conclusion is that a Fregean theory of the semantics of attitude contexts is from the structural point of view the best that is available. Its ultimate viability depends of course on how successful the efforts to develop a detailed theory of the nature of modes of presentation will be.

Such a theory is not developed in Forbes' paper.

5. In Salmon [1986], a belief report 'x believes that S' is analyzed as $B(x, p)$ (where p is the Russellian proposition denoted by the sentence S). But this in turn is equivalent to $\exists y (BEL(x, p, y))$, where y is something like a mode of presentation of the proposition p.

6. Near the end of [1986], we find (p. 126):

> The major problem remaining for the sort of theory I have advocated here is to provide a more complete account of the things corresponding to propositional recognition failure, the things that serve as the third relatum for the *BEL* relation.

When canvassing the possibilities (p. 120), Salmon suggests that this third relatum could be a 'way of taking' the proposition, a 'mode of presentation', or a 'mental file'.

7. In [1998] (25), Crimmins writes:

> The pretense account employs the notion of a mode of presentation, and nothing could be more important in assessing the account than determining the prospects for satisfying explanations of what modes of presentation are, and of the access to them that speakers and hearers rely on in producing and understanding attitude reports.

Crimmins then refers us to his earlier work on this question. See the following footnote.

8. In [1998] (25, note 17), Crimmins refers us his [1992] for more discussion about modes of presentation. But the discussion in [1992] is about 'representations' (i.e., notions and ideas), which Crimmins takes to be concrete mental particulars. He says explicitly there ([1992], 78) that these are not ways of thinking or modes of presentation. But in [1998], he seems to be talking about Fregean modes of presentation, not concrete particulars. See, for example, the first paragraph of Section 2 ([1998], 8).

9. This will contrast with analyses which treat such reports as asserting 3-place relations. See, for example, Crimmins and Perry [1989], or Perry [1979] and Fitch [1987].

Our analysis will also contrast with the 2-place Russellian analyses found in McKay [1981], Salmon [1986], and Soames [1989], since we shall treat belief reports as ambiguous.

10. The intensional logic for abstract objects was developed in its most sophisticated form in my [1988]. However, readers familiar with Zalta [1983], [1989], or [1993a] should be in a good position to understand the material in this paper.

11. I have revised Schiffer's example from 'Ralph believes Fido is a dog' to 'Ralph believes that Fido is a woodchuck'. To discuss further aspects of the case, Schiffer introduces the fictional species name 'schmog', as a second name for the species *dog*. In case we have to remark on the further aspects of the case, I prefer to use the real example of 'woodchuck' and 'groundhog', which are names of the same species.

12. Some philosophers might claim that this assumption is too strong. They argue that there is a very weak kind of sense on which each proper name has a single sense that is shared by all the competent speakers of a language. But if this is true, the present theory could still offer an account of such senses. These weak senses could be identified as abstract objects that encode the minimally informative properties involved. For example, the universal sense of 'Madonna' could be an abstract object which encodes such properties as being a name, being a name of Madonna, or being a name of someone called 'Madonna', etc. No circularity worries accompany such an view, since we would not use the sense of a term to determine the denotation of a term. But I shall not pursue this alternative theory of sense in what follows.

13. See Zalta [1983], Chapter VI, and [1988], Chapters 9–12. To handle more complex examples, such as Kripke's [1979] 'Paderewski' case, ILAO is designed so that the sense of a term can vary from time to time for any given person. But I will not examine such complicated cases here. See Zalta [1988], 195-6.

14. These are not on the list of suspects that Schiffer ([1990], 254-265) rejects as answers to the question 'What are modes of presentation?'.

15. On this typing scheme, $F^{\langle t_1, \ldots, t_n \rangle} x^{t_1} \ldots x^{t_n}$ is a well-formed exemplification formula and $x^t F^{\langle t \rangle}$ is a well-formed encoding formula. For any logical type t (whether individual, relation, or proposition), the theory postulates abstract things of type t as follows:

$$\exists x^t (A!^{\langle t \rangle} x^t \,\&\, \forall F^{\langle t \rangle} (xF \equiv \phi)), \text{ where } \phi \text{ has no free } xs.$$

The domain of each type t therefore divides up into ordinary things of that type (which do not encode properties) and the abstract things of that type. The abstract things of a type will encode and exemplify the same kinds of properties that the ordinary things of that type just exemplify.

16. Consider, then, how this stands in contrast to the typing schemes in Church [1951] and Montague [1974]. On those schemes, the sense or intension of a term is always an entity of higher or different type than that denoted by the term.

17. Note that this distinction between the objective content and cognitive content of the mental token **d** is the same distinction which we developed in previous work ([1988], 158) with respect to the terms of natural language. A term of natural language has both an objective content (its denotation) and a cognitive content (its sense) for the person using or hearing the term.

18. Ordinary properties and relations have precise existence and identity conditions. Their existence conditions are governed by a comprehension principle ([1983], 31; [1988], 46; [1993b], 405; [1999], 623), while their identity conditions have

been defined in terms of the notion of encoding. The identity conditions for properties are quite easy to state: ordinary properties F and G (of any complex type $\langle t \rangle$) are identical just in case necessarily, F and G are encoded by the same objects (of type t).

19. In addition, our theory of modes of presentation does not suffer from Schiffer's 'regress problem' ([1990], 68). The reason is that they serve to characterize the cognitive contents of mental tokens. Our mental tokens exist in a finite network in which tokens are are linked to one another: tokens of individuals are linked to tokens of properties, tokens of properties are linked to tokens of properties of properties, etc. But there is no regress because the structure of tokens is a finite one. So there is a finite set of logical types of A-objects that serve to characterize the contents of the various tokens. The structure branches only into those higher-typed entities of which we have actual conceptions.

20. The function **PLUG** is an algebraic operation that semantically corresponds to exemplification predication. It has been defined in numerous technical publications. Compare the *pred* and **PLUG** functions in the following publications: Bealer [1979], Parsons [1980], McMichael and Zalta [1980], Bealer [1982], Zalta [1983], and Menzel [1986].

21. On the present usage, 'Russellian proposition' and 'state of affairs' are used interchangeably. Some philosophers may wish to reserve the word 'proposition' to refer to complexes consisting of *concepts* of individuals and relations. Those philosophers will have to remember that in what follows, our usage of 'Fregean thought' corresponds to their usage of 'proposition'.

22. Though Frege would say that the sense of the predicate 'F' maps the sense of the individual term 'a' to a thought, in ILAO, it is the **PLUG** function that maps the sense of 'F' and the sense of 'a' to the thought expressed by the sentence 'a is F'. Moreover, each of the senses involved is relativized to a person and **PLUG** maps those senses to the thought the sentence expresses for that person.

23. Note that Forbes is assuming that the sense of a predicate does not vary from person to person.

24. The distinction between the truth of the belief report and the truth of the belief reported was defined precisely in [1983] (130), [1988] (175), and [1989] (462).

25. Consider the remarks that Crimmins makes about the connection between modes of presentation and pretense in [1998] (10, 26). He talks about manners of speaking and our access to certain modes of presentation.

26. The logical complexes can be described semantically in terms of **PLUG** and the **NEG** operations as:

$$\textbf{NEG}(\textbf{PLUG}(\textbf{P}, \textbf{a})), \text{ and}$$
$$\textbf{NEG}(\textbf{PLUG}(\textbf{Q}, \textbf{b})),$$

where '**P**' is a semantic name of the mode of presentation denoted by '$\underline{W}_b$', '**Q**' is a semantic name of the mode of presentation denoted by '$\underline{H}_b$', and '**a**' is a semantic name of the mode of presentation denoted by '$\underline{h}_b$' and '**b**' is a semantic name of the mode of presentation denoted by '$\underset{=}{p}_b$'. See Zalta [1983] or [1988] for the semantic definition of **NEG**.

27. Recently, S. Boër (1994, 1995) has begun to modify and extend ILAO in new ways, in an attempt to clarify the idea of a language of thought and to interpret such a language. It is not yet clear to me how the work in the present paper aligns with

358 / Edward N. Zalta

Boër's work. He has attempted to develop the syntax and semantics of Mentalese within an enhanced version of ILAO.

References

Bealer, G., 1982, *Quality and Concept*, Oxford: Oxford University Press
Bealer, G., 1979, 'Theories of Properties, Relations, and Propositions', *The Journal of Philosophy*, **76**: 634-648
Boër, S., 1994, 'Propositional Attitudes and Formal Ontology', *Synthese*, **98**: 187–242
Boër, S., 1995, 'Propositional Attitudes and Compositional Semantics', *Philosophical Perspectives* **9**, Atascadero: Ridgeview, pp. 341-380.
Church, A., 1951, 'A Formulation of the Logic of Sense and Denotation', *Structure, Method, and Meaning* New York: The Liberal Arts Press
Crimmins, M., 1998, 'Hesperus and Phosphorus: Sense, Pretense, and Reference', *Philosophical Review*, **107**/1 (January): 1-47
Crimmins, M., 1992, *Talk About Beliefs*, Cambridge, MA: MIT Press
Crimmins, M., and Perry, J., 1989, 'The Prince and the Phone Booth: Reporting Puzzling Beliefs', *Journal of Philosophy* **86**/12: 685–711
Fitch, G., 1987, *Naming and Believing*, Dordrecht: D. Reidel
Forbes, G., 1987, 'Indexicals and Intensionality: A Fregean Perspective', *The Philosophical Review* **96** (January): 3–31
Forbes, G., 1990, 'The Indispensability of *Sinn*', *The Philosophical Review* **99** (October): 535–563
Frege, G., 1892, 'Über Sinn und Bedeutung', *Zeitschrift für Philosophie und philosophische Kritik*, **C** (1892): 25–50.
Kaplan, D., 1969, 'Quantifying In', in *Words and Objections: Essays on the Work of W. V. Quine*, D. Davidson and J. Hintikka (eds.), Dordrecht: D. Reidel, 1969, pp. 178–214; reprinted in *Reference and Modality*, L. Linsky (ed.), Oxford: Oxford University Press, 1971, pp. 112–144. (Page reference is to the reprint.)
Kripke, S., 1979, 'A Puzzle About Belief', in *Meaning and Use*, A. Margalit (ed.), Dordrecht: D. Reidel, pp. 239–283
Menzel, C., 1986, 'A Complete, Type-free 'Second-order' Logic and Its Philosophical Foundations', Technical Report No. CSLI–86–40, STANFORD, CA: CSLI PUBLICATIONS
McKay, T., 1981, 'On Proper Names in Belief Ascriptions', *Philosophical Studies* **39**, pp. 287–303
McMichael. A. and Zalta, E., 1980, 'An Alternative Theory of Nonexistent Objects', *Journal of Philosophical Logic*, **9**, 297–313
Montague, R., 1974, *Formal Philosophy*, R. Thomason, ed., New Haven: Yale University Press
Parsons, T., 1980, *Nonexistent Objects*, New Haven: Yale University Press
Perry, J., 1979, 'The Problem of the Essential Indexical', *Nous* **13**: 3–21
Salmon, N., 1986, *Frege's Puzzle*, Cambridge, MA: MIT/Bradford
Schiffer, S., 1992, 'Belief Ascriptions', *The Journal of Philosophy*, 89, 499–521
Schiffer, S., 1990, 'The Mode-of-Presentation Problem', in C. A. Anderson and J. Owens, eds., *Propositional Attitudes: The Role of Content in Logic, Language, and Mind*, Stanford: CSLI Publications, 1990, pp. 249–268
Soames, S., 1989, 'Direct Reference and Propositional Attitudes', in
Themes from Kaplan, J. Almog, J. Perry, and H. Wettstein, eds., Oxford: Oxford University Press, 1989, pp. 393–419
Walton, K., 1990, *Mimesis as Make-Believe*, Cambridge, MA: Harvard University Press
Zalta, E., 2000a, 'A (Leibnizian) Theory of Concepts', *Philosophiegeschichte und logische Analyse / Logical Analysis and History of Philosophy*, **3**: 137–183
————, 2000b, 'The Road Between Pretense Theory and Object Theory', in *Empty Names, Fiction, and the Puzzles of Non-Existence*, A. Everett and T. Hofweber (eds.), Stanford: CSLI Publications, pp. 117–147

————, 1999, 'Natural Numbers and Natural Cardinals as Abstract Objects: A Partial Reconstruction of Frege's *Grundgesetze* in Object Theory', *Journal of Philosophical Logic*, **28**/6: 619–660

————, 1993a, 'Replies to the Critics', *Philosophical Studies*, **69**, 231–242

————, 1993b, 'Twenty-Five Basic Theorems in Situation and World Theory', *Journal of Philosophical Logic*, **22**, 385–428

————, 1989, 'Singular Propositions, Abstract Constituents, and Propositional Attitudes', in *Themes from Kaplan*, J. Almog, J. Perry, and H. Wettstein, eds., Oxford: Oxford University Press, pp. 455–478

————, 1988, *Intensional Logic and the Metaphysics of Intentionality*, Cambridge, MA: MIT/Bradford

————, 1983, *Abstract Objects: An Introduction to Axiomatic Metaphysics*, Dordrecht: D. Reidel

CAUSAL STRUCTURALISM[1]

John Hawthorne
Syracuse University

How should we think as metaphysicians about the nature of properties? A promising place to begin, perhaps, is with the following observation: Properties confer causal powers upon the things that have them. Being spherical confers a capacity to roll. Being hot confers a capacity to make ice melt. Being possessed with mass confers a capacity for gravitationally attracting other massy things. But what is the relationship between properties and the causal powers that they confer?

On one view, it is no part of the essence of a property that it confers the causal powers that it does. Properties have a causal role all right, but the role is utterly contingent. God could have bestowed a very different role upon, say, the property of being negatively charged. Such a view has been embraced, notably, by David Lewis. According to his conception of reality, the causal powers of a property are constituted by its patterned relations to other properties in the particular Humean mosaic that is the actual world.[2] In other worlds, that property will be combined differently. In those worlds, then, the laws of nature governing it and thus the causal role it enjoys may be utterly different. In this regard, Lewis is largely following David Hume. Hume clearly thinks of the nature of simple impressions as given by how they are intrinsically and not by their patterned connection to other elements in reality: hence the denial of necessary connections between simple existences. What is missing in Hume is a robust realism about properties.[3] Simple impressions of a certain shade of red do not, literally, have some shade in common. Let us then call Lewis' view the 'neo-Humean view'.

On a second view, some or all of the causal powers of a property are essential to it. It does not go so far, though, as to insist that the causal powers of a thing exhaust its nature. Two possible properties may be distinct and yet the same causal powers be essential to each. Those powers do not, then, constitute an individual essence (where an 'individual essence' is a profile that is necessary and sufficient for some particular thing). Like the first view, this view holds that there is something more to the nature of a property than the causal powers that it confers—the intrinsic nature of the property if you will—holding that two different internal natures might necessitate the same causal profile.[4] Call this the 'double aspect view'.

On a third view there is, for each fundamental property, a causal profile that constitutes the individual essence of a property. That is, the profile is both necessary and sufficient for each property. (The relevant profile, we should note, may include facts about how a property figures as an effect as well as how it figures as a cause.) Let us call this view 'causal structuralism'. The first two views but not the third holds that there is something to a property—call it its quiddity—over and above its causal profile.[5] Causal structuralism holds that quiddities are a will-o'the-wisp.[6]

Note that causal structuralism is not intended to be applied directly to properties that are neither vehicles of genuine change nor serious causal explanation. As such, it does not offer a theory of mathematical and logical properties—such as the successor relation and the identity relation. (Also excluded, perhaps are such properties as overlap and part of, codified by the mereologist.) Nor does it, in the first instance, offer a theory of mere Cambridge properties, whose change does not intuitively amount to real change and which are not, intuitively, the conferrers of bona fide causal powers.[7] Call the candidate domain of properties for which causal structuralism is intended the 'natural properties'. I shall for the purposes of this paper assume that this category is reasonably well understood.

Note also that the causal structuralist needn't hold that all of a thing's causal profile is essential to it. She could consistently claim that some property A has the power to bring about both B and C, but that only the power to bring about B is part of its individual essence. But, prima facie, it would seem that to distinguish the essential from the accidental in this way would be to draw lines in an arbitrary way. For now, then, lets focus on a version of causal structuralism according to which the whole causal profile of a property is essential to it.

In what follows, I shall be looking at arguments for and against the following two key theses of causal structuralism: (i) That for any given natural property, there is some causal profile such that having that profile is sufficient for being that property and (ii) that for any given natural property, there is some causal profile such that having that profile is necessary for being that property. I can't imagine anyone liking the first thesis but not the second.[8] Meanwhile, if one likes the second thesis but not the first, one will likely find the double aspect theory attractive. Finally, if one eschews both theses, one will likely find the neo-Humean position attractive.

Views on quiddities have rough analogues in debates about haecceities. The neo-Humean view on properties resembles a radical haecceitism according to which all the qualities of a particular are contingent to it: only its haecceity is essential. (I could have been a poached egg so long as my haecceity was present.) The double aspect view also has an analogue in the metaphysics of individuals: There are those who believe that certain kind-properties (and perhaps other origin-theoretic properties) are essential to individuals but that one cannot construct an individual essence out of such properties. Any such list would leave out the thisness or haecceity which distinguishes a particular individual from other possibilia of the same kind (and origin). Meanwhile, causal structuralism about properties is analogous to a view according to which some qualitative profile is both necessary and sufficient for being a particular individual and hence that haecceities are a fiction.[9] I shall be exploiting these analogies in due course.

In part one, I shall briefly explore various arguments for causal structuralism, considering semantic, metaphysical, epistemological and methodological considerations that offer prima facie support for one or both of its key theses.

In part two, I shall consider five kinds of considerations that apparently militate against causal structuralism, suggesting that none of them are decisive.

In part three, I shall consider an especially worrying kind of objection to causal structuralism, in response to which I shall offer a fresh way to think about that view.

Part One: Arguments for Causal Structuralism

1 Semantic: Referring to Properties

One might think that if a pair of properties are alike in causal role, then one would be unable to single one of them out. And if that is right, then it will be incoherent to think of, say, 'redness' as singling out a property whose causal profile is exactly like some other actual property. In his 'Causal and Metaphysical Necessity', Sydney Shoemaker endorses something like this line of thought, viz: "And what epistemological considerations show, in the first instance, is that if there are sets of properties whose members are identical with respect to their causal features, we necessarily lack the resources for referring to particular members of these sets."[10]

This doesn't secure causal structuralism. But it is fair to say that it at least goes part of the way, by undermining the idea that, say, the property of being negatively charged might be distinct from some other property whose actual causal profile is just the same.

The argument's plausibility trades on an equivocation on 'causal feature'. Suppose A and B have the same causal powers. To simplify, lets suppose the following profile is exhaustive: 'A' and 'B' are both 50 percent probable on C and both, if instantiated, bring about D. Suppose John has C. It is compatible with the profile of C that John has A and not B. Supposing John has A, can John uniquely refer to A? Surely he can. He can do this not by exploiting an asymmetry in the laws governing A and B but rather by an asymmetry in the pattern of instantiation. Thus he can say: "Let 'Jones' pick out the property that C just caused to be instantiated in me."

Response: But in the case described, A and B do differ in causal features, viz: A but not B caused the state of affairs 'John's being D'.

Reply: But this isn't the sense of 'causal feature' in question. The causal structuralist does not think it essential to A that it causes John to be D. What is essential to A, according to the causal structuralist, are the causal powers it confer upon whatever thing instantiates it. As the example shows, even if two properties have the same causal profile in the sense relevant to causal structuralism, we may have the capacity to single one of them out. The key point is that a pair of properties may have equivalent causal profiles and yet asymmetrical patterns of instantiation, the latter affording a perfectly good basis for unique reference to one of the pair. The line of thought we are considering is not all that much better than one which claims that if I have the same qualitative profile (relational and non-relational) as some other guy, then I can't single myself out.

2 Metaphysical: Intra-World and Inter-World Variation

It seems to me a general feature of our thought about possibility that how we think that something could have differed from how it in fact is [is] closely related to how we think that the way something is at one time could differ from the way that same thing is at a different time. In possible worlds jargon, the ways one and the same thing of a given sort can differ across worlds correspond to the ways one and the same thing of that sort can differ at different times in the same world. Could I have been a plumber or an accountant instead of a philosopher? The answer seems to be yes—and this goes with the fact that we acknowledge the possibility of a scenario in which something who was exactly as I was at some point in my life undergoes a series of changes resulting in his eventually being a plumber or accountant. Could I have been a poached egg? Pace Lewis, the answer seems to be no—and this goes with the fact that our principles of trans-temporal identity rule out the possibility of a scenario in which something starts off as a human being of a certain description and ends up a poached egg.[11]

This line of thought, taken from Shoemaker's 'Causal and Metaphysical Necessity' and aired earlier in his 'Causality and Properties' takes off from the idea that in the case of particulars, the possibility of something's being F is of a piece with the possibility of a world which branches from the actual world where that thing is F. It then generalizes that thought to all things. Combine this generalization with the thesis that a property cannot change its causal powers over the course of time and then it follows that there is no world where some property enjoys some power that it actually lacks—since there is no world branching from the actual world where that property enjoys that power.

Here's the motivating principle—call it the 'Branch Principle':

> If x exists at a world w^1 and x could have been F then there is a world w^2 which is exactly like w^1 up to some point in time where x is F (call such a world a 'branch world').[12]

Given that properties can't change their causal powers over the course of time, we can use the Branch Principle to secure at least one of the two key causal structuralist theses (that the causal powers of a property are essential to it).

Should we agree with Shoemaker that, at least in the case of particulars, the Branch Principle is right? If determinism is true, there is no branch world with the same history and the laws of nature but where I am a plumber. So, according to Shoemaker, if determinism is true, things could not have been such that I was a plumber. Even if one thinks that the laws of nature are metaphysically necessary, it does not seem that one wants to say that it is impossible that I be a plumber: for why not admit a world which is a bit different to ours all along where I am a plumber? To focus our intuitions, we might do well to consider a simple world, one where two particles have always existed (either since the beginning of time or for all eternity). Call them A and B. Intuitively, it seems that A could have existed alone. But there is no branch world where A exists alone. So Shoemaker is committed to the thesis that A could not have existed alone. At the very best, such modal commitments are extremely tendentious. It thus does not seem that a promising way to motivate causal essences for properties is by the Branch Principle.

3 Epistemological: An Argument from Recognition

Suppose a property is something over and above its causal profile. We then seem to have conceptual space for something like the following: There is negative charge 1 and negative charge 2 that have exactly the same causal powers. What we call an instance of negative charge is sometimes an instance of negative charge 1, sometimes an instance of negative charge 2. Since 1 and 2 have the same propensities to affect all possible detection mechanisms, there is no way of discriminating 1 and 2. We would now be unable to tell, it seems, whether two groups of particles that we call "negatively charged" had the same property or else distinct but indistinguishable properties. But this is absurd: We can recognize property sharing. So we had better not allow properties to have an individual essence that transcends causal features. Here is Sydney Shoemaker:

> ....if two property can have exactly the same potential for contributing to causal powers, then it is impossible for us even to know (or have any reason for believing) that two things resemble one another by sharing a single property.[13]

I myself am not much moved by arguments of this form. We are all familiar with arguments with the following structure: If metaphysics M is right, then there are unlucky worlds where our judgments are way off with respect to subject matter S. Further, there is a natural sense in which, if M is right, we can't tell whether we are in an unlucky world. But we are very knowledgeable about subject matter S. If we can't tell whether we are in an unlucky world, we are not knowledgeable about subject matter S. So metaphysics M is all wrong.

Examples: (i) If possible worlds are Humean mosaics then there are unlucky worlds where everything is just like this and then the world stops altogether at some point in the very near future. Supposing the world is a Humean mosaic, we can't tell whether we are in a world like that. But we know a whole lot about the future. So the world is not a Humean mosaic.

(ii) If metaphysical realism about physical objects is true, then there are unlucky worlds where we are brains in vats. Supposing realism is true, we can't tell whether we are in a brain in a vat world. But we know a whole lot about tables. So we should not be metaphysical realists about physical objects.

(iii) If qualia are superadded features of the world then there are unlucky worlds where everyone else but me is a zombie. ...

Now its true that there is no stable consensus concerning how to react to these kinds of arguments. We haven't come as far as we'd like when it comes to epistemology. Some of us will go reliabilist and say that so long as we in fact don't live in an unlucky world and unlucky worlds are not nearby, then our knowledge is not under threat. Applied to the case at hand, we will say that so long as there are is not in fact any real risk of pairs of properties being presented to us that are role indiscernible, then our knowledge that certain things share certain properties is safe. Some of us will go contextualist and say that once we start doing serious philosophy then we should all be sceptics when it comes to the deployment of 'know' but that the standards are far lower in ordinary contexts—when truth plus moderate credentials are sufficient for the proper applicability of 'know'. Applied to the case at hand, we will say that so long as scientists are lucky enough to be right when they say that the same feature is being presented over and over again and so long as they rule out alternatives that are relevant to them, they can say 'I know that is the same feature as that', but that we philosophers, having gotten all worried about duplication of role by different quiddities should hesitate to claim to know.[14] Some of us will go abductionist and say the simpler and more elegant hypothesis is evidence enough for knowledge, so long as there is belief and truth. Applied to the case at hand, we will say that it is reasonable to believe in the simpler hypothesis—that there is only one quiddity there, not several—when presented with the negative charge role.

I don't know what to say of these various epistemological reactions. But I do admire a common thread—namely, "Don't throw out a metaphysical hypothesis on the basis of unlucky world arguments".[15]

There is one further thing to be said. Once one takes unlucky world arguments seriously then one sees soon enough that causal structuralism doesn't help all that much. Consider the following sceptical scenario. There is negative charge 1 and negative charge 2 that are exactly alike except that were property

P which is in fact uninstantiated to be instantiated, charge 1 would interact with it in a different way than charge 2.[16] Such an unlucky world is perfectly possible even if causal structuralism is true. By hypothesis, charge 1 and charge 2 would engage with our sensory mechanisms and other detection devices in the same way. How then can we *know* that there is one property, negative charge, rather than a pair of properties whose causal differences are inscrutable? Insofar as causal structuralism is designed to offer respite against scepticism, its comforts may be largely illusory.

4 Epistemological: Getting to Know a Property.[17]

We distinguish, intuitively, between being able to refer to a property and knowing what that property is. Only in the latter case is the nature of the property genuinely revealed to us. One way to try to flesh out this intuitive contrast is via George Bealer's distinction between semantically stable and semantically unstable expressions:

> An expression is semantically stable iff, necessarily, in any language group in an epistemic situation qualitatively identical to ours, the expression would mean the same thing. An expression is semantically unstable iff it is possible for it to mean something different in some language group whose epistemic situation is qualitatively identical to ours. ...
>
> Semantic instability has to do with the effects of the external environment. An expression is semantically unstable iff the external environment makes some contribution to its meaning. Natural kind terms are paradigmatic—'water', 'gold', 'heat', 'beech,' 'elm', etc. Logical, mathematical, and a great many philosophical terms, by contrast, are semantically stable: the external environment makes no such contribution. For example, 'some', 'all', 'and', 'if', 'is identical to', 'is' 'necessarily', 'possibly', 'true', 'valid'; '0' '1' '+' '÷', '∈; 'property', 'quality', 'quantity', 'relation', 'proposition', 'state of affairs', 'object', 'category', etc. It seems clear that all these are semantically stable: any language group in an epistemic situation qualitatively identical to ours would mean what we mean by these "formal" expressions."[18]

The following seems rather natural as a necessary condition on knowing what a property is:

K1: One knows what a property is only if one has a semantically stable way of referring to it.

On this gloss, users of the term 'water' that are altogether ignorant of chemistry succeed in referring to the property of being H_2O, but, lacking a semantically stable way of referring to that property, do not know what property it is that they are referring to. It is tempting, meanwhile, to suppose that many of us are now in a position to know what property it is that 'water' refers to—thanks to modern chemistry. Indeed, it is tempting in general to suppose that the advance of science has enabled us in many cases not merely to refer to causally efficacious properties but to know what they are. Thus:

> K2: For a large range of causally efficacious properties we are in a position to know what those properties are.

Accept K1 and K2 and we are in a good position to argue against quidditism. For suppose, as the quidditist admits, that a different quiddity could have played the hydrogen role. Then there would seem to be a community whose epistemic situation is qualitatively identical to ours but who refer to a different property by 'hydrogen'. Moreover, there seems to be no imaginable way of achieving a semantically stable way of referring to the property of being hydrogen, given quidditism. Any sort of role-description (whether rigidified or not[19]) will, in a qualitatively identical situation, be used by a counterpart community to pick out a different property. Does this spell real trouble for quidditism? I doubt it. Notice that we do not appear to have a semantically stable way of referring to any given person, say Saul Kripke. I can't take a cognitive photograph of his haecceity. My ability to refer to him will exploit either intrinsic features that he happens to possess, or else relations that he stands to myself and others, or both. Whatever the means I have of referring to him, it seems clear that there will be a counterpart community that uses the same reference-fixing devices to refer to a different individual. So 'Saul Kripke' is not semantically stable in the relevant sense. Nor is a semantically stable way of referring to Saul Kripke available, even in principle. Does this mean that in the ordinary sense, people do not know Saul Kripke? Surely not. By analogy, the preceding reflections should not be taken to show that, in the ordinary sense, people do not know which property is picked out by 'hydrogen'. It remains very unclear why it should count as a cost of a theory that it reckons most or all causally efficacious properties to fail the demanding standards of knowability set by K1.[20]

5 Methodological: Don't Invoke What You Don't Need

The best case for thinking that the causal profile of a property exhausts its nature proceeds not via the thought "Well otherwise we wouldn't know a whole lot of what we do know" but rather via the thought "We don't need quidditative extras in order to make sense of the world." Let us return to negative charge. All scientific knowledge about negative charge is knowledge about the causal role it plays. Science seems to offer no conception of negative charge as something over and above "the thing that plays the charge role". If there were a quiddity that were, so to speak, the role filler, it would not be something that science had any direct cognitive access to, except via the reference fixer "the quiddity that actually plays the charge role". Why invoke what you don't need?

Unless certain logical considerations forced one to suppose that properties are individuated by something over and above their causal role, then why posit mysterious quiddities?

Bertrand Russell was certainly onto the idea that science reveals nothing beyond causal structure when it comes to fundamental properties when he tells us that while introspection reveals the intrinsic quality of percepts, "... .we know nothing of the intrinsic quality of the physical world," adding that "We know the laws of the physical world, in so far as these are mathematical, pretty well, but we know nothing else about it."[21] Supposing we are unpersuaded by Russell's idea that role transcendent qualities are required to accommodate the facts of introspection, we can easily generate an argument for causal structuralism: Why posit from the armchair distinctions that are never needed by science?

I recommend the current line of thought as the most promising for the causal structuralist to pursue. But one should be aware of a trade off: Perhaps science doesn't need a robust conception of causation and can get by with thinking of causal laws in a Humean way, as the simplest generalizations over the mosaic. If so, it seems that one needs an independent characterization of the mosaic's pixels. It hardly seems plausible to be a deflationary Humean about causation and yet a causal structuralist about properties. To eschew quiddities on the basis of considerations of scientific economy may serve to saddle us with a view of causality that is far from economical.

Part Two: Arguments Against Causal Structuralism

1 The Circularity Argument

Suppose we define A in terms of its capacity to bring about B and then go on to define B in terms of its capacity to be brought about by A. Isn't the definition circular? Perhaps Bertrand Russell was moved by something like this concern when he wrote:

> There are many possible ways of turning some things hitherto regarded as "real" into mere laws concerning the other things. Obviously there must be a limit to this process, or else all the things in the world will merely be each other's washing.[22]

Its not so clear that the problem is very serious. We avoided circularities in the functional analysis of belief and desire in the philosophy of mind by defining belief and desire together. Perhaps we can do the same in the functional analysis of properties. Suppose with David Armstrong that causal laws are relations between universals.[23] Assume, then, that a causal necessitation relation N that holds between certain universals. At the risk of oversimplification, let us look a simple world where the lawbook for properties instantiated in that world is very small. There are five properties A, B, C, D, E. Here are the laws in the lawbook: ANB, ANC, BND and DNE. Just as functionalism in the philosophy of mind was helped by aid of the Ramsey-Lewis technique for functional analysis, so the same is true of causal structuralism about properties. Take the laws of the lawbook and conjoin them. Replace each property name by a distinct variable (F^1... .F^n) and prefix each variable by a quantifier. So we have $\exists F^1 \exists F^2 \exists F^3 \ \exists F^4 \exists F^5 \ (F^1{}_N F^2 \ \wedge F^1{}_N F^3 \ F^3{}_N F^4 \ \wedge F^4{}_N F^5)$. The lawbook was supposed to be exhaustive. To capture this, we can add such clauses as $\forall F^6 \ (F^4{}_N F^6 \supset F^6 = F^5)$. Call this the Ramsified lawbook. We can now articulate causal structuralism very easily, and whatever its merits, we cannot be accused of vicious circularity. Since the variable 'F^1' replaced A, we can give a theory of the individual essence of A by the open sentence you get by dropping the existential quantifer prefixing 'F^1'. According to causal structuralism, it is a necessary truth that anything that satisfies that open sentence is identical to A. Generalizing, the causal structuralist will say that any natural property can be defined by a suitable open sentence delivered by the Ramsified lawbook for that property.

(Note that, according to the causal structuralist, one Ramsifies the lawbook and not the worldbook to get the essence of a property. If I am tall, that does not go into the definition of tallness. What goes into the definition are the laws concerning how tallness relates causally—as cause and effect—to other properties. Note also that the approach assumes what the Humean abhors—that the causal relation is fundamental. But that is to be expected of causal structuralism in any case. Note finally that the laws in the lawbook may be considerably more complicated that the simple single property to single property laws discussed above: but this makes little difference to the viability of the Ramsification strategy.)

2 Combinatorialism.

On one attractive picture of modality, you get possible worlds by mixing and matching the fundamental natural properties. Call this Humean combinatorialism. Here is David Lewis' version of that view: "To express the plenitude of possible worlds, I require a principle of recombination according to which patching together parts of different possible worlds yields another possible world."[24]

Lewis goes on to deploy this principle against the thesis that is common to causal structuralism and double aspect theory:

> Another use of my principle is to settle—or as opponents might say, to beg—the question whether laws of nature are strictly necessary. They are not; or at least laws that constrain what can coexist in different positions are not. Episodes of bread-eating are possible because actual; as are episodes of starvation. Juxtapose duplicates of the two, on the grounds that anything can follow anything; here is a possible world to violate the law that bread nourishes. So likewise against the necessity of more serious candidates for fundamental laws of nature.[25]

The principle of recombination offers a very elegant theory of possibility space. Pity to abandon it if there is nothing elegant to put in its place by way of expressing the plenitude of possibilities. But there is.

Let us replace Humean combinatorialism by Structural Combinatorialism. I sketched a simple lawbook above, containing five properties and four laws. Consider the Ramsified lawbook corresponding to that simple lawbook, the former sufficing to capture the content of the latter according to the causal structuralist. That Ramsified lawbook expresses five possible properties. What other properties are possible? According to the Structural Combinatorialist, any logically consistent Ramsified lawbook expresses a possible set of properties. The structural combinatorialist can work with his own fundamental principle of plenitude—one that governs properties: it corresponds to the plenitude of consistent lawbooks. He can then build a theory of possible worlds upon that principle of plenitude. I see no reason for thinking that the result will be inelegant or unsatisfying.

3 Experience

One might instinctively react to causal structuralism by worrying that it fails to capture the color of the world. Taken literally, the problem is not so pressing. After all, it is not so unreasonable to suppose that a property counts as redness so long as it has the appropriate capacity to cause sensations of the right sort. But how about the sensations themselves? One might think that, say, pain (or phenomenal red), is constituted by an intrinsic *thusness* and not simply by its causal role. On this way of thinking, something could duplicate the causal role of pain in its entirety and yet not *be* pain.

Clearly, part of what held Russell back from full blooded causal structuralism are considerations such as these, as is evidenced by his view that while "we do not know their laws so well as we would wish," we do know the intrinsic quality of percepts (which are in turn "part of the physical world") by introspection.[26] One way to push this line of thought is via zombie thought experiments: There are, it seems, possible worlds with zombies that are structurally isomorphic to us. The zombies possess states with the right causal role but which lack any qualitative character. The difference between a zombie and us, on the current conception, is that the quiddities have been switched. Quiddity switching is what turns the light on and off, so to speak.[27] If that is right, only the neo-Humean and double aspect views remain as serious options.

It would be silly to try and engage at length with this objection in a survey paper such as this one. It is clear enough, though, what the causal structuralist should say in broad outline: How is one so sure that it is some intrinsic, role-transcendent quiddity that is responsible for consciousness? Consider me, and suppose I am in pain. Assume that I do have evidence-transcendent quiddities and that God were now to switch the quiddity that underlies my pain for another one—makes the quiddities dance, as it were. I would still believe that I am in pain, as the causal propensities with respect to my belief system would be unchanged. There are two perspectives here. On one perspective, the experiences dance with the quiddities—its just that we don't notice that pain has been replaced by ersatz pain. On another perspective, the experiences do not dance with the quiddities: we remain in pain and hence do not start making introspective mistakes when the quiddity switch occurs. Is it so clear that the first perspective is correct? I believe that the jury is still very much out on this issue.

(Note that even if one does believe in role-transcendent properties— as, say, Lewis does—this needn't be because one thinks that experience is role-transcendent. Lewis' perfectly natural properties are role-transcendent— but Lewis' reason for positing role transcendent properties has far more to do with his combinatorialism than with any deep intuition that introspection brings us into acquaintance with something role-transcendent. Analogy—there are plenty of people who believe in haecceities but who don't believe that self-consciousness brings us into special acquaintance with a peculiar sort of me-ness that serves as the individual differentium.)

4 Categorical and Dispositional Properties

We've all learned that dispositional properties have a categorical basis. But isn't this violated by causal structuralism? Frank Jackson rejects the view that properties are defined by causal role for exactly this reason: "This, to my way of thinking, is too close to holding that the nature of everything is relational cum causal, which makes a mystery of what it is that stands *in* the causal relations." [28]

I find it hard to see how to make the worry compelling. Suppose, to parody Jackson, we worried about a necessity of origins thesis for substances in the following way: "This to my way of thinking, is too close to holding that the nature of particulars is relational cum causal, which makes a mystery of what it is that stands *in* the causal relations." That objection doesn't seem very compelling at all.

Its true enough that we wish to distinguish between the second order property of, say, being a property that causes headaches and those first order properties which instantiate that second order property. But the causal structuralist has no reason to deny distinctions like that. Consider, for example, the open sentence from a Ramsified lawbook that defines a property. There is a property that the open sentence expresses. And there is a different property that is the unique realizer of that open formula. No need for collapse.

Perhaps the worry is that categorical bases are supposed to be without any relational features essentially. It is true enough that if this is a requirement, then both the double aspect theorist and the causal structuralist are in trouble. But it seems that the requirement needs some sort of motivation rather than being put forward as an unargued axiom. Note also that the categorical basis would, prima facie, be a poor explanans for the disposition as explanandum, if the categorical basis did not drag any causal powers along with it.[29]

5 Argument Five: Hyperstructuralism

According to the hyperstructuralist, one defines a property by taking a law-book and Ramsifying through the whole thing entirely, so that every relational and non-relational predicate is replaced by a variable. This means that the relation of causal necessitation is itself replaced by a variable. The hyperstructuralist claims that the resulting Ramsified sentence (which, note, says nothing explicitly to the effect that its subject matter is causality) is sufficient to provide definitions of each predicate in the original vocabulary that figured in the lawbook, including the relation of causal necessitation.

I take it that none of us are hyperstructuralists.[30] None of us think that the truth conditions of the original lawbook are given by the purely formal sentence that the hyperstructuralist obtains by comprehensive Ramsification. So it looks like the content of the predicate 'causes' cannot be recovered by Ramsifying through the theory in which 'causes' figures. Why then believe—as the causal structuralist believes—that other predicates can be defined by the Ramsey-Lewis technique? What's so special about causality?

The question is fair enough. But it is not clear that the causal structuralist is devoid of an answer. After all, it is part of the metaphysical picture of causal structuralism that the structural properties of a system have a different status than the nodes of the structure. Causality is not the only property that turns out to be primitive and indefinable—probably the same goes for identity and for various mathematical and mereological properties. You may not like the picture. But it does not seem altogether arbitrary or ad hoc to treat the structure of the world (the "form" of the world) in a different way to the nodes in the structure (the "matter" of the world). It thus does not seem to me then to be altogether ad hoc or arbitrary to endorse causal structuralism but to resist hyperstructuralism.

Part Three. Symmetrical Roles: Two Varieties of Causal Structuralism

The following seems to me to be a perfectly possible causal structure: There are four properties, call them A, B, C, D . Here are the laws governing them: A N C, B N C, A and B N D. It is crucial to this structure, note, that A and B are distinct. Their coinstantiation has different effects (the addition of D to the world) than is produced by either being instantiated alone. Not only are such causal structures intuitively possible; the structural combinatorialism that I sketched and which seems to me to be an elegant principle of plenitude for properties militates in favor of their possibility.[31]

Suppose such a structure is possible. That spells trouble for causal structuralism. According to that view, the individual essence of a property can be given via the Ramsified lawbook. But there is no way for that to work here. Ramsify the lawbook and there is nothing to distinguish the pair of properties corresponding to 'A' and 'B' even though the structure does require that there *be* a pair and not just one. The situation is similar to that besetting the most straightforward version of anti-haecceitism, according to which some purely qualitative profile provides the individual essence of each individual substance. That view famously got into trouble when confronted with Max Black's symmetrical world[32] (and Scotus' duplicate angels[33]), which seemed to require that there be two substances whose qualitative profile is exactly the same. Anti-haecceitism of that sort is troubled by intra-world duplication of qualitative profiles. Causal structuralism of Shoemaker's sort is troubled by intra-world duplication of causal profiles. If causal structuralism is the view that each property has a unique individual essence consisting of a causal profile, then that view seems to be wrong.

David Lewis has provided an alternative way of thinking about anti-haecceitism than the one adumbrated above: Here is his favored conception of haecceitism:

> If two worlds differ in what they represent *de re* concerning some individual, but do not differ qualitatively in any way, I shall call that a *haecceitistic difference*. Haecceitism, as I propose to use the word, is the doctrine that there are at least some cases of haecceitistic difference between worlds.[34]

Lewis is clear that on this gloss, anti-haecceitism can allow intra-world duplication of things with the same qualitative profile. Max Black's world is perfectly possible according to this brand of anti-haecceitism. What is not possible is the existence of two qualitatively indiscernible worlds such that the *de re* truths concerning one are different from the *de re* truths concerning the other.

One might think that once the possibility of Black's world has been conceded, haecceitism quickly follows. For isn't there one world where one of the balls exists alone and a different world where the other ball exists alone in a qualitatively duplicate state? Here is Lewis:

> I might have been one of a pair of twins. I might have been the first-born one, or the second-born one. These two possibilities involve no qualitative difference in the way the world is. Imagine them specified more fully: there is the possibility of being the first-born twin in a world of such-and-such maximally specific qualitative character. And there is the possibility of being the second-born twin in exactly such a world. The haecceitist says: two possibilities, two worlds. They seem just alike, but they must differ somehow. They differ in respect of 'cross-identification'...I say: two possibilities, sure enough. And they do indeed differ in representation de re: according to one, I am the first-born twin, according to the other I am the second-born. But they are not two worlds. They are two possibilities within a single world. The world contains twin counterparts of me, under a counterpart relation determined by intrinsic and extrinsic qualitative similarities (especially, match of origins). Each twin is a possible way for a person to be, and in fact is a possible way for me to be.[35]

Lesson: Utilizing Lewisian counterpart theory we can resist multiplying worlds whenever we have multiple possibilities for a thing to be. In so resisting we can allow intra-world qualitative duplication without taking on haecceitism.

What is interesting is that there is a version of causal structuralism that exactly mimics Lewis' approach. Let a structural description of a world be a description which describes the world using certain structural primitives—like part/whole and causal necessitation—and which otherwise uses merely the resources of logic (if you want to be a haecceitist about things but causal structuralist about properties, then throw in all the individual constants corresponding to each thisness). The causal structuralist can map out his position in the following way:

> If two worlds differ in what they represent *de re* concerning some property, but do not differ structurally in any way (i.e. have the same structural description), I shall call that a quidditistic difference. Anti-structuralism is the doctrine that there are at least some cases of quidditistic difference between worlds. I say that there are no quidditistic differences between worlds.

Lewis' anti-haecceitist can allow that there is intra-world duplication of some qualitative profile. My causal structuralist can allow that there is intra-world duplication of a causal profile. One might think that one can generate quidditistic differences out of such duplication. Take the symmetric structure that I described earlier. Isn't there the possibility that there are two things that instantiate A and one thing instantiates B and another possibility where two things instantiate B and one thing instantiates A? The lesson learned earlier can be applied here: don't multiply possible worlds whenever one has a multiplication of possibilities.

Lewis' anti-haecceitism does not either require a deep answer to the question: "Which elements of a thing's qualitative profile are essential to it?" His counterpart theory allows context-sensitive flexibility when responding to such questions. Neither does my causal structuralist need treat as deep the question "Which element's of a property's causal profile are essential to it?" A counterpart theory can allow context-sensitive flexibility here too. What is crucial to this brand of causal structuralism is that it does not allow that worlds can be alike structurally and yet different concerning what is true *de re* of the properties in them.

Suppose one doesn't like counterpart theory and yet does believe in the possibility of Black's world of two numerically distinct but qualitatively duplicates balls. As I see it, there is then no resisting haecceitism. Suppose one doesn't like counterpart theory and yet does believe in the possibility of pairs of properties with symmetrical causal roles. As I see it, there is then no resisting anti-structuralism. But symmetric structures do seem eminently possible. So counterpart theory combined with a rejection of quidditistic differences between worlds is certainly the best way to pursue the causal structuralist's vision of reality. I leave it to the reader to judge whether that vision is worth pursuing.

Appendix: Modest Structuralism

In replying to a version of this paper, Sydney Shoemaker noted the availability of a more modest version of causal structuralism than any discussed in the body of this paper (evincing some temptation to embrace it rather than any of the more radical versions of causal structuralism). Lest readers assume that his writings are unequivocally committed to full-blooded causal structuralism, let me sketch the modest view. Let the Shoemaker sentence for a target property P be obtained as follows: Take the lawbook, conjoin it, and replace each occurrence of P by a variable v, (leaving the other property names as they are). The result is an open sentence. The modest structuralist claims that the open sentence produced by this procedure individuates the target property. Notice that the symmetric causal structure that I described is no problem at all for the modest structuralist. After all, the Shoemaker sentence for B (as it figures in that structure), will include some such clause as 'in combination with A, suffices for D', while the Shoemaker sentence for A will not say that. Thus we have a kind of "anti-reductive" structuralism that is much more tolerant in that it can make room for symmetric structures. This modest version of causal structuralism will still put some constraints on possibility space: It will not allow the following pairs of lawbooks: (1) A N B, B N C (and that's all) (2) A N D, D N C (and that's all), since the Shoemaker sentence associated with B and D would be the same. Insist that these are different and genuinely possible lawbooks and the thesis of modest structuralism—that the Shoemaker sentence for a property individuates it—is violated. From the perspective of the causal structuralism examined in this paper, modest structuralism risks being far too permissive with regard to possible structures of properties. After all, modest structuralism can allow a distinction between the following pairs of lawbooks: F N G (and that's all), H N I (and that's all), since each of the properties F, G, H and I will have a different Shoemaker sentence associated with them. The radical structuralist will think that there is no such multiplicity of possibilities.

If one were to put an intuitive gloss on what modest structuralism amounts to, I would suggest it is this: There are quiddities, though one can get a necessary and sufficient condition for being a particular quiddity in terms of its causal relations to other quiddities. Whether this attempt to find a middle ground between the merits of causal structuralism and a metaphysic of quiddities has much going for it, I leave as a question for another time.

Notes

1. Thanks to Tamar Gendler, David Lewis, Ted Sider, Zoltan Szabo, Dean Zimmerman and audiences at Cornell and Notre Dame for helpful discussion.
2. See, for example, his introduction to *Philosophical Papers Volume II*, Oxford University Press, 1986.
3. Lewis himself wavers on whether to endorse a full-blooded commitment to universals, conceived as more than set-theoretic entities. In this paper, I shall not be call-

ing the existence of universals into question. I shall leave the reader to judge to what extent the issues are significantly affected by a shift to a set-theoretic conception of properties.

4. Such a view was not uncommon, I believe, in scholastic philosophy. For example, while William of Ockham shows little willingness to think that a thing's nature is exhausted by some causal profile, he claims in Reportatio IV q2 that it is part of the very nature of an effect that it can be produced by one kind of efficient cause and not another.

5. I am not requiring of the 'quidditist' that he be ontologically serious about quiddities, considered as something metaphysically distinct from the properties themselves.

6. The causal structuralist will thus see something deeply misleading in Hilary Putnam's distinction between 'a causal description' and 'a canonical description' of a property, where a canonical description is of the form 'the property of being F' while the causal description picks out a property via its causal role. For the causal structuralist, it is the causal description that most deserves the label 'canonical'. See 'On Properties' in *Mathematics, Matter and Method, Philosophical Papers Volume 1* (Cambridge University Press, 1975), p. 316.

7. Cf. Shoemaker 'Causality and Properties,' in *Identity, Cause and Mind* (Cambridge University Press, 1984), p. 207.

8. For one thing, if a number of profiles were sufficient, it would seem that the disjunction of them would be necessary. For another, I wouldn't know how to motivate the thesis that a pair of distinct possible properties could not share some profile once one has denied that the profile is necessary to either.

9. Cf. Thomas Aquinas, who thought that form in the case of angels, and that form plus a certain originating quantity of matter in the case of corporeal substances (where 'quantity of matter' was not conceived of haecceitistically) was sufficient for individuation. See his *On Being and Essence*.

10. 'Causal and Metaphysical Necessity,' *Pacific Philosophical Quarterly* 1998, Volume 79 p. 66.

11. 'Causal and Metaphysical Necessity,' p. 69–70.

12. Cf 'Causality and properties,' p. 218: 'the assertion that a certain particular might have had different properties than it does in the actual world...implies that there is a possible history 'branching off' from the history of the actual world in which it acquires those properties...'

13. 'Causality and Properties,' p. 215.

14. Cf David Lewis 'Elusive Knowledge,' *Australian Journal of Philosophy* 74 (1996), p. 549–567.

15. Similar considerations apply to the spectre that there are lots of inert properties that bear heavily on what really resembles what, falsifying most of our overall resemblance judgments as between particulars. See p. 215 of 'Causality and Properties'.

16. Alternatively: negative charge 1 and negative charge 2 are exactly alike except that negative charge 1 causes epiphenomenon 1 (which is itself causally inert viz a viz our detection devices) and negative charge 2 causes epiphenomenon 2 (which is similarly inert).

17. I am grateful to David Lewis here, who proposed something like the argument that follows in discussion at Notre Dame, 1999.

18. 'On The Possibility of Philosophical Knowledge', *Philosophical Perspectives 10: Metaphysics, 1996*, p.23.

19. In the lingo made popular by David Chalmers' *The Conscious Mind* (Oxford University Press, 1986), the issue is whether there is a primary intension that always delivers the same property for any world, considered as actual, not whether there is a secondary intension that delivers the same property for any world considered as counterfactual.

20. Though it may make trouble for the philosophical idea, in circulation since antiquity, that forms are more fully knowable than particulars, at least where the forms concerned are the causally efficacious properties that are found in the natural world.

21. *The Analysis of Matter* (Kegan Paul, 1927), p. 264.

22. Russell's concern, taken from *The Analysis of Matter*, p. 325, is voiced by Simon Blackburn ('Filling in Space' in *Essays in Quasi-Realism*, pp. 255–258), who adds that the point is particularly pressing if one uses a possible worlds account of powers).

23. See his *What is a Law of Nature?* (Cambridge University Press, 1983).

24. *On The Plurality of Worlds* (Blackwell, 1986), p. 87–88.

25. *On The Plurality of Worlds* p. 91.

26. *The Analysis of Matter*, p. 264.

27. Note that if one wishes to suppose that the quiddity of a property is always something like experiential character, then one will be driven to a sort of panpsychism and will not tolerate the possibility of zombies after all. Quiddity switching may make for spectrum inversion but cannot, on this view, turn the lights off.

28. *From Metaphysics to Ethics* (Clarendon Press, 1998), pg 24.

29. On this last point, see Blackburn's 'Filling in Space'. It is of course not decisive against the Humean—what the latter thinks as the appropriate explanation for some dispositional property is a combination of one or more perfectly natural properties *together with* some suitable set of laws.

30. Especially if identity, mathematical relations (such as the successor relation) and mereological relations (such as being a part of) disappear into variables.

31. Admittedly, what would be nicer still would be a sketch of how circumstances in the actual practice of science might compel the positing of a symmetrical structure such as the one above (embedded, presumably, in a more complex structure that preserves the symmetry between A and B.) Mill's methods of agreement and difference certainly have no straightforward bite here, since the reidentification of circumstances is in this context epistemologically problematic. We normally discriminate properties by their differential impact on our sensory organs or on some detection instrument. But in the case described there is no straightforward basis for such discrimination. Where I posit a structure like the one above, you may posit a structure whereby there are four properties such that A N C and B N C and B N D. Nevertheless, the symmetrical structure does seem perfectly possible and well-motivated by proper principles of plenitude. It strikes me as ad hoc to deny its possibility.

32. 'The Identity of Indiscernibles,' in *Problems of Analysis*, Routledge and Kegan Paul, 1954, p. 80–92.

33. See *Ordinatio* II d3 p1 q7

34. *On The Plurality of Worlds*, p. 221.

35. *On The Plurality Of Worlds*, p. 231.

Philosophical Perspectives, 15, Metaphysics, 2001

ON THEORETICAL IDENTIFICATIONS

G. W. Fitch
Arizona State University

Ever since Saul Kripke argued that certain statements are both necessary and known only a posteriori, there has been widespread discussion and debate over both the arguments that Kripke offers and the conclusion he derives.[1] There are two kinds of statements that are examples of necessary *a posteriori* truths; those involving the use of ordinary proper names such as "Hesperus is Phosphorus" and those statements that Kripke refers to as theoretical identifications. The latter statements can be further divided into different sorts of identifications. There are what I call the 'physical substance identities' such as "Water is H_2O" and "Gold is the element with atomic number 79"; the 'event kind identities' such as "Heat is the motion of molecules" and 'Lightning is an electrical discharge"; and the species identities such as "Tigers are the species *felis tigris*." Of course, Kripke is not the only philosopher who holds such views. Hilary Putnam, for instance, independently developed the view that such theoretical identifications are necessary *a posteriori* truths. However, Putnam has retreated from his original position and he now holds that such identifications are only physically necessary and not necessary "in the highest degree" as Kripke claimed.[2] In this paper I shall defend one of Kripke's arguments for the conclusion that physical substance identities are indeed necessary (in the highest degree) *a posteriori* truths.

The argument we shall focus on in this paper that Kripke offers for the necessity of theoretical identifications is the following: "Theoretical identities, according to the conception I advocate, are generally identities involving two rigid designators and therefore are examples of the necessary *a posteriori*." (Kripke p. 140) One might critically respond to Kripke by saying that true identities between rigid designators are not generally necessary *a posteriori* truths. I shall not defend this premise here since for the most part those who reject theoretical identifications as examples of necessary *a posteriori* truths do not reject this premise. Instead, one might agree with Kripke that true identities between rigid designators are, in general, necessary *a posteriori* truths but argue that theoretical identifications are not identity statements between rigid designators because they are not identity statements at all. This is Mark Johnston's view and it is discussed in section I. Or one might accept that such identifications are identity statements but reject the claim that they are necessary because either the natural kind term is not a rigid designator (as Donnellan seems to claim—see section II) or the scientific kind term is not a rigid designator (see section III) or there is something wrong with attempting to apply the notion of a rigid designator to natural kind terms (as Putnam came to believe—see section IV). I shall defend Kripke's argument against all of these kinds of objections. There are, I believe, important lessons to be learned here.

I

Mark Johnston is an example of a philosopher who argues that theoretical identifications should be viewed as claims of constitution and not identity.[3] The claim that

(W) Water is H_2O,

should be understood to mean that water is constituted by H_2O, according to Johnston. His argument that the statement that water is H_2O should not be viewed as an identity statement is relatively straightforward. Assume that it is an identity statement. That is, assume

(1) Water $= H_2O$.

Next Johnston asserts

(2) If water $= H_2O$ then water vapor $= H_2O$ and snow $= H_2O$.

From (1) and (2) we can derive

(3) Water vapor $= H_2O$ and snow $= H_2O$.

Clearly (3) is false (since it implies that water vapor $=$ snow), so either (1) or (2) must be false. But Johnston argues that any reason you have for rejecting (2) is a reason to reject (1). Hence (1) is false.

One reason for thinking that (2) is true is that if the kind water is the kind H_2O then certainly the kind water vapor (or snow) is also the kind H_2O. For what else could the kind water vapor be if not the kind H_2O? However, this reasoning assumes that water vapor is itself a kind as opposed to a state of the kind water. So, Johnston holds that terms like 'snow' and 'water vapor' designate kinds just as 'water' and 'gold' designate kinds. But is snow a *kind* in the *same* sense that water is a kind? Johnston holds that expressions such as 'water', 'gold', 'snow' etc. denote *manifest* kinds whereas 'H_2O' denotes a chemical kind. Chemical kinds, or scientific kinds in general, are what are denoted by those expressions that are embedded in current scientific theory such as 'H_2O' and 'the element with atomic number 79'. A manifest kind according to Johnston is "a kind whose instances we identify and re-identify on the basis of their manifest properties". Kripke, however, does not use the phrase 'manifest kind' but rather talks about the manifest properties of natural kinds. Clearly part of the issue here is what sort of kind are we talking about. The term 'kind' itself can be used to refer to various sorts of categories. There are different *kinds* of chairs, different *kinds* of hair styles, different *kinds* of wine, and different *kinds* of philosophy. But these kinds of *kinds* are not relevant to our discussion. We are interested in kinds of substances. If Johnston is to be read as attempting to provide an objection to Kripke's argument, then we need to understand Johnston as dealing with the kinds that Kripke considers. But the problem is if we do look at (1) as an identity between kinds of *substances*, it is difficult to find any plausibility for (2). Neither 'water vapor' nor 'snow' designate kinds of substances—they designate a substance in a given state.

Although we use manifest properties and scientific characteristics to individuate kinds for the purposes of naming, it does not follow that the predicates used to express those properties and characteristics are analytically linked to the names we introduce. This is one of the features of Kripke's view of reference. It is possible for a given object or kind to lack the very characteristics and features we used to individuate that object or kind and it is possible for something other than the object or kind to have the characteristics and features that we used to individuate that object or kind. Putnam's well known Twin Earth examples are designed in part to show this. The manifest properties of water are present on Twin Earth, but H_2O is not present there.

Now we do not normally identify a sort or type of item with a version of that type. Hence, we would not identify the tea with ice tea, a milkshake with a strawberry milkshake, flower with yellow flower. This is not to say that ice tea is somehow more than just tea or a yellow flower is a flower plus some other type of thing. Another way to look at it is that expressions 'ice tea' and 'yellow flower' do not really designate kinds distinct from the expressions 'tea' and 'flower' respectively. What they do is describe a kind in a certain state (having a certain property). The expression 'water vapor' seems to function like the expression 'ice tea'. It describes a kind in a certain state or form.

Johnston considers this response to his argument (or a least something like this response) and argues that it will not work on the grounds that we can re-instate the objectionable conclusion (i.e., water vapor = snow) by adding the following premises:

(4) H_2O = H_2O in a vaporous condition.

(5) H_2O = H_2O in a powdery condition.

Of course, someone who rejects (3) is going to reject (4) and (5) as well and for the same reason. But Johnston claims that if we reject (4) we must do it with the constraint that water vapor is essentially vaporous. But why must we? He asks us to consider a certain fog (water vapor) and then comments:

> I do not mean to ask whether the fog could solidify into a block of ice or liquefy into a puddle of water. I know that it could. I mean to ask whether the fog could *be* either of these things. It seems to me that the fog could not be either of these things. For when the fog solidifies or liquefies, that is the end of the fog. (Johnston p. 568)

Of course, if a fog liquefies then we no longer have a fog. But has anything gone out of existence? If I paint my red car blue, then I no longer have a red car. But I still have a car. And if the fog liquefies I still have the water albeit in a different form. Or consider the same point with respect to the ice tea. Suppose the tea warms up and is no longer ice tea. Is this the end of the ice tea in your glass? Could this very ice tea *be* warm tea? Unlike Johnston, I am inclined to think that it could be warm tea and given enough heat, it might even *be* a tea fog. Of course, on a hot day warm tea is not as refreshing as ice tea and you cannot really drink tea fog. But it does not seem to follow from this that the tea itself is gone. It is simply in a different state. A change in the state of something, whether it is warm, cold, hot, etc., does not imply a substantial change. No new entities come into existence or go out of existence.

One might hold that the differences between being a solid, being a liquid, or being a gas are such that moving from one state to another involves substantial change. This is why the ice tea case, one might claim, is not really relevant. The difference between tea that is iced and warm tea is only a different between liquids and not a difference between a liquid and a gas. But consider a bowl of ice cream for a moment. Suppose I dish out a bowl of ice cream but then someone calls on the phone and I forget about the ice cream and by the time I get back what I find is a bowl of cream. Is the ice cream gone or is it there in a melted state? I'm inclined to the latter answer while Johnston is inclined to the former. I do not know if there is a nice knock down argument to prove that I am correct and that Johnston is not. I certainly think that if we supply enough energy to a sample of water such that the bonding among the atoms breaks down then the resulting gas is not water but a mixture of hydrogen and oxygen in a two to one ratio. In this case I am inclined to say that a substantial change occurred—even though the very same atoms exist in the very same region of space (we might suppose) as existed prior to our applying the energy. One reason why I am inclined to think that a substantial change has occurred is that if we were to simply cool the resulting gas we would not thereby have water but rather liquid hydrogen and liquid oxygen. And this brings up another point.

If I were to sufficiently cool a quantity of oxygen I would have a quantity of a liquid. Is *this* liquid *essentially* a liquid, as Johnston would have us believe? Consider an analogy, is *this* bachelor essentially unmarried? In both cases I think the answer is no. If I am correct that an instance of water vapor is not essentially vaporous (even though it is necessary that for all x, if x is water vapor then x is vaporous), then we can see why (2) is false. And if (2) is false, then Johnston's argument does not provide us with a reason to reject (1).

This being said, it does not follow that Johnston's suggestion to treat theoretical identifications as statements of constitution as opposed to identity statements is mistaken.[4] But just how plausible is Johnston's suggestion?

Johnston's suggestion is that we should understand the identification (W) (Water is H_2O) as expressing the statement

(6) Water is constituted by H_2O,

where we are to understand that constitution is *not* identity. Yet, there is something odd here. If water is not identical to H_2O but is only constituted by H_2O then water is something more than H_2O. But what more is there? Johnston says:

> Kinds are identical only if they have just the same instances. Modal arguments precisely paralleling the argument about the statue and its matter apply to the instances of manifest kinds and the instances of the chemical kinds that make them up...If a statute is not identical to the matter that makes it up, then an instance of a manifest kind like water is not to be identified with the instance of H_2O that makes it up (Johnston p. 570–1).

But those who, for example, hold that a given statue, S, is constituted by, but is not identical to, a certain hunk, H, of matter do so by arguing that S essentially has the property of being a statue but H lacks this property.[5] So what more there is of S is explained by S's having the essential property of being a statue. So what essential property does water have that H_2O lacks? In this case we cannot, without further argument, say that water has the essential property of being water, but H_2O lacks that property.[6] On the face of it, it seems as though H_2O has that property.[7] The argument about fog, ice, etc. is unconvincing. Of course, part of the issue here is the general question about the relationship between constitution and identity. A discussion of this issue would take us beyond the scope of our present inquiry. Nonetheless, consider the other examples of theoretical identifications. Does it really make sense to replace 'Gold = the element with atomic number 79' with 'Gold is constituted by the element with atomic number 79'? Is gold made of the element with atomic number 79? Can we apply a statue/hunk of matter modal argument to gold and the element with atomic number 79? (See section II below) Or consider heat and the motion of molecules. What sense is there to be made of the claim that heat is made of the motion of molecules? Is water made of H_2O?[8] You might say that water is made of oxygen atoms bonded with hydrogen atoms. But water is not made of H_2O, it just *is* H_2O.

II

Keith Donnellan, in his paper "Kripke and Putnam on Natural Kind Terms," says with respect to Kripke's use of kind terms "Thought of in this way, kind terms are in one way like proper names: they designate a single entity, albeit an abstract entity—a species or a substance in these cases."[9] If they are like proper names as Donnellan suggests, then Kripke's argument that such identifications are necessary *a posteriori* truths seems all the more compelling. However, Donnellan, like Johnston, rejects Kripke's argument, although his reasons are different from those of Johnston.

Donnellan grants that (1) is the correct form of the statement (W), but he argues that (1) is false. The reason (1) is false, according to Donnellan, is that the kind that our ordinary term 'water' refers to is *not* the kind that our scientific term 'H_2O' refers to. Of course, the extensions of the two kinds are the same on Earth, but that is not sufficient to show that the kinds are the same. It is possible, Donnellan argues, that the two kinds have different extensions. This is in part because the extensions of such ordinary terms are not fully determined by their use and hence allow for different ways of being more specific depending upon the discoveries of science. Donnellan's argument for this is based on a Twin-Earth type example. He says

> I imagine then that on Twin Earth not only do elements usually have several isotopes, but also it is a general rule that one of the isotopes on a particular element makes up the bulk of the element as it occurs in nature—the other isotopes being fairly rare...it seems to me not psychologically implausible for my Twin-Earthlings to be more taken with, so to speak, the isotope number of a bit of substance rather than with its atomic number and also not implausible for them to diverge from our practice and to identify the substance designated by some of their vernacular natural kind terms not with a certain element, but with the isotope which makes up the bulk of what had been previously called by that term ... If you accept that my story of Earth and Twin-Earth contains no inconsistencies or other mistakes, then I do not see how we can accept Putnam's [and presumably Kripke's] view that it is clear that natural kind terms in ordinary language have the same extension before and after scientific discoveries and the mapping of those terms on to those discoveries. (Donnellan pp. 99–103)

The idea is that if the extensions of our ordinary terms such as 'water' vary with scientific discovery then whatever kind (if any) they refer to, it will not be the same as the kind referred to by the scientific term.

While I do agree to some extent with Donnellan that there is a kind of "slackness" in our ordinary use of kind terms[10], I do not agree that the conclusion we should draw from this is that statements such as (1) are, strictly speaking, false. The reason why Donnellan's Twin-Earthians might appear to reject our claim that gold *is* the element with atomic number 79 is because the term 'gold' in Twin-English refers to a kind that is distinct from the kind that is referred to by the term 'gold' in English. The kind referred to by the Twin-Earthians is a kind identical to the isotope of the element with atomic number 79. To make the case clear suppose that the stuff called 'gold' on Twin-Earth is **Au**-195. That is, upon investigation the chemists on Twin-Earth find that most of the samples of what they call 'gold' are **Au**-195 (as oppose to our samples which are **Au**-197).[11]

So, Donnellan worries that our ordinary terms such as 'water' or 'gold' designate different substances in different possible worlds if those worlds are similar enough to our world. So in world, *w*, with the isotope **Au**-195, that gold-ly stuff might very well be what our word 'gold' designates at *w*. His argument for this is based on the idea that had our world been like the **Au**-195 world we would have designated **Au**-195 with our term 'gold.' But even if Donnellan is correct about what we *would have* designated had our world been different, it does not follow that we do designate **Au**-195 with our use of the term 'gold' when speaking about *w*. It is true that **Au**-195 is an isotope of gold and all the isotopes of a given element are included in our chemical description of the element. But this should not cause a problem for the view.

There are, at least, two ways of viewing the relationship between an element and its isotopes that are consistent with Kripke's overall claims. First, one can view each isotope as a different kind of substance (call this the 'unity of substance' view) or second, one can view the element as a general kind and the isotopes as subclasses or sub-kinds standing in a relation similar to the genus-species relation. In neither case do we get the result that *our* term 'gold' designates the **Au**-195 kind on *w*. Since the element with atomic number 79 happens to actually be **Au**-197, on the unity view, 'gold' designates that isotope and the other isotopes (including **Au**-195) simply do not have ordinary names (only scientific names). On the subclass view, 'gold' designates a general kind of which the kinds **Au**-195 and **Au**-197 are sub-kinds. On this view *our* term gold does not designate either the **Au**-195 or the **Au**-197 kinds but what we might describe as the general kind of being the element with atomic number 79.

Donnellan's example is not really analogous to Johnston's examples. In Johnston's case we are considering different states or forms of a single substance (water or carbon). Donnellan, on the other hand, is asking us to consider isotopes of an element. Distinct isotopes of a given element are not different states of a single substance; they are either sub-kinds of a given kind or distinct kinds. This response to Donnellan can also serve to handle some other objections that have been raised against Kripke's argument.

III

Helen Steward, like Donnellan, questions whether scientific kind terms are rigid designators and hence whether (1) is necessary.[12] In her example she imagines that we discover that there are two types of protons—the ordinary proton and the rare proton-B. In addition, when we have a large concentration of H_2O

molecules whose atoms all have proton-B we have an opaque pink solid. She then comments:

> What would happen to the claim that necessarily, water H_2O in such a case as this? Would we continue to insist that all the range of substances, from the pink and opaque to the clear and colorless, which are chemically composed of H_2O are in fact different kinds of water? Surely not; surely we would use different names for the widely varying kinds of substance produced by the substitution of protons-B for ordinary protons. (Steward p. 390)

The conclusion Steward draws from her example is that 'H_2O' is not a rigid designator since it *can* designate both water and the opaque pink solid made up of proton-B atoms. So Steward rejects one of Kripke's premises.

Given my comments concerning Donnellan's example, it is probably clear to the reader what is the correct response to this example. Our term 'H_2O' does not designate compounds primarily composed of proton-B atoms and hence it does not designate the pink solid substance. Steward anticipates this response and replies to it as follows:

> It simply ignores the fact that there is descriptive complexity in a term like 'H_2O', that it is a shorthand for a chemical structure and not just an arbitrary name, so that while that chemical structure (two atoms of hydrogen to one atom of oxygen, arranged in the particular way characteristic of the water molecule) remains intact, the term must continue to apply. (Steward p. 391 note 7)

The expression 'H_2O' is a chemical formula and as such carries with it a certain amount of information. Hence, there is a kind of descriptive complexity associated with any such formula. But it does not follow from this that any combination of two hydrogen atoms with one oxygen atom is designated by 'H_2O'. For example, we do not use 'H_2O' to designate heavy water (which is designated by 'D_2O') which contains two atoms of hydrogen to one atom of oxygen even though there is a certain amount of D_2O in all of our samples of (pure) water. So what reason do we have to suppose along with Steward that *our* expression 'H_2O' does designates compounds composed of two hydrogen B-atoms and one oxygen B-atom in any world? It is highly unlikely, given the reason and way we introduce chemical formulas, that if we discovered B-protons we would not distinguish between compounds containing such protons from those that do not in our chemical formulas. But even if we would not so distinguish them were we to discover B-protons, given that there are no such protons our chemical formulas do not designate any compounds containing them— since *our* chemical formulas designate *our* chemical kinds. Putting the point in a slightly different way, *our* chemical symbol **O** designates ordinary oxygen atoms—not oxygen B-atoms.

A similar point can be made in response to David Barnett's objection to the necessity of (1).[13] Barnett asks us to imagine a world where there are toxic "mushrooms" and then adds the following comment:

> Ironically, these "mushrooms" are composed entirely of H_2O molecules. (For those travelers interested in the chemistry of this toxic H_2O, see the recently published article, 'Packing Neutrons into Oxygen Packs a Mean Punch in H_2O'.) (Barnett p. 100)

If the case that Barnett wants us to consider is a case where there is some counterfactual isotope of oxygen (say O-27 or something), then there is little difference between Barnett's argument and Steward's argument. It does not matter whether we have a pink solid as a result of different proton types or a toxic mushroom as a result of counterfactual isotopes. In neither case would *our* term 'H_2O' designate the required compound.

However, Barnett does not emphasize the physical chemistry of the example. Indeed, Barnett says

> Regardless of whether it is physically possible for H_2O to form the previously envisaged toxic mushroom-like substance, it is intuitively possible for H_2O to form *something* other than water. I find it intuitively possible that in some world H_2O could form nasty mushroom-type stuff and that this stuff would not be water, and many people I ask, who do not have a philosophical axe to grind, share this intuition. (Barnett p.102)

This comment suggests we really should ignore the aside about isotopes and focus on the general claim about the metaphysical possibility of there being a mushroom-like substance composed entirely of H_2O molecules.

However, when we try and consider what H_2O molecules could form in a world that has different natural laws from our own (as suggested by Barnett's comment about physical possibility), a not so subtle issue emerges. Not doubt there are possible worlds with different natural laws that have elements that combine to form molecules that combine in various ways to form substances. But if the laws that govern the behavior and properties of the basic constituents of elements (if they even have constituents) are different from our corresponding laws, then it is not so clear that the elements of such a world are our elements and hence it is not clear that there is any H_2O in such worlds. This is true even if the people in those worlds would designate their mushroom molecules with their chemical formula 'H_2O'. This is a kind of Twin-World case where there are elements, molecules, etc. but they are not *our* elements, molecules, etc. since they have different (dare I say essential) properties from ours. So to avoid this sort of problem it is best to consider only those worlds that do contain *our* H_2O molecules.[14]

So, do collections H_2O molecules form something other than water in other possible worlds? Barnett takes it as almost obvious to anyone who lacks a philosophical axe to grind that it is possible and hence (1) is not necessary. I say 'almost obvious' because Barnett offers an analogy as a reason to accept that it is possible. As we have already noted above carbon comes in different forms or allotropes. The same can be said for silica or silicon dioxide (SiO_2). Suppose that the only form on Earth had been the crystalline form quartz and not the other crystalline forms nor lechatelierite (natural vitreous silica) (nor any of the other forms though the three crystalline and vitreous silica are the principle forms of silica). In such a situation wouldn't we have simply identified quartz with SiO_2. I.e., in such a situation, it is plausible to imagine us asserting the following as a true identity along the lines of (1):

(S) Quartz $= SiO_2$.

But the fact is that SiO_2 can take many forms (just as carbon can take many forms) and hence not only is (S) false but it would have been false in our imagined situation. Why, Barnett asks, should we think that H_2O is radically different from SiO_2. Since SiO_2 has different forms, it certainly seems possible for H_2O to have different forms (as oppose to just having different naturally occurring states) as well.

Barnett's analogy between H_2O and SiO_2 raises again an issue that Johnston raises with his diamond/graphite case, namely what is the correct way to describe the relationship between a substance and the form of a substance? It is not the case that graphite and diamond are different kinds of *substances* nor are quartz and lechatelierite. They are, in effect, different arrangements of the same substance in much the same way that one can arrange the same kind of clay into a statue of a horse or into a statue of a dog. Clearly, horse statues and dog statutes are not the same kind of statue and diamond and graphite are not the same kind of form (of a substance). Moreover, we may very well value one form over the other for various reasons. We may simply like dog statutes over horse statutes or we may like diamond over graphite because one occurs more rarely in nature than the other or because we simply like the way it looks. They are not different substances because we value them differently or because they have different properties. The difference in properties comes from a difference in arrangements, but the substance remains the same. Since terms like 'diamond' designate the arrangement of the substance (and not just the kind of substance), we do not identify diamonds with the kind carbon.

The same is true for quartz and silica. Silica is identical to SiO_2, not quartz. But consider Barnett's supposition. Suppose quartz were the only form of SiO_2 in the way that water is the only form of H_2O.[15] If there were only one form of SiO_2, then it is plausible (but not necessary) to imagine us as identifying the kind designated by the natural kind term with the kind designated by chemical formula. So, in such a case the assertion of (S) is one natural outcome. But we now run into what Donnellan called the "slackness" of our ordinary use of kind terms. In the case that Barnett describes, it is not clear that 'quartz' designates a kind of substance *in a certain arrangement* (as we use the word) or whether it just designates the kind of substance (i.e., it is synonymous with our word 'silica'). We say, pointing to a number of samples of quartz, let's call the kind of substance that all these samples are members of 'quartz'. Have we named the substance or have we named a form of the substance? Even though there is no practical difference if we live in a world where the substance only comes in one form between the two interpretations, there can be reasons (even in such a world) that suggest one of the interpretations is the correct one.

Suppose the world we are considering is one where carbon and other substances come in many forms. Or consider a world where all substances have a single form, i.e., water, carbon, silica, etc. are present in a single form. Depending on details of our suppositions we would find evidence to support one or the other interpretations of (S). In the case where the evidence leads us to translate 'quartz' as silica, (S)(so translated) is true. In the case where all substances come in a single form, I would argue that 'SiO_2' designates the specific form of the substance (as would all the chemical formulas). Again in that case (S) (so translated) would also be true.

But what about (W)? If we came across some mushroom like stuff on some planet and we found out that it was nothing but H_2O molecules in a very unusual arrangement, would we not say that we had discovered some spongy water? We did not discover some new *substance* since all we have here are water molecules. Of course, before we found out the chemical composition of 'wamushrooms' (as we may call them), we would not think that we had found a new form of water. But after investigation we would discover that water comes not only the usual liquid or solid state but it comes in a spongy form as well. We would not say that we had discovered a new substance any more than we think diamonds are a substance distinct from carbon.

IV

Finally, I turn to a brief comment concerning Putnam's change of heart. Putnam was one of developers along with Kripke of the view that theoretical identifications are example of necessary *a posteriori* truths. But Putnam changed his mind. The problem, according to Putnam, is that it makes no sense to talk about water in all possible worlds. He says:

> I do not think that a criterion of substance identity that handles "Twin Earth" cases will extend handily to "possible worlds". In particular, what if a hypothetical "world" *obeys different laws*? Perhaps one could tell a story about a world in H_2O exists (H still consists of one electron and one proton, for example), but the laws are slightly different in such a way that what is a small difference in the *equations* produces a very large difference in the *behavior* of H_2O. Is it clear that we would call a (hypothetical) substance with quite different behavior *water* in these circumstances? I now think that the question, "what is the necessary and sufficient condition for

being water *in all possible worlds*?" makes no sense at all. And this means I reject "metaphysical necessity". (Putnam p. 443)

Putnam's concern is over what 'water' designates in worlds that have different natural laws. This is something that we touched on in our discussion of Barnett. In that case we said that if the laws were different there was no reason to suppose that there were any H_2O molecules. Putnam, however, asks us to consider a world where there are H_2O molecules with only a very small difference in the laws—one where the equations that describe the behavior of basic particles and forces are only slightly different from the equations that describe our physical world. But this slight difference in our description of the laws, has "a very large difference in the *behavior* of H_2O."

However, I question Putnam's assumption here. It may (for all I know) be possible for some changes in the natural laws not to impact the existence of certain elements and substances. For example, suppose the degree of repulsiveness between like particles of the same mass and charge in world w is slightly different than it is in our world. This fact leads to a difference between our world and w in the freezing and boiling points of the liquid state of H_2O. It is *perhaps* acceptable to say that there is water in such a world.

But even this case worries me. If the degree of repulsiveness between what we describe as positively charged particles is different between our world and w, why would we think that there is a single property of being positively charged that is exemplified in both worlds. It would seem to me that we have two properties here—being positively-charged-in-α (our world) and being positively-charged-in-w. And this is confirmed by the fact that the degree of repulsiveness between objects having those properties is different (even if only slightly so). But now it is no longer obvious that the atoms of w are the atoms of our world. What goes as a hydrogen atom in w has a "proton" which has the property of being positively-charged-in-w, but our protons do not have this property. So, after further consideration we should conclude that there is no water in w. w is, after all, like Twin-Earth. It contains some water-like stuff, but it does not contain water.

One might say, in response to the above, that my example only works because of the particular feature that I choose to distinguish between w and our world—namely the degree of repulsiveness between like charges. But if we are to use examples where the natural laws are different we need to pick a difference that could have an impact on the water-like stuff. For if the water-like stuff is exactly like our water, then it does not represent a problem for Kripke's argument. And if the natural laws under consideration are wildly different from our laws, then there will be no water or H_2O in such a world. Again there is no problem for Kripke's argument.

So I do not think that the fact that some possible worlds have different natural laws from ours requires one to give up on metaphysical necessity. If we describe our counterfactual circumstances carefully enough, it will become reasonably clear, after reflection, whether or not we have described a circumstance where there is water and H_2O. Hence, it seems to me that Putnam ought not to reject metaphysical necessity for the reasons considered here. Moreover, after careful reflection on the various arguments presented here against Kripke's argument that (1) is a necessary *a posteriori* truth, we find that Kripke's argument still stands.[16]

Notes

1. Kripke, Saul (1972,1980) *Naming and Necessity* Harvard University Press.
2. Putnam, Hilary (1992) "Is Water Necessarily Identical to H_2O?" in *The Philosophy of A. J. Ayer* (ed) Hahn, L. E. Open Court 429–454.
3. Johnston, Mark (1997) "Manifest Kinds" *The Journal of Philosophy* 94, 564–583.
4. Johnston is not alone in thinking our claim that water is H_2O is not an identity claim. Alan Sidelle is also concerned that to the extent that it is an *a posteriori* claim (as Kripke asserts it is) it can only be considered a claim of constitution or supervenience. See Sidelle, Alan (1992) "Identity and the Identity-like" *Philosophical Topics* 20, 269–292
5. See, for just one example of this, Baker, Lynnne R. (1997) "Why Constitution is not Identity" *The Journal of Philosophy* 94, 599–621. Perhaps I should add that while I am uncertain as to whether or not the relation of constitution constitutes identity, I am not convinced by Baker's argument to the contrary. One of Baker's premises is that a given statute (*Discobolus*) is essentially a statue. Baker argues for this claim on the grounds that if it is false, all the other artworks that do exist could exist without being artworks (p.620). But this is a mistake. The most one could claim (if one denies that *Discobolus* is essentially a statue) is that all the other items that are statues could exist without there being any statues (perhaps this is all Baker meant by the phrase 'artworks'). Novels, poems, and other forms of art need separate consideration. So suppose some aliens who just didn't like statues melted down all the statues (without causing the loss of any parts). Have any objects or things disappeared? It seems (to me anyway) more reasonable to describe the situation as one where a number of things underwent accidental change as opposed to substantial change. In this case I am disagreeing with Kripke who seems to hold that statues are essentially statues.
6. In this connection see Michael D. Rocca's discussion of heat and the motion of molecules in "Essentialists and Essentialism" (1996) *The Journal of Philosophy* 93, 186–202.
7. However, see the discussion of H. Steward's and D. Barnett's objection to the identity claim below (section III).
8. I realize that some philosophers do talk as if water is *made of* H_2O (e.g., James Pryor "What Do We Know *A Priori* About Water?" (Unpublished) p. 2) but I interpret all such talk as not being exact.
9. Donnellan, Keith (1983) "Kripke and Putnam on Natural Kind Terms" in *Knowledge and Mind Philosophical Essays* eds. C. Ginet and S. Shoemaker Oxford University Press 84–104 .
10. This may simply be part of the general problem about how to follow a rule in circumstances unforeseen by the rule. David Lewis also holds that there is no truth to

matter, prior to Kripke and Putnam producing their various examples, as to whether or not our word 'water' includes compounds other than H_2O. See "Reduction of Mind" reprinted in *Papers in Metaphysics and Epistemology* Cambridge University Press 291–324

11. I am going to ignore an obvious problem with this example, namely that **Au**-195, while the most stable of the other isotopes of **Au**, only has a half life of 186 days.

12. Steward, Helen (1990) "Identity Statements and the Necessary A Posteriori" *The Journal of Philosophy* 87, 385–398. For a somewhat different response to Steward and others who reject the view that 'water' and/or 'H_2O' are rigid designators see Joseph LaPorte "Rigidity and Kind" (2000) *Philosophical Studies* 97, 293–316.

13. Barnett, David (2000) "Is Water Necessarily Identical to H_2O?" *Philosophical Studies* 98, 99–112.

14. Putnam also raises concerns about worlds that have different natural laws. See the discussion of Putnam's later views in section IV below.

15. I do not think this is actually correct. There are, for instance, different forms of ice in addition to the hexagonal form that occurs naturally. But we may assume there is only one such form for purposes of the argument.

16. I have not argued directly for the claim that 'water' and 'H_2O' are rigid designators. Kripke and (early) Putnam have provided us with some arguments in favor of the claim that natural kind terms are rigid. Here, I have only defended Kripke's claim against some of the objections that have been raised. I only hope that this discussion can help remove some misunderstandings.

I would like to thank Ted Guleserian for our endless discussions of these issues and Tom Blackson for his very helpful comments on an earlier version of this paper.

References

Baker, Lynnne R. (1997) "Why Constitution is not Identity" *The Journal of Philosophy* 94, 599–621.

Barnett, David (2000) "Is Water Necessarily Identical to H_2O?" *Philosophical Studies* 98, 99–112.

Bolton, C. J. (1996) "Proper Names, Taxonomic Names, and Necessity" *The Philosophical Quarterly* 46, 145–157.

Donnellan, Keith (1983) "Kripke and Putnam on Natural Kind Terms" in *Knowledge and Mind Philosophical Essays* eds. C. Ginet and S. Shoemaker Oxford University Press 84–104.

Johnston, Mark (1997) "Manifest Kinds" *The Journal of Philosophy* 94, 564–5.

Kripke, Saul (1972,1980) *Naming and Necessity* Harvard University Press.

LaPorte, Joseph (2000) "Rigidity and Kind" (2000) *Philosophical Studies* 97, 293–316.

Lewis, David (1994) "Reduction of Mind" reprinted in *Papers in Metaphysics and Epistemology* (1999) Cambridge University Press 291–324.

Pryor, James (2000) "What Do We Know *A Priori* About Water?" Unpublished p. 2.

Putnam, Hilary (1992) "Is Water Necessarily Identical to H_2O?" in *The Philosophy of A. J. Ayer* (ed) Hahn, L. E. Open Court 429–454.

Rooca, Michael D. (1996) "Essentialists and Essentialism" *The Journal of Philosophy* 93, 186–202.

Sidelle, Alan (1992) "Identity and the Identity-like" *Philosophical Topics* 20, 269–292.

Steward, Helen (1990) "Identity Statements and the Necessary A Posteriori" *The Journal of Philosophy* 87, 385–398.

THE CONCEIVABILITY ARGUMENT AND
TWO CONCEPTIONS OF THE PHYSICAL*

Daniel Stoljar
The Australian National University
The University of Colorado at Boulder

I

The conceivability argument (CA) against physicalism[1] starts from the premises that:

(1) It is conceivable that I have a zombie-twin, i.e., that there is someone who is physically identical to me and yet who lacks phenomenal consciousness; and

(2) If it is conceivable that I have a zombie-twin, then it is possible that I have a zombie-twin.

These premises entail that physicalism is false, for physicalism is the claim—or can be assumed for our purposes to be the claim[2]—that:

(3) For any subjects S and $S*$ and worlds W and $W*$, if S in W and $S*$ in $W*$ are physically identical, then they are psychologically identical.

If (3) is true, it is not possible that I have a zombie twin: anybody physically identical to me is psychologically identical, and must therefore also have phenomenal consciousness. If (1) and (2) are true, however, it *is* possible that I have a zombie twin. Hence, if physicalism is true, either (1) or (2)—or both—is false.

One response for the physicalist is to reject (1). The notion of conceivability that is at issue in (CA) is most usefully thought of as a kind of rational intuition or intellectual presentation of a possibility: a clear and distinct idea that something could be physically identical to me and yet psychologically different.[3] But the problem is that such ideas are very hard to pin down. It's not at issue that we sometimes *have* these intuitions—that we have them is an assumption of many discussions in philosophy, and will not be questioned here. It is rather that introspective judgments concerning the character and content of these intuitions are notoriously subject to influence. As Descartes says in the *Meditations*, in order to be clear that we are having the intuitions we say we are, we need to withdraw to a quiet place and meditate. Physicalists who respond to (CA) by rejecting its first premise are in effect saying that we haven't meditated enough.

A different response for the physicalist is to reject (2). In general it is plausible to suppose that intuition or conceivability should be thought of as a guide to possibility—just as perception is a guide to actuality—in the following sense: if I conceive that *p* is possible (or have the rational intuition that *p* is possible) then I am prima facie justified in believing that *p* is possible. But the trouble is that conceivability is not an infallible guide. From the mere fact that you conceive that *p* is possible it does not *follow* that *p* is possible.[4] In effect, then, what (2) says is that in the zombie case there are no defeating conditions for the inference. However, it is open to physicalists to reply that there *is* a defeating condition. They might say that inferences from conceivability to possibility are always subject to defeat, and thus never legitimate—this would be to endorse a form of skepticism about knowledge of modality. More plausibly, they might say that such inferences are not legitimate in certain important cases, some of which are the cases relevant to (CA).

In this paper I defend a third response. I will argue that (CA) involves a fallacy of equivocation: there is a sense of 'physical' according to which the premises of (CA) are true, and there is a sense of 'physical' according to which physicalism is true; the trouble for (CA) is that these are distinct senses. In my view, this sort of response captures what is attractive in the previous two responses but evades what is controversial. What it captures and what it evades will become clearer as we proceed.

II

I will begin by making a two preliminary remarks about the strategy I want to consider. First, our strategy raises a set of considerations which are distinct from, but might be confused with, those raised by what is often called Hempel's Dilemma.[5] Hempel's Dilemma is that if the notion of the physical is defined via reference to contemporary physics, then physicalism is false; but if it is defined via reference to future or ideal physics then physicalism is trivial. The conclusion of Hempel's Dilemma is supposed to be either that there is no notion of the physical, or that there is no clear notion, or that there is no notion that can play the role that philosophers want to the notion of the physical to play.

Now, the strategy I want to consider here presupposes that this conclusion is mistaken. I will assume not only that there is *a* clear notion of the physical but that there are *two* clear notions (or that there are two spellings out of a single clear notion). What then has gone wrong in Hempel's Dilemma? This question demands a paper in its own right, but to put it rather briefly, Hempel's

Dilemma forgets that we all have and understand an ordinary or commonsensical concept of the physical. What Hempel's Dilemma shows, if it shows anything, is that a particular proposal about how to analyse this concept—viz., that it should be analysed via reference to scientific physics at a particular stage of its development—is mistaken.[6] But from this one cannot conclude that one has no clear concept at all. After all we all have and understand plenty of concepts that we don't know how to analyse (Lewis 1970). Indeed, in this paper, I will not attempt to analyse the notion of the physical at all. Rather, I will simply present two ways in which that concept might be understood. Whether that means that we in fact have two rather different concepts, or that we have two spellings out of the same concept, is a question I will set aside.

The second preliminary is this. One interesting aspect of the strategy I want to consider is that, if successful, it allows us to answer (CA) in a way that avoids taking up controversial issues in the epistemology of modality. Many philosophers are attracted by the idea that the right answer to (CA) appeals to necessary a posteriori truths such as those discussed by Kripke (1980). Such truths, it is widely held, make available the possibility that the second premise of the conceivability argument—(2)—is false. Now, the mere existence of such truths is not controversial or at least should not be. Hence there should be nothing controversial if a response to (CA) appeals to necessary a posteriori truths—indeed, as I will note briefly later on, our strategy is at one point naturally paired with such an appeal (cf. fn. 13).

Nevertheless, there *is* a large controversy over the correct *theory* of the necessary a posteriori. According to one side of this controversy, every necessary a posteriori truth is a logical or a priori derivation from a contingent a posteriori truth and a necessary a priori truth; according to the other side, at least some necessary a posteriori truths are not derived in this way. Many contemporary philosophers who appeal to necessary a posteriori truths—*a posteriori physicalists*, as I will call them—are committed not only to the idea that necessary a posteriori truths can be marshalled in a response to (CA), they are committed to the stronger claim that such truths must be underived. But this *is* to take up a controversial position; indeed, the question of whether there are underived a posteriori necessary truths is one of the most controversial questions in the epistemology of modality. So an advantage of our approach to (CA) is that it allows us to sidestep this issue.[7]

III

Having made these preliminary points, we can now turn to the distinction between the two conceptions of what it is to be a physical property. According to the first—which I will call *the theory-based conception*—a physical property is a property which *either* is the sort of property that physical theory tells us about *or* else is a property which logically (or a priori) supervenes on the sort of property that physical theory tells us about. According to this conception, for example, if physical theory tells us about the property of having mass, then having mass is a physical property. Similarly, if physical theory tells us about the property of being a rock—or, what is perhaps more likely, if the property of being a rock supervenes on properties which physical theory tells us about—then it too is a physical property. Let us say that any property which is physical by the lights of the theory-based conception is a *t-physical property*.[8]

According to the second conception of the physical—which I will call *the object-based conception*—a physical property is a property which *either* is the sort of property required by a complete account of the intrinsic nature of paradigmatic physical objects and their constituents *or* else is a property which logically (or a priori) supervenes on the sort of property required by a complete account of the intrinsic nature of paradigmatic physical objects and their constituents.[9] According to this conception, for example, if rocks, trees, planets and so on are paradigmatic physical objects, then the property of being a rock, tree or planet is a physical property. Similarly, if having mass is a property of paradigmatic physical objects—or if the property of having mass is required in a complete account of the intrinsic nature of such objects—having mass is a physical property. Let us say that any property which is physical by the lights of the object-based conception is an *o-physical property*.

Since the concept of the physical is one of the most fundamental in our conceptual scheme, many philosophical issues arise in connection with it. But for our purposes, the important thing is that the two conceptions are not coextensive: some o-physical properties are not t-physical. The following passage from Frank Jackson provides a convenient way to develop the point:[10]

> When physicists tell us about the properties they take to be fundamental, they tell us about what these properties *do*. This is no accident. We know about what things are like essentially through the way they impinge on us and on our measuring instruments. It does not follow from this that the fundamental properties of current physics, or of 'completed' physics, are causal cum relational ones. It may be that our terms for the fundamental properties pick out the properties they do via the causal relations the properties enter into, but that at least some of the properties so picked out are intrinsic. They have, as we might put it, relational names but intrinsic essences. However, it does suggest the possibility that i) there are two quite different intrinsic properties, P and P^*, which are exactly alike in the causal relations they enter into, ii) sometimes one is possessed and sometimes the other, and iii) we mistakenly think that there is just one property because the difference does not make a difference (as the point is put in information theory). An obvious extension of this possibility leads to the uncomfortable idea that we may know next to nothing about the intrinsic nature of our world. We know only its causal cum relational nature ... I think we should acknowledge as a possible, interesting position one we might call Kantian physicalism. It holds that a large part (possibly all) of the intrinsic nature of our world is irretrievably beyond our reach, but that all the nature we know about supervenes on the (mostly or entirely) causal cum relational nature that the physical sciences tell us about. (1998, p. 26-7)

This description of Kantian physicalism allows us to distinguish two classes of properties. The first class comprises the causal cum relational properties that physical sciences tell us about—to put things in our terms, these are the t-physical properties. The second class comprises the properties that duplicate physical objects will share—to put things in our terms, these are the o-physical properties. As Jackson in effect points out, it is easy to imagine two objects O and O^* which are identical in respect of their causal cum relational properties but differ in their intrinsic properties. To put things in our terms, it is easy to imagine two objects O and O^* which are alike in respect of their t-physical properties, but differ in respect of (some of) their o-physical properties. But this is just to say that there are some o-physical properties which are not t-physical, and that the two conceptions of what it is to be a physical property are not co-extensive.

In suggesting that there are two conceptions of the physical, I do not mean to suggest that there are no controversial assumptions at play in the argument for their distinction suggested in this passage from Jackson. On the contrary, there are at least three such assumptions. First, there is the issue of why physical theory should tell us only about causal cum relational properties. Second, there is the issue of why, in addition to the causal cum relational properties, there are the intrinsic properties which underlie them. Third, there is the analysis of the notion of 'tells us about'—clearly, for a theory to tell us about a property cannot simply mean for the expressions of the theory to refer to that property, since (as Jackson points out) it is clear that expressions of physical theory could refer to the intrinsic properties if there are any.

However, while these assumptions are certainly controversial, I will not attempt to defend them here. I have three reasons for this. First, so far as I am aware, proponents of (CA) accept the assumptions, so there can in the context be nothing objectionable about the procedure of adopting them so as to draw the distinction at issue.[11] Second, the assumptions have nothing at all to with philosophy of mind, so one can appeal to them without begging any of the questions that arise in the context of (CA). Finally, and most importantly, the metaphysical picture described by Jackson, and our development of that picture, is in the end only the scaffolding of our answer to the conceivability argument. As I will argue in §VI, we can do without the scaffolding and nevertheless defend the view at issue.

IV

In addition to the two conceptions of the physical, there is one further piece of machinery that is required before we can turn our full attention to the conceivability argument. This is a distinction, due in its modern form to James Van Cleve (1983), between weak and strong conceivability. As I noted earlier, the notion of conceivability that is in play in (CA) is the notion of a clear and distinct idea or presentation of a possibility. Now, this is a very hard notion to clarify. The Cartesian phrase 'clear and distinct idea' is obviously only a gesture at a fuller treatment. I will not attempt any fuller treatment here beyond endorsing Van Cleve's remark that "there is such a thing as just 'seeing'—by a kind of intellectual vision—that a proposition is true. Each of us can 'see' in this way that $2 + 3 = 5$, that nothing is both round and square, and much else besides" (1983, p. 36).

However, it *is* possible to distinguish a stronger and a weaker claim of what conceivability might consist in, as follows:

(4) *S* strongly conceives that *p* just in case *S* has a clear and distinct idea that *p* is possible.

(5) *S* weakly conceives that *p* just in case it is not the case that *S* has a clear and distinct idea that *p* is impossible.[12]

One might bring out the distinction here by pursuing the analogy between conceiving and perceptual experience. There is a difference between being visually under the impression that there is a lamp on the table, on the one hand, and *not* being visually under the impression that there is *not* a lamp on the table on the other. Likewise, there is a difference between conceiving that something is possible, on the one hand, and *not* conceiving that it is *not* possible on the other. The first of these is strong, the second weak, conceivability.

Weak and strong conceivability differ from each other in a number of ways, but only two of these are important for us. First, the slogan 'conceivability is a guide to possibility' is only plausible when the notion of conceivability at issue is strong conceivability. If it visually appears to me that there is a lamp on the table, I seem thereby to be prima facie justified in believing that there is; hence one might reasonably say being visually appeared to is a good guide to actuality. But suppose it *is not* the case that it visually appears to me that there is *no* lamp on the table. We would not normally say that that in such cases I am thereby prima facie justified in believing that there *is* a lamp on the table. Perhaps if episodes of this kind were repeated often enough I would have some sort of justification. But this is not what we mean when we say that perceptual experience is a guide to actuality. Likewise, while it is true that if I conceive that *p* is possible I am thereby prima facie justified in believing that *p* is possible, it is not true that if I do *not* conceive that *p* is *not* possible I am thereby prima facie justified in believing that p is possible. And this means that it is safe to assume that (2) of (CA) is only plausible if 'conceivability' means 'strong conceivability'.

Second, strong conceivability is an epistemically more demanding notion than weak conceivability. One can strongly conceive a proposition—that is, have a clear and distinct idea that the proposition is possible—only if one has a sufficiently rich understanding of the proposition in question. But one can weakly conceive a proposition even in the absence of such understanding. Thus, for example, one cannot strongly conceive that there might be creatures with eyes that are not creatures with ears (a Van Cleve example) unless one has a sufficiently rich understanding of what it is to be a creature with eyes and a creature with ears. To take a different example, suppose the ontological argument is sound, and the honest and sincere atheist says that he can conceive of a Godless universe (cf. Yablo 2000). A conceivability report of this kind cannot be taken as a report of strong conceivability. For, if the ontological argument is sound, Godlessness is self-contradictory—you cannot conceive that it is possible if you understand it.

It is sometimes said that the distinction between strong and weak conceivability is, while real enough, one which is likely to be of considerably less interest once we factor in a different distinction, namely, that between ideal and prima facie conceivability (Chalmers 2000a). The idea is that if we consider conceivability in ideal conditions, then negative conceivability *can* be taken to be a guide to possibility, or, anyway, can be taken to be as good a guide as strong conceivability. I want to set this consideration aside, however. For one thing, the idealizations involved in this suggestion are extremely tricky. For another, and more importantly, our argument will go through even if we stick to positive conceivability. Again, I will return to this issue in §VI.

V

So far, I have introduced two conceptions of the physical, and a distinction between strong and weak conceivability. The point to be developed now is that these distinctions provide an answer to the conceivability argument.

The first step is to define, on the basis of our two conceptions of what a physical property is, two conceptions of what it is for a subjects S and S^* to be physically identical. This of course is a simple matter. In general, S is physically identical to S^* iff S and S^* share every physical property. Hence S is t-physically identical to S^* iff S and S^* share every t-physical property; *mutatis mutandis* for o-physical identity. Given our assumption that the class of o-physical properties is distinct from the class of t-physical properties, it follows that the notion of t-physical identity is distinct from o-physical identity.

The next step is to distinguish two versions of both the premises of (CA) and the statement of physicalism with which it operates. The two versions of the premises are:

(1-t) It is conceivable that I have a t-zombie-twin, i.e. that there is someone who is t-physically identical to me and yet who lacks phenomenal consciousness;

(1-o) It is conceivable that I have an o-zombie-twin, i.e. that there is someone who is o-physically identical to me and yet who lacks phenomenal consciousness.

(2-t) If it is conceivable that I have a t-zombie-twin, then it is possible that I have a t-zombie-twin.

(2-o) If it is conceivable that I have an o-zombie-twin, then it is possible that I have an o-zombie-twin.

And the two versions of physicalism are:

(3-t) For any subjects S and S^* and worlds W and W^*, if S in W and S^* in W^* are t-physically identical, then they are psychologically identical.

(3-o) For any subjects S and S^* and worlds W and W^*, if S in W and S^* in
       W^* are o-physically identical, then they are psychologically identical.

We might say that (3-t) articulates a version of physicalism called t-physicalism,
while (3-o) articulates a version of physicalism called o-physicalism.

The problem for the proponent of (CA) can now be stated with some precision. There are two versions of the conceivability argument. The first version
takes you from (1-t) and (2-t) to the falsity of (3-t)—let us call this (CA-t). The
second version takes you from (1-o) and (2-o) to the falsity of (3-o)—let us
call this (CA-o). But neither version is a threat to physicalism.

The reason (CA-t) is not a threat to physicalism is that, even if it is sound,
it only establishes that (3-t)—t-physicalism—is false. However, since there are
some o-physical properties which are not t-physical, (3-t) can be false while
(3-o) is true. It follows that the soundness of (CA-t) does not contradict physicalism, for that argument does not rule out the possibility of o-physicalism.
The most (CA-t) shows is that, if one wants to be a physicalist one should
endorse o-physicalism rather than t-physicalism, (3-o) and not (3-t). It does not
show that one should give up physicalism altogether.[13]

The reason (CA-o) is no threat to physicalism a little more complicated,
and depends on the distinction between weak and strong conceivability. Given
this distinction we can further differentiate between two readings of the initial
premise of (CA-o). These are:

(1-o-w) It is weakly-conceivable that I have an o-zombie-twin, i.e. that
         there is someone who is o-physically identical to me and yet who
         lacks phenomenal consciousness.
(1-o-s) It is strongly-conceivable that I have an o-zombie-twin, i.e. that
         there is someone who is o-physically identical to me and yet who
         lacks phenomenal consciousness.

As we pointed out in §IV, if (2)—the premise of the original conceivability
argument taking us from conceivability to possibility—is to have any force, it
had better be interpreted in terms of strong, rather than weak, conceivability.
What this means is that it is (1-o-s) rather than (1-o-w) which is the relevant
premise of (CA-o). In other words, the success or failure of the argument turns
on whether it is strongly conceivable that I have an o-zombie twin.

However, this claim can be reasonably denied by the physicalist. The reason, as we also noted in §IV, is that strong conceivability is an epistemically
more demanding notion than weak conceivability. One can only strongly conceive of a proposition if one has a sufficiently good understanding of the proposition. On other hand, on the Kantian picture, I know next to nothing—as
Jackson puts it—about the intrinsic physical nature of our world. But if I know
next to nothing about the physical nature of my world, then I know next to
nothing of *my* physical nature and thus have no genuine understanding of what
this nature consists in. However, if I have no understanding of my own o-physical

nature, I cannot truthfully be said to strongly conceive the possibility of something which is o-physically identical to me. But then it cannot truthfully be said that I can strongly conceive of an o-zombie, because an o-zombie is something that is o-physically identical to me *and* who lacks phenomenal consciousness. However—and this is the last step—if I fail to strongly conceive an o-zombie, there is no reason why (1-o-s) cannot be denied by the physicalists. But if (1-o-s) is denied, (CA-o) is no threat to physicalism.

Earlier we saw that (CA-t) is no threat to physicalism because even if it is successful it only refutes one version of physicalism. What we have just seen is that (CA-o) is likewise no threat to physicalism. These two points together constitute our response to the conceivability argument.

Before moving on, I want to pause to introduce an analogy[14] that I hope will make clear the basic shape of the view that I am pursuing. Imagine a mosaic *M* constituted only by two sorts of tiles, triangles and pieces of pie. *M* may of course have many different shapes in it, so long as those shapes are constructed by transparent principles from the basic ones: diamonds, circles, half-moons, and so on. Now imagine that our only epistemological access to *M* is via two shape-detecting systems, a triangle-detecting system and a circle-detecting system. In other words, given our epistemological access to *M*, it would be natural to think that it was constituted *only* by triangles and circles—of course this is a mistake, but it would be a natural one in the situation I am imagining.

Now, in that situation one might well develop a conceivability argument concerning *M* to the effect that circles are something over and above the rest of the mosaic. This argument would proceeds from two premises:

(1-m) It is conceivable that there is a zombie-mosaic-twin, that is, a mosaic exactly like *M* in non-circle respects but which lacks circles.

(2-m) If it is conceivable that there is a zombie-mosaic-twin, it is possible that there is zombie-mosaic-twin.

On the basis of these two premises one might argue that, since it is possible that there is a zombie-mosaic-twin, circles must be something quite over and above the non-circular aspects of *M*. When God created *M*, he first had to build it out of non-circular respects, and then he had to add circles—circles are (as Descartes might have said) a special creation.

It is obvious that this argument is a bad one. It is palpably *not* possible that there be a zombie-mosaic-twin in the sense we have defined. A mosaic exactly like *M* in non-circular respects would be exactly like it both in terms of triangles *and* pieces of pie—but such a mosaic would *also* be exactly like the actual mosaic in terms of circles. In other words, circles are *not* a special creation of God, and we stand in need of a plausible diagnosis of what has gone wrong in this argument. I think it is plausible to say that in the first premise we are at most *weakly* conceiving of a zombie-mosaic. Since we clearly do not understand central aspects of *M*, we cannot be said to strongly conceive of a zombie mosaic, to have a clear and distinct idea of zombie mosaic. So what is wrong with the argument is that it is invalid: (1-m) is only true if 'conceivable' means weakly conceivable, but (2-m) is only true if 'conceivable' means strongly conceivable.

In effect, my proposal is that the same thing goes for (CA-o). In both (CA-o) and the mosaic argument, the first premise is only plausible if conceivability means 'weak conceivability': (CA-o) is only plausible if (1-o) is interpreted as (1-o-w). Interpreted in that way, however, no troubling modal conclusion will follow.

V

Our conclusion to this point is that, if the two conceptions of the physical can be kept apart, the conceivability argument fails to refute physicalism. The most that is refuted is t-physicalism. But o-physicalism emerges unscathed. In this section of the paper I want to consider a number of objections to our proposal. In the course of responding to these objections, we will be able to expand on and develop what has gone before.[15]

Objection #1: Are o-Zombies only Weakly Conceivable?

The first objection takes up our suggestion that o-zombies are only weakly conceivable. Is this really true? Perhaps one *can* strongly conceive of o-zombies? After all, many people report that they can conceive of the possibility of zombies. Why am I so sure that these reports of conceivability should not be interpreted as reports of strong conceivability of o-zombies?

As I have said, I think it is doubtful that one can strongly conceive of the possibility of an o-zombie. It needs to be appreciated that conceivability reports such as (1-o) are empirical reports about what people can and cannot conceive. But if we interpret those claims as involving strong conceivability, they will have the consequence that people have a rich understanding of their own physical nature. On the other hand, if the Kantian picture or something like it is true, this consequence is false: people who report themselves as conceiving zombies may know next to nothing about it.

However, even if one insists that one *can* strongly conceive of o-zombies, and hence that (1-o-s) is true, our argument will still go through. The central consideration so far has been that ignorance of various aspects of the physical world makes it implausible to suppose that we can strongly conceive that o-zombies are possible. But a similar consideration will serve to show, that even if we can strongly conceive of the possibility of o-zombies, the inference from this to their genuine possibility will fail.

In order to illustrate this, it is useful to have before us a model of how ignorance can defeat the inference from (strong) conceivability to possibility. The best account that I know of is that developed in a number of papers by Stephen Yablo. Yablo writes:

> If X finds it conceivable that E, then she is prima facie justified in believing that E is possible. That justification is defeated if someone can provide her with reason to suspect the existence of a D such that (i) D is true, (ii) if D is true, then E is impossible, and (iii) that X finds E conceivable is explained by her failing to realize (i) and/or (ii). (2000, p. 121)

On this model of modal error, it is clear that ignorance ("failing to realize") can sometimes defeat the inference from conceivability to possibility. To see this, look again at the example of the mosaic. Suppose you insist that, in the case I imagined, you *can* strongly conceive a zombie-twin-mosaic, that is, that you can strongly conceive of a mosaic identical to *M* in non-circular respects but which lacks circles. In that case you are prima facie justified in believing that the zombie-twin-mosaic is possible. But now suppose you come to suspect the existence of the pieces of pie. Then it seems true both that what you conceived to be possible is in fact not possible, and also that you only conceived it to be possible because you did not know about the pieces of pie. More generally, if you insist that you can strongly conceive of a zombie-twin-mosaic, the pieces of pie will defeat the inference from this to the genuine possibility of such a mosaic. In sum, then, we seem to be faced with two possible suggestions about what has gone wrong in the mosaic argument. On the one hand we can say what we said before, that we can only weakly conceive of a zombie-twin-mosaic, and that in consequence the argument is invalid. On the other hand, we can say that we *do* strongly conceive of zombie-twin-mosaic but that this does not support the inference to the possibility of a zombie-twin-mosaic.

Once again, my suggestion is that parallel remarks apply in the case of the (CA-o). On the one hand, one might say what we said before: that the argument is invalid because the first premise can only be read as involving weak conceivability. On the other hand, one might concede that the first premise involves strong conceivability, but insist that, in that case, the second premise false. The second premise is false because the inference from conceivability to possibility is subject to defeat. The defeaters are the o-physical properties which are distinct from t-physical. Suppose *D* is the statement which specifies the o-physical properties which are distinct from my t-physical properties. Then *D* will be true of my (putative) zombie-twin as much as me, and will also (if physicalism is true) entail that my zombie-twin does not lack consciousness. From this point of view, our suggestion is that one only finds o-zombies conceivable because we don't know the nature of the relevant o-physical properties. But if that is so, the second premise of (CA-o) is false, and again the physicalist has an answer to the conceivability argument.

Objection #2: What role does the distinction between the two conceptions of the physical play in this account?

The second objection asks what role the distinction between the two conceptions plays in the account. We have just seen that the idea that we are ignorant of the physical world plays an important role in our response to (CA). But one might point out that we are certainly ignorant of many t-physical properties as well. For example, why couldn't the defeater suggested by Yablo's account of modal error simply be a t-physical truth, and not an o-physical truth? Or, again, why couldn't one simply argue against the strong conceivability of t-zombies?

One thing to say about this objection is that it seems to miss an important feature of the dialectical situation. Suppose somebody says that they clearly and distinctly conceive of the Eiffel Tower painted yellow (a Yablo example). It does not follow from this that they have to imagine every *detail* of the Eiffel Tower.[16] It is not to the point to ask whether they imagined every rivet yellow, for example. Nevertheless, it seems clear that they must conceive of the Eiffel Tower as being yellow to *some* degree of detail, otherwise their conceivability claim seems at best forced. Now, how much detail is required? To answer to this question fully would doubtless be extremely difficult, but in general, it seems reasonable to say that one needs to imagine situations in sufficient detail so that we are reasonably confident that further detail will not defeat the initial conceivability claim or the inference from conceivability to possibility. Thus, in the case of the Eiffel Tower, we can imagine it painted yellow not because we can imagine it in every detail, but because we can imagine it in enough detail that we are confident that further detail does not defeat the conceivability claim.

Now, in the case of the conceivability argument the situation is the same. If somebody says that they clearly and distinctly conceive of having a zombie-twin you cannot defeat that by pointing out that they haven't conceived of it down to the last detail. For it doesn't matter that they haven't conceived of it in every detail. All that matters is that they have conceived of it in sufficient detail that they can be confident that further detail will not defeat the claim.

However, once it is clear that we do not need to conceive of every detail of conceivable situations, the role of the two conceptions of the physical in our account becomes clear. If you say that you can conceive of the possibility of a t-zombie, it is certainly true that you do not need to conceive of this possibility in every detail. Nevertheless, in the absence of further information, it is plausible to say that further detail will not defeat the conceivability claim, for further detail will simply be roughly similar to the same sort that we have now. On the other hand, if you say you can conceive of the possibility of an o-zombie, it is open to you to say that further detail will or might defeat the conceivability claim, for in that case the further detail is detail about which we have no knowledge. If it is really true that the sort of knowledge we derive from physical science does not tell us anything about the intrinsic properties of physical objects, then further knowledge of that sort won't help us. In short, the distinction between the o-physical and t-physical properties of physical objects is crucial in our account because while we are certainly ignorant of both, our ignorance of o-physical properties is of a different order, and it is this different sort of ignorance that is in play in our response to (CA).

Of course, I certainly do not want to rule out the possibility that our ignorance of the t-physical properties might be as extreme as, or of the same order as, our ignorance of the o-physical properties. If that were so, then I certainly think that we could operate with only t-physical properties. But the important point is that, in that case, the essential structure of the account remains the same. We have two conceptions of physical properties, one which introduces a class of properties that are fairly familiar and one which introduces a class of properties some of which we do not understand. And recognizing this fact affords a response to the conceivability argument.

Objection #3: Rejecting the Kantian Picture

The final objection I want to consider focuses more directly on the plausibility of the Kantian picture that we took over from the passage from Jackson. So far we have been presuming that the picture is right, and pursuing its consequences. However, there is a certain frame of mind from which the picture seems preposterous. Why should we believe that there are these strange properties underlying ordinary physical properties? And, even if we do believe this why should we believe that these properties have anything to do with consciousness? (Notice that Jackson makes no such assumption.) Finally, even if there are such properties, and even if they have something to do with consciousness, the proposal seems to have a devastating epistemological consequence: since we are never going to know the nature of these intrinsic properties, we will never be able to give a scientific account of consciousness. In short, the account seems to be simply a metaphysical fantasy, and, worse, a fantasy with disastrous results.

One way to respond to this objection is to confront it directly—defend the metaphysics of the Kantian picture, and downplay its epistemological import. Another response is to bite the bullet—the world is a strange place, one might say, you've just got to learn to live with it. I have some sympathy with these responses, but I think that there is a better response available. The better response is to show that the Kantian picture is in the end only the scaffolding for our account. The picture makes very vivid a certain account of what physical objects and our access to them are like, and this account is very useful in the expression and development of our view. But the structure and plausibility of view survives, even if that account is dispensed with.

The best way to illustrate that our account does not require the Kantian picture is to consider another famous conceivability argument: Descartes' argument about language in section 5 of the *Discourse*. There we find Descartes' arguing that a certain version of physicalism is false given certain obvious facts about what we would nowadays calls linguistic competence—the ability to effortlessly and appropriately speak a language in the way that typical humans do. He writes:

> ...we can certainly conceive of a machine so constructed that it utters words, and even utters words which correspond to our bodily actions causing a change in its organs (e.g. if you touch it in one spot, it asks what you want of it, if you touch it in another it cries out that you are hurting it, and so on). But it is not conceivable

that such a machine should produce different arrangements of words so as to give an appropriately meaningful answer to whatever is said in its presence, as the dullest of men can do. (AT VI 56: CSM I I40, 1988, p. 44).

There is no doubt a number of different themes lying below the surface of this passage. But in general it seems reasonable to interpret Descartes as mounting a conceivability argument here that is very similar in structure to the one we have been considering from the outset. One may present this argument as proceeding from two premises:

(6) It is conceivable that I have a machine-twin, that is, something like me in all physical respects but which lacks linguistic competence.

(7) If it is conceivable that I have a machine-twin, then it is possible that I have a machine-twin.

On the basis of this argument Descartes concludes that physicalism is false. If a machine in the sense defined is possible, competence cannot in the end be a physical matter. However, since we *are* linguistically competent, physicalism is false.

Now, how should one react to Descartes' argument? In my view, the best response is to say that Descartes was right *given his understanding of physicalism*. According to John Cottingham (1992), Descartes' argument in this passage "starts from the observation that a machine, or a *bête machine*, is essentially a stimulus and response device" (p.247) and combines this with the further observation that "the human language-user has the capacity of respond appropriately to an indefinite range of situations, and this capacity seems *toto caelo* different from anything that could be generated by a "look-up tree...correlating inputs and outputs" (p. 248). It seems fair to summarize this by saying that Descartes' argument against physicalism assumes a certain conception of physical identity, namely that, at least as far as language goes, physical identity just is *behavioral identity*, i.e. identity in terms of actual and potential stimulus and response. On this interpretation, in other words, the first premise of Descartes argument appears to be more properly rendered as:

(6*) It is conceivable that I have a machine-twin, that is, something like me in all (actual and potential) behavioral respects but which lacks linguistic competence.

However, this premise *is* plausible. For the fact is it *does* seem plausible to suppose that someone identical to me in terms of actual and potential stimulus and response might lack linguistic competence. Moreover, *if* one were assuming, as Descartes apparently is, that behavioral identity just is physical identity, then reasoning from this premise does plausibly support Descartes' overall conclusion, namely, that physicalism is false.

Why is the first premise of the Cartesian argument so plausible once it is rendered as (6*)? The answer is that, on this interpretation, the premise looks strikingly similarly to the first premise of arguments which we *know* (or at least justifiedly believe) to be plausible, namely the refutations of behaviorism suggested by Ned Block (1981, 1998) and others. Block invites us to imagine a machine so designed that it mimics the linguistic dispositions of his Aunt Bubbles, but which operates only on the basis of a giant look-up tree. If the mimicry is clever and complete enough, the machine will be identical to Aunt Bubbles in terms of actual and potential behavior—in short, it will be Aunt Bubbles' machine-twin. But, as Block points out, if the causal transactions which mediate this behavior are of the wrong sort, the Aunt Bubbles' machine-twin will have no linguistic competence at all—"the intelligence of a toaster", as Block famously put it (1981, p. 21). Block convincingly argues on this basis that behaviorism, even in its most sophisticated form, is false. And once again the structure of Block's argument is exactly the same as the conceivability argument we have been considering from the outset: If I can conceive of myself (or Aunt Bubbles) having a machine-twin, then I am prima facie justified in believing that this is possible. But if it possible that I have a machine-twin then behaviorism is false. For if behaviorism in the form Block means to discuss it is true, then, necessarily, anything behaviorally identical to me would have to be psychologically identical.

Of course, the difference between Block and Descartes is that Block is aiming only to refute behaviorism, while Descartes is aiming to refute physicalism. Nevertheless, there remains an important sense in which their arguments are the same, and hence that if Block's argument is convincing (and I think we should agree that it is) there is an important sense in which Descartes' argument is convincing also. Given Descartes assumption that physical identity just is behavioral identity (an assumption obviously denied by Block) his argument has whatever plausibility Block's has.

But of course, even if Descartes' argument in the *Discourse* is successful given his understanding of physicalism, it does not follow that the argument is successful *tout court*. Looking back on Descartes' argument we can see that he was operating with what is from our point of view a greatly impoverished conception of the physical world. From our point of view, what Descartes is missing, among other things, is the idea that internal information processing can assume highly complex computational forms. With that notion in place the whole idea that I can conceive of something physically identical to me but which lacks linguistic competence seems quite unmotivated. Something physically identical to me *would* be identical to me in terms of internal information processing. And, in turn, something identical to me in terms of information processing *would* be identical to me in terms of linguistic competence. In other words, with the monumental advantage of hind-sight, one might suggest that the reason that Descartes' argument seemed plausible to him is only that he lacked certain concepts of the physical world, namely the idea of internal information processing. Moreover, the reason that his argument seems to us fine as a refutation of behaviorism which anticipates Block, but hopeless as a refutation of physicalism is precisely that the concept of internal information processing seems to be a physical notion broadly construed, even if it is not a behaviorist one.

Now, however, we are finally in a position to say why our account does not require the Kantian picture. We need to sharply distinguish two aspects of the Kantian picture that we have so far been running together. On the one hand, there is the claim that, if that picture is true, we are ignorant of certain aspects of the physical world. On the other hand, there is the claim that this ignorance can be recruited to answer the conceivability argument. But for our purposes it is really only this *second* claim that is important. The Kantian picture presents to us a certain vivid model of what our ignorance might be like, but it is really the ignorance, and not the model, that matters. To put it slightly differently, there are a number of different ways of making it plausible that we are ignorant of certain features of the physical world, and that this ignorance can induce conceivability arguments. One way is to appeal to the Kantian picture. But a different way is to appeal to historical cases such as that of Descartes' discussion of linguistic competence. In that case our answer to the conceivability argument is simply to suggest that our position with respect to consciousness is rather like Descartes's position with respect to linguistic competence. Just as he was ignorant with respect to features of the physical world, and just as this ignorance allowed him to formulate a conceivability argument concerning language, so too we are ignorant with respect to features of the physical world, and this allows us to formulate conceivability arguments concerning phenomenal consciousness. But in neither case is the denial of physicalism plausible.

If our proposal can be effectively de-coupled from the Kantian picture, then the final objection to our position can be answered. It remains true on our account that we can distinguish two conceptions of the physical, one which introduces a class of properties of which are ignorant, and another which does not. But it is mistaken to confuse this claim about ignorance with the full-blown Kantian picture. In particular, the claim that we are ignorant with respect to the physical world does not entail that any view about the metaphysics of relational or intrinsic properties, nor that our ignorance concerns or is limited to intrinsic properties, nor does it entail that our ignorance is chronic, in the way that the Kantian picture suggests. Indeed, for all our proposal requires, our ignorance might simply be a function of the present state of science. But of course, it is a mistake to infer from this ignorance that physicalism is false.[17]

VI

My argument has been that, if we distinguish between two conceptions of the physical, the physicalist has nothing to fear from the conceivability argument. Operating with the theory-conception of the physical, one might concede that the argument is successful, but on that interpretation, it does not refute physicalism in its most general form. Operating on the object-conception, on the other hand, the argument does not go through. For on the object-conception it is open to the physicalist to say that we are ignorant of various features of the physical world, and this ignorance will block the conceivability argument. But of course, even if what I have suggested is right, this only shows that our account is one way to answer the conceivability argument. It does not show that it is the best or the only way. In this final section, therefore, I will make some very brief remarks how our proposal fairs when compared to the alternatives.

At the heart of the proposal is a certain hypothesis which one might call *the missing concept hypothesis*. This hypothesis says that we are missing certain concepts of the physical world, and that this fact explains our present predicament with respect to consciousness. It is hard of course to defend this hypothesis directly. In the nature of the case, one cannot say what the concepts are, or even what they are like. One must appeal to made-up analogies (such as the mosaic example) or analogies from history of philosophy and science (such as the Kantian picture and the Cartesian argument about linguistic competence). Moreover, the hypothesis is a theoretical one and may of course be wrong. Nevertheless, if it explains the data in way which is less costly than alternatives then it should be preferred. So the crucial question is whether the missing concept hypothesis is more attractive on balance than the alternatives.

Contemporary philosophy seems to present us with three main alternatives to the missing concept hypothesis.[18] One option is eliminativism, according to which there are no experiences as we usually think of them, but there might of course be replacement concepts. Another option is primitivism or dualism, which says that experiences are a primitive or non-supervenient feature of the world. And a third option is a posteriori physicalism—the position I considered briefly in §II. According to this view, statements connecting phenomenal consciousness and the physical are necessary and a posteriori but irreducibly so, in the sense that involves a controversial issue in the epistemology of modality. Demonstrating the superiority of our account over these accounts would require an extensive comparative analysis. Obviously no such analysis can be undertaken here. What I will do, however, is suggest one consideration which favors our alternative over the others.

The consideration looks again the Cartesian argument about language that we considered in the previous section. It is important to see that analogues to all four positions (our own plus the three alternatives) are available as responses to Descartes' argument. A primitivist response would say that linguistic competence is an irreducible fact. (Descartes himself opted for something like this with his postulation of a rational soul.) An eliminativist response says that there is no linguistic competence as we usually conceive of it, and articulates a substitute notion. The a posteriori physicalist would say that the truths about linguistic competence are necessarily connected to truths that involve actual and potential stimulus and responses. Finally, the missing concept view says that we are missing certain concepts of the physical world, and that these concepts will defeat the argument at issue.

Now, in the case of the Cartesian argument, it is obvious in hindsight that the missing concept view is the right view, though of course it is not the view taken by Descartes. Both primitivism and eliminativism are positions which to contemporary philosophers seem obvious overreactions in the case of linguistic competence. And it is not usually thought that an appeal the necessary a posteriori is going to help in this case. Notice, for example, that in discussions of Ned Block's argument against behaviorism, it was never assumed to be open to the behaviorist to appeal to the necessary a posteriori, and say that linguistic competence is only a posteriori related to behavioral dispositions. That would be regarded as an unmotivated departure from usual practice. Since we do not pursue such options when other conceivability arguments are at stake it is not clear why we should pursue such options when considering the argument with which we began.

On other hand, if the missing concept hypothesis is obviously the right answer in the case of the Cartesian argument about language, we are confronted with a powerful reason for supposing that it is likewise the right answer in the case of the conceivability argument that concerns phenomenal consciousness. In fact, the analogies here are rather uncanny. Of course we have a natural tendency to think that, at least in principle we know everything, and that that it is unlikely that new concepts of the physical world will be developed. But I assume that that tendency was strong in Descartes also.

Notes

*A version of this paper was given to the Metaphysics and Consciousness in Philosophy of Mind Conference, Chateau Hotel, Sydney. Thanks to all who took part on that occasion. For comments and discussion about previous drafts, I am also indebted to Andrew Botterell, David Chalmers, Frank Jackson, and Philip Pettit.

1. For the most prominent recent defence of the conceivability argument, see Chalmers 1996. By phenomenal consciousness, I mean the property experiences have when there is something is like to have those experiences. For more on this terminology and for a good discussion of the relation between consciousness in this sense and other senses, see Block 1995. The first premise of the conceivability argument has variations that might be more plausible to some philosophers—for example, one might claim only to conceive someone physically identical to me who is phenomenally *different* (e.g because of inverted or alien experiences). But I will concentrate on the simplest version of the argument here.

2. Strictly speaking physicalism is not quite (3). First, physicalism is usually thought of as a contingent thesis whereas (3) is necessary. Second, physicalism is better stated as a global supervenience thesis; but (3) is not a global supervenience thesis. I will ignore these differences here. For some further discussion, see Jackson 1998 and the references therein.

3. For a very good discussion of the different senses of conceivability, see Van Cleve 1983, Yablo 1993, 2000, and Chalmers 1999.

4. But see Chalmers 2000a for arguments that, at least in some cases, conceivability *does* entail possibility. Here I will stick with the more standard assumption that allows modal error.

5. See Hempel 1970. For a more recent discussion see Crane and Mellor 1990, and Melnyk 1997.

6. The idea that the notion of the physical should be defined via reference to physical theory at a particular stage of its development is mistaken for another reason. Whether

a physical theory is true or not is a function of the contingent facts; but whether a property is physical or not is a not function of the contingent facts. For example, consider medieval impetus physics. Medieval impetus physics is false (though of course it might not have been) and thus it is irrational to suppose it true. Nevertheless, the property of having impetus—the central property that objects have according to impetus physics—is a physical property, and a counterfactual world completely described by impetus physics would be a world in which physicalism is true. But it is hard to see how any of this could be right if physicalism were defined by reference to the physics that we have now or by the physics that happens to be true in our world.

7. For more on this controversy, see Chalmers 1996, Jackson 1998, Stoljar 2000, and in particular the exchange on Chalmer's book in *Philosophy and Phenomenological Research*, Vol. LIX, No. 2, June 1999.

8. The theory-based conception bears some relation to the notion of physical$_1$ discussed in Feigl 1967; more explicit defense is found in Smart 1978, Lewis 1994, Braddon-Mitchell and Jackson 1996, and Chalmers 1996. For further discussion and defense of this notion of the physical, see Stoljar 2001.

9. The best example of a philosopher who operates with the object-conception of the physical is Feigl 1967; it is also a position that one encounters regularly in discussion. For further discussion and defense of the notion, see Stoljar 2001.

10. For a similar recent development of the themes articulated in this passage from Jackson, see Langton 1998.

11. See, e.g., Chalmers 1996, pp. 153–4, and n.29 on p.375.

12. For further discussion, see Bealer 1999, Chalmers 2000a, Van Cleve 1983, and Yablo 1993.

13. It is important to note that I have not here assumed that (CA-t) is sound, only that, even if it is, it would not defeat physicalism in all its forms. In fact, it is quite possible for us to deny that (CA-t) is sound by taking a leaf out of the book of the a posteriori physicalist—the position I considered briefly in §II. If we suppose that the connection between the t-physical truths and the phenomenal truths is a necessary and a posteriori one, then (CA-t) will not go through. However, this response to the argument does not mean that we need to take up any controversial position in the theory of necessary truths—for the o-physical truths which are not also t-physical will supply the truths from which the a posteriori necessary truths are logically derived.

14. This analogy is also discussed in Stoljar 2001.

15. In Stoljar 2001 I develop a similar strategy as a response to the knowledge argument. In that paper I also consider three further objections to the strategy under discussion. I am not supposing that the objections discussed either here or in that paper amount to all of the objections one might bring against the strategy I am pursuing.

16. This point is well made in Chalmers 2000a.

17. It is interesting to note that this way of stating our proposal makes it vivid that the concepts of the physical world that we are missing need not be concepts of the structure of matter itself. One problem with the Kantian picture is that it encourages the idea that our ignorance is limited to the very small, that is, to matters that pertain the structure of matter itself. To the extent that one might be sceptical that ideas drawn from this level of reality are applicable to consciousness, our answer to the conceivability argument will seem misguided. However, as the example of Des-

cartes makes clear, there is no reason to assume that our ignorance is limited in this way. Notions such as computation and information processing, for example, are notions which apply to the physical world, and are physical notions broadly construed, but they are not about the ultimate structure of matter.

18. One might think that there are many more options that this. However, as far as I can see, most of the apparently different options resolve themselves into one or other of the options discussed in the text. To take one example, a common idea in contemporary philosophy of mind is representationalism, the doctrine that the phenomenal truths supervene on intentional truths. When this position deals explicitly with arguments such as the conceivability argument it usually becomes a version either of eliminativism (as in Harman 1990) or a posteriori physicalism (as in Tye 1999).

References

Bealer, G. 1998. 'A Theory of Concepts and Concept Possession". In Villanuava, E. (ed.) Concepts: Philosophical Issues, Vol. 9, Ridgeview, pp. 261–301.

Block, N 1981. 'Psychologism and Behaviorism', *Philosophical Review*, XC, 1, 1981, pp.5–43.

Block, N. 1995: 'On A Confusion about a Function of Consciousness', *Behavioural and Brain Sciences*. Reprinted in Block et alia (eds) 1997. *The Nature of Consciousness*. MIT Press. References to the reprinted version.

Block, N. 1998. 'The Mind as the Software of the Brain'. In Osherson, D et al. (eds.) *Invitation to Cognitive Science Vol 3*. (2nd Ed.), Cambridge, MA: MIT Press.

Block, N. and Stalnaker, R. 1999. 'Conceptual Analysis, Dualism, and the Explanatory Gap', *Philosophical Review*, Forthcoming.

Braddon-Mitchell, D and Jackson, F. 1996. *Philosophy of Mind and Cognition*. Blackwell.

Chalmers, D 1996 *The Conscious Mind*, Oxford.

Chalmers, D. 1999. 'Materialism and the Metaphysics of Modality', *Philosophy and Phenomenological Research*, Vol. LIX, No. 2, June 1999 Web version at: *http://www.u.arizona.edu/~chalmers/papers/modality.html*

Chalmers, D 2000. 'The Content and Epistemology of Phenomenal Belief'. Forthcoming Web version at: *http://www.u.arizona.edu/~chalmers/papers/belief.html*

Chalmers, D 2000a. 'Does Conceivability Entail Possibility'. Forthcoming. Web version at: *http://www.u.arizona.edu/~chalmers/papers/conceivability.html*

Cottingham, J. 1992. 'Cartesian Dualism: Theology, Metaphysics and Science'. In Cottingham, J. (ed.) 1992 *The Cambridge Companion to Descartes*, Cambridge: Cambridge University Press, pp. 236–257.

Crane, T. and Mellor, D.H. 1990. 'There is no Question of Physicalism', *Mind* 99:185.

Descartes, R. 1988. *Selected Philosophical Writings* (ed. J. Cottingham) Cambridge: Cambridge University Press.

Feigl, H. 1967. 'The "Mental" and the "Physical"' (Minneapolis: University of Minnesota Press. Original Publication: 1958)

Harman, G. 1990. 'The Intrinsic Quality of Experience', in Tomberlin, J. (ed.) 1990 *Philosophical Perspectives*, Vol. 4, Ridgeview, pp.xx-51. Reprinted in Block et alia, (eds.) 1997 *The Nature of Consciousness: Philosophical Debates*, MIT Press.

Hempel, C (1970) 'Reduction: Ontological and Linguistic Facets'. In Morgenbesser et al. (eds) *Essays in Honor of Ernest Nagel*. New York: St Martin's Press.

Hill, Christopher S. and McLaughlin, B 1999. 'There are Fewer Things in Reality than are Dreamt of in Chalmers' Philosophy', *Philosophy and Phenomenological Research*, forthcoming.

Jackson, F. 1998. *From Metaphysics to Ethics: A Defense of Conceptual Analysis*, Oxford.

Kripke, S 1980. *Naming and Necessity*, Harvard.

Langdon, R. 1998. *Kantian Humility* Oxford: Clarendon.

Lewis, D. 1970 'How to Define Theoretical Terms' *Journal of Philosophy* 67:427–46.

Lewis, D. 1994 'Reduction of Mind'. In Guttenplan, S 1994 (ed) *A Companion to the Philosophy of Mind* Oxford: Blackwell.

Loar, B. 1997. 'Phenomenal States'. In Block N. et. alia (eds.) 1997. *The Nature of Consciousness*, MIT Press, pp. 597–616.

Melnick A "How To Keep The 'Physical' in Physicalism", *Journal of Philosophy*, XCIV, (1997), 622–637.

Searle, J. 1992. *The Rediscovery of the Mind*, Cambridge, MA: MIT Press.

Smart J.J.C. 'The Content of Physicalism', *Philosophical Quarterly* 28 (1978) pp. 239–41.

Strawson, G. 1994. *Mental Reality*. Cambridge, MA: MIT Press.

Stoljar, D 2000. 'Physicalism and the Necessary A Posteriori', *Journal of Philosophy*, XCVII, 1, (January 2000), pp. 33–54.

Stoljar, D 2001. 'Two Conceptions of the Physical', *Philosophy and Phenomenological Research*, forthcoming.

Tye, M. 1999. 'Phenomenal Consciousness: The Explanatory Gap as a Cognitive Illusion', *Mind*, Vol.108, 432, October 1999.

Van Cleve, J. 1983. 'Conceivability and the Cartesian Argument for Dualism', *Pacific Philosophical Quarterly* 64 (1983) 35–45.

Yablo, S. 1993. 'Is Conceivability a Guide to Possibility?', *Philosophy and Phenomenological Research* 53 (1993), pp. 1–42

Yablo, S. 2000 'Textbook Kripkeanism & the Open Texture of Concepts'. *Pacific Philosophical Quarterly* 81 (2000), pp. 98–122

Philosophical Perspectives, 15, Metaphysics, 2001

SUSTAINING ACTUALISM

Michael Devitt
Graduate Center, CUNY

In "Naturalism, Actualism, and Ontology" (1998), James Tomberlin's challenges actualists to show how

(1) Ponce de Leon searched for the fountain of youth

can be true without Ponce de Leon being related to some nonactual individual. I responded in "Putting Metaphysics First" (1998b) by drawing on the representational theory of the mind ("RTM") and the Quinean view that sentences like (1), involving intentional verbs, are similar to propositional attitude ascriptions. In "How Not to be an Actualist" (this volume) Tomberlin takes me to be parsing the opaquely construed (1) as

(1*) Ponce de Leon searched for the mental token with the meaning of purportedly referring by the mode of 'fountain of youth',

thus identifying *searching for* with a relation that holds between agents and mental tokens. Tomberlin's objection then is, in effect, that just as (1) is true even though the *object* that its definite description purports to refer to is nonactual, we can, as he ingeniously shows, come up with a sentence along the lines of (1*) that is true even though the *mental token* its definite description purports to refer to is nonactual. (His example concerns *wanting to study* not *searching for*, but that is of no significance.) So we have not really answered his challenge: all we have done is turn the problem of apparently searching for a nonactual object into the problem of apparently searching for a nonactual mental token.

Tomberlin has misinterpreted me in two ways. First, my view is that (1) is made true by Ponce de Leon being in a functional relation to *a* mental token—not *the* mental token—with the meaning of purportedly referring by the mode of 'fountain of youth'. Second, and more important, I do not identify the functional relation in question with the relation of *searching for* (p. 500–1). Indeed, the view that *searching for is* a relation between agents and mental tokens seems implausible if not absurd. Surely when I search for my pen, even in the opaque sense, I am not searching for a mental token! So (1*) is not my parsing of (1), Tomberlin's objection fails, and actualism is sustained.

Still, his objection has made two things apparent. First, I should have been more explicit that my view was not the identity-of-relation view he criticizes. My claim that it is "doubtless inappropriate to *call*...[the functional relation] "the searching relation" (p. 501) is too weak. If it *were* appropriate to call it "the searching relation" then it would *be* the searching relation and then the view would be open to Tomberlin's objection. Second, since *searching for* is not the functional relation, what is it? This is an interesting question that RTM needs to address.

The question generalizes. If we reject the identity-of-relation view for *searching for* then presumably we must also reject it for propositional attitudes, given the claimed similarity between sentences involving intentional verbs and propositional attitude ascriptions. So we must dismiss the view that *believing is* a functional relation between agents and mental tokens. Of course, the identity view does not seem as implausible for *believing* as it does for *searching for* but it surely does for other propositional attitudes. Thus it is just as implausible to think that when I expect that the Yankees will win I am expecting a mental token as it is that when I search for Mary I am searching for a mental token; or, indeed, as it is that when I expect Mary I am expecting a mental token. It seems then that we should reject the identity-of-relations view for attitudes. Then RTM needs to say what the attitudes are.

At the core of my RTM view is the claim that the psychological reality underlying the truth of (the opaquely construed) (1) is: Ponce de Leon stands in a certain functional relation to a mental token with a certain meaning. Analogously, the psychological reality underlying the truth of

(2) Ralph believes that Ortcutt is a spy

is: Ralph stands in a certain functional relation to a mental token with a certain meaning.[1] Call the former relation "*S*" and the former meaning "*M1*"; call the latter relation "*B*" and the latter meaning "*M2*". So:

(1S) Ponce de Leon *S*s an *M1* token
(2B) Ralph *B*s an *M2* token.

What has (1S) got to do with (1), and (2B), with (2)? More generally, what have the facts according to RTM got to do with what we ordinarily ascribe to the mind with the likes of (1) and (2)? I think that the actualist has to choose between three answers.

1. One answer takes *searching for* and *believing* to be relations to intentional objects that hold *in virtue of* relations to mental tokens. So, (1) asserts

that Ponce de Leon searches for a certain intentional object, <the fountain of youth>. He does so in virtue of (1S). (2) asserts that Ralph believes a certain intentional object, the proposition <Ortcutt is a spy>. He does so in virtue of (2B). This is neat but it raises three worries.

First, the answer is committed to intentional objects. What are they? Obviously we cannot claim that they are merely *possible* objects, for that would abandon actualism. The usual view is that they are actual objects but abstract, outside space and time. But many of us think that such objects are "creatures of darkness." Second it is unclear, to say the least, *how* a person's relation to such an abstract object can hold in virtue of a relation to a mental token. Third, the answer demands that transparent ascriptions be treated very differently from opaque ones. If (1) is to be true, it must be opaque. But sentences containing intentional verbs can be transparent. Consider, for example,

(3) Bob searched for his missing daughter.

This can be construed transparently so that it would not be true if Bob had no daughter and could be true whatever the description under which he saught his daughter. The natural thing to say is that the transparent (3) ascribes a relation between Bob and his daughter. Yet, on the answer we are considering, the opaque (3) ascribes a relation between Bob and an intentional object. Transparent ascriptions must of course be different from opaque ones but this difference seems too great to be plausibly explained.

2. I prefer an answer that denies that 'searching for' and 'believing' are simply relative terms and that *searching for* and *believing* are relations. Rather, we should think of (1S) and (2B) as paraphrases for (1) and (2) respectively, paraphrases that demonstrate the dual function of 'searching for' and 'believing' (cf. Quine 1960: 154). One function is to specify the appropriate relation, S or B, and is therefore the function of a relative term. But the other function is that of a quantifier, "supplying the indefiniteness" of 'an $M1$ token' and 'an $M2$ token'.[2] The meanings $M1$ and $M2$ are, of course, specified by 'the fountain of youth' and 'that Ortcutt is a spy', respectively.

From this perspective, although it is appropriate enough to ask about the natures of S and B, it is not appropriate to ask about the natures of *searching for* and *believing*. Asking that reflects the mistaken view that they are relations.

How does this view handle the difference between opaque and transparent ascriptions? Take (3) as our example. If (3) is opaque then it is true if Bob Ss a token with the meaning of purportedly referring by the mode of 'his missing daughter'. If it is transparent then it is true if Bob Ss a token with the meaning of referring to his missing daughter. On my preferred answer, the only difference between the two construals of (3) lies in the meaning specified by 'his missing daughter', hence in the meaning of the token that Bob has to be related to for (3) to be true. 'Searched for' is univocal, part relative term and part quantifier on both construals. On the opaque construal (3) affirms a relation to a token than could hold even if Bob has no missing daughter; see (1). On the transparent construal (3) affirms a relation to a token that could hold only if Bob has a missing daughter, for the token could not have the meaning of referring to a missing daughter unless Bob had one. Although the transparent (3) does not *primarily* affirm a relation between Bob and his daughter, we can take it as *derivatively* doing so, for it could not be true unless a token in his head referred to her.

3. The previous two answers each allow the facts according to RTM to support what we ordinarily ascribe to the mind; so (1) and (2) can be true. I conclude by mentioning an answer that removes that support, making (1) and (2) false. The answer follows answer 1 in taking *searching for* and *believing* to be relations to intentional objects. So (1) would be true if Ponce de Leon stood in the *searching for* relation to <the fountain of youth> and (2) if Ralph stood in the *believing* relation to <Ortcutt is a spy>. The answer differs from 1 in not supposing that (1) holds in virtue of (1S) nor (2) in virtue of (2B). Rather the answer claims that (1) and (2) do not hold because there are no intentional objects. (1) and (2) are convenient manners of speaking but, when the chips are down, must be abandoned in favor of (1S) and (2B). This is revisionist but it does not seem objectionably so to me. It is an acceptable fall-back if linguistics tells us that answer 2 does not work.[3]

My original response to Tomberlin's challenge sustains actualism but showing how it does has raised an interesting question about the relation between RTM and what we ordinarily ascribe to the mind.[4]

Notes

1. Strictly speaking this applies only to "core" beliefs not to beliefs one has but one has not entertained.
2. I aired this idea in my 1996, p. 216. The view that the underlying structure of a sentence might contain a quantifier not visible on the surface is not surprising. There is so much underlying syntax. Thus linguists find an underlying quantifier in 'He ate' (as Georges Rey reminded me) and Lepore and Ludwig (2000) have argued that complex demonstratives (like 'that dog') have underlying quantifiers.
3. The three answers parallel suggestions made by Eugene Mills in his critical discussion (1998) of my *Coming to Our Senses* (1996). The present discussion shows that my response to his criticism (1998a: 397–8) was far too harsh. He was right to be puzzled by RTM. And I was wrong to say that "nothing much hinges" on whether we call the functional relation that I am here calling "*B*" "believing."

   The discussion raises the question: What is the *common* view of where RTM stands on this issue? I don't know but I suspect that my earlier failure to address the issue carefully is typical. Georges Rey's masterly presentation (1997) of RTM, under the name "CRTT" (short for "Computational/Representational Theory of Thought"), includes remarks that are suggestive of the identity-of-relation view. Thus, he talks of CRTT attempting "to *analyze* propositional attitudes" (p. 209; my emphasis), and claims that "hoping, imagining, wishing, dreading, believing, and preferring that p *consist in* different computational relations to a sentence that expresses the proposition [that p]" (p. 210; my emphasis). Still, there is no clear commitment to the identity view. And he talks often of CRTT "*capturing*" the attitude states which could well be answer 1 or 2.

4. I am grateful to Hartry Field and Georges Rey for comments.

References

Devitt, Michael. 1996. *Coming to Our Senses*. New York: Cambridge University Press.

————. 1998a. "Responses to the Maribor Papers." In Jutronic 1998: 353–411.

————. 1998b. "Putting Metaphysics First: A Response to James Tomberlin." *Philosophical Perspectives, 12, Language, Mind, and Ontology, 1998* 499–502.

Jutronic, Dunja ed. 1998. *The Maribor Papers in Naturalized Semantics*, Maribor: Pedagoska fakulteta Maribor.

Lepore, E, and K. Ludwig. 2000. "The Semantis and Pragmatics of Complex Demonstratives." *Mind* 109: 199–240.

Mills, Eugene. "Devitt on the Nature of Belief." In Jutronic 1998: 310–17.

Quine, W. V. O. 1960. *Word and Object*. Cambridge, MA: MIT Press.

Rey, Georges. 1997. *Contemporary Philosophy of Mind: A Contentiously Classical Approach*. Cambridge, MA: Blackwell Publishers.

Tomberlin, James E. 1998. "Naturalism, Actualism, and Ontology." *Philosophical Perspectives, 12, Language, Mind, and Ontology, 1998*: 489–98.

Tomberlin, James E. "How Not to be an Actualist." This volume.

HOW NOT TO BE AN ACTUALIST

James E. Tomberlin
California State University, Northridge

1. The Background: Intentional Verbs

Actualism, as I understand the view here, is minimally the position that there are no objects that do not actually exist.[1] According to actualism, there are no philosophical problems whose solution calls for or requires an ontological commitment to nonactual objects. Now I harbor a deep and ongoing skepticism as regards this ontological stance, a skeptical concern increasingly extended and sharpened in my (1993, 1996, 1998a, 1998b, 1998c) and Tomberlin and McGuinness (1994).

In (1998b), my contribution to an exchange with Michael Devitt and Terence Horgan concerning the merits of actualism, I set out two challenges for actualism, one dealing with deontic matters, the other framed around intentional verbs. Devitt (1998), after declining a treatment of the first challenge, proffers a fascinating resolution to the challenge about intentional verbs.[2] In what follows, I seek to undermine Devitt's proposal. But first, what exactly is the challenge at issue?

Like Chisholm (1986), assume an actualism with these key ingredients: an ontology confined to actual individuals and attributes (some exemplified, others not); a relational account of believing and the other psychological attitudes; and a Russellian treatment of definite descriptions. Since a position of this sort demands that no person ever has genuine *de re* attitudes towards nonactual individuals, how exactly does this view treat items such as

(1) Ponce de Leon searched for the fountain of youth?

To deny that Ponce de Leon entertained any *de re* attitudes towards the fountain of youth, after all, dictates one of two alternatives as regards (1); (a) deny the truth of (1); or (b) interpret (1) in such a way that its truth does not place Ponce de Leon in a genuine *de re* relation to the nonactual fountain of youth.

To his credit, Chisholm rejects option (a). Instead, armed with a theoretically elegant account of believing as a relation between a believer and an attribute,[3] Chisholm theorizes that (1) is to be understood as expressing a dyadic *searched for* relation between Ponce de Leon and an attribute. That is, Chisholm would parse (1) as follows (Chisholm, 1986, pp. 56–57):

(1a) Ponce de Leon searched for the attribute of being a unique site of a unique fountain of youth.

By the lights of Chisholm's actualism, because there *is* such an attribute even though it fails to be exemplified, (1a) does not require that Ponce de Leon bear a *de re* relation to the fountain of youth.

A similar version of actualism is advanced independently by David Kaplan in his classic essay "How to Russell a Frege-Church" (1975). To begin with, Kaplan rightly observes that Russell's own primary-secondary scope distinction for eliminating descriptions within intentional contexts fails in the case of (1) inasmuch as the intentional verb on duty takes no sentential compliment. Why not, Kaplan proposes, model (1) semantically (and ontologically) as the bearing of a dyadic relation between Ponce de Leon and an attribute? Kaplan's resulting paraphrase of (1) turns out essentially like (1a) above (Kaplan 1975, p. 729).

In (1998b), I argued that the Chisholm-Kaplan model for intentional verbs fails.[4] (I return to this model for additional critique in section 3 below.) And consequently, my challenge to Devitt (and any actualist) was framed as follows:

Challenge. Tender a credible treatment of (1) meeting this constraint: (1) is true but its truth does not entail that Ponce de Leon stands in a *de re* relation to some nonactual individual.

Against this background, let us now turn to Devitt's intriguing response.

2. Devitt's Proposal

In Devitt (1996), after Quine(1960), items such as

(2) Ralph believes that Orcutt is a spy

are declared ambiguous, sometimes *opaque* but sometimes *transparent*. With Devitt, this opaque-transparent ambiguity receives a distinctive theoretical unpacking: under an opaque construal, (2) ascribes the *functional* relation of belief between Ralph and the property of purportedly referring to Orcutt by the mode of 'Orcutt'. As such, (2) may be true even if there is no actual Orcutt. In the transparent case, however, (2) ascribes the same dyadic relation of belief between Ralph and (the actual individual) Orcutt. So read, of course, (2) won't be true unless Orcutt is indeed actual.

How exactly does this view of attitude ascriptions bear on the puzzle as regards intentional verbs? Well, in Devitt (1998), we are presented with the proposal that sentences containing an intentional verb like 'search for' should be treated in a similar vein. Like (2), that is,

(1) Ponce de Leon searched for the fountain of youth

is either transparent or opaque. Since there is no (actual) fountain of youth, if (1) is to be true, the opaque reading must be on duty. By the latter, however, the dyadic relation (1) ascribes is between Ponce de Leon and a *mental token* with the meaning of purportedly referring by the mode of 'the fountain of youth'. As such, given that *searched for* is a functional relation, if (1) is true (and hence opaque), the mental token in question causes "searching behavior" in Ponce de Leon even though there is no actual fountain of youth. In this way, Devitt finds, (1) may be true without requiring Ponce de Leon to stand in a *de re* relation to some nonactual individual (Devitt, 1998: 500–501).

3. *A Rebuttal*

Consider:

(α) x searched for y.

According to Devitt, if the singular term replacing 'y' does not refer, as in (1), the resulting instance of (α) is true only if it is parsed as the appropriate instance of (the opaque):

(β) x searched for the mental token m of type t.

Now in counting Devitt as an actualist I take this to imply actualism across the board: there are no non-actual items of any sort in his ontology. By this view, therefore, there are in particular *no* possible but non-actual mental tokens. So, let ϕ be the set of all and only those actual mental tokens. Then Devitt's actualism requires that the description 'the unique non-member of ϕ most admired by Al' does not refer to any mental token.

As it happens, we may suppose, owing to Bob's keen esteem for Al, his desire to pursue Al's own endeavors, and whatever else, (3) is true:

(3) Bob wanted to study the unique non-member of ϕ most admired by Al.

By Devitt's program for intentional verbs, however, (3) won't be true unless the description in question picks out some actual mental token. And consequently, true (3) is not true, after all. This, I submit, is no way to preserve actualism.

(To close out the present discussion, I here observe that the above objection against Devitt carries over *mutatis mutandis* to the Chisholm-Kaplan model. By this model, it should be recalled, our troublesome (1) is parsed as

(1a) Ponce de Leon searched for the attribute of being a unique site of a unique fountain of youth.

Let ψ be the set of all and only those actual attributes. Then the Chisholm-Kaplan model dictates that 'the unique non-member of ψ most admired by Al' does not refer to any attribute.

As with (3), however, we may assume that (4) is true:

(4) Bob wanted to study the unique non-member of ψ most admired by Al.

And yet, according to the Chisholm-Kaplan model for intentional verbs, if (4) is true, there *is* such an actual attribute as the attribute of being a unique non-member of ψ most admired by Al. By this model, therefore, true (4) won't be true, after all.[5])

Notes

1. There are, it should be observed, *grades* of actualism. Alvin Plantinga (1985), for example, endorses actualism as the view that there neither are nor could have been objects that do not actually exist. But Nathan Salmon (1987) embraces actualism only by affirming the first half of Plantinga's characterization while explicitly rejecting the second (and modal) half. There are more technical characterizations of actualism in Menzel (1990) and Fitch (1996). For extensive references on actualism see the bibliographies of Tomberlin and McGuinness (1994) and Tomberlin (1996).
2. In Horgan (1998), my other symposiast, a tantalizing response is offered to both challenges. The response in each case is pivotally centered around Horgan's *contextual semantics* as formulated in his (1986, 1991, and elsewhere). As I take it, Horgan insists on the following: (a) a statement of the sort $(\forall X)B$ may be true; (b) an instance $B(T/X)$ may be true; (c) and hence the truth of $(\exists X)B$ follows, all of this despite the fact that there is no ontological commitment to any actual individual picked out by the term 'T'. (See, for example, Horgan (1998), pp. 508–509.) This strongly suggests that Horgan's contextual semantics is his version of *substitutional quantification*. If so, I firmly decline the view inasmuch as I have argued extensively against substitutional quantification in my (1990, 1993, 1997, and 1998a). Still, if I understand Horgan correctly, he intends contextual semantics to be neither objectual nor substitutional quantification. I hope to critically assess Horgan's view in future work.
3. There is an extensive critique of Chisholm's ingenious version of self-ascription for the psychological attitudes in Tomberlin (1991).
4. The objections of Tomberlin (1998b) to the Chisholm-Kaplan model serve to both extend and correct the main criticism of this model in Tomberlin and McGuinness (1994) and Tomberlin (1996).

5. Linsky and Zalta (1994) contains an original and important version of actualism. I critically examine their view in Tomberlin (1996). Linsky and Zalta reply in (1996). In future work, I plan to assess the novel and intriguing versions of actualism in Almog (1998a, 1998b), Bealer (1998a, 1998b), Fitch (1996), and Salmon (1998).

References

Almog, Joseph, 1998a, "The Subject Verb Object Class I," *Philosophical Perspectives* 12: 39–76.

Almog, Joseph, 1998b, "The Subject Verb Object Class II," *Philosophical Perspectives* 12: 77–104.

Bealer, George, 1998a, "A Theory of Concepts and Concept Possession," *Philosophical Issues* 9: 261–302.

Bealer, George, 1998b, "Concept Possession," *Philosophical Issues* 9: 331–338.

Chisholm, Roderick M., 1986, "Self-Profile," in R. Bogdan, ed., *Roderick M. Chisholm*, Profiles Dordrecht, D. Reidel.

Devitt, Michael, 1981, *Designation*, New York, Columbia University Press.

Devitt, Michael, 1996, *Coming to Our Senses*, New York, Cambridge University Press.

Devitt, Michael, 1998, "Putting Metaphysics First: A Response to James Tomberlin," *Philosophical Perspectives* 12: 499–502.

Fitch, G.W., 1996, "In Defense of Aristotelian Actualism," *Philosophical Perspectives* 10: 53–72.

Horgan, Terence, 1986, "Truth and Ontology," *Philosophical Papers* 15: 1–21.

Horgan, Terence 1991, "Metaphysical Realism and Psychologistic Semantics," *Erkenntnis* 34: 297–322.

Horgan, Terence, 1998, "Actualism Quantification, and Contextual Semantics," *Philosophical Perspectives* 12: 503–509.

Kaplan, David, 1975, "How to Russell a Frege-Church," *Journal of Philosophy* 72: 716–729.

Linsky, Bernard and Zalta, Edward N., 1994, "In Defense of the Simplest Quantified Modal Logic," *Philosophical Perspectives* 8: 431–458.

Linsky, Bernard and Zalta, Edward N., 1996, "In Defense of the Contingently Nonconcrete," *Philosophical Studies* 84: 283–294.

Menzel, Christopher, 1990, "Actualism and Possible Worlds," *Synthese* 85: 355–389.

Plantinga, Alvin, 1985, "Self-Profile," in J.E. Tomberlin and P. Van Inwagen, eds., *Alvin Plantinga*, Profiles, Dordrecht, D. Reidel.

Quine, W.V., 1960, *Word and Object*, Cambridge, MA, MIT Press.

Salmon, Nathan, 1987, "Existence," *Philosophical Perspectives* 1: 49–108.

Salmon, Nathan, 1998, "Nonexistence," *Noûs* 32: 277–319.

Tomberlin, James E., 1990, "Belief, Nominalism, and Quantification," *Philosophical Perspectives* 4: 573–579.

Tomberlin, James E., 1991, "Belief, Self-Ascription, and Ontology," *Philosophical Issues* 1: 233–259.

Tomberlin, James E., 1993, "Singular Terms, Quantification, and Ontology," *Philosophical Issues* 4: 297–309.

Tomberlin, James E., 1996, "Actualism or Possibilism," *Philosophical Studies* 84: 263–281.

Tomberlin, James E., 1997, "Quantification: Objectual or Substitutional?," *Philosophical Issues* 8: 157–167.

Tomberlin, James E., 1998a, "Actualism and Quantification," in F. Orelia and W.J. Rapaport, eds., *Thought, Language, and Ontology*, The Netherlands, Kluwer Academic Publishers.

Tomberlin, James E., 1998b, "Naturalism, Actualism, and Ontology," *Philosophical Perspectives* 12: 489–498.

Tomberlin, James E., 1998c, "Concepts and Ontology: A Query for Bealer," *Philosophical Issues* 9: 311–316.

Tomberlin, James E. and McGuinness, Frank, 1994, "Troubles with Actualism," *Philosophical Perspectives* 8: 459–466.